The Brew- master's Bible

THE BREW-MASTER'S BIBLE

THE GOLD STANDARD FOR HOMEBREWERS

STEPHEN SNYDER

HarperPerennial

A Division of HarperCollinsPublishers

HarperCollins books may be purchased for educational, business, or sales promotional use. For information please write: Special Markets Department, HarperCollins Publishers, Inc., 10 East 53rd Street, New York, NY 10022.

FIRST EDITION

Designed by Joel Avirom & Jason Snyder

Library of Congress Cataloging-in-Publication Data

Snyder, Stephen, 1961–
     The brewmaster's bible: the gold standard for
     homebrewers/by Stephen Snyder.
          p.   cm.
     Includes bibliographical references and index.
     ISBN 0-06-095216-4
     1. Brewing—Handbooks, manuals, etc.
     I. Title.
     TP570.S66   1997
     641.8'73—dc21   96-46877

09 ❖RRD 30

To Melissa, for years of inspiration,
support, and boundless optimism
=

CONTENTS

Acknowledgments viii

Preface ix

Introduction x

How to Use This Book xi

The World of Beer xiv

BASIC BREWING PROCEDURES

An Introduction to Brewing:
    Your First Batch 2

Basic Tips for Better Homebrewing 9

PARTIAL MASH AND ADVANCED BREWING

Partial Mash Ale Brewing 14

Partial Mash Lager Brewing 16

All-Grain Brewing: An Introduction
    to Advanced Techniques 19

Single-Temperature Infusion Mashing 25

Step-Mashing 27

Decoction Mashing 31

Fermentation and Lagering 34

Bottling Procedures 35

General Conditioning Procedures 38

General Kegging Procedures 39

Brewing Record & Evaluation Form 41

Carbonation Chart 43

Advanced Tips for Better Homebrewing 44

UNDERSTANDING BEER

The Major Beer Styles 48

Beer Styles at a Glance 56

Malt, Adjunct, and Specialty
    Grain Profiles 59

Malts, Adjuncts, and Specialty
    Grains at a Glance 67

Hop Profiles 68

Hops at a Glance 73

Yeast Profiles 74

Water 84

Additives 90

Sanitizers and Cleansers 91

RECIPE FORMULATION

Beer Design 95

ALE RECIPES

Brown Ale 108

Old Ale 117

Mild Ale 121

Pale Ale 124

Irish Red Ale 132

India Pale Ale 135

Bitter 142

Porter 150

Stout 163

Oatmeal Stout 175

Scottish and Scotch Ale 182

Barley Wine 189

Altbier 197

Kölsch 204

Weizenbier 206

Witbier 218

Abbey Beers 225

Lambic 237

Oud Bruin 241

North American Ales 243

LAGER RECIPES

Pilsner 272

Dortmunder Export 282

Munich Helles 285

Vienna 288

Märzen/Oktoberfest 293

Bavarian Dark 300

Bock 304

Mai/Helles Bock 310

Doppelbock 312

North American Lagers 317

SPECIALTY BEER RECIPES

Bavarian Specialty Beers 330

Christmas and Holiday Beers 334

Fruit- and Spice-Flavored Beers 338

WEIGHTS AND MEASURES 352

FORMULAS 353

DIRECTORY 355

CONTRIBUTORS 357

GLOSSARY 359

BIBLIOGRAPHY 361

INDEX 363

ACKNOWLEDGMENTS

I would like to extend a special word of thanks to my agents Susan Urstadt and Jeanne Fredericks for their hard work and enthusiasm, my editor Sharon Bowers for making this book better than I had ever thought possible; Susan Friedland for her great faith in this project; all the Bards of Beer for sharing their vast knowledge; and for their immeasurable contributions to this book's growth along the way, Paul White, Al Korzonas, and Dr. Alfred Haunold for technical direction; Bruce Fiene and Tracy Wheeler for photography and moral support, Byron Burch and Nancy Vineyard, Carlos and Rico Perez for their generous help in this project's infancy, Daniel S. McConnell, David Logsdon, Dr. Paul Bosken-Diebels, Iain Loe, James and Vera Melton for their undying interest in beer facts, and last but not least, the creator of saccharomyces.

PREFACE

Initially, this book started out as a resource for my own personal use, but as I began collecting helpful brewing data to put in a notebook with my own recipes, I realized how much more I needed to learn, and also how much contradiction existed in the information available on brewing products. By soliciting information from over two hundred homebrew supply shops and dozens of professional craft brewers in an effort to gather information, I was finally able to resolve many discrepancies, and in the process found that these shops had a lot of great recipes that they were graciously willing to share. It was then that I realized that this was information other homebrewers might find useful as well.

My hope is that this information will help you have more fun and grow as a brewer, but remember, these recipes are not sacred and do not have to be strictly adhered to. Feel free to use them as an outline for your own recipes; they are a map to guide you in discovering what works and tastes best for you. Don't forget that the foundations of homebrewing lie in trusting your own instincts, expressing your creativity, and most of all, exercising your freedom to brew the beer you want.

Last, but not least, I want to preface this manual by thanking the many beer writers who shared their vast knowledge, but especially the professional craft brewers and homebrew shops who generously lent their recipes and expertise for the creation of this book. They, as my aunt Ethel would say, "didn't know me from a sack of turnips," but they took the time to send me recipes and other information, often during their busiest time of year, proving the old adage, "If you want to get something done, ask a busy person to do it." I owe them a huge debt of gratitude.

INTRODUCTION

There is an old saying, "The truth is rarely pure and never simple." This is nowhere more appropriate than in the world of beer, despite the fact that all beer has roots in just four simple ingredients: water, malt, hops, and yeast. Even the name of our beloved beverage is a source of contention and confusion. Many people prefer to call warm-fermented beers "ales" and cool-fermented beers "lagers." Others take issue with this, however, because *lager* merely comes from the German verb meaning "to store" and has nothing to do with color, content, or method of brewing. German altbiers are ales, after all, yet they are cold-lagered; German wheats are often fermented with ale yeast then bottle-conditioned with lager yeast. Furthermore, some even feel the word *beer* should be used only to identify products where the yeast settles to the bottom during fermentation (bottom-fermented) and "ale" should be used exclusively for a product where the yeast rises to the top during fermentation (top-fermented). In fact, "beer" itself was once a term specifically used to differentiate malt beverages flavored with hops from ales, which were once flavored exclusively with other bitter herbs and spices.

The long and short of all this is that the lines between beer styles cross and crisscross, have two or more names, or have varying fermentation and conditioning methods from country to country and region to region. Therefore, in order to simplify matters for the practical purposes of homebrewing, I refer to all beverages herein as "beer" and have divided the recipes (for five gallons, unless otherwise noted) into three main sections: Top-fermented beers will be termed "ales" and bottom-fermented beers will be classified as "lagers." There is also a shorter third section of "Specialty Beers" that includes rare Bavarian styles, seasonal "Holiday Beers," or beers that use fruit or spices as flavoring agents; this section includes both ales and lagers.

You'll notice some of the recipes may fit into more than one category, particularly American versions of the classic styles. Some of these are included in the appropriate "American" sections, others in the "European" sections; in most cases, the ingredients used, especially the yeast and hops, were the deciding factors in where the recipes would be placed. You'll also see that brand names or specific products are recommended in some recipes. This is not for promotional purposes or because we've received a kickback from the manufacturer but because it was the product used in the original recipe, it is the best one for the job in the brewer's humble opinion, or it is true to the style of the beer due to the physical properties of its ingredients (that is, a "continental" American malt for a steam beer or a "maritime" German malt for a helles). The same is true for the hop alpha acid percentages given. Since it may be difficult in future years to find hops with the exact alpha acid percentage (AA%) as given, use the HBU/AAU/IBU formulas on pages 353 to adjust what alpha acid percentage you have to the ones given in the recipe. Otherwise, use whatever you have available and what suits your personal taste. Good luck and happy homebrewing!

How to Use This Book

This book was designed as a collection of recipes in the classic beer styles, a reference tool to the myriad homebrewing ingredients, and as a recipe formulation tool. To that end, a working knowledge of classic beer styles, their ingredients, and the brewing methods should be obtained by studying all the preliminary sections of this book before formulating an entirely new recipe of your own. By providing you with a solid background in the component parts and the techniques for bringing them together, you will be able to create a successful brew and to master a variety of brewing methods and beer styles. If you are an experienced brewer, you can skip this beginner's section and get right to the recipes, although a glance at the ingredient profiles and the formulation tables may be a good refresher.

You could brew for years following the recipes in this book to the letter and not be disappointed, but few brewers can resist the great joy in putting their own unique stamp on an existing formulation or in developing their own completely new recipe. Those that are not fully described can be supplemented by the basic instructions provided in the reference section if you are ever in doubt about the finer details of reproducing a recipe. The recipe formulation tables provide an outline of the classic ingredients used in the major styles. This general information should be supplemented by the more descriptive texts of the ingredient profiles.

For beginning brewers and for a vast majority of the world's homebrewers, "malt extracts" will form the basis for all your beers. Malt extracts are simply the sweet liquid derived from malt that has been processed into a concentrated syrup or powder form. All they need is the addition of water to create the "wort" (pronounced "wert") professional or all-grain brewers spend hours carefully crafting through the labor-intensive mashing process. Malt extracts are valuable not only for their ease of use but because they save the brewer vast amounts of time and effort, and don't require an intricate understanding of brewing processes to create good beer. The sophistication of malt extracts has progressed so rapidly over the past decade that there is a malt extract for almost every style of beer that you would like to brew.

Obviously, some of the ingredient choices are simple, especially with the extract recipes: You wouldn't choose a dark malt extract kit to create a pilsner or an extra light German extract kit to create an Irish stout. Other choices, such as the proper hop varieties to employ or the most appropriate commercial yeast require more information as your recipes become more advanced.

The first decision to make is which style of beer you want to brew and whether you will be using malt extracts as your base or be brewing entirely from grain. If you are brewing an extract-based beer, this will determine the type of liquid or dry malt extract to purchase and whether you want it with or without hops added for bitterness. There are so many malt extract selections available now, many of which are style-specific in design, that it would be impossible to catalog them all here. Your homebrew supply shop can guide you in choosing the best extract if the product names are not totally self-explanatory. If you are brewing an extract recipe supplemented with specialty grains, examine the formulation charts and the recipe section to determine the proper choices and quantities. If you are brewing all-grain, refer to the beer styles section, the formulation tables, and the section of recipes for that style to determine what base malts, water treatment, specialty malts, and techniques are recommended and frequently employed.

Your second decision will be your choice of hops. Hop selection is as style-specific as the other ingredients, and the proper amounts and the timing of their addition in the brewing process are critical. The wide array of hop varieties makes it easy to substitute and experiment with modern cultivars, but it also makes it very important to know which varieties are employed in the classic styles and which hybrids drawn from them are suitable for use in which beers. Extract brewers can forgo the choosing of hops and use prehopped kits, but the addition of your own hops is so easy and rewarding it warrants consideration even for the first-time brewer. Examine the hop profiles section, the styles at a glance, the recipe formulation tables, and the recipes to determine the proper variety, quantity, and purpose of the hops for the style you have chosen.

The next step is to choose the proper yeast. This is crucial, especially when brewing beers with a distinctive yeast signature such as a Bavarian weizenbier or an English bitter. Until a few years ago, only a handful of quality brewing yeasts were available to homebrewers, and most of those were in dried form. Today, there is a large and ever increasing number of high-quality liquid brewing yeasts. Most are tailored to one or two specific styles. Novice brewers are often encouraged to just sprinkle dry yeast into their fermenter the first time out, but this method often does not produce results equal to liquid yeast and, like the use of fresh hops, it can be incredibly easy to use. Study the yeast profiles section to determine which yeast fits the style you have chosen to brew. You'll be astounded at how much proper selection and attention to careful yeast management improves the quality and authenticity of your brew.

Next, you need to examine the water needs of your planned brew. For the brewer creating entirely from extract, this is of little concern as long as the water is free of contaminants and offensive tastes and odors. For the all-grain brewer or the extract brewer using large quantities of mashed or steeped grains, the profile of the brewing water (liquor) must be taken into account. First, determine the makeup of the intended water to be used, then compare and adjust as required, using the same methods as for the prior ingredients. The water section, the recipe formulation charts, and the individual recipe sections will help guide you.

The recipes are coded with a number of beer mugs beneath the name ranging from one to five. These numbers represent ascending degree of difficulty as follows:

1 *Easy.* These malt extract recipes use the most basic methods and techniques and may require either a simple addition of hops, a liquid yeast, or one or two types of specialty grains.

2 *Slightly more difficult.* These are primarily centered around the use of malt extracts but add

a few more intermediate ingredients such as grains, hops, and yeast in combination.

3 *Difficult extract-based.* This indicates a very involved recipe usually containing many specialty grains, multiple hop additions, and the use of a liquid yeast. These recipes may also require more advanced fermentation, lagering, or packaging methods. These recipes are perhaps the type used by most American homebrewers and, therefore, constitute the majority of those included in this book.

4 *All-grain.* These recipes require mashing of grain and use no malt extracts in the primary recipe, although they may be used for priming purposes.

5 *Difficult all-grain.* These are all-grain recipes of very large volume and ones that require advanced brewing methods.

Once you have studied the style to be brewed and all of your ingredients have been assembled, you are ready to put them all together. If you are brewing one of the recipes exactly or merely patterning your recipe after a particular one in this book, much if not all of that information will be provided by the original brewer. If required, additional brewing data can drawn from the basic brewing instructions of the reference section, the recipe formulation charts, and the individual style recipe sections. With all of these, you can control the proper form, temperature, and length of fermentation, lagering, and conditioning of your brew.

The World of Beer

O ne cannot speak of the history of human-
kind without discussing the history of
beer, for the two are inextricably linked. Civiliza-
tion seems to have always enjoyed fermented
grain beverages, and the love of them may actually have helped give rise to human society itself.
Some anthropologists now theorize that the
need to maintain an adequate and reliable supply of barley and wheat caused nomadic,
hunter-gatherer tribes of the Fertile Crescent to
settle into villages, domesticate livestock, and
take up agriculture. All, perhaps, for the sake of
a steady supply of beer. It seems ironic that we
should now at the end of the twentieth century
be forced to reeducate ourselves about this earliest of human inventions, which, in fact, facilitated our society's development.

A BRIEF HISTORY

To pinpoint the brewing of the first beer would
be nearly impossible, since the paper trail is
written on cuneiform tablets and papyrus scrolls
and stretches beyond the reach of recorded history. What is known for certain is that from
beer's first mention in history it was held in high
esteem, reserved for kings, priestesses, and
pharaohs. As a magical beverage that facilitated
religious ecstasy and an entry into a state of
euphoria, the production and consumption of
beer was afforded ceremonial status.

The most likely scenario for the invention,
or rather the discovery, of beer was a fortunate
accident, whereby wild barley or wheat in some
stage of germination became immersed in

water and began to ferment with the action of
wild, airborne yeasts. The resulting liquid was
imbibed by some brave soul who soon realized
that not only was this sweet beverage tasty and
satisfying as a food source but it also produced
a gentle sense of exhilaration. This event must
have occurred many millennia ago because six
thousand years ago Babylonians had already
developed sophisticated brewing processes and
had integrated beer into their religious cere-
monies. Two thousand years later their society
boasted more than a dozen styles of beer
brewed from a variety of ingredients. In all the
great civilizations throughout the world, beer
has ancient roots; from India to Peru and Per-
sia some form of fermented grain beverage was
an important part of everyday life. One might
dismiss the quality of these ancient drinks in
the light of modern mass marketing and health
standards, but it seems unlikely that societies
that built pyramids and ziggurats and developed astronomy and mathematics would have
tolerated bad brew.

In Egypt, men were strictly prohibited from
brewing, selling, or serving beer, presumably as
a means of quality control, and the female
"brewsters," as they were called, held extremely
high social status. Whether this tradition was
intentionally perpetuated or not no one knows,
but women were the primary brewers of beer as
late as colonial times in America, where it was a
standard household chore as integral as baking
bread. Beer, because of its alcohol content, pH
level, and CO_2 content, is an environment
inhospitable to bacteria. In fact, no organisms

that can live in beer are harmful to humans. Because of this, beer has provided a safe source of liquids for centuries when water, especially in populated areas, was rife with contamination. It seems ironic and unfair that the average beer, which has no fat and fewer calories than an éclair, is now considered unhealthy in many parts of the "civilized" world.

The benefits reaped from the pursuit of the more perfect beer did not end in the ancient civilizations either; quite the contrary. The pH scale now indispensable to the scientific world was developed by Danish chemist S. P. L. Sørenson for more accurate control of wort production, and Louis Pasteur's pioneering work in microbiology was largely at the behest of the brewing industry in determining the role of yeast in fermentation. It is almost as if the mystical processes of beer making were nudging the human race gently into the future. This may seem an outrageous leap of logic to the uninformed, but anyone who brews or greatly appreciates this beverage will readily understand how it serves to excite and inspire the search for greater knowledge, understanding, and appreciation. Largely because the search is so richly rewarded.

The first significant shift from brewing as a household necessity to a commercial enterprise began with the rise of the merchant class and the steady decline of the feudal societies of medieval Europe. As the monastic communities led Europe out of the Dark Ages that followed the fall of the Roman Empire, they developed not only sophisticated agricultural, educational, and religious systems but advanced brewing techniques as well. The beers of the abbeys were originally intended to sustain the nutritional needs of the monks and the pilgrims traveling between shrines in an increas-ingly prosperous and devout Europe. The reputation of the superior quality of monastic brews soon became widespread, and rapidly developed as an important source of revenue to finance monastery upkeep. It seems equally ironic that in the twentieth century a beverage fostered and perfected by priests might now be considered sinful.

As trade routes crisscrossed Europe from Genoa to Gaul and from Hamburg to Lisbon, great fortunes were made, and with wealth came power and autonomy for the countless towns and cities along the way. As these towns developed their power and independence, they also developed trade guilds to protect the consumer and to provide sophisticated, reliable services to the townspeople that for many centuries before had been performed by individual households. Breweries for making beer, bakeries for bread, butcher shops for providing meat—all developed as more specialized trades than they had been in the past. The growing merchant class had less time for messy, daily chores, and in areas such as Germany where beer was as vital as bread in the daily diet, a rather large industry grew into place. Large, communal brewhouses sprang up, forming the basis for the industrial breweries to come.

With the coming of the Industrial Revolution many centuries later came railways for transporting mass-produced beer and improved methods of malting, roasting, and milling grain, as well as steam power for mashing and boiling wort. But most importantly came refrigeration. The theories behind artificial refrigeration had been understood for some time, but it wasn't until the mid-1800s that the technology existed to put that knowledge into large-scale practice. Refrigeration quickly gave rise to industrial lager brewing and the birth of pilsner, the world's newest but most popular beer style.

Manufacturing enterprises stressed uniformity and consistency in beer making as in all their other commercial products, and the major modern styles such as pale ale, stout, and pilsner began to coalesce into the forms we know today, while the older regional styles of mild, brown, and altbier faded in popularity. The growing homogeneous nature of beer cannot be laid entirely at the doorstep of capitalistic industry, however, because two world wars, Prohibition in America, and an economic depression devastated small breweries in the industrialized world and forced larger ones to consolidate and downsize.

Perhaps equally devastating was the sanction these calamities gave in the 1940s and 1950s to the use of cheap, inferior ingredients such as corn and rice, and the additives now necessary to make these adjunct-heavy beers drinkable. A steady and rapid decline into paler, thinner, and blander lagers persisted until 1971 when in England, the only country in the world to remain primarily an ale-drinking nation after the lager revolution, consumers rebelled in the form of the grassroots group called the Campaign for Real Ale (CAMRA). CAMRA's original aim was to halt regional and national breweries from phasing out casked "real ale" naturally conditioned in the pub cellar in favor of keg beer, which is filtered, pasteurized, and forced to the tap by CO_2 pressure. CAMRA's efforts gave new life to England's heritage of living beer and soon spurred the birth of dozens of microbreweries producing rich, traditional brews. This rebellion slowly began to stem the tide of international brewing groups increasingly bent on producing pale lagers. Beer-loving traditionalists around the world began to take notice.

The birth of microbreweries in the United States was greatly influenced by the work of CAMRA and the inspired writings of Michael Jackson, but also by less dynamic factors. Many Americans had been stationed in Europe during the cold war and were introduced to quality German lagers and British ales there. A third and perhaps equally valid factor was the strength of the dollar in the early to mid-1980s that gave legions of young Americans easy access to the great brewing culture of western Europe. Many of these young people returned from Europe with an almost religious zeal and took up homebrewing as their only source of fresh, traditional beer. Paired with the growing interest in imported beers, particularly on college campuses, a new generation of sophisticated palates was awakening and it was thirsty for change.

In America, the one influence that spurred the craft-beer movement more than any single factor was homebrewing, and the two are inextricably linked. It is doubtful that any recent hobby has caused such a profound and rapid change in cultural, economic, and social forces in the way this pastime has. It schooled dozens of future microbrewers and propelled them into leadership roles of artisanal brewing. With roots in the Prohibition practices of homemade spirits, the hobby gained impetus with the legalization of homebrewing in 1979. Under the tutelage of homebrewing pioneers like Charlie Papazian, Byron Burch, and Fred Eckhardt, many of today's American microbrewers began developing the skill and artistry in their kitchens that we are enjoying the fruits of today. Who knows, perhaps you too will have planted the seeds of a new career by purchasing this book.

BEER:
THE COMPONENT PARTS

MALT

Barley is an ancient and extremely hardy cereal grass that has all but vanished from our diets except in beer. Long before advanced agricultural techniques developed, barley became a staple of the human diet because of its ability to flourish under adverse conditions, particularly in Europe. Its hardiness quickly made it a favorite of ancient societies, and there is evidence that its use as a fermentable even predates the baking of bread.

The rudimentary basics of barley's use in beer start with "malting," a process where the seeds of the harvested barley grass are soaked in water until they sprout (germinate) and begin to activate enzymes that can convert starch to sugars. Beer yeast will later eat and convert those sugars to alcohol and carbon dioxide (aka carbonic acid gas or CO_2). The barley is then gently dried—halting the conversion process—the acrospires (or sprouts) are removed, and the dried malt is then cured at least one month before use. When the malted barley is mashed, the enzymes created in the malting process go to work, converting the remaining starches in the malt and producing the sugars that the yeast will ingest.

Modern barley for homebrewing is available in two-row and six-row varieties. Six-row is preferred by large U.S. breweries because it has a higher starch-degrading enzyme content than two-row, thereby making it a better choice when using inexpensive adjuncts such as rice and corn. Two-row barley is preferred by most microbrewers, continental European, and British brewers because it yields higher extract and less husk material. Four-row barley is considered unsuitable for brewing and is grown as a decorative landscaping grass or for cattle feed.

Besides extract yield and enzyme content, the other significant aspect of malted barley to be considered is modification. *Modification* is defined as the level to which the starchy endosperm of the barley kernel is allowed to be altered, or "modified," into the growing acrospire during the germination process. Like a chicken embryo in an egg replacing the yolk, the acrospire will continue to grow into a barley plant until all the starch is consumed, unless the maltster halts the process by heating and drying the malt. By permitting higher levels of the starch to be modified during the malting process, the mashing stage that comes later is made simpler. Starch-degrading enzymes that occur naturally in malt are activated during this process, as well as yeast nutrients that will become very valuable later in the brewing process. These "highly modified malts" are valued not only for their ease of mashing but because they tend to create a clearer beer, and the abundant yeast nutrients lead to a more complete fermentation and a shorter "lag time" after the yeast is pitched. The downside is that during this growth process, the acrospire eats up more of the endosperm, and therefore, the level of sugar that you'll be able to extract into the wort is reduced.

Conversely, "undermodified malts," whose growth process is halted early in the germination stage, will give higher degrees of specific gravity per pound but require more sophisticated mashing schedules and a protein rest. These issues, however, are mostly of concern to all-grain brewers and primarily with the malt that makes up the bulk of the grain bill, or "grist" (the coarsely ground grains), not the specialty malts. Almost all American malts are highly modified, as are most English pale ale malts. Undermodification or moderate modification is becoming increasingly rare and is usually encountered in European two-row pilsner malts. If in doubt about the modification of a malt you're using, consult your supplier.

HOPS

Hops (*Humulus lupulus*) are a prolific, long-lived, climbing perennial herb whose flowers grow into cone-shaped structures (strobiles) on the female plant. These cones are composed of bracts and bracteoles—leaflike structures attached to a central axis. The bracteoles carry the lupulin glands that provide the aroma, flavor, and astringent bitterness that balances the sweetness of the malt and acts as a preservative and natural clarifier. The word *hop* comes from the Anglo-Saxon *hoppan*, which means "to climb," a reference to the dramatic climbing nature of this vine.

According to Native American and folk medicine, the hop plant is also a proven sedative, tonic, diuretic, painkiller, hypnotic, blood purifier, intestinal cleanser, sedative, and fever reducer, as well as a treatment for jaundice, skin disease, venereal disease, tuberculosis, sleeplessness, nervous tension, anxiety, worms, dandruff, and bladder problems. Hops were used in continental Europe for beer making at least as early as the eighth century, but not in Britain until they were introduced in the 1500s by Flemish immigrants. Fierce resistance to the use of this flavoring and preservative agent in ale persisted for more than two hundred years in England before the use of herbs such as bog myrtle, horehound, ground ivy (alehoof), and buckbean finally diminished.

The bitterness of hops comes primarily from the alpha acids contained in the resins of the lupulin glands located at the base of the strobiles of the hop flowers. The alpha acids also provide the preservatives that retard spoilage. When boiled, the alpha acids are converted (isomerized) into isoalpha acids, which are then water soluble. Hops also contain other acids known as beta acids, but these provide only negligible bitterness. The flavor and aroma come from the essential oils and are not measured by the alpha acid percent (AA%) figure listed by the hop merchant. Alpha acid percent is only a measure of the percentage of the flower's weight that is composed of the alpha acid resin, a measure of bittering potential and preservative power.

Hops for homebrewing come primarily in these forms: loose whole flowers, whole compressed flower plugs, pelletized powder, and extracts. The form you choose will be determined by your own need to balance availability, convenience, expense, and freshness. It is important to note that there are no "fresh" hops in the same sense as you would purchase vegetables from the grocery store. All hops are dried before they are packaged to prevent spoilage. However, whole flower hops are generally freshest if purchased when they are less than a year old, but hops that are kept cold, airtight, and dark can retain their bittering, flavoring, and aromatic qualities for well over a year. Try to buy plugs or pellets that are sealed in oxygen-proof or nitrogen-purged bags, and if possible, check the crop year and packaging date, as hops degrade over time, especially if left unrefrigerated.

For brewing purposes, hops are classified primarily as "bittering/kettle" or "finishing/aroma." Hops with high alpha acid percentages are generally used for bittering, and hops with lower alpha acid percentages are usually considered the best for aroma and flavor (collectively referred to as "finishing"). This is a very oversimplified categorization, as most hops can serve both purposes if the correct quantities are used or they are properly blended with other varieties. See "Tips for Better Homebrewing—Hops" on page 10 and the formulas for calculating hop utilization on page 353.

Whole flowers are often considered the freshest. They are packaged in large, tight bales, which the hop merchant then splits up and sells to homebrew shops or breweries in various quantities. These flowers are often repackaged in bags that are not oxygen-proof and, because of their bulkiness, are not refrigerated. As a result, they are more subject to the detrimental effects of heat and oxidation than are gas-purged pellets and plugs. They also require longer boils to fully utilize their bittering qualities—for example, ninety minutes to achieve full utilization. However, they are ideal as flavoring and/or aroma hops and provide a good filter bed when straining wort into the primary fermenter. These whole hops are often called "fresh," "loose," or "leaf," because the petals (bracts and bracteoles) of the hop flower resemble small green leaves. "Leaf" is a misnomer because the actual leaves of the hop plant are not used in brewing. Although it may be impossible to know what condition hops will be in when mail-ordering, try to buy whole hops that are green or pale greenish gold if you have the chance to examine them before purchase. Hops that are brown are old and no good for most brewing purposes and should be avoided. (Note: Belgian brewers often use "stale" hops in order derive the preservative qualities without adding significant hop bitterness, aroma, or flavor.) However, almost every bag of whole hops will have a few brown petals; this is normal and should not cause concern—just remove them before use. Few shops will risk their reputation by selling stale hops; nevertheless, try to buy whole flowers that are sealed in oxygen-barrier bags. Note that there are now machines on the market for home vacuum-sealing.

Plugs (aka type 100 pellets) are whole hop flowers compressed into half-ounce round disks, then sealed in nitrogen-purged aluminum or Mylar bags. When added to the boil, these expand to resemble whole flowers. Although some of the delicate aroma may be lost in the compression process, this form of hops is a good middle ground between the freshness of whole flowers and the convenience of pellets. If you are able to examine them before buying, look for "CO_2-purged, oxygen-barrier packaging" and similar terms. As with all hops, keep them refrigerated.

Pellets (type 45 and type 90) are hops that are ground very fine into powder, then formed into pellets under intense pressure. This process greatly increases the shelf life of the hops and helps to increase the utilization of bittering acids by crushing the tiny lupulin glands. However, some argue that this destroys the more delicate oils and resins responsible for aroma and flavor, but this has not been proven. Despite this controversy, pellets are in wide use in the microbrewing industry for all purposes. Pellets also have the added bonus that practically all varieties are available in this form. Type 90 pellets are the form most commonly used in homebrewing. Type 45 pellets are enriched with additional lupulin for increased bittering capabilities.

Hop oils are created by a variety of distillation processes and are used for adding aroma to fermented beer just before packaging. Hop extracts are hop products derived from whole hops by cooking or with chemical or liquid CO_2 solvents. These products have the advantage of long life, accurate measurement, and consistent quality. They usually contain only the vital alpha acids necessary for bittering and less flavor or aroma compounds. In isomerized extracts, the isomerization that normally occurs during boiling is already completed, thereby allowing more complete and accurate utilization in achieving desired bitterness after fermentation is complete. Nonisomerized extracts must be added to the brew kettle for boiling.

The two most popular ways of achieving proper hopping rates in homebrewing are by calculating homebrew bittering units (HBUs), a measure of hop quantity in ounces multiplied by alpha acid percentage; and international bittering units (IBUs), a measure of actual bitterness utilized during brewing. These two methods work well together in allowing the brewer to achieve not only the appropriate level of bitterness but also to estimate the quantity of hops needed in designing and planning a recipe. For more information on HBUs, IBUs, and their applications, see page 353. It is important to reiterate that hops are primarily meant to balance the sweetness of the malt. Therefore, try to keep in mind how attenuative your yeast is and where your original gravity (OG) is on the scale of a particular style. In other words, if you shoot for the upper end of a particular style's OG but the lower end of the style's IBUs,

and vice versa, you probably won't achieve proper bitterness and balance.

YEAST

Beer yeasts (primarily *Saccharomyces cerevisiae* and *Saccharomyces uvarum*) are simple, single-celled microscopic fungi that transform malt sugar into alcohol, carbon dioxide (CO_2), and other by-products that give beers their varied flavors. For centuries, the importance of yeast in brewing was not fully understood. In fact, the original "Reinheitsgebot" Bavarian Beer Purity Law did not even recognize yeast as one of the primary ingredients, and monks, who knew only that a potful of this stuff pitched into fresh wort made a great beer, euphemistically referred to it as "God is good." Now we know that yeast is the most important factor in determining a beer's flavor. Although it is probably the least glamorous ingredient in beer, yeast is quickly becoming the homebrewer's greatest concern, especially for those interested in accurately brewing a classic style, where proper yeast selection is imperative.

The primary differences between the two main beer yeasts are: (1) *Saccharomyces cerevisiae,* or "ale yeast," prefers warmer temperatures and tends to settle in clumps (flocculate) on top of the beer during fermentation; and (2) *Saccharomyces uvarum,* or "lager yeast," prefers cooler temperatures and flocculates to the bottom of the vessel during fermentation. Neither really ferments only at the top or bottom, but throughout the beer. Each yeast species has a variety of unique strains that give each beer style its characteristic flavor, body, and aroma.

In the past, controlling flavor was hindered by the scarcity of pure liquid yeast cultures, a situation that has rapidly changed. Dry yeasts have a somewhat bad reputation because many dry yeasts included with English malt extract kits were mixed with cheap baker's yeast and/or were contaminated with wild or mutant yeasts, not to mention the fact that they were often very old. Most of these problems have been eliminated because homebrewers are becoming more sophisticated and are demanding higher quality. Seven to fourteen grams are recommended for five U.S. gallon recipes, and rehydration with warm (90–110°F) water is now universally advised. Although liquid yeasts are currently very popular with serious homebrewers, to their credit, dry yeasts are drastically cheaper and tend to be longer lived. For these reasons, several microbreweries now use dry yeasts with excellent results. However, this applies only to quality name-brand yeasts; generic ones included in malt extract kits (for example, marked "beer yeast") still should be avoided. Some popular dry yeast brands available to homebrewers include Nottingham, Windsor, Munton & Fison, Red Star, Amsterdam (aka European), Whitbread, and Coopers.

WATER

The main reason that the properties of brewing water (called "liquor") are considered at all by brewers is because of the effect its various ions have on the vital starch-degrading enzymes in malt. The levels of the six main ions directly affect the water's pH, which in turn determines the effectiveness of the enzymes to do their job of making maltose. Therefore, achieving the correct balance among these ions will greatly influence the extract yield of the malt. In malt extract–based brewing, the concerns of water used in mashing and brewing down the wort into syrup or powder are taken care of by the manufacturer. However, if you are adding your own malts, specialty grains, or hops, the water you use *is* of importance.

The second major consideration of water is perhaps the most obvious—flavor. As long as your water is free of organic or man-made contaminants, its flavor will in large part be influenced by the same six ions that influence enzyme activity. If you've been plagued by unsatisfactory "house flavors," these may relate to an imbalance in the ions of the water you are using.

The third consideration of a particular water's makeup is its ability to provide necessary nutrients to the yeast that will ferment the wort. This is definitely the least of a homebrewer's concern, as yeast requires only trace amounts of these ions, which are generally present in more than sufficient quantities in well-modified malts and in all water sources except, of course, distilled water.

BASIC
BREWING
PROCEDURES

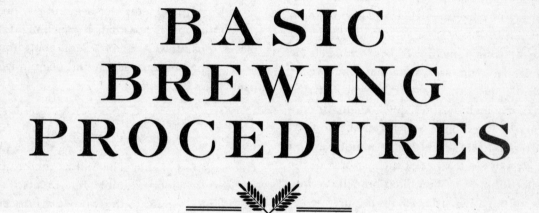

AN INTRODUCTION TO BREWING

Your First Batch

As we discussed earlier, brewing from malt extract, especially malt extract syrup in a can, is how most of us began as homebrewers because it is the simplest, fastest, and most reliable way to make great beer. Using a simple malt extract–based recipe you will learn to make a terrific homebrewed beer with a classic American microbrewery taste that will be ready to drink in just three weeks. After you've tasted your first homebrew you'll quickly gain the confidence to brew again and no doubt be fired with a zeal to brew and learn as much as you can. Brew a few batches of this or some of the simpler recipes to follow, then branch out into some of the other styles. You'll be surprised at how fun this turns out to be and perhaps a little nervous about how enthusiastic you get about your new hobby. Don't be alarmed, you're just feeling the excitement that has captivated brewers for at least ten thousand years

EQUIPMENT YOU WILL NEED

Below are the essential pieces of equipment needed for homebrewing. Most of these common items you already have around your kitchen and can be employed in your brewery. However, it is a good practice to either buy new equipment or to relegate utensils you have to the exclusive use of your brewery. Keeping the things you use in brewing away from everyday kitchen duty will help keep them clean, grease-free, easily sanitized, and in good shape for years to come. Items specifically intended for

brewing such as a bottling bucket or a hydrometer should be purchased from a homebrew supply store. There are over one thousand of these stores in the United States, and they can provide complete setups for beginning brewers, usually for much less than if you bought the pieces separately. A list of several good homebrew supply shops can be found beginning on page 357.

BREWING EQUIPMENT YOU WILL NEED

One large brew kettle. This will be used to boil the wort (it's not beer until it is fermented) and should be a twenty- to thirty-two-quart stockpot made of stainless steel or enamel. This needs to be physically clean but does not need to be sanitized, since you will be boiling in it for an hour.

Two hop bags. These will hold your two portions of hops in the boiling. They can be nylon or muslin bags purchased from a homebrew supply shop or simply pieces of cheesecloth tied around the hops with a piece of twine.

Sanitizing solution. In a new plastic bucket, prepare several gallons of sanitizing solution according to the instructions for the product you have chosen, or simply mix five teaspoons of bleach and five gallons of cold water in your primary fermenter. It is helpful to reserve a few pints of this solution in a measuring cup or glass jar in case you need to resanitize equipment sometime during the brewing process.

One primary fermenter with lid. Homebrewers have used everything from stockpots to plastic garbage pails to ferment their beer over the years, but I would recommend purchasing a new, 6.5–7.5-gallon "food-grade" plastic fermenter or a 6-gallon glass carboy. Although food-grade plastic, unlike glass, is porous enough to allow air to enter the beer over an extended time, it is significantly cheaper and can confidently be used for the short period needed for a primary ferment. If you do use a carboy, make sure there is plenty of "head space," the open area above the beer, to allow for the foaming that occurs during fermentation.

Airlock. These come in a variety of designs, but all are basically one-way valves created when you add a little water. Airlocks allow the escape of CO_2 from the fermenter but don't allow airborne beer-spoiling microorganisms to enter from the outside.

Floating thermometer. You will use this to read the temperature of your wort when you take your specific gravity readings. This can be any type of immersible thermometer for kitchen use such as a candy thermometer but should be able to read temperatures between 60° and 212°F.

Hydrometer. These are often called "triple-scale" hydrometers because they have three different scales of measurement on them. One is to measure liquid density with the specific gravity scale; one is to measure the percentage of sugar in the solution with the Balling scale; and the third is calibrated to measure the potential alcohol that will exist in your beer. The hydrometer is one item that you will probably not have lying around the house and will need to purchase from a homebrew supply shop. Your hydrometer is most likely set to measure accurately at 60°F. By measuring the wort temperature with your floating thermometer and adjusting for temperature variances from 60° using the chart on page

354, you will be able to measure the original gravity and eventually how strong your beer will be.

Two long-handled spoons. A long wooden spoon is ideal for stirring your boiling wort; a long plastic or stainless-steel spoon that can be easily sanitized is ideal for stirring in your yeast and aerating the wort after it is cooled.

Two measuring cups. These are always handy to have around to hold spoons, thermometers, and various brewing gadgets. One will be used later to draw a sample of your wort for testing.

One egg timer. This will be used to time your boil and the addition of your hops.

BOTTLING EQUIPMENT YOU WILL NEED

One bottling bucket with tap installed. This bucket will be used to hold your fermented beer while it is being siphoned into your bottles. By having a bottling bucket, you avoid the risk of transferring any of the thick residue at the bottom of the fermenter into your bottles. For the beginner, this is another piece of equipment that is best bought from a homebrew supply store with a tap already installed. You can transfer your beer from the fermenter to any sanitized five-gallon vessel, but the addition of the tap keeps you from having to siphon again when you fill the bottles. Once you start brewing you'll quickly learn the value of this.

One long-handled spoon. This will be used to stir in the corn sugar priming solution that will condition your beer and give it carbonation. This should ideally be plastic or stainless steel. Wooden spoons are porous and therefore nearly impossible to sanitize, making them a prime breeding ground for bacteria.

Sanitizing solution. This is the same as used above in the fermenting process. This will be used to sanitize your bottling bucket, bottles, caps, racking cane, siphon hoses, bottle filler, and anything that touches the beer.

One saucepan. Use this to boil your three-fourths of a cup of corn sugar and two cups of water for five minutes to make a priming solution.

Siphon hose. This should be clear plastic food-grade hose obtainable from any home-brew supply shop. The three-eighths-inch inside diameter hose fits most bottle fillers and racking tubes.

Racking stem and tip. Although not absolutely necessary for siphoning beer from one container to another, these great little gadgets help hold your siphon tube steady and keep you from drawing sediment from the bottom of your fermenter. The small plastic tip is place on the end of the racking cane, holding it off of the sediment and preventing the cane from getting clogged with debris. Remove the tip and replace with the bottle filler described below when you are ready to bottle.

Bottle filler. This little gadget slides onto the end of your racking cane when you are siphoning from your bottling bucket into your bottles. A spring-loaded device, the bottle filler releases beer from the hose when you press down against the bottom of the bottle and stops the flow when you lift it up. It cuts down on the amount of beer wasted and gives you control over the flow without having to manually pinch the siphon hose.

Forty sixteen-ounce _or_ fifty-three twelve-ounce bottles. These should be returnable brown glass beer bottles or Grolsch-type swing-top bottles. Do not use returnable screw-top (twist off) bottles. Screw-top returnable bottles cannot be capped properly with the standard homebrew capping device and are usually not strong enough to withstand homebrew CO_2 pressure and will explode. A five-gallon batch of beer typically results in three or four bottles less than the amount I have suggested due to losses from spillage or beer trapped in the sediment, but it is better to have more than you need than not enough. Don't be greedy, though; leave that last little bit if it is full of sediment. The bottles with all the bitter sludge may end up being the ones you accidentally send to a competition!

Bottle caps (or Grolsch gaskets if using swing-top bottles). These should be unused, plastic-lined crown caps sold at any homebrew store. They should be sanitized and rinsed with boiled water or air-dried just prior to use. I do not recommend boiling these to sanitize them, as it may weaken the seal. Consider purchasing oxygen-absorbing caps. They cost a little more but will deter air in the bottle from deteriorating your hop aroma.

Bottle capper. This device will be used to crimp the edges of the bottle caps around the mouth of your bottles. There are a variety of these available in different styles and price ranges. My stock advice, as with all homebrewing gear, is to buy the best you can afford, but even the cheapest versions work perfectly well.

INGREDIENTS YOU WILL NEED

Below are the ingredients you will need to brew your inaugural batch of craft beer. These are all simple, inexpensive, and easily obtainable ingredients that have proven themselves through years of homebrewing.

Two 3.3-pound cans of amber malt extract syrup (hopped) or 5.5 pounds of amber dried

malt extract (hopped). You can use any brand of extract you choose and there are dozens to choose from. I would recommend as simple a malt extract as possible, not one designed for a particular style of beer such as wheat, brown, or pilsner. Make sure it is "hopped," that is, with bittering hops already added. You will add the flavor and aroma, or "finishing," hops. If someone gave you cans of unhopped malt extract as a gift or you cannot find hopped kits at your local homebrew store, simply add one and one-half ounces of Cascade hop pellets at the beginning of the boil.

One pack of Wyeast 1056 American ale yeast or two packs of dried ale yeast. As noted earlier, I recommend that novices begin by using liquid yeast "slap packs" because they are almost as easy to use as simply opening dry yeast packets and usually produce better and more consistent results. Don't use the liquid yeast that requires a "starter." That is a more advanced technique that you'll learn later. The most popular yeast brand for homebrewers is sold by Wyeast in a self-containing foil pouch that only requires a few simple steps a few days before brewing to prepare your yeast.

Two ounces of Cascade hop pellets. A favorite of homebrewers and microbrewers alike, these hops will give your brew that classic American microbrewery flavor and aroma. Because you are using pellet form, you won't have to worry about straining out bulky hop whole hops. That will come later.

Six gallons of cold, pure water. You will be making five gallons of beer, but remember that some of it will be lost as steam during the wort boiling stage. Since you will only be boiling two or three gallons in an extract brew, the rest will go directly into your fermenter and therefore needs to be clean and sanitary. I like to use bottled spring water for this because the water will most likely be germ- and chlorine-free. However, if you feel good about your water and it lacks strong chemical odors, go ahead and use it. Water concerns are something you'll encounter as a more advanced brewer.

Three-quarters cup corn sugar for priming. Corn sugar has proven itself over the years as the most reliable and efficient priming ingredient for brewers. It works fast and leaves no detrimental flavors or effects on the beer in small quantities. It is also very easy to measure out. I recommend making a solution by dissolving it in two cups of water so that it can be evenly distributed throughout the beer in your bottling bucket. Make it sanitary by boiling your solution for five minutes before stirring it gently into your finished beer.

INSTRUCTION FOR BREWING YOUR FIRST BEER

The aim of the brewer is to sanitize rather than sterilize. By "sanitize" I mean to thoroughly clean and to destroy the vast majority of microorganisms that can infect beer. It will be unnecessary and nearly impossible to completely sterilize, that is, kill all unwanted organisms, in your homebrewery. You just need to neutralize most of the beer-spoiling bugs on anything that comes into contact with your beer. Once fermentation is under way, the likelihood of infection begins to decrease as the beer yeast takes hold and gobbles up the available nutrients. Begin by cleaning and sanitizing all of the brewing equipment in either a commercial sanitizing agent or a dilute solution of one ounce of chlorine bleach per gallon of cold water. You can also use one of the more environmentally friendly sanitizers available from homebrew supply shops such as One-Step. Keep some sanitizing solution handy to resanitize equipment throughout the brewing process if necessary. Sanitation is one of the most important concerns of the brewer, and it is imperative that careful sanitation is practiced throughout the brewing process.

Before sanitizing, visually inspect your equipment for cleanliness. If it is very dirty, wash with hot soapy water and rinse repeatedly to remove soap residue. Otherwise, I like to prewash my equipment with a B-Brite solution and a hot water rinse before sanitizing. Depending on the type of sanitizing method you choose, mix the appropriate proportions in your fermenting vessel or a separate plastic bucket. It is sometimes a good idea to have a separate "catch-all" bowl or measuring cup sanitized to use as a place to hold small brewing equipment once it has been sanitized. To sanitize simply soak the equipment in the solution or scrub down well with a new sponge or rag and let them sit for twenty to thirty minutes. If your sanitizer requires rinsing—for example, if you've used One-Step or chlorine solution—rinse with boiling water and allow to drip dry. Once a piece of equipment is clean and sanitary, keep it from coming in contact with anything that is not. You may find that it is best to do all of your sanitizing and cleaning operations in a small and enclosed space such as a bathroom. This allows you to scrub down and sanitize all of the surfaces that will come in contact with your brewing gear. One word of caution, though; overuse of disinfectants such as Lysol or Pine Sol in the presence of your fermenter can leave

a detectable chlorophenol taste in your beer. I give the bathroom a good cleaning, then rinse it down with B-Brite or an iodine-based sanitizer. When all of your equipment is cleaned and sanitized, rinse it well and put the equipment not to be used in the boiling stage inside the fermenter and cover with the lid. If possible keep this equipment in a clean and sanitary place such as a bathroom until it is ready to be used.

Immerse the cans of malt extract syrup in a sink filled with hot water for one-half hour. This will make the heavy, rich liquid more fluid and easier to pour into your brew kettle. If you are using dried malt extract in powder form, this step can be eliminated. During the thirty minutes you are soaking your malt cans, fill your brewing kettle with three gallons of good-quality brewing water (called "liquor"). Bring this water to a rolling boil. Water having a strong chlorine aroma or taste should be boiled vigorously for ten minutes before continuing on to the next stage.

When your water reaches a boil, remove it from the heat, open the cans of malt extract, and stir the syrup into the water. When it is thoroughly dissolved in the water, return it to the heat (uncovered) and resume a hard, rolling boil. Watch the kettle carefully from now on, as it is likely to foam up and boil over when the "wort," as it is now called, reaches a boil. To control a boilover, simply shut off the heat, move the kettle off of the burner, or stir in a pint of cold tap water. Boil vigorously for one hour, keeping a close watch on your kettle all the while. Add one-half of the Cascade hops tied in one of the muslin bags after forty minutes; these will produce hop flavor. Add the other half tied in the second muslin bag after fifty-eight minutes; these will produce hop aroma. When the sixty minutes are up, shut off the heat, cover your brew kettle with a tight-fitting lid, and set it in a sink filled with cold water and ice cubes. Set the egg timer for thirty minutes. Change the water halfway through if it feels warm.

While you are cooling your wort, remove the sanitizing solution from your fermenter, give it a good rinse, and fill it with the remaining three gallons of cold water. A large, heavy, and sanitized measuring cup is a good place to hold all the brewing gadgets you will need. When the wort has finished cooling, remove the hop bags and pour the wort into the fermenter. The cold water in the fermenter will help lower the wort temperature even further. Mix the wort gently with a sanitized spoon and check the temperature with your thermometer. Remember to keep your hands and other unsanitary things out of the wort. Use the second measuring cup to draw a few ounces of wort out of the fermenter. Pour the sample into your hydrometer tube or test jar and make a note of the reading. If the temperature of the wort is above or below the hydrometer's desired reading temperature of 60°F, be sure to adjust your reading using the chart on page 354. Your "original gravity," as this first reading is called, should be approximately 1.046. If it is off a few points, don't worry; variances in malt extracts can be expected. It is a good idea to keep good notes of your brews, in your own notebook, or on the chart on pages 41–42. Good notes can help you repeat past successes and correct past mistakes.

When the wort is below 75°F, it is safe to add your yeast. If you are using the liquid yeast, be sure to prepare it one to two days in advance per the package instructions. Carefully cut off one corner of the package with sanitized scissors and pour gently into your beer. Now stir vigorously with one of your sanitized spoons. If you are using the dried yeast, simply sprinkle it evenly onto the wort, wait ten minutes for it to rehydrate into a thick pasty sludge, then stir it in vigorously with a sanitized spoon. It is important to get plenty of air into the cooled wort for the yeast to properly ferment the beer.

Cover the fermenter as quickly as possible and fit with the airlock. Add about an ounce of water to your airlock and attach the cap. The beer can now be moved to a dark, quiet, room-temperature place to ferment for the next five to seven days. Active fermentation should be evident in one to two days. After five days check the airlock. If bubbles are still rising through the airlock, wait a few more days and recheck before transferring the beer to your bottling bucket. (All bottles and bottling equipment should be sanitized just like the brewing equipment.) Boil the three-quarters cup of corn sugar in a pint of water for five minutes, then pour into the bottling bucket. (Make sure the tap is closed.)

Place the fermenter in a position several inches above the bottling bucket to facilitate siphoning. Remove the lid, check the gravity and the temperature, and make a note of the figure. Don't forget to adjust your reading for temperature variances from 60°F. Your hydrometer should read approximately 1.012. If your specific gravity reading is above 1.014, let the beer ferment for two more days, then recheck. If your reading is below 1.012, that is fine. This is your "final gravity" reading. You are ready to bottle.

As mentioned earlier you will need approximately forty sixteen-ounce bottles or fifty-three twelve-ounce bottles and new crown caps to match. These bottles should be washed, rinsed, and sanitized prior to bottling and should not be the screw-top kind, but the variety that requires an opener. Generally, the bottles should be filled with the sanitizer and allowed to soak for the amount of time specified for the particular product you are using. These tend to vary quite a bit and range from one minute for an iodine solution to half an hour for some of the chlorine-based products. If you are using an iodine-based solution, rinsing is not necessary, but the bottles, bottling bucket, caps, and equipment should be allowed to air-dry before being used. If you are using a chlorine-based sanitizing solution, all bottles and equipment that will come into direct contact with your beer should be rinsed two or three times with hot water before filling. They do not need to dry before use, but your rinse water should be sanitary; otherwise you may contaminate your beer with microorganisms residing in your water. It is often advised that rinse water be boiled for three minutes prior to use. Bottles can also be sanitized by cleaning them first, then running them through the heated drying cycle of your dishwasher. Do not use the air-dry cycle, do not put your bottles in along with dirty dishes, detergent, or rinsing agents, and be sure your dishwasher has no food residue in its filters. Once your bottles and caps are clean, sanitized, and rinsed, you are ready to fill.

Attach the stem tip to the stem and the racking stem to the siphon hose, fill with water, hold your thumbs over the ends, and insert the stem end into the fermenter. Insert the other end into the bottling bucket and release your thumbs. The siphon should begin automatically. Being careful not to disturb the yeast sediment on the bottom of the fermenter, siphon the beer very gently until only about half an inch remains. Remove the siphon hose, rinse it well, and remove the stem tip. Replace the tip with the bottle filler and attach the other end to the tap on your bottling bucket. Gently stir the beer to mix the priming sugar evenly, then begin filling your bottles by inserting the stem down to the bottom of the bottles and exerting gentle pressure. Fill each bottle to within one inch of the top, cap, rinse off any spills, and move them to a room-temperature spot (65–70°F) for one week to condition.

After the first week, chill one of the bottles in the refrigerator. Sample by pouring slowly at eye level, keeping the yeast sediment on the bottom of the bottle but not so slowly as to keep a nice one-inch head of foam from forming. Having at least a little head is important in releasing the beer's aroma. Don't worry, if you don't get it right the first time, you'll get lots of practice. As the bottle empties you will notice a thin stream of yeast move toward the mouth of the bottle. At this point, quickly draw the bottle upright, leaving the dregs behind. Inclusion of this yeast sediment is inappropriate for most beers, except for some notable exceptions such as Bavarian weissbier. If you accidentally allow some of this yeast sediment into your beer, the worst it will do is make the beer slightly cloudy and perhaps a little bitter in large amounts, but it won't hurt you and is actually rich in B vitamins. Evaluate the carbonation level, taste, aroma, and overall quality of the beer, and continue to test the beer over the next two weeks. Notice how it matures with age. The tastes become more organized and mellow. You'll sense complexity and depth never dreamed of in a mass-market lager. Congratulations are now in order on successfully brewing your first beer. Welcome to the wonderful world of brewing!

BASIC TIPS FOR BETTER HOMEBREWING

ALCOHOL LEVEL AND BEER BODY

- You may notice that the liquid malt extract instructions (hopped or unhopped) call for the use of corn or cane sugar in large quantities. I strongly urge that you ignore this and use only pure (dried or liquid) barley malt extract, except for purposes of carbonating, where it is appropriate to the style (for example, high-alcohol Belgian ales), or where it is to be used in small amounts to lighten body.

BOILING

- Except where noted, it is advised that the wort be boiled for at least one hour in all of the recipes, regardless of the malt extract manufacturer's instructions.
- Remove the brew kettle from the heat source prior to adding malts to avoid burning or sticking of ingredients, which may impart a burnt flavor and darker color to your beer.
- Stir in extracts before applying heat to kettle water. This will keep the wort color lighter. Another way is to place a diffuser under the kettle to distribute heat evenly.

BEER CLARITY

- A very effective method for achieving brilliantly clear beer is the addition of fining agents. One of the best (besides using high-quality malts and proper sanitation) is *Irish moss,* which should be added for ten to twenty minutes at the end of your boil. Another very good product, especially for light lagers, is *Polyclar,* which can be stirred into your secondary two to five days prior to bottling or kegging. *Gelatin* and *isinglass* are two other popular and effective means of achieving clarity without the expense of filtration.

WATER

- Most tap water in the United States is suitable for homebrewing, whether on a city water line or taken from a private well. The common wisdom is, "If it tastes good, it's OK." However, municipal/public water that has a strong chlorine taste or smell should be corrected by a vigorous boil before adding specialty grains or extract. Just make sure the water is cooled again to the proper temperature for grain treatment (150–170°F). (Remember that carbonate hardness will be removed after ten minutes of boiling, then decanting the water off the precipitated sediment.)
- Your city water board can provide you with a detailed analysis of your water, usually for free. If you live in a rural area with a private well, the health department in your county can do a water sample, but this will almost always require a fee.
- Another easy, though slightly costlier, solution to water worries is to use *bottled water.* Bottled water is freer of contamination and can be chilled in bulk if you have the refrig-

erator space, and you also have the freedom to purchase the water that tastes best to you. Nevertheless, always sterilize water used in yeast starters or for priming.

- The two most popular forms of bottled water for brewing are *spring water* and *distilled water*. Unless you insist on only the best from the French Alps, spring water can be had for fifty cents to one dollar per gallon.

- Spring water is usually soft to medium soft and small additions of water salts or gypsum can be made without great concern. (A sampling of spring water parameters is listed on page 89.)

- Distilled water is created by boiling water to steam; the steam condenses in a still, then is collected again as a liquid, leaving the precipitated water salts behind. Distilled water is the softest water available and therefore makes a good starting point for creating the exact water profile you desire for a particular beer style. Distilled water costs approximately a dollar per gallon.

- Mineral water will usually be prohibitively expensive and should be avoided unless you know its ion content.

HOPS

- Regardless of the form in which you purchase hops, always keep them in the refrigerator or freezer (for long-term storage) until you are ready to use them.

- Always tightly rewrap and refrigerate opened packages of hops. Aluminum foil and plastic bags used together will offer some protection against oxidation and freezer burn.

- To be sure of maximum freshness, many experts advise against purchasing *whole* hops later than eight months after the most recent harvest, particularly since most whole hops are not packaged in oxygen-barrier gas-purged bags. In most hop-rowing regions, this would be eight months after late August/early September, that is, around April 30. Properly stored hops in *unopened* gas-purged oxygen-barrier bags will stay fresh for well over a year.

- Bittering hops should be added ninety to sixty minutes before the end of the boil when using plugs or whole hops; sixty to forty-five minutes before the end of the boil when using pellets.

YEAST

- Use liquid yeast or quality name-brand dry yeast whenever possible. The dry yeasts included with cans of malt extract may be old or damaged by exposure to temperature extremes, and even when fresh, they rarely compare with the consistent quality and variety of liquid cultures. Besides, the vast majority of award-winning brews are made with liquid yeast. Name-brand dry yeasts will give satisfactory results, but should be rehydrated.

YEAST REHYDRATION

- Yeast Lab suggests this method for rehydrating yeast. (1) Dissolve the dry yeast in a half cup of warm water (105°F/40°C) without stirring. (2) After fifteen minutes, mix well to suspend all the yeast before adding to the wort. (3) Do not keep the yeast in the water longer than recommended.

YEAST QUANTITY

- The homebrewer should consider using two packs of liquid yeast (100 ml) or seven to fourteen grams of rehydrated dry yeast when brewing higher-gravity beers (that is, seven pounds or more total malt extract). A better alternative is to prepare a yeast starter of one to two liters.

PREPARING A YEAST STARTER

- Fill a one quart jar ¾ full with water. Mix in 5 tablespoons of dry malt extract. Place a lid loosely on the jar, then put the jar into a large stockpot. Add three inches of water to the pot and cover. Bring to a boil, then reduce heat and simmer covered for 30 minutes. Remove from heat. Tighten the jar lid and cool to room temperature. Shake the jar to aerate the wort, then add your yeast and shake again. Loosen the lid slightly and put in a warm place. When a head of yeast develops in the wort, it is ready to pitch into your beer or add to a larger amount of sterile wort.

COOLING

- An easy way to quickly cool your wort to yeast-pitching temperatures if you don't have a wort chiller is to put two and a half to three gallons of commercially bottled spring water in the refrigerator at its lowest setting overnight, then pour into the fermenter just prior to adding wort.
- Another way to cool down your wort before adding it to the fermenting vessel is to let the brew kettle sit *covered* in a sink or tub of ice-cold water for up to thirty minutes.
- REMEMBER! A basic scientific principal states: Liquids cool faster in ice-cold water than in ice (or snow) because more surface area is covered, resulting in faster, more efficient heat transfer.

FLAVOR

- Ideally, specialty grains should be mashed or steeped at 150–170°F in a separate pot when extract brewing, and only the wort derived from them should be added to your brewpot and boiled. Boiling draws out tannins from grain husks, which may impart harsh flavors to your brew.
- Avoid violent stirring of wort or mashed grains. Also avoid violent "casting out" of *hot* wort into your fermenter. Oxidation of malt components results in sherrylike or wet cardboard aromas in the finished beer.

FERMENTATION

- Keep fermentation temperatures steady. Fluctuations of only 5°F can cause off-flavors and premature yeast settling, which will curtail fermentation; and always keep fermenting beer in the dark.
- Whenever possible use a secondary fermenter. Even when crafting the fastest turnaround British ales, a day or two in a secondary can greatly improve a beer's maturation time and smoothness of character. In lager brewing, a secondary is mandatory in achieving clarity and clean flavor profiles without the use of artificial aids.

BOTTLING

- Brown versus green bottles: Although it's hard to beat the convenience and beauty of those Grolsch bottles, serious homebrewers should consider weaning themselves off of green bottles. Green glass does not filter out the harmful high-energy (ultraviolet) rays that exist in sunlight and fluorescent light. This leads to a chemical reaction with the hops resulting in a skunky taste and aroma—sometimes after only a few minutes of exposure. If at all possible, use brown bottles, but try to keep all beer away from direct light until it is served, and if you must hold it up to a light to check the clarity and so forth, use incandescent light.

- Since most homebrew competitions will not accept entries in anything except green or brown twelve-ounce bottles with no raised lettering, designs, or identifying features, make sure you always put at least half a dozen of your beers in twelve-ounce bottles just in case you come up with a real winner!

CONDITIONING, LAGERING, AND AGING

- One of the hardest parts of homebrewing is waiting for the beer to be ready to drink. Although some ales mature very quickly and can be enjoyed after one to two weeks of conditioning, you've no doubt noticed how your beer improves with age. Many lagers slowly turn more golden and less red as they age, and hop bitterness mellows as the beer evolves from week to week. Most experts agree that ales require a *minimum* of five weeks from start to finish: one week to ferment, one week to condition, and three weeks to mature. Lagers generally require a *minimum* of ten weeks: two weeks in the primary, two weeks in the secondary, two weeks to condition, and four weeks to mature. Higher-gravity beers such as bock usually require at least eight weeks of maturing; and barley wine, from six months to several years. Homebrewed lambics can require one to three years to reach maturity. Maturation time can be reduced by minimizing tannin extraction and by the use of low-alpha boiling hops instead of high-alpha varieties.

SERVING TEMPERATURE

- British ales are generally served at "cellar" temperatures (that is, 50–57°F). Quality lagers, wheat beers, and most other ales should be served in the 45–50°F range. Ice-cold beer deadens the taste buds and detracts from the flavor. The internationally accepted definition of "room temperature" is 68°F/20°C. Dry stout is served at this temperature, but usually only in Ireland. Generally, it is served at cellar temperatures or colder.

PARTIAL MASH AND ADVANCED BREWING

PARTIAL MASH ALE BREWING

By borrowing a few of the ingredients and techniques of advanced all-grain brewing you can make a quantum leap in the quality of your homebrew. Sometimes called mini-mashing, or mash extract brewing, partial mashing uses a small portion of specialty malts or roasted grains to make the beer more complex. This step into intermediate brewing is usually accompanied by the use of your own hops for bittering, aroma, and flavor rather than using prehopped kits. In addition to the use of unhopped malt extracts and hops, partial mash brewing incorporates the use of liquid yeast or rehydrated dry yeast. Here are a few simple and easy methods of improving the flavor, authenticity, and freshness of a mostly extract ale.

If using a liquid yeast or yeast starter, prepare two to three days before brewing (see instructions for preparing a yeast starter on page 11). Clean and sanitize all equipment and areas to be used in brewing just prior to starting. Equipment and surfaces left overnight will not be free of germs. It is also a good idea to keep some sanitizing solution in reserve to resanitize contaminated equipment or work areas.

Crush any malts, adjuncts, or specialty grains, such as crystal malt, roasted barley, or toasted malt, and place loose or in a nylon, muslin, or cheesecloth bag. Place this bag in one to four quarts of cold water (preferably chlorine-free), depending on the quantity of grains to be used. If undermodified or unmalted grains are being used, a few tablespoons of highly enzymatic pale malt can be added to the water to provide the necessary enzymes. Although this process can be carried out in your brew kettle, it is highly preferable to steep in a separate pot so the crushed husk particles can be filtered out before the boil.

There are two popular ways of doing a steep/partial mash. The first is to add the crushed grains to the water (in a separate pot), slowly bring the temperature up to just below a boil, then turn off the heat and let them steep for twenty to thirty minutes; the second, and preferable, method is to heat the water to 150–160°F, then add the grains and let them steep for twenty to thirty minutes. Some grains, such as crystal malt, require no mashing, and their wort can be rinsed immediately into your brew kettle. At no point should the specialty grains be boiled. Harsh, grainy, and astringently bitter flavors may be imparted to the beer that will be nearly impossible to mask or lager out.

When the steep is completed, remove the grain bag or strain the liquid into your main brewpot, being careful to minimize aeration and catch any solid particles such as grain husks. Add any additional water as is necessary. The higher the percentage of your total batch size that can be boiled the better (that is, 2.5–5 gallons). This will greatly improve the quality of your beer, but will require a wort chiller to reduce the wort to pitching temperature in the recommended time frame of thirty to sixty minutes.

Remove the brewing kettle from the burner to prevent sticking and/or burning of residue on the bottom, then add any liquid or dry malt extract. Cans or bags of liquid extract should be soaked in hot water for fifteen to thirty minutes to facilitate easier pouring. Rinsing the can with hot water helps remove all of the extract. Stir the ingredients to dissolve completely before returning to the heat. For most ales, a hard rolling boil is best. This will result in better clarity, greater hop utilization, and lowered levels of dimethyl sulfide (DMS). The presence of DMS is considered a fault in most beer styles and is characterized by a cornlike aroma and a cooked vegetable taste. Covering the wort to speed up the boil is not recommended since a boilover can occur in seconds, and without warning, when the hydrostatic (surface) tension is broken. Covering also reduces the removal of DMS compounds.

When the boil commences, add your first addition of kettle (boiling) hops and any necessary yeast nutrients or water salts. (Yeast nutrients are required only in high-adjunct beers and are not necessary in all malt beers.) Pellet hops can be added loose; their particles will sufficiently settle out in the sediment in your primary. Whole hops or plugs can be placed in a hop bag or added loose to act as a filter bed later when the cooled wort is strained into the primary. Begin timing your boil at this point. Forty-five to sixty minutes may be sufficient if pellets are used for bittering; sixty to ninety minutes is preferable when using whole hops or plugs.

If using whole hops or plugs for bittering, it is sometimes recommended that you stagger their addition throughout the boil. Often this is done at ninety, sixty, forty-five, and thirty minutes remaining in a ninety-minute boil, in amounts that will yield the proper IBUs. (See page 353.) Pellets used for bittering can be staggered or added all at once at the beginning of the boil.

Flavoring hops should be added ten to twenty minutes before the end of the boil, with fifteen minutes being the recognized norm to avoid flavor components being boiled away. To avoid boiling off the fragile aromatic components, hops should either be added one to five minutes before the end of the boil, steeped for thirty minutes when the heat is shut off and the wort is cooling, placed in the fermenter for one to three weeks prior to racking, or even added directly to the cask when making "real ale" (the last two methods are referred to as "dry-hopping").

When the boil is finished, cool the wort with a wort chiller (this will lend better clarity and stability) or as a less desirable alternative, place in a bath of ice-cold water for twenty to thirty minutes. Be careful not to overfill the cooling bath, as the kettle will tip over or water will leak into your wort. The wort must be cooled to below 80°F before aerating or oxidation of malt compounds will occur.

During this time, pour enough cold water into your sanitized primary fermenter so that total volume, including wort, will equal five gallons. This will further ensure that your wort will quickly reach yeast-pitching temperature. (Jugs of bottled spring water are ideal for this, since they are more likely to be freer of bacteria, chemical contaminants, and chlorine than tap water. They are also easier to place in your refrigerator or freezer for cooling. Reserve some of the spring water for rinsing if you used whole hops or plugs in your boil.) Never pour hot wort into a cold carboy unless there is cold water in it to absorb the thermal shock; it will shatter!

If you are using dry yeast, you can use this time to rehydrate your yeast in some water that has been boiled for five minutes to sterilize, then cooled to between 90º and 110°F. This rehydration should be carried out in a sanitary place and in a sanitized vessel. After thirty minutes have elapsed since the end of the boil, place a sanitized strainer (and funnel if using a carboy) above your primary. Gently strain the wort into your primary, rinsing the hop filter bed with some of the spring water to remove the wort. Stir gently to mix the cooled wort, then take hydrometer and temperature readings.

If the wort has cooled to 75°F, add your yeast. If the wort is still too hot, place it in a tub or somewhere it can be immersed in cold water, but do not add ice unless you are absolutely certain it is sanitary. Stir the wort thoroughly to mix with the yeast and to aerate enough for a healthy aerobic phase of fermentation. Some yeasts require greater aeration than others (see "Yeast Profiles" section.)

Cover the fermenter, fit it with airlock filled with one inch of water, and move to a dark, quiet place at the temperature recommended for the yeast you are using (typically 60–72°F). If using a carboy, fit it with a blow-off hose with one end placed in a jug containing clean water.

Partial Mash Lager Brewing

If you are attempting to brew a lager, you are probably beyond the novice brewer stage and on your way to intermediate and advanced brewing. As in ale partial mashing, a few more slightly involved techniques in lager brewing can open up a whole new world of authentic bottom-fermented styles.

If using a liquid yeast, prepare one to three days before brewing according to the manufacturer's suggestions. A large yeast starter is highly recommended for all lager recipes and will also require one to three days to culture up to pitching levels. A one-liter starter for five gallons of beer would not be too large. See "Basic Tips for Better Homebrewing—Yeast."

Clean and sanitize all equipment and areas to be used in brewing just prior to starting. Surfaces left overnight will not remain germ-free.

Also, keep a few quarts of sanitizing solution in reserve in case a piece of equipment has to be resanitized.

Prepare any malts, adjuncts, or specialty grains and place loose or in a nylon, muslin, or cheesecloth bag. Place this bag in one to four quarts of cold (preferably chlorine-free) water, depending on the quantity of grains to be used. If undermodified or unmalted grains are being used, a few tablespoons of crushed, highly enzymatic pale malt can be added to the water to provide the necessary enzymes. It is highly recommended that you mash/steep in a separate pot so the crushed husk particles can be filtered out before the boil.

There are two popular ways of doing a steep/partial mash. The first is to add the crushed specialty grains such as dextrine malt to the water, slowly bring the temperature up to just below a boil, then turn off the heat and steep the grains for twenty to thirty minutes. The second, and preferable, method is to heat the water to 150–160°F, then add the grains and let them steep for twenty to thirty minutes. Some grains, such as crystal malt, require no mashing and their wort can be rinsed immediately into your brew kettle. At no point should these specialty grains be boiled. Harsh, grainy, and astringently bitter flavors will be imparted to the beer that will be nearly impossible to mask or lager out.

When the steep is completed, remove the grain bag or strain the liquid into your main brewpot, being careful to minimize aeration and catch any solid particles such as grain husks. Add any additional water as is necessary. The higher the percentage of your total batch size that can be boiled, the better (that is, 2.5–5 gallons). This will greatly improve the quality of your beer, but will require a wort chiller to reduce the wort to pitching temperature in the recommended time frame of thirty to sixty minutes.

To avoid darkening the finished product, dissolve all extracts into the brewing water before bringing to a boil. Cans or bags of liquid extract should be soaked in hot water for thirty minutes to facilitate easier pouring. Rinsing the can with hot water helps remove all of the extract. For most light lagers, a short, gently rolling boil of sixty minutes is best (as opposed to one and a half to two hours or more for ales). This will also result in lighter color. Covering the wort to speed up the boil is not recommended since a boilover can occur in seconds and without warning when the hydrostatic (surface) tension is broken. Covering also reduces the removal of DMS compounds.

When the boil commences, add your first addition of kettle (boiling) hops and any necessary yeast nutrients or water salts. (Yeast nutrients are not needed except in high-adjunct beers.) Pellet hops can be added loose; their particles will sufficiently settle out in the sediment in your primary. Whole hops or plugs can be placed in a hop bag or added loose to act as a filter bed later when the cooled wort is strained into the primary. Begin timing your boil at this point. Sixty minutes may be sufficient if pellets are used for bittering; sixty to ninety minutes is often necessary when using whole hops or plugs. Alternatively, you can compensate for reduced utilization with whole hops by adding more. It is also advantageous to skim the brown resinous scum (hot-break) at the beginning of the boil. This haze-forming coagulated protein can detract from the clarity and delicate flavor of lagers.

If using whole hops or plugs for bittering, it is often suggested that you stagger their addition throughout the boil. Usually, this is done with ninety, sixty, forty-five, and thirty minutes remaining in a ninety-minute boil, in amounts that will yield the proper IBUs. (See page 353.) Pellets can be added all at once at the beginning of the boil.

Flavoring hops should be added ten to twenty minutes before the end of the boil, with fifteen minutes being the recognized norm. Aromatic hops should be added one to five minutes before the end of the boil, steeped for thirty minutes when the heat is shut off and the wort is cooling, or placed in the secondary fermenter one to three weeks prior to bottling or kegging.

When the boil is finished, cool the wort with a wort chiller or as an alternative, place in a bath of ice-cold water for twenty to thirty minutes. Be careful not to overfill the cooling bath, as the kettle may tip over or water will leak into your wort.

During this time, pour enough cold water into your sanitized primary fermenter so that total volume, including wort, will equal five gallons. This will further ensure that your wort will quickly reach yeast-pitching temperature. (Jugs of bottled spring water are ideal for this, since they are more likely to be freer of bacteria, chemical contaminants, and chlorine than tap water. They are also easier to place in your refrigerator or freezer for cooling. Reserve some of the spring water for rinsing if you used whole hops or plugs in your boil.) Never pour hot wort into a cold carboy unless there is cold water in it to absorb the thermal shock; it will shatter!

If you are using dry yeast, you can use this time to rehydrate your yeast in some water that has been boiled for five minutes, then cooled to 90–110°F. This rehydration should be carried out in a sanitary place and in a sanitized vessel. After thirty minutes have elapsed since the end of the boil, place a sanitized strainer (and funnel if using a carboy) above your primary. Strain the wort into your primary, rinsing the hop filter bed with some of the spring water to remove all wort. Stir well to mix the wort, then take hydrometer and temperature readings.

If the wort has cooled to 75–80°F, add your yeast. Stir the wort thoroughly to mix the wort and yeast and to aerate enough for a healthy aerobic phase of fermentation. If the wort is still too hot, place it in a tub or somewhere it can be immersed in cold water, but do not add ice unless you are absolutely certain it is bacteria-free.

Cover the fermenter and fit it with an airlock, then fill the airlock with one inch of water or vodka—do not overfill. An ample 500–1,000 ml starter will generally allow you to move to fermentation temperatures immediately; otherwise keep at room temperature until fermentation is visually evident (approximately twelve to twenty-four hours, depending on the quantity of yeast pitched), then move to the temperature recommended for the yeast you are using. However, be aware that this method may adversely affect the flavor of your beer. If you are using a carboy as your primary, fit with a blow-off hose with one end placed in a jug containing clean water.

ALL-GRAIN BREWING

An Introduction to Advanced Techniques

Pretty soon after extract brewers see how easy partial mash brewing is, they begin to contemplate all-grain brewing. Weeks, months, or years may pass before you put aside your lack of confidence and finally make the decision to take the plunge. With few exceptions, most brewers will regret not starting all-grain brewing sooner. You may have read this many times before, but I must repeat that advanced brewing really isn't that difficult and only involves more time and a minimal amount of additional equipment. The rewards are many as your kinship with the professional brewer grows and you begin to realize the honest pleasures of a centuries-old craft. At the very least, all-grain brewing will save you lots of money on ingredients and, most likely, you'll notice a cleaner, fresher taste to your brew—a brew over which you have complete control.

Advanced brewery training is not needed. After brewing extract recipes with a variety of specialty grains, multiple hop additions, and yeast starters, you are well equipped to juggle the many elements of all-grain brewing. The methods we will be discussing are single-temperature infusion, stepped, and decoction mashing.

This chapter lists the basic equipment commonly used by all-grain homebrewers, the special ingredients all-grain brewing requires, a general description of the mashing process, some basic points about advanced brewing to keep in mind, and finally, a few simple schedules for applying basic principles to specific recipes. If you are interested in learning more about the science and more intricate details of mashing, several excellent books are available:

Dave Miller's *The Complete Handbook of Home Brewing* (Garden Way, 1988), George Fix's *Principles of Brewing Science* (Brewers Publications, 1989), and Gregory Noonan's *Brewing Lager Beer* (Brewers Publications, 1986).

EQUIPMENT YOU WILL NEED

Mash tuns. For a single-temperature infusion mash an insulated cooler, Styrofoam box, or any similar container may be suitable as long as the temperature can be kept stable for sixty to ninety minutes. However, I like to use one or two large stainless-steel stockpots or enamel kettles even for single-temperature infusions because they allow easy upward adjustment of temperature without having to dilute the mash with hot water. For low or standard-gravity five-gallon batches, a four-gallon kettle will be sufficient to hold your grains and mash water. For medium- to high-gravity beers and large batches as frequently encountered in this book, a kettle with a seven- or eight-gallon capacity will be required. An alternative is to use two separate four-gallon pots with the mash divided equally between them.

Hot liquor/boiling kettle. This should be a stainless or enamel vessel or two vessels capable of boiling a total of at least seven gallons of liquid. This will be first used to heat your mash water and then to boil your wort when the sparge is finished.

Mash paddle. A sturdy, long-handled stirring spoon or paddle for mixing the mash. This can be wood, stainless steel, or plastic, but should be strong enough to turn large volumes of grain and fifteen to twenty inches in length.

Wire screen, strainer, or colander. These are placed atop the grain bed in order to deflect the flow of sparge water and force it to spread more gently and evenly through the grains. Slowly pour the water through one of these using a large Pyrex measuring cup, saucepan, or ladle. A violent introduction of water can disturb the settled grains and promote channels forming in the grain bed. These channels will direct sparge water directly to the bottom of the tun and away from the rest of the grains where wort is trapped.

Lauter tun. This sophisticated-sounding device is nothing more than a bucket in which to sparge your grains after they have been mashed. The only requirement is that a tap be installed at the bottom, which can be turned on and off to control the flow of sweet wort as it flows out of the grain, and that a false bottom of some sort be installed to keep the grains an inch or two above the tap. Because most of us already have such a bucket that we use for bottling, it can double as a lauter tun. The false bottom can be achieved by the use of a sparge bag hung inside of the bucket and held in place by a drawstring. A false bottom can also be engineered by drilling dozens of small holes into the bottom of a second food-grade plastic bucket (an old fermenting vessel, for example) and inserting it into the bucket fitted with a tap. This "Zapap" lauter tun design by Charlie Papazian has seen wide use by homebrewers, but should be wrapped in a blanket or foam padding to retain heat during the sparge. Cylindrical picnic coolers are another popular choice because not only do they have a tap at the bottom, but their insulation helps keep the mash hot and fluid and they can double as a mash tun. Homebrewing sophistication has also led to the development of several commercial lauter tuns with many improvements over the homemade variety.

Probe thermometer. This may be the most vital instrument for the all-grain brewer, as it allows you to precisely predict the character of your beer. As noted previously, temperature control is the most important means of determining the body and strength of the finished product. An easy-to-read metal dial thermometer that can read at a minimum from 32° to 212°F is suggested because a candy thermometer often must be removed from the mash for a reading. The popularity of digital thermometers is growing because of their pinpoint accuracy, but they can be sensitive to the messy liquid environment of a brewing session. One accidental drop into hot sparge water can destroy your $20 investment. The metal probe thermometers intended for meat cooking generally read only from 130° to 190°F in wide 10° increments and therefore may not be appropriate if you are trying to obtain a very precise saccharification temperature, especially if you are starting your mash with a protein rest at 122°F or an acid rest at 95°F.

Wort chiller. This can be an immersion type or a counterflow chiller, but the use of one is imperative for the all-grain brewer because of the large volume of wort being boiled. Failure to chill the wort quickly to proper yeast-pitching temperature will darken the wort and increase the chance of an airborne infection by wild yeast. The immersion type of wort chiller consists of several feet of copper tubing bent into a spiral. On each end, flexible tubing is attached so that cold water can flow into and out of the copper coil. The coil is completely "immersed" in the wort at the end of the boil and because copper is an excellent conductor of heat, rapidly cools the wort. By attaching one end to a continuous flow of cold water, a kitchen tap for example, a stream of cold water passes through the coil, drawing heat out. Immersion chillers should be cleaned and sanitized before submerging into the wort or should be immersed in the wort for the last five to ten minutes of the boil to sanitize them. The more efficient but complicated and more expensive "counterflow"-type wort chiller cools by passing the hot wort through a copper pipe coiled inside a flexible hose (such as a garden hose) filled with cold water. As the cold water flows through the hose it passes over the surface of the copper coil, drawing heat from the wort as it is pumped or siphoned into the fermenter.

pH test papers. These should be able to test inside of the pH 4–7 range and will tell if you if your mash is in the proper pH 5–5.5 range for optimum enzyme activity. Mashes that are to be decocted or for beers to be subjected to a long lagering phase may begin with a higher pH of up to 5.8, but infusion-mashed beers generally should begin at no higher than pH 5.5. The mash should not be continued unadjusted if your initial pH reading is above 6.2 or below 4.7. Variations from this range should be adjusted up or down with water salts stirred into the mash in small increments until a pH of approximately 5.2 to 5.3 is achieved. Note that pH values will appear slightly lower at mash temperatures than they actually are at room temperature. Expect a 0.2 to 0.3 downward drop in the pH measurement when the mash is in the 122–150°F range.

Iodine tincture. Bavarian brewmasters used to judge the conversion of a mash by how well their leather trousers stuck to a bench covered with the wort, and after you have several all-grain batches under your belt you'll probably be able to dip your finger into the mash and tell by taste alone that it's ready. Until then, you need a way of determining that the starches in your mashed grain have been converted to fermentable sugars and it's time to proceed with sparging. To use the tincture, simply place a dropperful of wort on a clean white plate, then add a drop or two of iodine. When there is little or no change in the color of the tincture, conversion is complete and you are ready to mash out. If the tincture turns blue-black, unconverted starches remain. Continue the mash for twenty to thirty minutes, then recheck with the tincture. Note: Iodine is poisonous and should never be consumed or reintroduced into the mash.

Grain mill. Beginning all-grain brewers may wish to buy their malts precrushed from their homebrew supply store. This is fine if you plan to mash within a day or two. After that the cracked malt will absorb moisture from the atmosphere and become "slack," a term referring to grains with noticeable stale flavors. If you aren't able to brew immediately after the purchase of your grains, invest in a grain mill and grind your own. A variety of models exist on the market ranging in price and efficiency. Most homebrewers begin with the simple Corona mill. This works well, but since it is designed for grinding corn, is notoriously hard to master when crushing malt.

Pound scale. Unless your homebrew shop has delivered your grain packaged precisely in the quantities you will be using, you will need to weigh your grains before mashing. If you insist on estimating, or if your mill breaks mid-crush, one pound of dry, uncrushed malt equals approximately twenty-eight ounces by volume or roughly three and a half cups.

INGREDIENTS YOU WILL NEED SPECIFICALLY FOR ALL-GRAIN BREWING

Eight to twelve pounds of malted grains. As the term "all-grain" implies, you will be using only whole grains and perhaps a few flaked adjuncts but no malt extract. The standard-gravity five-gallon batch uses between eight and twelve pounds of malts and specialty grains. These malts and grains make up the "grain bill" of your recipe and when crushed are called the "grist."

Water treatments. Unlike most extract-based brews, all-grain batches require more attention to proper water chemistry, principally in regulating the pH of the mash and the sparge water. If your mash water, or "liquor," is around pH 7, your mash will more than likely fall within the proper range once the crushed grains are stirred in. If water with low temporary hardness and/or a large percentage of dark malts is used, an acidic mash may result. Upward adjustment may then be required with calcium carbonate until a pH between 5 and 5.5 is achieved. Conversely, if your mash is too alkaline, additions of calcium chloride or calcium sulfate may be needed to lower the pH to the suggested optimum around 5.2.

MASHING

Mashing in, or "doughing in," as it is also called, is the process of mixing the crushed malts with the hot mash water, properly called "liquor." To professional brewers, "water" is something you wash your equipment with. In a brewery, the grain is often cracked in a roller mill and augered into the mash tun while simultaneously being mixed with hot water. In home brewery practice the crushed grains, or "grist," is carefully sprinkled onto the hot water in the mash tun, then gently stirred in. As in every arena of brewing techniques, some suggest adding water to the grain instead of grain to the water. The main thing is to mix the grain thoroughly so that it is evenly saturated with water and stir throughout the mash to equalize temperature and promote better enzyme activity. Water is generally added at a ratio of between one and two quarts per pound of grain, depending on the type of mashing schedule and the ingredients being used. Less water produces a thicker mash and better breakdown of proteins in the malt as well as higher extraction rates from the grain. Larger amounts of water will naturally produce a thinner mash and better starch-degrading enzyme activity, subsequently yielding a wort high in maltose. On the surface it may seem logical to have the mash as thin as possible to produce as much sugar as possible, especially when a well-attenuated beer is planned. Unfortunately, thinner mashes take much longer to convert and enzyme activity may be halted altogether. It is better to err on the side of thick mash, using one to one and a third quarts per pound of grain. To determine the amount of water in gallons to prepare for your mash-in, simply multiply the total pounds of crushed grain by quarts of water. For example, if you decide to use 1.33 quarts per pound in a batch with a grist of 12 pounds of base malt and specialty grains, $1.33 \times 12 = 15.96$ quarts;

15.96 quarts divided by 4 (to give you the amount in gallons) = 3.99 gallons. It is OK to round up or down a little for convenience. In this instance, four gallons is a good amount of water to heat to mash "strike" temperature.

Strike heat is a term used to define the temperature of the mash liquor before the grist is mixed in. Because the grains are cooler than the liquor, they will reduce the temperature of the water a good eight to twelve degrees or more, depending on the temperature and volume of the grist. The differentiation between this temperature and the "initial" temperature required for mashing is important, since a difference of just a few degrees can dramatically affect the outcome of the wort. Therefore, you need to heat your mash liquor to a temperature higher than what you want your mash to be. Although no one can tell you exactly how much higher without knowing your equipment or brewing conditions, a good rule of thumb is to have your strike temperature 10°F above what you have decided will be the initial temperature of your mash. If the planned mash temperature is 153°F, as in a single-temperature infusion, simply heat the liquor in your hot liquor kettle or mash tun to 163°F before adding the grist. Experience will teach you the exact variation from your target "rest" temperature to plan for.

Rest is another bit of brewer's jargon that is largely self-explanatory. This is merely a period when the mash is left alone at a particular temperature for a predetermined length of time. These "rests" allow temperature-specific enzymes to operate and normally range in duration from fifteen minutes to an hour and a half. The most common rests used by modern homebrewers are the "protein rest" and the "saccharification" or "sugar" rest. The protein rest generally occurs at 122–140° for twenty to forty-five minutes and is employed to break down large protein molecules by the protein-degrading protease enzymes. This rest is primarily to produce yeast nutrients and to reduce haze potential in the finished beer when using high-protein malts. Smaller proteins are broken down by proteolytic enzymes in the 113–122° range. In a mash using well-modified barley malts, a protein rest is unnecessary. When step or decoction mashing, one protein rest temperature of 122°F is more than adequate for both types of protein-degrading enzymes to work, but a mash pH no higher than 5.2 is recommended for their optimum performance for infusion mashing and no higher than 5.5 for decoction mashing. The sugar rest is simply the phase where the main conversion of starches to fermentable sugars and dextrines occurs. In this rest, the primary diastatic enzymes in malt, beta-amylase and alpha-amylase, work on the glucose in the malt, breaking it down into smaller molecules that the yeast will be able to metabolize. Beta-amylase works best at temperatures ranging from 126° to 149° and is responsible for producing the fermentable sugars in the wort. Alpha-amylase works best from 149° to 153° and produces the dextrines that give beer its sweetness and body. The dextrines in beer are only partially fermentable by yeast and at a very slow rate, so they are generally labeled "unfermentable."

Mashing out stops the mashing process by raising the heat to a level that will destroy the starch-degrading enzymes. Resting the mash at higher temperatures of 165–170°F reduces the viscosity of the mash, making the wort flow more easily from the grains during the sparging phase.

Sparging is simply brewer's jargon for rinsing with 160–168° water to extract residual wort held by the grains. In the lauter tun the mashed grains are stirred and allowed to sit undisturbed for ten to fifteen minutes so that the bed of grain is loosely settled and the cracked barley husks can act as a filter medium and keep the grains separated from compacting when running off. German brewers often sparge with 172°F water, and Belgian lambic brewers commonly sparge with 200°F water. However, it is safer for homebrewers to stay below 170° to avoid extracting harsh and astringent tannins from the grain husks. Sparge water ideally should be added in a gentle spray and at the same rate that you are running off to ensure thorough extraction of the wort and to keep the grain bed loose and separated. The sparge water should cover the grain bed at all times or the grains will settle, trapping much of the wort in the grains. The main thing to remember above all else is to sparge slowly. A typical five- to six-gallon batch should use five or six gallons of sparge water, or a half gallon per pound of grain, and should take about forty-five minutes to an hour to complete. Simply place your colander, strainer, or wire screen on top of the grains and gently pour the hot sparge water onto it.

Running off is basically letting the sweet wort run out of the bottom of the lauter tun and into your brew kettle for boiling. This final phase of the mashing and lautering process should be done slowly to keep the grain bed from drying out and becoming compacted. Try to avoid splashing the wort as you run off into your kettle to minimize the detrimental oxidation effects of aeration. A short length of siphon hose attached to the lauter tun tap and running to the bottom of your kettle can help accom-

plish this. A common practice is to recirculate the cloudy "first runnings" from the mash tun through the mash to remove some of the sediment. In a typical five-gallon batch, a gallon of the first wort runoff is collected, then gently trickled on top of the grain bed before sparging is begun. Running off too quickly will lower the yield from your mash and pull the grains toward the bottom, possibly resulting in a "stuck mash." If your mash becomes stuck—that is, prematurely stops yielding wort—you may introduce some more sparge water and gently stir the mash to lift it off of the false bottom. Let the mash rest for five to ten minutes, then resume running off. Otherwise, do not disturb the grain bed once sparging has begun. Sparge and run off until you have collected about one gallon more than you intend to ferment. Remember that your wort will get a one-and-a-half- to two-hour boil and approximately a half gallon per hour will be lost to evaporation. This loss may be more if you are using more than one kettle for boiling. The common brewery practice is to continue to run off until the specific gravity of the wort is around 1.008–1.010. Remember to adjust for temperatures higher than 60°F. If you have the amount of wort you require but your wort gravity is much higher than 1.010, you can continue to collect and brew a larger batch or you can save the excess for yeast starters. Once your kettles are full, you are ready to begin boiling your wort just as in an extract brew, except that it may need to go a little longer. I like to boil for a total of two hours when using whole hops; one-half hour to force formation of hot-break before adding hops, then another ninety minutes once the first bittering hops have been added.

SINGLE-TEMPERATURE INFUSION MASHING

Single-temperature infusion mashing is by far the most popular all-grain mashing method with homebrewers, microbreweries, and brewpubs because of its simplicity and relative ease. It is the predominant method used by ale breweries in Great Britain, and has gained considerable popularity in traditional lager-brewing countries because of the drastic reduction in time, energy, cost, and labor a single-temperature mash affords. Once thought of as a mashing technique primarily for brewing with well-modified ale malts, single-temperature mashing is now widely used in brewing lager beer as well, thanks to the advances in malting science that have allowed the production of very pale, yet well-modified lager malts.

As its name implies, the single-temperature infusion mash uses just one rest at a constant saccharification temperature for the entire time needed for starch conversion. The brewer generally chooses a temperature somewhere in the 149–158°F range, depending on the fermentability and body desired in the finished beer. Malts that will convert easily and leave no haze-forming proteins, e.g., well-modified malts such as English and Belgian two-row, are a necessity. To perform a single-temperature infusion, the brewer simply stirs in the precrushed grains to the heated mash liquor ten to fifteen degrees above the temperature where starch conversion is intended. Because there is no need to change the temperature during the course of the mash, an insulated vessel such as a Styrofoam box or picnic cooler is often used by homebrewers to maintain a constant temperature. A kettle can be used, but these do not hold heat well and often require constant attention to maintain proper temperature. However, using a large kettle has the advantage of allowing heat to be applied if the temperature falls.

Infusion mashes generally have saccharification rests running from thirty to ninety minutes, depending mainly on the modification level of your malt and the temperature of your mash. After the mash is well stirred, check that the temperature is where it should be. You have about ten minutes to adjust up or down with hot or cold water or bottom heat before significant enzyme activity takes place. Simply check the conversion of your mash with the iodine test described earlier and proceed with mashing out when conversion is complete. Most brewers allow the mash to continue for at least an hour even if conversion is complete in order to extract more flavor from the grains. However, it is recommended that the mash not exceed 120 minutes unless absolutely necessary to avoid extracting harsh tannins from the grain husks.

Because a single-temperature infusion mash is often carried out in a vessel that cannot be placed directly on a burner to raise the temperature to mash out, simply add pints of 200°F water slowly over ten to fifteen minutes until the mash reaches 165–170°F. Allow the mash to rest for ten minutes at this temperature, then proceed with the transfer to your lauter tun.

BASIC POINTS TO REMEMBER

- Highly modified two-row malts are preferred for this mashing method because their lower protein content will cause fewer haze problems.

- Because two-row malts are lower in enzymes, single-temperature infusion mashing is not advised when using a high percentage of adjuncts (such as 15–30 percent or more).

- The mash should be fairly thin for optimum starch conversion and higher fermentability, using from 1 to 1.75 quarts of brewing liquor (water) per pound of grain.

- Mash temperatures typically range from 148° to 158°F (65–70°C). Mash pH should be in the 5.0–5.7 range. Adjust upward or downward by stirring in small additions of water salts as appropriate.

- Keep your mash tun well insulated against heat loss.

- Mashing at the lower end at 150°F requires a longer mash (up to ninety minutes) and will produce a lighter-bodied beer.

- Mashing at the higher end of 158°F converts faster (thirty to sixty minutes) but will produce a fuller-bodied beer with a higher degree of "unfermentables."

- The "strike heat" of the mash liquor should be 8–10°F (6–7°C) above what you want the initial heat to be.

- Recirculate cloudy first runnings from the mash tun back through the mash until the wort runs fairly clear.

- Add grist to mash liquor, not mash liquor to grist, in a gentle sprinkling motion. Stir gently but thoroughly.

- Sparge slowly and do not oversparge. Typically, sparging is stopped when the wort gravity drops to around 1.010–1.008, in order to avoid harsh tannins being extracted into the wort.

- When sparging, keep the grain bed covered with hot liquor at all times to keep it from becoming compacted.

- All-grain brews ideally should be mashed and sparged with enough brewing liquor for a full wort boil, that is, enough to yield 6 to 6.5 gallons for a 5-gallon batch.

Advantages: Infusion is a cheaper and easier method than stepped or decoction mashes, and requires less time and equipment.

Disadvantages: The higher temperatures of 155–158°F (70°C) used to produce greater extract yield also produce a wort high in slowly fermenting dextrines, which may result in more sweetness and mouthfeel than desired.

TYPICAL SINGLE-TEMPERATURE INFUSION MASH SCHEDULE

First Step: Saccharification rest. Mash in ("dough in"), carefully stirring to mix the liquor and grist. Rest sixty to ninety minutes at 148°F/65° C (for a thinner, stronger beer) to 158°F/70°C (for a richer, less alcoholic beer). Stir occasionally.

Second Step: Test for remaining starches with an iodine tincture by adding one drop to a tablespoon of wort on a white saucer. If negative (wort no longer turns blue-black), mash out.

Third Step: Mash out. Raise mash temperature to 165–170°F (74–77°C) by adding doses of hot water. Rest five to ten minutes to decrease wort viscosity.

Fourth Step: Transfer to lauter tun if a separate vessel is being used. Slowly sparge with 165–168°F (74–76°C) water over forty-five to sixty minutes and collect wort into brew kettle.

STEP-MASHING

Seen as an alternative to the traditional, labor-intensive decoction method, the stepped-mash, "upward infusion," or "temperature-controlled mash," as it is also called, is better suited for malts with few surplus enzymes, which would be destroyed by boiling, but that still require a protein rest prior to starch conversion. This "programmed" method is most beneficial for recipes containing higher-protein malts, starchy adjuncts and/or "raw" grains, or beers with low serving temperatures.

As the various names used to describe this mashing method indicate, temperatures are stepped upward to specific temperatures to facilitate the action of a particular enzyme before culminating in the sugar rest. This method can be accomplished by raising the temperature by the infusion of measured amounts of hot water or applying bottom heat to a stovetop kettle. The stovetop method is probably the best for new entrants into this mashing method, as it removes the necessity of learning through experience amounts and temperatures of water your mashing system requires to raise the mash quickly and accurately to a given rest without producing an overly thin wort. Coincidentally, the infusion method of step-mashing lends itself well to the optimum activity of each enzyme, since you begin with a thick mash (around one quart per gallon of grain), which favors the protein-degrading enzymes, and raise the temperature with the addition of water. The subsequent thinning of the mash as the temperature is elevated favors the starch-degrading enzymes.

In a typical five-gallon batch for a standard-gravity beer approximately one gallon of hot water is required to raise the temperature of the mash from protein rest temperature to starch conversion temperature. Craft brewers use and some brewing texts suggest water temperatures of 212°F, but to avoid the possibility of extracting unwanted flavors from the malt, I recommend using water at 200°F added one quart at a time and stirred in well before the temperature is checked. Remember that the temperature will continue to rise for several minutes after the initial infusion, so make additions slowly when you near your target temperature.

The typical step mash begins with a strike heat around 132°F to give an initial protein temperature rest of 122°F to reduce the larger proteins that cause haze and foam instability in the finished beer. The protein rest may last from ten minutes to an hour depending on the protein level of the grist or the style of beer being brewed. The standard protein rest lasts for around thirty minutes. Rests lasting longer increase the risk that the proteins will be too thoroughly degraded, resulting in poor head formation. The longer protein rests of forty-five to sixty minutes are generally reserved for grists containing high levels of haze-producing adjuncts such as rolled oats. After the protein rest, the mash is usually raised quickly to one or two rests within the starch conversion range. The simplest method is to go directly to the chosen sugar rest temperature between 150° and 158°F until conversion is complete. A more involved method steps up to a temperature in the lower end of the starch conversion range to facilitate a high degree of fermentables in the wort, followed by raising the mash to the upper range of starch conversion temperatures to yield a good balance of dextrines in the wort.

If you are using the infusion method of step-mashing, proceed with mash-out by adding pints of 200°F water to raise the mash temperature to 165–170°F. If you are mashing in a large kettle, simply apply high heat while stirring until mashing-out temperature is achieved. Rest for ten to fifteen minutes to stop enzyme activity and decrease wort viscosity, then proceed with lautering.

BASICS TO REMEMBER

- Choose the right type of malt for the beer you're brewing. Step-mashing is a good method for well-modified, domestic two-row malt and for well-modified six-row malts with high tannin levels in their husks that might be extracted in a decoction mash.

- Use fresh grains that are milled properly.

- Experts often advise having a thick mash during the protein rest at 122°F (50°C), which favors the protein-converting proteolytic enzymes, followed by the addition of hot water to give a thinner mash when raising the temperature to 150–158°F, which favors the starch-converting diastatic enzymes. This method allows both types of enzymes to work in their optimum environment.

- Step-mashing elevates the amino acid level of the wort, a factor important to yeast nutrition. However, high-malt grists using modern, well-modified barley will naturally have plenty of amino acids; only in high-adjunct beers will amino acid deficiency be a problem.

- Step-mashing lends greater colloidal stability (less haze potential) when using higher-protein malts such as six-row, and possibly even American two-row.

Advantages: Greater extract yields. Allows more control over the balance between fermentable sugars and dextrines than in a single-temperature mash. It also allows the use of somewhat cheaper, high-protein malts and adjuncts.

Disadvantages: Energy costs, more time is required, lower foam formation may result if your protein rest is too long. Diminished foam formation and stability may also occur when brewing high-adjunct/low-gravity beers.

TYPICAL STEPPED-MASH SCHEDULES

FOR A LIGHT-BODIED BEER

First Step: Protein rest. Mash in, stir well. Rest thirty minutes at 122°F (50°C).

Second Step: Saccharification rest. Rest twenty to thirty minutes at 150°F (65°C). Stir occasionally. Test for remaining starches with iodine tincture by adding one drop to a tablespoon of wort. If negative (wort no longer turns blue-black), mash out.

Third Step: Mash out. Raise to 165–170°F (74–77°C). Rest five to ten minutes to decrease viscosity.

Fourth Step: Transfer to lauter tun. Slowly sparge with 165–168°F (74–76°C) water over forty-five to sixty minutes and collect wort into brew kettle.

FOR A MEDIUM-BODIED BEER

First Step: Protein rest. Mash in, stir well. Rest thirty minutes at 122°F (50°C).

Second Step: Saccharification rest. Rest ten minutes at 150°F followed by twenty minutes at 158°F. Stir occasionally. Test for remaining starches with iodine tincture by adding one drop to a tablespoon of wort on a white dish. If negative (wort no longer turns blue-black), mash out.

Third Step: Mash out. Raise to 165–170°F (74–77°C). Rest five to ten minutes to decrease viscosity.

Fourth Step: Transfer to lauter tun. Slowly sparge with 165–168°F (74–76°C) water over forty-five to sixty minutes and collect wort into brew kettle.

FOR A FULL-BODIED BEER

First Step: Protein rest. Mash in, stir well. Rest thirty minutes at 122°F (50°C).

Second Step: Saccharification rest. Rest twenty to thirty minutes at 158°F (70°C). Stir occasionally. Test for remaining starches with iodine tincture as noted above. If negative (wort no longer turns blue-black), mash out.

Third Step: Mash out. Raise to 165–170°F (74–77°C). Rest five to ten minutes to decrease viscosity.

Fourth Step: Transfer to lauter tun. Slowly sparge with 165–168°F (74–76°C) water over forty-five to sixty minutes and collect wort into brew kettle.

WHEN MASHING WITH PRECOOKED ADJUNCTS

First Step: Protein rest. Mash in, stir well. Rest thirty minutes at 104°F (40°C).

Second Step: Protein rest. Add precooked adjuncts and the water they are cooked in. Rest forty-five minutes at 122°F (50°C). Stir occasionally.

Third Step: Saccharification rest. Rest sixty minutes at 150°F (65°C). Test for remaining starches with iodine tincture as noted above. If negative (wort no longer turns blue-black), mash out.

Fourth Step: Mash out. Raise to 165–170°F (74–77°C). Rest five to ten minutes to decrease viscosity.

Fifth Step: Transfer to lauter tun. Slowly sparge with 165–168°F (74–76°C) water over forty-five to sixty minutes and collect wort into brew kettle.

WHEN USING WELL-MODIFIED PILSNER MALT

First Step: Protein/saccharification rest. Mash in, stir well. Rest fifteen minutes at 140°F (60°C).

Second Step: Saccharification rest. Rest fifteen minutes at 148°F (65°C). Stir occasionally.

Third Step: Saccharification rest. Rest thirty to forty-five minutes at 150–158°F (65–70°C), depending on attenuation desired in beer. Test for remaining starches with iodine tincture as noted above. If negative (wort no longer turns blue-black), mash out.

Fourth Step: Mash out. Raise to 165–170°F (74–77°C). Rest five to ten minutes to decrease viscosity.

Fifth Step: Transfer to lauter tun. Slowly sparge with 165–168°F (74–76°C) water over forty-five to sixty minutes and collect wort into brew kettle.

COMMON MASH TEMPERATURES

	94° F/35°C	122° F/50°C	140° F/60°C	149° F/65°C	158° F/70°C	168° F/76°C	172° F/77°C
Optimum Activity	Phytase optimum —Acid rest temperature for under-modified lager malts	Proteolysis optimum —Protein rest temperature	Beta-amylase optimum —Starch converts to sugars	Diastase optimum —Alpha- & beta-amylase work equally well	Alpha-amylase optimum —Starch converts to dextrins	Beta-amylase stopped/ alpha-amylase curtailed	Maximum sparge liquor temperature
Typical Duration	1-24 hours	15-60 minutes	15-90 minutes	45-90 minutes	15-30 minutes	5-15 minutes	45-60 minutes
Effect on Mash/Wort	Lowers mash pH when using low calcium brewing liquor	Malt proteins and adjunct starches broken down	Yields wort very low in dextrins, high in fermentables	Produces wort with well-balanced ratio of dextrins to fermentables	Produces wort high in dextrins, low in fermentables	Reduces viscosity, aids run-off of mash	Possible tannin extraction from mash if 170° F exceeded

DECOCTION MASHING

This is the traditional German method devised in the mid-nineteenth century to deal with undermodified malts and is rarely needed with today's homogenous, well-modified malts. However, decoction is still considered the preferred (but not mandatory) method for certain German beer styles because of the character it lends to the finished product. It is often recommended in brewing Bavarian weissbiers because the boiling physically breaks down the wheat starch. It is also recommended in bock and Märzen brewing because the boiling lends a deeper color and a maltier flavor and aroma without requiring large quantities of the specialty grains that can sometimes impart harshness. In my own experience, decoction mashing does produce greater extract yields and clearer wort from a single decoction even when using well-modified two-row malts. There are single-decoction, double-decoction, and triple-decoction programs. It is rare that a triple decoction will absolutely be required except when mashing poorly modified lager malts or when perhaps brewing an authentic Bavarian doppelbock; nevertheless, a triple-decoction schedule has been included for the adventurous brewer.

To conduct a decoction mash you will need a spare kettle, since you will be drawing off a portion of the mash from your primary mash tun and bringing it to a boil. You will also be using more water per pound of grain, typically two to three quarts per pound as opposed to one to one and a half in an infusion mash. Decoction mashes often start by mashing in at initial temperatures much lower than for step-mashing.

This acid rest, typically in the 95–105°F range, is intended to acidify the mash mainly by action of phytase enzymes. This rest may not be necessary unless you have high-carbonate mash water and the pH is not lowered sufficiently by the high percentage of acidic dark malts in a dunkel or bock grist. Besides, only undermodified malts have phytase enzymes available for acidification of the mash. Phytase enzymes are destroyed during the kilning of well-modified malts. If after mashing in with a high percentage of dark malts the pH is too low, stir in small amounts of calcium carbonate to raise the pH to an acceptable 5.3–5.8 level.

After mashing in at around 100°F, a tightly covered acid rest is performed in a triple-decoction mash for about thirty minutes before pulling the first decoction. In single and double decoctions, the acid rest is usually skipped and the mash is quickly raised from 100° to the protein rest at 122°F for fifteen to thirty minutes. After the appropriate rest time, the thickest 30–40 percent of the mash is ladled out into a second kettle and quickly brought to sugar rest temperatures with bottom heat. The amount of decocted mash needed to raise the main mash to the next rest will be learned from experience and is determined largely by your equipment and mash thickness. The main mash from which the smaller mash portion is decocted must be checked frequently to ensure that the temperature remains constant. After resting ten to fifteen minutes at 153–158°F, the decocted portion is brought to a boil for twenty to thirty minutes before being gradually stirred back into

BASIC POINTS TO REMEMBER

- Decoction mashing requires a larger water-to-grain ratio of up to three parts liquor to one part grist (three quarts of water per pound of grain).

- Two-row malts are preferable, since six-row malts may yield high levels of tannins when boiled.

- Decoct the thickest part so the majority of the enzymes residing in the thinner, liquid portion will be preserved.

- Stir the mashes frequently and thoroughly to prevent scorching.

- Lauter especially gently and slowly when using wheat to avoid a set mash.

- Use fewer coloring grains than you would in an extract brew.

- Remember that you may achieve greater hop utilization in the full wort boil of an all-grain beer.

the main mash to elevate its temperature. The main mash is then rested for a time before another decoction is pulled in the case of double and triple decoctions and the whole process is repeated until a dextrinous starch conversion temperature of 155–160° is achieved. When complete starch conversion has been achieved, mashing out, lautering, and sparging can commence just as in the other methods of mashing.

Advantages: Decoction often provides higher extract yields, better mash pH, less hot-break, and a clearer runoff from the lauter tun. Decoction also provides more complete breakdown of starches when mashing adjuncts or malted wheat. It also provides smoother, fuller malt flavors and a traditional deep color to German dark lagers without the use of high percentages of dark malts. These dark malts often lend harsh tannic and astringent flavors to the finished beer.

Disadvantages: There are many. Decoction mashing requires greater time, energy consumption, and skill, as well as more equipment; not to mention the risk of tannin extraction and the likelihood of scorching in a direct-fired homebrew setting. Decoction darkens the

wort, which may not be desirable for the beer style that you are brewing.

TYPICAL DECOCTION MASH SCHEDULES

SINGLE DECOCTION

1. Mash in at 100°F (38°C) with a three-to-one liquor-to-grist ratio.

2. Immediately raise the temperature 2°F (1°C) per minute to 122°F (50°C).

3. Maintain protein rest twenty to thirty minutes (thirty to forty-five minutes is sometimes suggested for wheat beers).

4. Pull first thick decoction of roughly 40 percent of the mash with a two-to-one ratio of liquor to grist.

5. Ladle into second kettle and bring to 158°F (70°C).

6. Maintain saccharification rest ten to fifteen minutes.

7. Bring to boil for thirty to forty minutes.

8. Recombine with the "rest mash" to yield a

temperature of 147°F (64°C), applying bottom heat if necessary.

9. Rest ten to twenty minutes.

10. Raise to 158°F (70°C) and rest for ten to fifteen minutes or until iodine test is negative.

11. Raise to 170°F (77°C) and mash out.

12. Sparge with 165–170°F (74–77°C) water.

DOUBLE DECOCTION

1. Mash in at 100°F (38°C) with a three-to-one liquor-to-grist ratio.

2. Raise the temperature 2°F (1°C) per minute to 122°F (50°C).

3. Maintain protein rest ten to fifteen minutes before pulling first decoction.

4. Pull first thick decoction of roughly 40 percent of the mash with a two-to-one ratio of liquor to grist.

5. Ladle into second kettle and raise heat 2°F (1°C) per minute to 158°F (70°C).

6. Hold saccharification rest for ten to fifteen minutes.

7. Bring to a boil over ten to fifteen minutes and boil for twenty to forty minutes (depending on desired darkness of wort).

8. Recombine decocted portion slowly into pot with main mash over ten to fifteen minutes, while stirring.

9. The main mash should now be around 147°F (64°C). Adjust with bottom heat if necessary.

10. Immediately pull a second decoction and perform exactly as in the first.

11. Recombine with main rest mash. Raise temperature with bottom heat to 158°F (70°C).

12. Hold for ten to fifteen minutes or until iodine test is negative.

13. Mash out. Raise to 165–170°F (74–77°C). Rest five to ten minutes to decrease viscosity.

14. Transfer to lauter tun and sparge as normal.

TRIPLE DECOCTION

1. Mash in at 95°F (35°C) with a three-to-one liquor-to-grist ratio. Stir well. Hold rest thirty to sixty minutes.

2. Pull first thick decoction of roughly 33 percent of the mash with a two-to-one ratio of liquor to grist.

3. Ladle into second kettle and raise heat 2°F (1°C) per minute to 150°F (66°C).

4. Hold saccharification rest for thirty minutes.

5. Bring to a boil over ten to fifteen minutes and boil for twenty minutes.

6. Recombine decocted portion slowly into pot with main mash over ten to fifteen minutes, while stirring.

7. The main mash should now be around 122°F (50°C). Adjust with bottom heat if necessary. (Carefully maintain correct temperature in main "rest" mash while performing all decoctions.)

8. Hold protein rest for sixty minutes.

9. Pull a second decoction and perform exactly as in the first.

10. Recombine slowly with main rest mash. Raise temperature with bottom heat to 155°F (68°C) if necessary.

11. Hold saccharification rest for sixty minutes.

12. Pull a third decoction and bring to a boil.

13. Recombine with main rest mash. Raise temperature with bottom heat to 158°F (70°C) if necessary.

14. Hold for ten to fifteen minutes or until iodine test is negative.

15. Mash out. Raise to 165–170°F (74–77°C). Rest five to ten minutes to decrease viscosity.

16. Transfer to lauter tun and sparge as normal.

FERMENTATION AND LAGERING

First and foremost, keep fermenting beer in the dark. Light reacts badly with hops, creating off-flavors.

Second, keep the fermentation temperature constant as much as possible. Studies indicate that fluctuations of 10°F, and sometimes as little as 5°F, can result in off-flavors and poor yeast performance.

In most cases, beer should be kept sealed from outside air via an airlock, one-way valve, or blow-off hose system. However, when fermenting certain wheat beers, British ales, and Belgian beers, some believe open fermentation works best in accurately brewing these styles, but this is very risky when homebrewing. Because of the change in pH and the production of alcohol and CO_2, fermenting beer produces an environment unfriendly to most bacteria; nevertheless, keep all fermenting beer in a dark, draft-free area, preferably one that can be sanitized beforehand and kept undisturbed throughout the fermentation process.

If using a blow-off hose system during the primary stages of fermentation, always immerse the free end of the blow-off hose under several inches of clean water. A blow-off hose of at least a half-inch (one inch for fruit beers) inside diameter is recommended.

For brewers using an open fermenter or a covered primary fermenter with an airlock, fusel oils and resins that can impart harsh flavors to your beer can be removed during the period known as "high kräusen." This is the stage approximately thirty-six to seventy-two hours into your fermentation when the yeast forms billowing clumps called "rocky heads." If you lift the lid of your fermenter, you will see these rocky heads topped with the brown resinous scum that should be removed. This residue can be skimmed off the yeast, but only with a sanitized implement and under strictly sanitary conditions! The yeast itself should be left on the beer.

Follow the directions for proper fermentation temperature provided by the yeast manufacturer, *not* the extract manufacturer. Exceeding these limits may speed up fermentation but will most likely result in unacceptably high diacetyl and ester levels, unwanted higher alcohol levels, and generally poor flavor.

Most beers should be allowed to complete their *primary* fermentation in a single vessel. It is safe to assume that if kept at the proper temperature, the beer will have finished its primary fermentation when the hydrometer readings stay constant for two to three days. This will take approximately five to ten days for ales and two to four weeks for lagers, aiming for a final gravity of about 25 percent of your original gravity. If you prefer not to expose your beer to bacterial risk by repeatedly taking readings, let your ales ferment a full ten days before bottling and your lagers fourteen days before racking to the secondary for at least two more weeks of secondary fermentation.

Longer ale fermentation times (ten to fourteen days), when the beer is allowed to sit on its yeast sediment for a few extra days, will help reduce the diacetyl that gives beer a buttery flavor note that is inappropriate for many styles. But it is advised that, if the fermentation extends beyond fourteen days, the beer be transferred off the yeast sediment to another container.

For ales, the beer can now be racked to a bottling bucket and packaged. For lagers, it is highly recommended that the beer be racked to another vessel for an extended period of "secondary fermentation" at temperatures slowly brought down to 32°F. Because plastic fermenters are permeable to oxygen, this stage should be done in a glass carboy. This secondary fermentation can last for one to eight weeks (depending on temperature used—beer conditions faster at warmer temperatures, but lagers should not exceed 45°F) and allows more complete settling of the yeast and other haze-causing matter, resulting in a clearer and cleaner-tasting finished product.

Lagers universally require a *minimum* of three weeks of cold lagering at 32–45°F to achieve their best flavor. Temperatures higher than this have been shown to deteriorate flavor and aroma. Light lagers with a higher malt content, such as Munich helles or Czech pilsner, require a minimum of four weeks of lagering, and preferably seven to eight weeks, as noted by

George Fix in *Vienna, Märzen, Oktoberfest* (Brewers Publications, 1991). Many experts agree that darker lagers, such as Oktoberfest and bock, benefit from even greater lagering periods ranging from eight weeks to a year.

Clarifying aids can be added to the beer during its final week in the secondary, as well as any aroma hops. Dry hops can be placed in your secondary either loose or in a hop bag. The hop bag will keep loose bracts from clogging your racking tube and bottle filler, but may be difficult to remove through a narrow carboy neck. Longer dry-hopping times (two to three weeks) and careful movement of your carboy will promote better settling of loose hops.

A possible, although unlikely, side effect to very long periods of secondary fermentation is that too much of the yeast may settle out or die, making bottle or keg conditioning with priming sugar unsuccessful or sluggish. Homebrewers can rectify this by force-carbonating the flat beer with CO_2 or by adding a fresh dose of the yeast you used for primary fermentation along with the priming solution at bottling time (see next section).

BOTTLING PROCEDURES

Before starting any bottling procedure, it is best to check your beer's final gravity to be sure it is ready to be bottled, ideally within .002 specific-gravity points of what your recipe predicted. If you have no clear guidelines for

the style or a particular recipe, a good rule of thumb is to shoot for a final gravity of 25 percent of your original specific gravity. Sometimes yeast will stop fermenting if it has been exposed to adverse conditions such as sudden temperature changes, then begin fermenting again when the bottles are filled or the fermenter is disturbed. Bottling with too high a gravity may result in an inappropriately unattenuated beer or a bottle that resembles the "Old Faithful" geyser when opened.

The first thing to do is collect enough bottles and caps/Grolsch gaskets to hold all your beer. If you brewed five gallons, that will equal fifty-three twelve-ounce bottles, forty sixteen-ounce pints, or thirty-seven half-liters. Rarely will you be able to package a full five gallons from a five-gallon batch, but it's better to be prepared. Screw-cap, nonreturnable bottles require special caps and a different type of bottle capper than what homebrew shops sell.

The next step is to make sure the bottles are visually clean—that is to say, free from sediment, visible dirt, and so forth. If they are not clean, they should be thoroughly washed and rinsed.

Finally, the bottles should be carefully sanitized. You can use any of the popular sanitizers on the market, or stick with the standard thirty-minute chlorine bleach and water soak (one tablespoon per gallon). Another alternative is to sterilize the bottles in a household dishwasher—if it has a sanitary cycle. However, it is important to make sure there are no food particles in the drain that might be splashed onto or inside the bottles. This sterilizing should be done without soap and rinsing agents.

If you used the chlorine bleach method or other harsh chemicals, it is recommended that you thoroughly rinse the bottles two or three times with hot water to remove the residual chlorine.

All instruments—gadgets, containers, hoses, buckets, and so forth—that will come in contact with the beer in any way should also be thoroughly sanitized and rinsed, as well as the area to be used for the bottling procedure. (Bathrooms are usually the most convenient.) The room should also be free of drafts carrying airborne germs.

At this point, unless you will be force-carbonating your beer with CO_2, you need to prepare a priming solution of corn sugar or dried malt extract dissolved in water. For added security, this water should be boiled at least five minutes to kill any germs and to remove chlorine odors. The recommended amount of water is one or two pints, with one-half to three-quarters cup of corn sugar or 1.2 to 1.5 cups dried malt extract. Adding individual doses to each bottle is highly discouraged. Note: For packaging beer in bulk such as casks, kegs, or minikegs, it is recommended that you reduce the amount of priming sugar or dried malt extract by one-third. This equates to a half cup corn sugar or a maximum of one cup dried malt extract.

Another popular method of priming is one in which sterile, unfermented wort (called "speise"—German for "food") is added to the beer. In homebrewing, this speise can be taken from your wort before the yeast is pitched, then kept refrigerated in a sterile, airtight container until ready for use, or it can be made up fresh on bottling day (but this requires removal of the trub). This method is sometimes incorrectly called "kräusening," a method German brewers use whereby a portion of actively fermenting beer (containing a high yeast cell count and unfermented sugar) in the kräusen stage is added to fully fermented beer in order to facilitate carbonation. With ales, the addition of new yeast is usually not necessary, so a sterile, filtered malt extract and water solution can be used. However, with lagers that have been subjected to very long periods of cold conditioning, the initial yeast colony may be dead or completely settled out. A new yeast addition to lagers is considered by some to be a measure of security for ensuring adequate fermentation in the bottle or keg and a more rapid absorption of air in the head space.

Rates for five gallons equal roughly 1.5 quarts of speise for high OG beers (>1.060) and three quarts for lower OG beers (<1.030). The approximate amount of speise needed (depending on fermentability of the malt you use) is listed below (in quarts):

OG	SPEISE NEEDED
1.070	1.00–1.50 quarts
1.060	1.50–1.75 quarts
1.050	1.75–2.00 quarts
1.040	2.00–2.50 quarts
1.030	2.50–3.00 quarts
1.020	3.00–3.50 quarts

Although this method of adding wort may make your beer "all malt" and in accordance with the Reinheitsgebot, it does have its drawbacks: (1) Malt takes longer to be processed by the yeast than sugar, resulting in slower conditioning. (2) This new malt has not fermented and aged as long as the rest of the beer, and, therefore, may contribute minor "new beer" characteristics that will require slightly more time to dissipate. (3) This method is less exact because of the variable nature of malt extracts and may require more trial and error than simply dosing out three-quarters of a cup of corn sugar. (4) This method often results in residue in your bottles if the trub from the speise is not filtered out.

Now that you've prepared your priming solution, you can add it to your bottling bucket. This solution may be very hot, so be careful not to pour it directly onto a fresh dose of yeast. Set your fermenter above the bottling bucket, insert one end of the racking tube into the beer, and begin your siphon.

The safest way to start a siphon is to fill the siphon tube with water, pinch the "out" end, then first insert the "in" end in the beer and then the "out" end in the bottling bucket. When you release the bottling bucket end, the siphon will begin.

Try not to aerate or splash the beer during any racking procedure. This will result in oxidation of the hops, resulting in a possible loss or deterioration of aroma and stale flavors in the beer. When the siphoning is complete, gently mix the priming sugars, new yeast, and beer.

From here you can begin filling your bottles. Most bottling buckets now have spigots from which to run a racking hose. If yours doesn't or you're siphoning directly from the fermenter, you'll have to pinch the tube between fills. If you have a rigid racking cane and bottle filler, insert it into the bottle and fill until the beer reaches the top rim. When the racking tube is removed, proper head space will be created.

Cap the bottles, rinse to remove spilled beer, then dry and move to a dark space for conditioning.

GENERAL CONDITIONING PROCEDURES

Most ales require about five to seven days to produce CO_2 in the bottle at normal fermentation temperature when corn sugar is used as the priming agent, longer with malt extract or speise. This process of bottle or cask refermentation is known as "conditioning." The term "carbonated" is used to refer the process where CO_2 is injected artificially into the beer from an outside source.

Lagers usually require a few days more to condition, especially if they are primed with malt extract or speise, and depending on the temperature of the room where they are stored. Lagers should be conditioned as close to the fermentation temperature as possible, typically in the 46–58°F range, for a minimum of ten to fourteen days to let the slower-acting lager yeasts work.

When you are satisfied with the CO_2 level of your beer, you can now move it to a cooler environment for maturation. This is a period where any "green beer" flavor qualities in hops or malt can mellow. Traditional English cask-conditioned ales often receive as little as two days of "cellaring" before being served up in a pub, but it is accepted wisdom that three weeks is best for standard-gravity homebrewed ales. Ideally, this should be done at temperatures in the 50–55°F range—and as cold as 32°F for German ales such as alt or American cream ale. Higher-gravity ales, such as barley wine, strong ale, and Belgian tripel, for example, benefit from even longer aging times of six months to several years. Some off-flavors and aromas in lagers can take four months to dissipate, and

beers using bacteria, such as Berliner weisse, often require long six- to twelve-month aging times. The time needed is very dependent on yeast strain.

After CO_2 has been produced in the packaged beer, the main purposes of lagering beer are for clarification and to allow the flavor to mature, especially in regards to the mellowing of hop bitterness. Although this may be considered unnecessary in filtered, artificially carbonated lagers brewed with sophisticated techniques, this time is absolutely vital for "living beers" with active yeast sediment.

CARBONATING WITH RESIDUAL SUGARS

A simpler method of priming can be used with casked beers, which involves racking the beer while it is still fermenting and allowing the residual sugars to provide carbonation. One disadvantage is that the original and final gravities must be precisely known; another is that the transfer must occur when the proper level of sugars (approximately 20 percent) remain. Excess CO_2 can be bled off if the pressure gets too high in a Cornelius keg, but other bulk systems, such as five-liter minikegs, will require guesswork and experience. As with other natural carbonation methods, avoid excessive head space above the beer.

The formula for this method involves subtracting the projected final gravity from the original gravity, then calculating 80 percent of the result and subtracting that figure from original gravity. For example, a beer with a 1.050 original gravity and a 1.014 final gravity would be calculated 1.050 – 1.014 = 1.036; 1.036 × 80% = 1.029; 1.050 – 1.029 = a gravity of 1.021 when the beer is racked. This translates roughly to 1.007 specific-gravity points above expected final gravity for lagers and well-carbonated ales. Less-carbonated British ales are typically racked to cask when there are roughly 1.004 points remaining.

General Kegging Procedures

—

Most serious brewers will consider a kegging system at some time. The best, but most expensive, is the "Cornelius" type. They are five-gallon stainless-steel kegs with a CO_2 cylinder, regulator, and in and out hoses. Kegs may be either ball lock or pin lock. Ball-lock kegs usually have a pressure relief valve that you can operate manually. Pin-lock keg relief valves usually cannot be manually operated.

6. Depress the "out" poppet to drain sanitizer from the pickup tube.
7. Rinse once, then fill halfway with clean, hot water. Reseal, pressurize, and run some water through the dispensing line, then remove the line.
8. Relieve the pressure, open the keg, and drain. Keep the keg upside down until cooled. It's now ready to fill.

CLEANING
—

1. Rinse the keg with hot water and inspect. Put the lid in a pan of hot water.
2. Fill keg halfway with hot water then add one-quarter ounce of BTF. Install the lid and shake the keg to coat all surfaces.
3. Pressurize the keg with 5 psi of CO_2, shake again to recoat surfaces.
4. Run about a cup of sanitizer out through the dispensing line. Shake again.
5. When the keg has had twenty minutes of contact with the sanitizer, remove all lines, relieve the pressure, open the keg, and pour off the sanitizer. It may be saved and reused.

FILLING
—

Siphon your finished beer into the keg. Be sure your hose is long enough to reach the bottom of the keg. While the beer is running, put the lid in a small pan of water and bring to a boil. This sanitizes the lid and softens the O-ring for a better seal. Do not fill the keg so full that the short "in" stem is in the beer. Install the lid and pressurize with 5–10 psi. Check for leaks. Then pull the relief ring or lever in the center of the lid. This removes air from the keg and replaces it with CO_2. Do this three times, waiting a few minutes each time. To remove air from pin-lock kegs, remove the disconnect and depress the poppet with a blunt tool.

CARBONATING

Method 1: Treat the keg like one big bottle, but use a third of a cup of corn sugar boiled in one cup of water. Add this to the keg before filling. Pressurize to 5 psi, leaving the pressure on for the first two days. Store at 70°F for seven days.

Method 2: After sealing and bleeding the air out, raise the regulator pressure to 25 psi. Shake the keg for twenty seconds, take a break, then shake again. Repeat a third time. Disconnect the CO_2 line, shake, then store in a cool, dry place.

Method 3: You will need a place that has a constant temperature below 60°F—the colder the better. On the carbonation chart find your temperature and desired carbonation level (usually 2.5 to 3.0). Set the regulator to the proper psi and leave connected. Allow two weeks for conditioning.

TIPS

- Check poppets for leaks anytime you disconnect. A drop or two of beer on a leaker will foam. Flick the poppet with a fingernail to stop most leaks.
- If carbonating by Method 1, you may want to shorten the pickup tube by one-half inch.
- The clearer the beer going in, the clearer the finished product will be. I use Irish moss in the boil, four to eight days in a secondary at 55°F, and if it's not clear by then, I add some gelatin finings.
- A new toilet brush works well for getting to the bottom of kegs when cleaning.
- All types of faucets come apart. Clean them and beer lines regularly.

- Bleach is not recommended for sanitizing kegs as it corrodes stainless steel, especially at the weld.

GADGETS

Jumper cable—This allows you to move clear, carbonated beer from one keg to another under pressure. Your second keg ends up with sediment-free beer that can be transported without getting cloudy. You can also blend beers.

Pressure checker—A pressure gauge connected to an "in" side disconnect. Just pop the checker onto the keg to check pressure.

Pressure bleeder—A disconnect with a bleeder valve connected. Used with a jumper cable to keep flow going.

Combination pressure checker/bleeder—The two units above on one disconnect.

Counter-pressure bottle filler—A device for filling bottles from the keg under pressure.

OTHER SYSTEMS

There are several optional kegging systems on the market. I will do a short description of them based on my order of preference.

The five-liter party kegs—Four five-liter plastic-lined metal kegs that will hold a five-gallon batch. Tappers are either air pump or CO_2 bulb injectors.

The party ball—Two-and-a-half- or five-gallon plastic balls. May be tapped by full CO_2 system, CO_2 bulb injectors, or air pumps.

The party pig—A two-and-a-quarter-gallon brown plastic ball. The beer is dispensed by an inside bladder filled with a special soda and salt combination that swells as the keg empties.

Pressure kegs by Edme, Rotokeg, and others—White plastic barrels in various sizes and shapes. Beer is dispensed by CO_2 bulb injectors or natural pressure.

Headpacks—A five-gallon plastic bag in a cardboard box. Beer is drawn off a spigot at the bottom by natural pressure and gravity.

Note: The information in this section is courtesy of Paul White, Head Brewer, Seven Barrel Brewery, West Lebanon, New Hampshire.

BREWING RECORD & EVALUATION FORM

Batch Name/Number: _____ Volume: _____

Original Gravity/°Plato: _____ Final Gravity/°Plato: _____

Style: _____ Sub-style: _____

MALTS/ADJUNCTS & QUANTITY	MASH TEMPERATURE & TIME	MASH METHOD
_____	_____	_____
_____	_____	_____
_____	_____	_____
_____	_____	_____
_____	_____	_____

Mashing Notes: _____

Malt Extracts:

_____	_____	_____
_____	_____	_____

Malt Extract Notes: _____

Sugars/Miscellaneous Kettle Ingredients:

_____	_____	_____
_____	_____	_____

Wort Boil Notes: _____ Boil Time: _____

_____

continued

Primary Fermentation Ingredients/Techniques: _____

Apparent Attenuation: _____

_____

_____

Hops/Form: _____AA%: _____Quantity: _____Purpose: _____Time: _____

Hops/Form: _____AA%: _____Quantity: _____Purpose: _____Time: _____

Hops/Form: _____AA%: _____Quantity: _____Purpose: _____Time: _____

Hops/Form: _____AA%: _____Quantity: _____Purpose: _____Time: _____

Yeast: _____Brand/No.: _____Liquid/Dry/Rehydrated _____Quantity: _____

Length of Ferment: _____Special Ingredients/Brewing Procedures:_____

Secondary Fermentation and Lagering Ingredients/Techniques: Date: _____

_____

_____

Dry Hops/Form:_____AA%: _____Quantity: _____Time:_____

Length of Secondary Ferment/Lagering: _____Notes: _____

Bottling Date: _____Priming Method: _____

Number of Pints/12 Ounce Bottles: _____

Other (Party Pig, RotoCask, Cornelius Keg, etc.): _____

	6 pts.	10 pts.	19 pts.	5 pts.	10 pts.	50 pts.	
Date	Appearance	Aroma	Taste	Condition	Overall	Total	Comments

CARBONATION CHART

Pounds per Square Inch

Temperature of Beer (degrees F.)

0	1	2	3	4	5	6	7	8	9	10	11	12	13	14	15	16	17	18	19	20	21	22	23	24	25	26	27	28	29	30
30	1.82	1.92	2.03	2.14	2.23	2.36	2.48	2.60	2.70	2.82	2.93	3.02																		
31	1.78	1.88	2.00	2.10	2.20	2.31	2.42	2.54	2.65	2.76	2.86	2.96																		
32	1.75	1.85	1.95	2.05	2.16	2.27	2.38	2.48	2.59	2.70	2.80	2.90	3.01																	
33		1.81	1.91	2.01	2.12	2.23	2.33	2.43	2.53	2.63	2.74	2.84	2.96																	
34		1.78	1.86	1.97	2.07	2.18	2.28	2.38	2.48	2.58	2.68	2.79	2.89	3.00																
35			1.83	1.93	2.03	2.14	2.24	2.34	2.43	2.52	2.62	2.73	2.83	2.93	3.02															
36			1.79	1.88	1.99	2.09	2.19	2.29	2.39	2.47	2.57	2.67	2.77	2.86	2.96															
37				1.84	1.94	2.04	2.15	2.24	2.34	2.42	2.52	2.62	2.72	2.80	2.90	3.00														
38				1.80	1.90	2.00	2.10	2.20	2.29	2.38	2.47	2.57	2.67	2.75	2.85	2.94														
39					1.86	1.96	2.05	2.15	2.25	2.34	2.43	2.52	2.61	2.70	2.80	2.89	2.98													
40					1.82	1.92	2.01	2.10	2.20	2.30	2.39	2.47	2.56	2.65	2.75	2.84	2.93													
41						1.87	1.97	2.06	2.16	2.25	2.35	2.43	2.52	2.60	2.70	2.79	2.87	2.96												
42						1.83	1.93	2.02	2.12	2.21	2.30	2.39	2.47	2.56	2.65	2.74	2.82	2.91	3.00											
43						1.80	1.90	1.99	2.08	2.17	2.26	2.34	2.43	2.52	2.60	2.69	2.78	2.86	2.95											
44							1.85	1.95	2.04	2.13	2.21	2.30	2.39	2.47	2.56	2.64	2.73	2.81	2.90	2.99										
45							1.82	1.91	2.00	2.08	2.17	2.26	2.34	2.42	2.51	2.60	2.68	2.77	2.85	2.94	3.02									
46								1.88	1.96	2.04	2.13	2.22	2.30	2.38	2.47	2.55	2.63	2.72	2.80	2.89	2.98									
47								1.84	1.92	2.00	2.09	2.18	2.25	2.34	2.42	2.50	2.59	2.67	2.75	2.84	2.93	3.02								
48								1.80	1.88	1.96	2.05	2.14	2.21	2.30	2.38	2.46	2.55	2.62	2.70	2.79	2.87	2.96								
49									1.85	1.93	2.01	2.10	2.18	2.26	2.34	2.42	2.50	2.58	2.66	2.75	2.82	2.91	2.99							
50									1.82	1.90	1.98	2.06	2.14	2.21	2.30	2.38	2.45	2.54	2.62	2.70	2.78	2.86	2.94	3.02						
51										1.87	1.95	2.02	2.10	2.18	2.25	2.34	2.41	2.49	2.57	2.65	2.73	2.81	2.89	2.97						
52										1.84	1.91	1.99	2.06	2.14	2.22	2.30	2.37	2.45	2.54	2.61	2.69	2.76	2.84	2.93	3.00					
53										1.80	1.88	1.96	2.03	2.10	2.18	2.26	2.33	2.41	2.48	2.57	2.64	2.72	2.80	2.88	2.95	3.03				
54											1.85	1.93	2.00	2.07	2.15	2.22	2.29	2.37	2.44	2.52	2.60	2.67	2.75	2.83	2.90	2.98				
55											1.82	1.89	1.97	2.04	2.11	2.19	2.25	2.33	2.40	2.47	2.55	2.63	2.70	2.78	2.85	2.93	3.01			
56												1.86	1.93	2.00	2.07	2.15	2.21	2.29	2.36	2.43	2.50	2.58	2.65	2.73	2.80	2.88	2.96			
57												1.83	1.90	1.97	2.04	2.11	2.18	2.25	2.33	2.40	2.47	2.54	2.61	2.69	2.76	2.84	2.91	2.99		
58												1.80	1.86	1.94	2.00	2.07	2.14	2.21	2.29	2.36	2.43	2.50	2.57	2.64	2.72	2.80	2.86	2.94	3.01	
59													1.83	1.90	1.97	2.04	2.11	2.18	2.25	2.32	2.39	2.46	2.53	2.60	2.67	2.75	2.81	2.89	2.96	3.03
60													1.80	1.87	1.94	2.01	2.08	2.14	2.21	2.28	2.35	2.42	2.49	2.56	2.63	2.70	2.77	2.84	2.91	2.98

To use this chart, look up the temperature of the beer; and read across to the desired level of carbonation. Follow up the line to find what pressure to set your regulator. ©1994 Byron Burch, The Beverage People.

ADVANCED TIPS FOR BETTER HOMEBREWING

BOILING

- A technique once used in brewing dark, heavy German beers is to boil the wort for up to three or four hours. Using this method, the protein coagulated in the hot-break is eventually dissolved back into the wort, resulting in an extremely smooth, velvety, and full-bodied beer. A longer boil also lends a darker color and more toasted/caramel flavors. The bittering hops should be added just ninety to sixty minutes before the end of such a boil.

BEER CLARITY

- Use of a secondary fermenter, preferably a five-gallon glass carboy for five-gallon recipes, is practically mandatory in successful lager brewing. In two-stage fermenting, the beer is racked off the sediment formed in the fermenter after primary fermentation is complete, therefore reducing the time that dead yeast and trub stay in contact with the beer, as well as lessening the chance that this sediment will make it into your bottling bucket.
- In his book *Continental Pilsener* (Brewers Publications, 1989), David Miller suggests racking your homebrew off the cold trub before pitching your yeast (or eight to twelve hours afterward) to further eliminate unwanted sediment. According to Miller, this procedure lowers fusel alcohol production and eliminates the need to skim the residue off the kräusen. A simple method for home-

brewers is described in the following paragraph. Note: This trub sediment is not the same as the yeast sediment that forms during fermentation. Fermenting beer should not be racked off this yeast sediment until fermentation is complete, except where specifically called for in a recipe.

- For added beer clarity, you can perform a homebrewer's version of what the commercial brewers call cold trub removal. They do it in a whirlpool or by floating these coagulated proteins out with forced air; you can do it by racking your beer into another fermentation vessel anytime before active fermentation begins (less than twelve hours is best). Simply put your wort and yeast in a vessel other than what you'll use for primary fermentation (preferably a glass carboy so you can see when the layer of sediment forms at the bottom). In as little as an hour you'll see the trub settle to form a whitish layer about a half inch thick. You can now very carefully siphon off the beer into your primary, leaving the trub behind.

FLAVOR

- Avoid pulverizing specialty grains or malts that will be used in your brew. Turning the husks into flour will greatly increase the possibility that tannins will make their harsh flavor presence known in your final product.
- Avoid oversparging of grains. This can wash out the dreaded tannins in the husks that lend a harsh, bitter flavor. One good rinse is

usually enough for specialty malts. Also, do not use water above 172°F except where specifically called for in a recipe. One of the rare examples is in sparging Belgian lambic where the astringent flavors extracted by a high-temperature sparge are an integral part of the flavor profile.

HOPS

- Use of a carboy/blowoff hose system for primary fermentation may reduce your beer's bitterness because many of the bitter hop resins will be ejected with the foam. Save the carboy for secondary ferments or increase your IBUs in the boil.

BOTTLING

- PureSeal bottle caps (aka "Smartcaps") absorb oxygen in the head space and have been proven to make hop aroma last much longer. It is important to note that boiling these caps in order to sanitize them will ruin their oxygen-absorbing capabilities.

CASK CONDITIONING AND CELLARMANSHIP

- Leave casks well secured and undisturbed in serving position until empty. Once in this position, allow to settle at least one day before serving. Use only whole or plug hops to dry-hop. Place in a sanitized hop bag and leave for seven to ten days.
- Select the correct cask size, that is, for the quantity of beer to be consumed in one or two days once tapped.
- Maintain a temperature in the cellar between 50° and 57°F. Temperature significantly affects the CO_2 level, which for a traditional cask-conditioned ale should be 0.75–1.5 volumes. High temperatures will result in flat beer and a degradation of finings. Excessively low temperatures may result in a permanent chill haze or an overly gassy beer.
- Cellars should be ventilated, but devoid of any drafty areas. Sudden temperature changes (hot or cold) can cause sediment-disturbing convection currents to be set up in your cask.

REFRIGERATION

- Regardless of whether you prefer ales or lagers, the serious homebrewer should also seriously consider obtaining a second "beer-designated" refrigerator. Even a small fridge with constant temperatures can vastly improve the conditioning of ales and is absolutely essential for brewing and storing lagers in warm weather—when they are most appropriate. Check your local yellow pages for used appliance dealers. Second-hand refrigerators can be had for as little as $50 to $100.

UNDER-STANDING BEER

THE MAJOR BEER STYLES

Learning the history and development of a beer you love is one of the great joys of home brewing. Following is a brief description of most of the world's great beer styles. A more thorough description of these follows in their respective recipe sections. A solid understanding of the major styles is an important base for any brewer and will help you not only understand why these beers taste the way they do but also greatly increase your ability to design your own recipe formulations. At the end of this section is a listing of the major recognized beer styles and their technical parameters for easy reference. Attention to the general guidelines seen in commercial styles and expected by beer judges at competitions will greatly increase the authenticity of your brew.

Abbey Beer—Although there are no rigid guidelines for what constitutes an abbey beer, it is generally accepted as a rich, full-flavored Belgian ale patterned after one of the Trappist beers (see "Trappist Ale"), often with a vinous quality due to high alcohol content. These beers are called "abbey" simply because they often have the name of an old monastery attached—usually by a commercial brewery that pays a royalty for the privilege. Abbey beers run the gamut from deep gold to dark reddish brown and are generously carbonated. Esters, malt aroma, and some phenols usually dominate. Abbeys classified as "dubbel" or "tripel" sometimes have hop aroma. Alcohol averages 6 to 8 percent v/v.

Altbier—Also known as Düsseldorfer alt. "Altbier" means "old" or "traditional beer" in German, referring to the old way that beers (that is, ales) were top-fermented prior to the lagering revolution of the nineteenth century. These ales were originally lagered for long periods in ice-filled caves after a warm primary ferment, which served to subdue the fruitiness. These beers have intense hop bitterness but subdued hop flavor and aroma. They are full-bodied, bitter, and a deep, reddish amber to brown color, but drier and more carbonated than an English-style ale. It should be noted that altbier is not an appellation and, therefore, the term "alt" can be incorporated in the brand names of various beers not in the Düsseldorfer style—for example, Münster Alt, Altmünchener, Kloster Altbier, Alt Bayerische—and often merely indicates an older style of ale or a dark lager.

American Microbrewed Ale—In the wake of the revival of craft brewing in North America, microbrewed or, more accurately, "craft-brewed" beers are now exemplified by full-bodied, fruity, moderately strong, and well-hopped variations of classic British, Belgian, and German ales. Often craft brewers strive to compromise between the American taste for a drier, livelier beer and the freshness and character of European beers previously unavailable in America. A perfect example of this type of beer is American amber ale, a beer that began as a brewpub interpretation of an English-style ale using domestic ingredients, but has evolved into a distinct and recognizable style of its own.

American Microbrewery Lager—In the earliest days of the craft-brew revolution, microbrews were patterned after hard-to-obtain English-style ales using simple, single-step infusion mashing, as opposed to the more complex and expensive methods of stepped and decoction mashing used in lager brewing, but now scores of American lagers that borrow from modern European temperature-controlled mashing methods are being brewed in a wide variety of German and pre-Prohibition styles. As in American ale brewing, American lager brewers often rely heavily on homegrown hop varieties such as Cascade, Willamette, Mt. Hood, Eroica, Chinook, as well as American yeast strains, which tend to be more neutral than their European counterparts.

American Pilsner—Also referred to as "American Premium Lager." Lightly colored and hopped, these often include adjuncts such as corn and rice for their character, and bear little resemblance to Czech pilsner. They are usually highly carbonated and served ice-cold. These generally are the products of the "giants" (such as Coors, Budweiser, and Miller) that have grown progressively lighter and blander over the past thirty years but still dominate the marketplace. American pre-Prohibition pilsners did have a small portion of adjuncts in their makeup, but are a much more palatable brew with a fuller, richer malt flavor and hop presence.

Australian/New Zealand Ales and Lagers—These beers tend to be light straw to amber colored, are often dry, full-bodied, and well hopped with the locally grown Pride of Ringwood or Sticklebract. Although they have a reputation for being very strong, Australian beers are usually moderately alcoholic, and draw from both British and German brewing traditions. After a promising start in the 1980s, the craft-brewing movement has faltered somewhat in Australia and an overwhelming majority of the brewing is done by international brewing giants.

Barley Wine—Perhaps this strong ale of England gained its moniker from its elevated, often winelike alcohol content. Barley wines range from deep amber in color to copper. High final gravities give barley wine a residual sweetness balanced by high hop bitterness. Barley wine is well suited to cellaring and often reaches its peak when matured at least one year.

Belgian Red Ale—A West Flanders ale deriving its reddish color from large portions of Vienna malt, and its trademark tartness, spiciness, and acidity from more than a year of maturation in oak tuns. Belgian red (aka "old red" or "Flanders red") is frequently blended with younger ale to reduce the acidity level. Michael Jackson has called this Belgian specialty the world's most refreshing beer.

Belgian Strong Ale—As the name suggests, Belgian strong ale is an alcoholically strong ale akin to the barley wines and strong ales of Britain that ranges in color from deep gold to reddish brown. The use of highly fermentable sugars lends alcoholic strength and a vinous nature, but without the malty heaviness associated with Scotch ale, stout, or doppelbock.

Bière de Garde/Bière de Paris—French country and Parisian brewed beers, respectively, featuring moderate levels of body and maltiness. The hop bitterness, flavor, and aroma are also generally mild to moderate. Bière de garde is especially characterized by a clean, satisfying, and mature personality with hints of musty cellar notes. These beers borrow heavily from Belgian brewing traditions. Bière de Paris is usually fermented with lager yeast, and the color for both beers is amber to reddish brown. Bières de garde are brewed primarily in the area near the Belgian border, cork-finished in 750 ml wine bottles, and well aged to mellow their intense flavor profile.

Bière de Mars—Light-bodied seasonal French ales homebrewed from the choicest barley and hops. After an extended fermentation over the winter, Bière de Mars is consumed in celebration of the arrival of spring following a tradition that goes back five hundred years. Unlike the commercially extinct Mars beer of Belgium, the French Bière de Mars is meant to be alcoholically strong yet balanced and mature.

Bitter—This popular British pub beer includes three substyles classified according to original gravity: ordinary bitter, special bitter, and best bitter, which is also called extra special bitter (ESB) or strong bitter. These well-hopped ales are often cask-conditioned and served on draft, but bottled versions abound as well. Bitter is not as bitter as the name implies, but more often aromatic and spicy from English hops and only slightly drier than standard pale ale. Bitters range in color from bronze to deep copper and often have a pronounced fruitiness and a touch of butterscotch in their flavor profile.

Bock—Bock is a rich, malty, brown German lager of 6.5 percent or more alcohol by volume that was traditionally brewed in fall and winter for enjoyment in spring. Originally bock was consumed by monks, as these beers provided a good source of nutrition during Lenten fasts. Craft-brewed American bocks are usually lighter in body and color than the original Bavarian bocks. Doppelbocks, or "double bocks," start with original gravities of around 1.075 (and alcohol at 7.5 percent by volume) and feature intense maltiness. Bock can also be homebrewed with top-fermenting yeast at cooler temperatures while still remaining fairly true to style. Weizenbock is a Bavarian wheat beer that ranges from a deep, reddish amber to black in color, but these are usually much lighter in body and malt intensity than the standard all barley malt bocks.

Brown Ale—Brown ales from the south of England typically are darker, sweeter, and lower in alcohol than their northern counterparts. American brown typically has more pronounced hop bitterness, flavor, and aroma—masking any diacetyl/estery qualities. All are brewed with softer water than that used for pale ales and from a wide range of ingredients and original gravities. Brown ales have enjoyed a notable resurgence in their popularity in the wake of craft brewery revival.

California Common Beer—A uniquely American lager style fermented at the lower range of ale fermenting temperatures or at the upper range for lagers (that is, 55–60°F) with a clean lager yeast strain, then cold lagered—resulting in low esters and diacetyl. Pale to dark straw or copper in color, medium-full flavor and body, and usually well-hopped in bitterness, flavor, and aroma, these well-carbonated lagers were nicknamed "steam beer" in the nineteenth century, most likely after the fascinating new source of brewery power, steam.

Canadian Ales and Lagers—Beers similar to U.S. versions in the use of adjuncts and so forth, but usually with much more hop character. The ales have clean, crisp, lager characteristics, but exported megabrewery versions of both ales and lagers are often considered inferior to those found close to home in Canada. Canadian microbrews, however, can boast the same success as their American counterparts.

Cream Ale—An American or Canadian mild, golden, and full-bodied pale ale generally brewed with North American–grown barley and hops, and with an alcohol content of around 4.5–5.75 percent by volume. Typically cream ales are top-fermented, then cold-aged like a lager or even blended with lager beer to produce a smooth, clean flavor.

Czech/Bohemian Pilsner—Czech pilsner is possibly the world's most ubiquitous beer style, invented in the Bohemian city of Plzen (Pilsen) in 1842. This classic lager ignited the nineteenth-century lager brewing revolution. Pilsner is pale straw to deep golden colored and features a flowery bouquet and bitterness of Saaz hops balanced by a clean maltiness. Czech pilsner is generally more complex and malty than the European or American versions.

Dortmunder Export—Originally brewed in the area around the city of Dortmund in western Germany, Dortmunder, or export, as it is also called, is typified by a full-bodied and robust character derived in large part from the hard water around Dortmund used to brew it. Dortmunder lager is maltier than a German pils, yet drier than a Munich helles. Because the term "export" is not an appellation, it can often be applied to other "premium" beers not in the style such as export-dunkel, a dark Bavarian lager.

Dubbel (Double)—A more clearly defined substyle of the Belgian Trappist/abbey style that perhaps gained its designation because it originally had approximately twice the original gravity of the "simple" beers of Belgium in the Middle Ages. With moderately high original gravities, these fairly sweet, dark, reddish brown beers fall below tripel in strength, are usually bottle-conditioned, and are suitable for cellaring.

Eis Bock—German for "ice bock." A Bavarian lager beer created by freezing doppelbock after completion of fermentation. The resulting ice is removed and, therefore, much of the water, resulting in a much sweeter, heavier, and alcoholically strong beer.

Erlanger—A dark German lager originating in the Bavarian city of Erlangen that is both heavier and darker than Munich dunkel but has lower gravity and lighter color than Kulmbacher.

Faro—A style of Belgian lambic that is pale to brown in color, spontaneously fermented, of course, and refermented with candi sugar. The result is a lively, faintly sweet, but lactic and acidic ale with a soft, winelike character. Originally served exclusively on draft in and around Brussels, faro is hard, but not impossible, to find in bottles outside of Belgium and France. Frank Boon's Pertotale Faro is aged for two years in oak casks, then blended with wheat ale before bottling. It is also spiced with Curaçao orange peel and the prehops bitterer, gentian root.

Framboise—The term "framboise" generally indicates a bottle-conditioned Belgian fruit lambic or gueuze flavored with fresh raspberries. Framboise should be minimally hopped, sour and cloudy, with lively carbonation.

German/North European Pils—Created as an answer to the original Czech pilsner, German pils is dramatically paler, more attenuated, hoppier, and more effervescent than the original Bohemian-brewed versions of pilsner.

Grand Cru—A vague designation for a Belgian beer in no particular style that is often given to a strong seasonal beer. Originally brewed for weddings, village celebrations, and other important events, grand cru is usually high in alcohol but pale in color.

Gueuze—Old lambic (two to four years old) and young lambic (three months to one year old) that are blended, then refermented and aged at least one more year in the bottle before being released.

Ice Beer—The result of a fermentation process developed by Labatt's Brewery of Canada. The lager is force-fermented with specially designed yeasts engineered to work at low temperatures in order to produce a very clean, dry, and smooth product. The subsequent removal of ice crystals from the chilled beer similar to the method of creating eis bock is meant to produce less of the watery flavor found in "dry" or "light" beers (in some brands, water is put back in). Alcohol is typically 5–5.6 percent by volume.

India Pale Ale (IPA)—A substyle of English pale ale whose textbook definition has traditionally been of a premium, high-gravity, extremely well-hopped ale, although there are many commercial brands that do not fit this description. IPA gained its name because of its popularity with the British troops in colonial India. Its alcoholic strength and high hopping rates helped it withstand the long ocean voyage from England. However, another legend exists that the name was dreamed up by a merchant who wanted to unload ale bound for Russia but was stranded onboard a ship moored at London's "India Dock" during a political crisis. This is a beer now found mostly in bottled form, although it was originally cask-conditioned for several months (and with estimated hopping rates well over 100 IBUs).

Irish Red Ale—A reddish (from the use of roasted barley) Irish cousin of English pale ale/bitter exhibiting slightly more sweetness and body. Greatly influenced by the Scottish ales, Irish reds are malty, lightly hopped, light- to medium-bodied, and have a slight buttery quality. Top- or bottom-fermented versions can be found, although the most traditional ones are ales.

Kellerbier—Defined as a roughly filtered, fruity, dry Bavarian lager, kellerbier is brewed primarily in Franconia around Buttenheim and Bamberg. Kellerbier averages 4.5 to 5 percent alcohol by volume, and is highly hopped and lightly carbonated and bears many similarities to homebrewed lagers and those found in brewpubs in America. Bottled versions do exist, but this unfiltered or minimally filtered beer is usually served on draft in local village "bräustüberls."

Klosterbier—Literally translated, a "cloister beer," indicating that the beer is or was brewed in a monastery or convent, usually in Germany.

Kölsch—A blond-colored, often cloudy "old-style" German ale originally brewed in Köln (Cologne). Kölsch has moderate or low hop bitterness, is dry from a thorough fermentation, and features a slight lactic quality. Kölsch is also moderately high in alcohol at 4–5.5 percent by volume.

Kriek—Belgian lambic or gueuze subjected to a lengthy secondary fermentation on sour cherries in an oak cask.

Kulmbacher—Originally from the town of Kulmbach in northern Bavaria, this lager is considered to be heavier and darker than the Bavarian dark beers brewed in Erlangen and Munich.

Lambic—Spontaneously fermented Belgian ale that draws its character from wild yeasts found in the area around Brussels and from bacteria residing in the wooden casks where it is fermented. The style originated in the town of Lembeek in the Pajottenland and by law must contain a minimum of 30 percent wheat, traditionally raw. It is cloudy yellow, very lightly hopped, frothy, and slightly sour or citric in taste. Lambic is often flavored with macerated fruits such as peaches ("pêche"), cherries ("kriek"), or raspberries ("framboise") and occasionally with grapes ("muscat"), currants ("cassis"), and recently with various others. The lambic wort is exposed to the local microorganisms overnight in large, open "coolships," then fermented in used wine casks for up to three years.

Märzen—A German lagered "festbier." Similar to the Vienna style, but now generally regarded to have evolved into a slightly darker, stronger beer. True Märzen, by the traditional Bavarian definition, is brewed in March and aged until late September/early October harvest festivals. Märzen should be amber, smooth, and malty, but well balanced by German or Czech hops.

Mexican Beer—Originally, these were basically German or Vienna-style lagers brewed by German immigrants. Most modern varieties, however, have moved closer to American megabrewery lagers in body, flavor, carbonation, and alcohol content due in large part to the recent popularity of Corona, a high-adjunct beer originally brewed in the 1920s to be an inexpensive, blue-collar beer.

Mild Ale—Mild ales are low-alcohol, medium- to light-bodied English ales with a subtle residual sweetness. Mild ale color varies from deep copper to dark brown but almost all are brewed from low original gravities. They were originally immature beers of normal or even high gravity, but are now "mild" in terms of strength and hop bitterness, not age.

Munich Dunkel—Dunkel (German for "dark") might be considered the southern Bavarian version of a larger category of continental dark lagers that also includes schwarzbier, Kulmbacher, and Erlanger as well as the dark beers brewed in eastern Europe and the Netherlands. Mastery of this beer style is credited to the lager-brewing pioneer Gabriel Sedlmayr II in the last century. His initials can still be found on the Spaten label. The smooth and restrained dunkel is characterized by a malty aroma and flavor gently balanced by Bavarian hops varieties.

Munich Helles—Munich helles was developed in response to consumer demand for pilsner lagers at a time when Munich's claim to fame was dunkel. Helles is often considered merely a pale version of the renowned Munich dunkel. Helles, which means "pale" in German, is not particularly low in calories or alcohol, but medium-bodied, malty, and with a gentler hop presence than is found in pilsner.

Oktoberfest—An American term denoting the style of beer traditionally served at Oktoberfest celebrations in Bavaria. Bavarians generally refer to this beer as "Märzen."

Old Ale—Today's old ales are often thought of as a warming winter specialty or nightcap, as many approach barley wine strength. This English ale was dubbed "old" because it was aged a year or more before being sold. The combination of the more costly old ale and the more affordable mild ale evolved into what we know today as porter.

Oud Bruin (Old Brown)—Also commonly called "Flanders brown," this Belgian specialty ranges from deep garnet brown to nearly black in color. Oud bruin is given extended primary and secondary fermentations and traditionally often in casks where it picks up a lactic tang from bacteria residing in the wood. What emerges is a malty, mature, slightly sour, and acidic beer with a mellow winelike quality. Some oud bruins are also flavored with raspberry or cherry, but almost all are low in hop bitterness, flavor, and aroma.

Pale Ale—The classic British ale developed in the eighteenth century and made famous by the pale ales of Burton Pale Ale is hoppy, robust, and bronze, amber, or burnished copper in color with a balance of malt sweetness, hop bitterness, and fermentation fruitiness. By modern standards, these ales are far from pale, but the name was first used in comparison to the really dark stouts and porters. Pale ales are brewed from harder waters than most ales and typically with OGs of 1.040–1.055. (See "India Pale Ale" and "Bitter.") A full-bodied, light, amber to copper ale with a pronounced hop character emphasized by the sulfate-rich waters of Burton.

Porter—Often considered London's claim to brewing fame, porter is dark, moderately strong ale created as a blend of mild and/or brown ale with old ale. Porter is noted for having a spicy, chocolatey flavor profile balanced by generous English hop bitterness. Although a stout predecessor, porter is lighter in body and malt character than stout but still features substantial roast malt character. After decades of decline, this slightly bitter, dark ale has regained widespread popularity among microbreweries and homebrewers alike.

Rauchbier—German "smoke beer." Made famous by the breweries of Bamberg in northern Bavaria, rauchbiers go well with the intensely flavored sausages made there or with any smoked foods. The smoky quality originated from the old method of curing malts over oak or beechwood fires, but authentic flavor can be achieved by homebrewers through the use of "liquid smoke" flavoring, by home-smoking lager malt, or by purchasing the increasingly available rauch malts imported from Bavaria.

Roggenbier/Rye Beer—A rare specialty beer made from 60 percent malted and roasted rye in one Bavarian version to produce a dry, grainy, and weizenbier-like brew. Several American craft brewers also produce beers with rye as a principal ingredient. The traditional Finnish "farmhouse" brew, sahti, is often brewed with rye and juniper, then fermented with wild yeasts.

Saison—A complex and earthy ale brewed in the French-speaking region of Belgium around the town of Liège. These mellow, smooth, thirst-quenching ales are brewed by traditional farmhouse breweries in the cold-weather months and matured for long periods before being released for summer consumption. Saisons are generally top-fermented, dry-hopped, and refermented in cork-finished wine bottles.

Schwarzbier—Literally translated as "black beer" in German, schwarzbier is a dark east German lager noted for the presence of bittersweet chocolate flavors. Schwarzbier is more assertive than the more popular Munich dunkel and is noticeably darker in color. Ironically, few examples of this style are brewed in Germany, but several prime examples are brewed in Japan.

Scottish/Scotch Ale—The normal-strength Scottish ales include the beers designated light, heavy, and export (aka 60 shilling, 70 shilling, and 80 shilling, respectively). Scottish ale is historically low in hop bitterness, flavor, and aroma. A fourth category, strong (90 shilling) is a dark, rich, complex ale of varying strengths that is often called "Scotch ale" or "wee heavy" and approaches barley wine strength.

Steam Beer—Although the name "Steam" now belongs to Anchor Brewing Company of San Francisco, it is widely used colloquially in the homebrewing community to refer to California common beer (see above). The origin of the name "steam" is subject to many theories ranging from the source of brewery power in the 1800s to the relatively high temperature of fermentation, and even the sound released when the beer was tapped. Several Bavarian brewers have also revived a style called dampfbier (German for "steam beer") in the past two decades. Produced mainly around the Bavarian towns of Bayreuth and Zweisel, these are fruity, top-fermented, but cold-lagered beers.

Steinbier—A top-fermented wheat beer brewed in Altenmünster, Germany, whose character is drawn from an ancient method of bringing large quantities of wort to a boil in a wooden vessel by dropping in superheated rocks. "Steinbier" literally means "stone beer" in German, and refers to the fact that porous graywacke stones are heated to 1,200°C, then are dunked into the wort (or more recently, have the wort poured over them), causing the sugars to crystallize on the stone. The stones are allowed to cool, then immersed into the beer so the caramelized sugars can be fermented. The result is a beer with a sweet, smoky flavor.

Stout—Another beer style with its roots in English mild, this descendant of porter is a dark, malty, and opaque ale brewed with 5–10 percent roasted unmalted barley for a flavor that suggests roasted coffee. Stouts may be "sweet," "dry," or "imperial" and range in strength from a low 3.5 percent alcohol to 10 percent by volume. Dry or "Irish" stout is often dispensed with a high-pressure nitrogen/CO_2 mixture to give it a moussy, tan head without overcarbonating the beer itself. In Ireland, dry stout is often served at room temperature and is usually lower in alcohol than in the rest of the world to make it a better "session beer." The sweet stout category also includes oatmeal stout.

Trappist Ale—As an "appellation," only beers produced by Trappist monasteries (the five in Belgium and the one in the Netherlands) have the right to attach the name "Trappist" to their beers. Although the term "Trappist" is more indicative of a brewery location than an actual style, they are mostly top-fermented, bottle-conditioned, and (usually) lightly hopped ales and are generally strong (alcohol 6–10 percent v/v), estery, phenolic, and complexly malty, with higher alcohol flavors often in evidence. The higher-gravity Trappist beers typically use adjuncts such as invert or candi sugar to provide increased alcohol without the heavy maltiness associated with bock. See the subcategories "Dubbel," "Tripel," and "Belgian Strong Ale."

Tripel—A substyle of Belgian beers with Trappist origins and original gravities that are approximately triple the original specific gravities of the "simple" beers of medieval Belgium. These beers are typically in the 1.070–1.095 original-gravity range and are brewed from very pale malt and a generous quantity of candi or invert sugar. The pale gold to amber tripel is alcoholically stronger, but drier and paler than dubbel, as well as English ales of comparable strength, such as old ale or barley wine.

Vienna—Vienna emerged as a style of lager beer in Vienna, Austria, during the mid-nineteenth century. This commercially produced lager evolved from the old tradition of brewing a special, higher-gravity beer in March and cold-aging it until the autumn harvest celebrations. Vienna is deep amber to light garnet in color, only moderately strong, modestly hopped for balance, and predominantly malty.

Wheat/Weizen Beer—Made from widely varying percentages of malted wheat and barley; depending on substyle and country of origin, "wheat beer" is an enormous style category encompassing vastly differing beers ranging from the tart, refreshing Berliner weisse to the dark, malty Bavarian weizenbock. Colors range from pale, whitish gold to ruddy orange to dark brown. Bavarian-style wheats, particularly hefe-weizen, are now enjoying a dramatic comeback worldwide after more than a century of near extinction. American wheat is much milder in flavor and usually lacks the distinctive clove and banana notes of the Bavarian-style varieties, but has the same refreshing taste and generous carbonation. Other major substyles include kristall, a clear, filtered wheat beer kräusened with bottom-fermenting yeast for more lagerlike character,

and dunkelweizen, a maltier, darker variation of hefe-weizen.

Witbier—A yellow-gold wheat beer originally from around Leuven (Louvain) and Hoegaarden, Belgium, witbier is cloudy, frothy, and pale, with a light and mellow flavor and aroma profile. Known variously as "white beer," "bière blanche," or simply "wit," lactobacillus bacteria, special ale yeast strains, unmalted ("raw") wheat, and spices such as coriander, cumin, and Curaçao bitter orange peel contribute to witbier's unique flavor and thirst-quenching qualities.

Zoigl—Rarely produced by commercial breweries, but mainly "homebrewed" in small towns in the Oberfalz region of northern Bavaria, zoigl may be top- or bottom-fermented, but it is usually amber to dark brown, full-bodied, unfiltered, dry, and served *vom fass* (on draft). Zoigl's availability is heralded when the farmhouse brewer displays an ancient, six-pointed alchemist's sign resembling the Star of David. The commercial bottled version from the village of Friedenfels has an alcohol level of 5.2 percent v/v.

BEER STYLES AT A GLANCE

Use these general guidelines demonstrated by modern commercial beers in creating your own recipes, but bear in mind that these numbers are merely averages and cannot tell of the quality ingredients, proper balance of flavor, and attention to detail needed for success. Sample some good microbrews or fresh imported versions to guide you in crafting your own recipes. (See explanation of column headings below.)

Style	OG	FG	IBUs	SRM	ABV percent
Altbier	1.043–48	1.008–14	28–50	10–16	4.5–5
American Amber Ale	1.050–60	1.012–14	30–40	8–18	5–6
American Lager (pre-Prohibition)	1.044–60	1.010–16	20–40	2–5	5–6
Barley Wine	1.065–1.120+	1.024–32	50–100	8–22	7–12
Belgian Pale Ale	1.044–54	1.008–14	20–30	3.5–12	4–6.2
Berliner Weisse	1.028–32	1.004–06	3–8	2–4	2.5–3.4
Bière de Garde	1.055–75	1.010–12	25–30	8–12	6.0–8.5
Bitter (Extra Special)	1.042–60	1.010–16	30–55	12–15	4.5–6
Bitter (Ordinary)	1.035–38	1.006–12	20–30	8–12	3–3.5
Bitter (Special)	1.038–42	1.006–12	25–30	12–14	3.5–4.5
Bock	1.064–72	1.018–24	20–25	9.5–22	6.6–7.5
Brown Ale (American)	1.038–55	1.010–18	25–55	15–25	3.5–5.5
Brown Ale (English)	1.040–50	1.008–14	14–35	18–34	3.5–4.5
California Common	1.040–55	1.012–18	30–45	8–17	3.6–5
Cream Ale	1.044–55	1.004–10	10–22	2–4	4.5–5.75
Czech Pilsner	1.043–49	1.014–20	30–43	4–4.5	4–4.5
Doppelbock	1.072–80	1.020–28	17–27	12–30	6.5–8
Dortmunder Export	1.048–55	1.010–14	20–30	3–5	5–6
Dubbel	1.063–70	1.012–16	18–25	10–14	6–7.5
Dunkel	1.049–54	1.014–18	20–30	14–20	5–6
Dunkelweizen	1.048–56	1.008–16	10–15	17–22	4.8–5.4
Eis Bock	1.066–1.110	1.018–26	28–40	18–50	8.6–14.4
Faro	1.044–56	1.000–10	11–23	6–13	5–6
German Pils	1.044–50	1.006–12	30–40	2.5–4	4–5
Gueuze	1.044–56	1.000–10	11–23	6–13	5–6
Imperial Stout	1.072–80	1.020–30	50–80	20–50	7–9
India Pale Ale	1.050–65	1.010–16	40–60	8–14	5–6.5
Japanese-style Dry	1.040–50	1.004–08	15–23	2–4	4–5
Kölsch	1.044–48	1.006–10	25–30	3.5–5.5	4.5–5
Kristall-Weizen	1.045–55	1.016–20	10–19	3.5–5	5–5.5
Lambic (Fruit)	1.042–72	1.008–16	15–21	5–10	5–7
Lambic	1.047–54	1.004–10	15–21	5–10	5–6.5
Light Beer	1.024–40	1.002–08	8–15	2–4	2.9–4.2
Mai/Helles Bock	1.064–72	1.012–20	20–35	4.5–6	6–7.5
Märzen/Oktoberfest	1.050–60	1.012–20	20–25	8–12	5–6
Mild Ale	1.030–38	1.004–08	10–25	10–26	3–3.5

STYLE	OG	FG	IBUs	SRM	ABV PERCENT
Munich Helles	1.044–47	1.008–12	20–25	3–4.5	4.5–5.5
Old Ale	1.055–95	1.008–22	30–40	10–16	6–9
Oud Bruin	1.044–56	1.008–10	15–25	12–18	4.8–5.2
Pale Ale (American)	1.044–56	1.008–16	20–40	4–11	4.5–5.5
Pale Ale (English)	1.045–55	1.008–16	25–45	6–12	4.5–5.5
Porter	1.045–60	1.008–16	25–45	20–40	5–6
Rauchbier	1.048–52	1.012–16	20–30	10–20	4.3–4.8
Saison	1.044–54	1.006–12	20–30	3.5–12	4–6
Schwarzbier	1.044–52	1.012–16	22–30	25–30	3.8–5
Scotch Ale	1.072–85	1.016–25	25–35	15–50	6–8
Scottish Export	1.040–50	1.010–18	15–20	10–20	4–4.5
Scottish Heavy	1.035–40	1.010–14	10–15	10–20	3.5–4
Scottish Light	1.030–35	1.006–12	8–18	7–18	3–4
Stout (Dry)	1.040–50	1.008–14	30–50	35–70	4–5.5
Stout (Oatmeal)	1.044–48	1.008–20	27–31	30–40	3.7–4.5
Stout (Sweet)	1.045–56	1.012–20	15–25	40+	3–6
Strong Ale (Belgian)	1.063–95	1.012–24	20–50	3.5–20	7–12
Tripel	1.070–95	1.016–24	20–25	3.5–5.5	7–10
U.S. Pilsner (megabrewery)	1.044–48	1.010–14	11–16	2–2.5	4–5
Vienna	1.048–56	1.012–18	22–28	8–12	4.4–6
Weizen (Helles Hefe-Weissbier)	1.048–55	1.008–16	10–18	3–10	4.5–5.5
Weizenbock	1.065–80	1.026–32	15–25	7–30	6.5–7.5
Witbier	1.044–50	1.006–10	15–20	2–4	4.5–5.2

OG—*Original Gravity. A measure of the fermentables in the wort prior to fermentation.*

IBUs—*International Bittering Units. See page 360.*

SRM—*Standard Reference (Research) Method. See page 59.*

ABV—*Alcohol by Volume (v/v). Expressed as a percentage, this figure is often confused with the Alcohol by Weight (w/v) figure used by U.S. breweries.*

MALT, ADJUNCT, AND SPECIALTY GRAIN PROFILES

Below is a list of the malts commonly used in brewing, the traditional specialty grains, and the adjuncts used to adjust color, body, and head retention. There are three coloring scales used throughout this book. I have chosen not to use just one for the primary reason that all three are still widely used in homebrew supply catalogs and in beer literature, and there are strong loyalties to each. They are as follows:

SRM—The acronym for "Standard Research (or Reference) Method," a term used by the American Society of Brewing Chemists (ASBC) to denote degrees of color. They range on a scale of approximately 1 to 600; higher numbers are progressively darker. SRM/Lovibond figures are roughly one-half the EBC values.

Lovibond—An older form of color measurement, usually seen with British products, that is close enough to the SRM designation to be used interchangeably for homebrewing purposes. Expressed as "degrees Lovibond," "°Lovibond," or "°L." As with the SRM scale, Lovibond ranges from approximately 1 (e.g., pilsner malt) to 550 (e.g., black patent malt) in beer usage.

EBC—The acronym for the European Brewing Convention (Congress), whose measurements are used primarily in continental Europe. Numbers are usually seen ranging from 3.5 (e.g., Belgian pils malt) to 1,400 (e.g., Belgian roasted malt) and are roughly double the SRM/Lovibond rating.

Acid Malt—Malt containing high levels of lactic acid that is used by brewers who want to adjust malt pH without having to "sour mash" or add lactobacillus. Originally designed by brewers of pale or pilsner beer to doctor high-carbonate mash water. This malt is rarely available to (or needed by) homebrewers and is used mostly by German breweries. Color 2–4 SRM. Typically yields 1.030–35 degrees of specific gravity per pound in one gallon of 60°F water.

Amber Malt—A roasted specialty malt used primarily by British brewers for coloring and biscuity taste in old ale, mild, brown ale, and the occasional bitter. Created by heating cured mild ale malt quickly to 212°F then slowly up to 300°F. Because of its low diastatic power, it should be mashed with a diastatic malt to yield fermentable extract. It is rarely available in the United States. Color 15–25 SRM. Typically yields 1.025–28 degrees of specific gravity per pound in one gallon of 60°F water.

Aromatic Malt—A mildly kilned Belgian barley malt that adds a strong malt aroma and deep color when used as a specialty malt. Can be used as 100 percent of the grist in recipes, but since it is fairly low in surplus diastatic enzymes, keep adjunct usage to below 10 percent of the total grist. Color 20–25 SRM. Typically yields 1.030–35 degrees of specific gravity per pound in one gallon of 60°F water.

Barley Syrup—A mixture of barley, corn, and wheat malt extracts used as a cheap substitute for pure malt. Rich in carbohydrates and yeast nutrients, it is highly fermentable, but should never exceed 50 percent usage and is generally not recommended for high-quality beers.

Belgian Pils—A European two-row malt rapidly gaining popularity because it makes a good base malt for almost any all-grain beer style, particularly continental lager and, because it is extremely well modified, can be easily mashed with a single-temperature infusion. Color 1–2 SRM. Typically yields 1.035–39 degrees of specific gravity per pound in one gallon of 60°F water.

Biscuit Malt—The darker Belgian version of victory malt. This toasted malt provides a warm bread or biscuit flavor and aroma. Also lends a garnet to brown coloring. Use 5–15 percent maximum. No enzymes. Must be mashed with malts having surplus diastatic power. Color 20–25 SRM. Typically yields 1.033–37 degrees of specific gravity per pound in one gallon of 60°F water.

Black Barley—Roasted unmalted barley that lends color properties similar to black patent malt, but the two are not interchangeable in your recipes. A much darker form of roasted barley, black barley provides sharp, dry stout flavor. Ideal for hearty brews. Drier than black patent or chocolate malts. Color 500–550+ SRM. Typically yields 1.022–27 degrees of specific gravity per pound in one gallon of 60°F water.

Black Patent Malt (Black Malt)—Malted barley roasted at very high temperatures using the same process as chocolate malt except it is kilned much longer. These high temperatures destroy enzymes and much of the starch, which results in low extract yield. Black patent malt has no enzymes and is generally not used for its aroma, which is very aggressive. Small amounts

add brown coloring, large amounts add black color and a charcoal/burnt/smoky or nutty taste that is less dry than roasted barley. Use sparingly. Good for porters, stouts, and dark lagers. German versions and the trademarked Briess version are often called "black prinz" in supply catalogs. The Belgian version is called "roasted malt." Color 475–550 SRM. Typically yields 1.023–26 degrees of specific gravity per pound in one gallon of 60°F water.

Brewer's Sugar—See "Corn Sugar/Dextrose" and "Glucose."

Brown Malt—An old style of a roasted malted barley that was once the staple of European beer brewing, particularly in England and Germany, where it formed the basis of the famous London porter and the brown beers of the Bavarian monasteries before nineteenth-century innovations using coal as a heat source made "pale malt" more affordable. Technically, brown malt should be a smoked malt kilned over an oak, beech, ash, or hornbeam fire, resulting in a rich, spicy/smoky flavor. This brand of malt is now rarely used in commercial brewing outside of the United Kingdom or Bamberg, Germany. It is still sometimes used by U.K. homebrewers primarily as a specialty malt, but is sold by only a few supply shops in the United States, where home brewers have taken to smoking their own malts for authenticity. Color 50–70 SRM. Typically yields 1.030–33 degrees of specific gravity per pound in one gallon of 60°F water.

Brumalt—A dark German malt developed by German breweries to darken and improve the malt flavor and aroma of Märzen/Oktoberfest and altbiers without having to decoction mash. Rarely available to homebrewers. Color 15–30 SRM. Typically yields 1.030–35 degrees of specific gravity per pound in one gallon of 60°F water.

Candi Sugar—A very pure, slowly crystallized dextrose/sucrose mixture used in traditional Belgian brewing that adds its own special flavor and aroma. Corn sugars are considered the nearest substitute for the light versions, caramel sugar for the darker styles. Candi ranges in color from approximately 10 to 750 SRM. Typically yields 1.035–40 degrees of specific gravity per pound in one gallon of 60°F water.

Cane/Beet Sugar—A 100 percent fermentable refined sugar (99.5 percent sucrose) made from sugar cane or sugar beets that is primarily used to raise gravity and lighten body. Also known as table sugar. Should be dissolved before adding to the boil. Use sparingly (i.e., less than or equal to one pound per five U.S. gallons). Beet sugar must be totally refined, but partially refined cane sugar is available as "raw sugar." Typically yields 1.042–45 degrees of specific gravity per pound in one gallon of 60°F water.

Caramel—Cooked sugar (usually sucrose) used primarily in commercial brewing to darken beer and to lend a slight caramel flavor. Its use has been suggested as a possible alternative to dark candi sugar.

Caramel Malt/Crystal Malt—Made by heating wet germinated barley (high-nitrogen "green malt") to around 150°F until the enzymes in the malt convert the starches; then it is kilned at around 500°F. There are no enzymes and few fermentables, but crystal malt's dextrines and other nonfermentables add enhanced mouthfeel, body, reddish color, head retention, caramel/nutty flavor, and sweetness to differing degrees, depending on

SRM/EBC rating, country of origin, brand, and amount used. For example, the German "light crystal" version adds little sweetness. To avoid harsh flavors, use of no more than 20–30 percent or less than one pound per five U.S. gallons is recommended. Crystal malts can be added to the main mash or steeped alone prior to the wort boil and range in color from 10 to 120 SRM. Typically yields 1.020–30 degrees of specific gravity per pound in one gallon of 60°F water.

CaraMunich—A medium-amber Belgian crystal malt. No enzymes. Imparts a rich, caramel-sweet aroma and full flavor, as well as intense color. Not synonymous with Munich malt. Color 53–75 SRM. Typically yields 1.030–35 degrees of specific gravity per pound in one gallon of 60°F water.

CaraPils—The brand name of a dextrine malt made by the Briess Malting Company. See "Dextrine Malt" below. Color 1–2 SRM. Typically yields 1.025–35 degrees of specific gravity per pound in one gallon of 60°F water.

CaraVienne—A Belgian light caramel malt. Originally used by Belgian breweries in lighter abbey- or Trappist-style ales, but it is appropriate for any recipe that calls for crystal malt. Not synonymous with Vienna malt. Color 12–25 SRM. Typically yields 1.030–35 degrees of specific gravity per pound in one gallon of 60°F water.

Chocolate Malt—A high-nitrogen malt that is roasted at temperatures up to 450°F, then rapidly cooled when the desired color is achieved. "Chocolate" refers primarily to the malt's color, not its flavor. Similar to black patent, but lighter and is most often used in milds and porters. Lends various levels of aroma, deep red color, and a nutty/roasted taste, depending on the amounts used. Color varies for country of origin but averages 350–450 SRM. Typically yields 1.025–30 degrees of specific gravity per pound in one gallon of 60°F water.

Corn Sugar (Dextrose-Glucose)—Also commonly referred to as "brewer's sugar." The most fermentable and commonly used adjunct, often added in lieu of the more expensive barley malts, and commonly used for priming (bottle/keg conditioning). Will lend cidery flavors and thin body if overused (i.e., >15 percent or more than one or two pounds per five U.S. gallons). Increases alcohol level without increasing body. Typically yields 1.035–40 degrees of specific gravity per pound in one gallon of 60°F water.

Dark Crystal Malt—The darkest version of the caramel malts, this term is sometimes used specifically to refer to the dark German version of caramel malt. Adds a deep reddish amber color and a rich caramel sweetness. Steep or mash. Color usually 80–120 SRM (the German version averages 40–90 SRM). Typically yields 1.020–30 degrees of specific gravity per pound in one gallon of 60°F water.

Demerara—A British term for an aromatic and softly flavored "raw" brown sugar sometimes used in English ales. Less refined than "table" cane sugars. Slightly subtler in flavor than the American equivalent, "turbinado." Typically yields 1.038–42 degrees of specific gravity per pound in one gallon of 60°F water.

Dextrine Malt—Very light caramel malt made by drying barley malt at low temperatures. Lends body, smoother mouthfeel, and foam stability, without adding a red color or crystal malt flavor. Dextrine malts include the popular six-row Briess CaraPils and the DeWolf-

Cosyns' two-row Belgian version. No enzymes. No mashing required. Use as 5 to 20 percent of the grist. Color 1–2 SRM. Typically yields 1.025–35 degrees of specific gravity per pound in one gallon of 60°F water.

Dried Malt Extract (DME)—Malted barley, and often other coloring grains according to intended style, cooked down to a thick syrup then spray-dried to a powder form. Available with or without hop extracts added. Except for "diastatic" malt extracts, the presence of enzymes is negligible. Color 10–55 SRM. Typically yields 1.035–45 degrees of specific gravity per pound in one gallon of 60°F water.

English Pale Malt—Fully modified and easily converted by a single-temperature mash (e.g., 150–158°F for one hour). The preferred malt for English ales. Usually higher kilned than U.S. two-row pale malts (i.e., Klages and Harrington) and lower in enzymes. Keep use of adjuncts to less than 15 percent. Color 2–4 SRM. Typically yields 1.027–33 degrees of specific gravity per pound in one gallon of 60°F water.

Flaked Barley—Unmalted barley often added directly to the main mashes of bitter, dark mild, porter, and stout to lend a rich, grainy taste and to increase head retention, creaminess, and body. Does not need to be precooked, but mashing is required to avoid haze formation in the finished beer. Color 1–3 SRM. Typically yields 1.025–35 degrees of specific gravity per pound in one gallon of 60°F water.

Flaked Maize—A virtually nitrogen-free adjunct widely used in moderate quantities to provide more depth of character to lighter beers. Contributes alcohol, but no flavor, color, or body. Overuse will impart a distinct corn taste. Must be mashed with pale malt, and as with other flaked products, doesn't need cooking beforehand. Color 0–1 SRM. Typically yields 1.030–35 degrees of specific gravity per pound in one gallon of 60°F water.

Flaked, Rolled, and Steel Cut Oats—Used primarily in brewing oatmeal stouts and Belgian ales. All must be mashed, and steel cut oats should be well cooked beforehand. Adds a distinct full-bodied flavor and "chewy" texture, and can also counteract the harshness caused by hard brewing water. A long protein rest must be done to avoid a haze in pale-colored beers. Color 1–3 SRM. Typically yields 1.030–35 degrees of specific gravity per pound in one gallon of 60°F water.

Flaked Rye—Lends a dry, crisp character and strong, unique flavor that is inappropriate and overpowering in most classic beer styles. Must be mashed, preferably with highly modified malts. (See "Rye.") Color 1–3 SRM. Typically yields 1.030–35 degrees of specific gravity per pound in one gallon of 60°F water.

Flaked Wheat—Increases head retention and body. Must be mashed, preferably with a highly modified malt. As with other flaked products, the grain is steamed, then rolled flat. Color 1–3 SRM. Typically yields 1.025–30 degrees of specific gravity per pound in one gallon of 60°F water.

German Crystal Malt—Usually found in only two varieties: "light" (10–20 SRM) and "dark" (40–90 SRM). The lower SRM ratings provide body without the drastic color and sweetness of British crystal malt. No enzymes. Steep or mash. Typically yields 1.020–30 degrees of specific gravity per pound in one gallon of 60°F water.

German Roasted Raw Wheat—Imparts a deep brown color and a unique flavor to dunkelweizens and other dark beers. Color 200–650 SRM. Typically yields 1.020–30 degrees of specific gravity per pound in one gallon of 60°F water.

Glucose—This is term used most often in British homebrewing to refer to what Americans know as corn or brewer's sugar. A monosaccharide created through hydrolysis of vegetable starch (usually corn) with acid. One hundred percent fermentable. Typically yields 1.035–40 degrees of specific gravity per pound in one gallon of 60°F water.

Grits—Cereal grains (usually corn and rice) milled to small granules, giving them a larger surface area in water—making them more easily converted in one-step infusion mashes. Should be cooked beforehand.

Invert Sugar—A highly fermentable brewing/priming sugar composed of a mixture of fructose and dextrose formed when sucrose is split by acid or an enzyme. Sweeter and more soluble than sucrose. Popular in Belgian brewing because it contributes alcoholic strength without heaviness. Not generally available to homebrewers, but corn sugar is often recommended as a substitute. Color 10–190 SRM. Typically yields 1.036–39 degrees of specific gravity per pound in one gallon of 60°F water.

Lager Malt—Malt that is kilned at low temperatures for lighter color and to preserve high enzyme levels. Usually two-row German, Canadian, or American pale malt is available to homebrewers in catalogs if not specifically called pilsner malt. Modern lager malts are more highly modified than the traditional lager malts, which allows single-temperature infusion mashing. High levels of adjuncts can be used, but this will require more complicated stepped or decoction mashing. Appropriate as a base malt for all lagers. Color 1–2 SRM. Typically yields 1.027–35 degrees of specific gravity per pound in one gallon of 60°F water.

Malt Extract Syrup—Malted barley and/or wheat and other grains mashed and cooked down to a thick syrup to which water is added by the brewer to create wort. The recipe basis for beginning and intermediate homebrewing. When hopped and a yeast packet is included, packaged malt extract is referred to as a "kit." Color 4–120 SRM. Typically yields 1.027–38 degrees of specific gravity per pound in one gallon of 60°F water.

Mild Ale Malt—Two-row British barley of higher nitrogen content that is malted the same as pale ale malt, but is then kilned at higher temperatures and for slightly longer to yield a deeper color and lower moisture content. Mild ale malt has lower extract yields than pale ale malt, but its somewhat higher diastatic enzyme levels allow the use of greater percentages of adjuncts. Yields a malty flavor and aroma, good for English-style mild and brown ales. Mashing required. Color 2–3 SRM. Typically yields 1.025–30 degrees of specific gravity per pound in one gallon of 60°F water.

Molasses—A thick, aromatic, and uniquely flavored syrup made from sorghum or as a residue of cane sugar refinement. Available "sulfured" or "unsulfured" and in varying degrees of intensity and fermentability as light, medium, and blackstrap. Use sparingly. See "Treacle."

Munich Malt—So named because this is the malt long used by Munich brewers for their dark lagers. German, Belgian, American, and Canadian varieties are now available. Higher kilning than pale malts provides a full, grainy, malty flavor and aroma, sweetness, and orange-amber color. Can make up to 100 percent of the grain bill, but low diastatic power makes it unsuitable for use with adjuncts. Mashing required. Color 5–8 SRM for imported varieties and usually 10 SRM for domestic. Typically yields 1.025–35 degrees of specific gravity per pound in one gallon of 60°F water.

Pale Ale Malt (Two-Row Belgian)—Interchangeable with British pale ale malt except that it has slightly more diastatic power. Color 2–4 SRM. Typically yields 1.035–38 degrees of specific gravity per pound in one gallon of 60°F water.

Pale Ale Malt (Two-Row British)—The quintessential fully modified British malt slowly kilned at low temperatures to a 3 percent moisture level. Easily mashed by a single-temperature infusion, two-row pale is suitable for both ales and lagers, but keep adjuncts to under 15 percent of the total grist because it has lower diastatic power than U.S. two-row. There are fewer tannins and higher extract yields than with six-row malt, but because of reduced husk material, great care must be taken when crushing to avoid a sluggish runoff in the mash. Mashing is required. Color 2–3 SRM. Typically yields 1.035–38 degrees of specific gravity per pound in one gallon of 60°F water.

Pale Malt (Two-Row American)—Highly modified and highly enzymatic for a two-row variety. Suitable for ales and lagers. Mashing required. Color 2.5–4 SRM. Typically yields 1.030–35 degrees of specific gravity per pound in one gallon of 60°F water.

Pale Malt (Six-Row American)—High in enzymes, proteins, but also tannins from the greater amount of husk material (avoid oversparging). A protein rest is recommended in all-grain brewing. Will yield less extract per pound than two-row varieties, but is ideal for use with adjuncts (up to 50 percent). Suitable for ales and lagers. Mashing required. Color 1–2 SRM. Typically yields 1.025–30 degrees of specific gravity per pound in one gallon of 60°F water.

Pilsner Malt—German/Eastern European/ Belgian two-row. Also known as German pale malt. Popular strains include "Moravian" and DeWolf-Cosyns' "Pils." Light color, easily mashed, and produces very malty flavor, but it is weaker in enzymes than U.S. six-row. Large amounts of adjuncts in the mash will require addition of amylase enzyme or other highly enzymatic malts. Color 1–2 SRM. Typically yields 1.035–40 degrees of specific gravity per pound in one gallon of 60°F water.

Raw Barley—An adjunct that can compose up to 15 percent of the grist, but extremely skillful milling is required to preserve husk integrity while sufficiently crushing the endosperm. Raw barley performs best when decoction mashed, but it can be infusion mashed by the experienced brewer. Because it is cheaper than malted barley, it is sometimes used in large commercial breweries in conjunction with industrial enzymes as a malted barley substitute. Typically yields 1.025–30 degrees of specific gravity per pound in one gallon of 60°F water.

Rice Extract Syrup—The ingredient that gives some American and Japanese lagers (especially "dry" lagers) their crisp, clean taste and light body. Use instead of corn sugar and in small quantities (i.e., less than or equal to 15 percent). Typically yields 1.030–35 degrees of specific gravity per pound in one gallon of 60°F water.

Roasted Barley—This is unmalted barley gently and gradually roasted to a rich, dark brown, but it is generally lighter than black barley and smoother and drier than black malt. It is produced in Britain, Belgium, and the United States and is most often used in porters, stouts, Scottish ales, and milds. No enzymes. Improves head retention and also adds reddish color when used sparingly. Imparts bitterness, roast aroma, dark color, and coffee flavor when used in greater quantities (1–4+ cups). Steep or add to main mash. Color 300–500+ SRM. Typically yields 1.024–27 degrees of specific gravity per pound in one gallon of 60°F water.

Roasted Malt—The Belgian version of black patent malt (see above). Color 500–700 SRM. Typically yields 1.025–30 degrees of specific gravity per pound in one gallon of 60°F water.

Rye—(aka "roggen" in German). This traditional bread grain is occasionally used to lend rye's uniquely dry flavor to beer styles. However, because of a lack of husk material and a high water-absorption rate, rye is a difficult grain to mash. A long protein rest is recommended. Available raw, malted (2–5 SRM), or roasted unmalted (400–600 SRM). Typically yields 1.025–35 degrees of specific gravity per pound in one gallon of 60°F water.

Special B—The darkest of the Belgian caramel malts; on par with the darkest English or German crystal malts. Imparts a heavy caramel taste and is often credited with the raisinlike flavors of some Belgian abbey beers. Larger percentages, that is, greater than 5 percent, contribute a dark brown to black color and fuller body. Color 110–225 SRM. Typically yields 1.025–30 degrees of specific gravity per pound in one gallon of 60°F water.

Spray Malt—The British term for dried malt extract. (See above.)

Toasted Malt—Toasting of pale malted barley is easily done by the homebrewer (10–15 minutes in a 350°F oven); or it can be purchased as "biscuit" or "victory" malt. These add a reddish/orange color and improved body without the sweetness of crystal malt. Mashing required to avoid starch haze. Color averages 25–30 SRM. Typically yields 1.030–35 degrees of specific gravity per pound in one gallon of 60°F water.

Torrefied Grains—Usually wheat and rice that have been puffed like breakfast cereal or popcorn, exploding the endosperm and gelatinizing the starches. They need no further cooking, but these adjuncts used for head retention and improved mouthfeel should be mashed. Torrefied barley reportedly improves mash tun runoff and lends a drier taste than flaked barley. It is used by some British breweries in bitters and milds. Color 1–1.5 SRM Typically yields 1.025–30 degrees of specific gravity per pound in one gallon of 60°F water.

Treacle—A heavy, sweet British-style mixture of molasses, invert sugar, and corn syrup. Treacle is intensely flavored, but has a very different taste from American-style molasses so the two are not interchangeable in recipes. "Golden syrup" is a milder, clarified molasses derivative. Both are popular in the United Kingdom as food products and in the brewing of some stouts.

Turbinado—A light "raw" brown sugar made from sugarcane that is minimally refined and coarsely granulated. It is usually found in vegetarian groceries and health-food stores. Good for homebrewed British-style pale ales and possibly high-gravity Belgian ales. Use sparingly or a cloying sweetness may result. See "Demerara." Typically yields 1.041–44 degrees of specific gravity per pound in one gallon of 60°F water.

Victory Malt—A lightly toasted aroma and flavoring malt. Provides a warm biscuit aroma to dark lagers and ales such as porter. Also lends a garnet to brown coloring, but not the sweetness of dark crystal. Use 5–15 percent maximum. Similar to Belgian biscuit malt, but lighter. Color 3–5 SRM. Typically yields 1.030–35 degrees of specific gravity per pound in one gallon of 60°F water.

Vienna Malt—A two-row German or six-row American malt with high acidity levels. Lends a full flavor and deep amber color. Rich and aromatic, Vienna malt is the flavorful basis for the Vienna/Märzen/Oktoberfest-style beers. Mashing required. Domestic varieties are generally darker. Color 3–10 SRM. Typically yields 1.025–35 degrees of specific gravity per pound in one gallon of 60°F water.

Wheat Malt—Made primarily from winter wheat, malted wheat is used in various amounts generally ranging from 30–70 percent of the grist in creating the many styles of wheat beer, and in smaller amounts (i.e., 5–10 percent) to aid in head retention of other beers such as Münster alt. Mash with two-row or six-row barley malt to compensate for wheat's lack of husk material. Wheat malt extracts are often a combination of barley and wheat malt. Used in combination with barley, wheat malt is believed to lighten mouthfeel, improve yeast activity, and heighten thirst-quenching properties. Color 0–3 SRM. Typically yields 1.035–40 degrees of specific gravity per pound in one gallon of 60°F water.

Malts, Adjuncts, and Specialty Grains at a Glance

(One pound per gallon of water at 60°F)

———

Variations from these figures will depend on a variety of factors including the vigorousness and length of the boil, efficiency of your mashing/brewing techniques, and the quality and modification of your ingredients. A homebrewing extract efficiency of 75–80 percent is assumed here for malt and grain adjunct values.

Ingredient	Color (SRM)	S.G. Yield
Acid Malt	2–4	1.030–35
Amber Malt	15–25	1.025–28
Aromatic Malt	20–25	1.030–35
Belgian Pils	1–2	1.035–39
Biscuit Malt	20–25	1.033–37
Black Barley	500–550+	1.022–27
Black Patent Malt	475–550	1.023–26
Brown Malt	50–70	1.030–33
Brumalt	15–30	1.030–35
Candi Sugar	10–750	1.035–40
Cane/Beet Sugar	0–1	1.042–45
Caramel Malt/Crystal Malt	10–120	1.020–30
CaraMunich	53–75	1.025–30
CaraPils®	1–2	1.020–30
CaraVienne	12–25	1.020–30
Chocolate Malt	350–450	1.020–25
Corn Sugar (Dextrose)	0–1	1.035–40
Corn Syrup	0–1	1.034–37
Dark Crystal Malt	80–120	1.020–30
Demerara	5–20	1.038–42
Dextrin Malt	1–2	1.025–35
Dried Malt Extract	10–55	1.035–45

Ingredient	Color (SRM)	S.G. Yield
English Pale Malt	2–4	1.027–33
Flaked Barley	1–3	1.025–30
Flaked Maize	0–1	1.030–35
Flaked Rye	1–3	1.030–35
Flaked Wheat	1–3	1.025–30
Flaked, Rolled, and Steel Cut Oats	1–3	1.030–35
German Dark Crystal Malt	40–90	1.020–30
German Light Crystal Malt	10–20	1.020–30
German Roasted Raw Wheat	200–650	1.020–30
Invert Sugar	10–190	1.036–39
Lager Malt	1–2	1.027–35
Malt Extract Syrup	4–120	1.027–38
Mild Ale Malt	2–3	1.025–30
Munich Malt (European)	5–10	1.025–30
Pale Ale Malt (2-row Belgian)	2–4	1.030–35
Pale Ale Malt (2-row British)	2–3	1.030–35
Pale Malt (2-row American)	2.5–4	1.030–35

Ingredient	Color (SRM)	S.G. Yield
Pale Malt (6-row American)	1–2	1.025–30
Pilsner Malt	1–2	1.035–40
Raw Barley	1–2	1.025–30
Rice Extract Syrup	4–10	1.030–35
Roasted Barley	300–500+	1.024–27
Roasted Malt	500–700	1.025–30
Rye (malted)	2–5	1.025–35
Rye (roasted)	400–600	1.025–35
Special B	110–225	1.025–30

Ingredient	Color (SRM)	S.G. Yield
Toasted Malt	25–30	1.030–35
Torrefied Grains	1–1.5	1.025–30
Turbinado	5–15	1.041–44
Victory Malt	3–5	1.030–35
Vienna Malt	3–10	1.025–35
Wheat Flour	0–2	1.026–29
Wheat Malt	0–3	1.035–40
Wheat Malt Extract Syrup	8–15	1.025–35

Hop Profiles

Commonly used brewing hops are listed below, with countries that are the major producers, the hop's typical alpha acid percentage, usage (bittering or finishing), characteristics, and the styles of beer most often used in. More than twenty varieties, such as Columbia, Comet, Magnum, and Talisman, have been omitted because either they are generally not yet available for homebrewing or have decreased in production to the point of being unobtainable. It should be noted that many of the finishing or "aroma" hops are often used by traditional craft brewers for bittering purposes. The reverse is not true. Hops intended for bittering purposes rarely make good finishing hops.

Bramling Cross (Canada & Britain) (5–7 percent)—Finishing and bittering but primarily an aroma hop. A decreasingly popular hop developed in the 1960s as a wilt-resistant replacement for East Kent Goldings. Not widely available in the United States. Ales and lagers.

Brewers Gold (Britain & Germany) (6–10 percent)—Second only to Northern Brewer production numbers in Germany, Brewers Gold is a good bittering hop traditionally used for German lagers and English ales but is versatile enough for bittering usage in most recipes.

British Columbia Goldings (B.C.) (Canada & America) (4–6 percent)—North American version of the classic British aromatic finishing hop. Identical to "East Kent Goldings" below. Pale ales, bitter, porters, and stouts, especially dry-hopped ales.

Bullion (Britain & America) (5–10 percent)—Primarily bittering, strong flavors, spicy, and pungent. A sister selection of Brewers Gold and virtually identical to it in agronomic characteristics (except maturity), brewing performance, and quality. The America-grown Bullion usually has higher AA percents. A homebrewer's favorite as a good general-purpose hop. Stouts and dark ales.

Cascade (America) (4–7 percent)—A Fuggles cross. Versatile, citrusy, and primarily a flavor- and aroma-finishing hop, but also an acceptable bittering hop that is a favorite of microbrewers as well as homebrewers. American ales and lagers.

Centennial (America) (9–11 percent)—Aka CFJ–90. Bittering, but also very acceptable for aromatic purposes. Medium to dark American ales.

Challenger (Britain) (7–10 percent)—A popular seeded or seedless hop second only to Target in annual production. Because of the overwhelming use of traditional aroma varieties such as East Kent Goldings, it is used primarily in the United Kingdom for bittering, despite the fact that it has a nice aroma. A favorite of British homebrewers as a multipurpose hop, but only recently available in the United States. British and Belgian ales.

Chinook (America) (11–14 percent)—Bittering, similar to Bullion, but stronger. Sometimes used for its intense aroma. A U.S. hybrid suited for practically all American ales and lagers.

Cluster (America) (5–8 percent)—Primarily a mild bittering hop but with a nice floral aroma and fair to good flavor. Light and dark American lagers.

Columbus (America) (12–16 percent)—Engineered primarily as a Centennial substitute. Like Centennial, Columbus is high in both alpha acids and essential oils. Very pungently aromatic, but also an economical and clean-tasting bittering hop. American amber ale, American pale ale, porter, and stout.

Crystal (America) (2–5 percent)—A newer hop cultivar released in 1993 derived from Hallertauer Mittelfrüh and Cascade as a further improvement over Mt. Hood and Liberty in approximating Hallertau Mittelfrüh aroma. German and American lagers.

East Kent Goldings (Britain, Canada, & America) (4–6 percent)—The classic aromatic ale finishing hop. Unfortunately, availability is spotty and these hops store poorly. Nitrogen-purged plugs are recommended. Like Fuggles, this hop is produced mainly in the English counties of Kent, Sussex, Hereford, and Worcester but is rapidly expanding in Oregon to an estimated eighty bales (16,000 pounds) in 1995. Pale ales, bitter, porters, and stouts, especially dry-hopped ales.

Eroica (America) (10–14 percent)—Bittering and acceptable aroma for a high-alpha variety (use sparingly). Now decreasing in popularity among growers because it matures very late, is difficult to harvest, has lower alpha acid content than Galena or Nugget, and doesn't keep as well. Pale ales, dark ales, and stouts.

Fuggles (Britain & America) (4–6 percent)—A classic finishing hop. Very versatile and popular, with a rounded, mild, and woody aroma. The British varieties have higher alpha acid percentages. Well suited for all English ales, especially pale ales, porters, and stouts.

Galena (America) (11–14 percent)—Very bitter. Very popular because, as a bittering hop, it is said to blend well with finishing hops. American ales and lagers.

Green Bullet (New Zealand) (9–11 percent)—Bittering. When available it is usually in pellet form. Australian-style ales and lagers.

Hallertau (Germany) (4–6 percent)—The Hallertau is an area in Bavaria extending north of Munich bounded by the rivers Isar, Vils, Rott, and Inn that is the largest single hop-production region in Europe. Although there is a variety of German hop called Hallertau Hallertauer, hops of unknown origin simply labeled "Hallertau" are likely to be American-grown Mittelfrüh. Imported hops labeled only "Hallertau" are most likely Hallertau Hallertauer but technically could be any hop from the Hallertau region. Mellow, spicy fragrance, a good all-around bittering and finishing hop for altbiers, Belgian ales, and all continental-style lagers.

Hallertauer Hersbrucker (Germany) (2–6 percent)—The Hersbrucker hops grown near Nürnberg and along the "Hopfen Strasse" are one of Germany's most popular aroma varieties. Most are now grown in the Hallertau region. Often used interchangeably with the superior but scarcer Mittelfrüh. Mildly aromatic, with a crisp, spicy fragrance; a versatile bittering and herbal finishing hop. Wheats, altbiers, pilsners, Belgian ales, American and German lagers.

Hallertauer Mittelfrüh (Mittelfrueh) (Germany & America) (4–6 percent)—Bittering, flavor, and aroma. The legendary Mittelfrüh's share of Germany's hop production has dropped from around 90 percent twenty-five years ago to less than 5 percent today, largely due to low yields and susceptibility to verticillium wilt. More pungent, assertive, and herbal than Hersbrucker, but the two have been used interchangeably by brewers. This hop is usually bought up by commercial brewers and is rarely available to homebrewers. Domestic Hallertauer is an American-grown version of Hallertau Mittelfrüh and is much more readily available. Continental lagers and German ales.

Hallertauer Tradition (Germany) (5–7 percent)—A newer aroma variety developed as a higher-yielding and wilt-resistant derivative of the noble Mittelfrüh. This hop has found very favorable response from growers and merchants and is likely to find its way into increasing numbers of German ales and lagers.

Liberty (America) (4–5 percent)—A very good, low-alpha-acid improvement of the Mt. Hood variety developed to closely approximate Hallertauer Mittelfrüh aroma. Primarily a finishing hop. American and German ales and lagers.

Lublin (Poland) (3–5 percent)—A fine aroma variety grown in Poland that reportedly is merely transplanted Czech Saazer. Relatively new and scarce in homebrewing circles, but ideal for pilsners or Belgian ales.

Mt. Hood (America) (4–6 percent)—An excellent American derivative of Hallertauer Mittelfrüh with a light, delicate aroma. "Half-sister" to the Liberty. Primarily for aroma and flavor in American and German ales and lagers.

Northdown (Britain) (8–11 percent)—Developed by the famous Wye College, Northdown is a versatile flavor and aroma hop that also performs well as a bittering hop. Available seeded or seedless, this derivative of the Northern Brewer variety is one of Great Britain's most popular hops.

Northern Brewer (America, Britain & Germany) (7–11 percent)—Each country produces a distinctly different version of this versatile hop—the British variety, for example, can have as much as a 4 percent higher alpha acid content than the German (approximately 7 percent AA), and the American version has a rougher flavor and aroma than the German. Primarily for bittering, but with strong flavors and very fragrant. Available seeded or seedless, this is a favorite bittering hop for California common beers, dark English ales, and German lagers, but is also acceptable for aroma when used very sparingly.

Nugget (America) (11–16 percent)—Extremely bitter, a Brewer's Gold derivative with a distinct herbal/spicy aroma and good storage stability. Rapidly gaining popularity among microbrewers for its economy. Medium to dark American ales and lagers.

Omega (Britain) (9–11 percent)—A newer variety of high-alpha-acid bittering hop quickly gaining favor with British commercial brewers and homebrewers alike. Available in seeded or seedless varieties.

Perle (Germany & America) (6–11 percent)—A Hallertau/Northern Brewer hybrid. American varieties generally have higher alpha-acid ratings and are used primarily for bittering, but it also has good "green hop" aromas when used sparingly. The lower-alpha-acid German varieties are considered more of an aroma hop. Lagers, wheats, and pilsners.

Pride of Ringwood (Australia) (8–10 percent)—An acclaimed bittering hop grown primarily in Tasmania. Availability spotty in the United States. British ales, Australian-style ales, and lagers.

Progress (Britain) (6–7 percent)—A disease-resistant derivative of Whitbread Goldings. Primarily an aroma variety, Progress has declined drastically since its introduction in the mid-1960s.

Saaz (Zatec) (Czech Republic & America) (3–6 percent)—Production of this 150-year-old strain has declined in recent years, but it is still considered one of the finest varieties ever used in beer. Aromatic, spicy, and flavorful. Higher-yielding, disease-resistant American varieties are currently being tested. Saaz, the German word for Zatec, is the quintessential Czech pil-

sner hop, but is also exceptionally good in other continental lagers and wheats.

Spalter (Germany & America) (4–5 percent)—Another aromatic and flavorful hop that has been suggested as an alternative to Saaz because it is a member of the Saazer "Formenkreis" (or group of varieties). Although Spalter production quantity is second only to Hersbrucker in terms of aroma hops, this pungent and spicy hop is not widely available to homebrewers, and it is often found only in pellet form—so stock up when you can. Ideal for all German lagers.

Spalter Select (Germany) (4–6 percent)—A new disease-resistant version of Spalter bred to produce higher yields. Primarily an aroma hop, but also suitable for rounded bittering. German lagers and ales, Belgian ales.

Sticklebract (New Zealand) (9–10 percent)—A reliable and popular bittering hop among Australian and New Zealand breweries. Not widely available in America and then often only in pellet form. Australian-style ales and lagers.

Strissel Spalt (France) (3–5 percent)—An aroma hop popular in France but rarely seen in the United States. Grown primarily in the Alsace region, it's mellow, rounded, and delicate bitterness and aroma are often considered on par with the "noble" varieties and is commonly employed in the brewing of bière de garde, but is well suited to pilsner and saison or any Belgian ale.

Styrian (Savinja) Goldings (Slovenia) (3–7 percent)—Basically, Fuggles that were brought to the Austro-Hungarian Empire from England at the turn of the century. Styria is a region of southeast and central Austria. The term "Goldings" was arbitrarily attached by merchants years ago, but these are not a predecessor of

East Kent Goldings. Strong, warm aroma, but like many aroma varieties, it is often used by traditional brewers to provide a "rounded" bitterness as opposed to the so-called "harsh" bitterness of some high-alpha varieties. For finishing English-style ales and often suggested for bittering Vienna/Märzen lagers, Belgian ales, and pilsners.

Target (Britain) (9–13 percent)—A robust and disease-resistant bittering hop developed at Wye College in Kent. This is the U.K.'s most popular bittering hop because of its low seed count and high alpha percentage, and it accounts for nearly half of British hop production. Used primarily by British brewers; not widely available to U.S. homebrewers. British ale and lagers.

Tettnanger (Germany & America) (3–5 percent)—A member of the Saazer "Formenkreis" primarily grown in the Swabian region of southern Germany around the Bodensee (Lake Constance). Can be used interchangeably with Spalter. Tettnanger is often used by traditional German brewers in aroma blends with Saazer and Spalter. Mild, floral, and very aromatic. Also grown on a small scale in the United States. Traditionally used in Bavarian wheats and German lagers.

Ultra (America) (3–4 percent)—A newly released aroma variety developed from Hallertauer Mittelfrüh and a Saaz clone. Praised for its pronounced floral aroma, Ultra is ideal for delicate pilsners and light lagers.

Whitbread Golding Variety (WGV) (Britain) (5–7 percent)—Not actually a Golding, but an aroma hybrid developed with Golding as a parent strain. Generally considered a Fuggles replacement. WGV is not generally available to U.S. homebrewers and is diminishing in popularity in the U.K. British ales.

Willamette (America) (4–6 percent)—A spicy, aromatic finishing hop. A popular, high-quality American derivative of Fuggles with a slightly higher AA content. American and British ales.

Yeoman (Britain) (9–14 percent)—A popular, disease-resistant bittering hop developed in the United Kingdom that is similar to the Target variety. Not generally available to U.S. homebrewers. British ales and Continental lagers.

Zenith (Britain) (9–10 percent)—A newer bittering hop with fairly good aroma developed in the United Kingdom in the 1980s. Not generally available to U.S. homebrewers. British ales and continental lagers.

Note: Hops, like wine grapes, are greatly influenced by climatic conditions such as rainfall, temperature, and days of sunshine, and whether the hops are grown seeded or seedless, etc. Therefore, alpha acid percentage varies slightly from year to year.

HOPS AT A GLANCE

VARIETY	ORIGIN	ALPHA ACID	PRIMARY PURPOSE
Bramling Cross	Canada & U.K.	5–7 percent	Finishing
Brewers Gold	U.K. & Germany	6–10 percent	Bittering
British Columbia Goldings	Canada & U.S.	4–6 percent	Finishing
Bullion	U.K. & U.S.	5–10 percent	All-Purpose
Cascade	U.S.	4–7 percent	Finishing
Centennial	U.S.	9–11 percent	All-Purpose
Challenger	U.K.	7–10 percent	All-Purpose
Chinook	U.S.	11–14 percent	Bittering
Cluster	U.S.	5–8 percent	Bittering
Columbus	U.S.	12–16 percent	All-Purpose
Crystal	U.S.	2–5 percent	Finishing
East Kent Goldings	U.K., Canada, & U.S.	4–6 percent	Finishing
Eroica	U.S.	10–14 percent	All-Purpose
Fuggles	U.K. & U.S.	4–6 percent	Finishing
Galena	U.S.	11–14 percent	Bittering
Green Bullet	New Zealand	9–11 percent	Bittering
Hallertau	Germany	4–6 percent	All-Purpose
Hallertauer Hersbrucker	Germany	2–6 percent	All-Purpose
Hallertauer Mittelfrüh	Germany & U.S.	4–6 percent	All-Purpose
Hallertauer Tradition	Germany	5–7 percent	All-Purpose
Liberty	U.S.	4–5 percent	Finishing
Lublin	Poland	3–5 percent	Finishing
Mt. Hood	U.S.	4–6 percent	Finishing
Northdown	U.K.	8–11 percent	All-Purpose
Northern Brewer	U.S., U.K., & Germany	7–11 percent	Bittering
Nugget	U.S.	11–16 percent	Bittering
Omega	U.K.	9–11 percent	Bittering
Perle	Germany & U.S.	6–11 percent	All-Purpose
Pride of Ringwood	Australia	8–10 percent	Bittering
Progress	U.K.	6–7 percent	Finishing

Variety	Origin	Alpha Acid	Primary Purpose
Saaz (Zatec)	Czech Republic & U.S.	3–6 percent	Finishing
Spalter	Germany & U.S.	4–5 percent	All-Purpose
Spalter Select	Germany	4–6 percent	All-Purpose
Sticklebract	New Zealand	9–10 percent	Bittering
Strissel Spalt	France	3–5 percent	Finishing
Styrian Goldings	Slovenia	3–7 percent	All-Purpose
Target	U.K.	9–13 percent	Bittering
Tettnanger	Germany & U.S.	3–5 percent	All-Purpose
Ultra	U.S.	3–4 percent	Finishing
Whitbread Golding Variety (WGV)	U.K.	5–7 percent	Finishing
Willamette	U.S.	4–6 percent	Finishing
Yeoman	U.K.	9–14 percent	Bittering
Zenith	U.K.	9–10 percent	Bittering

Yeast Profiles

Following is a glossary of popular liquid yeasts tailored to the major beer styles. Some of the advanced Wyeast brands require a starter, as do all of the Yeast Lab products. The BrewTek yeasts are "slants" and require the use of a yeast culturing kit to produce quantities suitable for fermentation.

ALE YEASTS (SACCHAROMYCES CEREVISIAE)

Except where specifically noted, these generally perform best when fermenting at 60–72°F and aging at 40–55°F. Common names include Wyeast Brewer's Choice, BrewTek, Yeast Culture Kit Company, or Yeast Lab number, and a brief supplier's/manufacturer's description:

Ale Yeast Blend (Wyeast 1087)—A highly concentrated blend of superior ale yeasts for large volumes of beer. Designed to ensure quick starts, good flavor, and good flocculation. Apparent attenuation 71–75 percent. Optimum fermentation temperature 64–72°F.

Altbier (The Yeast Culture Kit Co. A37)—Appropriate styles: altbier. Origin: Bavaria. Description: The strain used by many alt breweries. Distinct profile.

American (Chico) Ale (Wyeast 1056)—Used commercially for several classic American ales.

Dry, neutral-flavored. Finishes soft, smooth, clean, and well balanced. A long secondary fermentation yields a dry, lagerlike beer. Apparent attenuation 73–77 percent, low to medium flocculation. Optimum fermentation temperature 60–72°F.

American Ale (The Yeast Culture Kit Co. A01)—Appropriate styles: barley wine, brown ale, IPA, pale ale, porter, stout. Origin: California. Description: Clean, crisp, and neutral. Easy to use.

American Ale (Yeast Lab A02)—This clean strain produces a very fruity aroma, with a soft and smooth flavor when fermented cool. Medium attenuation and low flocculation. This is an all-purpose ale yeast. Optimum fermentation temperature 65–66°F.

American Ale II (Wyeast 1272)—Fruitier and more flocculant than 1056, slightly nutty, soft, clean, and slightly tart in the finish. Apparent attenuation 72–76 percent, high flocculation. Optimum fermentation temperature 60–72°F.

American Microbrewery Ale #1 (BrewTek CL–10)—A smooth, clean, strong-fermenting ale yeast that works well down to 56°F. The neutral character of this yeast makes it ideal for cream ales and other beers in which you want to maintain a clean malt flavor.

American Microbrewery Ale #2 (BrewTek CL–20)—Gives an accentuated, rich, and creamy malt profile with detectable amounts of diacetyl. Use it in lower-gravity beers where the malt character should not be missed or in strong ales for a robust character.

American White Ale (BrewTek CL–980)—A smooth, American-style wheat beer yeast with an exceptionally round, clean malt flavor. The poor flocculation of this yeast leaves a cloudy hefe-weizen, yet its smooth flavor makes it an integral part of a true unfiltered wheat beer.

Australian Ale (BrewTek CL–270)—Produces a malty, bready, nutty character with a pleasant honeylike finish. This yeast emphasizes malt nuances and is very forgiving in warmer fermentations for those who cannot ferment under controlled conditions.

Australian Ale (Yeast Lab A01)—An all-purpose strain that produces a very complex, woody, and flavorful beer. Australian origin. Medium attenuation, medium flocculation. Great for brown ales and porters. Optimum fermentation temperature 65–68°F.

Bavarian Weizen (The Yeast Culture Kit Co. A50)—Appropriate styles: weizen, weizenbock (was M01). Origin: Bavaria. Description: Clove and banana esters blend well with the sweet fruitiness of wheat malt to produce a classic weizen. Recommended fermentation temperature 64–66°F.

Bavarian Weizen (Yeast Lab W51)—This strain produces a classic German-style wheat beer, with moderately high, spicy, phenolic overtones reminiscent of cloves. Medium attenuation, moderate flocculation. Optimum fermentation temperature 66–70°F.

Bavarian Wheat (Wyeast 3056)—Blend of *S. cerevisiae* and *S. delbrückii* for producing mildly phenolic and estery wheat beers. Apparent attenuation 73–77 percent, medium flocculation. Optimum fermentation temperature 64–70°F.

Belgian Abbey (Wyeast 1214)—Estery abbey-style top-fermenting yeast suitable for high-gravity beers. Apparent attenuation 72–76 percent, medium flocculation. Optimum fermentation temperature 58–68°F.

Belgian Abbey II (Wyeast 1762)—High-gravity yeast with a distinct warming character from ethanol production. Slightly fruity with a dry finish. Apparent attenuation 73–77 percent, medium flocculation. Optimum fermentation temperature 65–75°F.

Belgian Ale #1 (BrewTek CL–300)—Produces a truly classic Belgian ale flavor. Robust and estery with big notes of clove and fruit. Recommended for general-purpose Belgian ale brewing, but this yeast also ferments high-gravity worts well.

Belgian Ale #2 (BrewTek CL–320)—A traditional Trappist strain that is particularly good in dubbels and tripels. This strong-fermenting yeast attenuates well and produces a complex, dry, fruity, and estery malt profile sought after in fine Belgian ales.

Belgian Ale #3 (BrewTek CL–340)—Slightly more refined than the CL–300, this yeast also produces a classic Trappist character, with esters of spice and fruit. Mildly phenolic, this is a strong-fermenting yeast, well suited to Trappist and other Belgian ales.

Belgian Ale (The Yeast Culture Kit Co. A36)—Appropriate styles: Belgian ales. Origin: Houffalize, Belgium. Description: Distinct yeast signature. Estery and fruity.

Belgian Strong Ale (Wyeast 1388)—Robustly flavored yeast with moderate to high alcohol tolerance. Fruity nose and palate with a dry, tart finish. Apparent attenuation 73–77 percent, low flocculation. Optimum fermentation temperature 65–75°F.

Belgian Trappist (Wyeast 3787)—A robust top-cropping yeast with phenolic character. Alcohol tolerance to 12 percent. Ideal for bière de garde. Ferments dry with a rich estery profile and a malty palate. Apparent attenuation 75–80 percent, medium flocculation. Optimum fermentation temperature 64–78°F.

Belgian Wheat (BrewTek CL–900)—A top-fermenting yeast that produces a soft, breadlike flavor and leaves a sweet, mildly estery finish. Lends its delicious Belgian character to any beer, especially when brewing with Belgian pils malt, and finishing with coriander and orange peel.

Belgian Wheat (Yeast Lab W52)—Yeast used in the production of Belgian white beer (wit). This strain provides a soft, elegant finish with moderate esters and mild, spicy phenols. Optimum fermentation temperature 66–70°F.

Belgian Wheat (Wyeast 3942)—Estery, low phenol-producing yeast from a small Belgian brewery. Features an apple- and plum-like nose with a dry finish. Apparent attenuation 72–76 percent, medium flocculation. Optimum fermentation temperature 64–74°F.

Belgian Wit (The Yeast Culture Kit Co. A35)—Appropriate styles: Belgian wit. Origin: central Belgium. Description: Spicy, slight phenolic character complements orange and coriander.

Belgian White Beer (Wyeast 3944)—A tart, slightly phenolic character capable of producing distinctive witbiers and grand cru–style ales alike. Alcohol tolerant. Apparent attenuation 72–76 percent, medium flocculation. Optimum fermentation temperature 60–75°F.

British (Whitbread) Ale (Wyeast 1098)—For the classic English pale or bitter ale. Slightly tart, slight diacetyl. Dry, crisp, fruity, and well balanced. Complex, but more neutral than Wyeast 1028-London. Apparent attenuation 73–75 percent, medium flocculation. Optimum fermentation temperature 64–72°F.

British Ale (Yeast Lab A04)—This strain produces a great light-bodied ale, excellent for pale ales and brown ales, with a complex estery flavor. Ferments dry with a sharp finish. Medium attenuation and medium flocculation. Optimum fermentation temperature 65–68°F.

British Ale II (Wyeast 1335)—Typical of British and Canadian ale fermentation profile with good flocculating and malty flavor characteristics. Crisp finish, clean, fairly dry. Apparent attenuation 73–76 percent, high flocculation. Optimum fermentation temperature 63–75°F.

British Draft Ale (BrewTek CL–160)— Gives a full-bodied, well-rounded flavor with a touch of diacetyl. Emphasizes malt character. Highly recommended for porters and bitters.

British Microbrewery Ale 1 (BrewTek CL–110)—Provides a complex, oaky, fruity ester profile and slightly full-flavored finish suitable to low- and medium-gravity British ale styles. Very distinct, this classic, old-fashioned yeast is great for traditional bitters and is a rare find for mild ale fans.

British Pale Ale #1 (BrewTek CL–120)— Produces a bold, citrusy character that accentuates mineral and hop flavors. The distinctive character of this yeast makes it well suited for use in your classic British pale ales or bitters.

British Pale Ale #2 (BrewTek CL–130)—A smooth, full-flavored yeast. Mildly estery, this yeast is a strong fermenter and is highly recommended for strong or spiced ales. This yeast is smooth, well rounded, and accentuates caramel and other malt nuances.

British Real Ale (BrewTek CL–150)—For those longing for the character of a real pub bitter. This yeast has a complex, woody, almost musty ester profile that characterizes many "real ales." Typically underattenuating, the malt profile is left intact with a mild sweetness in the finish.

California Pub Brewery Ale (BrewTek CL–50)—For that classic U.S. small brewery flavor. This yeast produces terrific American red and pale ale styles. While attenuation is normal, this yeast produces a big, soft, well-rounded malt flavor that accentuates caramel malt flavors and a silky smooth profile, even in well-hopped beers. Produces threshold levels of diacetyl and mild esters.

Canadian Ale (BrewTek CL–260)—A clean, strong-fermenting, and well-attenuating ale yeast that leaves a pleasant, lightly fruity, complex finish. Well suited for light Canadian ales, as well as fuller-flavored porters and other British styles such as bitter and pale ale.

Canadian Ale (Yeast Lab A07)—This strain produces a light-bodied, clean, and flavorful beer—very fruity when fermented cool. High attenuation, medium flocculation. Good for light and cream ales. Optimum fermentation temperature 65–66°F.

Classic British Ale (BrewTek CL–170)— Creates a very complex British-style ale with fruity esters for draft bitter or porter; it also produces a classic Scottish heavy and plays well in high-gravity worts.

Dusseldorf Ale (Yeast Lab A06)—German altbier yeast strain that finishes with full body, complex flavor, and spicy sweetness. Medium attenuation, high flocculation. Optimum fermentation temperature 65–68°F.

English Ale (The Yeast Culture Kit Co. A15)—Appropriate styles: IPA, pale ale, brown ale, English bitter. Origin: England. Description: Complex with strong, yeasty flavors.

English Ale (Yeast Lab A09)—An old English brewery strain, this clean yeast is fairly neutral in character, producing a fruity, soft, and estery finish. A vigorous fermenter. Optimum fermentation temperature 64–66°F.

English Barleywine Ale (The Yeast Culture Kit Co. A08)—Appropriate styles: barley wine. Origin: Dorchester, England. Description: Tends to leave a high residual sweetness.

European Ale (Alt) (Wyeast 1338)—This Wissenschaftliche strain from Munich typifies the old prelager style of ale. Complex, full-bodied, and sweet, finishing very malty. Produces a dense, rocky head during fermentation. Apparent attenuation 67–71 percent, high flocculation. Optimum fermentation temperature 60–72°F.

German Ale (The Yeast Culture Kit Co. A04)—Appropriate styles: Kölsch, cream ale. Origin: Germany. Description: Clean and fruity, produces exquisitely flavorful light-bodied ales.

German Ale (Wyeast 1007)—Ferments dry and crisp, leaving a mild and complex flavor. Produces an extremely rocky head, ferments well down to 55°F. Apparent attenuation 73–77 percent, low flocculation. Optimum fermentation temperature 55–66°F. Often confused with 1338 above.

German Weiss (BrewTek CL–930)—Milder than the German Wheat 920, the 930 strain from a famous German yeast bank still produces the sought-after clove and phenol characters, but to a lesser degree, with a fuller, earthier character underneath.

German Wheat (BrewTek CL–920)—A true, top-fermenting weizenbier yeast. Intensely spicy, clovey, and phenolic. This yeast is highly attenuative and flocculates in large, loose clumps. Use for all weizen recipes—it is particularly good in weizenbocks.

German Wheat (Wyeast 3333)—Features a subtle flavor profile for a wheat yeast with a sharp, tart crispness and a fruity, sherrylike palate. Apparent attenuation 70–76 percent, high flocculation. Optimum fermentation temperature 63–75°F.

Irish Ale (The Yeast Culture Kit Co. A13)—Appropriate styles: porter, stout, imperial stout. Origin: Dublin, Ireland. Description: The real thing from Ireland. Nutty, woody, and complex.

Irish Ale (Wyeast 1084)—Dry, complex, slight residual diacetyl and fruitiness, good for stouts and strong ales. Soft, smooth, clean, and full-bodied. Apparent attenuation 71–75 percent, medium flocculation. Optimum fermentation temperature 62–72°F.

Irish Ale (Yeast Lab A05)—This top-fermenting strain is ideal for stouts and porters. Slightly acidic, with a hint of butterscotch in the finish. Soft and full-bodied. High attenuation, high flocculation. Optimum fermentation temperature 65–66°F.

Irish Dry Stout (BrewTek CL–240)—A true, old-fashioned, top-fermenting yeast that leaves a very recognizable, slightly woody character to dry stouts. Has a vinous, almost lactic character that blends exceptionally well with roasted malts. Highly attenuative.

Kölsch (BrewTek CL–450)—Produces an astonishing clean lagerlike flavor at ale temperatures. Smooths with time into a clean, well-attenuated flavor. Mineral and malt character comes through well, with a clean, lightly yeasty flavor and aroma in the finish.

Kölsch (Wyeast 2565)—A hybrid of ale and lager characteristics. This strain develops excellent maltiness and subdued fruitiness with a crisp finish. Ferments well at moderate temperatures. Apparent attenuation 73–77 percent, low flocculation. Optimum fermentation temperature 56–64°F.

London Ale (Wyeast 1028)—Rich, minerally profile, bold and crisp—with some diacetyl production. Apparent attenuation 73–77 percent, medium flocculation. Great for porters; often confused with Wyeast 1098. Optimum fermentation temperature 60–72°F.

London Ale (Yeast Lab A03)—A classic pale ale strain, very dry. A powdery yeast with a hint of diacetyl and a rich, minerally profile, crisp and clean. Medium attenuation and medium flocculation. Optimum fermentation temperature 65–68°F.

London Ale III (Wyeast 1318)—From a traditional London brewery with a great malt and hop profile. A true top-cropping strain that is fruity, very light with a soft, balanced palate. Finishes slightly sweet. Apparent attenuation 71–75 percent, high flocculation. Optimum fermentation temperature 64–74°F.

Old German Ale (BrewTek CL–400)—For traditional altbiers, a strong fermenter that leaves a smooth, attenuated, yet mild flavor. Use in your favorite German ale recipes. This yeast also makes a slightly dry but clean, quenching wheat beer.

Pale Ale (The Yeast Culture Kit Co. A17)—Appropriate styles: brown ale, English bitter, mild, IPA, pale ale. Origin: London, England. Description: Very smooth and mellow with a distinct yeast signature.

Saison (BrewTek CL–380)—A pleasant yeast best used to recreate country French and Belgian ales, as well as grand cru styles. This yeast leaves a smooth, full character to the malt with mild yet pleasant esters and flavors reminiscent of apple pie spices.

Scotch Ale (The Yeast Culture Kit Co. A34)—Appropriate styles: barley wine, Scotch ale, Scottish bitter, strong ale. Origin: Edinburgh, Scotland. Description: Clean, ferments well at cool temperatures.

Scottish Ale (BrewTek CL–200)—This is a truly unique yeast for the classic Scottish heavy, 90 shilling, or strong ale. This yeast produces a soft, fruity malt profile with a woody, oaky ester reminiscent of malt whisky. A mild, mineral-like dryness in the finish makes this a very complex yeast strain.

Scottish Ale (Wyeast 1728)—Rich, smoky, peaty character ideally suited for Scottish-style ales, smoked beers, and high-gravity ales of all types. Apparent attenuation 69–73 percent, high flocculation. Optimum fermentation temperature 55–70°F.

Scottish Bitter (BrewTek CL–210)—Will produce a unique style of bitter. The soft, yeasty, fruity nose yields to a well-attenuated malt flavor and big ester complex of ripe fruit, apricots, and rose petals. This yeast has a teasing finish with a dry and complex, yet smooth, fruity character.

Special London (Wyeast 1968)—Highly flocculant ale yeast with rich, malty character and balanced fruitiness. Its high degree of flocculation makes it an excellent strain for cask-conditioned ales. So flocculant that additional aeration and agitation is needed. Apparent attenuation 67–71 percent, high flocculation. Optimum fermentation temperature 64–72°F.

Stout Ale (The Yeast Culture Kit Co. A06)—Appropriate styles: porter, stout, imperial stout. Origin: Ireland. Description: Low attenuation, slight diacetyl.

Swedish Ale (Wyeast 1742)—Stark beer Nordic-style yeast of unknown origin with a floral nose and malty finish. Apparent attenuation 69–73 percent, medium flocculation. Optimum fermentation temperature 69–73°F.

Thames Valley (Wyeast 1275)—Produces classic British bitters. Features a rich, complex flavor profile and a clean, light malt character. Low fruitiness, low esters, well balanced. Apparent attenuation 72–76 percent, medium flocculation. Optimum fermentation temperature 62–72°F.

Trappe Ale (The Yeast Culture Kit Co. A16)—Appropriate styles: Trappist-style ales. Origin: Belgian monastery. Description: Typical Trappist esters and aromas.

Trappist Ale (Yeast Lab A08)—This is a typical Belgian strain, producing a malty flavor with a balance of fruity, phenolic overtones when fermented warm. Alcohol tolerant, high attenuation, and high flocculation. Optimum fermentation temperature 64–70°F.

Weihenstephan Wheat (Wyeast 3068)—Unique top-fermenting yeast that produces the unique and spicy weizen character, rich with clove, banana, and vanilla esters. Best results are achieved when fermentations are held around 68°F. Apparent attenuation 73–77 percent, low flocculation. Optimum fermentation temperature 64–70°F.

LAGER YEASTS (SACCHAROMYCES UVARUM)

Except where specifically noted, these generally perform best when fermenting at 46–55°F and aging at 32–45°F.

American (New Ulm) Lager (Wyeast 2035)—For steam beers and other American lagers—bold, complex, and aromatic. Ferments dry, crisp, clean, and light, producing flavors characteristic of the Midwest breweries' pre-Prohibition beers. Slight diacetyl. Apparent attenuation 73–77 percent, medium flocculation. Optimum fermentation temperature 48–58°F.

American Megabrewery Lager (BrewTek CL–620)—A smooth yeast with a slightly fruity character when fresh, which lagers into a smooth, clean-tasting beer. Use for your lightest, cleanest lagers or those in which you want an unobtrusive yeast character.

American Microbrewery Lager (BrewTek CL–630)—A strong fermenter leaving a clean, full-flavored, malty finish despite its strong attenuation. This is a very old strain commonly used by pre-Prohibition American breweries. This yeast is very versatile for most lager styles requiring a clean, full flavor.

Bavarian Lager (Wyeast 2206)—Used by many Bavarian breweries to produce rich, full-bodied, malty beers. Excellent for bocks and Vienna/Oktoberfest/Märzen. Apparent attenuation 73–77 percent, medium flocculation. Optimum fermentation temperature 48–58°F.

Bavarian Lager (Yeast Lab L32)—Use this classic strain for medium-bodied lagers and bocks, as well as Vienna and Märzen styles. Rich in flavor with a clean, malty sweetness. Medium attenuation and medium flocculation. Optimum fermentation temperature 48–52°F.

Bohemian Lager (Wyeast 2124)—A pilsner yeast from Weihenstephan. Ferments clean and malty with a rich, residual maltiness in full-gravity pilsners. Apparent attenuation 69–73 percent, medium flocculation. Optimum fermentation temperature 46–54°F.

California Gold (BrewTek CL–690)—Use to recreate California common beers, leaves a slightly estery, well-attenuated finish. The character of this yeast is quite distinct; try it in American or robust porters for a new and unique flavor profile.

California Lager (Wyeast 2112)—Particularly suited for producing nineteenth-century-style West Coast beers. Retains lager characteristics at temperatures up to 65°F and produces malty, brilliantly clear beers. Apparent attenuation 67–71 percent, high flocculation. Optimum fermentation temperature 58–68°F.

California Lager (Yeast Lab L35)—A California common beer strain. Malty with a sweet, woody flavor and a subtle fruitiness. Medium attenuation and high flocculation. Optimum fermentation temperature 64–66˚F.

Czech Pils (Wyeast 2278)—Classic pilsner strain from the home of pilsners for a dry but malty finish. The perfect choice for pilsners and bock beers. Sulfur produced during fermentation dissipates with conditioning. Apparent attenuation 70–74 percent, medium to high flocculation. Optimum fermentation temperature 48–64˚F.

Danish Lager (Wyeast 2042)—Continental European/North German–style with a soft profile accentuating hop character. Rich, Dortmund style, crisp, dry finish. Produces strong fermentation odors that soon fade. Apparent attenuation 73–77 percent, low flocculation. Optimum fermentation temperature 46–56˚F.

Danish Lager II (Wyeast 2247)—Clean, dry flavor profile often used in aggressively hopped pilsners. Clean, very mild flavor, slight sulfur production, dry finish. Apparent attenuation 73–77 percent, low flocculation. Optimum fermentation temperature 46–56˚F.

East European Lager (BrewTek CL–680)—From a very old European brewery, imparts a smooth, rich, almost creamy character, emphasizing malt flavor and clean finish. For brewing lagers in which the malt character should be full and smooth as in Märzen/Oktoberfest and dunkels.

German Lager (The Yeast Culture Kit Co. L09)—Appropriate styles: German lagers and bocks, most other lager styles. Origin: Bavaria. Description: Common strain used in many German lager breweries.

Lager Yeast Blend (Wyeast 2178)—A blend of the Brewer's Choice lager strains for the most complex flavor profiles. Apparent attenuation

71–75 percent. Optimum fermentation temperature 48–56˚F.

Munich Lager (Wyeast 2308)—Well-rounded, malty, smooth, full-bodied, and soft, but sometimes unstable Wissenschaftliche 308. Recommended for dunkels, bocks, and heavier German beers, but also makes a nice Vienna/Oktoberfest. Apparent attenuation 73–77 percent, medium flocculation. Optimum fermentation temperature 48–56˚F.

Munich Lager (Yeast Lab L33)—German brewing strain for medium-bodied lagers and bocks. Produces subtle and complex flavors, and a smooth and soft profile, with a hint of sulfur when fresh. Medium attenuation and medium flocculation. Optimum fermentation temperature 50–52˚F.

North American Lager (Wyeast 2272)—Traditional culture of North American and Canadian lagers and light pilsners. Malty finish. Apparent attenuation 70–76 percent, high flocculation. Optimum fermentation temperature 48–56˚F.

North German Lager (BrewTek CL–660)—Exhibits a clean, crisp, traditional northern German lager character. A strong fermenting and forgiving lager yeast. Excellent for general-purpose lager brewing of German pils, as well as Mexican and Canadian lagers.

Old Bavarian Lager (BrewTek CL–650)—Well rounded and malty with a subtle ester complex and citrus undertones. This distinct, southern German yeast strain is great for full-flavored, classic German lagers such as bock, dunkel, and helles styles.

Original Pilsner (BrewTek CL–600)—Leaves a full-bodied lager with a sweet, mildly underattenuated finish and subdued diacetyl character. Use in classic Czech pilsners or any lager in which you want to emphasize a big, malty palate.

Pilsen Lager (Wyeast 2007)—Aka St. Louis. A classic American pilsner strain that produces a malty smooth palate. Ferments dry and crisp. For American pilsners and "steam" beers. Apparent attenuation 71–75 percent, medium flocculation. Optimum fermentation temperature 48–56°F.

Pilsen Lager (The Yeast Culture Kit Co. L17)—Appropriate styles: American lager, pilsner. Origin: Plzen. Description: Extremely clean, malty, and full-bodied. Ferments well to 48°F.

Pilsner Lager (Yeast Lab L31)—This classic strain produces a lager that is light in both flavor and body, fermenting dry and clean. High attenuation and medium flocculation. Optimum fermentation temperature 50–52°F.

St. Louis Lager (Yeast Lab L34)—This strain produces a rounded, very crisp and clean, fruity flavor, with medium body that is good for American-style lagers. High attenuation and medium flocculation. Optimum fermentation temperature 50–52°F.

Swiss Lager (BrewTek CL–670)—A unique strain that has both a clean, crisp lager flavor and a soft, smooth maltiness. Perfect for European pilsners. An excellent all-purpose lager yeast for those wanting a fuller, rounder palate.

SPECIAL-PURPOSE YEASTS AND BACTERIA

Belgian Lambic Blend (Wyeast 3278)—Belgian lambic-style yeast blend with lactic bacteria. Produces a rich, earthy aroma and acidic finish. Suitable for lambic, gueuze, and faro. Apparent attenuation 65–75 percent, low to medium flocculation. Optimum fermentation temperature 63–75°F.

Brettanomyces Lambicus (BrewTek CL–5200 & Yeast Lab 3220)—"Wild yeast" added during various stages of fermentation (depending on your opinion of what works best) in the creation of Belgian lambics. *Brettanomyces* is a slow-growing yeast used in the production of Belgian lambic-style beers. This strain produces an odd horselike aroma and flavor, an integral part of the lambic profile. A sterile starter should be made approximately one week prior to use. At the peak of fermentation, this strain will produce very little carbon dioxide.

Champagne (The Yeast Culture Kit Co. W06)—Appropriate styles: mead, strong beers, wine. Origin: Montreal. Description: A vigorous and thorough fermenter, very alcohol tolerant.

Pasteur Champagne Yeast (Wyeast 3021)—"Prisse de Mousse." Sold on the Vintner's Choice label. Institut Pasteur's Champagne yeast race bayanus. Crisp and dry. Can be used for high-gravity beers, meads, and barley wines. A good flocculating, low-foaming, excellent barrel fermenter. Ferments well at 55–65°F.

Pediococcus Cerevisiae (Yeast Lab 3200)—One of the many bacterial cultures used in the production of Belgian lambic-style beers. This slow-growing organism is responsible for some of the intense lactic sourness present in these beers. A sterile starter should be made one week prior to use.

Pediococcus Damnosus (BrewTek CL–5600)—A lactic-acid- and diacetyl-producing bacteria usually added prior to or in conjunction with *Brettanomyces lambicus* in the secondary fermentation of Belgian lambics and oud bruins.

TIPS FOR A SUCCESSFUL FERMENTATION

Use the freshest yeast possible. Yeast is very sensitive to temperature extremes and light. Keep refrigerated and use within thirty days of manufacture date.

Culture up yeast that isn't at peak freshness. Yeast more than one month old should be rejuvenated with a 1.020–1.025 SG half-liter starter, sterilized, then cooled to exactly 75°F before pitching in yeast.

Use sufficient quantities. Yeast quantities provided by manufacturers are generally for standard-gravity beers. Wyeast recommends doubling the pitching rate for every 0.008 increase above 1.048.

Pitch at the right time. The high-kräusen stage of yeast reproduction thirty-six to seventy-two hours after making your starter or activating your "slap pack" is the optimum time to pitch into wort or a larger starter.

Use the proper yeast for the beer you are brewing. Select the appropriate yeast not only for the style you want but also for the actual temperature at which you'll be fermenting. More flocculant ale yeast produces maltier, clearer beers. Less flocculant ale yeast produces drier beers, but they are often more estery and fruity. More flocculant lager strains produce clearer, fuller-bodied beers, and ferment best at 48°F or above. Less flocculant lager yeasts usually produce drier, colder fermenting beers, but take longer to drop bright.

Use the correct fermentation temperature. Culture yeast at 75°F, not at fermentation temperature. Introduce this starter into your wort when both are at 75°F, then adjust to proper fermentation temperature.

Perform appropriate aeration. Lack of aeration increases lag time, prolongs fermentation, results in high final gravities, and causes off-flavors. As long as wort is cooled to 75°F, there is no threat of oxidation from vigorous aeration. The CO_2 produced during fermentation will purge any oxygen. Highly flocculant yeasts need greater aeration, medium and low flocculators need less.

Keep your fermentation temperature constant. Changes in fermentation temperature (at night, for example) can result in premature flocculation and stuck fermentation, particularly with high flocculators.

Don't rack prematurely. Transferring beer too early can result in a high final gravity. Wait until 90 percent of the sugars are attenuated before racking to a secondary fermenter. Also, top-fermenting yeast should not be harvested before at least 50 percent of the sugars are attenuated.

WATER

The main reason that the properties of brewing water (called "liquor") are considered at all by brewers is because of the effect its various ions have on the vital starch-degrading enzymes in malt. The levels of the six main ions directly affect the water's pH, which in turn determines the effectiveness of the enzymes in doing their job of making maltose. Therefore, achieving the correct balance among these ions will greatly influence the extract yield of the malt. In malt-extract-based brewing, the concerns of water used in mashing and brewing down the wort into syrup or powder are taken care of by the manufacturer. However, if you are adding your own malts, specialty grains, or hops, the water you use *is* of importance.

The second major consideration of water is perhaps the most obvious—flavor. As long as your water is free of organic or man-made contaminants, its flavor will in large part be influenced by the same six ions that influence enzyme activity. If you've been plagued by unsatisfactory "house flavors," these may relate to an imbalance in the ions of the water you are using.

The third consideration of a particular water's makeup is its ability to provide necessary nutrients to the yeast that will ferment the wort. This is definitely the least of a home brewer's concern, as yeast requires only trace amounts of these ions, which are generally present in more than sufficient quantities in well-modified malts and in all water sources except, of course, distilled water.

Below is a list of the six main ions and their effects on brewing liquor:

Carbonate/Bicarbonate (CO_3 or HCO_3)—The ions that determine temporary or "carbonate" hardness. Expressed as "total alkalinity" on most water analysis sheets, the presence (or lack of) bicarbonate is considered the most crucial factor in brewing liquor. Too little and the mash acidity will be too high, especially when using darker malts. (High levels in Munich's water are largely responsible for the famous softness of Münchner dunkel). Too much counteracts the calcium ion acidification process, resulting in poor extract yields from malted grain. Levels should generally be no higher than 25–50 mg/l for pale beers, 100–300 mg/l for dark beers.

Sodium (Na)—Contributes body, full mouthfeel, and character. Overuse of sodium in liquor treatment will lead to a noticeable "seawater" taste. Levels generally range from 10–70 mg/l in good brewing liquor.

Chloride (Cl)—Found in common table salt, this ion brings out malt sweetness, and like sodium, contributes to the overall mouthfeel and complexity of the beer. Levels generally can range from 1–100 mg/l in good brewing liquor, but should always stay below 150 mg/l to avoid salty flavors.

Sulfate (SO_4)—Although secondary to calcium in lowering pH, this is the main water element influencing hopping rates as it brings out a sharp, dry bitterness if IBUs are too high. Levels below 10 mg/l are recommended for pilsners, around 25–50 mg/l for most light or amber lagers, and 30–70 mg/l for most ales.

Notable exceptions include Burton-on-Trent–style pale ales (500–700 mg/l), and Dortmunder and Vienna lagers (100–130 mg/l).

Calcium (Ca)—This most important "permanent hardness" element in brewing liquor helps lower pH to the optimum 5.0–5.5 range and encourages the precipitation of proteins ("the break") during the boiling process. A good level for most ales and lagers is generally considered to be around 100 mg/l. Too much will create a harsh, bitter taste, especially in amber lagers.

Magnesium (Mg)—Valued primarily as a yeast nutrient, this ion is usually increased by the addition of Epsom salts, but addition of magnesium is usually advised against by many experts, especially when brewing light lagers. Levels above 30 mg/l will lend a dry, astringent bitterness to your brew. Levels in the great brewing waters of the world usually hover around 20–30 mg/l.

All of the above ions, along with other trace elements, determine the water's total hardness and total dissolved solids (TDS). TDS and total hardness are arrived at by complex laboratory methods of titration and filtration and generally cannot be calculated at home if you only know the free ion levels. In the United States, water is generally grouped according to its TDS into one of the four categories below:

Soft—0 to 75 mg/l (ppm) TDS
Moderate—75 to 150 mg/l (ppm) TDS
Hard—150 to 300 mg/l (ppm) TDS
Very Hard—Above 300 mg/l (ppm) TDS

Temporary Hardness: Also referred to as "carbonate hardness," this refers to the level of carbonates/bicarbonates in a water sample. Temporary hardness can be removed by boiling your brewing liquor for ten minutes, but the liquor should then be transferred off the powdery, white salts precipitated behind. Water high in temporary hardness is good for porter, stout, Munich dunkel, and schwarzbier.

Permanent Hardness: This pertains to the levels of calcium and magnesium ions that contribute to a water sample's "total hardness." These cannot be removed by boiling and, therefore, are called "permanent." Water with a high degree of permanent hardness is good for brewing Burton-style ales and Dortmund-style lagers.

Note: You can obtain a water analysis from your local water board or health department, or you can test your own water to a certain degree with kits purchased from local hot tub and swimming pool suppliers, and some hardware stores.

WATER TREATMENTS

These additives, commonly sold by homebrew supply shops, can help you adjust your ion concentrations and pH levels.

Burton Water Salts—A combination of gypsum, magnesium sulfate, and sodium chloride added in the mash tun or brew kettle.

Gypsum ($CaSO_4$)—Increases calcium and sulfate ions, primarily used to lower the pH in the mash. Not generally recommended in large amounts for lager brewing.

Table Salt (NaCl)—Increases sodium and chloride ions. Addition is usually advised against unless you are certain of the results. In any event, addition should be below one teaspoon per five U.S. gallons.

Epsom Salts ($MgSO_4$)—Increases magnesium and sulfate ions. For permanent hardness in the brew kettle or mash tun to imitate Burton-on-Trent water.

Calcium Carbonate (CaCO$_3$)—Increases temporary hardness in the mash and raises pH (increases alkalinity/lowers acidity). One teaspoon raises the carbonate level 60 ppm and the calcium level 36 ppm (per five U.S. gallons). This may also be referred to in water analysis sheets as bicarbonate (aka HCO$_3$).

Calcium Chloride (CaCl$_2$)—Increases calcium and chloride ions. Preferable to calcium sulfate for pH adjustment because of the side effect of harshness contributed by sulfate.

"Water Salts" are often sold as additives containing the above ingredients alone, in combination, or sometimes with other products such as supplementary yeast nutrients and haze reducers added. Several books contain information on the use of water salts to achieve proper ion concentrations, particularly Clive La Pensee's *The Historical Companion to House-Brewing,* Gregory Noonan's *Brewing Lager Beer,* and Charlie Papazian's *The New Complete Joy of Homebrewing.* It is recommended that you first learn what your water contains, then determine what additions will yield the proper results. Consulting works on a particular style, such as the Brewers Publications' Beer Style Series, is highly recommended for this.

It is usually safe to add the standard prepackaged dosage of water-hardening salts in brewing a Burton-style pale ale or a Dortmunder, since most of us start with treated municipal water that is fairly soft, but when brewing other styles where water hardness should be in the medium or soft range, adjustment will be trickier. Above all else, remember that homebrewing is more of an art than a science when compared to commercial brewing, so use the tried-and-true "artistic methods" of (1) trial and error; and (2) practice, practice, practice!

BASIC THINGS TO KNOW ABOUT BREWING LIQUOR

- pH is measured on a scale of 1–14; 7 is neutral, the accepted ideal for brewers *prior* to adding malt, which should lower the pH to the 5.0–5.5 range. The numbers below 7 indicate increasing acidity, the numbers above 7 indicate increasing alkalinity. The brewing process only deals with pH levels in the 4–8 range.

- Dark malts counteract the effects of alkaline water, and vice versa. This also includes lower Lovibond-rated malts such as Vienna and Munich. Therefore, beers with more than 5–15 percent dark malt in the grist should have some level of temporary hardness.

- Chlorine in public drinking-water supplies lends significant off-flavors to beer, especially light lagers. Boiling is the most effective means of removing chlorine from water, but it also reduces temporary hardness, which may not be desirable. Aerating cold water, then waiting twenty-four hours before using, reduces chlorine without reducing temporary hardness.

- Reduce hops if using water with temporary hardness greater than 100–150 mg/l.

- Add water treatments to the mash or to the wort, not raw water. Some salts, like NaCl, will dissolve in plain water, but CaCO$_3$, for example, will not.

- These basic water principles apply not only to the mash liquor but to sparge liquor as well.

- Top-fermenting yeasts are not as sensitive to improper wort pH as bottom-fermenting yeasts and, therefore, can tolerate a wider range of water salt levels.

The International Bottled Water Association gives these definitions for the major bottled water products and processes, all of which must meet FDA standards.

- *Spring water* is defined as coming from an underground formation and flowing naturally to the earth's surface. Like most bottled waters, spring water is disinfected with ozone (O_3), a form of oxygen that leaves no chemical residue, aftertaste, or aroma.
- *Natural water* is spring, mineral, artesian well, or well water that is derived from an underground formation and is not taken from a municipal or public water supply nor modified by the addition or deletion of dissolved solids, except for ozonation (non-chlorine disinfecting).
- *Mineral water* is defined as coming from a geologically or physically protected underground source. It should be clearly distinguishable from other water types by the level of minerals and trace elements. Total dissolved solids must appear on the label stated in milligrams per liter.
- *Distilled water* is vaporized, then condensed, leaving the water free of dissolved minerals. Also known as "purified water."
- *Deionization* is a process in which water is filtered through resins that remove most of the dissolved minerals. This also creates "purified water."
- *Reverse osmosis* is a process in which water is forced under pressure through membranes that remove 90 percent of the dissolved minerals. This also creates "purified water."

WATER ANALYSES OF SELECTED U.S. CITIES

These are *average* figures (often from combined groundwater and surface water sources) that indicate the approximate levels at the consumer's faucet.

These will often be quite different from the raw, untreated levels. (All numbers expressed in milligrams per liter, which is equivalent to parts per million.)

	TH	SODIUM	CHLORIDE	SULFATE	CALCIUM	MAGNESIUM	pH	TDS	HARDNESS
Atlanta, GA	19	3	NA	7	6	1	7.2	37	24
Boston, MA	10	10	14	8	4	1	7.9	NA	15
Charlotte, NC	17	9	6	8	8	1	8.8	NA	28
Chicago, IL	106	6	11	25	34	11	8.1	NA	131
Cleveland, OH	70	11	16	25	33	8	7.3	176	7
Dallas, TX	45	17	34	44	24	3	9.0	150	74
Hackensack, NJ	87	69	120	0	40	7	8.4	310	133
Las Vegas, NV	105	103	92	279	80	30	7.7	NA	329
Los Angeles (East)	NA	84	99	151	63	22	7.9	531	256
L.A. (West & S.F. Valley)	105	68	85	75	32	14	7.8	347	139
Memphis, TN	53	8	4	7	8	5	7.2	74	46
Milwaukee, WI	107	7	16	26	96*	47*	7.5	NA	143
New York City	29	11	21	12	13	4	7.2	102	47
Pittsburgh, PA	252	5	7	12	145	17	7.9	200	238
Portland, OR	9	2	2	0	2	1	6.7	24	9
Richmond, VA	29	NA	13	NA	15	3	8.0	94	49
Salt Lake City, UT	252	5	7	12	30	17	7.9	238	145
Seattle, WA	18	4	4	2	17*	1	7.8	41	21
S. San Francisco	NA	28	39	39	24	15	8.2	212	143

TH—Temporary Hardness: A term used primarily in brewing texts as a measure of the carbonate/bicarbonate level. Temporary hardness is usually expressed on a water analysis as bicarbonate hardness or total alkalinity (as CaCO$_3$).

TDS—Total Dissolved Solids.

NA—Levels not tested, levels too low for current testing methods, or current data not available.

Hardness—Total Hardness, a measure of calcium (as CaCO$_3$) and magnesium (as CaCO$_3$). This will be significantly different from the free ion totals of calcium and magnesium alone.

*Expressed as CaCO$_3$, which can be three times higher than the "free ion" level.

ANALYSES OF SELECTED BOTTLED SPRING WATERS

(Expressed in milligrams per liter, which is equivalent to parts per million.)

	TH	SODIUM	CHLORIDE	SULFATE	CALCIUM	MAGNESIUM	pH	TDS
Deer Park®	32.9	2.8	0.5	6.0	3.8	1.17	7.6	50.0
Great Bear®	110.0	3.9	5.6	14.0	42.0	7.3	7.0	153.0
Naya®	243.0	6.0	1.0	14.0	38.0	22.0	7.0	NA
White Rock®	2.0	0.6	0.7	5.4	1.2	0.9	5.7	19.0
Poland Spring®	22.0	3.0	5.1	5.0	19.0	1.2	6.5	38.0
Vermont Pure®	NA	1.6	1.5	12.5	58.3	5.3	7.0	97.0

Note: The FDA classifies "sodium-free" as less than 5 milligrams per 8-ounce serving.

TH—Temporary Hardness: A term used primarily in brewing texts as a measure of the carbonate/bicarbonate level. Temporary hardness is usually expressed on a water analysis as bicarbonate hardness or total alkalinity (as CaCO₃).

NA—Levels not tested, levels too low for current testing methods, or current data not available.

ANALYSES OF FAMOUS BREWING WATERS

(Expressed in milligrams per liter, which is equivalent to parts per million.)

Unlike the U.S. city numbers, these figures generally represent the approximate raw, untreated, and unfiltered sources.

	TH	SODIUM	CHLORIDE	SULFATE	CALCIUM	MAGNESIUM
Burton-on-Trent	200	40	35	660	295	55
Dortmund	180	69	106	260	261	23
Dublin	319	12	19	54	117	4
London	156	99	60	77	52	16
Munich	152	10	2	8	75	18
Pilsen	14	2	5	5	7	2

TH—Temporary Hardness: A term used primarily in brewing texts as a measure of the carbonate/bicarbonate level. Temporary hardness is usually expressed on a water analysis as bicarbonate hardness or total alkalinity (as CaCO₃).

ADDITIVES

Below are products intended to improve the overall quality of your beer *or* to solve common problems such as poor head retention, thin body, or haze.

Amylase Enzyme—One of the diastatic enzymes (naturally occurring in malted barley) that converts starch to maltose (sugar) and allows better conversion when using low-enzyme malts or high percentages of adjuncts. Produces light and dry characteristics in beer. Use in the mash.

Ascorbic Acid (Vitamin C)—Reduces oxidation in the bottle. Overuse will lend citrusy flavors.

Burton Water Salts—Used to harden brewing liquor for creating Burton-on-Trent–style pale ales or "hard water" beers. (See "Water" section.)

Calcium Carbonate (Powdered Chalk)—Used in mash to add "temporary hardness" and to raise pH. (See "Water" section.)

Citric Acid—Antihaze and pH balance.

Epsom Salts—Magnesium sulfate (sulphate), used in mash or kettle to provide "permanent hardness." (See "Water" section.)

Fermax—A yeast nutrient/dietary supplement for meads and low-gravity/low-malt beers.

Gelatin—Promotes clearing by settling yeast and reduces haze by removing suspended proteins. Added before bottling—colorless and tasteless.

Gypsum (Calcium Sulfate)—Used to harden soft brewing liquor and settle out suspended particulate matter, specifically in pale ales. Lowers pH. (See "Water" section.)

Heading Agents—Helps beers develop and retain a creamy head, especially low-gravity and high-adjunct beers.

Irish Moss—A negatively charged, dried seaweed that attracts positively charged suspended beer proteins in the final (fifteen to twenty) minutes of a wort boil to aid clearing. Active ingredient carrageenan deters chill-haze. "Red" Irish moss is a similar but more finely powdered version. One teaspoon per five gallons is recommended.

Isinglass—A yeast-settling, gelatinous fining agent made from the linings of fish swim bladders. Aids in clarification. Use of isinglass during the secondary fermentation or conditioning stage is permitted under the Reinheitsgebot.

Juniper Berries—Good for flavoring holiday beers, stouts, and porters. Use sparingly.

Lactic Acid—For lowering pH when brewing with hard water. (See "Water" section.)

Lactose (Milk Sugar)—A mildly sweet, nonfermentable carbohydrate found only in milk. It is used primarily in stouts and porters to lend residual sweetness. Lactose has approximately 17 percent of the sweetness of table sugar.

Licorice Sticks—Add a special, smooth flavor to stouts, porters, and flavored beers. Chop up two to five inches, then boil in brew kettle for twenty minutes.

Malto-Dextrin—Nonfermentable, tasteless carbohydrate that adds smoothness to beer. Can cause haze in light beers. Primarily for extract-based recipes to improve mouthfeel.

Oak Chips—A flavoring additive used to add hints of spiciness—as in India pale ale or Belgian ale—to simulate oak cask conditioning. One ounce per five gallons is typical. Sanitize by steaming or baking in a 350˚F oven for thirty minutes or by boiling for five minutes in one cup of water.

Papain—Derived from the juice of unripe papaya. Usually seen as a meat tenderizer. Prevents chill-haze in beer.

Pectic Enzyme—Removes the haze caused by the pectin carbohydrates contained in fruits and berries. Used primarily in winemaking, but can be used in fruit-flavored beers.

Polyclar—A polymer (plastic powder) that prevents chill-haze and oxidation.

Spruce Essence—Adds a unique flavor to porters, holiday beers, and honey lagers. Use sparingly!

Water Crystals/Water Salts (Magnesium Sulfate & Gypsum)—Water hardener used for imitating Burton-on-Trent brewing liquor. Aids enzymes during the mash. Often contains other haze-preventing ingredients. (See "Water" section.)

Yeast Nutrient—Aids fermentation in low-gravity worts and meads by providing essential foods for rapid yeast growth.

Sanitizers and Cleansers

Sanitation is probably the single most crucial factor in the final outcome of your beer. Some of the more popular and widely available products for cleaning and sanitizing your equipment are as follows:

B-Brite—Product name of a cleaner/sanitizer that removes beer stone (hardened yeast) and other fermentation residues, but needs thorough rinsing. Its active oxygen cleans without chlorine or bisulfite and is especially useful in cleaning hard-to-reach places like carboy necks, but this may require an overnight soak. One tablespoon per gallon of water is recommended. Environmentally friendly.

BTF-Iodophor—Sanitizer. Product name of an iodine solution used in many breweries as a line cleaner because it won't corrode stainless steel or kegs. Requires no rinsing if properly diluted. Often recommended after using B-Brite. One-half ounce per five gallons is recommended. Not environmentally friendly and can permanently stain clothing.

Campden Tablets (Potassium or Sodium Metabisulfite)—Inhibits harmful bacteria and yeast. Use only *in* wine. One tablet per gallon is recommended. Allow to air-dry for twenty-four hours. Contains sulfites, which many people are extremely allergic to. It is recommended that asthmatics avoid sulfite- (sulphite-) based products.

Chlorine/Household Bleach—Although very effective in cleaning and sanitizing, it is very environmentally unfriendly. One tablespoon per gallon of water is recommended for cleaning purposes. One teaspoon per gallon of water is recommended for sanitizing. When using chlorine, soak for twenty to thirty minutes, then rinse thoroughly with boiled or sterile water. Adequate ventilation is highly recommended.

CL–9 Sanitizer—Concentrated chlorine-based sanitizer in a granular form.

One-Step—Product name of a nontoxic, environmentally friendly sanitizer. No rinsing required after washing bottles or equipment. A good iodophor substitute, but extended soaking can leave a residue. One tablespoon per gallon of warm water is recommended.

Potassium Metabisulfite—Antibacterial agent that produces bacteria/yeast-inhibiting sulfur dioxide gas. Same uses as sodium metabisulfite, but adds no sodium. Use in wine "must" only; should not be put into beer wort.

Soda Ash (Sodium Carbonate)/Washing Soda—Cleaner used primarily in winemaking to "sweeten" new oak barrels, but also for cleaning primary and secondary fermenters, and for "beer clean" glassware.

Sodium Metabisulfite—Sanitizer. Inhibits bacterial and yeast growth. No longer widely used because many consider it dangerous and ineffective. See "Campden Tablets."

Straight-A—Product name of a cleaner similar to B-Brite. Environmentally friendly. One tablespoon per gallon of water is recommended. Rinsing required.

RECIPE
FORMULATION

BEER DESIGN—HOW TO USE THESE TABLES

On the following pages are tables containing outlines for brewing thirty-six classic beer styles. These easily referenced charts of the ingredients and techniques used in brewing these styles will help you construct accurate formulations for your own recipes. Preferred ingredients as demonstrated by historical or commercial brewing are listed, although there are certainly ingredients that may on occasion have been used in commercial versions of these recipes but are not included here in order to simplify matters. Figures are calculated for a five and a half U.S. gallon volume at the end of the wort boil to allow for transfer loss, sediment and trub removal, and spillage so that a full five U.S. gallons can be packaged. Be sure to adjust the amount of priming if your final volume is significantly more or less than five gallons.

Entries used in the tables are explained as follows:

Primary Grist. These are the malts used to make up the bulk of the grain bill for a five and a half gallon batch listed in order of preference. Adjuncts are usually listed separately except in the case of beers such as lambic where adjuncts make up a significant portion of the grist. The weight in pounds given refers to the total weight of all the grains of the primary grist, not for each grain listed. A conservative average yield of 1.025 to 1.030 SG points per pound/per gallon is used for most base malts to accommodate new all-grain brewers, a wide range of mash temperatures, and the realities of rudimentary mashing and sparging equipment. If your results are different, adjust accordingly. The specific gravity contributions from a typical 5–15 percent use of specialty malts and other fermentables noted has been taken into account in calculating the weight of the primary grist.

Specialty Malts. These are the coloring malts often seen in this particular recipe. Most often all of the possibilities are given. The quantities listed for these malts are in addition to the total weight given for the primary grist. Rarely does a recipe require all of the specialty malts when four or five are listed, and generally the total specialty malts used is kept to 15 percent or less of the total grist. A conservative average yield of 1.020 to 1.025 SG points per pound/per gallon is used for the specialty malts. As with the primary grist, if you achieve greater yields, adjust accordingly.

Malt Extracts. Quantities are given for both malt extract syrup (syrup) and for dried malt extract (DME). The quantities given are the total if you are using either one or the other, not both. A conservative average yield of 1.035 SG points per pound/per gallon is used for the syrup, 1.040 is assumed for the DME.

Hops. These are the traditional and most widely used varieties for the style. Traditional international bitterness unit levels are given and their proper usage for bittering, flavor, aroma, or dry-hopping are indicated by the letters B, F, A, and D. Substitutions are not given because most hops should be readily obtainable due to the growing availablity, variety, and sophistication of home-brewing supplies.

Adjuncts and Additives. These include unmalted grains, sugars, clarifying agents, spices, water treatment, or any ingredient traditionally used in the style.

Water Hardness. This indicates the water hardness typical of the brewing liquor for this particular style. Only where very narrow or specific ion counts are required are they given, otherwise a general hardness and carbonate range are indicated.

Mashing Method. This provides a general note of the mashing method traditionally employed for this beer style. It should be noted that, except in the case of beers such as bocks, dunkels, and weizens, decoction mashing has been largely supplanted with step-mashing by modern brewers because of the higher modification of modern malts. Feel free to exercise your judgment on which method to use. Refer to the appropriate mashing schedules beginning on page 25 for more detailed instruction for each mashing method.

Wort Boil. The average length of the traditional wort boil. The shorter times noted are generally favored for the partial wort boils often used in extract brews, the longer times given are recommended for full wort boils with extract or all-grain brews.

Yeast. These are my recommendations for the commercially available liquid yeast strains best suited for the beer style. They are identified by manufacturer and catalog number as listed in the yeast profiles section on pages 74–82. Wyeast™, BrewTek™, Yeast Lab™, and The Yeast Culture Kit Company™ cultures are abbreviated W, BT, YL, and YC, respectively.

OG/FG The lower and upper ranges of typical original and final gratives aimed for in this particular style. Although there may be variances from these parameters in the commercial brewing world, they have been narrowed here to facilitate easier recipe planning.

Primary Fermentation. The type and temperature of the primary ferment is noted here. Open fermentation is often recommended because it has seen traditional use in the professional brewing industry. Realities of homebrewing equipment and sanitation dictate that closed fermentation can be substituted in all instances. If the traditional fermentation temperature differs from the optimum fermentation temperature of your yeast, defer to the manufacturer's recommended temperature.

Secondary Fermentation. This includes the brief secondary ferment or the long bulk maturation period for ales as well as the bulk lagering of bottom-fermented beers. Recommended temperatures in degrees Fahrenheit and length of time are given.

Priming/Conditioning. These are the traditional or recommended methods of producing CO_2 in the packaged beer after lagering/maturation. By all means, feel free to substitute your tried and true methods of conditioning, such as forced carbonation or refermentation with corn sugar, for the more difficult residual sugar or kräusening techniques if necessary.

Serving Temperature. The traditionally recommended optimum serving temperature of the finished beer.

*Delete when extract brewing.
**Delete when all-grain brewing.

	Altbier	American Amber Ale	American Lager (pre-Prohibition)	Barleywine (Dark)
Primary Grist*	7-9 lbs. (80-90%) German 2-row Pale Malt Belgian 2-row Pils. Malt	10-12.5 lbs. 2-row Harrington or Klages Pale Malt	9-10 lbs. Domestic 6-row Pale Malt Domestic 2-row Pale Malt	12-23 lbs. 2-row Pale Ale Malt Mild Ale Malt
Specialty Malts	0-2 lbs. Light and/or Dark Munich or Vienna Malt 0.25-1 lb. Light or Dk German Crystal Malt 0-0.25 lb. Chocolate Malt 0-0.25 lb. Black Prinz Malt	40° F Crystal Malt Dextrine Malt Victory Malt Munich Malt Special Roast Malt	0.25-0.5 lb. Light Crystal Malt 0-1 lb. Dextrine Malt	0-1 lb. Dextrine Malt 0.25-1 lb. Crystal Malt 0-0.5 lb. Chocolate Malt 0-0.25 lb. Black Malt
Malt Extracts** Syrup DME	Light to Amber 6.5-7.5 lbs. Syrup 6-7 lbs. DME	Light to Amber 7.5-9 lbs. Syrup 6.5-8 lbs. DME	Ex Light 7-8 lbs. Syrup 6-7 lbs. DME	Light to Amber 10-20 lbs. Syrup 9-17 lbs. DME
Hop Bitterness, Varieties & Uses: Bittering (B) Flavor (F) Aroma (A) Dry Hopping (D)	28-50 IBU Spalt Tettnang Hallertau Mittelfrüh Hersbrucker Saaz (B)(F)	30-40 IBU Mt Hood Chinook Cascade Willamette (B)(F)(A)(D)	20-40 IBU Cluster Northern Brewer Saaz Perle Mt Hood Liberty Galena Eroica Hallertau (B)	50-70 IBU Kent Goldings Fuggles Challenger Cascade Willamette (B)(F)(A) (D)
Adjuncts and Additives	None	Irish Moss	10-25% Flaked Maize, Rice, Corn Sugar, Flaked Wheat and Barley Polyclar, Gelatin finings	0-0.5 lb. Roasted Barley Treacle Corn Sugar Brown Sugar Molasses
Water Hardness	Soft to Medium-Soft 250-300 ppm hardness	Soft to Moderate Low to Moderate Temporary Hardness	Moderate to Hard Low to Moderate Temporary Hardness	Medium to Hard Moderate Temporary Hardness (see London and Burton profiles)
Mashing Method	Single Temp Infusion Double Decoction or Step Mash w/rests at 122° F, 140-149° F, 155-158° F	Single Temperature Infusion @ 149-155° F or Step Mash	Protein rest highly recommended Step Mash or Single Decoction w/ high temp saccarification rest to increase body	Single Temperature Infusion Mash (1st runnings are often used exclusively)
Wort Boil	1.5-2 hours	1.5 hours	1-1.5 hours	1.5-3 hours
Yeast	YC A37 YL A06 W 1338/1007 BT 400	W 1056/1087 YL A02 YC A01 BT 10/20	W 2035/2007/2178 BT 620/360 YL L34 YC L17	YC A01/A08/A34 W 1084/1728/1214 BT 20/130/170
OG/FG	1043-48/1008-14	1.050-60/1.012-14	1044-60/1010-16	1065-125/1024-32
Primary Fermentation	Open or Closed 5-7 days @ 57-72° F	Closed 5-7 days @ 65-70° F	Closed 10-14 days @ 46-48° F	Open or Closed 1-2 weeks @ 60-70° F
Secondary Fermentation/ Lagering	3-8 weeks Conditioning @ 32-46° F	5-7 days @ 60-65° F	Closed 7-10 days @ 46-48° F Lager @ 31-35° F 3-4 weeks	4-16 weeks @ 55-60° F Yeast Rousing Sometimes Used
Priming/ Conditioning Methods/ Rates /Temperatures Volumes of CO₂	1.75-2 qts. Speise Residual Sugar Kräusening w/ 1-2 weeks @ 60-70° F	3/4 cup Corn Sugar w/ 1 week @ 65-70° F & 2-3 weeks @ 55° F	Filtered and Force Carbonated or 3/4 cup corn sugar w/ 2-3 weeks @ 45-50° F	1/2-3/4 cup Corn Sugar Fresh Yeast 4-36 months @ 50-55° F
Serving Temperature	45-50° F	50-55° F	42-47° F	50-60° F

	Belgian Strong Ale	Berliner Weisse	Bière de Garde	Bitter (Ordinary)
Primary Grist*	10-15 lbs. Belgian 2-row Pils. Malt Munich Malt Vienna Malt	5-6 lbs. total 25-75% German 2-row Pale Malt 25-75% Wheat Malt	12-16 lbs. 4 °L Vienna Malt 2-row Pale Malt 5-10 °L Munich Malt	7.5-8.5 lbs. 2-row Pale Ale Malt
Specialty Malts	0-0.75 lb. Crystal Malt Aromatic Malt Caravienne Malt Caramunich Malt Biscuit Malt	None	Light or Dark Crystal Malt Roasted Malt	0.25-.50 lbs. 20-40 °L Crystal Malt
Malt Extracts** Syrup DME	Light to Amber 10-15 lbs. Syrup 8.5-13 lbs. DME	Extra Light and Wheat 4.5-5 lbs. Syrup 4-4.5 lbs. DME	Light to Amber 9-11 lbs. Syrup DME	Ex Light to Light 5-5.5 lbs. Syrup 4.5-5 lbs. DME
Hop Bitterness, Varieties & Uses: Bittering (B) Flavor (F) Aroma (A) Dry Hopping (D)	20-50 IBU Saaz Hallertau Lublin Styrian Goldings Kent Goldings (B)	3-8 IBU Northern Brewer Hallertau Tettnang Spalt Perle (B)	25-30 IBU Poperinge Hersbruck Aurora Tettnang Perle Strissel Spalt Saaz Brewers Gold Styrian Goldings (B) (F) (A)	20-30 IBU Fuggles Kent Goldings Northern Brewer Challenger Target (B) (F) (A) (D)
Adjuncts and Additives	White or Brown Candi Sugar Cane or Corn Sugar Spices (e.g., coriander, ginger, cardamom, cumin, nutmeg, curaçao)	None	0-0.75 lb. Brewing Sugar	Torrefied Wheat Flaked Barley Brewing Sugar Irish Moss/ Isinglass
Water Hardness	Soft to Medium Spring Water	Medium Hard to Hard High Carbonate Level	Medium to Soft	Hard- High Sulfate, Low Bicarbonate Gypsum/Burton Salts often used
Mashing Method	Single Temp Infusion or Single Decoction w/ low temp sugar rest	Infusion mash with Low mash temp to favor high fermentables	Single Temp Infusion or Step Mash w/low to medium temp sugar rest	Single Temp Infusion 60-90 min.@ 150°F
Wort Boil	2-3 hours	15-120 minutes @ 185- 212° F	60-90 minutes	60-90 minutes
Yeast	BT 300/320/340 YL A08 W 1214/3944 YC A36	BT 980/450/400 W 1338/1007/2565 YC A04 w/ ratio of 15-25% lacto- bacillus culture	Lager (@ warm temps) or Ale W 3787/1762/1388/2112 BT 320/340/380/ 690 YL A08/L35	W 1098/1028/1968 BT 160/120/170 YC A15/A17 YL A04/A09/A03
OG/FG	1063-95/1012-24	1028-32/1004-06	1055-75/1010-12	1035-38/1006-12
Primary Fermentation	5-7 days @60-68° F open or closed	4-7 days @ 68-77° F	10-14 days @ 55-65° F	3-5 days @ 60-72° F
Secondary Fermenta- tion/Lagering	2 months to 2 years @ 50- 55° F	3-12 mos. @ 59-77° F	8-12 Weeks @ 32-35° F	5-7 days @ 55-60° F
Priming/Conditioning Methods/ Rates /Tem- peratures Volumes of CO_2	Bottle Condition w/ 1/2- 3/4 cup candi, corn, cane or invert sugar @ 68-75° F for 1 week Mature 6-36 mos. @ 50-55° F	3-4 vols CO_2 kräusened w/ or w/o fresh lactobacillus @ 65-75° F then @ 50-55° F 3-4 wks	Bottle Condition w/ 3/4 cup Priming Sugar and Fresh Yeast Cellar 3-36 months @ 50- 55° F	1-2 weeks in cask w/dry hops and finings or 1-2 weeks in bottle w/ 1-2 cup corn sugar @ 60-70° F
Serving Temperature	50-55° F	45° F w/raspberry or woodruff syrup	50-55° F	50-55° F

	Bitter (ESB)	Bock	Brown Ale (Northern English)	California Common
Primary Grist*	9-12 lbs. 2-row Pale Ale Malt	14-16 lbs. Munich Malt German 2-row Pale Malt Vienna Malt	8.5-10.5 lbs. Mild Ale Malt Amber Malt Brown Malt 2-row Pale Ale Malt	8.5-11.5 lbs. 2-row or 6-row Pale Malt
Specialty Malts	0.5-.1 lb. Crystal Malt 0.5-.1 lb. Dextrine Malt	0-.75 lb. German Dark or Light Crystal Malt 0-0.25 lb. Black Prinz or Chocolate Malt	0.5-1 lb. Crystal Malt Chocolate Malt Dextrine Malt	0.25-1 lb. Dextrine Malt 0-0.75 lb. 10-40 °L Crystal Malt
Malt Extracts** Syrup DME	Light to Amber 6-9 lbs. Syrup 5.5-8 lbs. DME	Amber to Dark 10-11 lbs. Syrup 8.5-10 lbs. DME	Amber to Dark 6-7.5 lbs. Syrup 5.5-6.5 lbs. DME	Light to Amber 6- 8 lbs. Syrup 5.5-7 lbs. DME
Hop Bitterness, Varieties & Uses: Bittering (B) Flavor (F) Aroma (A) Dry Hopping (D)	30-55 IBU Fuggles Kent Goldings Challenger Target (B)(F)(A)	20-25 IBU Mittelfrüh Tettnang Hersbrucker Spalt Northern Brewer Perle Saaz Liberty (B)(F)	14-35 IBU Kent Goldings Fuggles Challenger Bramling Cross Northdown Target Willamette Cascade(B)	30-45 IBU Northern Brewer Brewers Gold BC or East Kent Goldings (B)(F)(A)(D)
Adjuncts and Additives	Flaked Maize Brewing Sugar Flaked/Torrefied Wheat and Barley Gypsum/ Burton Salts Irish Moss Isinglass	None	0-0.5 lb Treacle Brown Sugar Molasses Malto-Dextrin	Corn Sugar historically, but not currently used
Water Hardness	Hard Sulfate ~300 ppm Low Temporary Hardness	Soft to moderate w/ High Temporary Hardness	High Bicarbonate Hardness High Sodium Chloride	Moderate Hardness Low to Moderate Temporary Hardness
Mashing Method	Single Temp Infusion @ 150-154° F 60-90 min.	Single, Double, or Triple Decoction or Intensive Step Mash w/ rests @ ~100°, 122°, 150°, 160° F	Single Temp Infusion @ 150-160° F	Step Mash w/ 122° protein rest and sugar rest @ 149-151° F
Wort Boil	60-90 minutes	90-180 minutes Minimum of 120 minutes for nondecoction mashes	60 minute extract 90 minute all-grain	60 minute extract 90 minute all-grain
Yeast	W 1098/1028/1968 BT 130/120/170 YC A15/A17 YL A04/A09/A03	W 2206/2278/ 2308 YL L32/33 BT 680 YC L09	YC A01/A15/A17 YL A04 W 1084	W 2035/2112/2007 BT 690 YL L35
OG/FG	1042-60/1010-16	1064-73/1018-24	1040-50/1008-14	1040-55/1012-18
Primary Fermentation	Open or closed 5-7 days @ 60-70° F	Closed 10-14 Days @ 48-54° F (2-2.5 Liters of Yeast Starter advised)	Open or closed 5-7 days @ 60-68° F	Open or closed 7-14 days @ 56-72° F
Secondary Fermentation/Lagering	(Cask) 7-10 days @ 50-60° F w/finings 1/2 cup corn sugar, dry hops	3-6 months @ 30-33° F	3-5 days at 55-65° F	2-3 weeks @60-65° F in glass
Priming/Conditioning Methods/ Rates /Temperatures Volumes of CO_2	(Bottle) 1 week @ 60-70° F w/ 3/4 cup corn sugar and 2-3 weeks to mature	Residual Sugar or Wort Priming w/ fresh yeast and 2 weeks @ primary fermentation temp	1/3-1/2 cup Corn Sugar Priming 1-2 weeks @ 60-65° F	1.5-2 qts. kräusen 1-2 weeks @ 50-55° F or w/ 3/4 cups corn sugar 2.8-3 vols CO_2
Serving Temperature	50-55° F	45-50° F	50-55° F	45-50° F

	Cream Ale	Czech Pilsner	Doppelbock	Dortmunder
Primary Grist*	9.5-12 lbs. 2-row or 6-row Domestic Pale Malt 0-5 lbs. Munich or Vienna Malt	9.5-11 lbs. Belgian Pils. Malt German 2-row Pale Malt	15.5-17 lbs. German 2-row Pale Malt Munich Malt Vienna Malt	10.5-13 lbs. German 2-row Pale Malt Belgian Pils. Malt (may include 2-3 lbs. Domestic 6-row or 1-2 lbs. Pale Munich Malt)
Specialty Malts	0.25-.75 lb. Light Crystal Malt	0.25-.75 lb. Light Crystal Malt	0.25-.75 lb. Dark German Crystal Malt 0.25-.50 lb. Chocolate Malt	0.25-0.5 lb. Dextrine Malt Light German Crystal Malt
Malt Extracts** Syrup DME	Ex Light to Light 6.5-8.5 lbs. Syrup 6-7.5 lbs. DME	Ex Light to Light 6.5-7.5 lbs. Syrup 6-6.5 lbs. DME	Amber to Dark 11-12.5 lbs. Syrup 9.5-11 lbs. DME	Ex Light to Light 7.5-9 lbs. Syrup 6.5-8 lbs. DME
Hop Bitterness, Varieties &Uses: Bittering (B) Flavor (F) Aroma (A) Dry Hopping (D)	10-22 IBU Cluster Cascade Willamette Northern Brewer Perle Bullion Kent Goldings (B)	30-40 IBU Saaz Styrian Goldings Hallertau Tettnang Lublin (B) (F) (A)	17-27 IBU Hallertau Hersbrucker/ Mittelfrüh Perle Spalt Tettnang Northern Brewer Saaz Liberty Mt Hood (B) (F)	20-30 IBU Hallertau Hersbrucker/ Mittelfrüh Perle Spalt Tettnang Saaz Northern Brewer (B) (F) (A)
Adjuncts and Additives	0.5-1.5 lbs. Corn Sugar Flaked Maize or Rice Rolled oats	Gelatin or Polyclar Finings	None	None
Water Hardness	Hard to Very Hard Low Temporary Hardness	Soft w/ low Temporary Hardness	Soft-Moderate w/ High Temporary Hardness	Hard to Very Hard Water High Sulfate High Temporary Hardness
Mashing Method	Step Mash w/ rests @ 122° and 149° F	Step Mash w/ Intensive Protein Rest and Sugar Rest @ 150-155° F or Double or Triple Decoction	Double or Triple Decoction w/ Sugar rest @ 153-158° F Step Mash	Decoction w/ Sugar Rest @ 150-155° F
Wort Boil	60 minutes	60 -90 minutes extract 90 -180 minutes all-grain	90-180 minutes 60 minutes extract	90 minutes all-grain
Yeast	W 1056 YL A02/A07 BT 10/260 (Lager yeast may also be used in a 55-60° F ferment)	W 2124/2278 BT 600 YC L17 YL L31	W 2206/2278/2308 YL L32/33 BT 680 YC L09	W 2042/2272/2247 BT 660 YC L09
OG/FG	1044-55/1004-10	1043-50/1014-16	1074-80/1020-28	1048-55/1010-14
Primary Fermentation	Closed 5-7 days @ 58-70° F	Open or Closed 2 weeks @ 39-48° F	Closed 2 weeks @ 48-54° F	Closed 2 weeks @ 46-56° F
Secondary Fermentation/Lagering	2-4 months @ 32-34° F	2-3 months @ 32-34° F	6-9 months @ 30-33° F	4-6 weeks @ 32-34° F
Priming/Conditioning Methods/ Rates /Temperatures Volumes of CO_2	3/4 cup Corn Sugar for 1 week @ room temp. and 2 weeks @ 30-35° F	3/4 Cup Priming Sugar 2 qts. Wort Priming or Kräusen	Residual Sugar Kräusen or Wort Priming w/ fresh yeast for 2 weeks @ 48-54° F	Wort Priming Kräusen Residual Sugar 1-2 weeks @ 48-55° F and 4-6 weeks @ 30-35° F
Serving Temperature	45-50° F	45-50° F	45-50° F	45-50° F

	Dubbel	Dunkel	India Pale Ale	Kölsch-Style Ale
Primary Grist*	10.5-14.5 lbs. 2-row Belgian Pils. Malt 2-row Pale Ale Malt Munich Malt	10.5-11.5 lbs. 66-99% Munich Malt 0-4 lbs. Vienna German 2-row Pale Malt or 2-row Belgian Pils. Malt	10.5-14 lbs. 2-row Pale Ale Malt	9-10.5 lbs. German 2-row Pale Malt Vienna Malt Pale Munich Malt 0-20% Wheat Malt
Specialty Malts	0.25-1 lb. each: CaraVienne CaraMunich Special B Malt Aromatic Malt Biscuit Malt Dextrine Malt	0.25-0.75 lb. Chocolate Malt Dark Crystal Malt Aromatic Malt Black Prinz Malt 0-0.25 lb. Caramunich Brumalt	0.25-0.5 lb. 10-20 °L Crystal Malt	0.25-0.5 lb. German Light Crystal Malt 0-0.75 lb Dextrine Malt
Malt Extracts** Syrup DME	Light to Dark 7.5-10.5 lbs. Syrup 6.5-9.5 lbs. DME	Light to Dark 7.5-9.5 lbs. Syrup 6.5-8 lbs. DME	Ex Light to Light 7.5-10 lbs. Syrup 6.5-9 lbs. DME	Ex Light to Light 6.5-7.5 lbs. Syrup 6-6.5 lbs. DME
Hop Bitterness, Varieties & Uses: Bittering (B) Flavor (F) Aroma (A) Dry Hopping (D)	18-25 IBU Hallertau Northern Brewer Styrian Saaz Lublin Tettnanger Fuggles Kent Goldings Cascade Mt Hood Liberty (B)(A)	20-30 IBU Hallertau Hersbrucker/ Mittelfrüh Tettnang Spalt Perle Liberty Mt Hood (B)(F)(A)	40-60 IBU Fuggles Kent Goldings Northern Brewer Brewers Gold Challenger Northdown Target Bramling Cross Progress (B)(F)(A)(D)	25-30 IBU Spalt Tettnang Perle Hallertau (B)(F)(A)
Adjuncts and Additives	Light and/or Dark Candi Sugar Corn, Cane, Brown, Invert Sugar	None	0-1 lb. Corn Sugar 0-0.25 lb. Flaked Maize/ Wheat Irish Moss Isinglass Burton Salts < 1 oz. Oak Chips	None
Water Hardness	Soft to Hard Moderate to High Temporary Hardness	Soft to Moderate High Temporary Hardness	Hard to Very Hard Sulfate 300-400 ppm Low Temporary Hardness	Soft Low Temporary Hardness
Mashing Method	Step Mash w/ rests @ 122, 140, 150, 160° F Single Temp Infusion @ 150-155° F Single or Double Decoction	Double or Triple Decoction with sugar rest @ 153-160° F Stepped w/ rests @ 100°, 122°, 149°, 158° F	Single Temp Infusion 60-90 minutes @ 149-153° F	Step Mash w/ Protein Rest at 122° F 30-60 minutes Saccharification rest at 150° F 60-90 minutes
Wort Boil	90-180 minutes	90 minutes extract 90-120 minutes all-grain	60 minutes extract 90-180 minutes all-grain	60 minutes extract 90 minutes all-grain
Yeast	BT 300/340 W 1214 YC A36/A16 YL A08 W 2206/2308/ 2124	YL L32/33 BT 680 YC L09 BT 10/120/170 W 1098/1028/ 1968	YL A09/A03 YC A15/A17 YC A04 W 2565/1007	BT 450
OG/FG	1063-70/1012-16	1049-54/1014-18	1050-65/1010-16	1044-48/1006-10
Primary Fermentation	Open or closed @ 65-75° F 3-7 days	Open or closed 1-2 weeks @ 40-50° F	Open or closed 5-7 days @ 60-68° F	Open or closed 3-5 days @ 64-72° F
Secondary Fermentation/Lagering	1-3 months in glass under airlock @ 45-65° F	1-2 weeks @ 35-40° F and/or 2-3 Months@ 30-35° F	5-7 days @ 55-60° F 3-6 months @ 50-55° F	5-7 days @ 55-65° F 2-6 weeks @ 32-40° F
Priming/Conditioning Methods/ Rates /Temperatures Volumes of CO_2	3/4-1 cup Corn Sugar @ 65-75° F 1-2 weeks Mature 1-5 years @ 50-55° F 2-3 vols CO_2	Residual Sugar Kräusening Wort Speise	(Bottle) 1 week @ 60-70° F w/ 3/4 cup corn sugar and 2-3 weeks to mature	Wort Primed Kräusened Residual Sugar Generally Filtered
Serving Temperature	55-60° F	45-50° F	50-55° F	45-50° F

	Lambic	Mai Bock	Märzen/Oktoberfest	Mild Ale (Dark)
Primary Grist*	9-11.5 lbs. 60-65% high-enzyme 2-row or domestic 6-row Pale Malt 35-40% Raw Wheat	14-15.5 lbs. German 2-row Pale Malt Belgian 2-row Pils. Malt	10.5-12.5 lbs. German 2-row Pale Malt Munich Malt Vienna Malt	6.5-8 lbs. Mild Ale Malt Brown Malt 2-row Pale Ale Malt
Specialty Malts	None	0.25 lb. Light German Crystal Malt	0.25-0.75 lb. German Light or Dark Crystal Malt Brumalt Dextrine Malt	0.25-0.75 lb. Amber Malt Crystal Malt Chocolate Malt
Malt Extracts** Syrup DME	Ex Light Barley and Wheat Extracts 6.5-8.5 lbs. Syrup 5.5-7.5 lbs. DME	Ex Light to Light 10-11.5 lbs. Syrup 9-10 lbs. DME	Light to Amber 7.5-9 lbs. Syrup 6.5-8 lbs. DME	Amber to Dark 4.5-6 lbs. Syrup 4-5-5 lbs. DME
Hop Bitterness, Varieties & Uses: Bittering (B) Flavor (F) Aroma (A) Dry Hopping (D)	15-21 IBU derived from 2-3 yr. old Hops or Low Alpha Acid Aroma Hops (B)	20-35 IBU Hallertau Mittelfrüh/ Hersbrucker Spalt Tettnang Perle Mt Hood Liberty (B) (F) (A)	20-25 IBU Saaz Hallertau Spalt Perle Styrian Goldings (B) (F) (A)	10-25 IBU Fuggles Progress Bramling Cross Challenger Kent Goldings (B)
Adjuncts and Additives	40% Flaked Wheat (as a raw wheat substitute) 8-10 lbs. macerated: Sour Cherries Peaches Raspberries	None	None	Caramel or Corn Sugar Torrefied Wheat and Barley Black Malt Isinglass Irish Moss
Water Hardness	Soft to Moderate Low Temporary Hardness	Soft Low to Very Low Temporary Hardness	Medium-Soft Temporary Hardness 100-150 ppm	High Sulfate and Chloride Moderate Temporary Hardness
Mashing Method	Pre-boil Adjuncts Step mash or Double Decoction w/rests @ 117°, 135°, 150°, and 162° F 200° F Sparge	Single or Double Decoction	Decoction or Step Mash w/ rests at 122°, 147°, and 158° F	Single Temp Infusion 60-90 minutes @ 150-155° F
Wort Boil	3.5-6 hours Turbid mash favors a long boil	60 minutes extract 90 minutes all-grain	60 minutes extract 90 minutes all-grain	60 minutes extract 90 minutes all-grain
Yeast	W 1056-primary YC A01-primary BT 5600 YL 3200 W 3273/3220/3200	W 2206/2278 /2308 YL L32/33 BT 680 YC L09	W 2206/2308 YL L32/33 BT 680/600 YC L09	YC A01/A15/ A17 BT 20 YL A01/04
OG/FG	1042-54/1001-10	1064-72/1012-20	1050-60/1012-20	1030-38/1004-08
Primary Fermentation	Open and closed In oak cask 2-4 yrs. @ 63-68° F or 6 months in glass	3-6 months in glass Closed 2 weeks @ 40-49° F	Closed 7-10 days @ 46-55° F	Closed 3-5 days @ 60-65° F
Secondary Fermentation/Lagering	18 mos. in casks @ 50-60° F then 4-6 mos. w/ fruit in cask or glass	2 weeks @ 40-49° F 2-6 months @ 31-35° F	3-6 months @ 32-35° F	3-5 days @ 60-70° F
Priming/Conditioning Methods/ Rates /Temperatures Volumes of CO_2	3/4 cup Corn Sugar @ 65-75° F 4-8 weeks or blended w/ Young Lambic Mature 6-12 months in bottles	2.8-3.0 vols. Wort Primed w/ fresh Yeast 2 weeks @40-49° F Residual Sugar 2.5-2.7 vols.	Wort Primed w/ fresh Yeast 2 weeks @ 46-55° F Kräusened Residual Sugar 2.4-2.6 vols.	Traditonally on Draft but also in Bottles w/ 1/2-3/4 cup Corn Sugar Priming 1 week @ 65-70° F and 1 week @ 50-55° F
Serving Temperature	45-55° F	45-47° F	45-47° F	50-55° F

	Munich Helles	Oud Bruin	Pale Ale (American)	Porter
Primary Grist*	8.5-10.5 lbs. German 2-row Pale or Domestic 6-row Pale Malt	9-12 lbs. Belgian 2-row Pale Ale or Pils. Vienna Munich	9-12 lbs. 2-row Domestic 6-row Pale 2-row Belgian Pils. 0-5% Wheat	9.5-12.5 lbs. 2-row Mild Ale 2-row Brown 2-row Pale Ale Vienna
Specialty Malts	0.25-0.75 lb. German Light Crystal Malt Dextrine Malt	0.25-0.75 lb. CaraMunich CaraVienne Dextrine Biscuit Aromatic Roasted Special B	0.25-0.75 lb. Dextrine Light Crystal	0.5-1 lb. 2-row Amber Black Patent Chocolate Dark Crystal Dextrine
Malt Extracts** Syrup DME	Ex Light to Light 6.5-8 lbs. Syrup 6-7 DME	Light to Amber 6.5-8.5 lbs. Syrup 6-7.5 DME	Ex Light to Amber 6.5-8.5 lbs. Syrup 6-7.5 lbs. DME	Amber to Dark 6.5-9 lbs. Syrup 6-8 lbs. DME
Hop Bitterness, Varieties & Uses: Bittering (B) Flavor (F) Aroma (A) Dry Hopping (D)	20-25 IBU Tettnang Spalt Saaz (B) (F) (A)	15-25 IBU Saaz Hallertau Kent Goldings Fuggles Styrian Goldings (B)	20-40 IBU Cascade Cluster Mt Hood Willamette Eroica BC Goldings Perle Chinook Nugget (B) (F) (A) (D)	25-45 IBU Cluster Fuggles Willamette Kent Goldings Cascade Chinook Challenger (B) (F)
Adjuncts and Additives	None	0-0.25 lb. Roasted Barley 8-10 lbs.-optional Sour Cherries or Raspberries in Secondary	Burton Salts Irish Moss 0-5% Flaked Barley/Maize/ Wheat Polyclar or Gelatin	Roasted Barley Flaked Barley Molasses Brown Sugar Licorice Root
Water Hardness	Soft Low Temporary Hardness	Moderate to Hard Moderate Temporary Hardness	Moderate to Hard Low Temporary Hardness	Moderate to Hard High Calcium and Chloride Low Sulfate High Temporary Hardness
Mashing Method	Step Mash or Single decoction w/ Sacch. rest @ 153-158° F	Step Mash or Single Temp Infusion w/ Sacch. rest @ 153-158°	Single Temp Infusion @ 149-153° F or Step Mash w/ rests @ 122°, 150°, 158° F	Single Temp Infusion @ 149-155° F
Wort Boil	60 minutes extract 90 minutes all-grain	1.5-2 hours extract 2-3 hours all-grain	60 minutes extract 90 minutes all-grain	60 minutes extract 90 minutes all-grain
Yeast	BT 630/680/600 W 2206/2308 YL L32/L33 YC L09/L17	BT 320 W 1056/1272 YC A01 YL A02/A09/A05 Optional-W 3278 BT 5600/5200 YL 3200/3220	W 1056/1098/1087 YL A02/A07/A09 YC A01/A15 BT 10/120/260 Cultured up Sierra Nevada Yeast	YC A01/A13/A06 YL A01/A05 BT 160/170 W 1028
OG/FG	1044-47/1008-12	1044-56/1008-10	1044-56/1008-16	1045-60/1008-16
Primary Fermentation	Closed 10-14 days @ 46-55° F	Open 5-7 days @ 65-70° F	Closed 5-7 days @ 65-70° F	Open or Closed 5-7 days @ 60-68° F
Secondary Fermentation/Lagering	2-10 weeks @32-35° F	3-12 Months w/ Fruit (optional)	5-7 days @ 55-65° F	2-3 weeks @ 50-55° F
Priming/Conditioning Methods/ Rates /Temperatures Volumes of CO2	Wort Primed w/ fresh yeast Kräusen Residual Sugar 1-2 weeks @ 46-55° F Mature 2-3 weeks @ 32-35° F	3/4 cup Priming Sugar and Fresh Yeast. Mature 1-3 months @ 50-60° F (Often Blended w/ young Brown) 1.5-3 vols.	3/4 cup Corn Sugar Kräusen 1 week @ 65-70° F Force Carbonate Mature 1-3 weeks @ 50-55° F	3/4 cup Corn Sugar 1 week @ 65-70° F Force Carbonate Mature 1-3 weeks @ 50-55° F 1-2.5 vols.
Serving Temperature	45-47° F	50-55° F	50-55° F	50-55° F

	Scotch Ale	Scottish 80/- Ale (Export)	Stout (Dry)	Tripel
Primary Grist*	15-17.5 lbs. Scottish 2-row Pale Ale Malt 1-2 lbs. Brown or Munich Malt	8.5-11 lbs. Scottish 2-row Pale Ale Malt 0.25-1 lb. Brown Malt	8.5-11 lbs. UK 2-row Pale Ale Malt Belgian 2-row Pale Ale Malt	15-20 lbs. Belgian 2-row Pils Malt German 2-row Pale Malt
Specialty Malts	Amber Malt 2-14 oz. Peat Smoked Malt Dextrine Malt Crystal Malt	5-10 oz. 10-40 °L Crystal or Dextrine Malt 1-4 oz. Amber or Black Patent Malt	0.5-1 lb. dark Crystal Black Patent Chocolate Malt	0.5-1 lb. Crystal Malt Caravienne Dextrine Malt
Malt Extracts** Syrup DME	Amber to Dark 11-13 lbs. Syrup 9.5-11 lbs. DME	Light to Amber 6-7.5 lbs. Syrup 5.5-6.5 lbs. DME	Dark to Ex Dark 6-7.5 lbs. Syrup 5.5-6.5 lbs. DME	Ex Light to Light 10.5-14.5 lbs. Syrup 9-12.5 lbs. DME
Hop Bitterness, Varieties & Uses: Bittering (B) Flavor (F) Aroma (A) Dry Hopping (D)	25-35 IBU Fuggles Kent Goldings WGV Bramling Cross Target Yeoman (B)	15-20 IBU Fuggles Kent Goldings WGV Bramling Cross Target Yeoman (B)	30-50 IBU Challenger Goldings Fuggles Target (B) (F)	20-25 IBU East Kent Goldings Saaz Fuggles Hallertau Hersbrucker Styrian Poperinge (B) (F)
Adjuncts and Additives	1-5 oz. Roasted Barley	1-2 oz. Roasted Barley	0.75-1.5 lbs. Roasted Barley 0-3 lbs. Flaked Barley	1-4 lbs. White Candi Corn Cane or Invert Sugar
Water Hardness	Soft to Moderate 125-150 ppm Temporary Hardness	Soft to Moderate 125-150 ppm Temporary Hardness	Soft to Moderate Low Sulfate High Calcium and Chloride High Temporary Hardness	Soft to Moderate Low Temporary Hardness
Mashing Method	Thick Single Temp Infusion w/ Sacch. rest @ 154-158° F	Thick Single Temp Infusion w/ Sacch. rest @ 154-158° F	Single Temp Infusion @ 153-158° F or Step Mash	Single Temp Infusion @ 149-153° F or Step Mash w/ low Sacch. rest
Wort Boil	90-120 minutes	90-120 minutes 60 minutes extract	90 minutes all-grain 60 minutes extract	90-120 minutes all-grain 60 minutes extract
Yeast	2-4 liter starter BT 170 YC A34 W 1728/1084	1-4 liter starter BT 170 YC A34 W 1728/1084	YC AO6/A13/A01 BT 240 YL A05 W 1084	BT 300/340 W 1214 YC A16/A36 YL A08
OG/FG	1072-85/1016-25	1040-50/1010-18	1040-50/1008-14	1070-95/1016-24
Primary Fermentation	Closed 10-14 days @ 60-68° F	Closed 5-7 days @ 60-68° F	Open or closed 7-10 days @ 55-60° F	Open @ 64-68° F
Secondary Fermentation/Lagering	2-3 months @ 40-50° F in glass or oak	3-4 weeks in glass @ 40-50° F	2-4 weeks @ 55-60° F	4-5 weeks @ 45-50° F
Priming/Conditioning Methods/ Rates /Temperatures Volumes of CO_2	1/2 (cask)-3/4 (bottles) cup Corn Sugar 1 week @ 60-65° F Mature 2-3 weeks @ 40-50° F 1-2 vols.	1/2 (cask)-3/4 (bottles) cup Corn Sugar 1 week @ 60-65° F Mature 1-2 weeks @ 40-50° F 1-2 vols.	3/4 cup Corn or Cane Priming Sugar in Cask or Bottles Force Carbonate High CO_2	2-3 weeks @ 65-70° F w/ 3/4 cup Corn or Cane Sugar Mature 1-36 months @ 50-55° F 2-2.5 vols.
Serving Temperature	55-65° F	50-55° F	55-65° F	45-55° F

	Vienna	Weizen Bier (Helles Hefe)	Weizenbock	Witbier
Primary Grist*	10-12 lbs. Vienna Malt 5-10 °L Munich Malt German 2-row Pale Belgian 2-row Pils.	10-12 lbs. 30-50% German 2-row Pale Belgian 2-row Pils. or Domestic 6-row Malt 50-70% Wheat Malt	14-17.5 lbs. 30-50% German 2-row Pale Belgian 2-row Pils. or Domestic 6-row Malt 50-70% Wheat Malt	9.5-11 lbs. 45-50% 2-row Belgian Pils. Malt 40-50% Raw or Flaked Wheat 5-10% Flaked or Rolled oats
Specialty Malts	0.25-1 lb. Dextrine Malt or Light Crystal Malt	0.25-0.5 lb. German Light Crystal Malt	0.25-0.75 lb. German Dark Crystal Malt	None
Malt Extracts** Syrup DME	Ex Light to Amber 7-8.5 lbs. Syrup 6.5-7.5 lbs. DME	Ex Light to Light Barley and Wheat Extracts 7-8.5 lbs. Syrup 6.5-7.5 lbs. DME	Amber to Dark Barley and Wheat Extracts 10-12.5 lbs. Syrup 8.5-11 lbs. DME	Ex Light to Light 6.5-7.5 lbs. Syrup 6-6.5 lbs. DME
Hop Bitterness, Varieties & Uses: Bittering (B) Flavor (F) Aroma (A) Dry Hopping (D)	22-28 IBU Saaz Lublin Styrian Perle Tettnang Hallertau Hersbrucker Mittelfrüh (B) (F) (A)	10-18 IBU Hallertau Hersbrucker Mittelfrüh Perle Spalt Tettnang (B)	15-25 IBU Hallertau Perle Spalt Tettnang (B)	15-20 IBU Styrian Hallertau Saaz Lublin Cascade Kent Goldings Willamette (B)
Adjuncts and Additives	None	None	None	0-1 oz. Sweet and 0.5-1 oz. Curaçao Bitter Orange Peel 0.5-1 oz. Coriander 5-10% oats
Water Hardness	Soft to Moderate 50-100 ppm Temporary Hardness	Soft to Moderate Low to Moderate Temporary Hardness	Soft to Moderate Moderate to High Temporary Hardness	Soft Water Low Temporary Hardness
Mashing Method	Single or Double Decoction w/ Sacch. rest @ 149-153° F Step Mash w/ rests @ 140 and 150° F	Protein Rests @ 95° F and 122° F Recommended Single or Double Decoction w/ Sacch. rest @ 158-162° F	Protein Rests @ 95° F and 122° F Recommended Double or Triple Decoction w/ rests @ 95°, 122°, 149°, 158° F	Single or Double Decoction (or if using Flaked Adjuncts) Step Mash w/ Protein rest at 104° F (30 min.) Sacch. rest at 150° F (60 minutes)
Wort Boil	60 minutes extract 90-120 minutes all-grain	60 minutes extract 90-120 minutes all-grain	60 minutes extract 90-120 minutes all-grain	60 minutes extract 90 minutes all-grain
Yeast	W 2206/2278/2308 YL L32/L33 BT 680/600 YC L09/L17	YL W51 YC A50 W 3056/3068 BT 930/920	YL W51 YC A50 W 3056/3068 BT 930/920	BT 900 YL W52 W 3944 YC A35
OG/FG	1048-56/1012-18	1048-55/1008-16	1065-80/1026-32	1044-50/1006-10
Primary Fermentation	Closed 10-14 days @ 46-55° F	Open or closed 5-7 days @ 55-68° F	Open or closed 5-7 days @ 55-68° F	Open or closed 5-7 days @ 65-75° F
Secondary Fermentation/Lagering	2-6 months @ 32-40° F	1-4 weeks @40-45° F	1-4 weeks @40-45° F	2-4 weeks @ 55-60 F
Priming/Conditioning Methods/ Rates /Temperatures Volumes of CO_2	3/4 cup corn sugar Kräusening Residual Sugar Wort Priming w/ fresh yeast 2 weeks @ 46-55° F	Kräusening Residual Sugar Wort Priming-1.25 cups DME 1-2 weeks @ 65-70° F Mature 2-3 weeks @ 45-50° F 2.4-2.6 vols.	Kräusening Residual Sugar Wort Priming-1.25 cups DME 1-2 weeks @ 65-70° F Mature 2-3 weeks @ 45-50° F 2.4-2.6 vols.	Bottle-condition w/ fresh yeast and Corn Sugar 7-10 days @ 68-75° F Mature 2-3 weeks @ 50-55° F
Serving Temperature	45-47° F	45-50° F	45-50° F	45-50° F

ALE
RECIPES

BROWN ALE

These sweet, full-bodied, and moderately alcoholic British ales are a venerable old style that represents what most beer was like for centuries: simple, wholesome, and easy to make at home. Ales called "nut brown" are often seen in this category, although sometimes light-colored mild is also called nut brown ale. Original gravities for modern versions of this beer hover around 1.040 for the southern English version, 1.050 for the northern; English hops such as East Kent Goldings, Fuggles, and so forth are recommended, and the use of small amounts of refined sugar is also acceptable. Water high in temporary hardness and sodium chloride is traditional, but overall, the water should be softer than for Burton-style ales. Good versions to enjoy while waiting for yours to ferment include Watney's Brown Ale, Newcastle Brown, and Samuel Smith's Nut Brown Ale. North American microbrewed varieties of English brown include Pyramid Best Brown Ale and Griffon Brown Ale.

BROWN ALE BASICS

ORIGINAL GRAVITY: 1.040–50

FINAL GRAVITY: 1.008–14

IBUs: 14–35

COLOR (SRM): 18–34

ALCOHOL BY VOLUME: 3.5–4.5%

SCOTS BROWN ALE

THE HOME BREWERY—OZARK, MISSOURI
This is a very simple recipe for the novice brewer. The bittering hops are already there for you; all you have to do is add a little Irish moss and some finishing hops and you've got a great strong brown ale. If you are feeling adventurous, experiment with one of the liquid yeasts designed for brown ale brewing.

ORIGINAL GRAVITY: 1.060

FINAL GRAVITY: 1.016

POTENTIAL ALCOHOL: 5.6% ABV

INGREDIENTS

   3.3 pounds (1 pack) Home Brewery hopped light malt extract

   3.3 pounds (1 pack) Home Brewery hopped dark malt extract
   1.7 pounds (½ pack) Yellow Dog malt extract
   No bittering hops
   ½ teaspoon Irish moss added 15 minutes before the end of the boil
   ½ ounce Willamette hop pellets (finishing)
   2 packs Doric ale yeast
   ¾ cup corn sugar for priming

BREWING PROCEDURES

1. Heat 5 gallons of water in a large kettle. Many people don't have a kettle that large, but heat as much as you can (at least 2 gallons). When the water is boiling, turn off the heat and add the malt extract to the water. Use a spoon and stir until you are sure no

malt extract is sticking to the bottom of the kettle. Then turn the heat back on.

2. Bring the kettle back to a boil and stir occasionally so the ingredients won't burn on the bottom of the kettle. Watch out for a boilover. In the early part of the boil, the kettle usually tries to boil over once or twice, so control this by adjusting the heat. Later in the boil, the surface tension changes and boiling over is not a problem. Keep stirring occasionally, and let the beer (wort) boil hard for 1 hour. Stir in the ½ teaspoon of Irish moss in your recipe about 15 minutes before the end of the boil.

3. Stir finishing hops in 2 minutes before the end of the boil. Using finishing hops at the end of the boil adds a fresh aroma and flavor to the beer, and the use of finishing hops is appropriate in most beer styles.

4. Pour the hot beer (wort) into the primary fermenter. It is not necessary to strain the wort if you used hop pellets. Add cold water to bring the total volume up to 5 gallons. Cover the fermenter and wait until the temperature is down to 75°F. If you have a wort chiller, use it to bring the temperature down quickly. At 75° or less, add the yeast in your recipe. Just tear open the pack(s) and sprinkle it on the wort. Close the fermenter with the lid, stopper, and airlock. Remember to put water (or vodka) in the airlock. Vodka evaporates more quickly, but bacteria won't live in it.

5. Fermentation should start within 24 hours, and may continue for between 1 day and 2 weeks, depending on the type of yeast, the recipe, and the temperature. Leave the beer alone and don't open the lid. When the airlock has not bubbled for several days and the beer is flat, still, and clearing, it is ready to bottle.

6. To bottle, siphon about 1 pint of beer into a pan and warm it on the stove. Add exactly ¾ cup of corn sugar to the pan and stir until it is dissolved. Pour this back into the beer and stir gently but well to distribute the sugar. Siphon or tap into clean, sanitized bottles and cap. Keep the bottles at room temperature. After a week, put a bottle in the refrigerator and try it. It will be best in about 3 weeks.

NUT BROWN ALE

🍺 🍺 🍺

STEPHEN SNYDER

This is a simple extract-based recipe using a pre-hopped kit with the easy addition of some crystal malt for sweetness and body, and some authentic English hops for a subtle, woody bitterness. This brown ale is medium-full in body and has a deep reddish brown color, good clarity, aroma, and balance. The flavor could be a little more malty by using Wyeast 1968 Special London yeast.

ORIGINAL GRAVITY: 1.050

FINAL GRAVITY: 1.015

POTENTIAL ALCOHOL: 4.5% ABV

INGREDIENTS

One 3.3-pound Telford's Nut Brown Ale kit
3.25 pounds English light DME
¾ pound English 40 °L crystal malt
¼ ounce Fuggles plug 4.2% AA (boil) 60 minutes
½ ounce Fuggles plug 4.2% AA (boil) 30 minutes
½ ounce Fuggles plug 4.2% AA (flavor) 10 minutes
½ ounce Fuggles plug 4.2% AA (aroma) steep 30 minutes

Wyeast 1028 London Ale yeast
½ to ¾ cup corn sugar for priming

BREWING PROCEDURES

1. Add cracked crystal malt to 3 gallons of cold water. Bring slowly to 158°F. Steep for 20 minutes. Remove from heat immediately and strain spent grains.
2. Bring to a boil.
3. Remove brew kettle from heat before adding extract and DME to avoid sticking or burning.
4. Boil for 60 minutes, adding hops as noted above.
5. Let hot wort sit for 30 minutes (covered) in an ice-water bath before pouring into single-stage fermenter containing 2.5 gallons ice cold water (33–40°F).
6. Wort should be below 75°F before pitching yeast. Stir vigorously to aerate. Fit with blowoff hose for carboy and move to dark, quiet, draft-free space and ferment at 60–65°F.
7. Fit carboy with airlock after blowout ceases. Ferment for 5–7 days or until final gravity is reached. Prime with either ½ or ¾ cup corn sugar, depending on your desired level of carbonation, and bottle.
8. Warm-condition 7 days at room temperature (68–72°F). Store cold (45°F) for 1–2 weeks and serve at 50°.

BROWN ALE
🍺🍺

DICK FOEHRINGER, THE BREWMEISTER—FAIR OAKS, CALIFORNIA

"Our brown ale features a strong, rummy flavor from the brown sugar. Mild and sweet with a medium hoppiness in between Newcastle and Watney's Brown Ale."

ORIGINAL GRAVITY: 1.050

FINAL GRAVITY: 1.012

POTENTIAL ALCOHOL: 4.9% ABV

INGREDIENTS

6 pounds amber malt extract syrup
14 ounces crystal malt
2 ounces black patent malt
½ teaspoon citric acid
1 teaspoon calcium carbonate
4 ounces lactose
8 ounces dark brown sugar
1½ ounce Northern Brewer hops (boiling)
½ ounce Northern Brewer hops (aromatic)
1 teaspoon Irish moss
1 package ale yeast
1 teaspoon gelatin
¾ cup bottling sugar

BREWING PROCEDURES

1. Put the crushed crystal and black patent malts in a grain bag. Place bag and 1½ to 2½ gallons of cold water in your brewpot. Bring to a near boil (160°F). Shut off heat and steep the grain for 30 minutes.
2. Remove grains.
3. Stir in extract and thoroughly dissolve. Return to heat and add lactose, brown sugar, citric acid, and calcium carbonate. Bring to a boil for 15 minutes.
4. Add boiling hops and boil 30 minutes. Add Irish moss and boil 15 minutes. Turn off heat and add the aromatic hops. Steep 15 minutes.
5. Cold-break by placing the pan into a sink full of cold water. When wort is below 100°F, strain the wort into your primary fermenter.

Add enough cold water to make 5½ gallons. Rehydrate yeast by dissolving in 1 cup warm water. Let stand for 15 minutes. When wort is cool (below 85°F), pitch yeast.

6. Ferment in a cool place (70°F). When fermentation is complete, rack into secondary, leaving all sediment behind. Prepare gelatin by dissolving in 1 cup hot water and stir into secondary. When clear (3–5 days) rack again, leaving sediment behind.

7. Prepare bottling sugar by dissolving in 1 cup hot water. Stir dissolved bottling sugar into clear beer, bottle, and cap.

8. Age a minimum of 2–3 weeks.

NUT BROWN ALE
▥ ▥

JOE AND BRYAN TIMMONS

BOSTON BREWERS SUPPLY CO.—
JAMAICA PLAIN, MASSACHUSETTS

"Our nut brown ale is sure to be a favorite. It is designed to replicate the northern English brown ales with a low level of bitterness and carbonation. These combined qualities allow the sweetness of the malt to come through beautifully. It's also quick maturing, you'll be able to enjoy this one in just about four weeks after brewing."

ORIGINAL GRAVITY: 1.040–42

FINAL GRAVITY: 1.008–10

POTENTIAL ALCOHOL: 4.2% ABV

IBUs: 20–22

INGREDIENTS

    6 pounds English amber extract syrup
    8 ounces English crystal malt

    8 ounces dextrine malt
    4 ounces English chocolate malt
    1 ounce Fuggles hop pellets
    1 ounce Kent Goldings hop pellets
    1 teaspoon Irish moss flakes
    1 package dry ale yeast
    4 ounces corn sugar for priming

BREWING PROCEDURES

1. Secure the grains in the muslin straining bag. Pour 2 gallons of cold water into your brewpot, apply heat, and add the grain bag. Heat to a near boil (about 155° F), turn off the heat, cover the pot, and allow the grains to steep for 20 minutes. Remove the grain bag, drain, and discard.

2. Thoroughly dissolve the malt extract, apply heat, and bring to a boil. While you are waiting for the boil to commence, open both packages of hop pellets and as accurately as possible divide each ounce in half. As soon as the wort (unfermented beer) begins to boil, add ½ ounce of the Fuggles hops and ½ ounce of the Goldings hops. Start timing the boil, the total elapsed time will be 45 minutes. Maintain a good rolling boil.

3. After 20 minutes, add all of the remaining hops and the Irish moss flakes. Continue to boil for an additional 25 minutes, then cover and remove the pot from the heat.

Remember that after the wort has cooled, it is highly vulnerable to contamination; everything that comes into contact with it from this point on must be thoroughly sanitized!

4. Cool the wort as quickly as possible. A wort chiller works best, but if you haven't got one yet a cold water bath will do the trick. Place the covered pot in your kitchen sink and fill

with ice and cold water. When the temperature has fallen to about 75°F, transfer the wort, through a strainer if possible, into your fermenter. Top off with enough cold water to reach a 5-gallon level and stir or shake well. Draw off a small sample and take both a hydrometer and a temperature reading; always discard the sample used.

5. When the wort has cooled to 65° to 70°F, you are ready to add the yeast. Once the yeast has been added, attach an airlock and keep the fermenter in a cool, dark location where temperature fluctuations are minimal, ideally 68°F. Active fermentation should become visible in the next 12 to 24 hours and will continue for about 3 to 5 days.

6. When visible signs of fermentation have ceased, gently transfer the beer to a sanitized secondary fermenter (ideally a 5-gallon glass carboy), leaving all sediment behind. Attach an airlock and allow the beer to settle for an additional 5 to 7 days at the same temperature as primary fermentation. At the end of this period, draw off a small sample and check the final gravity. By now it should be within the range stated above; if not, wait another couple of days and check again. Prepare to bottle.

BOTTLING AND CONDITIONING

1. Sanitize all of your siphoning and bottling equipment, bottles, and caps.
2. Boil the 4 ounces of corn sugar in about a cup of water and pour it into your bottling bucket. Gently siphon the beer out of the fermenter into the bucket, making sure the flow is directed to the bottom of the bucket; avoid splashing or agitating the beer.
3. Using your siphon tubing and bottle filler,

fill each bottle to within an inch from the top and cap immediately. Store the bottles upright for 3 to 4 weeks, chill, and enjoy.

PIRATES BREW NUT BROWN ALE

JAY GARRISON, HEAD BREWER, PIRATE BREWERY

BREWBUDDYS—REDONDO BEACH, CALIFORNIA

This is a heavier-bodied, brownish beer with a well-rounded, malty taste, though a slightly hoppy taste is present in the background. This ale might be described as a strong brown ale given its high gravity. You might also try brewing this with Wyeast 1098 or 1728.

ORIGINAL GRAVITY: 1.061

FINAL GRAVITY: 1.015

POTENTIAL ALCOHOL: 6.1% ABV

INGREDIENTS

> 7.5 pounds amber liquid extract
> 1 pound 120 °L crystal malt
> 1 pound Munich malt
> 2 ounces chocolate malt
> 1½ ounces Perle hops
> ½ ounce Willamettte hops
> ½ ounce Mt. Hood hops
> 1 teaspoon Irish moss
> 2 packs Windsor ale yeast or Wyeast 1084 Irish Ale
> ¾ cup corn sugar for priming

BREWING PROCEDURES

1. If you selected the Wyeast liquid yeast, you must break the inner packet before you

begin to brew. Allow 1 day for each month after the manufacture date printed on the front. If you're using dry yeast, go ahead and get to it.

2. Prepare the grains. The grains should be crushed; if you did not get the grains crushed at the shop, crush them with some sort of rolling pin. You can either mix the grains with 2 quarts of water and slowly heat it until it just starts to boil, or heat it to about 155°F and steep for about 30 minutes.

3. Strain the grains, collecting the liquid into your brewpot. Rinse the grains (sparge) with 2 quarts of hot (170°F) water.

4. Add the bag and can of extract and 1 gallon of water to the brewpot. (You might want to rest the bag of extract in hot water for a while to soften it up.) Bring the wort to a soft rolling boil.

5. Add the Perle hops to the wort and boil for 40 minutes. Stir occasionally.

6. Add the Willamette hops and Irish moss to the wort and boil for 20 minutes. Stir occasionally.

7. Add the Mt. Hood hops to the wort and turn off the heat; stir and let sit (covered, if possible) for 10 minutes.

8. Add the boiled wort to your sanitized, rinsed fermenter. Add ice-cold water to make 5 gallons. When the temperature drops to 75°F or less, add the yeast.

9. If you use liquid yeast, open the swollen packet and add to the wort. If you use dry yeast, add the yeast to 1 cup of 90°F water for a few minutes before adding to the wort. (You can add the yeast directly to the wort and let it sit for a few minutes also, but rehydrating the yeast in warm water will improve the fermentation.) Stir the wort thoroughly with a sanitized spoon.

10. Put the lid on the fermenter tightly, insert the fermentation lock with the stopper into the hole in the lid, and fill it up about ³⁄₄ of the way with water or vodka. Let the wort ferment for a week or two until the fermentation ceases.

11. When fermentation is complete, siphon the beer into a sanitized bottling bucket. Boil the corn sugar in about a cup of water; cool; stir gently into the beer. This provides the nutrients necessary for the yeast to carbonate the beer in the bottle.

12. Insert one end of the sanitized and rinsed hose into the bottling spigot and the other end to the bottle filler. Push the bottle filler down onto the bottom of the bottle and open the bottling spigot. Five gallons of beer will make about 2 cases, so make sure you sanitize this amount beforehand. Leave about ¹⁄₂–³⁄₄ inch of space at the top of the bottle. Cap the bottles.

13. Let the beer age for 2 weeks to 6 months. Chill and enjoy.

How Now Brown Ale
The Cellar Homebrew—Seattle, Washington

"Following the English brown style, the combination of roasted grains, Kent Goldings hops, and brown sugar or molasses yields a moderately sweet, alcoholic beer with a hint of caramel. Named from the now meaningless cliché, 'How now, brown cow?' Back in the days of yore (and beer in wooden kegs), this phrase was the equivalent of 'What now, friends, shall we have another beer (before leaving)?'"

ORIGINAL GRAVITY: 1.050

FINAL GRAVITY: 1.015

POTENTIAL ALCOHOL: 4.5% ABV

INGREDIENTS (FOR 5.5 GALLONS)

> 6 pounds Alexander's amber bulk malt syrup
>
> 1 pound dark brown sugar or molasses
>
> ¼ pound English crystal malt (crushed)
>
> 1 ounce chocolate malt (crushed)
>
> ½ pound toasted malt (follow roasting directions in step 1)
>
> 1½ ounces Kent Goldings hops (boiling)
>
> ½ ounce Kent Goldings hops (finishing)
>
> Edme dry ale yeast or Wyeast European Ale liquid yeast
>
> ¾ cup priming sugar

BREWING PROCEDURES

Note: If you are using the European Ale liquid yeast with this recipe, be sure to start that yeast at least 1 to 3 days before doing any of the brewing steps below. Follow the package directions and use the yeast in step 5 below.

1. Place uncrushed grains onto a cookie sheet into an oven preheated to 350°F. Toast for about 10 minutes. Remove from oven and then crack the toasted grain with a rolling pin.

2. Place the crushed English crystal, toasted, and chocolate malt grains in a strainer bag. Add this bag to your brewing kettle, which contains 2 to 2½ gallons of brewing water. Bring that water to a boil, then remove the grain bag. It is a good idea not to boil these specialty grains for any length of time as they may contribute a bitter or grainy taste to the finished beer.

3. Sparge (rinse) the bag of grains with about 1 quart of hot tap water into the brewing kettle; dispose of spent grains.

4. Remove the brewing kettle from the burner and add the 6 pounds of Alexander's amber malt syrup and the 1 pound of dark brown sugar or molasses. The syrup is easier to pour if the jar has been previously placed in hot water. Also, rinse the jar with hot water to ensure that all the syrup goes into the kettle. Stir the mixture, now called "wort," until it boils. Watch carefully at this time, for the wort may boil over. You can stop a wort boilover by pouring in a cup of cold water.

5. At this point add the Kent Goldings boiling hops. Hops can be placed in a hop bag or added loose, to be strained out after the boil using a strainer bag. Time the boil for about 1 hour, stirring occasionally. After the first 10 minutes of this boil, remove 2 cups of wort in a measuring cup and cover with foil or plastic. Cool to 90°F for use in step 6 below.

6. Making the yeast starter: For dry yeast, use ½ cup warm tap water (90–100°F). Sprinkle the contents of yeast packet into that water, cover for at least 15 minutes, and then add to the 2 cups of wort you prepared in step 5. Cover and set aside for use in step 10 below. For liquid yeast, prepare 1 to 3 days ahead of brewing time per package instructions. Add the contents to the 2 cups of wort as prepared in step 5.

7. After the wort has boiled for that 1 hour, it is time to add the Kent Goldings finishing hops. Place them in the hop bag, which has been emptied of the spent boiling hops, and place them in the boiling kettle. Otherwise, just add the finishing hops directly to the brewing kettle. They will be strained later in step 9.

8. Let the boil continue for 5 minutes. This step gives the beer its hop aroma. Remove the pot from the burner and let it cool, cov-

ered, for about 20 minutes before going to step 9.

9. Pour 3 gallons of cold water into the sanitized open fermenter fitted with strainer bag. If loose finishing hops were used in step 7, strain the warm wort from step 8 into the cold water. Top up the fermenter to 5½ gallons using cold tap water, if necessary. Cover the fermenter and cool the wort as rapidly as possible.

10. When the wort has cooled to about 80°F, add the yeast starter and ferment as you usually do.

BROWN & BRITISH
⫟ ⫟ ⫟

THE HOME BEER, WINE, & CHEESEMAKING SHOP—WOODLAND HILLS, CALIFORNIA

This rich and hearty ale owes its character to the wide diversity of brewing ingredients, particularly the English treacle, which provides a unique, mellow sweetness that blends perfectly with the character of the English hops.

ORIGINAL GRAVITY: 1.058

FINAL GRAVITY: 1.013

POTENTIAL ALCOHOL: 5.9% ABV

IBUs: 18

COLOR: 15 SRM

INGREDIENTS

8 ounces Gambrinus honey malt

4 ounces Belgian biscuit malt

4 ounces Belgian aromatic malt

8 ounces Scottish 80 °L crystal malt

4 ounces chocolate malt

6 pounds Royal light DME

2 pounds English treacle

0.5 ounce Bramling Cross hop pellets at 7.1% AA (60 minutes)

0.5 ounce Kent Goldings hop pellets at 4.1% AA (20 minutes)

0.5 ounce Challenger hop pellets at 7.2% AA (0 minutes—at knockout)

1 teaspoon Irish moss

1 teaspoon gypsum

Wyeast 1275 Thames Valley Ale yeast

¾ cup corn sugar for priming

BREWING PROCEDURES

1. Steep (soak) the grains in 2 quarts of 150°F water for 30–40 minutes. Sparge (rinse) with 2.5 quarts of 150°F water into your boiling pot. Discard grain. No water over 170°F with grain. Do not oversparge. Do not squeeze grain bag.

2. After adding 2.5 gallons of water and dissolving the malt, bring pot to a gentle but rolling boil. Skim all foam before starting the hop sequence. Add Irish moss the last 20 minutes to remove the protein missed in steps 1 and 2. Add the gypsum into the boil. It adds hardness, accentuating the crisp hop character.

3. Ferment at an average of 62–66°F. This keeps the fruity esters to a minimum. Pitch (add) yeast when your water bath around the fermenter reads 70–80°F. Maintain this temperature until the first signs of fermentation (about 10–12 hours). If using a yeast starter (highly recommended), fermentation can start in 2–3 hours. Use ¾ cup sugar for priming.

LONDONER'S BROWN ALE
⫽⫽ ⫽⫽ ⫽⫽

E. C. KRAUS HOME WINE AND BEER MAKING SUPPLIES—INDEPENDENCE, MISSOURI

"This particular recipe is for the sweeter southern version of English brown ales as opposed to the northern brown ales, which are dryer and more assertive. The hops tend to be light, but strong enough to compete with the nutty-chocolate character."

ORIGINAL GRAVITY: 1.040–43

FINAL GRAVITY: 1.010–12

POTENTIAL ALCOHOL: 3.8–4% ABV

IBUs: 15–25

COLOR: 15–22 SRM/26–44 °L

INGREDIENTS

- 3.3 pounds light unhopped malt syrup
- 1.4 pounds light dried malt extract (3.4 cups)
- 8 ounces crystal malt
- 6 ounces chocolate malt
- 12 ounces malto-dextrin (5-minute boil time)
- 1½ ounces Fuggles hop pellets (30-minute boil time)
- ½ ounce Cascade hop pellets (finishing)
- 1 tablespoon Irish moss (15-minute boil time)
- 14 grams Whitbread Ale yeast or Wyeast 1968
- 1 cup corn sugar

BREWING PROCEDURES

1. Lightly crack malted barleys and put with 1½ gallons of cold water in a cooking pot. Slowly bring to a boil over a 30–45-minute period.
2. Once boiling, strain the grains out by the use of a colander or the like and discard.
3. Bring liquid back to a boil and add both the liquid and dried malt extracts. Bring back to a boil again.
4. Once boiling, add Fuggles hops and boil for 30 minutes. During the last 15 minutes of the boil, add the Irish moss. During the last 5 minutes of the boil, fold in the malto-dextrin.
5. Once the boiling is complete, add the Cascade hops for finishing; turn off the burner and allow to steep for 15 minutes with a lid on.
6. Now add the wort to your fermenter along with cold tap water up to 5 gallons. Make sure the wort has cooled to below 80°F and pitch yeast.
7. Attach airlock to fermenter and allow to ferment for 7–10 days or until finished and bottle with priming sugar as normal.

EAST COAST NEWCASTLE BROWN ALE
⫽⫽ ⫽⫽ ⫽⫽ ⫽⫽

EAST COAST BREWING SUPPLY—STATEN ISLAND, NEW YORK

This all-grain recipe employs the advanced techniques of souring a portion of the mash for a unique tangy character and requires the equipment to handle a 12-gallon batch size. Otherwise, reduce all ingredients by half, except for the yeast, and you will have a more easily workable 6-gallon batch. Either way, your efforts will be rewarded with a fresh, complex ale using American hops of English pedigree.

ORIGINAL GRAVITY: 1.044

FINAL GRAVITY: 1.012

POTENTIAL ALCOHOL: 4.1% ABV

INGREDIENTS (FOR 12 GALLONS)

- 1 pound Klages 2-row soured 2 days at 120°F (sour mash)
- 12 pounds Klages 2-row
- 1 pound 40°L crystal
- 0.5 pound chocolate
- 0.25 pound black patent
- 0.25 pound roast barley
- 2.0 ounces Centennial hops for 60 minutes
- 1.5 ounces Willamette hops for 20 minutes
- 4 teaspoons gypsum in the boil
- 2 teaspoons Irish moss for 30 minutes
- Wyeast 1028 London Ale yeast
- Wyeast 1098 British Ale yeast
- 1.2 cups priming sugar (½ cup per 5 gallons)

BREWING PROCEDURES

Main Mash:

1. Dough in the crushed grains and sour-mashed malt, then perform a protein rest at 122°F for 30 minutes.

2. Raise the temperature of the mash to 150–152°F and perform a saccharification rest for 60 minutes.

3. Mash out by raising the temperature of the mash to 168°F for 10 minutes. Transfer to your lauter tun, sparge with 12 gallons of 168° water, and collect approximately 13 gallons of wort as normal.

4. Boil the wort for 90 minutes, adding hops as noted above. After the boil, cool the wort with a wort chiller and transfer to your fermentation vessels.

Fermentation:

1. Ferment in the primary for 4 days at 64–75°F. Transfer to the secondary fermenter.

2. Ferment in the secondary for 2 weeks at 54–59°F.

3. Keg or bottle with 1.2 cups corn sugar and condition 2–3 weeks at cellar temperatures.

OLD ALE

In the world of beer, "old" is perhaps as nebulous and overused a word as "amber." To attempt to classify what fits into the modern style of Old English ale is territory suited for only the best beer experts, as the definition of what an old ale seems to have evolved over the years. Michael Jackson has made the work much easier by identifying what brands belong in this category, but many of the commercial beers lumped in this category have dramatic differences and often push the boundaries of what might be classified as a barley wine.

The most obvious requirement for making these beers is that they be well aged—up to a year before bottling, with five or more years in the bottle. More often than not they are strong and brewed with traditional English two-row pale malt, hops such as Target and Challenger, and English ale yeast. These ales are often deep, reddish brown from the use of dark caramel and black patent malts and may contain adjuncts such as sugar and unmalted grains. The basic parameters below are for the more or less standard-gravity beers of this style. There are beers of much greater strength that may fit into this category because of their age or may also fall into the barley wine group because of their original gravity. Eldridge Pope's Thomas Hardy's Ale is a prime example of one of those. Commercial examples of old ales whose classification is less in doubt include Greene King's Strong Suffolk, Young's Winter Warmer, Gale's Prize Old Ale, Marston's Owd Rodger, and Theakston's Old Peculier.

OLD ALE BASICS

ORIGINAL GRAVITY: 1.055–95

FINAL GRAVITY: 1.008–20%

IBUs: 30–40

COLOR (SRM): 10–16

ALCOHOL BY VOLUME: 6–8%

OLD PICK & MULER

🍺🍺🍺

MOUNTAIN MALT AND HOP SHOPPE—
  LAKE KATRINE & POUGHKEEPSIE,
  NEW YORK

"The following recipe was created for those who love a rich, dark ale. The brewer and all those who partake will enjoy the taste of roast toffee in the mouth combined with a subtle hopping and a bittersweet finish."

ORIGINAL GRAVITY: 1.061

FINAL GRAVITY: 1.014

POTENTIAL ALCOHOL: 6% ABV

INGREDIENTS

  1 pound amber crystal malt
  1 ounce Challenger hop pellets at 7.3% AA
    (bittering)
  ¼ pound roasted barley
  1 ounce Fuggles hop pellets at 3.6% AA
    (bittering)
  3 pounds English amber DME
  ½ ounce Fuggles hop plug (flavor)
  3 pounds English dark DME
  2 teaspoons gypsum
  ¼ pound malto-dextrin
  1 teaspoon Irish moss
  ¼ pound black treacle
  2 packages Nottingham Ale yeast
  ¾ pound brown sugar
  ¾ cup priming sugar

BREWING PROCEDURES

1. In a 12-quart or larger stainless-steel pot, heat 1 gallon of water to 160°F and add 1 teaspoon of gypsum. Stir until dissolved and turn off heat. Place cracked grains in a nylon bag and immerse in water. Cover pot and allow grain to steep for 30 minutes. Remove grain bag and bring the "tea" to a boil. (If you do not have a nylon bag, add grains directly to water and strain.)

2. When boil is attained, turn off heat and add the dry malt. (Putting DME in a bowl first makes it easier to add.) Then add the ¼

pound of black treacle. Turn on heat and return to a boil.

3. When the danger of a messy boilover has passed, add the 1 ounce of Challenger and 1 ounce of Fuggles hop pellets. Cook at a low, rolling boil for 45 minutes.

4. Add ¾ pound brown sugar and ¼ pound malto-dextrin and stir until dissolved. Then add 1 teaspoon of Irish moss and boil for 5 more minutes.

5. Take the ½ ounce Fuggle hop plug and slice it up. Place pieces in a muslin hop bag and immerse in wort. Boil for 10 more minutes, then turn off heat and remove both hop bags.

6. Take the brewpot from the stove and place it in a sink partially filled with cold water. Add 1 gallon of sanitary, refrigerated water (40°F) to the brewpot, then cover and place ice in the water around the brewpot. Never add ice directly to the wort! Let stand 15 minutes. Place 2 gallons of refrigerated water into the fermenter, then add the wort. Check the temperature (65–75°F is ideal). Top off to 5½ gallons with either more cold or room-temperature water.

7. With a sanitized measuring cup, scoop out ¾ cup and take a hydrometer reading. Discard sample.

8. Add the packages of yeast to the fermenter when the temperature of the wort is between 65–75°F, let sit 10 minutes, then stir vigorously to aerate. Snap the fermenter lid on, fill the airlock halfway with water, and place in lid. Place fermenter in a spot where the temperature will remain a constant 65–70°F.

9. Ferment in the primary for 5–6 days, then rack into a glass carboy for 2 weeks.

10. When brew is clear, siphon into a bottling bucket. Dissolve priming sugar into 1 cup boiling water, cool, and gently stir into beer with a sanitized spoon. CAUTION: If finished volume is less than 5 gallons, scale proportionately (e.g., 4½ gallons = 2/3 cup sugar).

11. Keep in a warm place for 7–10 days, then move to a cool place to age for 2 weeks.

HAPPY JERRY STRONG ALE

🍺 🍺 🍺

NOELLE AURIEMMA

MOUNTAIN MALT AND HOP SHOPPE— LAKE KATRINE & POUGHKEEPSIE, NEW YORK

This recipe uses a very traditional list of ingredients for a rich English strong ale, but gains a very unique vanilla-ish personality from the late addition of crème de cacao.

ORIGINAL GRAVITY: 1.063

FINAL GRAVITY: 1.013

POTENTIAL ALCOHOL: 8.3% ABV (estimated— after addition of crème de cacao)

INGREDIENTS

1 pound amber crystal malt

4 ounces Lyle's Black Treacle

½ pound dextrine malt

1.1 pounds demerara sugar

½ pound chocolate malt

2 ounces Willamette (9 HBU)

3 pounds dark DME

1 tablespoon gypsum

3 pounds amber DME

Wyeast 1056 American Ale
750 ml crème de cacao
¾ cup corn sugar for priming

BREWING PROCEDURES

1. In a 12-quart or larger stainless-steel pot, heat 1 gallon of water to 160°F and add 1 teaspoon of gypsum. Stir until dissolved and turn off heat. Place cracked grains in a nylon bag and immerse in water. Cover pot and allow grain to steep for 30 minutes. Remove grain bag and bring the "tea" to a boil. (If you do not have a nylon bag, add grains directly to water and strain.)

2. When boil is attained, turn off heat and add the dry malts, treacle, and demerara. (Putting DME in a bowl first makes it easier to add.) Turn on heat and return to a boil.

3. When the danger of a messy boilover has passed, add 2 ounces of Willamette hops (9 HBU) and cook at a rolling boil for 30 minutes.

4. Add 1 teaspoon of Irish moss and boil for 15 more minutes.

5. Take the brewpot from the stove and place it in a sink partially filled with cold water. Add 1 gallon of sanitary, refrigerated water (40°F) to the brewpot, then cover and place ice in the water around the brewpot. Never add ice directly to the wort! Let stand 15 minutes. Place 2 gallons of refrigerated water into the fermenter, then add the strained wort. Check the temperature (65° to 75°F is ideal). Top off to 5½ gallons with either more cold or room temperature water.

6. With a sanitized measuring cup, scoop out ¾ cup and take a hydrometer reading. Discard sample.

7. Save 1 quart of wort for priming. This measure is based on an original gravity of 1.063.

8. Add the package of yeast to the fermenter when the temperature of the wort is 65–75°F, then stir vigorously to aerate. Snap the fermenter lid on, fill the airlock halfway with water, and place in lid. Place fermenter in a spot where the temperature will remain a constant 65–70°F.

9. Ferment in the primary for 5–6 days, then rack into a glass carboy for 2 weeks. Add the crème de cacao into the secondary fermenter and ferment out as usual.

10. When brew is clear, siphon into a bottling bucket. Dissolve priming sugar into 1 cup boiling water, cool, and gently stir into beer with a sanitized spoon. CAUTION: If finished volume is less than 5 gallons, scale proportionately (e.g., 4½ gallons = 2/3 cup sugar).

11. Keep in a warm place for 7–10 days, then move to a cool place to age for 2 weeks.

MILD ALE

—

One of the oldest styles of British ale, mild (an archaic term denoting a "new" or "fresh" ale) in its original form was merely an immature ale as opposed to an ale that would be cellared for a year or more before it was sold. For reasons no one is completely sure of, probably an expanding population and the growing demand for beer, mild beers began to be sold before they were ready, and at a considerably lower cost than mature beer. Eventually, this led to the harsh, sour mild being mixed with a small portion of the old (or "stale") ale in order to make it more palatable. This nine-to-one mixture was the origin of an ale called "porter's ale," because it was a good-tasting beer still affordable by the working class, particularly London's porters.

As porter developed into a distinct style of its own, brewers began to formulate recipes of mild that didn't require the addition of matured ale to improve the taste. These recipes included the addition of chocolate malt, torrefied barley, black malt, oatmeal, and roasted barley. Mellower hop varieties were used, hopping rates were reduced, more flocculant yeast was developed, and finings were employed to evolve mild into its present form.

"Mild" now means lightly hopped and can be considered a mellower, lighter bodied, but darker version of English brown ale—many experts consider mild to be nothing more than the draft version of brown ale. In any event, traditional milds had original gravities of 1.060 or greater, but have fallen in the last century to 1.037–1.030, mainly to avoid high excise taxes. Although this lightly carbonated beer style is far less popular than the pub-dominating bitter, it can be widely found in Wales and northwestern England and seems to be making a comeback throughout Britain in the wake of the "real ale" movement. Its low alcohol strength (around 3.5% ABV) makes this an excellent "session" beer.

Modern milds are often crafted from Maris Otter malt, amber malt, black malt, torrefied wheat, and caramel malts, as well as Fuggles, Challenger, and Goldings hops. Historically, waters rich in calcium sulfate and calcium chloride were used, but the water should be softer than for brewing an English pale ale. Popular commercial examples include Bass Highgate Dark, Theakston Traditional, Tetley Mild, Brain's Dark, McMullen's AK, and Grant's Celtic Ale.

MILD ALE BASICS

ORIGINAL GRAVITY: 1.030–38

FINAL GRAVITY: 1.004–08

IBUs: 10–25

COLOR (SRM): 10–26

ALCOHOL BY VOLUME: 3–3.5%

PUBLIC HOUSE MILD
▥ ▥

STEPHEN SNYDER

This is the type of easy-drinking session mild you might be served in a homey English pub in the country. This is a wonderful accompaniment to simple traditional foods such as a ploughman's lunch or chips with malt vinegar.

ORIGINAL GRAVITY: 1.037

FINAL GRAVITY: 1.010

POTENTIAL ALCOHOL: 3.4% ABV

IBUs: 25 (bitterness for amber and dark hopped kits is usually 20–30 IBUs)

INGREDIENTS

> 1 Telford's English Ale kit
> 2 pounds English Amber Spray malt
> ¼ cup 40 °L English crystal malt
> ½ ounce Fuggles Plug at 4.2% AA (flavor)
> ½ ounce East Kent Goldings plug (aroma)
> 1 teaspoon Irish moss
> Wyeast 1098 (British) or 1084 (Irish) ale yeast with starter
> ½ cup corn sugar for priming

BREWING PROCEDURES

1. Fill brewpot with 3 gallons cold water. Crack crystal malt and place into a muslin bag. Place bag into brewpot and heat to a boil.
2. Remove grains when boil commences, add malt extracts, and boil vigorously for 1 hour.
3. Add the flavor hops and Irish moss 15 minutes before the end of the boil.
4. Add the aroma hops 2 minutes before the end of the boil. After 1 hour, cover the brewpot and place in a sink filled with ice-cold water for 30 minutes.
5. Pour wort into fermenter through a sanitized kitchen strainer to remove hops and filter trub. Pitch yeast and stir vigorously to aerate.
6. Cover, fit with airlock or blowoff hose, and ferment at 55–65°F for 5–7 days.
7. Rack to bottling bucket and prime with ½ cup corn sugar, then bottle and leave at room temperature for 1 week.
8. Condition at cellar temperatures between 50–60°F for 1–3 weeks.

CARDIFF DARK
▥ ▥ ▥ ▥ / ▥ ▥

DUNCAN HOOK

THE CELLARS—CARDIFF, WALES

"This recipe is for a mild ale (only in the Cardiff area are milds referred to as "darks"). Hop variations—Liberty is obvious, Willamette should be good. U.K. Northern Brewer has also been used with success."

ORIGINAL GRAVITY: 1.046

FINAL GRAVITY: 1.013

POTENTIAL ALCOHOL: 4.3% ABV

If possible you should use fresh brewer's yeast from your local brewery, as your beer will tend to develop the character of the beer from that brewery. If liquid yeast is unobtainable, you can use a good commercial dried variety. This will produce a good beer but will lack some of the traditional "Cardiff" character. The first recipe shown is the ideal way to produce this distinctive dark beer, but if you do not feel confident enough to try mashing, follow our second recipe for a very acceptable brew using malt extract. For both recipes you should use fairly soft water to which has been added a good rounded teaspoon of common salt (5 ml).

TRADITIONAL BREWING METHOD AND RECIPE: INGREDIENTS (FOR 5 IMPERIAL GALLONS)

> 5 pounds cracked pale malt
> 5 ounces cracked black malt
> 5 ounces cracked crystal malt
> 1 pound demerara sugar
> 2 ounces whole (or plug) Fuggle hops
> Fresh ale yeast
> ½ cup priming sugar

BREWING PROCEDURES

1. Mash the grains in about 2 gallons of salted water. Keep the temperature at a constant level of 145–148°F for 3 hours. This is important, especially for the first half hour. Sparge the grain with water at 170°F to collect 5½ gallons of wort.

2. Bring the wort to the boil. Add sugar and hops, fast boil for 2 hours, and add the Irish moss ½ hour before the end of the boil. Allow the wort to settle for ½ hour after the boil is completed. Open the boiler tap to draw off the clear wort, using the settled bed of hops as a filter. If the wort does not run clear, return the liquid to the boiler and draw off again until clear wort is obtained.

3. Make quantity back up to 5 gallons with cold water (use sanitary ice if possible) and cool as rapidly as you can. Pitch yeast when temperature has dropped below 80°F. When the fermentation is under way, reduce temperature to, and maintain at, an ideal of 60° to 65°F. A heavy yeast deposit will form on top of the beer. Do not disturb this yeast cap, but remove any brown scum that forms on the sides of the vessel.

4. Stir the brew daily, taking care not to disturb the yeast cap too much. After 5 days skim off the yeast. Retain some of the yeast (about the size of a walnut will do) for pitching your next brew.

5. Transfer the beer to a sterile, closed 5-gallon container and fit with an airlock. Leave beer to drop bright. Use beer finings if necessary. This should take a week to 10 days. When beer is clear, rack off.

6. Prime the beer with 4 ounces white sugar (made into a syrup) and put in cask or bottle to mature (2 weeks in cask or 4 weeks in bottle). This beer continues to mature and improve, being superb after 3 months.

MALT EXTRACT EQUIVALENT RECIPE AND METHOD

> 4 pounds pale dried malt extract
> 8 ounces cracked crystal malt
> 5 ounces cracked black malt
> 1½ pounds demerara sugar
> Hops, Irish moss, yeast, and water as in first recipe
> ½ cup priming sugar

PROCEDURE

1. Put all the ingredients except the yeast and Irish moss into the boiler. Pour on 5½ gallons of boiling water (salted). Boil for 2 hours. Add the Irish moss ½ hour from the end of boil as above to produce bright wort. If you do not have a proper boiler, a large saucepan can be used.

2. Boil using as much water as possible, strain the wort through the hops in a straining bag, and make up the quantity to 5 gallons with cold water. Once the bright wort is obtained, proceed as in first recipe above.

PALE ALE

This English-born beer is the world's most popular style of ale, and deservedly so. A good pale ale represents everything a beer should be: malty but not too sweet, refreshing but not too bitter, lively but not overcarbonated, full-bodied but not heavy.

Unlike the Germans, the British are more liberal in their categorization of beers and you'll be hard pressed to scientifically pin down exactly what separates a pale ale from an India pale ale and what separates these two from bitter, except that the latter is usually served on draft and the former are usually bottled. In reality, these ales are simply what the brewer arbitrarily decides to name them. For this same reason, there may be some pale ale recipes here that are closer to the American version of pale ales included in the "North American Ale" section, and vice versa, but we have tried to put them in the category they fit the closest. These beers are generally made from hard water that is rich in calcium, sulfate, and bicarbonate. A study of Burton-on-Trent's water will give you a good idea of proper levels.

Some of the many fine examples of English-style pale ale include Eldridge Pope's Royal Oak Pale Ale, Samuel Smith's Old Brewery Pale Ale, Lord Granville Pale Ale, Fuller's London Pride, Young's Special London Ale, Pike Place Pale Ale, and Great Lakes Brewing Company's Burning River Ale.

PALE ALE BASICS

ORIGINAL GRAVITY: 1.045–55

FINAL GRAVITY: 1.008–16

IBUs: 25–45

COLOR (SRM): 6–12

ALCOHOL BY VOLUME: 4.5–5.5%

SPRING PALE ALE
▥ ▥ ▥
THE VINEYARD–UPTON, MASSACHUSETTS
This full-bodied pale ale recipe employs not only the traditional hops and yeast often used in British pale ale brewing but also brown sugar, an ingredient often used to increase strength and to add a subtle, unique flavor.

ORIGINAL GRAVITY: 1.050–52

FINAL GRAVITY: 1.010–12

POTENTIAL ALCOHOL: 5.1% ABV

INGREDIENTS

5.4 pounds Alexander's pale malt extract

1 pound light dry malt extract

$\frac{1}{3}$ cup light brown sugar

1 pound pale malt grain

$\frac{1}{2}$ pound crystal malt grain

$1\frac{1}{2}$ ounces Northern Brewer hop pellets (boiling)

$\frac{1}{2}$ ounce Kent Goldings hop plug (10 minutes)

$\frac{1}{2}$ ounce Kent Goldings hop plug (5 minutes)

1 teaspoon Burton water salts

1 teaspoon Irish moss

1 package Wyeast 1098 British (Whitbread)
Ale yeast

¾ cup corn sugar for priming

BREWING PROCEDURES

1. Crush and put all grains into 1½ gallons cold water with 1 teaspoon Burton water salts for 10 minutes, then raise temperature to 158°F slowly. Remove from heat and steep for 30 minutes.

2. Strain liquid into boiling pot. Add ½ gallon water, bring to boil, and add 5.4 pounds Alexander's malt extract, 1 pound dry malt, and ⅓ cup light brown sugar. Bring back to a boil and add 1½ ounces Northern Brewer hops; start timing 30 minutes. Add Irish moss last 15 minutes of boil. Add Goldings hops last 10 minutes of boil. Add ½ ounce Goldings hops last 5 minutes of boil.

3. Strain into sanitized primary fermenter and add cold water to make 5 gallons and let cool. Pitch yeast when temperature drops below 75°F. Primary fermentation: 4 days at 70°F. Secondary fermentation: 8 days at 70°F.

4. At bottling time boil ¾ cup priming sugar with 1 cup of boiled water for bulk priming.

ENGLISH REAL ALE

🍺 🍺 🍺

BEER & WINE HOBBY—WOBURN, MASSACHUSETTS

This medium-bodied ale stays true to the English "pub pint" tradition and features the warm, rounded bitterness of Fuggles and the classic Kent Goldings aroma hops. The unique use of victory lends a fresh, bready aroma and a wonderfully deep, amber reddish color.

ORIGINAL GRAVITY: 1.040–44

FINAL GRAVITY: 1.009–13

POTENTIAL ALCOHOL: 4% ABV

INGREDIENTS

1 can English light malt, 3.3 pounds

1 can English amber malt, 3.3 pounds

½ pound English crystal malt

½ pound victory malt

1 cup brown sugar

4 ounces malto-dextrin

1½ ounce Fuggles hop pellets (boil)

1 ounce Kent Goldings hop plug, last 2 minutes

1 package Burton water salts

1 teaspoon Irish moss

Wyeast Special London Ale or Yeast Lab A09 English Ale yeast (starter required)

¾ cup corn sugar

BREWING PROCEDURES

1. Crush grains, place in muslin bag, and tie. Add grains to 2 gallons of cold water and bring to a boil. When water comes to a boil, remove from heat and discard grains.

2. Add 2 cans of liquid malt, 1 cup brown sugar, 4 ounces malto-dextrin, 1½ Fuggles hop pellets. Put back on heat and return to a boil; boil for 20 minutes. Add 1 teaspoon Irish moss and package of Burton water salts; put back on heat and return to boil. Continue to boil for 15 minutes more. During the last 2 minutes add 1 ounce Kent Goldings hop plug tied in muslin bag.

3. Remove from heat and add to primary fermenter containing enough cold water to bring total volume to 5¼ gallons. Remove hop bag and discard. When wort has cooled to between 65° and 75°F, pitch prepared

yeast (instructions included). Proceed as usual. Finish fermenting.

4. Prime with ¾ cup priming sugar and bottle.

Brass Rale
🍺🍺🍺

Mountain Malt and Hop Shoppe—Lake Katrine & Poughkeepsie, New York

This recipe produces a brew that is a very accurate duplication of the well-known Burton-on-Trent IPA, a classic British pale ale.

Original Gravity: 1.050

Final Gravity: 1.014

Potential Alcohol: 4.6% ABV

Ingredients

> 1 can of English extra light malt extract
>
> 1 teaspoon Irish moss
>
> 2 pounds English extra light dry malt
>
> 1 package Burton water salts
>
> 2 ounces Fuggles hop pellets at 3.6% AA (bittering)
>
> 1 package Whitbread ale yeast (Optional: Wyeast 1098)
>
> 1 ounce East Kent Goldings hop pellets at 5% AA (bittering)
>
> 1 ounce East Kent Goldings hop pellets at 5% AA (flavor/aroma)
>
> ¾ cup priming sugar
>
> ½ pound amber crystal malt
>
> 1 pound invert sugar

Brewing Procedures

1. In a 12-quart or larger stainless-steel pot, heat 1 gallon of water to 160°F and add 1 teaspoon of gypsum. Stir until dissolved and turn off heat. Place cracked grains in a nylon bag and immerse in water. Cover pot and allow grain to steep for 30 minutes. Remove grain bag and bring the "tea" to a boil. (If you do not have a nylon bag, add grains directly to water and strain.)

2. When boil is attained, turn off heat and add the can of English malt and the dry malt. (Putting DME in a bowl first makes it easier to add.) Turn on heat and return to a boil.

3. When the danger of a messy boilover has passed, reduce heat slightly and stir in the invert sugar. Then add 2 ounces of Fuggles hops and 1 ounce of East Kent Goldings and cook at a low, rolling boil for 30 minutes.

4. Add 1 teaspoon of Irish moss and boil for 5 more minutes.

5. Take ½ ounce East Kent Goldings hop plug and slice it up. Place pieces in a muslin hop bag and immerse in wort. Boil for 8 more minutes.

6. Take the remaining ½ ounce East Kent Goldings hop plug and repeat the same process. Boil for 2 more minutes, then turn off heat. Immediately remove both hop bags.

7. Take the brewpot from the stove and place it in a sink partially filled with cold water. Add 1 gallon of sanitary, refrigerated water (40°F) to the brewpot, then cover and place ice in the water around the brewpot. Never add ice directly to the wort! Let stand 15 minutes. Place 2 gallons of refrigerated water into the fermenter, then add the wort. Check the temperature (65° to 75°F is ideal). Top off to 5½ gallons with either more cold or room-temperature water.

8. With a sanitized measuring cup, scoop out ¾ cup and take a hydrometer reading. Discard sample.

9. Add the package of yeast to the fermenter when the temperature of the wort is between 65° and 75°F, let sit 10 minutes, then stir vigorously to aerate. Snap the fermenter lid on, fill the airlock halfway with water, and place in lid. Place fermenter in a spot where the temperature will remain a constant 65–70°F.

10. Ferment in the primary for 5–6 days, then rack into a glass carboy for 2 weeks.

11. When brew is clear, siphon into a bottling bucket. Dissolve priming sugar into 1 cup boiling water, cool, and gently stir into beer with a sanitized spoon. CAUTION: If finished volume is less than 5 gallons, scale proportionately (e.g., 4½ gallons = ⅔ cup sugar).

12. Keep in a warm place for 7–10 days, then move to a cool place to age for 2 weeks.

PALE ALE

BOSTON BREWERS SUPPLY CO.— JAMAICA PLAIN, MASSACHUSETTS

"This is a delightful, quick-maturing pale ale that closely resembles an English bitter. It is beautiful pale copper color with a delicate, somewhat spicy hop aroma. A full malty flavor that has some fruity, estery overtones is offset by a long, clean, lingering hop bitterness."

ORIGINAL GRAVITY: 1.040–42

FINAL GRAVITY: 1.008–10

POTENTIAL ALCOHOL: 4% ABV

IBUs: 38 to 40

INGREDIENTS

- 6 pounds English light extract syrup
- 8 ounces English crystal malt
- 3 ounces Fuggles hop pellets
- 1 package Burton water salts
- 1 teaspoon Irish moss
- 1 package Windsor ale yeast
- 6 ounces corn sugar for priming

BREWING PROCEDURES

1. Secure the grains in the muslin straining bag. Pour 2 gallons of cold water into your brewpot, apply heat, and add the grain bag. Heat to a near boil (about 160°F), turn off the heat, cover the pot, and allow the grains to steep for 15 minutes. Remove the grain bag, drain, and discard.

2. Turn off the heat and, while stirring constantly, dissolve all of the malt extract. As soon as the boil begins add the 2 ounces of Fuggles hops and start timing the boil; the total elapsed time will be 50 minutes. Maintain a good rolling boil and stir occasionally. After 35 minutes, add the Irish moss flakes; 5 minutes later add the remaining ounce of Fuggles hops. Continue to boil for an additional 10 minutes, then cover and remove the pot from the heat.

Remember that after the wort has cooled, it is highly vulnerable to contamination; everything that comes into contact with it from this point on must be thoroughly sanitized!

3. Cool the wort as quickly as possible. A wort chiller works best, but if you haven't got one yet a cold water bath will do the trick. Place the covered pot in your kitchen sink and fill with ice and cold water. When the temperature has fallen to about 90°F, transfer the

wort, through a strainer if possible, into your fermenter. Top off with enough cold water to reach a 5-gallon level and stir or shake well. If you are using a glass carboy for fermentation, it is a good idea to add the cold water first. Draw off a small sample and take both a hydrometer and a temperature reading; always discard the sample used.

4. When the wort has cooled to 65° to 70°F, you are ready to add the yeast. Once the yeast has been added, attach an airlock and keep the fermenter in a cool, dark location where temperature fluctuations are minimal, ideally 65–68°F. Active fermentation should become visible in the next 12 to 24 hours and will continue for about 3 to 5 days.

5. When visible signs of fermentation have ceased, draw off a small sample and check the final gravity, by now it should be within the range stated above; if not, wait another couple of days and check again. Prepare to bottle.

Bottling and Conditioning

1. Sanitize all of your siphoning and bottling equipment, bottles, and caps.

2. Boil the 6 ounces of corn sugar in about a pint of water and pour it into your bottling bucket. Gently siphon the beer (again leaving sediment behind) out of the fermenter into the bucket, making sure the flow is directed to the bottom of the bucket; avoid splashing or agitating the beer. Reserve the last remnants to take thermometer and hydrometer readings; this will be your final gravity.

3. Using your siphon tubing and bottle filler, fill each bottle to within an inch from the top and cap immediately. Store the bottles

upright at room temperature, about 65° to 70°F for 3 or 4 weeks, chill, and enjoy!

Pale Ale (Partial Mash)
🍺 🍺 🍺
Northeast Brewers Supply— Providence, Rhode Island

"Pale ale is stronger with more hop flavor than its cousin, English bitter. This partial mash recipe will provide more malt character than our all-extract kit of the same style. If you want to use liquid yeast for this brew, we recommend Wyeast 1056 or 1028."

Original Gravity: 1.046

Final Gravity: 1.012

Potential Alcohol: 4.4% ABV

Ingredients

- 3.3-pound can light malt extract
- 4½ pounds pale ale grain mix (3 pounds Harrington 2-row and 1½ pounds crystal malt)
- 2 ounces boiling hops
- 1½ ounces finishing hops
- ½ teaspoon Irish moss
- 1 pack ale yeast
- ¾ cup corn sugar (priming)

Brewing Procedures

1. Add 5 quarts of water to your mash tun. Heat the water to about 120°F. Crush the grains. Mix well and hold the temperature at 120° for about 20 minutes. Bring the temperature up to 152°. Maintain the temperature at 152° for 1 hour. Stir the mash every 5 minutes.

2. Carefully transfer the mash to the lauter tun (another 5-gallon bucket with a false bottom). Start draining the water off the mash. Initially, this water should be recirculated through the mash to "set" the filter bed. The idea is to let the small particles in the mash collect at the bottom and create a filter. Once the filter is set (you can tell when the runoff starts to look clean—without particles and sediment), it is very important not to disturb it by letting it dry out or by forcing the sparge water through it too quickly. It should take about 45 minutes to sparge 5½ gallons of water through the grain. Collect the runnings into your brewpot.

3. When you're finished sparging, it's time to start the boil. (If you're using the NBS Mashing Kit, you can start raising the temperature in the brewpot while you're waiting for the sparge to finish.) When the water starts to boil, add the malt extract and the boiling hops. To prevent scorching, turn off the heat before adding the extract and turn it back on after the extract is well mixed. Put the boiling hops into a boiling bag and drop into the pot. When the water starts boiling again, set your timer for *25 minutes.*

4. After 25 minutes have elapsed, add the Irish moss and set your timer for an additional *20 minutes.*

5. After you've boiled the wort for a total of 45 minutes, put the finishing hops into a bag, drop them in, and boil for an additional 2 minutes. Remove from heat.

6. Cool the wort. There are a couple of ways to do this. If you have a wort chiller, this process takes about 10 minutes. If you're boiling a small quantity of wort (1½ to 3 gallons), you can add it to cold water in your primary fermenter to make up 5 gallons. Whatever method you use, remember the time between the end of the boil and pitching the yeast is when your brew is most susceptible to contamination. Therefore, extra care is warranted during this time to protect the wort from exposure to undesirable microorganisms. Be sure to sanitize everything that comes into contact with your beer with boiling water, chlorine, or iodophor.

7. When the wort has been added to the primary fermenter and cooled to 70–80°F, add the yeast.

8. Ferment at 65–70°F (in a single- or two-stage fermenting system—your choice) until the specific gravity falls to below 1.015. This should take approximately 1–2 weeks.

9. When you're ready to bottle, dissolve the corn sugar in 2 cups of boiling water. Add to the brew and mix well without disturbing the sediment. This is easy if you first siphon your beer into a bottling bucket and then mix in the sugar solution.

10. Bottle, cap, and put in a warm (65–75°F) environment for at least 6 days. Your pale ale will be ready to drink in about 2 weeks and will improve with age. Cheers!

CLASSIC ENGLISH PALE ALE

⫢ ⫢

E. C. KRAUS—INDEPENDENCE, MISSOURI

"Classic English pale ale is a more hoppy, drier version of English bitter. It tends to be higher in alcohol. While it is called 'pale,' its color is closer to light amber. Its most prevalent character is the clean, dry, hoppy finish."

ORIGINAL GRAVITY: 1.044–46

FINAL GRAVITY: 1.010–12

POTENTIAL ALCOHOL: 4.4% ABV

IBUs: 20–40

COLOR: 4–11 SRM/5.5–13 °L

INGREDIENTS

> 3.3 pounds light unhopped malt extract
>
> 2.5 pounds light dried malt extract (6 cups)
>
> 8 ounces dark caramel malt
>
> 4 ounces malto-dextrin (5-minute boil time)
>
> 1¼ ounces Brewers Blend pelletized hops (60-minute boil time)
>
> ½ ounce Fuggles pelletized hops (finish-steep 15 minutes)
>
> 14 grams Whitbread ale yeast
>
> ¾ cup priming sugar

BREWING PROCEDURES

1. Lightly crack malted barley and put with 1½ gallons of cold water in a cooking pan. Slowly bring to a boil over a 30–45-minute period.

2. Strain the grain out by use of a colander and discard.

3. Bring the liquid back to a boil and add both the liquid and dried malt extracts. Bring back to a boil again.

4. Once boiling, add Brewers Blend hops and boil for 60 minutes. During the last 5 minutes of boil, fold in malto-dextrin.

5. Once the boiling is complete, add the Fuggles hops, turn off the burner, and allow to steep for 15 minutes with a lid on.

6. Now add the wort to your fermenter with cold water up to 5 gallons. Make sure it has cooled below 80°F and sprinkle on yeast.

7. Attach airlock to fermenter and allow to ferment for 7–10 days or until finished, then bottle with priming sugar as normal.

FOOLER'S WONTON PRIDE

🍺 🍺 🍺

MOUNTAIN MALT AND HOP SHOPPE— LAKE KATRINE & POUGHKEEPSIE, NEW YORK

This brew was designed to recreate a famous British beer, a classic example of a true bitter.

ORIGINAL GRAVITY: 1.044

FINAL GRAVITY: 1.012

POTENTIAL ALCOHOL: 4.1% ABV

INGREDIENTS

> 1 can of English extra light malt extract
>
> ½ pound crystal malt
>
> 2 pounds English extra light DME
>
> 1 teaspoon Irish moss
>
> 1 ounce Fuggles hop pellets at 3.6% AA (bittering)
>
> 1 package Burton water salts
>
> 2 ounces Kent Goldings hop pellets at 5% AA (bittering)
>
> 1 package Whitbread ale yeast
>
> 2 ounces Kent Goldings hop plugs (flavor and aroma)
>
> 1.1 pounds demerara sugar
>
> ¾ cup corn sugar for priming

BREWING PROCEDURES

1. In a 12-quart or larger stainless-steel pot, heat 1 gallon of water to 160°F and add 1 teaspoon of gypsum. Stir until dissolved and turn off heat. Place cracked grains in a nylon bag and immerse in water. Cover pot and allow grain to steep for 30 minutes. Remove grain bag and bring the "tea" to a boil. (If you do not have a nylon bag, add grains directly to water and strain.)

2. When boil is attained, turn off heat and add

the can of English malt and the dry malt. (Putting DME in a bowl first makes it easier to add.) Turn on heat and return to a boil.

3. When the danger of a messy boilover has passed, reduce heat slightly and stir in ¾ of the box of demerara sugar. Then add 1 ounce of Fuggles and 2 ounces of Kent Goldings and boil for 30 minutes.

4. Add 1 teaspoon of Irish moss and boil for 5 more minutes.

5. Take the remaining 1 ounce of Kent Goldings hop plugs and slice them up. Place pieces in a muslin hop bag and immerse in wort. Boil for 10 more minutes.

6. Take the brewpot from the stove and place it in a sink partially filled with cold water. Add 1 gallon of sanitary, refrigerated water (40°F) to the brewpot, then cover and place ice in the water around the brewpot. Never add ice directly to the wort! Let stand 15 minutes. Place 2 gallons of refrigerated water into the fermenter, then add the wort. Check the temperature (65° to 75°F is ideal). Top off to 5½ gallons with either more cold or room-temperature water.

7. With a sanitized measuring cup, scoop out ¾ cup and take a hydrometer reading. Discard sample.

8. Add the package of yeast to the fermenter when the temperature of the wort is 65–75°F, let sit 10 minutes, then stir vigorously to aerate. Snap the fermenter lid on, fill the airlock halfway with water and place in lid. Place fermenter in a spot where the temperature will remain a constant 65–70°F.

9. Ferment in the primary for 5–6 days, then rack into a glass carboy for 2 weeks.

10. When brew is clear, siphon into a bottling bucket. Dissolve priming sugar into 1 cup boiling water, cool, and gently stir into beer with a sanitized spoon. CAUTION: If finished volume is less than 5 gallons, scale proportionately (e.g., 4½ gallons = ⅔ cup sugar).

11. Keep in a warm place for 7–10 days, then move to a cool place to age for 2 weeks.

PALE ALE

ANDREW TVEEKREM, BREWMASTER, GREAT LAKES BREWING CO.— CLEVELAND, OHIO

"This a standard everyday beer that can be made with either English or American hops. This makes for a nice copper-colored ale with a hugely mouth-puckering bitterness and a long, lingering finish that leaves your palate begging for more. All of my recipes are for 10 gallons and use Wyeast 1028 in a thick slurry (usually a 1-quart jar per 10 gallons). All hops are pellets and are added by the handful (I gave up measuring several years ago)."

ORIGINAL GRAVITY: 1.056

FINAL GRAVITY: 1.012

POTENTIAL ALCOHOL: 5.8% ABV

INGREDIENTS (FOR 10 GALLONS)

- 21 pounds English pale malt
- 3 pounds English crystal malt
- 3 good-sized handfuls of Northern Brewer or 2 smaller handfuls of Galena
- 3 handfuls of Cascade hop pellets
- 3 handfuls of B.C. Goldings hop pellets
- 3 handfuls of Kent Goldings hop pellets
- A dash of Irish moss
- 1 quart thick yeast slurry of Wyeast 1028 London Ale
- 1.5 cups corn sugar for priming

BREWING PROCEDURES

1. Mash crushed malt at 154–156°F for 1 hour, stirring occasionally.
2. Lauter to collect 12 gallons of wort and bring to a boil.
3. Add 2 or 3 handfuls of Northern Brewer or Galena hop pellets at the beginning of the boil.
4. Boil for 75 minutes, adding 3 more handfuls of Cascade hop pellets at 30 minutes prior to the end. Add 3 more handfuls of B.C. Goldings hop pellets at 15 minutes prior to the end and a dash of Irish moss.
5. At the end of the boil add 3 handfuls of Kent Goldings hops.
6. Swirl, cool, and ferment at 65°F.
7. Rack, prime, and bottle as you normally do.

IRISH RED ALE

—

The reddish amber Irish variation of English pale ale has received a great deal of renewed interest recently in the wake of the craft beer renaissance. Like Scottish pale ales, Irish ale is typically less hoppy than its English counterpart and often exhibits a pronounced malty, buttery, and caramel character. Commercial versions rely primarily on well-modified two-row pale ale malt with just a touch of black malt or roasted barley for color. The caramel character, as in Scottish brewing, is more a result of the long wort boil and the light hopping than from the use of crystal malts. The use of adjuncts such as brewing sugar or flaked maize is not uncommon, and although most are top-fermented, Coors uses lager yeast and a warm ferment in its Killian's Irish Red. Prime commercial versions include Smithwick's Ale, Guinness's Kilkenny Irish Beer, Phoenix Beer, Big Rock's McNally's Extra, and George Killian's Irish Red.

IRISH RED ALE BASICS

ORIGINAL GRAVITY: 1.036–65

FINAL GRAVITY: 1.010–16

IBUs: 20–35

COLOR (SRM): 8–15

ALCOHOL BY VOLUME: 3.5–6.5%

ERIN-GO-BRAUGH PALE ALE
◫ ◫

BREW MASTERS, LTD.–ROCKVILLE, MARYLAND

This is an exceptional pale ale featuring a traditional Irish ale flavor with a nice malty start and a perfect balance of hop flavor and nose.

ORIGINAL GRAVITY: 1.046

FINAL GRAVITY: 1.013

POTENTIAL ALCOHOL: 4.3% ABV

INGREDIENTS

½ pound toasted Klages malt

⅓ pound crystal malt

6.6 pounds Northwestern Gold Unhopped malt extract

1 ounce Centennial hops (bittering) 20-minute boil

½ ounce Cascade hops (aroma) no boil

1 package English Ale yeast (dry) or Wyeast 1084 Irish Ale

¾ cup priming sugar

BREWING PROCEDURES

1. Toast your grain. Place Klages malt on cookie sheet and toast in 350° oven for 10–15 minutes.

2. Crack and steep your grain. Combine toasted grain with crystal malt and crush with a malt mill or in a sealed bag using a rolling pin. Place crushed grains in a muslin sack. In a 2- to 3-gallon stainless-steel or enamel pot (never use aluminum), bring 1 quart of water to a boil, add the grains, then turn off the heat, cover, and steep for 10–15 minutes. Remove grain bag and discard.

3. Rehydrate your dry yeast. Place contents of yeast package in ½ cup of water and stir to dissolve. Yeast will bubble and thicken slightly. Set aside.

4. Boil your wort. Add 3 quarts of water to your pot, then add the bittering hops and boil for 15–20 minutes. Add the liquid malt (2 pouches) and stir to dissolve. Continue to boil another 10 minutes. Watch the pot carefully so that it does not boil over. Add the finishing hops, stir in, and turn off heat.

5. Ferment. Place 2 gallons of cold water into a sanitized fermentation vessel (plastic or glass). Add the wort to the fermenter, then add additional cold water up to the 5-gallon mark on your fermenter. Stir. When it is approximately 80°, add the yeast and stir vigorously. Place the airlock in the lid and cover the fermenter. Fill the airlock ⅔ full with water. Place the fermenter in a 70–75° area and allow to ferment until the hydrometer reading shows a specific gravity reading of 1.010 (approximately 5 to 10 days).

6. Bottle. Sanitize 48 twelve-ounce returnable beer bottles. Siphon your fermented beer into a bottling bucket, leaving the sediment behind and being careful not to oxidize the beer by splashing. Add ¾ cup priming sugar to ½ cup of boiled water and stir to dissolve. Gently stir the sugar mixture into your beer and bottle immediately, leaving approximately 1 inch head space in the bottle. Cap with sanitized crown caps. Set beer aside for at least a week at room temperature for carbonation to form. Do not refrigerate!

7. Enjoy. Try a beer after it's been in the bottle a week. Try another one a week later. You will taste the difference aging has made. Never put this beer in the refrigerator until you want to serve it. Let it age at room temperature and drink it when you want to enjoy your own special beer!

IRISH RED ALE
⚐ ⚐

THE VINEYARD—UPTON, MASSACHUSETTS

This simple mash-extract recipe uses the addition of classic Bavarian aroma hops to lend a spicy, crisp aroma that marries nicely with the malty sweetness. You can also try this one with a liquid ale yeast, but choose one that has a slight diacetyl character for true Irish ale flavor.

ORIGINAL GRAVITY: 1.042

FINAL GRAVITY: 1.012

POTENTIAL ALCOHOL: 3.9% ABV

INGREDIENTS

> ½ pound light crystal malt
>
> 2 ounces roasted barley
>
> 6.6 pounds Northwestern hopped gold malt extract
>
> 1 teaspoon Irish moss (last 15 minutes)
>
> ½ ounce Hersbrucker hop plug (last 5 minutes)
>
> 1 package Whitbread ale yeast
>
> ½ cup corn sugar for priming

BREWING PROCEDURES

1. Crush and put grains into 1 gallon cold water for 10 minutes, then slowly raise temperature to a boil. Once boiling commences, remove from heat. Strain liquid and sparge grains with 1 gallon hot water into boiling pot.

2. Add ½ gallon water, 6.6 pounds malt extract, and bring to a boil. Once boil begins start timer for 40 minutes. Last 15 minutes add Irish moss. Last 5 minutes add Hersbrucker hops. Strain into sanitized primary fermenter and add cold water to make 5 gallons, and let cool.

3. Pitch yeast when temperature drops below 80°F. Primary fermentation: 4 days at 70°F. Secondary fermentation: 8 days at 70°F. At bottling time boil ½ cup priming sugar with 1 cup water for bulk priming.

"RED" ZEPPELIN ALE
⫿ ⫿ ⫿

DICK FOEHRINGER

THE BREWMEISTER—FAIR OAKS, CALIFORNIA

"Red Zeppelin Ale is reddish in color due to the roasted barley. The generous amount of crystal and Munich malts lends a residual sweetness that is well balanced with the hop bitterness. The Fuggles aromatics, along with moderate-high alcohol strength, will make you rock-on!"

ORIGINAL GRAVITY: 1.056

FINAL GRAVITY: 1.014

POTENTIAL ALCOHOL: 5.5% ABV

INGREDIENTS

> 7 pounds pale malt extract
>
> ¼ pound roasted barley
>
> 1 pound 20 °L crystal malt
>
> ½ pound Munich malt
>
> 1 ounce Northern Brewer hops (60 minutes) boiling
>
> 1 ounce Northern Brewer hops (30 minutes) boiling
>
> 1 ounce Fuggles hops (2 minutes) aromatic
>
> 1 teaspoon Irish moss (15 minutes)
>
> 1 package Doric dry ale yeast
>
> 1 teaspoon gelatin
>
> ¾ cup bottling sugar

BREWING PROCEDURES

1. Put the crushed roasted barley, crystal, and Munich malted grains into a grain bag. Place 1½ to 2 gallons of cold water in your brewpot. Place grain bag in water and bring to a near boil (160–170°F). Turn off heat and allow grains to steep for 30 minutes. Drain and remove grain.

2. Dissolve extract thoroughly and then return mixture to heat. Bring to a boil. Add the 1 ounce of hops and boil for 30 minutes. Add the second 1 ounce of hops and boil for 15 minutes. Add Irish moss and boil for 15 minutes. Add the remaining aromatic hops and boil for 2 minutes. Cold-break the wort to below 100°F by setting your pan of wort into a sink full of cold water.

3. Put the cooled wort into your primary fermenter and add cold water to make 5½ gallons. When cooled below 85°F, pitch your yeast. (Note: Rehydrate your yeast by dissolving it in 1 cup warm water and allowing it to sit for 10 minutes before pitching.) Ferment in a warm (65–75°F), dark place.

4. When fermentation has ceased, transfer to the secondary, leaving all the sediment behind. Dissolve gelatin in 1 cup hot water and stir into secondary. Allow beer to clear, typically 3–5 days.

5. Rack again, leaving sediment behind.

6. Dissolve bottling sugar in 1 cup of hot water and stir into beer. Bottle and cap. Allow to age/carbonate in the bottles for 2–4 weeks. Enjoy!

INDIA PALE ALE

India pale ale is so named because it was a pale ale brewed strong and heavily hopped in order to withstand the rigorous ocean voyage to the British troops stationed in colonial India. Modern special or best bitters are sometimes considered the "true" descendants of the original India pale ales. Oak chips are often added by homebrewers to create a spicy flavor obtained when beer is aged in oak casks. However, this should be done very sparingly (that is, 1 ounce or less) because the American and French oak chips available to homebrewers are very pungent. Some English beer authorities insist that oak flavor is inappropriate to IPA because pitch-lined English oak barrels impart little flavor to the beer. Others, however, assert that the barrels used to ship beer to India were probably not coated with pitch and, therefore, would have contributed some oak flavor notes. No matter which stance you take, IPAs should be in the original gravity range of 1.050–65, with IBUs at 40–60, alcohol 5–6.5% ABV, and equal to or lighter than standard pale ales in color.

Because of the American love affair with hops, India pale ale is enjoying a wide resurgence of popularity in the United States among homebrewers, microbrewers, and brewpubs alike. A few of the great examples, American and British, by which to judge your homebrewed IPA include: Brooklyn Brewery's East India Pale Ale, Marston's India Export Pale Ale, Harpoon IPA, Greene King IPA, and Anchor Liberty Ale.

INDIA PALE ALE BASICS

ORIGINAL GRAVITY: 1.050–65

FINAL GRAVITY: 1.010–16

IBUs: 40–60

COLOR (SRM): 8–14

ALCOHOL BY VOLUME: 5–6.5%

MARYLAND STYLE INDIA PALE ALE
⌸ ⌸

BOB FRANK

THE FLYING BARREL—FREDERICK, MARYLAND

The combination of Chinook hops and oak chips in the boil of this easy extract recipe will give you an exceptionally spicy and pungent beer with a robust hop character.

ORIGINAL GRAVITY: 1.049

FINAL GRAVITY: 1.012

POTENTIAL ALCOHOL: 4.8% ABV

INGREDIENTS

> 6.6 pounds Northwestern amber, unhopped
> ½ pound 40 °L crystal malt
> 4 ounces oak chips
> 2 ounces Chinook whole hops
> 1 package gypsum
> 1 teaspoon Irish moss
> 1 package Wyeast 1056 American Ale
> ¾ cup priming sugar

BREWING PROCEDURES

1. Break yeast pack a day before you are ready to brew.
2. Steep grains for 20 minutes at 155–160°F, then strain into boil pot, dispose of spent grains.
3. Add malt extract, hops (in straining bag), and gypsum.
4. Boil malt and hops for about 60 minutes in about 3 gallons of water.
5. In the last 15 minutes of the boil, put the Irish moss and oak chips in the wort.
6. Put boiling wort into a fermenter with 2½ gallons of cold water.
7. When temperature drops to below 75°F, pitch yeast.
8. Take hydrometer reading, airlock the fermenter, and watch the yeast do its thing.
9. After fermentation is complete, prime and bottle.

SNAKE ROCK IPA
⌸ ⌸ ⌸

PAUL HEALY

MOUNTAIN MALT AND HOP SHOPPE— LAKE KATRINE & POUGHKEEPSIE, NEW YORK

This strong IPA uses a unique blend of American high alpha and aroma hop varieties to produce a solidly bitter hop head's delight. The demerara helps keep the body light while lending a unique flavor profile and alcoholic strength.

ORIGINAL GRAVITY: 1.062

FINAL GRAVITY: 1.014

POTENTIAL ALCOHOL: 6.3% ABV

INGREDIENTS

> ⅓ pound amber crystal malt
> 1 ounce Cascade hop plugs
> ⅓ pound toasted malt
> 1 ounce Tettnang hop plugs

One 4-pound can Alexander's pale syrup

½ Eroica hops

3 pounds extra light DME

½ ounce Tettnang (for dry-hopping—optional)

½ pound demerara sugar

⅓ ounce Burton water salts

1 ounce Galena hops

1 teaspoon Irishmoss

Wyeast 1056 American Ale yeast

½ ounce Eroica hops

¾ cup priming sugar

BREWING PROCEDURES

1. In a 12-quart or larger stainless-steel pot, heat 1 gallon of water to 155°F and add 1 teaspoon of gypsum. Stir until dissolved and turn off heat. Place cracked grains in a nylon bag and immerse in water. Cover pot and allow grain to steep for 30 minutes. Remove grain bag and bring the "tea" to a boil. (If you do not have a nylon bag, add grains directly to water and strain.)

2. When boil is attained, turn off heat and add the liquid and dry malts. (Putting DME in a bowl first makes it easier to add.) Turn on heat and return to a boil.

3. When the danger of a messy boilover has passed, add the Galena and Eroica hops (20 HBU) and cook at a low, rolling boil for 45 minutes.

4. Add 1 teaspoon of Irish moss and boil for 5 more minutes.

5. Take one ½-ounce Tettnang hop plug and one Cascade hop plug and slice them up. Place pieces in a muslin hop bag and immerse in wort. Boil for 8 more minutes.

6. Take the remaining ½-ounce Tettnang and Cascade hop plugs and repeat the same process. Boil for 2 more minutes, then turn off heat and add ½ ounce Eroica hops. Immediately remove the boiling hops.

7. Take the brewpot from the stove and place it in a sink partially filled with cold water. Add 1 gallon of sanitary, refrigerated water (40°F) to the brewpot, then cover and place ice in the water around the brewpot. Never add ice directly to the wort! Let stand 15 minutes. Place 2 gallons of refrigerated water into the fermenter, then add the wort. Check the temperature (65° to 75°F is ideal). Top off to 5½ gallons with either more cold or room-temperature water.

8. With a sanitized measuring cup, scoop out ¾ cup and take a hydrometer reading. Discard sample.

9. Add the package of yeast to the fermenter when the temperature of the wort is 65–75°F, then stir vigorously to aerate. Snap the fermenter lid on, fill the airlock halfway with water, and place in lid. Place fermenter in a spot where the temperature will remain a constant 65–70°F.

10. Ferment in the primary for 5–6 days, then rack into a glass carboy for 2 weeks. Boil hop bag and six marbles to weight bag. Cut up ½ ounce Tettnang plug, place in bag, and knot close to open end. Allow hops to soak 1–2 weeks. Remove after racking beer to bottling bucket.

11. When brew is clear, siphon into a bottling bucket. Dissolve priming sugar into 1 cup boiling water, cool, and gently stir into beer with a sanitized spoon. CAUTION: If finished volume is less than 5 gallons, scale proportionately (e.g., 4½ gallons = ⅔ cup sugar).

12. Keep in a warm place for 7–10 days, then move to a cool place to age for 2 weeks.

"Colonial" IPA
▥ ▥ ▥

Joe & Bryan Timmons

Boston Brewers Supply Co.—
Jamaica Plain, Massachusetts

The creative addition of victory malt to this straightforward recipe lends a gentle bready character and a subtle reddish color to this well-hopped ale. The strength of this English classic will allow it to mature and evolve in the cellar for many months (if your willpower holds out).

Original Gravity: 1.058–62

Final Gravity: 1.015–18

Potential Alcohol: 6% ABV

IBUs: approximately 44

Ingredients

- 9 pounds English light extract syrup
- 8 ounces light crystal malt
- 8 ounces victory malt
- 1 ounce Chinook hop pellets
- 2 ounces English Kent Goldings hop pellets
- 1 ounce gypsum
- 1 teaspoon Irish moss
- 1 package dry ale yeast or Wyeast 1098 British Ale
- 6 ounces corn sugar for priming

Brewing Procedures

1. Secure the grains in the muslin straining bag. Pour 2 gallons of cold water into your brewpot, apply heat, and add the grain bag. Heat to a near boil (about 155°F), then remove the grain bag, drain, and discard.

2. Turn off the heat and, while stirring constantly, dissolve all of the malt extract. Bring to a boil and add the 1 ounce of Chinook hop pellets. Immediately start timing the boil; the total elapsed time will be 45 minutes. The following additions should be made according to the schedule below:

   15 minutes into the boil, add 1 ounce of Kent Goldings pellets.

   25 minutes into the boil, add the Irish moss flakes.

   20 minutes after the last addition, cover and remove the pot from the heat.

Remember that after the wort has cooled, it is highly vulnerable to contamination; everything that comes into contact with it from this point on must be thoroughly sanitized!

3. Cool the wort as quickly as possible. A wort chiller works best, but if you haven't got one yet a cold water bath will do the trick. Place the covered pot in your kitchen sink and fill with ice and cold water. When the temperature has fallen to about 90°F, transfer the wort, through a strainer if possible, into your fermenter. Top off with enough cold water to reach a 5-gallon level and stir or shake well. If you are using a glass carboy for fermentation, it is a good idea to add the cold water first. Draw off a small sample and take both a hydrometer and a temperature reading; always discard the sample used.

4. When the wort has cooled to 65–70°F, you are ready to add the yeast. Once the yeast has been added, attach an airlock and keep the fermenter in a cool, dark location where temperature fluctuations are minimal, ideally 65–70°F. Active fermentation should become visible in the next 12 to 24

hours and will continue for about 3 to 5 days.

5. When visible signs of fermentation have ceased, it is time to transfer and dry-hop the beer. Secure the remaining 1 ounce of Kent Goldings pellets in the second muslin bag and place it in your "secondary fermenter." Gently siphon the beer to the sanitized secondary fermenter (ideally a 5-gallon glass carboy), leaving all sediment behind. Attach an airlock and allow the beer to settle for an additional 5 to 7 days at the same temperature of primary fermentation.

6. At the end of this period, draw off a small sample and check the final gravity, by now it should be within the range stated above; if not, wait another couple of days and check again. Prepare to bottle.

Bottling and Conditioning

1. Sanitize all of your siphoning and bottling equipment, bottles, and caps.

2. Boil the 6 ounces of corn sugar in about a pint of water and pour it into your bottling bucket. Gently siphon the beer (again leaving sediment behind) out of the fermenter into the bucket, making sure the flow is directed to the bottom of the bucket; avoid splashing or agitating the beer.

3. Using your siphon tubing and bottle filler, fill each bottle to within an inch from the top, and cap immediately. Store the bottles upright for a minimum of 3 weeks, chill, and enjoy.

India Pale Ale

Ric Genthner

Wine Barrel Plus—Livonia, Michigan
"This India pale ale is a special variety of British ale and is a relative of the English bitter. The characteristic of the IPA makes this beer more hoppy and alcoholic (5.5–7%) than the English bitter. Use authentic varieties of British malt extracts, hops, and pure liquid brewing yeast."

Original Gravity: 1.050–55

Final Gravity: 1.014–16

Potential Alcohol: 4.6–5% ABV

Ingredients

6 pounds amber plain malt extract
1 pound crystal malt
½ pound toasted malt
2 ounces Northern Brewer hops (boiling)
1 ounce Kent Goldings hops (finishing)
1 teaspoon Irish moss
1 package of liquid ale yeast
¾ cup corn sugar (for bottling)

Brewing Procedures

1. Add the crystal and toasted malt to 1½ gallons of water and bring to a boil. Remove the grain when the boiling starts.

2. Add the malt extracts and the Northern Brewer hops and boil for 60 minutes.

3. Add the Cascade hops and the Irish moss to the boil for the last 15–20 minutes.

4. Pour immediately into primary fermenter with cold water and top up to make 5 gallons.

5. Add yeast when cool.

6. Bottle with ¾ cup of corn sugar when fermentation is complete.

RAINY DAY IPA

▥ ▥

THE CELLAR HOMEBREW—SEATTLE, WASHINGTON

"Based on the classic historical style developed to withstand the journey from England to the far reaches of the British Empire in India. By packing extra hops and an alcoholic punch, the brew would survive the three- to five-month ocean voyage to tropical climates. Light bodied and strong, our IPA is a hop lover's dream."

ORIGINAL GRAVITY: 1.054

FINAL GRAVITY: 1.014

POTENTIAL ALCOHOL: 5.3% ABV

INGREDIENTS (FOR 5.5 GALLONS)

> 6 pounds British light bulk malt syrup
> 2 pounds English light dry malt extract
> 2 ounces Chinook or Columbus hops (boiling)
> 1 ounce Kent Goldings hops (finishing)
> 1 teaspoon gypsum (optional, add during step 3)
> 1 package Whitbread dry ale yeast or British Ale liquid yeast
> ¾ cup corn sugar for priming

BREWING PROCEDURES

Note: If you are using the British Ale liquid yeast with this recipe, be sure to start that yeast at least 1 to 3 days before doing any of the brewing steps below. Follow the package directions and use the yeast in step 4 below.

1. Pour 2 to 2½ gallons of water into your brewing kettle and bring to a boil.

2. Remove the brewing kettle from the burner and add the 6 pounds of British light malt extract and the 2 pounds of English light dry malt. The syrup is easier to pour if the can has been previously placed in hot water. Also, rinse the can with hot water to ensure that all the syrup goes into the kettle. Stir the mixture, now called "wort," until it boils. Watch carefully at this time because the wort may boil over. You can prevent this by pouring a cup of cold water into the overboiling wort.

3. At boiling point, add the Chinook or Columbus boiling hops. Hops can be placed in a hop bag or added loose, to be later strained out after the boil using a strainer bag. Time the boil for about 1 hour, stirring occasionally. After the first 10 minutes of this boil, remove 2 cups of wort in measuring cup and cover with foil or plastic. Cool to 90°F for use in step 4 below.

4. Making the yeast starter: For dry yeast, use ½ cup warm tap water (90–100°F). Sprinkle the contents of yeast packet into that water, cover for at least 15 minutes, and then add to the 2 cups of wort you prepared in step 3. Cover and set aside for use in step 8 below. For liquid yeast, prepare 1 to 3 days ahead of brewing time per package instructions. Open the swollen package and add the contents to the 2 cups of wort as prepared in step 3.

5. After the wort has boiled for that 1 hour, add finishing hops. Place them in the hop bag, which has been emptied of the spent boiling hops, and place them in the boiling kettle, or just add the finishing hops directly to the brewing kettle. They will be strained later in step 7.

6. Let the boil continue for 5 minutes. This gives the beer its hop aroma. Remove the pot from the burner and let it cool, covered, for about 20 minutes.

7. Pour 3 gallons of cold water into the sanitized open fermenter fitted with strainer bag. If

loose finishing hops were used in step 5, strain the warm wort from step 6 into the cold water. Top up the fermenter to 5½ gallons using cold tap water. Cover the fermenter and cool the wort as rapidly as possible.

8. When the wort has cooled to about 80°, add the yeast starter and ferment as you usually do.

HAIL TO THE "INDIA PALE ALE"

🍺 🍺 🍺

THE HOME BEER, WINE, & CHEESEMAKING SHOP—WOODLAND HILLS, CALIFORNIA

Novice brewers should not be intimidated by the wide range of ingredients employed in this recipe. The mixture of Belgian malts, classic English hops, and a bit of honey malt yields a complexly malty, hoppy, and gently sweet brew that is worth the extra effort.

ORIGINAL GRAVITY: 1.058

FINAL GRAVITY: 1.013

POTENTIAL ALCOHOL: 5.8% ABV

IBUs: 58

COLOR: 11 SRM

INGREDIENTS

   4 ounces Belgian aromatic malt

   4 ounces Belgian biscuit malt

   8 ounces Gambrinus honey malt

   8 ounces English 80 °L crystal malt

   6 pounds Royal light DME

   1 ounce Phoenix hop pellets at 9% AA (60 minutes)

   1.5 ounces Challenger hop pellets at 7.2% AA (20 minutes)

   0.5 ounce Progress hop pellets at 6.1% AA (0 minutes—at knockout)

   1 ounce Northdown whole hops at 9.4% AA (dry-hopped)

   1 teaspoon Irish moss

   2 teaspoons gypsum

   Wyeast 1275 Thames Valley Ale

   ¾ cup corn sugar for priming

BREWING PROCEDURES

1. Steep (soak) the grains in 2 quarts of 150°F water for 30–40 minutes. Sparge (rinse) with 2.5 quarts of 150°F water into your boiling pot. Discard grain. No water over 170°F with grain. Do not oversparge. Do not squeeze grain bag.

2. After adding 2.5 gallons of water and dissolving the malt, bring pot to a gentle but rolling boil. Skim all foam before starting the hop sequence. Add Irish moss the last 20 minutes to remove the protein missed in steps 1 and 2. Add the gypsum into the boil. It adds hardness, accentuating the crisp hop character.

3. Ferment at an average of 62–66°F. This keeps fruity esters to a minimum. Pitch (add) yeast when your water bath around the fermenter reads 70–80°F. Maintain this temperature until the first signs of fermentation (about 10–12 hours). If using a yeast starter (highly recommended), fermentation can start in 2–3 hours. Use ¾ cup sugar for priming.

ELEPHANT CHASER INDIA PALE ALE

🍺 🍺 🍺

E. C. KRAUS HOME WINE AND BEER MAKING SUPPLIES—INDEPENDENCE, MISSOURI

"The first thing you notice about this IPA is its strong hoppy flavor and aroma. It has a good malty mouthfeel, but the flavors of the malt are subdued by the hops. The color is amber with a distinctly reddish hue. This is due to the toasting of the pale malt. There is some maltiness in the aroma, but it is dominated by hops."

ORIGINAL GRAVITY: 1.057–63

FINAL GRAVITY: 1.015–18

POTENTIAL ALCOHOL: 5.5–6% ABV

IBUs: 50–60

COLOR: 10–14 SRM/16–24 °L

INGREDIENTS

> 6.6 pounds light unhopped malt syrup
>
> 4 ounces pale malt (toasted)
>
> 1 pound dark caramel malt
>
> 8 ounces malto-dextrin (5-minute boil time)
>
> 1 ounce Galena pellet hops (60-minute boil time)
>
> 1 ounce Fuggles pellet hops (finishing)
>
> 1 tablespoon Irish moss (15-minute boil time)
>
> 2 teaspoons gypsum
>
> 10 grams Manchester ale yeast or Wyeast 1968
>
> ¾ cup priming sugar

BREWING PROCEDURES

1. Toast pale malt by placing on a cookie sheet and baking at 450°F for 10 to 20 minutes. Be careful not to let it burn.

2. Lightly crack malted barleys and put with gypsum in 1½ gallons of cold water in a cooking pot. Slowly bring to a boil over a 30–45-minute period.

3. Once boiling, strain the grains out by the use of a colander or the like and discard.

4. Bring liquid back to a boil and add the liquid malt extract. Bring back to a boil again.

5. Once boiling, add Galena hops and boil for 60 minutes. During the last 15 minutes of the boil, add the Irish moss. During the last 5 minutes of the boil, fold in the malto-dextrin.

6. Once the boiling is complete, add the Fuggles hops; turn off the burner and allow to steep for 15 minutes with a lid on.

7. Now add the wort to your fermenter along with cold tap water up to 5 gallons. Make sure the wort has cooled to below 80°F and pitch yeast.

8. Attach airlock to fermenter and allow to ferment for 7–10 days or until finished and bottle with priming sugar as normal.

BITTER

Technically a substyle of pale ale, this style of beer is the favorite of the British pubs. Like the textbook descriptions of pale ale, the term "bitter" is a little tough to pin down and is often used interchangeably with "pale ale." Northern English bitter is generally different from its southern counterpart in hopping rates, water profiles, and creamier heads provided by a different dispensing system. Yorkshire bitters traditionally also have a unique, yeasty, dry character derived from the use of "Yorkshire Stone Square" fermenters. Some Englishmen will insist that for a beer to qualify as a true bitter, it must be served on draft, but many of the Great British

Beer Festival's champions also appear in bottles. Bitter's subcategories include ordinary bitter, special bitter, extra special bitter (aka best bitter or strong bitter)—and practically every brewery interprets them somewhat differently. However, to make things easier, the American Homebrewers Association uses these guidelines for classifying English bitter:

ORDINARY: ORIGINAL GRAVITY: 1.033–1.038, 20–35 IBUs, and Alcohol 3–3.7% ABV

SPECIAL: ORIGINAL GRAVITY: 1.038–1.045, 28–46 IBUs, and Alcohol 4.1–4.8% ABV

EXTRA SPECIAL: ORIGINAL GRAVITY: 1.046–1.060, 30–55 IBUs, and Alcohol 4.8–5.8% ABV

The Campaign for Real Ale, on the other hand, categorizes bitter in this way:

BITTER: ORIGINAL GRAVITY: less than 1.040

BEST BITTER: ORIGINAL GRAVITY: 1.040–1.045

STRONG BITTER: ORIGINAL GRAVITY: 1.046–1.054

English malts, hops, and yeast strains are recommended, as is water rich in dissolved salts similar to that used for Burton-style ales. Brakspear's Bitter, Webster's Yorkshire Bitter, Timothy Taylor Landlord Best Bitter, Barnsley Bitter, St. Austell Bosun's Bitter, Riding Bitter, Mansfield Bitter, Adnams Bitter, Young's Ram Rod, Greene King Abbot Ale, Fuller's ESB, Marston's Pedigree Bitter, and Bateman XXXB are but a few of the many, many excellent commercial examples.

BITTER BASICS

ORIGINAL GRAVITY: 1.035–60

FINAL GRAVITY: 1.006–16

IBUs: 20–55

COLOR (SRM): 8–15

ALCOHOL BY VOLUME: 3–6%

BIG BEN'S BITTER

THE CELLAR HOMEBREW—SEATTLE, WASHINGTON

"You don't have to be a hop fan to love an English bitter. 'Bitter' has been used synonymously with 'pale ale' for centuries, and this quick, easy-to-brew ale has just a hint of spicy bitterness from Fuggles hops, along with a smooth, light body and golden color. Reduced priming sugar assures the low carbonation characteristic of the style."

ORIGINAL GRAVITY: 1.030

FINAL GRAVITY: 1.008

POTENTIAL ALCOHOL: 2.8% ABV

INGREDIENTS (FOR 5.5 GALLONS)

- 3.3 pounds John Bull light unhopped malt syrup
- 1 can Alexander's amber "Kicker"
- ½ ounce Fuggles hops (boiling)
- ½ ounce Fuggles hops (finishing)
- 1 package Edme dry ale yeast or London Ale liquid yeast
- ½ cup corn sugar for priming

BREWING PROCEDURES

Note: If you are using the London Ale liquid yeast with this recipe, be sure to start that yeast at least 1 to 3 days before doing any of the brewing steps below. Follow the package directions and use the yeast in step 4.

1. Pour 2 to 2½ gallons of water into your brewing kettle and bring to a boil.
2. Remove the brewing kettle from the burner and add the 3.3 pounds John Bull light unhopped malt syrup and the 1 can Alexander's amber "Kicker." The syrup is easier to pour if the can has been previously placed in hot water. Also, rinse the can with hot water to ensure that all the syrup goes into the kettle. Stir the mixture, now called "wort," until it boils. Watch carefully at this time because the wort may boil over. You can prevent this by pouring a cup of cold water into the overboiling wort.
3. At boiling point, add the Fuggles hops. Hops can be placed in a hop bag or added loose, to be later strained out after the boil using a strainer bag. Time the boil for about 1 hour, stirring occasionally. After the first 10 minutes of this boil, remove 2 cups of wort in a measuring cup and cover with foil or plastic. Cool to 90°F for use in step 4 below.
4. Making the yeast starter: For dry yeast, use ½ cup warm tap water (90–100°F). Sprinkle the contents of yeast packet into that water, cover for at least 15 minutes, and then add to the 2 cups of wort you prepared in step 3. Cover and set aside for use in step 8 below. For liquid yeast, prepare 1 to 3 days ahead of brewing time per package instructions. Open the swollen package and add the contents to the 2 cups of wort as prepared in step 3.

5. After the wort has boiled for that 1 hour, add the Fuggles finishing hops. Place them in the hop bag, which has been emptied of the spent boiling hops, and place them in the boiling kettle or just add the finishing hops directly to the brewing kettle. They will be strained later in step 7.
6. Let the boil continue for 5 minutes. This step gives the beer its hop aroma. Remove the pot from the burner and let it cool, covered, for about 20 minutes before going to step 7.
7. Pour 3 gallons of cold water into the sanitized open fermenter fitted with a strainer bag. If loose finishing hops were used in step 5, strain the warm wort from step 6 into the cold water. Top up the fermenter to about 5½ gallons using cold tap water, if necessary. Cover the fermenter and cool the wort as rapidly as possible.
8. When the wort has cooled to about 80°, add the yeast starter and ferment as you usually do.
9. If you desire the low carbonation characteristics of this style, use only ½ cup priming sugar at bottling time.

JOLLY BREWER'S BEST BITTER

PENELOPE S. J. COLES

JOLLY BREWER—WREXHAM CLWYD, WALES

This darkish Welsh bitter reflects the popularity in British brewing of using refined sugar to provide strength to higher-gravity bitters while keeping the body light and drinkable. The large quantity of classic English hops provides a nice contrast to the nutty sweetness of the dark malt.

ORIGINAL GRAVITY: 1.048

FINAL GRAVITY: 1.010

POTENTIAL ALCOHOL: 4.9% ABV

INGREDIENTS (FOR 5 IMPERIAL GALLONS)

> **6 pounds SFX dark malt extract**
> **1.5 pounds sugar**
> **3 ounces Kent Goldings hops**
> **1 teaspoon Irish moss**
> **1 pound crushed crystal malt**
> **5 gallons water**
> **Beer yeast**
> **¾ to 1 cup priming sugar**

BREWING PROCEDURES

1. Pour about 1 gallon of water into a 2-gallon-capacity pan. Bring to a boil.
2. Weigh the malt extract, add to the pan of water, stir very well.
3. Weigh 1.5 ounces of hops and 1 pound crystal malt, put them each in muslin bags, and tie the necks.
4. Drop the bags into the pan, bring the contents of the pan to a boil, simmer in the wort for 1 hour.
5. Weigh the sugar and put it into a clean, sterile fermenting bucket. Pour 2 pints of boiling water onto the sugar and stir to dissolve.
6. Pour 6 pints of cold water into the bucket, then add the boiling wort, retaining the muslin bags in the pan. Stir very well.
7. Pour 1 gallon of water into the pan, bring to a boil, give the muslin bags a good pummel, and stir.

8. Simmer for half an hour, then pour the wort into the fermenting bucket, leaving the muslin bag in the pan.
9. Weigh the remaining 1.5 ounces of hops, put them in a muslin bag, and drop them into the pan. Add 1 teaspoon of Irish moss. Top up the pan again with 1 gallon of water, bring to a boil, and simmer for half an hour.
10. Pour the wort into the fermenting bucket with cold water to the 5-gallon mark, stir, and leave to cool to 20°C.
11. Add the yeast and ferment, barrel, and prime as usual.

NEW YORK-SHIRE BITTER

🍺 🍺 🍺

STEPHEN SNYDER

I tried to design this recipe to capture the taste of the great bitters I enjoyed in Yorkshire, England. Although I did not have the traditional Yorkshire stone squares at my disposal for fermentation, this recipe produced a very authentic session beer with a lot of character.

ORIGINAL GRAVITY: 1.038–40

FINAL GRAVITY: 1.010–12

POTENTIAL ALCOHOL: 3.5–4% ABV

IBUs: 30

HBUs: 16

INGREDIENTS

> **2 pounds English amber DME**
> **2.5 pounds English light DME**
> **¾ pound English 40 °L crystal malt**

1 ounce Fuggles hop plugs at 4.2% AA
(boil) 60 minutes

1 ounce Fuggles hop plugs at 4.2% AA
(boil) 30 minutes

2 teaspoons Irish moss (boil 20 minutes)

1 ounce East Kent Goldings hop plugs at
5.0% AA (flavor) 7 minutes

½ ounce East Kent Goldings hop plug
(aroma) 1 minute

Wyeast 1098 British Ale liquid yeast

¾ cup corn sugar for priming

BREWING PROCEDURES

1. Place cracked crystal malt in muslin or
nylon hop bag and put in medium-sized pot
and add 1 quart of cold water. (I boiled,
then cooled 1 quart of water beforehand to
remove chlorine and temporary hardness.)
Dissolve in Burton salts by stirring. Bring
slowly to boil. Remove from heat immediately and strain liquid into brew kettle.
Sparge grains with hot (150–170°F) water
that has had chlorine and temporary (carbonate) hardness removed by boiling.

2. Add 2 gallons of cold water and bring to a
boil. (I also boiled, then cooled 3 gallons of
water beforehand to remove chlorine.)
Remove brew kettle from heat before
adding extract and DME to avoid sticking or
burning.

3. Boil vigorously for 60 minutes, adding hops
as noted above. Hot-break trub should be
skimmed at the beginning of the boil.

4. Let hot wort sit for 30 minutes (covered) in
ice-water bath before pouring into single-
stage fermenter (5-gallon carboy) containing approximately 2.5 gallons ice-cold water
(at 35–40°F). Wort should be below 75°F
before pitching yeast. Stir vigorously to aerate. Fit with airlock or blowoff hose and
move to a dark, quiet, draft-free space and
ferment at 68°F.

5. Fit carboy with airlock after blowoff ceases
(approx. 48–72 hours). Ferment for 5 more
days or until fermentation ceases.

6. Rack into bottling bucket, prime with ¾
cup corn sugar dissolved in 1 pint of boiling
water, and bottle.

7. Warm-condition 7 days at room temperature
(68°F). Store cool (55–60°F) for 1–3 weeks.

LONDON CALLING ORDINARY BITTER

🍺 🍺 🍺

AL KORZONAS
SHEAF & VINE BREWING SUPPLY— COUNTRYSIDE, ILLINOIS

"I call this an ordinary even though its original
gravity is in the special bitter range because the
Dutch and crystal malts keep the unfermentables
high (thereby putting the alcohol level down
around 3.3% ABV). A great session beer, but be
aware that it's meant to be consumed young. The
best way to enjoy this beer would be hand-pulled
(from a cask) using a beer engine. Barring that,
you could keg it (priming very lightly) and then
release all the pressure from the keg when you're
not serving. Despite the fact that this beer is low
in alcohol, it is not low in flavor."

ORIGINAL GRAVITY: 1.042

FINAL GRAVITY: 1.015

POTENTIAL ALCOHOL: 3.5% ABV

INGREDIENTS (FOR 15 GALLONS)

15.5 gallons Chicago water (see page 88)

3 pounds Belgian CaraVienne crystal malt

1 pound Belgian CaraMunich crystal malt

12 pounds Northwestern Gold extract syrup

2 pounds Dutch light dried malt extract

15 grams gypsum (added to boil)

4.25 grams noniodized sodium chloride (added to boil)

4.5 ounces Mt. Hood pellets (4.1% AA) (60 minutes)

2.25 ounces East Kent Goldings Plugs (4.1% AA) (15 minutes)

1.5-liter starter from Wyeast Irish Ale 1084

1 ounce Styrian Goldings Plugs (dry-hopped 2 weeks)

BREWING PROCEDURES

1. Boil 7.5 gallons of water the day before and add to the 20-gallon, sanitized fermenter to cool overnight.

2. On brewing day, steep the crushed grains in 3 gallons of water at 170°F, remove the grains and add the final 4.5 gallons of water, brewing salts, and extracts.

3. Bring to a boil. Boil 15 minutes. Add the boiling hops. Boil 45 minutes. Add the flavor hops. Boil 15 minutes. Remove hops (I used hops bags for easier cleanup) and chill with a wort chiller down to 70°F. Pour the wort and starter into the fermenter.

4. Ferment 2 weeks at 62–65°F.

Notes: "The brewing salt additions in the recipe are based upon Chicago water. You should adjust them for your own water. The target water I was trying to get was:

100 ppm of Ca

10 ppm of Mg

30 ppm of Na

225 ppm of SO₄

35 ppm of Cl

CO_3 should be kept as low as reasonable—if your water is high in carbonates, you should add some calcium chloride and boil the water to get the calcium carbonate to precipitate out. After boiling, decant the water off the precipitate. You see, if you just use the water, the carbonate will dissolve back into the wort."

FAR OUT ESB

THE HOME BEER, WINE, & CHEESEMAKING SHOP—WOODLAND HILLS, CALIFORNIA

This bitter recipe is "far out" in its use of ingredients from Canada, Australia, England, and Scotland, but the result is a classic malty and well-balanced beer with a low level of fruitiness and a complex flavor profile.

ORIGINAL GRAVITY: 1.062

FINAL GRAVITY: 1.015

POTENTIAL ALCOHOL: 6.5% ABV

IBUs: 37

COLOR: 11 SRM

INGREDIENTS

8 ounces Gambrinus honey malt

4 ounces Belgian biscuit malt

4 ounces Belgian aromatic malt

8 ounces Scottish 80 °L crystal malt

4 ounces flaked maize

6 pounds Royal light DME

4 ounces wheat solids

0.5 ounce Pride of Ringwood hop pellets at 8% AA (60 minutes)

0.5 ounce Phoenix hop pellets at 9% AA (60 minutes)

0.5 ounce Kent Goldings hop pellets at 4.1% AA (20 minutes)

0.5 ounce Progress hop pellets at 6.1% AA
(0 minutes)

1 teaspoon Irish moss

2 teaspoons gypsum

Wyeast 1275 Thames Valley Ale

¾ cup corn sugar for priming

BREWING PROCEDURES

1. Steep (soak) the grains in 2 quarts of 150°F water for 30–40 minutes. Sparge (rinse) with 2.5 quarts of 150°F water into your boiling pot. Discard grain. No water over 170°F with grain. Do not oversparge. Do not squeeze grain bag.

2. After adding 2.5 gallons of water and dissolving the malt, bring pot to a gentle but rolling boil. Skim all foam before starting the hop sequence. Add Irish moss the last 20 minutes to remove the protein missed in steps 1 and 2. Add the gypsum into the boil. It adds hardness, accentuating the crisp hop character.

3. Ferment at an average of 62–66°F. This keeps the fruity esters to a minimum. Pitch (add) yeast when your water bath around the fermenter reads 70–80°F. Maintain this temperature until the first signs of fermentation (about 10–12 hours). If using a yeast starter (highly recommended), fermentation can start in 2–3 hours. Use ¾ cup sugar for priming.

STOCKPORT STYLE BITTER
PETER HOOD
BREWING SUPPLIES—STOCKPORT & ALTRINCHAM, ENGLAND

This remarkably simple and straightforward all-grain recipe relies on just five ingredients to create an authentic English bitter. The secret is to use English hops and malt.

ORIGINAL GRAVITY: 1.049

FINAL GRAVITY: 1.013

POTENTIAL ALCOHOL: 4.6% ABV

INGREDIENTS (FOR 5 IMPERIAL GALLONS)

8 pounds pale malt, crushed (Maris Otter)

10 ounces crystal malt, crushed

5 ounces Kent Goldings hops

Dried ale yeast (or the cultured-up residue from a Coopers bottle works well)

¾ cup corn sugar for priming

BREWING PROCEDURES

1. Raise 3 gallons of water to 75° C.
2. Throw in the crushed pale malt and crystal. Cover and leave for 2 hours.
3. Jug wet grain through a sparge bag and sparge with 170°F water until you get 5.5 gallons of liquor.
4. Boil with 4 ounces hops for 1 hour, add 1 ounce hops and boil for 5 minutes.
5. Strain into bucket and ferment out as normal. Prime, bottle, and condition for 2–3 weeks.

STRONG ENGLISH BITTER
STEPHEN SNYDER

My all-grain recipes are designed to yield 5.5 gallons into the fermenter so ½ gallon can be lost in trub removal, racking, and bottling procedures with the traditional 5-gallon batch still going into the bottles. Nothing is more frustrating than working very hard on a great batch of beer and only ending up with 30–35 bottles. I have also indicated collecting 6.5 gallons in the kettle to compensate for the steam loss of a 90-minute boil and for hot-break removal during the boil. If you are using two kettles for your wort boil you may experience a greater loss of volume. Add additional water to the kettle if necessary and boil for at least 15 minutes. Do not compensate by over-sparging your mash. I have assumed an extract yield of 1.025 per pound per gallon for my base malts to allow for the use of the most basic mashing and sparging techniques of novice all-grain brewers. If your usual methods produce consistently better results, please adjust accordingly.

ORIGINAL GRAVITY: 1.051

FINAL GRAVITY: 1.016

POTENTIAL ALCOHOL: 4.5% ABV

IBUs: 42

INGREDIENTS (FOR 5.5 GALLONS)

> 10 pounds English 2-row pale ale malt (crushed)
>
> 1 pound English dextrine malt (crushed)
>
> 0.5 pound 40–60 °L crystal malt (crushed)
>
> 1 ounce Fuggles hop plugs at 4.1% AA (boil 60 minutes)
>
> 0.5 ounce Challenger hop pellets at 8.2% AA (boil 60 minutes)
>
> 0.5 ounce Bramling Cross hop pellets at 7.1% AA (boil 60 minutes)
>
> 2 teaspoons Irish moss
>
> 1 ounce East Kent Goldings aroma hop plugs (boil 3 minutes)
>
> 1 ounce East Kent Goldings aroma hop plugs (dry-hopped in fermenter 10 days)
>
> Wyeast 1968 Special London yeast in 1 liter starter
>
> ¾ cup corn sugar for priming

BREWING PROCEDURES

1. Saccharification rest. Mash in 3.25 gallons of 163°F brewing liquor, carefully stirring to mix the liquor and grist. Rest 90 minutes at 155°F. Stir occasionally.

2. Test for remaining starches with an iodine tincture by adding 1 drop to a tablespoon of wort on a white saucer. If negative (wort no longer turns purplish/black).

3. Mash out. Raise mash temperature to 165–170°F by adding doses of hot water or bottom heat. Rest 10 minutes to decrease wort viscosity.

4. Transfer to lauter tun if separate vessel is being used. Slowly sparge with 5.5 gallons of 165–168°F water over 45–60 minutes and collect wort into brew kettle.

5. Collect 6.5 gallons of wort.

6. Boil for 90 minutes, adding hops as noted above.

7. Force-cool with wort chiller.

8. Rack through sanitizer sieve or strainer bag into carboy or other fermenter.

9. Pitch 1 liter yeast starter. Aerate well.

10. Rest beer for 2–3 hours or until trub settles. (Optional.)

11. Rack into primary fermenter and ferment under airlock (or open ferment) at 64–72°F for 5 days. Rack to secondary and add dry hops in sanitized muslin bag. Ferment under airlock for 10 days.

12. Rack to bottling bucket, prime, add fresh yeast (optional), and bottle or keg.

13. Condition at 65–70°F for 5 to 7 days.

14. Cellar for 1 to 2 weeks.

15. Serve at 50–55 °F.

GLASTONBURY ESB

🎹🎹🎹🎹

DAVID GOURLEY

THE MAD CAPPER—GLASTONBURY, CONNECTICUT

Here's a large-quantity ESB recipe for the all-grain brewer who can't seem to keep a 5-gallon batch around very long. The gravity puts it in contention for being called an IPA, but the Munich malt makes it solidly malty in the strong bitter tradition. The yeast called for in this formulation produces a classically complex and well-balanced bitter with just a hint of butterscotch that in all likelihood will make this one of your favorite beers.

ORIGINAL GRAVITY: 1.064

FINAL GRAVITY: 1.016

POTENTIAL ALCOHOL: 6.4% ABV

INGREDIENTS (FOR 10 GALLONS)

15 pounds pale malt

1 pound Munich malt

1 pound crystal malt

½ pound wheat malt

2 ounces Kent Goldings hop pellets (boil 60 minutes)

1 ounce Cascade hop pellets (boil 30 minutes)

1 ounce Cascade hop pellets (finishing)

2 teaspoons Irish moss (boil 30 minutes)

Wyeast 1968 Special London yeast

1.5 cups corn sugar for priming (or force carbonate)

BREWING PROCEDURES

1. Mash in at 150°F for 90 minutes.
2. Mash out, lauter, and sparge as you normally do.
3. Boil wort for 90 minutes, adding hops and Irish moss as noted above. Add finishing hops with 2 minutes remaining.
4. Cool with wort chiller, rack to primary, then pitch yeast.
5. Ferment 7 days in the glass primary and 7 days in the glass secondary fermenter.
6. Keg or prime and bottle using your favorite methods.

PORTER

Born as a mixture of inexpensive mild and expensive old ale, porter is a full-bodied, dark ale accentuating crystal, black, and roasted malts and medium to high hop bitterness. Originally named "porter's ale" because of its popularity among London's market porters, this beer dominated the working-class market in the eighteenth and nineteenth centuries because it was cheap, and because it was one of the first beers to be available in sufficient quantities year-round—due in large part to the Industrial Revolution. Porter gave rise to an even stronger and heavier ale called "stout porter," which eventually was shortened to "stout." Porter became almost extinct when faster-maturing pale ales, stouts, and then lagers became more popular. The final blow came with Great Britain's Beer Orders of 1915 and 1916, which placed restrictions on specific gravities and the use of raw materials during World War I. Stout rebounded after the war, porter did not. However, recently renewed interest in the style has introduced porter to a whole new generation of craft-beer lovers in the United States.

Porters are generally brewed with large percentages of roasted malts and water rich in bicarbonates, sodium, and chloride. Just a few of the commercial versions include Harvey's 1859 Porter, Ushers Dark Horse Porter, Samuel Smith's The Famous Taddy Porter, and the American-brewed Edmund Fitzgerald Porter, Catamount Porter, Yuengling Porter, and Anchor Porter.

PORTER BASICS

ORIGINAL GRAVITY: 1.045–60

FINAL GRAVITY: 1.008–16

IBUs: 25–45

COLOR (SRM): 20–40

ALCOHOL BY VOLUME: 5–6%

LONDON PORTER
⫸⫸⫸

**BOSTON BREWERS SUPPLY CO.—
JAMAICA PLAIN, MASSACHUSETTS**

"Our London porter is designed to replicate one of the early versions of this wonderful beverage. The unhopped amber extract and blend of crystal, black, and chocolate malts produces a deep black-red ale with a smooth roasted malt flavor. A clean bitterness is achieved using traditional Fuggles hops with a late addition of Kent Goldings for their fine, subtle aroma."

ORIGINAL GRAVITY: 1.046–48

FINAL GRAVITY: 1.012–14

POTENTIAL ALCOHOL: 4.7% ABV

IBUs: 30 to 34

HBUs: 11 to 12

INGREDIENTS

7 pounds English amber extract syrup
1 pound English crystal malt
4 ounces English black malt
4 ounces English chocolate malt
2 ounces Fuggles hop pellets
1 ounce Kent Goldings hop pellets
1 teaspoon calcium carbonate
1 teaspoon Irish moss flakes
1 package dry ale yeast
6 ounces corn sugar for priming

BREWING PROCEDURES

1. Secure the grains in the muslin straining bag. Pour 2 gallons of cold water into your brewpot, apply heat, dissolve the calcium carbonate, and add the grain bag. Heat to a near boil (about 160°F), then remove the grain bag, drain, and discard.

2. Turn off the heat and, while stirring constantly, dissolve all of the malt extract. As soon as the boil begins, add all of the Fuggles hop pellets and start timing the boil; the total elapsed time will be 60 minutes. Maintain a good rolling boil and stir occasionally. After 45 minutes, add the Irish moss flakes; continue to boil for 15 minutes, then add the Kent Goldings hop pellets.

Remove the pot from the heat and steep for 10 to 15 minutes.

Remember that after the wort has cooled, it is highly vulnerable to contamination; everything that comes into contact with it from this point on must be thoroughly sanitized!

3. Cool the wort as quickly as possible. A wort chiller works best, but if you haven't got one yet a cold water bath will do the trick. Place the covered pot in your kitchen sink and fill with ice and cold water. When the temperature has fallen to about 90°F, transfer the wort, through a strainer if possible, into your fermenter. Top off with enough cold water to reach a 5-gallon level and stir or shake well. If you are using a glass carboy for fermentation, it is a good idea to add the cold water first. Draw off a small sample and take both a hydrometer and a temperature reading; always discard the sample used.

4. When the wort has cooled to 65–70°F, you are ready to add the yeast. Once the yeast has been added, attach an airlock and keep the fermenter in a cool, dark location where temperature fluctuations are minimal, ideally 68°F. Active fermentation should become visible in the next 12 to 24 hours and will continue for about 3 to 5 days. This porter can be bottled immediately but will benefit from a week of secondary fermentation. If you choose to bottle right away, take both a temperature and a hydrometer reading. If the final gravity is within the range stated above, proceed directly to the bottling instructions below; if not, wait another couple of days and check again.

5. When visible signs of fermentation have ceased, gently siphon the beer to the sani-tized secondary fermenter (ideally a 5-gallon glass carboy), leaving all sediment behind. Attach an airlock and allow the beer to settle for an additional 5 to 7 days at the same temperature of primary fermentation.

6. At the end of this period, draw off a small sample and check the final gravity. By now it should be within the range stated above; if not, wait another couple of days and check again. Prepare to bottle.

BOTTLING AND CONDITIONING

1. Sanitize all of your siphoning and bottling equipment, bottles, and caps.

2. Boil the 6 ounces of corn sugar in about a pint of water and pour it into your bottling bucket. Gently siphon the beer (again leaving sediment behind) out of the fermenter into the bucket, making sure the flow is directed to the bottom of the bucket; avoid splashing or agitating the beer. Reserve the last remnants to take thermometer and hydrometer readings; this will be your final gravity.

3. Using your siphon tubing and bottle filler, fill each bottle to within an inch from the top and cap immediately. Store the bottles upright at room temperature; about 65–70°F for a minimum of 3 weeks. Serve cool, but not cold. Enjoy!

LONDON PORTER

THE HOME BREWERY—OZARK, MISSOURI

Brewed purely from a base of liquid malt extract and hop pellets, this recipe couldn't be simpler for the novice brewer. The resulting beer is dark, rich, and complex with a nice nutty-roasty character.

ORIGINAL GRAVITY: 1.060

FINAL GRAVITY: 1.016

POTENTIAL ALCOHOL: 5.6% ABV

INGREDIENTS

> 3.3 pounds (1 pack) Home Brewery hopped dark malt extract
>
> 3.3 pounds (1 pack) Home Brewery unhopped dark malt extract
>
> 1.7 pounds (½ pack) Yellow Dog malt extract
>
> 1 ounce Cascade hop pellets (bittering)
>
> ½ teaspoon Irish moss added 15 minutes before the end of the boil
>
> ¾ ounce Tettnanger hop pellets (finishing)
>
> 2 packs Doric ale yeast
>
> ¾ cup corn sugar for priming

BREWING PROCEDURES

1. Heat 5 gallons of water in a large kettle. Many people don't have a kettle that large, but heat as much as you can (at least 2 gallons). When the water is boiling, turn off the heat and add the malt extract to the water. Use a spoon and stir until you are sure no malt extract is sticking to the bottom of the kettle. Then turn the heat back on.

2. Bring the kettle back to a boil, and stir occasionally so the ingredients won't burn on the bottom of the kettle. When your recipe calls for bittering hops, now is the time to add them and stir them in. Watch out for a boilover. In the early part of the boil, the kettle usually tries to boil over once or twice, so control this by adjusting the heat. Later in the boil, the surface tension changes and boiling over is not a problem. Keep stirring occasionally, and let the beer (wort) boil hard for 1 hour. Stir in the ½ teaspoon of Irish moss in your recipe about 15 minutes before the end of the boil.

3. When finishing hops are called for in your recipe, stir them in 2 minutes before the end of the boil. Using finishing hops at the end of the boil adds a fresh aroma and flavor to the beer, and the use of finishing hops is appropriate in most beer styles.

4. Pour the hot beer (wort) into the primary fermenter. It is not necessary to strain the wort if you used hop pellets. Add cold water to bring the total volume up to 5 gallons. If you are using our B3a Fermenter (the one in the kits), the 5-gallon mark is the bottom ring. Cover the fermenter and wait until the temperature is down to 75°F. If you have a wort chiller, use it to bring the temperature down quickly. At 75° or less, add the yeast in your recipe. Just tear open the pack(s) and sprinkle it on the wort. Close the fermenter with the lid, stopper, and airlock. Remember to put water (or vodka) in the airlock. Vodka evaporates more quickly, but bacteria won't live in it.

5. Fermentation should start within 24 hours, and may continue for between 1 day and 2 weeks, depending on the type of yeast, the recipe, and the temperature. Leave the beer alone and don't open the lid. When the airlock has not bubbled for several days and the beer is flat, still, and clearing, it is ready to bottle.

6. To bottle, siphon about 1 pint of beer into a pan and warm it on the stove. Add exactly ¾ cup of corn sugar to the pan and stir until it is dissolved. Pour this back into the beer and stir gently but well to distribute the

sugar. Siphon or tap into clean sanitized bottles and cap. Keep the bottles at room temperature. After a week, put a bottle in the refrigerator and try it. It will be best in about 3 weeks.

COLONIAL HONEY PORTER

⬤ ⬤ ⬤

BEER & WINEMAKING SUPPLIES, INC.— NORTHAMPTON, MASSACHUSETTS

"A dark, robust ale brewed with honey for a hint of sweetness to balance the roasted malt flavor. Color is deep amber-black. A commercial example is Boston Beer Co.'s Samuel Adams Honey Porter. Using liquid yeast 1028 London or 1084 Irish will give a drier profile, while 1098 British will leave it slightly sweet, and 1056 American will leave it clean and more neutral tasting."

ORIGINAL GRAVITY: 1.048–52

FINAL GRAVITY: 1.011–13

POTENTIAL ALCOHOL: 4.5–4.9% ABV

INGREDIENTS

> 6 pounds light malt extract
> ¾ pound Munich malt (cracked)
> 1 pound medium crystal malt (cracked)
> 6 ounces black malt (cracked)
> 3 ounces chocolate malt (cracked)
> 1 pound honey
> 10 HBUs bittering hops (Cluster or similar type)
> ½ ounce Mt. Hood, Liberty, or Hallertauer aroma hops

> 10–14 grams dry ale yeast or Wyeast 1028, 1084, 1056, or 1098
> ¾ cup corn sugar for bottling

BREWING PROCEDURES

Note: If using a liquid culture, activate 12–24 hours prior to brew session.

1. Place your three blended grains in a 4–6-quart pan and stir in 2.25 quarts of 168°F water. Mix well. Grain should bring temperature down to approximately 150–154°F. Steep for 45–60 minutes in oven, small insulated cooler, or on stovetop at that temperature. While grain is steeping, bring 2 gallons of water up to 165–170°F in an 8–12-quart pot. Place strainer or colander over large kettle, then pour and spoon all grains and liquid in. Rinse with 1.5–2 gallons of 165°F water. Allow liquid to drain into kettle. Discard grains and bring liquid to a boil. Momentarily remove from heat.

2. Pour the 6 pounds of malt extract and honey into the pot, making sure to rinse out the container to get all the malt. Stir well.

3. Resume boiling (total time: 1 hour). Split the bittering hops into two equal portions. At the 15-minute mark, add half; at the 30-minute mark, add the second half. At 60 minutes, add the aroma hops.

4. Shut off the heat and let stand for 15 minutes.

5. Put 2 gallons of very cold water into your sterilized primary fermenter, then carefully pour the hot wort into it. Top up to 5 gallons with more cold water if necessary. If still above 85°F, run a cold water bath around your fermenter. The fermenter should then be stirred or swirled to aerate the wort. Take a hydrometer reading and write it down.

6. Wort should now be 70–85°F. Activate dry yeast by putting in 1 cup of sterile water at 75–95°F for 15 minutes, then stir well.

7. Now add the yeast and stir or swirl to aerate. Pitch yeast solution into fermenter. Put lid and airlock on. Fill airlock halfway with water.

8. Ferment at room temperature (64–68°F) for 3–4 days, then siphon over to a glass secondary fermenter for another 4–7 days. Take a hydrometer reading, and if low enough, bottle the beer into 53 reusable bar bottles (12-ounce size) or equivalent.

9. Bottling procedure: Make a priming syrup on the stove with 1 cup water and ¾ cup corn sugar, bring to a boil, and then shut heat off immediately, stirring well. Transfer beer back to primary or bottling bucket, mixing the priming syrup in well to distribute evenly. Siphon into bottles and cap them.

10. Remember to sanitize everything you use after the boil with a good chlorinated alkaline cleanser.

11. Allow bottles to sit at room temperature for 1–2 weeks before cooling down.

Porter
🍺 🍺

The Vineyard—Upton, Massachusetts
This is an ideal recipe for the novice brewer venturing into mash-extract recipes for the first time with the simple addition of a few specialty grains and the use of an English hop plug for finishing.

Original Gravity: 1.052–54

Final Gravity: 1.010–14

Potential Alcohol: 5.1% ABV

Ingredients

> 3.3 pounds Superbrau amber malt extract unhopped
> 3 pounds amber dry malt extract
> 1 pound black malt grain
> 4 ounces crystal malt grain
> 2 ounces Northern Brewer hop pellets
> ½ ounce Fuggles hop plug (last 5 minutes)
> 1 packet Nottingham ale yeast
> ½ cup corn sugar for priming

Brewing Procedures

1. Crush and put all grains into 2 quarts cold water for 10 minutes, then slowly raise temperature to a boil. Once boiling commences, remove from heat.

2. Strain liquid into boiling pot. Add up to 2 gallons water. Add Superbrau malt and amber dry malt and bring to boil. Once boiling starts, add Northern Brewer hop pellets. Last 5 minutes add Fuggles hops.

3. At end of boil, strain into primary fermenter and add cold water to make 5 gallons. Pitch yeast when temperature drops below 90°F. Primary fermentation: 4 days at 70°F. Secondary fermentation: 8 days at 70°F.

4. At bottling time boil ½ cup priming sugar with 1 cup water for bulk priming.

PIRATES BREW PORTER
🍺 🍺

JAY GARRISON, HEAD BREWER, PIRATE
  BREWERY

BREWBUDDYS—REDONDO BEACH,
  CALIFORNIA

The purity and simplicity of this recipe is
revealed in its light, easy-drinking character
and distinct chocolate taste, making it ideal for
quaffing or as a companion to hearty pub fare.
This is a great recipe for the novice brewer
interested in trying a liquid yeast strain.

ORIGINAL GRAVITY: 1.040

FINAL GRAVITY: 1.010

POTENTIAL ALCOHOL: 3.8% ABV

INGREDIENTS

> **6 pounds dark liquid extract**
>
> **One 1.4-pound can Alexander's dark malt
>   extract**
>
> **7 ounces chocolate malt**
>
> **1 ounce Perle hops**
>
> **½ ounce Willamette hops**
>
> **Wyeast 1028 London Ale or dry ale yeast**
>
> **¾ cup corn sugar for bottling**

BREWING PROCEDURES

1. If you selected the Wyeast liquid yeast, you
   must break the inner packet before you
   begin to brew. Allow 1 day for each month
   after the manufacture date printed on the
   front. If you're using the dry yeast that came
   with the Pirates Brew Kit, go ahead and get
   to it.

2. Prepare the grain. The grain should be
   crushed; if you did not get the grain
   crushed at the shop, crush it with some sort
   of rolling pin. You can either mix the grain
   with 2 quarts of water and heat it until it

starts to boil, or heat it to about 165°F and
steep for about 15 minutes.

3. Strain the grain, collecting the liquid into
   your brewpot. Rinse the grain (sparge) with
   2 quarts of hot (170–180°F) water.

4. Add the bag and can of extract and 1 gallon
   of water to the brewpot. (You might want to
   rest the extract in hot water for a while to
   soften it up.) Bring the wort to a soft rolling
   boil.

5. Add the Perle hops to the wort and boil for
   40 minutes. Stir occasionally.

6. Add ½ of the Willamette hops (¼ ounce) to
   the wort and boil for 20 minutes. Stir occasionally.

7. Add ½ of the Willamette hops (¼ ounce) to
   the wort, turn off the heat; stir and let sit
   (covered, if possible) for 10 minutes.

8. Add the boiled wort to your sanitized,
   rinsed fermenter. Add ice-cold water to
   make 5 gallons. When the temperature
   drops to 75°F or less, add the yeast.

9. If you use liquid yeast, open the swollen
   packet and add to the wort. If you use dry
   yeast, add the yeast to 1 cup of 90°F water
   for a few minutes before adding to the wort.
   (You can add the yeast directly to the wort
   and let it sit for a few minutes also, but rehydrating the yeast in warm water will improve
   the fermentation.) Stir the wort thoroughly
   with a sanitized spoon.

10. Put the lid on the fermenter tightly, insert
    the fermentation lock with the stopper into
    the hole in the lid, and fill it up about ¾ of
    the way with water or vodka. Let the wort
    ferment for a week or two until the fermen-
    tation ceases.

11. When fermentation is complete, siphon the
    beer into a sanitized bottling bucket. Boil

the corn sugar in about a cup of water; cool; stir gently into the beer. This provides the nutrients necessary for the yeast to carbonate the beer in the bottle.

12. Insert one end of the sanitized and rinsed hose into the bottling spigot and the other end to the bottle filler. Push the bottle filler down onto the bottom of the bottle and open the bottling spigot. Five gallons of beer will make about 2 cases, so make sure you sanitize this amount beforehand. Leave about ½–¾ inch of space at the top of the bottle. Cap the bottles.

13. Let the beer age for 2 weeks to 6 months. Chill and enjoy.

Note: The normal phase of fermentation will be a lag phase, usually 2 hours to 1.5 days, followed by a steady increase in intensity, usually lasting anywhere from 1 to 4 days. Fermentation abruptly slows down after this and tapers off to an occasional bubble being pushed out of the fermentation lock every 30 seconds or so. The main contributing factors to these fluctuations are the strain and initial amount of yeast being used, sanitation, and temperature intensity and consistency. For ale yeast, try to maintain temperatures between 65° and 75°. For lagers, temperatures of 65° down to 32° work best to maintain lager characteristics.

BREWMASTER'S ENTIRE BUTT
⧉ ⧉ ⧉

PAUL HEALY

MOUNTAIN MALT AND HOP SHOPPE— LAKE KATRINE & POUGHKEEPSIE, NEW YORK

The name of this authentic recipe is not derived from a part of the brewer's anatomy but rather from "entire," an early description of porter, and from "butt," an 108-imperial-gallon cask. The addition of treacle lends a truly English personality to this rich brew.

ORIGINAL GRAVITY: 1.055

FINAL GRAVITY: 1.021

POTENTIAL ALCOHOL: 4.4% ABV

INGREDIENTS

⅔ pound amber crystal malt

1.5 ounces Challenger hops

¼ pound black patent malt

1 ounce Fuggles hops

¼ pound roasted barley

1.5 ounces Bramling Cross hops

1 can Coopers unhopped dark malt extract

1 teaspoon gypsum

3 pounds plain amber DME

4 ounces black treacle

Coopers ale yeast

¾ cup corn sugar

BREWING PROCEDURES

1. In a 12-quart or larger stainless-steel pot, heat 1 gallon of water to 160°F and add 1 teaspoon of gypsum. Stir until dissolved and turn off heat. Place cracked grains in a nylon bag and immerse in water. Cover pot and allow grain to steep for 30 minutes. Remove grain bag and bring the "tea" to a boil. (If you do not have a nylon bag, add grains directly to water and strain.)

2. When boil is attained, turn off heat and add the malt extracts and treacle. (Putting DME in a bowl first makes it easier to add.) Turn on heat and return to a boil.

3. When the danger of a messy boilover has passed, add 1½ ounces of Challenger hops

and 1 ounce Fuggles hops (15 HBU), then cook at a rolling boil for 60 minutes.

4. Add 1 teaspoon of Irish moss and boil for 7 more minutes.

5. Add 1 ounce Bramling Cross hops for flavor. Boil for 8 more minutes. Turn off heat.

6. Add ½ ounce of Bramling Cross for aroma.

7. Take the brewpot from the stove and place it in a sink partially filled with cold water. Add 1 gallon of sanitary, refrigerated water (40°F) to the brewpot, then cover and place ice in the water around the brewpot. Never add ice directly to the wort! Let stand 15 minutes. Place 2 gallons of refrigerated water into the fermenter, then add the strained wort. Check the temperature (65–75°F is ideal). Top off to 5½ gallons with either more cold or room-temperature water.

8. With a sanitized measuring cup, scoop out ¾ cup and take a hydrometer reading. Discard sample.

9. Add the package of Coopers yeast to the fermenter when the temperature of the wort is 65–75°F; let sit 10 minutes, then stir vigorously to aerate. Snap the fermenter lid on, fill the airlock halfway with water, and place in lid. Place fermenter in a spot where the temperature will remain a constant 65–70°F.

10. Ferment in the primary for 5–6 days, then rack into a glass carboy for 2 weeks.

11. When brew is clear, siphon into a bottling bucket. Dissolve priming sugar into 1 cup boiling water, cool, and gently stir into beer with a sanitized spoon. CAUTION: If finished volume is less than 5 gallons, scale proportionately (e.g., 4½ gallons = ⅔ cup sugar).

12. Keep in a warm place for 7–10 days, then move to a cool place to age for 2 weeks.

BLACK HEART PORTER
🍺 🍺 🍺

THE CELLAR HOMEBREW—SEATTLE, WASHINGTON

"A style steeped in tradition. During the eighteenth century, bartenders would blend three different beers from three different casks to create a more flavorful, complex beverage. Porter is rumored to have been brewed to replace these 'three thread' beers, and named for the workmen that guzzled them. A 'few grains' shy of a stout, our porter has a dark brown color, roasted/coffee taste, and a malty finish."

ORIGINAL GRAVITY: 1.053

FINAL GRAVITY: 1.014

POTENTIAL ALCOHOL: 5.1% ABV

INGREDIENTS (FOR 5.5 GALLONS)

- ½ pound English crystal malt (crushed)
- ¼ pound chocolate malt (crushed)
- ¼ pound black patent malt (crushed)
- 1 can of Alexander's amber "Kicker"
- 1½ ounces Fuggles hops and ½ ounce Tettnang hops (boiling)
- 1 ounce Tettnang hops and ½ ounce Fuggles hops (finishing)
- Burton water salts (optional; add during step 4)
- 1 package Whitbread dry ale or British Ale liquid yeast
- ¾ cup corn sugar for priming

BREWING PROCEDURES

Note: If you are using the British Ale liquid yeast with this recipe, be sure to start that yeast at least 1 to 3 days before doing any of the brewing steps below. Follow the package directions and use the yeast in step 5.

1. Place the crushed English crystal, chocolate, and black patent malts in a strainer bag. Add this bag of grain to your brewing kettle, which contains 2 to 2½ gallons brewing water. Bring the brewing water to a boil, then remove the bag of grains. It is not a good idea to boil these specialty grains for any length of time, as they may contribute a bitter or grainy taste to the finished beer.

2. Sparge (rinse) the bag of grains with about 1 quart of hot tap water into the brewing kettle; dispose of the spent grains.

3. Remove the brewing kettle from the burner and add the 6 pounds of British light malt syrup and the 1 can of Alexander's amber "Kicker." The syrup is easier to pour if the can has been previously placed in hot water. Also, rinse the can with hot water to ensure that all the syrup goes into the kettle. Stir the mixture, now called "wort," until it boils. Watch carefully at this time because the wort may boil over. You can prevent this by pouring a cup of cold water into the over-boiling wort.

4. At boiling point, add the Fuggles and Tettnang boiling hops. Hops can be placed in a hop bag or added loose, to be later strained out after the boil using a strainer bag. Time the boil for about 1 hour, stirring occasionally. After the first 10 minutes of this boil, remove 2 cups of wort in measuring cup and cover with foil or plastic. Cool to 90°F for use in step 5 below.

5. Making the yeast starter: For dry yeast, use ½ cup warm tap water (90–100°F). Sprinkle the contents of yeast packet into that water, cover for at least 15 minutes, and then add to the 2 cups of wort you prepared in step 4. Cover and set aside for use in step 7 below. For liquid yeast, prepare 1 to 3 days ahead of brewing time per package instructions. Open the swollen package and add the contents to the 2 cups of wort as prepared in step 4.

6. After the wort has boiled for that 1 hour, add the Fuggles and Tettnang finishing hops. Place them in the hop bag, which has been emptied of the spent boiling hops, and place them in the boiling kettle or just add the finishing hops directly to the brewing kettle. They will be strained later in step 8.

7. Let the boil continue for 5 minutes. This gives the beer its hop aroma. Remove the pot from the burner and let it cool, covered, for about 20 minutes.

8. Pour 3 gallons of cold water into the sanitized open fermenter fitted with strainer bag; if loose finishing hops were used in step 6, strain the warm wort from step 7 into the cold water. Top up the fermenter to 5½ gallons using cold tap water. Cover the fermenter and cool the wort as rapidly as possible.

9. When the wort has cooled to about 80°, add the yeast starter and ferment as you usually do.

BLACK DOG PORTER
⫴ ⫴ ⫴

THE HOME BREWERY—OZARK, MISSOURI
This strong porter pushes the upper range of common original gravities for the style, offering the drinker a balance of mellow European hops and a high final gravity, which will lend a satisfying malt sweetness.

ORIGINAL GRAVITY: 1.060

FINAL GRAVITY: 1.020

POTENTIAL ALCOHOL: 5.5% ABV

INGREDIENTS

- ½ pound dark crystal malt, crushed
- ¼ pound black patent malt, crushed
- ⅓ pound chocolate malt, crushed
- 6.6 pounds (2 packs) Yellow Dog malt extract
- ¾ ounce Northern Brewer pellets (8.1% AA) in boil
- ½ ounce Tettnanger hop pellets (5.0% AA) finishing
- ½ ounce Hallertauer hop pellets (5.1% AA) after heat is off
- ½ teaspoon Irish moss
- 2 packs Doric dry ale yeast *or* 1 Wyeast Liquid Ale yeast
- ¾ cup corn sugar for priming

BREWING PROCEDURES

1. Heat 5 gallons of water in a large kettle. Add crushed grains. Many people don't have a kettle that large, but heat as much as you can (at least 2 gallons). Remove grains from kettle at 170°. When the water is boiling, turn off the heat and add the malt extract to the water. Use a spoon and stir until you are sure no malt extract is sticking to the bottom of the kettle. Then turn the heat back on.

2. Bring the kettle back to a boil and stir occasionally so the ingredients won't burn on the bottom of the kettle. If your recipe calls for bittering hops, now is the time to add them and stir them in. Watch out for a boilover. In the early part of the boil, the kettle usually tries to boil over once or twice, so control this by adjusting the heat. Later in the boil, the surface tension changes and boiling over is not a problem. Keep stirring occasionally and let the beer (wort) boil hard for 1 hour. Stir in the ½ teaspoon of Irish moss in your recipe about 15 minutes before the end of the boil.

3. When finishing hops are called for in your recipe, stir them in 2 minutes before the end of the boil. Using finishing hops at the end of the boil adds a fresh aroma and flavor to the beer, and the use of finishing hops is appropriate in most beer styles.

4. Pour the hot beer (wort) into the primary fermenter. It is not necessary to strain the wort if you used hop pellets. Add cold water to bring the total volume up to 5 gallons. If you are using our B3a Fermenter (the one in the kits), the 5-gallon mark is the bottom ring. Cover the fermenter and wait until the temperature is down to 75°F. If you have a wort chiller, use it to bring the temperature down quickly. At 75° or less, add the yeast in your recipe. Just tear open the pack(s) and sprinkle it on the wort. Close the fermenter with the lid, stopper, and airlock. Remember to put water (or vodka) in the airlock. Vodka evaporates more quickly, but bacteria won't live in it.

5. Fermentation should start within 24 hours, and may continue for between 1 day and 2 weeks, depending on the type of yeast, the recipe, and the temperature. Leave the beer alone and don't open the lid. When the airlock has not bubbled for several days and the beer is flat, still, and clearing, it is ready to bottle.

6. To bottle, siphon about 1 pint of beer into a pan and warm it on the stove. Add exactly ¾ cup of corn sugar to the pan and stir until it is dissolved. Pour this back into the beer and stir gently but well to distribute the sugar. Siphon or tap into clean sanitized bottles and cap. Keep the bottles at room temperature. After a week, put a bottle in the refrigerator and try it. It will be best in about 3 weeks.

BRITISH PUB PORTER
⫿ ⫿ ⫿

THE HOME BEER, WINE, &
    CHEESEMAKING SHOP—WOODLAND
    HILLS, CALIFORNIA

As the name implies, this complex porter is
brewed to a lower gravity so that more than one
can be enjoyed without overpowering. The
Swedish yeast strain accentuates a malty finish.

ORIGINAL GRAVITY: 1.048

FINAL GRAVITY: 1.013

POTENTIAL ALCOHOL: 4.5% ABV

IBUs: 32

COLOR: 20 SRM

INGREDIENTS

   4 ounces Gambrinus honey malt

   4 ounces Belgian biscuit malt

   4 ounces Belgian aromatic malt

   8 ounces chocolate malt

   2 ounces black patent malt

   8 pounds Alexander's light malt extract

   0.75 ounce Target hop pellets at 8.1% AA
       (60 minutes)

   0.5 ounce Challenger hop pellets at 7.2%
       AA (20 minutes)

   0.75 ounce Fuggles whole hops at 4.3% AA
       (2 minutes)

   1 teaspoon Irish moss

   1 teaspoon gypsum

   Wyeast 1742 Swedish Ale yeast

   ¾ cup corn sugar for priming

BREWING PROCEDURES

1. Steep (soak) the grains in 2 quarts of 150°F
   water for 30–40 minutes. Sparge (rinse)
   with 2.5 quarts of 150°F water into your boiling pot. Discard grain. No water over 170°F

with grain. Do not oversparge. Do not
squeeze grain bag.

2. After adding 2.5 gallons of water and dissolving the malt, bring pot to a gentle but rolling
   boil. Skim all foam before starting the hop
   sequence. Add Irish moss the last 20 minutes
   to remove the protein missed in steps 1 and
   2. Add the gypsum into the boil. It adds hardness, accentuating the crisp hop character.

3. Ferment at an average of 62–66°F. This
   keeps the fruity esters to a minimum. Pitch
   (add) yeast when your water bath around
   the fermenter reads 70–80°F. Maintain this
   temperature until the first signs of fermentation (about 10–12 hours). If using a yeast
   starter (highly recommended), fermentation can start in 2–3 hours. Use ¾ cup sugar
   for priming.

ORFORDVILLE PORTER REVISITED
⫿ ⫿

PAUL WHITE, HEAD BREWER, THE SEVEN
    BARREL BREWERY—WEST LEBANON,
    NEW HAMPSHIRE

"You can change anything in this recipe except
the can of John Bull dark. It's a tried-and-true
ingredient that has always given the best flavor
in this recipe."

ORIGINAL GRAVITY: 1.051

FINAL GRAVITY: 1.014

POTENTIAL ALCOHOL: 4.8% ABV

INGREDIENTS

   8 ounces crystal malt

   4 ounces chocolate malt

2 ounces black patent malt

1 can John Bull dark-hopped syrup

1 can John Bull light-hopped syrup

1 package Edme ale yeast

¾ cup corn sugar for bottling

BREWING PROCEDURES

1. Put crushed grains into 2 quarts cold water and raise temperature to 160°F. Cover and steep for 20 minutes. Strain the grains and sparge with 1 quart of 170°F water.

2. Add more hot water and stir in extracts. Bring to a boil and boil for 15 minutes.

3. Cool and ferment with Edme ale yeast. Bottle when ready and age for as long as you can stand it (usually 1 week).

PORTER

BEER & WINE HOBBY—WOBURN, MASSACHUSETTS

This recipe allows the intermediate mash-extract brewer considerable latitude in choosing their favorite malt extract. The German-style hops provide a nice mild bitterness. The Australian yeast makes the international mix of ingredients complete by bringing a complex woodiness to this ale.

ORIGINAL GRAVITY: 1.040–44

FINAL GRAVITY: 1.009–13

POTENTIAL ALCOHOL: 4% ABV

INGREDIENTS

½ pound English crystal malt

½ pound chocolate malt

¼ pound biscuit malt

2 cans light malt extract

1 ounce Perle hops (boil)

½ ounce Tettnang hops (flavor)

½ ounce Tettnang hops (finishing)

1 teaspoon Burton water salts

1 teaspoon Irish moss

1 package liquid Australian or American Ale yeast

¾ cup corn sugar

BREWING PROCEDURES

1. Add 2 gallons of cold water to your pot; put ½ pound crushed English crystal malt, ½ pound crushed chocolate malt, and ¼ pound crushed biscuit malt into your muslin bag and tie. Place bag in cold water and bring almost to a boil. Remove from heat and let grains steep for 15 minutes. Remove grains and discard.

2. Add 2 cans of light malt extract, 1 ounce of Perle hops, 1 teaspoon Burton water salts and dissolve. Return to boil for 40 minutes. At this point add 1 teaspoon of Irish moss and ½ ounce of Tettnang hops, and boil for 20 more minutes. Add the remaining ½ ounce of Tettnang hops during the final 2 minutes of the boil. Remove from heat.

3. Put 3 gallons of cold water in your primary fermenter, add boiled wort, and top off to 5¼ gallons total volume. When wort has cooled to between 65–75°F, pitch prepared yeast starter and proceed as usual.

4. Ferment to completion.

5. Prime with ¾ cup of corn sugar and bottle.

STOUT

"Stout," an archaic term meaning "strong," was once used to describe high-alcohol beers in a variety of styles. Stout, as we know it today, originated from a porter of high gravity called "stout porter." The most famous is Guinness, which has dominated the market since its introduction in 1759. This "dry" (because of its hop bitterness) or "Irish stout" is served at room temperature (68°F) in Ireland and generally at cellar temperatures (50–57°F) or colder in the U.K. and elsewhere. Russian Imperial Stout is actually the trade name of a bottle-conditioned product of the Courage Ltd. company that was originally exported to the royal court of Czarist Russia. However, the term "imperial stout" is often used colloquially and by other breweries to describe a similarly sweet, high-alcohol ale that is technically a barley wine. So-called foreign export stout, such as those popular in Belgium and Africa, are merely more alcoholic versions of dry stout, and are usually contract-brewed around the world by British and Irish firms. Practically all stouts have been made less assertive in recent years to accommodate what marketing directors feel are the tastes of younger drinkers and women.

Noteworthy commercial examples in the dry stout category include Murphy's Irish Stout, Guinness Extra Stout, of course, and the microbrewed North Coast Old No. 38 Stout and Riverside's 7th Street Stout. In the sweet stout category: Mackeson's Sweet Stout and Young's Oatmeal Stout. In the imperial stout category: Courage Russian Imperial Stout and Samuel Smith's Imperial Stout. The rarer microbrewed example is well represented by Brooklyn Brewery's Black Chocolate Stout.

Homebrewers should aim for a full-bodied, black beer made from English or Scottish malts that is low in hop flavor and aroma but high *or* low in hop bitterness, depending on the substyle. Emphasize the malty, caramel, and roasted barley qualities, but use water with enough temporary hardness to counteract the acidity of the dark malts. A long primary fermentation in the cooler range of ale temperatures is advised to keep diacetyl levels low. Carbonation should be high, with a thick, lacy head that lasts until the end.

STOUT BASICS

ORIGINAL GRAVITY: 1.040–56

FINAL GRAVITY: 1.008–20

IBUs: 15–50

COLOR (SRM): 35–70

ALCOHOL BY VOLUME: 3–6%

FIRE BREATHING STOUT

⚔ ⚔ ⚔

PAUL HEALY

MOUNTAIN MALT AND HOP SHOPPE—
LAKE KATRINE & POUGHKEEPSIE,
NEW YORK

This is a strong stout like you are likely to find brewed in Belgium or Africa. It is bursting with roastiness and prominent malt flavors, but is held in check by the intensely flavored Bullion hops that are perfect for such a beer. The American Ale yeast keeps the hefty flavor profile clean and balanced.

ORIGINAL GRAVITY: 1.074

FINAL GRAVITY: 1.024

POTENTIAL ALCOHOL: 6.9% ABV

INGREDIENTS

> ½ pound dark crystal malt
>
> 8 pounds Mountmellick unhopped dark malt extract
>
> ¼ pound chocolate malt
>
> 1 ounce Northern Brewer hops
>
> ⅔ pound roasted barley
>
> 1 ounce Bullion hops
>
> 4 teaspoons gypsum
>
> Wyeast 1056 American Ale yeast
>
> ¾ cup corn sugar for priming

BREWING PROCEDURES

1. In a 12-quart or larger stainless-steel pot, heat 1 gallon of water to 160°F and add 4 teaspoons of gypsum. Stir until dissolved and turn off heat. Place cracked grains in a nylon bag and immerse in water. Cover pot and allow grain to steep for 30 minutes. Remove grain bag and bring the "tea" to a boil. (If you do not have a nylon bag, add grains directly to water and strain.)

2. When boil is attained, turn off heat and add the malt extract. Turn on heat and return to a boil.

3. When the danger of a messy boilover has passed, add 1 ounce Northern Brewer and 1 ounce of Bullion hops (15 HBU) and cook at a rolling boil for 45 minutes.

4. Add 1 teaspoon of Irish moss and boil for 15 more minutes.

5. Take the brewpot from the stove and place it in a sink partially filled with cold water. Add 1 gallon of sanitary, refrigerated water (40°F) to the brewpot, then cover and place ice in the water around the brewpot. Never add ice directly to the wort! Let stand 15 minutes. Place 2 gallons of refrigerated water into the fermenter, then add the strained wort. Check the temperature (65–75°F is ideal). Top off to 5½ gallons with either more cold or room-temperature water.

6. With a sanitized measuring cup, scoop out ¾ cup and take a hydrometer reading. Discard sample.

7. Add the package of yeast to the fermenter when the temperature of the wort is 65–75°F, then stir vigorously to aerate. Snap the fermenter lid on, fill the airlock halfway with water, and place in lid. Place fermenter in a spot where the temperature will remain a constant 65–70°F.

8. Ferment in the primary for 5–6 days, then rack into a glass carboy for 2 weeks.

9. When brew is clear, siphon into a bottling bucket. Dissolve priming sugar into 1 cup boiling water, cool, and gently stir into beer with a sanitized spoon. CAUTION: If finished volume is less than 5 gallons, scale proportionately (e.g., 4½ gallons = ⅔ cup sugar).

10. Keep in a warm place for 7–10 days, then move to a cool place to age for 2 weeks.

McCellar's Stout
⏣ ⏣ ⏣

The Cellar Homebrew—Seattle, Washington

A stout in the great tradition of the Irish pub draft. The sweetness of the residual sugars is carefully balanced by the appealing bitterness of roasted specialty grains.

Original Gravity: 1.060

Final Gravity: 1.016

Potential Alcohol: 5.9% ABV

Ingredients (for 5.5 Gallons)

> ¾ **pound English crystal malt (crushed)**
> ½ **pound roasted barley (crushed)**
> ¼ **pound black patent malt (crushed)**
> 3.3 **pounds English dark malt syrup**
> 3 **pounds English dark dry malt extract**
> 1 **can Alexander's amber "Kicker"**
> 1 **ounce Chinook hops (boiling)**
> 1 **ounce Fuggles hops (finishing)**
> 1 **teaspoon gypsum (optional, add during step 4)**
> **Edme dry ale yeast or Irish Ale liquid yeast**
> ¾ **cup corn sugar for priming**

Brewing Procedures

Note: If you are using the Irish Ale liquid yeast with this recipe, be sure to start that yeast at least 1 to 3 days before doing any of the brewing steps below. Follow the package directions and use the yeast in step 5 below.

1. Place the crushed English crystal, roasted barley, and black patent in a strainer bag. Add this bag of grain to your brewing kettle, which contains 2 to 2½ gallons brewing water. Bring the brewing water to a boil, then remove the bag of grains. It is not a good idea to boil these specialty grains for any length of time, as they may contribute a bitter or grainy taste to the finished beer.

2. Sparge (rinse) the bag of grains with about 1 quart of hot tap water into the brewing kettle; dispose of the spent grains.

3. Remove the brewing kettle from the burner and add the 3.3 pounds of English dark malt syrup, the 3 pounds of English dark dry malt, and the 1 can of Alexander's amber "Kicker." The syrup is easier to pour if the can has been previously placed in hot water. Also, rinse the can with hot water to ensure that all the syrup goes into the kettle. Stir the mixture, now called "wort," until it boils. Watch carefully at this time because the wort may boil over. You can prevent this by pouring a cup of cold water into the over-boiling wort.

4. At boiling point, add the Chinook boiling hops. Hops can be placed in a hop bag or added loose, to be later strained out after the boil using a strainer bag. Time the boil for about 1 hour, stirring occasionally. After the first 10 minutes of this boil, remove 2 cups of wort in measuring cup and cover with foil or plastic. Cool to 90°F for use in step 5 below.

5. Making the yeast starter: For dry yeast, use ½ cup warm tap water (90–100°F). Sprinkle the contents of yeast packet into that water, cover for at least 15 minutes, and then add to the 2 cups of wort you prepared in step 4. Cover and set aside for use in step 7 below. For liquid yeast, prepare 1 to 3 days ahead

of brewing time per package instructions. Open the swollen package and add the contents to the 2 cups of wort as prepared in step 4.

6. After the wort has boiled for that 1 hour, add the Fuggles finishing hops. Place them in the hop bag, which has been emptied of the spent boiling hops, and place them in the boiling kettle or just add the finishing hops directly to the brewing kettle. They will be strained later in step 8.

7. Let the boil continue for 5 minutes. This gives the beer its hop aroma. Remove the pot from the burner and let it cool, covered, for about 20 minutes.

8. Pour 3 gallons of cold water into the sanitized open fermenter fitted with strainer bag; if loose finishing hops were used in step 6, strain the warm wort from step 7 into the cold water. Top up the fermenter to 5½ gallons using cold tap water. Cover the fermenter and cool the wort as rapidly as possible.

9. When the wort has cooled to about 80° add the yeast starter and ferment as you usually do.

DEEP WINTER STOUT
⊞ ⊞ ⊞

THE VINEYARD—UPTON, MASSACHUSETTS

With 1½ pounds of roasted grains in the mix, this recipe is designed for the lover of a strong stout with a big, roasted coffee-chocolate character. The hops used provide a traditional mellow bitterness in a supporting role.

ORIGINAL GRAVITY: 1.056

FINAL GRAVITY: 1.014

POTENTIAL ALCOHOL: 5.5% ABV

INGREDIENTS

½ pound roasted barley

½ pound black malt

½ pound chocolate malt

1 pound crystal malt

3.3 pounds Northwestern Gold unhopped

3.1 pounds Superbrau dark unhopped

2 ounces Northern Brewer hop pellets (boiling)

½ ounce Fuggles hops plug (last 10 minutes)

1 packet Whitbread ale yeast

½ cup priming sugar

BREWING PROCEDURES

1. Crush and put all grains into 2 gallons cold water for 10 minutes, then slowly raise the temperature to a boil. Once boiling commences, remove from heat. Strain liquid into boiling pot.

2. Add ½ gallon water, Northwestern and Superbrau malt extracts, 2 ounces Northern Brewer hop pellets, and bring to a boil for 40 minutes. Add ½ ounce Fuggles during the last 10 minutes of the boil.

3. Strain into primary fermenter and add cold water to make 5 gallons and let cool.

4. Pitch yeast when temperature drops below 80°F. Primary fermentation: 4 days at 60–65°F. Secondary fermentation: 10 days at 60–65°F.

5. At bottling time boil ½ cup priming sugar with 1 cup water for bulk priming.

DRY IRISH STOUT
⊞ ⊞ ⊞

BOSTON BREWERS SUPPLY CO.—
JAMAICA PLAIN, MASSACHUSETTS

"The principal ingredient that distinguishes dry stout from porter is unmalted roasted barley, which contributes the opaque black color and the dry, roasted, coffeelike flavors associated with this style. Ours uses a high-quality English extract, a blend of roasted malts and traditional bittering hops that add authenticity. This is a quick-maturing stout that can be enjoyed just weeks after bottling."

ORIGINAL GRAVITY: 1.048–50

FINAL GRAVITY: 1.012–14

POTENTIAL ALCOHOL: 4.7% ABV

IBUs: 40 to 44

HBUs: 12 to 13

INGREDIENTS

> **8 ounces English crystal malt**
> **8 ounces English roasted malt**
> **8 ounces English black malt**
> **4 ounces flaked barley**
> **6 pounds English dark extract syrup**
> **1 pound English dark dry malt extract**
> **1 ounce Northern Brewer hop pellets**
> **1 ounce Kent Goldings hop pellets**
> **1 teaspoon Irish moss**
> **1 package dry ale yeast**
> **¾ cup corn sugar for priming**

BREWING PROCEDURES

1. Secure the grains in the muslin straining bag. Pour 2 gallons of cold water into your brewpot, apply heat, and add the grain bag. Heat to a near boil (about 155°F), then remove the grain bag, drain, and discard.

2. Turn off the heat and, while stirring constantly, dissolve all of the malt extract. As soon as the boil begins, add all of the Northern Brewer and Goldings hops and start timing the boil; the total elapsed time will be 45 minutes. Maintain a good rolling boil and stir occasionally. After 25 minutes add the Irish moss flakes; continue to boil for 20 minutes, then cover and remove the pot from the heat.

Remember that after the wort has cooled, it is highly vulnerable to contamination; everything that comes into contact with it from this point on must be thoroughly sanitized!

3. Cool the wort as quickly as possible. A wort chiller works best, but if you haven't got one yet a cold water bath will do the trick. Place the covered pot in your kitchen sink and fill with ice and cold water. When the temperature has fallen to about 90°F, transfer the wort, through a strainer if possible, into your fermenter. Top off with enough cold water to reach a 5-gallon level and stir or shake well. If you are using a glass carboy for fermentation, it is a good idea to add the cold water first. Draw off a small sample and take both a hydrometer and a temperature reading; always discard the sample used.

4. When the wort has cooled to 65–70°F, you are ready to add the yeast. Once the yeast has been added, attach an airlock and keep the fermenter in a cool, dark location where temperature fluctuations are minimal, ideally 68°F. Active fermentation should become visible in the next 12 to 24 hours and will continue for about 3 to 5 days. This stout can be bottled immediately but will benefit from a week of secondary fermenta-

tion. If you choose to bottle right away, take both a temperature and a hydrometer reading. If the final gravity is within the range stated above, proceed directly to the bottling instructions below; if not, wait another couple of days and check again.

5. When visible signs of fermentation have ceased, gently siphon the beer to the sanitized secondary fermenter (ideally a 5-gallon glass carboy), leaving all sediment behind. Attach an airlock and allow the beer to settle for an additional 5 to 7 days at the same temperature of primary fermentation.

6. At the end of this period, draw off a small sample and check the final gravity. By now it should be within the range stated above; if not wait another couple of days and check again. Prepare to bottle.

BOTTLING AND CONDITIONING

1. Sanitize all of your siphoning and bottling equipment, bottles, and caps.

2. Boil the 6 ounces of corn sugar in about a pint of water and pour it into your bottling bucket. Gently siphon the beer (again leaving sediment behind) out of the fermenter into the bucket, making sure the flow is directed to the bottom of the bucket; avoid splashing or agitating the beer. Reserve the last remnants to take thermometer and hydrometer readings; this will be your final gravity.

3. Using your siphon tubing and bottle filler, fill each bottle to within an inch from the top and cap immediately. Store the bottles upright at room temperature; about 65–70°F for a minimum of 3 weeks. Serve cool, not cold. Enjoy!

PIRATES BREW IRISH STOUT

🍺 🍺

JAY GARRISON, HEAD BREWER, PIRATE BREWERY

BREWBUDDYS—REDONDO BEACH, CALIFORNIA

This is a good recipe for the intermediate brewer wanting to experiment with an American hop variety in an Irish stout context. The mild bitterness of Cluster marries nicely with the highly roasted flavor of this brew.

ORIGINAL GRAVITY: 1.049

FINAL GRAVITY: 1.013

POTENTIAL ALCOHOL: 4.6% ABV

INGREDIENTS

1 pound 120 °L crystal malt

5 ounces roasted barley

2 ounces black patent malt

6 pounds dark liquid malt extract

2½ ounces Cluster hops

Wyeast 1084 Irish Ale or dry ale yeast

¾ cup corn sugar for priming

BREWING PROCEDURES

1. If you selected Wyeast liquid yeast, you must break the inner packet before you begin to brew. Allow 1 day for each month after the manufacture date printed on the front. If you're using the dry yeast that came with the Pirates Brew Kit, go ahead and get to it.

2. Prepare the grains. The grain should be crushed; if you did not get the grains crushed at the shop, crush them with some sort of rolling pin. You can either mix the grain with 2 quarts of water and heat it until it starts to boil, or heat it to about 165°F and steep for about 15 minutes.

3. Strain the grains, collecting the liquid into your brewpot. Rinse the grain (sparge) with 2 quarts of hot (170–180°F) water.

4. Add the bag of extract and 1 gallon of water to the brewpot. (You might want to rest the bag of extract in hot water for a while to soften it up.) Bring the wort to a hard rolling boil.

5. Add 2 ounces of the Cluster hops to the wort and boil for 40 minutes. Stir occasionally.

6. Add the remaining ½ ounce of the Cluster hops to the wort and boil for 20 minutes. Stir occasionally.

7. Add the boiled wort to your sanitized, rinsed fermenter. Add ice-cold water to make 5 gallons. When the temperature drops to 75°F or less, add the yeast.

8. If you use liquid yeast, open the swollen packet and add to the wort. If you use dry yeast, add the yeast to 1 cup of 90°F water for a few minutes before adding to the wort. (You can add the yeast directly to the wort and let it sit for a few minutes also, but rehydrating the yeast in warm water will improve the fermentation.) Stir the wort thoroughly with a sanitized spoon.

9. Put the lid on the fermenter tightly, insert the fermentation lock with the stopper into the hole in the lid, and fill it about ¾ of the way with water or vodka. Let the wort ferment for a week or two until the fermentation ceases.

10. When fermentation is complete, siphon the beer into a sanitized bottling bucket. Boil the corn sugar in about a cup of water; cool; stir gently into the beer. This provides the nutrients necessary for the yeast to carbonate the beer in the bottle.

11. Insert one end of the sanitized and rinsed hose into the bottling spigot and the other end to the bottle filler. Push the bottle filler down onto the bottom of the bottle and open the bottling spigot. Five gallons of beer will make about 2 cases, so make sure you sanitize this amount beforehand. Leave about ½–¾ inch of space at the top of the bottle. Cap the bottles.

12. Let the beer age for 2 weeks to 6 months. Chill and enjoy.

Note: The normal phase of fermentation will be a lag phase, usually 2 hours to 1.5 days, followed by a steady increase in intensity, usually lasting anywhere from 1 to 4 days. Fermentation abruptly slows down after this and tapers off to an occasional bubble being pushed out of the fermentation lock every 30 seconds or so. The main contributing factors to these fluctuations are the strain and initial amount of yeast being used, sanitation, and temperature intensity and consistency. For ale yeast, try to maintain temperatures between 65° and 75°. For lagers, temperatures of 65° down to 32° work best to maintain lager characteristics.

BLACK DRAGON EXPORT STOUT
▦ ▦ ▦

THE HOME BEER, WINE, & CHEESEMAK-
ING SHOP—WOODLAND HILLS,
CALIFORNIA

The Belgian ingredients of this stout bring a strong bready malt aroma and flavor to this complex brew in addition to the traditional roasted malt. Its strength makes it the type of stout popular in Belgium.

ORIGINAL GRAVITY: 1.064

FINAL GRAVITY: 1.015

POTENTIAL ALCOHOL: 6.5% ABV

IBUs: 47

COLOR: 40 SRM

INGREDIENTS

> 8 ounces Gambrinus honey malt
>
> 4 ounces Belgian biscuit malt
>
> 4 ounces Belgian aromatic malt
>
> 8 ounces chocolate malt
>
> 1 pound flaked barley
>
> 1.5 pounds roasted barley
>
> 6 pounds Royal light DME
>
> 4 ounces wheat solids
>
> 1 ounce Target hop pellets at 8.1% AA (60 minutes)
>
> 0.5 ounce Bramling Cross hop pellets at 7.1% AA (45 minutes)
>
> 1 ounce Kent Goldings hop pellets at 4.1% AA (20 minutes)
>
> 2 teaspoons Irish moss
>
> 2 teaspoons calcium carbonate
>
> Wyeast 1084 Irish Ale
>
> ¾ cup corn sugar for priming

BREWING PROCEDURES

1. Seep (soak) the grains in 2 quarts of 150°F water for 30–40 minutes. Sparge (rinse) with 2.5 quarts of 150°F water into your boiling pot. Discard grain. No water over 170°F with grain. Do not oversparge. Do not squeeze grain bag.

2. After adding 2.5 gallons of water and dissolving the malt, bring pot to a gentle but rolling boil. Skim all foam before starting the hop sequence. Add Irish moss the last 20 minutes to remove the protein missed in steps 1 and 2. Add the calcium carbonate into the boil. It adds softness and neutralizes the acidic quality of the dark grains.

3. Ferment at an average of 68–72°F. The resulting buttery/diacetyl flavors are appropriate for Irish ales. Pitch (add) yeast when your water bath around the fermenter reads 70–80°F. Maintain this temperature until the first signs of fermentation (about 10–12 hours). If using a yeast starter (highly recommended), fermentation can start in 2–3 hours. Use ¾ cup sugar for priming.

INSPIRATION STOUT

JEFF PZENA

THE MODERN BREWER CO. INC.— SOMERVILLE, MASSACHUSETTS

Using a German altbier yeast may seem odd in brewing a stout, but this strain actually works quite well. Its dry, crisp, and complex character perfectly matches the complex nature of the diverse ingredients used. It balances the sweetness of the crystal malt and accentuates the dryness brought by the wheat malt.

ORIGINAL GRAVITY: 1.060

FINAL GRAVITY: 1.013–1.017

POTENTIAL ALCOHOL: 5.6–6.1% ABV

INGREDIENTS

> 1 pound roasted barley
>
> 8.5 pounds pale barley malt
>
> 0.125 pound black patent malt
>
> 0.5 pound wheat malt
>
> 0.5 pound steel cut oats
>
> 0.5 pound crystal malt
>
> 0.5 pound dark brown sugar
>
> 1.25 ounces Chinook hops (boil) 11.9% AA (50 minutes)

1 ounce Cascade hops (flavor) 5.9%AA (20 minutes)

0.5 ounce Mt. Hood hops (aroma) (5 minutes)

0.5 ounce water crystals

1 tablespoon Irish moss for fining

Wyeast 1007 liquid ale yeast (German Ale/Mild Alt)

1¼ cups dried malt for priming

BREWING PROCEDURES

1. Add cracked grains to 3.5 gallons of 173° water and stir thoroughly. Put in oven on hold (warm) and let mash for 90 minutes (mash temperature settles to 151–153°F).

2. Put mash on stove and slowly heat to 165°F. Sparge with 4.25 gallons of 168° water. Bring to boil, add brown sugar. When boil resumes, begin the hop additions and add water crystals and Irish moss.

3. At end of boil, chill as quickly as possible (wort chiller or ice water bath). Funnel into fermenter and add prestarted yeast culture.

4. Ferment 7 days at approximately 67°F, then rack into clean carboy and let sit as cold as possible (refrigerate) for 7 days.

5. Rack, prime, bottle, and let condition for 4 weeks at 67°F.

IRISH CREAM STOUT
⬛ ⬛ ⬛
BEER & WINE HOBBY—WOBURN, MASSACHUSETTS

This intermediate recipe introduces a great traditional brewing ingredient used in British brewing—lactose. This unfermentable milk sugar lends a smooth mellow sweetness that is a wonderful complement to malt roastiness and hop bitterness.

ORIGINAL GRAVITY: 1.045–50

FINAL GRAVITY: 1.010–14

POTENTIAL ALCOHOL: 4.6% ABV

INGREDIENTS

½ pound English crystal malt

¼ pound chocolate malt

¼ pound roasted barley

2 cans of Mountmellick dark plain malt

2½ ounce Bullion whole hops (boil) (15 HBU) or 1½ ounce pellets

½ ounce Kent Golding hops (last 10 minutes)

1½ ounce Kent Golding Plug (dry hop)

½ pound lactose

1 package Burton water salts

Yeast Lab A03 London Ale yeast—starter required

¾ cup priming sugar

BREWING PROCEDURES

1. Add 2 gallons of cold water to your pot. Put ½ pound of crushed English crystal, ¼ pound chocolate malt, and ¼ pound crushed roasted barley into muslin bag and tie. Place bag in cold water and bring to a boil. When water comes to a boil, remove from heat and let steep for 5 minutes.

2. Remove grains and discard, return pot to heat, and bring to a boil. Add 2 cans of Mountmellick dark plain malt and 2½ ounces of Bullion loose hops (in muslin bag) and boil for 45 minutes. During the last 10 minutes of the boil, add ½ ounce plug of Kent Golding hops tied into a muslin bag, ½ pound lactose, and 1 package of Burton water salts.

3. Remove from heat, discard hops, and cool.

In primary fermenter, add some cold water and boiled liquid; bring total volume of liquid to 5¼ gallons. When wort has cooled to 65–75°F, add prepared yeast (instructions included).

4. Prepare dry hops; place 1½ ounce of Kent Golding Plugs in muslin bag, tie, and place in primary fermenter, stir, and allow hops to float. After 3 days of fermentation, remove hops and gently siphon beer into secondary fermenter. Finish fermenting.

5. Prime with ¾ cup corn sugar, bottle, and cap. For best results age a minimum of 4 weeks.

Ms. Bessy's Moo-Moo Milk Stout
🍺 🍺 🍺
E. C. Kraus Home Wine and Beer Making Supplies—Independence, Missouri

"The name of this beer may be a slight exaggeration. Milk stouts do not have milk in them but rather milk sugar (lactose). This recipe does make a sweeter stout than usual. Stouts in general tend to have a coffeelike aftertaste that comes from the roasted barley. With this milk stout recipe you have a residual sweetness from the milk sugar and malto-dextrin to balance out the roasted bitterness."

Original Gravity: 1.050–55

Final Gravity: 1.013–14

Potential Alcohol: 4.8–5.3% ABV

IBUs: 30–40

Color: 40+ SRM/89+ °L

Ingredients

12 ounces dark caramel malt

8 ounces chocolate malt

8 ounces roasted barley

3.3 pounds dark unhopped malt syrup

2 pounds dark dried malt extract (4.8 cups)

8 ounces lactose (milk sugar)

8 ounces malto-dextrin (5-minute boil time)

1¼ ounces Bullion pellet hops (30-minute boil time)

1 tablespoon Irish moss (15-minute boil time)

10 grams Manchester ale or Wyeast 2565 Kölsch ale yeast

¾ cup priming sugar

Brewing Procedures

1. Lightly crack malted barleys and put with 1½ gallons of cold water in a cooking pot. Slowly bring to a boil over a 30–45-minute period.

2. Once boiling, strain the grains out by the use of a colander or the like and discard.

3. Bring liquid back to a boil and add both the liquid and dried malt extracts and lactose. Bring back to a boil again.

4. Once boiling, add Bullion hops and boil for 30 minutes. During the last 15 minutes of the boil, add the Irish moss. During the last 5 minutes of the boil, fold in the malto-dextrin.

5. Now add the wort to your fermenter along with cold tap water up to 5 gallons. Make sure the wort has cooled to below 80°F and pitch yeast.

6. Attach airlock to fermenter and allow to ferment for 7–10 days or until finished and bottle with priming sugar as normal.

SWEET STOUT
⫴ ⫴ ⫴

DICK FOEHRINGER

THE BREWMEISTER—FAIR OAKS,
  CALIFORNIA

This seems like a sweet stout to enjoy on a cold winter evening by a roaring fireplace, but considering these strong versions are wildly popular in Africa and the Caribbean, perhaps summertime is just as appropriate for their enjoyment.

ORIGINAL GRAVITY: 1.078

FINAL GRAVITY: 1.026

POTENTIAL ALCOHOL: 7% ABV

INGREDIENTS

- ¼ **pound black patent malt**
- ¼ **pound roasted barley**
- ¼ **pound flaked barley**
- ½ **pound dextrine malt**
- 7 **pounds amber malt extract syrup**
- 3.3 **pounds Telfords or Edme dark extract syrup**
- 1 **ounce Bullion hops (boiling)**
- 1 **ounce Fuggles (boiling)**
- ½ **ounce Cascade hops (aromatic)**
- 2 **ounces lactose**
- 1 **teaspoon Irish moss**
- 1 **package ale yeast**
- 1 **teaspoon gelatin**
- ¾ **cup bottling sugar**

BREWING PROCEDURES

1. Put grains in 1½ to 2½ gallons of cold water. (Use a grain bag if you have one.) Bring to a near boil and turn off heat. Steep grain for 30 minutes, then remove grain.
2. Dissolve malt extract syrups and lactose, and return to heat. Bring to a boil. Add boiling hops and boil 45 minutes. Add Irish moss; boil 5 minutes. Add aromatic hops; boil 10 minutes. Total boiling time of 60 minutes.
3. Cold-break and strain wort into primary fermenter. Add cold water to make 5½ gallons. When cool (below 85°F) pitch yeast.
4. Ferment in a cool, dark place. When fermentation stops, transfer to secondary. Stir in dissolved gelatin and allow to clear (3–5 days).
5. When cleared, rack again, stir in bottling sugar, bottle and cap.
6. Age a minimum of 2–4 weeks.

MARK'S RYE STOUT
⫴ ⫴ ⫴

MARK LARROW

BEER & WINEMAKING SUPPLIES, INC.—
  NORTHAMPTON, MASSACHUSETTS

If milk sugar and oyster flavors can work in a stout, then why not rye? Rye, whether roasted or malted as in this recipe, lends a unique, spicy dryness that blends well into a stout's complex flavor profile.

ORIGINAL GRAVITY: 1.050

FINAL GRAVITY: 1.014

POTENTIAL ALCOHOL: 4.6% ABV

INGREDIENTS

- 12 **ounces roasted barley (crushed)**
- 4 **ounces flaked barley**
- 2 **ounces roasted rye (crushed)**
- 2 **ounces malted rye (crushed)**
- 8 **pounds British pale malt extract**
- 2 **ounces Bullion/Northern Brewer hops**
- ½ **ounce Fuggles aroma hops**

10–14 grams dry ale yeast or 1 Wyeast liquid yeast

¾ cup corn sugar for bottling

Brewing Procedures

Note: If using a liquid culture, activate 12–24 hours prior to brew session.

1. Place your blended grains in a 4–6-quart pan and stir in 2.25 quarts of 168°F water. Mix well. Grain should bring temperature down to approximately 150–154°F. Steep for 45–60 minutes in oven, small insulated cooler, or on stovetop at that temperature. While grain is steeping, bring 2 gallons of water up to 165–170°F in an 8–12-quart pot. Place strainer or colander over large kettle, then pour and spoon all grains and liquid in. Rinse with 1.5–2 gallons of 165°F water. Allow liquid to drain into kettle. Discard grains and bring liquid to a boil. Momentarily remove from heat.

2. Pour the malt extract into the pot, making sure to rinse out the container to get all the malt. Stir well.

3. Resume boiling (total time: 1 hour). Split the bittering hops into two equal portions. At the 15-minute mark, add half; at the 30 minute mark, add the second half. At 60 minutes, add the aroma hops.

4. Shut off the heat and let stand for 15 minutes.

5. Put 2 gallons of very cold water into your sterilized primary fermenter, then carefully pour the hot wort into it. Top up to 5 gallons with more cold water if necessary. If still above 85°F, run a cold water bath around your fermenter. The fermenter should then be stirred or swirled to aerate the wort. Take a hydrometer reading and write it down.

6. Wort should now be 70–85°F. Activate dry yeast by putting in 1 cup of sterile water at 75–95°F for 15 minutes, then stir well.

7. Now add the yeast and stir or swirl to aerate. Pitch yeast solution into fermenter. Put lid and airlock on. Fill airlock halfway with water.

8. Ferment at room temperature (64–68°F) for 3–4 days, then siphon over to a glass secondary fermenter for another 4–7 days. Take a hydrometer reading, and if low enough, bottle the beer into 53 reusable bar bottles (12-ounce size) or equivalent.

9. Make a priming syrup on the stove with 1 cup water and ¾ cup corn sugar, bring to a boil, and then shut heat off immediately, stirring well. Transfer beer back to primary or bottling bucket, mixing the priming syrup in well to distribute evenly. Siphon into bottles and cap them.

10. Remember to sanitize everything you use after the boil with a good chlorinated alkaline cleanser.

11. Allow bottles to sit at room temperature for 1–2 weeks before cooling down.

Russian Imperial Stout

⫞ ⫞ ⫞

Mike Knaub, Head Brewer, Chickies Rock Beers–Starview Brewing Company

Starview Brew–Mt. Wolf, Pennsylvania

This is an easy mash-extract recipe for a great imperial stout, with a considerable dose of lactose thrown in for sweetness. This is a perfect dessert beer for a cold winter evening with complex layers of molasses and roasted malt complexity.

ORIGINAL GRAVITY: 1.087

FINAL GRAVITY: 1.018

POTENTIAL ALCOHOL: 9.1% ABV

INGREDIENTS

> 1 pound crystal malt
>
> ⅓ pound black patent malt
>
> ⅓ pound roasted barley
>
> Two 3.3 pound cans English extra light plain malt extract
>
> 4 pounds plain light Dutch DME
>
> 25 HBUs Chinook pellet hops (boil 60 minutes)
>
> ½ ounce whole Cascade hops (boil 5 minutes)
>
> 1 pound lactose
>
> 1½ cups molasses
>
> Yeast Lab Irish Ale yeast with 1½ pint starter
>
> ¾ cup corn sugar for priming

BREWING PROCEDURES

1. Add grains to 2 gallons of cold water. Raise to 160°F and steep for 30 minutes.
2. Sparge grains, add the other 4 gallons of water, and bring to a boil.
3. Add extracts, lactose, and molasses. Bring back to a boil, add boil hops, and boil for 60 minutes.
4. Cool down to 70°F and add active starter culture.
5. Ferment in primary for 10 days at 70°F. Ferment in secondary for 14 days at 70°F.
6. Prime, bottle, and condition as normal.

OATMEAL STOUT

Oatmeal stout is a member of the "sweet stout" subcategory that traces its roots back to mild ales that were brewed with a portion of oatmeal to cut the green beer harshness. Oatmeal stout's new popularity among homebrewers demands that it be given a section of its own. Oatmeal stout has more body than Irish stout, is smoother, slightly sweeter, and often stronger, with a clean, roasted, malty flavor, and a "chewy" texture from the rolled or steel-cut oats. Hops should be used only to bitter; otherwise, the full roasted malt and oatmeal flavors, which should prevail, will be masked. Low- to medium-carbonate water and fermentation temperatures between 60° and 66°F are recommended. Samuel Smith's Oatmeal Stout and the American microbrewed Anderson Valley Barney Flats Oatmeal Stout are good commercial examples of this style to enjoy while brewing your own.

OATMEAL STOUT BASICS

ORIGINAL GRAVITY: 1.044–48

FINAL GRAVITY: 1.008–20

IBUs: 27–31

COLOR (SRM): 30–40

ALCOHOL BY VOLUME: 3.7–4.5%

OATMEAL STOUT
🍺🍺

WILLIAM'S BREWING—SAN LEANDRO,
CALIFORNIA

"A rich and smooth stout in the English tradition. This recipe is not overly sweet, yet it lacks the roasted character of a dry stout. Hops are used minimally to balance the sweetness, and aromatic hops are not used, as they detract from the oatmeal and malt character."

ORIGINAL GRAVITY: 1.047

FINAL GRAVITY: 1.016

POTENTIAL ALCOHOL: 4% ABV

INGREDIENTS

> 6 pounds William's Oatmeal Dark
> 1 pound William's American Dark
> 4 ounces lactose
> ¼ ounce English Fuggle hops AA 6.7% (boil) 60 minutes
> 1 ounce English Fuggle hops AA 6.7% (flavor) 30 minutes
> 1 package liquid Burton ale yeast
> 4½ ounces corn sugar for priming

BREWING PROCEDURES

1. Boil for 1 hour with at least 3 gallons of water, adding hops as indicated. Add the lactose during the last 10 minutes of the boil. Cool and add to a fermenter, adding water if needed to make 5 gallons.

2. Add the swollen pack of Burton ale yeast (started 2 or 3 days in advance). Allow to ferment at 60–75°F (ideally 65°F) for 12 days before checking with a hydrometer to see if the finishing gravity has been reached.

3. After the finishing gravity has been reached, prime and bottle. Age 2 weeks in a dark place before drinking, ideally at 60–65°F.

PIRATES BREW OATMEAL STOUT
🍺🍺🍺

JAY GARRISON, HEAD BREWER, PIRATE BREWERY

BREWBUDDYS—REDONDO BEACH, CALIFORNIA

BrewBuddys highly recommends this recipe to all who inquire about brewing an oatmeal stout. Customer Steve Crawford took first place at the Los Angeles County Fair using this recipe.

ORIGINAL GRAVITY: 1.059

FINAL GRAVITY: 1.015

POTENTIAL ALCOHOL: 5.8% ABV

INGREDIENTS

> 6 ounces crystal malt 80 °L
> 5 ounces chocolate malt
> 4 ounces roasted barley
> 8 ounces flaked oatmeal
> 7.5 pounds dark liquid extract
> 1 ounce Chinook hops
> 1 ounce Perle hops
> ½ ounce Hallertau hops
> 1 teaspoon gypsum
> Wyeast 1084 Irish Ale or dry ale yeast
> ¾ cup corn sugar for bottling

BREWING PROCEDURES

1. If you selected the Wyeast liquid yeast, you must break the inner packet before you begin to brew. Allow 1 day for each month after the manufacture date printed on the front. If you're using the dry yeast that came with the Pirates Brew Kit, go ahead and get to it.

2. Prepare the grains. The grains should be crushed; if you did not get the grains crushed at the shop, crush them with some sort of rolling pin. You can either mix the

grains and oatmeal flakes with 2 quarts of water and heat it until it starts to boil, or heat it to about 165°F and steep for about 15 minutes.

3. Strain the grains and flakes, collecting the liquid into your brewpot. Rinse the grain (sparge) with 2 quarts of hot (170–180°F) water.

4. Add the bag and can of extract, the gypsum, and 1 gallon of water to the brewpot. (You might want to rest the bag of extract in hot water for a while to soften it up.) Bring the wort to a soft rolling boil.

5. Add the Chinook hops to the wort and boil for 30 minutes. Stir occasionally.

6. Add the Perle hops to the wort and boil for 30 minutes. Stir occasionally.

7. Add the Hallertau hops to the wort, turn off the heat; stir and let sit (covered, if possible) for 10 minutes.

8. Add the boiled wort to your sanitized, rinsed fermenter. Add ice-cold water to make 5 gallons. When the temperature drops to 75°F or less, add the yeast.

9. If you use liquid yeast, open the swollen packet and add to the wort. If you use dry yeast, add the yeast to 1 cup of 90°F water for a few minutes before adding to the wort. (You can add the yeast directly to the wort and let it sit for a few minutes also, but rehydrating the yeast in warm water will improve the fermentation.) Stir the wort thoroughly with a sanitized spoon.

10. Put the lid on the fermenter tightly and insert the fermentation lock with the stopper into the hole in the lid and fill it up about ¾ of the way with water or vodka. Let the wort ferment for a week or two until the fermentation ceases.

11. When fermentation is complete, siphon the beer into a sanitized bottling bucket. Boil the corn sugar in about a cup of water; cool; stir gently into the beer. This provides the nutrients necessary for the yeast to carbonate the beer in the bottle.

12. Insert one end of the sanitized and rinsed hose into the bottling spigot and the other end to the bottle filler. Push the bottle filler down onto the bottom of the bottle and open the bottling spigot. Five gallons of beer will make about 2 cases, so make sure you sanitize this amount beforehand. Leave about ½–¾ inch of space at the top of the bottle. Cap the bottles.

13. Let the beer age for 2 weeks to 6 months. Chill and enjoy.

Note: The normal phase of fermentation will be a lag phase, usually 2 hours to 1.5 days, followed by a steady increase in intensity, usually lasting anywhere from 1 to 4 days. Fermentation abruptly slows down after this and tapers off to an occasional bubble being pushed out of the fermentation lock every 30 seconds or so. The main contributing factors to these fluctuations are the strain and initial amount of yeast being used, sanitation, and temperature intensity and consistency. For ale yeast, try to maintain temperatures between 65° and 75°. For lagers, temperatures of 65° down to 32° work best to maintain lager characteristics.

QUAKER'S STOUT
THE CELLAR HOMEBREW—SEATTLE, WASHINGTON

"Full-bodied is an understatement for this dark stout. It's downright chewy. The oatmeal provides the unfermentable starches that give this beer its remarkable mouthfeel, while the use of specialty grains gives it a distinctive roasted quality. Perfect for those winter evenings in front of the fireplace."

ORIGINAL GRAVITY: 1.066

FINAL GRAVITY: 1.016

POTENTIAL ALCOHOL: 6.6% ABV

INGREDIENTS (FOR 5.5 GALLONS)

¾ pound English crystal malt (crushed)

½ pound chocolate malt (crushed)

¼ pound black patent malt (crushed)

½ pound roasted barley (crushed)

¾ pound rolled oats

6 pounds Alexander's amber bulk malt syrup

2 pounds English dark dry malt extract

½ stick of brewer's licorice

1 ounce Centennial hops and 1 ounce Willamette hops (boiling)

1 ounce Willamette hops (finishing)

Edme dry ale yeast or Irish Ale liquid yeast

¾ cup corn sugar for priming

BREWING PROCEDURES

Note: If you are using the Irish Ale liquid yeast with this recipe, be sure to start that yeast at least 1 to 3 days before doing any of the brewing steps below. Follow the package directions and use the yeast in step 5.

1. Place the crushed English crystal, chocolate, roasted barley, and black patent in a strainer bag. Add this bag of grain to your brewing kettle, which contains 2 to 2½ gallons brewing water. Bring the brewing water to a boil, then remove the bag of grains. It is not a good idea to boil these specialty grains for any length of time, as they may contribute a bitter or grainy taste to the finished beer. Continue to boil the rolled oats for 10 minutes. Remove kettle from the heat and pull out the bag of rolled oats.

2. Sparge (rinse) the bag of English crystal, chocolate, roasted barley, and black patent with about 1 quart of hot tap water into the brewing kettle; dispose of the spent grains. Rinse the bag of rolled oats with about 2 cups of cold water over the brew kettle to reduce heat, then squeeze the bag over the kettle to extract some of the murky liquid. Dispose of the spent rolled oats.

3. Remove the brewing kettle from the burner and add the 6 pounds of Alexander's amber malt syrup, the 2 pounds of English dark dry malt, and the ½ stick of brewer's licorice. The syrup is easier to pour if the can has been previously placed in hot water. Also, rinse the can with hot water to ensure that all the syrup goes into the kettle. Stir the mixture, now called "wort," until it boils. Watch carefully at this time because the wort may boil over. You can prevent this by pouring a cup of cold water into the overboiling wort.

4. At boiling point, add the Centennial and Willamette boiling hops. Hops can be placed in a hop bag or added loose, to be later strained out after the boil using a strainer bag. Time the boil for about 1 hour, stirring occasionally. After the first 10 minutes of this boil, remove 2 cups of wort in measuring cup and cover with foil or plastic. Cool to 90°F for use in step 5 below.

5. Making the yeast starter: For dry yeast, use ½ cup warm tap water (90–100°F). Sprinkle the contents of yeast packet into that water, cover for at least 15 minutes, and then add to the 2 cups of wort you prepared in step 4. Cover and set aside for use in step 7 below. For liq-

uid yeast, prepare 1 to 3 days ahead of brewing time per package instructions. Open the swollen package and add the contents to the 2 cups of wort as prepared in step 4.

6. After the wort has boiled for that 1 hour, add finishing hops. Place them in the hop bag, which has been emptied of the spent boiling hops, and place them in the boiling kettle or just add the finishing hops directly to the brewing kettle. They will be strained later in step 8.

7. Let the boil continue for 5 minutes. This gives the beer its hop aroma. Remove the pot from the burner and let it cool, covered, for about 20 minutes.

8. Pour 3 gallons of cold water into the sanitized open fermenter fitted with strainer bag; if loose finishing hops were used in step 6, strain the warm wort from step 7 into the cold water. Top up the fermenter to 5.5 gallons using cold tap water. Cover the fermenter and cool the wort as rapidly as possible.

9. When the wort has cooled to about 80°F, add the yeast starter and ferment as you usually do.

OATMEAL STOUT
🍺🍺

**BEER & WINEMAKING SUPPLIES, INC.—
NORTHAMPTON, MASSACHUSETTS**

"Extra dark, almost black in color, with a nice malt character and a slightly higher than normal alcohol content. Full-bodied, the oats round out the beer, giving a nice mouthfeel. Best typified by Samuel Smith's Oatmeal Stout from Yorkshire, England."

ORIGINAL GRAVITY: 1.056–60

FINAL GRAVITY: 1.013–15

POTENTIAL ALCOHOL: 5.85% ABV

INGREDIENTS

12 ounces flaked or rolled oats
10 ounces chocolate malt (cracked)
4 ounces flaked barley
4 ounces roasted barley (cracked)
2 ounces black malt (cracked)
8 pounds light or amber malt extract
1 ounce Eroica hop pellets (bittering)
10–14 grams dry ale yeast or Wyeast 1098 or 1335
¾ cup corn sugar

BREWING PROCEDURES

Note: If using a liquid culture, activate 12–24 hours prior to brew session.

1. Place your three blended grains in a 6-quart pan and stir in 2 quarts of 168°F water. Mix well. Grain should bring temperature down to approximately 150–154°F. Steep for 45 minutes in oven, small insulated cooler, or on stovetop at that temperature. While grain is steeping, bring 2 gallons of water up to 165°F in an 8–12-quart pot. Place strainer or colander over large kettle, then pour and spoon all grains and liquid in. Rinse with 1.5–2 gallons of 165°F water. Allow liquid to drain into kettle for about 10 minutes. Discard grains and bring liquid to a boil. Momentarily remove from heat.

2. Pour the 8 pounds of malt extract into the pot, making sure to rinse out the container to get all the malt. Stir well.

3. Resume boiling (total time: 1 hour). Split the Eroica hops into two equal portions.

Add half to the kettle; at the 30-minute mark, add the second half.

4. Shut off the heat and let stand for 15 minutes.

5. Put 2 gallons of very cold water into your sterilized primary fermenter, then carefully pour the hot wort into it. Top up to 4 gallons with more cold water if necessary. If still above 85°F, run a cold water bath around your fermenter. The fermenter should then be stirred or swirled to aerate the wort. Take a hydrometer reading and write it down. (This beer is a volatile bubbler, so only start off with 4 gallons, then top up to 5 gallons later with sterile water.)

6. Wort should now be 70–85°F. Activate dry yeast by putting in 1 cup of sterile water at 75–95°F for 15 minutes, then stir well.

7. Now add the yeast and stir or swirl to aerate. Pitch yeast solution into fermenter. Put lid and airlock on. Fill airlock halfway with water.

8. Ferment at room temperature (60–70°F) for 4 to 6 days, then siphon over to a glass secondary fermenter for another 4–7 days. Take a hydrometer reading, and if low enough, bottle the beer into 53 reusable bar bottles (12-ounce size) or equivalent.

9. Make a priming syrup on the stove with 1 cup water and ¾ cup corn sugar, bring to a boil, and then shut heat off immediately, stirring well. Transfer beer back to primary or bottling bucket, mixing the priming syrup in well to distribute evenly. Siphon into bottles and cap them.

10. Remember to sanitize everything you use after the boil with a good chlorinated alkaline cleanser.

11. Allow bottles to sit at room temperature for 1–2 weeks before cooling down.

SHOUT IT OUT OATMEAL STOUT

🍺 🍺 🍺

THE HOME BEER, WINE, & CHEESEMAKING SHOP—WOODLAND HILLS, CALIFORNIA

This strong version of an oatmeal stout is quintessentially British in its ingredient mix, except for the inventive addition of some Belgian Special B crystal malt, which adds a deep caramel flavor.

ORIGINAL GRAVITY: 1.062

FINAL GRAVITY: 1.016

POTENTIAL ALCOHOL: 6.3% ABV

IBUs: 40

COLOR: 42 SRM

INGREDIENTS

- 1 pound flaked oats
- 8 ounces roasted barley
- 12 ounces black patent malt
- 12 ounces Belgian Special B 220 °L malt
- 4 ounces chocolate malt
- 6.6 pounds John Bull light malt extract
- 8 ounces wheat solids
- 1.5 ounces Whitbread Goldings hop pellets at 6% AA (60 minutes)
- 1 ounce Northdown hop pellets at 6.1% AA (20 minutes)
- 1 teaspoon Irish moss
- 2 teaspoons calcium carbonate
- Wyeast 1084 Irish Ale
- ¾ cup corn sugar

BREWING PROCEDURES

1. Seep (soak) the grains in 2 quarts of 150°F water for 30–40 minutes. Sparge (rinse) with 2.5 quarts of 150°F water into your boil-

ing pot. Discard grain. No water over 170°F with grain. Do not oversparge. Do not squeeze grain bag.

2. After adding 2.5 gallons of water and dissolving the malt, bring pot to a gentle but rolling boil. Skim all foam before starting the hop sequence. Add Irish moss the last 20 minutes to remove the protein missed in steps 1 and 2. Add the calcium carbonate into the boil. It adds softness and neutralizes the acidic quality of the highly roasted grains.

3. Ferment at an average of 68–72°F. This promotes a slight buttery/diacetyl aroma, which is appropriate for this style of beer. Pitch (add) yeast when your water bath around the fermenter reads 70–80°F. Maintain this temperature until the first signs of fermentation (about 10–12 hours). If using a yeast starter (highly recommended), fermentation can start in 2–3 hours. Use ¾ cup sugar for priming.

OATMEAL STOUT
🏺🏺🏺/🏺🏺🏺

BREWERS RESOURCE—CAMARILLO, CALIFORNIA

"In an oatmeal stout recipe you will want to emphasize the roasted malt and thick oatmeal flavor. Keep it full and slightly sweet by using original gravity between 1.050 and 1.060. Balance the roast barley with chocolate malt for complexity. So as not to mask the malt flavor, use hops only to bitter. You should use a clean ale yeast, preferably one that will produce a full-bodied beer. Fermentation temperatures should be kept between 60° and 66°F to minimize excessive ester production, and use a low- to medium-carbonate water for brewing this style of beer."

ORIGINAL GRAVITY: 1.060

FINAL GRAVITY: 1.015

POTENTIAL ALCOHOL: 5.9% ABV

MASH-EXTRACT RECIPE: INGREDIENTS

> 8 ounces roast barley
>
> 6 ounces chocolate malt—crushed
>
> 8 ounces regular rolled oats, steeped with pale malt below
>
> 3 pounds crushed British pale ale malt, mashed in 4 liters of water at 152°F for 45 minutes
>
> 4½ pounds light dry malt extract or 5½ pounds pale malt extract syrup
>
> 38 IBUs Northern Brewer (i.e., 1¼ ounce at 7.5% AA)
>
> BrewTek American Microbrewery Ale #1 yeast (CL–10) or Wyeast 1056 American Ale
>
> ¾ cup (4 ounces) corn sugar to prime at bottling

BREWING PROCEDURES

1. Steep crushed grains in mini-mash bucket and sparge to collect 3 gallons of wort.

2. Add the malt extract and brew recipe as you normally would, or see Partial Mash Ale Brewing beginning on page 14.

ALL-GRAIN RECIPE: INGREDIENTS

> 9 pounds pale crushed Klages or, preferably, British pale ale malt
>
> 8 ounces roast barley
>
> 6 ounces chocolate malt—crushed
>
> 8 ounces regular rolled oats, steeped with pale malt below
>
> 38 IBUs Northern Brewer (i.e., 1¼ ounce at 7.5% AA)

BrewTek American Microbrewery Ale yeast (CL–10) or Wyeast American Ale 1056

¾ cup (4 ounces) corn sugar to prime at bottling

BREWING PROCEDURES

1. In mash/lauter bucket stir crushed malts into 10 liters of 168°F water to rest out at about 154°. Cover and rest for 45 minutes.
2. Sparge to 6 gallons into kettle. Bring to a boil and add hops. Brew to completion as you normally would, or see Fermentation and Lagering beginning on page 34.

Recipe variations: You may experiment with these recipes by increasing or decreasing the ratios of roasted malts and oatmeal, or try a touch of black patent malt. Experiment with different original gravities and hop varieties. We prefer a malty oatmeal stout, but you may experiment with different yeast strains or mash temperatures for more complexity and variety.

SCOTTISH AND SCOTCH ALE

Scottish ale is traditionally brewed rich, malty, dark, and smooth. Products of barley wine strength are often labeled "Scotch ale." Strong Scotch ale ("wee heavy") is compared to English strong or old ale but has no real equivalent in taste. The subcategories of Scotch ale are: Scottish light (60 shilling), which is light in gravity, not color; Scottish heavy (70 shilling); Scottish export (80 shilling); and wee heavy (90 shilling).

Originally, beers of the Scottish style were brewed mostly with brown malt, with bog myrtle for bitterness, a high-temperature mash, and a lengthy, cool ferment. Later, brewers began to use more pale malts with roasted malts or roasted barley for color. Scottish ales are low in hop bitterness, with noticeable fruitiness and diacetyl, and a subtle smoky taste. MacAndrew's Scotch Ale, McEwan's Scotch Ale, and Traquair House Ale represent some of the legendary Scottish versions—Auld Tartan Wee Heavy is a noteworthy American microbrewed versions.

The Scottish microbrewed Golden Promise is a prime example of the Scottish style of ale patterned after English pale ale.

SCOTTISH ALE BASICS

ORIGINAL GRAVITY: 1.030–50

FINAL GRAVITY: 1.006–18

IBUs: 8–20

COLOR (SRM): 7–20

ALCOHOL BY VOLUME: 3–4.5%

SCOTCH ALE BASICS

ORIGINAL GRAVITY: 1.072–85

FINAL GRAVITY: 1.016–25

IBUs: 25–35

COLOR (SRM): 15–50

ALCOHOL BY VOLUME: 6–8%

POLE-TOSSIN' SCOTTISH EXPORT

⟨▦⟩ ⟨▦⟩ ⟨▦⟩

E. C. KRAUS HOME WINE AND BEER MAKING SUPPLIES—INDEPENDENCE, MISSOURI

"This is a full-bodied malty brew with a hint of roasted flavor. The hops are not noticeable upon the first swallow, but show their presence clearly in the aftertaste. This gives the beer the impression of being remarkably well rounded and balanced. The color is a heavy amber with a slightly smoky tint. The aroma is exceptionally malty and inviting."

ORIGINAL GRAVITY: 1.044–47

FINAL GRAVITY: 1.011–12

POTENTIAL ALCOHOL: 4–5% ABV

IBUs: 15–20

COLOR: 14–19

SRM/25–35 °L

INGREDIENTS

- 1 pound crystal malt
- 2 ounces chocolate malt
- 3.3 pounds light unhopped malt syrup
- 1 pound light dried malt extract (2.4 cups)
- 8 ounces brown sugar
- 8 ounces malto-dextrin (5-minute boil time)
- 1 ounce Fuggles pellet hops (45-minute boil time)
- 1 tablespoon Irish moss (15-minute boil time)
- 2 ounces oak chips
- 10 grams London English ale yeast or Wyeast 1728
- ¾ cup priming sugar

BREWING PROCEDURES

1. Lightly crack malted barleys and put with 1½ gallons of cold water in a cooking pot. Slowly bring to a boil over a 30–45-minute period.

2. Once boiling, strain the grains out by the use of a colander or the like and discard.

3. Bring liquid back to a boil and add both the liquid and dried malt extracts and the brown sugar. Bring back to a boil again.

4. Once boiling, add Fuggles hops and boil for 45 minutes. During the last 15 minutes of the boil, add the Irish moss. During the last 5 minutes of the boil, fold in the malto-dextrin.

5. Now add the wort to your fermenter along with cold tap water up to 5 gallons. Make sure the wort has cooled to below 80°F and pitch yeast.

6. Attach airlock to fermenter and allow to ferment. On the second day of fermentation, add the boiled and strained oak chips to your fermenter.

7. In 7–10 days or when fermentation is complete, add priming sugar and bottle as normal.

SCOTTISH LIGHT 60°/-

⟨▦⟩ ⟨▦⟩

E. C. KRAUS—INDEPENDENCE, MISSOURI

"Scottish light is a lightly hopped but very full-bodied beer. Its color is a light translucent amber and has a lasting lacy head of foam. Its most prevalent character is its malty attack, but it still leaves a clean-tasting finish."

ORIGINAL GRAVITY: 1.030–35

FINAL GRAVITY: 1.008–10

POTENTIAL ALCOHOL: 3–4% ABV

IBUs: 9–15

COLOR: 8–17 SRM/12–30 °L

INGREDIENTS

>   8 ounces crystal malted barley
>
>   1 ounce chocolate malted barley
>
>   3.3 pounds light unhopped malt extract
>
>   0.5 pound light dried malt extract (1¼ cups)
>
>   4 ounces brown sugar
>
>   4 ounces malto-dextrin (5-minute boil time)
>
>   ¾ ounce Fuggles pellet hops (45-minute boil time)
>
>   2 ounces dried oak chips
>
>   14 grams ale yeast or Wyeast 1728 Scottish Ale
>
>   ¾ cup priming sugar

BREWING PROCEDURES

1. Lightly crack malted barley and put with 1½ gallons of cold water in a cooking pan. Slowly bring to a boil over a 30–45-minute period.
2. Strain the grains out by use of a colander and discard.
3. Add the liquid and dried malt extracts and the brown sugar to the mixture. Now bring back to a boil once again.
4. Once boiling, add Fuggles hops and boil for 45 minutes. During the last 5 minutes of boil, fold in malto-dextrin.
5. When the boiling is complete, add the wort to your fermenter with cold water up to 5 gallons.
6. Boil oak chips in a small amount of water for about 10 minutes. Strain the chips off the water, then add them to the wort.
7. Make sure the wort has cooled below 80°F and sprinkle yeast on top.
8. Attach airlock to fermenter and allow to ferment for 7–10 days or until finished.
9. Bottle with priming sugar as normal and condition 2–4 weeks.

OFF-KILTER ALE
🍺 🍺

THE CELLAR HOMEBREW—SEATTLE, WASHINGTON

"This beer of deep copper color has several typical characteristics of this style: malt and roasted flavor, high alcohol content, and a sweet, full body. The use of flaked barley gives this beer its richness. The Scottish ale liquid yeast will add a subtle smoky accent."

ORIGINAL GRAVITY: 1.054

FINAL GRAVITY: 1.016

POTENTIAL ALCOHOL: 5% ABV

INGREDIENTS (FOR 5.5 GALLONS)

>   1 pound English crystal malt (crushed)
>
>   ¼ pound chocolate malt (crushed)
>
>   ½ pound flaked barley
>
>   6 pounds British light bulk malt syrup
>
>   1 pound English light dry malt extract
>
>   1½ ounces Kent Goldings hops
>
>   ½ ounce Kent Goldings hops
>
>   Edme dry ale yeast or Scottish Ale liquid yeast
>
>   ¾ cup corn sugar for priming

BREWING PROCEDURES

Note: If you are using the Scottish Ale liquid yeast with this recipe, be sure to start that yeast at least 1 to 3 days before doing any of the brewing steps below. Follow the package directions and use the yeast in step 5 below.

1. Place the crushed English crystal and chocolate malt in a strainer bag. Place the flaked barley in its own strainer bag. Add these bags of grain to your brewing kettle, which contains 2 to 2½ gallons brewing water. Bring the brewing water to a boil, then remove the bag of grains. It is not a good idea to boil these specialty grains for any length of time as they may contribute a bitter or grainy taste to the finished beer. Continue to boil the flaked barley for 10 minutes.

2. Sparge (rinse) the bag of English crystal and chocolate malts with about 1 quart of hot tap water into the brewing kettle; dispose of the spent grains. Rinse the bag of flaked barley with about 2 cups of cold water over the brew kettle to reduce heat, then squeeze the bag over the kettle to extract some of the murky liquid. Dispose of the spent flaked barley.

3. Remove the brewing kettle from the burner and add the 6 pounds of British light malt syrup and the 1 pound of English light dry malt. The syrup is easier to pour if the can has been previously placed in hot water. Also, rinse the can with hot water to ensure that all the syrup goes into the kettle. Stir the mixture, now called "wort," until it boils. Watch carefully at this time because the wort may boil over. You can prevent this by pouring a cup of cold water into the over-boiling wort.

4. At boiling point, add the Kent Goldings boiling hops. Hops can be placed in a hop bag or added loose, to be later strained out after the boil using a strainer bag. Time the boil for about 1 hour, stirring occasionally. After the first 10 minutes of this boil, remove 2 cups of wort in measuring cup and cover with foil or plastic. Cool to 90°F for use in step 5 below.

5. Making the yeast starter: For dry yeast, use ½ cup warm tap water (90–100°F). Sprinkle the contents of yeast packet into that water, cover for at least 15 minutes, and then add to the 2 cups of wort you prepared in step 4. Cover and set aside for use in step 7 below. For liquid yeast, prepare 1 to 3 days ahead of brewing time per package instructions. Open the swollen package and add the contents to the 2 cups of wort as prepared in step 4.

6. After the wort has boiled for that 1 hour, add the Kent Goldings finishing hops. Place them in the hop bag, which has been emptied of the spent boiling hops, and place them in the boiling kettle or just add the finishing hops directly to the brewing kettle. They will be strained later in step 8.

7. Let the boil continue for 5 minutes. This gives the beer its hop aroma. Remove the pot from the burner and let it cool, covered, for about 20 minutes.

8. Pour 3 gallons of cold water into the sanitized open fermenter fitted with strainer bag; if loose finishing hops were used in step 6, strain the warm wort from step 7 into the cold water. Top up the fermenter to 5½ gallons using cold tap water. Cover the fermenter and cool the wort as rapidly as possible.

9. When the wort has cooled to about 80°F, add the yeast starter and ferment as you usually do.

PIRATES BREW BITTER
🍺 🍺

JAY GARRISON, HEAD BREWER, PIRATE
  BREWERY

BREWBUDDYS—REDONDO BEACH,
  CALIFORNIA

A Scottish-influenced bitter with a generous portion of crystal malt for a caramel maltiness and a base of amber malt extract that brings a traditional darker color to the brew. The light hopping reflects the Scottish tradition of emphasizing a complex malt character. A good dinner beer.

ORIGINAL GRAVITY: 1.045

FINAL GRAVITY: 1.012

POTENTIAL ALCOHOL: 4.3% ABV

INGREDIENTS

> **6 pounds amber liquid extract**
> **8 ounces Scottish crystal malt**
> **1 ounce Nugget hops**
> **1 ounce Willamette hops**
> **Wyeast 1098 British Ale or Edme dry ale yeast**
> **¾ cup corn sugar**

BREWING PROCEDURES

1. If you selected the Wyeast liquid yeast, you must break the inner packet before you begin to brew. Allow 1 day for each month after the manufacture date printed on the front. If you're using the dry yeast that came with the Pirates Brew Kit, go ahead and get to it.

2. Prepare the grain. The grain should be crushed; if you did not get the grain crushed at the shop, crush it with some sort of rolling pin. You can either mix the grain with 2 quarts of water and heat it until it starts to boil, or heat it to about 165°F and steep for about 15 minutes.

3. Strain the grain, collecting the liquid into your brewpot. Rinse the grain (sparge) with 2 quarts of hot (170–180°F) water.

4. Add the bag of extract and 1 gallon of water to the brewpot. (You might want to rest the bag of extract in hot water for a while to soften it up.) Bring the wort to a soft rolling boil.

5. Add the Nugget hops to the wort and boil for 40 minutes. Stir occasionally.

6. Add half of the Willamette hops to the wort and boil for 20 minutes. Stir occasionally.

7. Add half of the Willamette hops to the wort and turn off the heat; stir and let sit (covered, if possible) for 10 minutes.

8. Add the boiled wort to your sanitized, rinsed fermenter. Add ice-cold water to make 5 gallons. When the temperature drops to 75°F or less, add the yeast.

9. If you use liquid yeast, open the swollen packet and add to the wort. If you use dry yeast, add the yeast to 1 cup of 90°F water for a few minutes before adding to the wort. (You can add the yeast directly to the wort and let it sit for a few minutes also, but rehydrating the yeast in warm water will improve the fermentation.) Stir the wort thoroughly with a sanitized spoon.

10. Put the lid on the fermenter tightly and insert the fermentation lock with the stopper into the hole in the lid and fill it up about ¾ of the way with water or vodka. Let the wort ferment for a week or two until the fermentation ceases.

11. When fermentation is complete, siphon the beer into a sanitized bottling bucket. Boil the corn sugar in about a cup of water; cool; stir gently into the beer. This provides the nutrients necessary for the yeast to carbonate the beer in the bottle.

12. Insert one end of the sanitized and rinsed hose into the bottling spigot and the other end to the bottle filler. Push the bottle filler down onto the bottom of the bottle and open the bottling spigot. Five gallons of beer will make about 2 cases, so make sure you sanitize this amount beforehand. Leave about 1/2–3/4 inch of space at the top of the bottle. Cap the bottles.

13. Let the beer age for 2 weeks to 6 months. Chill and enjoy.

SCOTTISH ALE
🛢 🛢 🛢

BREWERS RESOURCE—CAMARILLO, CALIFORNIA

"In designing a Scottish ale you will want to emphasize the rich malt flavor. An original gravity between 1.055 and 1.065 is fine. It's important to use a strong, slightly estery ale yeast. Fermentation temperatures should be kept between 62° and 68°F to ensure a strong fermentation and allow some ester production. Use low- to medium-carbonate water for brewing this style of beer."

ORIGINAL GRAVITY: 1.063

FINAL GRAVITY: 1.016

POTENTIAL ALCOHOL: 6.3% ABV

INGREDIENTS

    10 ounces dark crystal malt (120 °L)—crushed and steeped with pale malt below

    3 pounds crushed British pale ale malt, mashed in 4 liters of water at 152°F for 45 minutes

    4 1/2 pounds light dry malt extract or 5 1/2 pounds pale syrup malt extract

    31 IBUs Fuggles (i.e., 1 1/2 ounces at 5% AA)

    BrewTek British Draft ale yeast (CL–26) or Wyeast American Ale 1056

    3/4 cup (4 ounces) corn sugar to prime at bottling

BREWING PROCEDURES

1. Steep crushed grains in mini-mash bucket and sparge to collect 3 gallons of wort.

2. Add malt extract and brew as you normally would, or see Partial Mash Ale Brewing beginning on page 14.

90 SHILLING SCOTCH ALE
🛢 🛢 🛢

BEER & WINEMAKING SUPPLIES, INC.—NORTHAMPTON, MASSACHUSETTS

A small addition of smoked malt (peat-smoked is best) gives this intermediate recipe a unique Scottish flavor. The variety of specialty grains will add an authentically complex character.

ORIGINAL GRAVITY: 1.070–72

FINAL GRAVITY: 1.016–18

POTENTIAL ALCOHOL: 7–7.5% ABV

INGREDIENTS

    8 ounces toasted malt (cracked)

    8 ounces U.K. dark crystal malt (cracked)

    2 ounces U.K. chocolate malt (cracked)

    1 ounce smoked malt (cracked)

    7 pounds British light malt extract

    2 pounds light dry malt powder

    2.5 ounces U.K. Challenger hop pellets

10–14 grams dry ale yeast or Wyeast 1728 (Scottish) or 1084 (Irish)

¾ cup corn sugar

BREWING PROCEDURES

Note: If using a liquid culture, activate 12–24 hours prior to brew session.

1. Place your three blended grains in a 4-quart or larger pan and stir in 1.25 quarts of 168°F water. Mix well. Grain should bring temperature down to approximately 150–154°F. Steep for 45 minutes in oven, small insulated cooler, or on stovetop at that temperature. While grain is steeping, bring 2 gallons of water up to 165°F in an 8–12-quart pot. Place strainer or colander over large kettle, then pour and spoon all grains and liquid in. Rinse with 1.5–2 gallons of 165°F water. Allow liquid to drain into kettle. Discard grains and bring liquid to a boil. Momentarily remove from heat.

2. Pour the 2 pounds of light dry malt and 7 pounds of malt extract into the pot, making sure to rinse out the container to get all the malt. Stir well.

3. Resume boiling (total time: 1 hour). Add half of the bittering hops. At 30 minutes, add the other half of bittering hops.

4. Shut off the heat and let stand for 15 minutes.

5. Put 3 gallons of very cold water into your sterilized primary fermenter, then carefully pour the hot wort into it. Top up to 5 gallons with more cold water if necessary. If still above 85°F, run a cold water bath around your fermenter. The fermenter should then be stirred or swirled to aerate the wort. Take a hydrometer reading and write it down.

6. Wort should now be 70–85°F. Activate dry yeast by putting in 1 cup of sterile water at 75–95°F for 15 minutes, then stir well.

7. Now add the yeast and stir or swirl to aerate. Pitch yeast solution into fermenter. Put lid and airlock on. Fill airlock halfway with water.

8. Ferment at room temperature (60–70°F) for 4 days, then siphon over to a glass secondary fermenter for another 4–7 days. Take a hydrometer reading, and if low enough, bottle the beer into 53 reusable bar bottles (12-ounce size) or equivalent.

9. Make a priming syrup on the stove with 1 cup water and ¾ cup corn sugar, bring to a boil, and then shut heat off immediately, stirring well. Transfer beer back to primary or bottling bucket, mixing the priming syrup in well to distribute evenly. Siphon into bottles and cap them.

10. Remember to sanitize everything you use after the boil with a good chlorinated alkaline cleanser.

11. Allow bottles to sit at room temperature for 1–2 weeks before cooling down.

SCOTCH ALE

MIKE KNAUB, HEAD BREWER, CHICKIES ROCK BEERS–STARVIEW BREWING COMPANY

STARVIEW BREW—MT. WOLF, PENNSYLVANIA

This simple all-grain recipe most definitely fits the description "wee heavy" and might best be savored slowly as a winter nightcap.

ORIGINAL GRAVITY: 1.088

FINAL GRAVITY: 1.028

POTENTIAL ALCOHOL: 8% ABV

INGREDIENTS (FOR 5.5 GALLONS)

- 13 pounds Hugh Baird pale malt
- 4 pounds Hugh Baird crystal malt
- 2 pounds German Munich malt
- 3 pounds German pilsner malt (toasted at 350°F for 20 minutes)
- 2 HBUs Kent Goldings whole hops
- 1 teaspoon Irish moss
- Yeast Lab Irish Ale yeast
- ¾ cup corn sugar for priming

BREWING PROCEDURES

1. Mash in grains in 5½ gallons of water at 180°F.

2. Perform saccharification rest for 85 minutes at 156°F.

3. Mash out for 10 minutes at 165°F.

4. Sparge with 6 gallons at 170°F.

5. Collect wort into brew kettle and boil for 30 minutes before adding hops.

6. Add 15 HBUs Kent Goldings whole bittering hops and boil for 60 minutes.

7. Add 5 HBUs Kent Goldings whole flavoring hops and boil for 20 minutes.

8. Boil Irish moss for 15 minutes.

9. Chill wort, pitch yeast, and ferment as you normally do, then transfer to secondary for 1 week before priming with corn sugar and bottling.

BARLEY WINE

Technically, these malty-sweet ales belong in the British strong ale category that includes winter warmers and strong Christmas ales, but their extremely high original and final gravities, not to mention their popularity among homebrewers in recent years, have earned them a style category of their own. The traditional ingredients have included, but are in no way limited to, British two-row pale ale malt, crystal malt, chocolate malt, roasted barley, and black malt. Adjuncts and sugars such as treacle are often used, but the color should be deep amber to deep copper and not dark brown/black as in the case of bock or stout. These beers should also be balanced with enough hop bitterness to avoid an overwhelming sweetness inappropriate for the style. An alcohol-tolerant yeast such as Wyeast 3021 Pasteur Champagne is sometimes recommended, especially in the conditioning phase. Thomas Hardy's Ale,

Young's Old Nick, Woodeford's Headcracker, Marston's Owd Rodger, and Gibbs Mew Brewery's The Bishop's Tipple are British standouts. There are also several excellent American microbrewed versions available, including Anchor Old Foghorn Barley Wine, Rogue Old Crustacean Barley Wine, Pike Place Old Bawdy Barley Wine, and Sierra Nevada Big Foot Barleywine.

BARLEY WINE BASICS

ORIGINAL GRAVITY: 1.065–1.120+

FINAL GRAVITY: 1.024–32

IBUs: 50–100

COLOR (SRM): 8–22

ALCOHOL BY VOLUME: 7–12%

WALT'S GNARLY BARLEY WINE

⫿ ⫿

CHETT SCHAFF & PAUL HEALY

MOUNTAIN MALT AND HOP SHOPPE—
   LAKE KATRINE & POUGHKEEPSIE,
   NEW YORK

This easy recipe is perfect for novice–intermediate brewers who have brewed their share of pale ales and porters and want to branch out into something with a little more strength. There are no specialty grains to worry about, just the simple addition of some hops and you will have a great strong ale. Don't forget to let it age.

ORIGINAL GRAVITY: 1.078

FINAL GRAVITY: 1.016

POTENTIAL ALCOHOL: 8.4% ABV

INGREDIENTS

> 3 cans (12 pounds) Alexander's pale malt
> 2 ounces Cascade hops
> 1 pound wheat DME
> 2 ounces Willamette hops
> 4 ounces Galena hops
> 1 tablespoon gypsum
> 2 ounces Chinook hops
> Wyeast 1098 Whitbread Ale
> ¾ cup corn sugar for priming

BREWING PROCEDURES

1. In a 12-quart or larger stainless-steel pot, heat 1 gallon of water to 155°F and add 1 tablespoon of gypsum. Stir until dissolved and turn off heat. Place cracked grains in a nylon bag and immerse in water. Cover pot and allow grain to steep for 30 minutes. Remove grain bag and bring the "tea" to a boil. (If you do not have a nylon bag, add grains directly to water and strain.)

2. When boil is attained, turn off heat and add the liquid and dry malt extracts. (Putting DME in a bowl first makes it easier to add.) Turn on heat and return to a boil.

3. When the danger of a messy boilover has passed, add the Galena and Chinook hops (69 HBU) and cook at a low, rolling boil for 45 minutes.

4. Add 1 teaspoon of Irish moss and boil for 5 more minutes.

5. Place Cascade hops in a muslin hop bag and immerse in wort. Boil for 8 more minutes.

6. Boil the Willamette hops for 2 more minutes, then turn off heat. Immediately remove both hop bags.

7. Take the brewpot from the stove and place it in a sink partially filled with cold water. Add 1 gallon of sanitary, refrigerated water (40°F) to the brewpot, then cover and place ice in the water around the brewpot. Never add ice directly to the wort! Let stand 15 minutes. Place 2 gallons of refrigerated water into the fermenter, then add the wort. Check the temperature (65–75°F is ideal). Top off to 5½ gallons with either more cold or room-temperature water.

8. With a sanitized measuring cup, scoop out ¾ cup and take a hydrometer reading. Discard sample.

9. Add the package of yeast to the fermenter when the temperature of the wort is 65–75°F, then stir vigorously to aerate. Snap the fermenter lid on, fill the airlock halfway with water, and place in lid. Place fermenter in a spot where the temperature will remain a constant 65–70°F.

10. Ferment in the primary for 5–6 days, then rack into a glass carboy for 2 weeks.

11. When brew is clear, siphon into a bottling

bucket. Dissolve priming sugar into 1 cup boiling water, cool, and gently stir into beer with a sanitized spoon. CAUTION: If finished volume is less than 5 gallons, scale proportionately (e.g., 4½ gallons = ⅔ cup sugar).

12. Keep in a warm place for 7–10 days, then move to a cool place to age for 2 weeks.

BACCHUS' ALE

🍺🍺

THE CELLAR HOMEBREW—SEATTLE, WASHINGTON

"This style normally achieves alcohol levels known to kill your average beer yeast. This style is unlike any other. Consider the benefits of aging this beer when planning your brew cycle. It will mellow into a sublime treat during long-term storage."

ORIGINAL GRAVITY: 1.079

FINAL GRAVITY: 1.021

POTENTIAL ALCOHOL: 7.7% ABV

INGREDIENTS (FOR 5.5 GALLONS)

- ¼ pound English crystal malt (crushed)
- ¼ pound chocolate malt (crushed)
- Two six-pound jars of Alexander's light bulk malt syrup
- 2 ounces Chinook hops
- 2 ounces Tettnang hops
- 2 packages dry Champagne yeast or Belgian Ale liquid yeast
- ¾ cup corn sugar for priming

BREWING PROCEDURES

Note: If you are using the Belgian Ale liquid yeast with this recipe, be sure to start that yeast at least 1 to 3 days before doing any of the brewing steps below. Follow the package directions and use the yeast in step 5.

1. Place the crushed English crystal and chocolate malts in a strainer bag. Add this bag of grain to your brewing kettle, which contains 2 to 2½ gallons brewing water. Bring the brewing water to a boil, then remove the bag of grains. It is not a good idea to boil these specialty grains for any length of time, as they may contribute a bitter or grainy taste to the finished beer.

2. Sparge (rinse) the bag of grains with about 1 quart of hot tap water into the brewing kettle, dispose of the spent grains.

3. Remove the brewing kettle from the burner and add the two 6-pound jars of Alexander's light malt syrup. The syrup is easier to pour if the can has been previously placed in hot water. Also, rinse the jars with hot water to ensure that all the syrup goes into the kettle. Stir the mixture, now called "wort," until it boils. Watch carefully at this time because the wort may boil over. You can prevent this by pouring a cup of cold water into the over-boiling wort.

4. At boiling point, add the Chinook boiling hops. Hops can be placed in a hop bag or added loose, to be later strained out after the boil using a strainer bag. Time the boil for about 1 hour, stirring occasionally. After the first 10 minutes of this boil, remove 2 cups of wort in measuring cup and cover with foil or plastic. Cool to 90°F for use in step 5 below.

5. Making the yeast starter: For dry yeast, use ½ cup warm tap water (90–100°F). Sprinkle the contents of yeast packet into that water, cover for at least 15 minutes, and then add

to the 2 cups of wort you prepared in step 4. Cover and set aside for use in step 7 below. For liquid yeast, prepare 1 to 3 days ahead of brewing time per package instructions. Open the swollen package and add the contents to the 2 cups of wort as prepared in step 4.

6. After the wort has boiled for that 1 hour, add the Tettnang finishing hops. Place them in the hop bag, which has been emptied of the spent boiling hops, and place them in the boiling kettle or just add the finishing hops directly to the brewing kettle. They will be strained later in step 8.

7. Let the boil continue for 5 minutes. This gives the beer its hop aroma. Remove the pot from the burner and let it cool, covered, for about 20 minutes.

8. Pour 3 gallons of cold water into the sanitized open fermenter fitted with strainer bag; if loose finishing hops were used in step 6, strain the warm wort from step 7 into the cold water. Top up the fermenter to 5½ gallons using cold tap water. Cover the fermenter and cool the wort as rapidly as possible.

9. When the wort has cooled to about 80°, add the yeast starter and ferment as you usually do.

BARLEY WINE
⫴ ⫴ ⫴

NORTHEAST BREWERS SUPPLY— PROVIDENCE, RHODE ISLAND

"A classic English style, this very strong ale offers a huge body that is dominated by a malty sweetness. Barley wines are often aged for months or years, allowing the hop character to fade away. To combat this tendency, this recipe calls for dry-hopping in the secondary fermenter. To avoid problems with stuck fermentation with this high gravity recipe, a yeast starter must be used for the liquid yeast. Prepare the yeast starter according to the instructions given on page 11."

ORIGINAL GRAVITY: 1.086

FINAL GRAVITY: 1.022

POTENTIAL ALCOHOL: 8.5% ABV

INGREDIENTS

1 pound crushed crystal malt

Two 3.3-pound cans light malt extract

3 pounds amber dry malt extract

½ pound malto-dextrin

3 ounces boiling hops (Northern Brewer)

1 ounce flavoring hops (Northern Brewer)

1½ ounces finishing hops for dry-hopping (Cascade)

1 pack liquid ale yeast

¾ cup corn sugar (priming)

BREWING PROCEDURES

1. About 2 days before you're ready to brew, take the liquid yeast out of the refrigerator and pop the inner bag (according to instructions on the package) to get it started. To improve performance of liquid yeast with this recipe, you must use a yeast starter.

2. When you're ready to brew, put the crushed grain mix into one of the boiling bags. Tie off the top of the bag and put it into the biggest stainless steel or enameled pot you can find. Add water to the pot, leaving space for the malt (approx. ¾ gallon) and a cou-

ple of inches at the top for the boil. Apply heat.

3. When the water starts to boil, remove the grains and discard. Add the 3 cans of malt extract (to prevent scorching, turn off heat before adding malt—turn it back on after the malt is well mixed). Put the boiling hops into a bag and drop them into the pot. When the water starts boiling again, set your timer for 30 minutes.

4. After 30 minutes have elapsed, put the flavoring hops into a boiling bag and drop them into the pot. Set your timer for an additional 30 minutes.

5. After you've boiled the wort for a total of 60 minutes, turn off the heat.

6. Cool the wort. There are a couple of ways to do this. If you have a wort chiller, this process takes about 10 minutes. If you're boiling a small quantity of wort (1½ to 3 gallons), you can add it to cold water in your primary fermenter to make up 5 gallons. Whatever method you use, remember the time between the end of the boil and pitching the yeast is when your brew is most susceptible to contamination. Therefore, extra care is warranted during this time to protect the wort from exposure to undesirable microorganisms. Be sure to sanitize everything that comes into contact with your beer with boiling water, chlorine, or iodophor.

7. When the wort has been added to the primary fermenter and cooled to 70–80°F, shake it up for about 5 minutes. After the wort is sufficiently cooled and aerated, add the yeast.

8. Ferment in the primary fermenter for at least a week at room temperature. Rack to the secondary fermenter. Before installing the airlock and stopper (or cover, if you're using a bucket), put the finishing hops into a hop bag and drop them into the fermenter. The finishing gravity is difficult to predict. Optimally, it should finish around 1.020. If it doesn't drop below 1.030, don't worry—it will still turn out great.

9. When you're ready to bottle, dissolve the corn sugar in 2 cups of boiling water. Add to the brew and mix well without disturbing the sediment. This is easy if you first siphon your beer into a bottling bucket and then mix in the sugar solution.

10. Bottle, cap, and put in a warm (65–75°F) environment for at least a week. Start enjoying your barley wine after it's been in the bottle for at least 3 months. You will find that it improves with age. Cheers!

CALIFORNIA BARLEY WINE
🏛 🏛 🏛

DICK FOEHRINGER

THE BREWMEISTER—FAIR OAKS, CALIFORNIA

"This is a barley wine–style beer noted for its malty richness and high alcohol strength. Its full, rich body is balanced with a higher hopping rate, making this a winter warmer that will light up your tree! Patterned after the celebrated Sierra Nevada Big Foot."

ORIGINAL GRAVITY: 1.074

FINAL GRAVITY: 1.019

POTENTIAL ALCOHOL: 7.3% ABV

INGREDIENTS

- 1 pound 20 °L crystal malt
- ½ pound dextrine malt
- ¼ chocolate malt
- 7 pounds pale malt extract
- 2 pounds light dry malt extract
- 2 ounces Northern Brewer hops (60 minutes) boiling
- 1 ounce Hallertauer hops (5 minutes) aromatic
- 2 teaspoons gypsum
- 1 teaspoon Irish moss (15 minutes)
- 1 teaspoon gelatin
- 1 dry ale yeast
- ¾ bottling sugar

BREWING PROCEDURES

1. Put the crushed crystal malt, dextrine, and chocolate malt grains into a grain bag. Place ½ to 2 gallons of cold water in your brewpot. Place grain bag in water and bring to a near boil (160–170°F). Turn off heat and allow grains to steep for 30 minutes. Drain and remove grain.

2. Dissolve extract thoroughly and then return mixture to heat. Bring to a boil. Add the Northern Brewer hops and boil for 45 minutes. Add Irish moss and boil for 10 minutes. Add the aromatic hops and boil for 5 minutes.

3. Cold-break the wort to below 100°F by setting your pan of wort into a sink full of cold water. Put the cooled wort into your primary fermenter and add cold water to make 5½ gallons. When cooled below 85°F, pitch your yeast. (Note: Rehydrate your yeast by dissolving it in ½ cup warm water and allowing it to sit for 10 minutes before pitching.) Ferment in a cool (65–75°F), dark place.

4. When fermentation has ceased, transfer to the secondary, leaving all the sediment behind. Dissolve gelatin in 1 cup hot water and stir into secondary. Allow beer to clear, typically 3–5 days. Rack again, leaving sediment behind.

5. Dissolve bottling sugar in 1 cup of hot water and stir into beer. Bottle and cap.

6. Allow to age/carbonate in the bottles for 2–4 weeks. Enjoy!

PLOUGHMAN'S BARLEYWINE

🍺 🍺 🍺 🍺

STEPHEN SNYDER

The English hop varieties in this recipe can easily be replaced by a fine American variety like Cascade, which will lend a decidedly West Coast character. That is where some of the world's most interesting barley wines are made, after all. Try using Wyeast 1056 American Ale or another American strain as well. Champagne yeast will not be needed if a large volume of a healthy starter is pitched.

ORIGINAL GRAVITY: 1.095

FINAL GRAVITY: 1.025

POTENTIAL ALCOHOL: 9.4% ABV

IBUs: 69

INGREDIENTS (FOR 3 GALLONS)

- 11 pounds 2-row pale ale malt (crushed)
- 0.5 pound 40 °L crystal malt (crushed)
- 1 ounce Bramling Cross hop pellets at 7.1% AA (boil 60 minutes)
- ½ ounce Challenger hop pellets at 8.2% AA (boil 60 minutes)

1 ounce Fuggles hop plugs at 4.1% AA (boil 15 minutes)

1 ounce East Kent Goldings hop plugs (boil 2 minutes)

1 ounce East Kent Goldings hop plugs (dry-hopped 2 weeks)

Wyeast 1098 British Ale or 1214 Belgian Ale yeast in 1 liter starter

0.33 cup corn sugar for priming

BREWING PROCEDURES

1. Saccharification rest. Mash in 3.25 gallons of brewing liquor, carefully stirring to mix the liquor and grist. Rest 90 minutes at 150°F. Stir occasionally.

2. Test for remaining starches with an iodine tincture by adding 1 drop to a tablespoon of wort on a white saucer. If negative (wort no longer turns purplish/black), mash out.

3. Mash out. Raise mash temperature to 165–168°F by adding doses of hot water or bottom heat. Rest 10 minutes to decrease wort viscosity.

4. Transfer to lauter tun if separate vessel is being used. Slowly sparge with 3 gallons of 165–168°F water over 45–60 minutes and collect wort into brew kettle.

5. Collect 4.5 gallons of wort.

6. Boil for 90 minutes, adding hops as noted above.

7. Force-cool with wort chiller.

8. Rack through sanitizer sieve or strainer bag into carboy or other fermenter.

9. Pitch 1 liter yeast starter. Aerate well.

10. Rest beer for 2–3 hours or until trub settles. (Optional.)

11. Rack into primary fermenter and ferment under airlock (or open ferment) at 58–68°F for 5 days. Rack to secondary and add dry hops in sanitized muslin bag. Ferment under airlock for 10–14 days.

12. Rack to stainless steel soda or minikegs and mature for 3–6 months.

13. Rack to bottling bucket, prime, add fresh yeast, and bottle or keg.

14. Condition at 65–70°F for 5 to 7 days.

15. Cellar for 6 months to 3 years.

16. Serve at 50–55°F.

TROUBLE

ANDREW TVEEKREM, BREWMASTER, GREAT LAKES BREWING CO.– CLEVELAND, OHIO

"This is the same recipe as my pale ale but with 3 quarts of thistle honey added. The gravity shoots up to the 1.080 range, yet most of the honey ferments out, leaving a highly quaffable beer with 7–8% alcohol. Trouble indeed!"

ORIGINAL GRAVITY: 1.080

FINAL GRAVITY: 1.020–28

POTENTIAL ALCOHOL: 7–8% ABV

INGREDIENTS (FOR 10 GALLONS)

21 pounds English pale malt

3 pounds English crystal malt

8 pounds (3 quarts) thistle honey

3 good-sized handfuls of Northern Brewer or 2 smaller handfuls of Galena

3 handfuls of Cascade hop pellets

3 handfuls of B.C. Goldings hop pellets

3 handfuls of Kent Goldings hop pellets

A dash of Irish moss

1 quart thick yeast slurry of Wyeast 1028 London Ale

1.5 cups corn sugar for priming

BREWING PROCEDURES

1. Mash crushed malt at 154–156°F for 1 hour, stirring occasionally.
2. Lauter to collect 12 gallons of wort and bring to a boil. Add the 3 quarts of honey.
3. Add 2 or 3 handfuls of Northern Brewer or Galena hop pellets at the beginning of the boil.
4. Boil for 75 minutes, adding 3 more handfuls of Cascade hop pellets at 30 minutes prior to the end. Add 3 more handfuls of B.C. Goldings hop pellets at 15 minutes prior to the end and a dash of Irish moss.
5. At the end of the boil add 3 handfuls of Kent Goldings hops.
6. Swirl, cool, and ferment at 65°F.
7. Rack, prime, and bottle as you normally do.

QUILTER'S IRISH DEATH
🍺 🍺 🍺 🍺

JIM QUILTER, ASSISTANT BREWMASTER, SIERRA NEVADA BREWING CO. INC.– CHICO, CALIFORNIA

If you have the facilities to handle nearly 50 pounds of grain, this simple infusion-mash recipe will provide you with enough barley wine to lay down for many years. Some suggest that most of these strong ales are at their peak after three years in the cellar.

ORIGINAL GRAVITY: 1.140

FINAL GRAVITY: 1.035

POTENTIAL ALCOHOL: 13.5% ABV

INGREDIENTS (FOR 10 GALLONS)

    30 pounds pale malt
    15 pounds wheat malt

    1½ pounds caramel malt
    1 pound black patent malt
    1 pound chocolate malt
    1½ cups molasses
    2 ounces Brewers Gold (⅓ at first boil, ⅔ after ½ hour)
    1 ounce Fuggles (2 hours into boil)
    2 ounces Hallertau (steep 10 minutes at end of boil)
    2 ounces Centennial whole hops
    1 ounce Cascade whole hops
    Ale yeast* or Wyeast 1056 American Ale yeast
    1½ cups corn sugar for priming

BREWING PROCEDURES

Propagate yeast from Sierra Nevada Pale Ale 4 days prior to brewing. Propagate and pitch at 64°F.

1. Mash at 154°F for 1 hour.
2. Boil for 2½ hours, adding hops as noted above.
3. Add 1½ cups molasses when heat is turned off; just before aromatic hops, stir well.
4. Rinse wort through Centennial and Cascade hops.
5. Ferment at 68°F.
6. Use your favorite priming and packaging methods. Age for 1 year or more.

BRUTUS
🍺 🍺 🍺 🍺

ANDREW TVEEKREM, BREWMASTER, GREAT LAKES BREWING CO.– CLEVELAND, OHIO

"Here is a great barley wine for midwinter consumption. It tastes great at six months and is astounding at one year."

ORIGINAL GRAVITY: 1.136–42

FINAL GRAVITY: 1.030–40

POTENTIAL ALCOHOL: 13.3–13.8% ABV

INGREDIENTS (FOR 10 GALLONS)

40 pounds English pale malt

36 pounds (3 gallons) thistle honey

Hops: "You cannot hop this monster enough. Use a bunch of Galena up front, then work down to Northern Brewer and Cascade. You should have about 4 gallons of trub left in the kettle if you did it right."

1 quart thick yeast slurry of Wyeast 1028 London Ale

1.5 cups corn sugar for priming

BREWING PROCEDURES

1. Mash crushed malt at 154–156°F for 1 hour, stirring occasionally.

2. Lauter to collect 12 gallons of wort and bring to a boil. Add the honey after boiling for 1 hour. Bring back to a boil and go for another hour—it takes a good 2-hour boil to develop the proper flavor on big beers like this.

3. Add Galena hop pellets at the beginning of the boil.

4. Boil for 120 minutes, adding Northern Brewer hop pellets at 30 minutes prior to the end. Add Cascade hop pellets at 15 minutes prior to the end.

5. Swirl, cool, and ferment at 65°F. Be sure to aerate the wort vigorously and pitch plenty of yeast.

6. Primary fermentation usually takes a week, sometimes two.

7. Rack to secondary for at least a month.

ALTBIER

I will leave the description of this beer style to Dr. Paul Bösken-Diebels of Privatbrauerei Diebels in Issum, Germany, who writes: "With the explanation given below, it will be possible for a well-trained homebrewer to produce a good Alt.

"'Alt,' the German word for 'old,' is a synonym for the traditional, old way of brewing beer. This type of dark, top-fermented beer has been brewed in the areas of mild climate in Germany since the very first days of brewing. Its brewing method has been kept unchanged in the lower Rhein region until today. In the past, in regions with cold winters brewers could control fermentation and storage temperatures of their lager-beer with ice cut with saws from frozen lakes. In the Rhein area, however, winters are too mild to produce enough natural ice.

"Alt is produced in a quantity of approximately 4 million hectoliters per annum—mainly in Nordrhein-Westfalen. Various little breweries share the market with the main brand, our Diebels Alt, brewed in Issum. Privatbrauerei Diebels Alt sales exceeded 1.7 million hectoliters in 1992.

"Alt is brewed according to the 'Reinheitsgebot' of 1516 from water, malt, hops, and yeast with an original gravity of 11.0–12.0 °P (1.044–1.048). Alt is always dark (30–35 EBC)

(12–14 SRM), quite contrary to Kölsch, another top-fermented beer being brewed in Cologne with light color. Alt is a dry and bitter beer with approximately 28–38 IBU. The color derives from roasted malt while the main quantity of the malt used is normal malt. The necessary quantity of roasted malt to be added depends on the color intensity of this malt.

"By an intensive mash program a complete saccharification is intended. Lautering and wort boiling will be made according to the existing facilities of the brewery. The starting fermentation temperature is higher than for lager type beers and varies between 14°C and 18°C (57–64°F). A special strain of top-fermenting *Saccharomyces cerevisiae* must be used [e.g., Wyeast's 1338 or 1007, BrewTek CL–400, or Yeast Lab A06—ed.].

"According to the high fermentation temperatures, the fermentation period is rather short. After diacetyl reduction, the beer will be cooled, separated from the yeast—the yeast will not settle—and lagered at temperatures of about 0°C (32°F) for approximately three weeks. When filtered and bottled, a tasty, wholesome beer is ready for the first trial."

Long Trail Ale, Harpoon Alt, August Schell Schmaltz's Alt, Widmer Alt, and St. Stan's Dark Alt represent notable American versions, although some experts argue that these generally have more hop aroma and flavor than the German originals, such as Diebels Alt and Hannen Alt.

ALTBIER BASICS

ORIGINAL GRAVITY: 1.043–48

FINAL GRAVITY: 1.008–14

IBUs: 28–50

COLOR (SRM): 10–16

ALCOHOL BY VOLUME: 4.5–5%

NEW ALT BIER
🍺 🍺 🍺

THE HOME BEER, WINE, & CHEESEMAKING SHOP—WOODLAND HILLS, CALIFORNIA

This an excellent formulation that uses fine aroma hop varieties virtually unknown to most homebrewers. The Strissel Spalt is a classic French aroma variety, the Select and Tradition are newer Bavarian varieties that produce the mellow and rounded bitterness imperative for this beer style.

ORIGINAL GRAVITY: 1.048

FINAL GRAVITY: 1.011

POTENTIAL ALCOHOL: 4.8% ABV

IBUs: 31

COLOR: 5 SRM

INGREDIENTS

- 4 ounces Belgian aromatic malt
- 4 ounces dextrine malt
- 4 ounces German 10 °L crystal malt
- 5 pounds light DME
- 1.5 ounces Select whole hops at 4.7% AA (60 minutes)
- 1 ounce Strissel Spalt whole hops at 2.5% AA (20 minutes)
- 0.5 ounce Hallertau Tradition whole hops at 6.3% AA (2 minutes)
- 1 teaspoon Irish moss
- 2 teaspoons gypsum

Wyeast 1338 European Ale yeast, 1 liter
starter
¾ cup corn sugar for priming

BREWING PROCEDURES

1. Steep (soak) the crushed grains in 2 quarts
   of 150°F water for 30–40 minutes. Sparge
   (rinse) with 2.5 quarts of 150°F water into
   your boiling pot. Discard grain. No water
   over 170°F with grain. Do not oversparge.
   Do not squeeze grain bag.
2. After adding 2.5 gallons of water and dissolving the malt, bring pot to a gentle but
   rolling boil. Skim all foam before starting
   the hop sequence. Add Irish moss the last
   20 minutes to remove the protein missed in
   steps 1 and 2. Add the gypsum into the boil.
   It adds hardness, accentuating the crisp hop
   character.
3. Ferment at an average of 58–62°F for minimal esters. Pitch (add) yeast when your
   water bath around the fermenter reads
   70–80°F. Maintain this temperature until
   the first signs of fermentation (about 10–12
   hours). If using a yeast starter (highly recommended), fermentation can start in 2–3
   hours. Use ¾ cup sugar for priming.

ALTBIER
🍺 🍺 🍺

BOSTON BREWERS SUPPLY CO.—
JAMAICA PLAIN, MASSACHUSETTS

"The differences between German and English
pale ales stem not only from the German hops
and malts used but from a unique yeast culture
and perhaps more significantly a cool secondary ferment that greatly reduces the esters
produced during the warm primary phase. This
process truly is the hallmark of an authentic
German altbier. This recipe uses a pure liquid
yeast culture that must be prepared in advance
of your brewing session. You'll be amazed how
much they contribute to the flavor and aroma
of the beer."

ORIGINAL GRAVITY: 1.046–48

FINAL GRAVITY: 1.012–14

POTENTIAL ALCOHOL: 4.5% ABV

IBUs: 32 to 36

INGREDIENTS

- 4 ounces Ireks Munich malt
- 4 ounces Ireks Vienna malt
- 4 ounces Ireks light crystal malt
- 4 ounces Ireks wheat malt
- 6.6 pounds Ireks light malt extract
- 2 ounces Spalt hop pellets
- 1 ounce Tettnang hop pellets
- 1 teaspoon Irish moss flakes
- 1 package Wyeast 1338
- 6 ounces corn sugar for priming

BREWING PROCEDURES

1. Secure the crushed grains in the muslin
   straining bag. Pour 2 gallons of cold water
   into your brewpot, apply heat, and add the
   grain bag. Heat to a near boil (about
   155°F), then remove the grain bag, drain,
   and discard.
2. Turn off the heat and, while stirring constantly, dissolve all of the malt extract. As soon
   as the boil begins, add the 2 ounces of Spalt
   hops and start timing the boil; the total
   elapsed time will be 60 minutes. Maintain a
   good rolling boil and stir occasionally. While
   the wort is boiling, divide the Tettnang hops

into 2 half-ounce portions. They will be added at separate time intervals. After 20 minutes add ½ ounce of the Tettnang hops. Twenty minutes later add the remaining Tettnang hops and the Irish moss flakes. Continue to boil for the remaining 20 minutes, then cover and remove the pot from the heat.

Remember that after the wort has cooled, it is highly vulnerable to contamination; everything that comes into contact with it from this point on must be thoroughly sanitized!

3. Cool the wort as quickly as possible. A wort chiller works best, but if you haven't got one yet a cold water bath will do the trick. Place the covered pot in your kitchen sink and fill with ice and cold water. When the temperature has fallen to about 90°F, transfer the wort, through a strainer if possible, into your fermenter. Top off with enough cold water to reach a 5-gallon level and stir or shake well. If you are using a glass carboy for fermentation, it is a good idea to add the cold water first. Draw off a small sample and take both a hydrometer and a temperature reading; always discard the sample used.

4. When the wort has cooled to 65–70°F, you are ready to add the yeast. Once the yeast has been added, attach an airlock and keep the fermenter in a cool, dark location where temperature fluctuations are minimal, ideally 65–70°F. Active fermentation should become visible in the next 12 to 24 hours and will continue for about 3 to 5 days.

5. When visible signs of fermentation have ceased, gently siphon the beer into a sanitized secondary fermenter (ideally a 5-gallon glass carboy), leaving sediment behind. Attach an airlock and allow the beer to con-

dition for 3 to 4 weeks as cool as you can get it, ideally 40–45°F. During the winter months a cold basement or hallway should get you close. Do the best you can; even at slightly warmer temperatures you'll still have a great-tasting beer.

BOTTLING AND CONDITIONING

1. Sanitize all of your siphoning and bottling equipment, bottles, and caps.

2. Boil the 6 ounces of corn sugar in about a pint of water and pour it into your bottling bucket. Gently siphon the beer (again leaving sediment behind) out of the fermenter into the bucket, making sure the flow is directed to the bottom of the bucket; avoid splashing or agitating the beer. Reserve the last remnants to take thermometer and hydrometer readings; this will be your final gravity.

3. Using your siphon tubing and bottle filler, fill each bottle to within an inch from the top and cap immediately. Store the bottles upright at room temperature—about 65–70°F for a minimum of 3 weeks. Chill and enjoy.

GERMAN ALTBIER
⫼ ⫼

DICK FOEHRINGER
THE BREWMEISTER–FAIR OAKS, CALIFORNIA

The beauty of alt lies in its simplicity of ingredients and brewing methods. This recipe is true to that tradition and produces a malty traditional altbier that will only improve with age and a little cold lagering. Prost!

ORIGINAL GRAVITY: 1.050

FINAL GRAVITY: 1.012

POTENTIAL ALCOHOL: 4.9% ABV

INGREDIENTS

> ½ pound Munich malt
> ½ pound 20 °L crystal malt
> 7 pounds amber malt extract
> 2 ounces Tettnanger (60 minutes) boiling
> 1 teaspoon Irish moss (15 minutes)
> 1 Wyeast 1007 German Ale liquid yeast
> 1 teaspoon gelatin
> ¾ cup bottling sugar

BREWING PROCEDURES

1. Put the crushed crystal malt and Munich malt grains into a bag. Place 1½ to 2 gallons of cold water in your brewpot. Place grain bag in water and bring to a near boil (160°F). Turn off heat and allow grain to steep for 30 minutes. Drain and remove grain.

2. Dissolve liquid extract thoroughly and then return mixture to heat. Bring to a boil. Add the 2 ounces of hops and boil for 45 minutes. Add Irish moss and boil for 15 minutes. Cold-break the wort to below 100°F by setting your pan of wort into a sink full of cold water.

3. Put the cooled wort into your primary fermenter and add cold water to make 5½ gallons. When cooled below 75°F, pitch your yeast. (Note: You must start the liquid yeast 1–2 days prior to brewing to allow it to culture up. Follow the instructions on the package for preparation.)

4. Ferment in a cool (65–75°F), dark place. When fermentation has ceased, transfer to the secondary, leaving all the sediment behind. Dissolve gelatin in 1 cup hot water and stir into secondary. Replace airlock and allow beer to clear, typically 3–5 days.

5. Rack again, leaving sediment behind. Dissolve bottling sugar in 1 cup of hot water and stir into beer. Bottle and cap.

6. Allow to age/carbonate in the bottles for 2–4 weeks. Enjoy!

GERMAN ALT

BEER & WINE HOBBY—WOBURN, MASSACHUSETTS

This is a good recipe to ease yourself into using specialty grains for added coloring and character. It primarily uses German malt extract and has the right hops and yeast for authenticity. Try giving this one 3 weeks at near freezing temperatures in a secondary or after conditioning in bottles for an even cleaner Düsseldorf flavor.

ORIGINAL GRAVITY: 1.040–45

FINAL GRAVITY: 1.010–14

POTENTIAL ALCOHOL: 3.8–4% ABV

INGREDIENTS

> ½ pound German dark crystal malt
> 2 ounces chocolate malt
> 2 cans Bierkeller light liquid malt
> 1 pound light dry malt
> 1 ounce Perle hop pellets (boil)
> 1 ounce Tettnang hop pellets (boil)
> 1 ounce Tettnang hop pellets (last 2 minutes)
> 1 package Burton water salts
> 1 teaspoon Irish moss

Yeast Lab AO6 Düsseldorfer Alt yeast
(starter required)
¾ cup priming sugar

BREWING PROCEDURES

1. Crush grains, place in muslin bag, and tie. Add grains to 2 gallons of cold water and bring to a boil. When water comes to a boil, remove from heat and discard grains.

2. Add 2 cans of German light malt, 1 pound light dry malt, 1 ounce Perle hop pellets, and 1 ounce Tettnang hop pellets. Put back on heat and return to a boil; boil for 20 minutes. Add 1 teaspoon Irish moss and package of Burton water salts; continue to boil for 15 minutes more. During the last 2 minutes add 1 ounce Tettnang hop pellets.

3. Remove from heat and add to primary fermenter containing enough cold water to bring total volume to 5 ¼ gallons. When wort has cooled to 65–75˚F, pitch prepared yeast.

4. Proceed as usual. Finish fermenting.

5. Prime with ¾ cup priming sugar and bottle.

RHINE CASTLE ALT
🍺 🍺 🍺

STEPHEN SNYDER

I used a mix of German malts to provide not only a deep copper color but also to lend a malty, bready aroma that makes alt so appetizing. If you like your alts drier, use an American or British extract exclusively, for the Dutch produces a lot of residual sweetness and a rich dextrinous beer. Using malt extract for priming instead of sugar enhances the full-bodied maltiness (and allows you to boast compliance with the Reinheitsgebot).

ORIGINAL GRAVITY: 1.047

FINAL GRAVITY: 1.015

POTENTIAL ALCOHOL: 4.5% ABV

IBUs: 28

HBUs: 8

INGREDIENTS

¼ pound (1 cup) German light crystal malt

¼ pound (1 cup) Vienna malt

¼ pound (1 cup) Munich malt

1 pound English light DME

4½ pounds Dutch light DME

½ ounce Spalter hop pellets 4.5% AA (boil) 60 minutes

1 ounce Hallertau Hersbrucker hop plugs 2.9% AA (boil) 60 minutes

1 ounce Hallertau Hersbrucker hop plugs 2.9% AA (boil) 30 minutes

Wyeast 1007 (German Ale/Mild Alt) liquid yeast with starter

¾ cup corn sugar

BREWING PROCEDURES

1. Place cracked crystal, Munich, and Vienna malts in hop bag and put into ½ gallon of cold water. (I boiled, then cooled ½ gallon of water beforehand to remove chlorine). Bring slowly to 158˚F. Rest for 45 minutes, then strain liquid into brew kettle. Sparge grains lightly with hot water.

2. Add 1 gallon of cold water and bring to a boil. (I also boiled, then cooled, 1 gallon of water beforehand to remove chlorine). Remove brew kettle from heat before adding extract and DME to avoid sticking or burning.

3. Boil for 60 minutes, adding hops as noted above. Hot-break trub should be skimmed throughout boil.

4. Use wort chiller or let hot wort sit for 30 minutes (covered) in ice-water bath before straining into a single-stage fermenter containing 2 gallons ice-cold water (33–40°F). Wort should now be ready for pitching yeast.

5. Make certain wort is below 75°F before pitching yeast. Stir vigorously to aerate. Cover and fit with airlock (or blowoff hose if using a carboy, then use an airlock after blowoff ceases) and move to dark, quiet, draft-free space and ferment at 68°F.

6. Ferment for 7–10 days or until fermentation ceases. (Longer fermentation in the primary [10–14 days] will further reduce diacetyl.)

7. Prime with sugar dissolved in 1 pint boiling water and bottle.

8. Warm-condition 7–14 days at room temperature (68°F). Store cold (32°F) 6 weeks and serve at 45–50°F.

EIN ALT BITTE*
🍺 🍺 🍺 🍺

PAUL WHITE, HEAD BREWER, THE SEVEN BARREL BREWERY—WEST LEBANON, NEW HAMPSHIRE

"(*Translation: An Alt Bier Please!) The name comes from all I needed to know how to say during a week in Germany."

ORIGINAL GRAVITY: 1.063

FINAL GRAVITY: 1.018

POTENTIAL ALCOHOL: 6% ABV

INGREDIENTS (FOR 5.5 GALLONS)

> 1 pound wheat malt
> 12 ounces crystal malt
> 4 ounces dextrine malt
> 8 ounces flaked barley
> 7½ pounds 2-row pale malt
> 12 AAUs of Northern Brewer whole flower hops
> 5–6 AAUs of Cascade whole flower hops
> 1 teaspoon of Irish moss
> German Ale culture or Edme ale yeast
> ¾ cup corn sugar for priming

BREWING PROCEDURES

1. Mash in 3 gallons at 148°F for 1½ hours. Mash out and sparge to collect 6 gallons.

2. Bring to a boil, and after 15 minutes add 12 AAUs of Northern Brewer flowers. Boil for 55 minutes, adding 1 teaspoon of Irish moss at 45-minute mark. Add 5–6 AAUs of Cascade flowers for 5 minutes.

3. End boil, cool to 70°F, pitch a German Ale culture or Edme ale yeast.

4. Ferment, bottle, and age at least 2 months.

KÖLSCH

A pale golden or blond German ale with a subdued malt flavor, moderate hop bitterness, and low hop flavor and aroma. Like alt bier, this is a beer from the "old" brewing tradition before lagers took over. Traditional German recipes include very hard water, Vienna malt, wheat malt, pilsner malt, crystal malt, and German hop varieties. Warm primary and secondary fermentations should be followed by three to six weeks of cold lagering, as with alt. Bottling with lager yeast will greatly improve clarity, but a slight cloudiness is normal. If you are interested in crafting your own Kölsch but are unsure that you'll like this unique taste, you'll have a hard time finding a German import, so sample the excellent microbrewed versions: Hart Brewing's Pyramid Kålsch, Long Trail Kölsch, or Goose Island's Kölsch Beer.

KÖLSCH BASICS

ORIGINAL GRAVITY: 1.044–48

FINAL GRAVITY: 1.006–10

IBUs: 25–30

COLOR (SRM): 3.5–5.5

ALCOHOL BY VOLUME: 4.5–5%

KÖLSCH
🛢🛢🛢

THE HOME BEER, WINE, & CHEESEMAKING SHOP—WOODLAND HILLS, CALIFORNIA

As in their alt bier recipe, The Home Beer, Wine, & Cheesemaking Shop demonstrates their ability to incorporate new and interesting hop varieties. The Crystal and Ultra have many of the wonderful aroma qualities of Hallertau Mittelfrüh, and Strissel Spalt is a highly regarded bière de garde hop with similarities to Saaz.

ORIGINAL GRAVITY: 1.047

FINAL GRAVITY: 1.009

POTENTIAL ALCOHOL: 4.9% ABV

IBUs: 16

COLOR: 4 SRM

INGREDIENTS

- 4 ounces victory malt
- 4 ounces dextrine malt
- 3 pounds light DME
- 2 pounds rice solids
- 1 ounce Crystal hop pellets at 3.2% AA (60 minutes)
- 0.5 ounce Ultra hop pellets at 2.5% AA (20 minutes)
- 0.5 ounce Strissel Spalt whole hops at 2.5% AA (2 minutes)
- 1 teaspoon Irish moss
- 1 teaspoon gypsum
- Wyeast 2565 Kölsch yeast
- ¾ cup corn sugar for priming

BREWING PROCEDURES

1. Steep (soak) the crushed grains in 2 quarts of 150°F water for 30–40 minutes. Sparge (rinse) with 2.5 quarts of 150°F water into

your boiling pot. Discard grain. No water over 170°F with grain. Do not oversparge. Do not squeeze grain bag.

2. After adding 2.5 gallons of water and dissolving the malt, bring pot to a gentle but rolling boil. Skim all foam before starting the hop sequence. Add Irish moss the last 20 minutes to remove the protein missed in steps 1 and 2. Add the gypsum into the boil. It adds hardness, accentuating the crisp hop character.

3. Ferment at an average of 58–62°F. This keeps the fruity esters to a minimum. Pitch (add) yeast when your water bath around the fermenter reads 70–80°F. Maintain this temperature until the first signs of fermentation (about 10–12 hours). If using a yeast starter (highly recommended), fermentation can start in 2–3 hours. Use ¾ cup sugar for priming.

KÖLSCH–GERMAN PALE ALE

🍺 🍺

DICK FOEHRINGER

THE BREWMEISTER—FAIR OAKS, CALIFORNIA

"Kölsch is a pale version of German alt beer from the region around Cologne. It is a light, fruity, medium-hopped dry ale, excellent for summer quaffing!"

ORIGINAL GRAVITY: 1.052

FINAL GRAVITY: 1.014

POTENTIAL ALCOHOL: 4.9% ABV

INGREDIENTS

   ½ pound Munich malt
   ½ pound 20 °L crystal malt

7 pounds pale malt extract
2 ounces Tettnanger hops (60 minutes) boiling
1 teaspoon Irish moss (15 minutes)
1 Wyeast 1007 German Ale yeast
1 teaspoon gelatin
¾ cup bottling sugar

BREWING PROCEDURES

1. Put the crushed crystal malt and Munich malt grains into a bag. Place 1½ to 2 gallons of cold water in your brewpot. Place grain bag in water and bring to a near boil (160°F). Turn off heat and allow grain to steep for 30 minutes. Drain and remove grain.

2. Dissolve liquid extract thoroughly and then return mixture to heat. Bring to a boil. Add the 2 ounces of hops and boil for 45 minutes. Add Irish moss and boil for 15 minutes. Cold-break the wort to below 100°F by setting your pan of wort into a sink full of cold water.

3. Put the cooled wort into your primary fermenter and add cold water to make 5½ gallons. When cooled below 85°F, pitch your yeast. (Note: You must start the liquid yeast 1–2 days prior to brewing to allow it to culture up. Follow the instructions on the package for preparation.)

4. Ferment in a cool (65–75°F), dark place. When fermentation has ceased, transfer to the secondary, leaving all the sediment behind. Dissolve gelatin in 1 cup hot water and stir into secondary. Replace airlock and allow beer to clear, typically 3–5 days.

5. Rack again, leaving sediment behind. Dissolve bottling sugar in 1 cup of hot water and stir into beer. Bottle and cap.

6. Allow to age/carbonate in the bottles for 2–4 weeks. Enjoy!

WEIZENBIER

Wheat beer in its modern form, also known as weizen (German for "wheat"), weisse, or weissbier (German for "white beer"), gained a fanatical following in Bavaria during the later part of the seventeenth century. Wheat beers are now enjoying a renewed popularity worldwide, especially in Germany (weizenbiers now account for 50 percent of Spaten Brewery's production). Beers typical of the style are made with roughly a fifty-fifty mixture of wheat and barley malt. They are also characterized by phenolic flavors and estery aromas provided primarily by special top-fermenting yeast strains. Weizenbiers are made from a wide range of brewing waters commercially and require no special parameters.

Freshness is more important to this style than any other, primarily due to the low hop content. In Germany, weizenbiers are usually full-flavored ales with hints of clove and spice esters. American wheat beers tend to be cleaner and softer in flavor without the wild yeast influences and are included with the "North American ales." All wheat beers should be well-carbonated and low in hop bitterness, aroma, and flavor. Franziskaner Hefe-Weissbier, Maisel's Weisse, Hübsch Hefe Weizen, Ayinger Ur-Weisse, August Schell Weizen, Schneider Weisse, and Paulener Hefe-Weissbier are among the multitude of good commercial brands.

WEIZENBIER BASICS

ORIGINAL GRAVITY: 1.048–55

FINAL GRAVITY: 1.008–16

IBUs: 10–18

COLOR (SRM): 3–10

ALCOHOL BY VOLUME: 4.5–5.5%

WEIZENBOCK BASICS

ORIGINAL GRAVITY: 1.065–80

FINAL GRAVITY: 1.026–32

IBUs: 15–25

COLOR (SRM): 7–30

ALCOHOL BY VOLUME: 6.5–7.5%

NORTHWESTERN WHEAT 🍺🍺

PAUL WHITE, HEAD BREWER, THE SEVEN BARREL BREWERY—WEST LEBANON, NEW HAMPSHIRE

Because of Weizenbier's lower hopping rates and low usage of specialty malts, the recipes are inherently simple. This is a perfect example. A simple recipe that nevertheless produces an exceptionally authentic brew in either the Bavarian or the American style.

ORIGINAL GRAVITY: 1.046

FINAL GRAVITY: 1.014

POTENTIAL ALCOHOL: 4.1% ABV

INGREDIENTS

> 6.6 pounds Northwestern Weizen malt extract
>
> 1½ ounces Hallertau hops (bittering) 5–6 AAUs
>
> ½ ounce Hallertau hops (flavoring)
>
> Yeast Lab W51 yeast (for German style) American Ale yeast (for American style)
>
> ¾ cup corn sugar for priming

BREWING PROCEDURES

1. Mix extract well with hot water, then bring to a boil. When the boil is under control, add bittering hops and start timing. Total length of boil will be 60 minutes.
2. If using Irish moss, add 2 teaspoons 20 minutes before the end of the boil.
3. Add flavoring hops 15 minutes before the end of boil.
4. Cool to achieve 70°–80°F degrees after topping up in the fermenter, and pitch yeast.
5. Ferment, prime, and bottle as normal.

WHEAT BEER

JOE & BRYAN TIMMONS

BOSTON BREWERS SUPPLY CO.– JAMAICA PLAIN, MASSACHUSETTS

"Our wheat beer is a great thirst quencher and a summertime favorite of ours. The six pounds of extract included yields a relatively low original gravity, which allows the tartness of the wheat (approximately 25 percent of the fermentables) and subtle spiciness of the hops to blend perfectly. A more authentic clovelike aroma can be achieved by using a liquid yeast culture."

ORIGINAL GRAVITY: 1.045–48

FINAL GRAVITY: 1.010–12

POTENTIAL ALCOHOL: 4.5% ABV

IBUs: approximately 12

INGREDIENTS

> 3 pounds plain light extract
>
> 3 pounds weizen malt extract
>
> 1 pound wheat malt
>
> 1 ounce Hallertau hop pellets
>
> 1 ounce Saaz hop pellets
>
> 1 teaspoon Irish moss
>
> 1 package dry ale yeast or Wyeast 3056 Bavarian Wheat
>
> ¾ cup corn sugar for priming

BREWING PROCEDURES

1. Secure the crushed grains in the muslin straining bag. Pour 2 gallons of cold water into your brewpot, apply heat, and add the grain bag. Heat to a near boil (about 155°F), then remove the grain bag, drain, and discard.
2. Turn off the heat and, while stirring constantly, dissolve all of the malt extract. Bring to a boil and add the 1 ounce of Hallertau hop pellets. Immediately start timing the boil; the total elapsed time will be 45 minutes. The following additions should be made according to the schedule below:

   30 minutes into the boil, add the Irish moss flakes.

   40 minutes into the boil add the 1 ounce of Saaz pellets.

   Remember that after the wort has cooled, it is highly vulnerable to contamination; everything that comes into contact with it from this point on must be thoroughly sanitized!

3. Cool the wort as quickly as possible. A wort chiller works best, but if you haven't got one

yet a cold water bath will do the trick. Place the covered pot in your kitchen sink and fill with ice and cold water. When the temperature has fallen to about 90°F, transfer the wort, through a strainer if possible, into your fermenter. Top off with enough cold water to reach a 5-gallon level and stir or shake well. Draw off a small sample and take both a hydrometer and a temperature reading; always discard the sample used.

4. When the wort has cooled to 65–70°F, you are ready to add the yeast. Once the yeast has been added, attach an airlock and keep the fermenter in a cool, dark location where temperature fluctuations are minimal, ideally 65–70°F. Active fermentation should become visible in the next 12 to 24 hours and will continue for about 3 to 5 days.

5. After 5 days of primary fermentation, carefully siphon the beer into a secondary fermenter, leaving as much sediment as possible behind. Attach an airlock and let settle and clarify for an additional 5 to 10 days.

6. At the end of this period, draw off a small sample and check the final gravity. By now it should be within the range stated above; if not, wait another couple of days and check again. Prepare to bottle.

BOTTLING AND CONDITIONING

1. Sanitize all of your siphoning and bottling equipment, bottles, and caps.

2. Boil the ¾ cup of corn sugar in about a pint of water and pour it into your bottling bucket. Gently siphon the beer (again leaving sediment behind) out of the fermenter into the bucket, making sure the flow is directed to the bottom of the bucket; avoid splashing or agitating the beer.

3. Using your siphon tubing and bottle filler, fill each bottle to within an inch from the top and cap immediately. Store the bottles upright for a minimum of 3 weeks, chill, and enjoy.

BAVARIAN WHEAT BEER

NORTHEAST BREWERS SUPPLY— PROVIDENCE, RHODE ISLAND

"Sometimes called the 'Champagne of Beer,' wheat beer is known for its crisp, refreshing character. Lightly hopped, this brew should be served cold and perhaps with a slice of lemon. We suggest liquid Bavarian wheat beer yeast from Wyeast with this recipe because it is the yeast, rather than the wheat, that provides this style with its unique character. As an ale, this recipe is a quick, easy, and satisfying beverage for the home brewer."

ORIGINAL GRAVITY: 1.052

FINAL GRAVITY: 1.013

POTENTIAL ALCOHOL: 5% ABV

INGREDIENTS

½ pound light crystal malt

One 4-pound can Alexander's pale malt extract

Two 1.5-pound cans Alexander's wheat "Kicker"

2 ounces boiling hops (Hallertau whole hops)

½ teaspoon Irish moss

1 package Wyeast 3056 Bavarian Wheat liquid yeast

¾ cup corn sugar for priming

BREWING PROCEDURES

1. About 2 days before you're ready to brew, take the liquid yeast out of the refrigerator and pop the inner bag (according to instructions on the package) to get it started. To improve performance of liquid yeast, it is recommended that you use a yeast starter. Instructions for preparing a yeast starter are given on page 11.

2. When you're ready to brew, put the crushed grain mix into one of the boiling bags. Tie off the top of the bag and put it into the biggest stainless steel or enameled pot you can find. Add water to the pot, leaving space for the malt (approx. ¾ gallon) and a couple of inches at the top for the boil. Apply heat.

3. When the water starts to boil, remove the grains and discard. Add the 3 cans of malt extract and kickers (to prevent scorching, turn off heat before adding malt—turn it back on after malt is well mixed). Put the boiling hops into a bag and drop them into the pot. When the water starts boiling again, set your timer for 25 minutes.

4. After 25 minutes, add the Irish moss and set your timer for an additional 20 minutes.

5. After you've boiled the wort for a total of 45 minutes, turn off the heat.

6. Cool the wort. There are a couple of ways to do this. If you have a wort chiller, this process takes about 10 minutes. If you're boiling a small quantity of wort (1½ to 3 gallons), you can add it to cold water in your primary fermenter to make up 5 gallons. Whatever method you use, remember the time between the end of the boil and pitching the yeast is when your brew is most susceptible to contamination. Therefore, extra care is warranted during this time to protect the wort from exposure to undesirable microorganisms. Be sure to sanitize everything that comes into contact with your beer with boiling water, chlorine, or iodophor.

7. When the wort has been added to the primary fermenter and cooled to 70–80°F, add the yeast.

8. Ferment at 65–70°F (in a single- or two-stage fermenting system—your choice) until the specific gravity falls to below 1.015. This should take approximately 1–2 weeks.

9. When you're ready to bottle, dissolve the corn sugar in 2 cups of boiling water. Add to the brew and mix well without disturbing the sediment. This is easy if you first siphon your beer into a bottling bucket and then mix in the sugar solution.

10. Bottle, cap, and put in a warm (65–75°F) environment for at least 2 days. Your wheat beer will be ready to drink in about 2 weeks and will improve with age. Cheers!

YEASTY BEASTY WHEAT
🍺🍺

THE CELLAR HOMEBREW—SEATTLE, WASHINGTON

"A unique German style recently revived and revised by American microbreweries. A highly carbonated, lightly hopped wheat beer with plenty of yeast, this beer goes well with a squeeze of lemon."

ORIGINAL GRAVITY: 1.058

FINAL GRAVITY: 1.015

POTENTIAL ALCOHOL: 5.8% ABV

INGREDIENTS (FOR 5.5 GALLONS)

> 1 pound German light crystal malt
>
> 1 pound German wheat malt
>
> 6 pounds Alexander's wheat bulk malt syrup
>
> 1 can Alexander's wheat "Kicker"
>
> 1 ounce Hallertauer hops (boiling)
>
> 1 package Edme dry ale or Bavarian Wheat liquid yeast
>
> ¾ cup corn sugar for priming

BREWING PROCEDURES

Note: If you are using the Bavarian Wheat liquid yeast with this recipe, be sure to start that yeast at least 1 to 3 days before doing any of the brewing steps below. Follow the package directions and use the yeast in step 5.

1. Place the crushed German light crystal and German wheat malts in a strainer bag. Add this bag of grain to your brewing kettle, which contains 2 to 2½ gallons brewing water. Bring the brewing water to a boil, then remove the bag of grains. It is not a good idea to boil these specialty grains for any length of time as they may contribute a bitter or grainy taste to the finished beer.

2. Sparge (rinse) the bag of grains with about 1 quart of hot tap water into the brewing kettle; dispose of the spent grains.

3. Remove the brewing kettle from the burner and add the 6 pounds of Alexander's wheat malt extract and the 1 can of Alexander's wheat "Kicker." The syrup is easier to pour if the can has been previously placed in hot water. Also, rinse the can with hot water to ensure that all the syrup goes into the kettle. Stir the mixture, now called "wort," until it boils. Watch carefully at this time because the wort may boil over. You can prevent this

by pouring a cup of cold water into the over-boiling wort.

4. At boiling point, add the Hallertau boiling hops. Hops can be placed in a hop bag or added loose, to be later strained out after the boil using a strainer bag. Time the boil for about 1 hour, stirring occasionally. After the first 10 minutes of this boil, remove 2 cups of wort in measuring cup and cover with foil or plastic. Cool to 90°F for use in step 5 below.

5. Making the yeast starter: For dry yeast, use ½ cup warm tap water (90—100°F). Sprinkle the contents of yeast packet into that water, cover for at least 15 minutes, and then add to the 2 cups of wort you prepared in step 4. Cover and set aside for use in step 8 below. For liquid yeast, prepare 1 to 3 days ahead of brewing time per package instructions. Open the swollen package and add the contents to the 2 cups of wort as prepared in step 4.

6. After the wort has boiled for that 1 hour, remove the pot from the burner and let it cool, covered, for about 20 minutes.

7. Pour 3 gallons of cold water into the sanitized open fermenter followed by the warm wort from step 6. Top up the fermenter to 5½ gallons using cold tap water. Cover the fermenter and cool the wort as rapidly as possible.

8. When the wort has cooled to about 80°F, add the yeast starter and ferment as you usually do.

9. OPTIONAL STEP: If you choose to add extra "hefe" (yeast) to your brew, save ⅓ of your yeast starter from step 5 in a sanitized beer bottle fitted with an airlock on top and place in the refrigerator until bottling time. Add this to your beer at the same time as you add the priming sugar.

SALZBURGER KRISTALL-WEIZEN

⑪ ⑪

STEPHEN SNYDER

Although technically not a true kristall weizen unless the yeast sediment is removed by counterpressure filling, etc., you can achieve excellent clarity in bottle-conditioned versions by careful pouring and the use of lager yeast for priming. Serve with a lemon slice if desired for a bright, spritzy summer refresher.

ORIGINAL GRAVITY: 1.042

FINAL GRAVITY: 1.012

POTENTIAL ALCOHOL: 4% ABV

IBUs: 9.25

INGREDIENTS

- 3.3 pounds Ireks weizen extract (½ can)
- 3¾ pounds Dutch extra light DME
- ½ ounce Hallertauer Hersbrucker plug at 2.9% AA (boil) 60 minutes
- ½ ounce Hallertauer Hersbrucker plug at 2.9% AA (boil) 30 minutes
- ½ ounce Hallertauer Hersbrucker plug at 2.9% AA (flavor) 10 minutes
- Wyeast liquid Bavarian weizen yeast with starter
- Liquid or dry lager yeast with a neutral flavor profile
- 1.2 cups Dutch light DME for priming

BREWING PROCEDURES

1. Bring 4 gallons of cold water to a boil.
2. Remove brew kettle from heat before adding extract and DME to avoid sticking or burning.
3. Boil for 60 minutes, adding hops as noted above.
4. Let hot wort sit for 30 minutes (covered) in ice-water bath before pouring into single-stage fermenters containing 1.5 gallons ice-cold water (33–40°F).
5. Stir to aerate. Move to dark, quiet, draft-free space and open-ferment at 70–72°F for the first 12 hours.
6. Fit bucket with lid and airlock. Ferment for 7 days or until fermentation ceases.
7. Cold-condition/settle 5 days at 45°F.
8. Prime with DME that has been boiled and strained off of its trub and lager yeast, then bottle.
9. Condition for 1 week at room temperature, then 4 weeks at 45°F.

WHEAT BEER

⑪⑪/⑪⑪⑪/⑪⑪⑪

BREWERS RESOURCE—CAMARILLO, CALIFORNIA

"In designing a wheat beer recipe you may want a clean malt flavor or a full, clovey beer like the Germans or Belgians brew. Concentrate on the yeast strain rather than the recipe for these differences. The yeast strain you choose is of the greatest importance in wheat beers. The original gravity should be kept between 1.040 and 1.050, while fermentation temperatures should be between 64° and 72°F, to promote a strong fermentation and to allow traditionally slow-working wheat strains to ferment."

ORIGINAL GRAVITY: 1.046

FINAL GRAVITY: 1.012

POTENTIAL ALCOHOL: 4.4% ABV

MALT EXTRACT RECIPE: INGREDIENTS

- 3.5 pounds dry wheat extract plus 2 pounds DME, or

3.3 pounds syrup wheat extract and 3.3 pounds pale syrup malt extract

19 IBUs Hallertau (i.e., 1 ounce at 4.5% AA)—bittering hops

¼ ounce Saaz finishing hops

BrewTek German Wheat (CL–6) or Belgian Wheat yeast (CL–60), or Wyeast 3056 Bavarian Wheat yeast

1 cup (5 ounces) corn sugar to prime at bottling

BREWING PROCEDURES

(Refer to An Introduction to Brewing Procedures beginning on page 2.)

MASH-EXTRACT RECIPE: INGREDIENTS

2 pounds crushed German pale malt

1 pound crushed wheat malt, mashed in 3 liters of water at 152°F for 45 minutes

3 pounds light dried wheat extract or 3.3 pounds syrup wheat extract

19 IBUs Hallertau (i.e., 1 ounce at 4.5% AA)—bittering hops

¼ ounce Saaz finishing hops

BrewTek German Wheat (CL–6) or Belgian Wheat yeast (CL–60), or Wyeast 3056 Bavarian Wheat yeast

1 cup (5 ounces) corn sugar to prime at bottling

BREWING PROCEDURES

1. Steep crushed grains in mini-mash bucket and sparge to collect 3 gallons of wort.
2. Continue with recipe as you normally would or see Partial Mash Ale Brewing Procedures beginning on page 14.

ALL GRAIN RECIPE: INGREDIENTS

3 pounds crushed wheat malt

3 pounds crushed Klages or, preferably. German pale malt

14 IBUs Hallertau (i.e., ¾ ounce at 4.5% AA)—bittering hops

BrewTek German Wheat (CL–6) or Belgian Wheat yeast (CL–60), or Wyeast 3056 Bavarian Wheat yeast

1 cup (5 ounces) corn sugar to prime at bottling

BREWING PROCEDURES

1. In mash/lauter bucket stir crushed pale malt into 8 liters of 166°F water to rest out at about 152°F.
2. Cover and rest for 45 minutes.
3. Sparge to 6½ gallons into kettle. Bring to boil and add hops.
4. Cool wort and transfer to fermenter.
5. Pitch yeast, ferment, and bottle.

Recipe Variations: You may experiment with these recipes by varying the wheat-to-malt ratio (try 40 to 70 percent wheat); add 4 ounces each of crystal and chocolate malt for a dark wheat beer. Add a teaspoon of crushed coriander seed for a Belgian wheat style and try different finishing hops (traditionally not used).

HEFE WEIZEN
🍺 🍺 🍺 🍺

STEPHEN SNYDER

I have included optional steps for open fermentation with this recipe because I have convinced myself that it produces a more authentic Bavarian weissbier flavor. It does entail significant risk of a wild yeast invasion, however, so don't try it unless you are sure that you have a sanitary fermentation environment. Don't forget to save a couple of quarts of unfermented wort for priming!

ORIGINAL GRAVITY: 1048

FINAL GRAVITY: 1.012

POTENTIAL ALCOHOL: 4.6% ABV

IBUs: 17

INGREDIENTS (FOR 5.5 GALLONS)

- 6 pounds malted wheat (crushed)
- 6 pounds 2-row pilsner malt (crushed)
- 0.5 pound German light crystal malt (crushed)
- 0.5 pound dextrine malt (crushed)
- 2 ounces Hallertau Hersbrucker hop plugs at 3% AA (boil 60 minutes)
- 2 teaspoons Irish moss (boil 15 minutes)
- 1 liter starter Wyeast 3068 Weihenstephan Weizen yeast
- 2 quarts of unfermented wort or 0.75 cup corn sugar for priming

BREWING PROCEDURES

1. Mash in at 100°F with 3.5 gallons of brewing liquor.
2. Immediately raise the temperature 2°F per minute to 122°F.
3. Maintain protein rest 30 minutes.
4. Remove the thickest 40% of the mash.
5. Ladle into second kettle and bring to 158°F. Keep original "rest mash" temperature constant at 122°F.
6. Maintain saccharification rest for 15 minutes.
7. Bring to boil and boil for 30 minutes.
8. Recombine with the "rest mash" to yield a temperature of 147°F, applying bottom heat or cold water if necessary to adjust temperature up or down.
9. Rest 15 minutes.
10. Raise to 158°F and rest for 45 minutes or until iodine test is negative.
11. Raise to 170°F for 10 minutes and mash out. Transfer to lauter tun.
12. Sparge with 5.5 gallons of 165–170°F water.
13. Collect 7 gallons of wort.
14. Boil for 90 minutes, adding hops as noted above.
15. Force-cool with wort chiller.
16. Rack through sanitized strainer bag or sieve into fermenter or carboy to remove hops.
17. Pitch 1 liter yeast starter. Aerate well. Cover and attach airlock.
18. Rest beer for 3–4 hours or until trub settles. (Optional.)
19. Rack off of trub into primary fermenter. Cover and attach airlock. Ferment for 5–7 days.
20. (Optional open fermentation steps.) Keep under airlock until a yeast head forms on the beer. Remove cover and/or airlock and open-ferment at 64–70°F for 3 days. If proper sanitation can be maintained, skim brown, resinous scum from top of kräusen when a thick layer has formed. Cover and attach airlock for an additional 2–4 days.
21. Rack to secondary. Cover and attach airlock. Ferment for 3 more days.
22. Rack to bottling bucket, prime, pitch fresh yeast (optional), and bottle.
23. Condition at 65–70°F for 10–14 days.
24. Cellar for 1–3 weeks at 55–65°F.
25. Serve at 45–50°F.

EAST COAST WEIZEN

EAST COAST BREWING SUPPLY—STATEN ISLAND, NEW YORK

East Coast Weizen is a large quantity formulation for the big-time lover of Bavarian wheat beers who wants more than the standard five-gallon batch. Once you've ground your way through nineteen pounds of malt, the rest is easy! The Mt. Hood hops lend a subtle bitterness and a hint of delicate Mittelfrüh aroma. Don't forget to use a large starter as recommended; you're fermenting a lot of beer here.

ORIGINAL GRAVITY: 1.046

FINAL GRAVITY: 1.012

POTENTIAL ALCOHOL: 4.4% ABV

INGREDIENTS (FOR 12.5 GALLONS)

- 9 pounds Klages malt
- 10 pounds Ireks wheat malt
- 3 ounces Mt. Hood hops (3.8% AA) 60 minutes
- 1 ounce Mt. Hood hops 2 minutes
- 2 teaspoons Irish moss
- Brewers Resource Weizen CL–920 (with 1.4 liter starter)
- 2 cups corn sugar for priming

Water Requirements:

- Mash: 4.75 gallons
- Raise: 2.38 gallons
- Sparge: 9.75 gallons

BREWING PROCEDURES

1. Protein rest: Dough in at 127°F for an initial rest at 118°F. Hold for 45 minutes.
2. Mash: Add raise water to bring temperature to 150°F. Hold for 90 minutes. Raise heat to 168°F, then mash out and start sparge at 170°F.
3. Boil: Collect about 13½ gallons of wort. Boil for 90 minutes, adding bittering hops after 30 minutes. Add finishing hops in the last 2 minutes.
4. Chill, ferment, and bottle using your favorite methods.

DUNKEL WEISSBIER
🍺 🍺

DICK FOEHRINGER

THE BREWMEISTER—FAIR OAKS, CALIFORNIA

"Dunkel Weissbier is a darker version of weizenbier. It is a wheat beer from southern Germany. Dunkel Weissbier is refreshing, light-bodied, lightly hopped, yeasty, highly effervescent, slightly sour, and with flavor and aroma suggestive of cloves and banana."

ORIGINAL GRAVITY: 1.056

FINAL GRAVITY: 1.014

POTENTIAL ALCOHOL: 5.5% ABV

INGREDIENTS

- ½ pound 60 °L crystal malt
- 8 pounds wheat malt extract syrup
- ½ ounce Northern Brewer hops (boiling) 60 minutes
- ½ ounce Cascade hops (boiling) 30 minutes
- ½ ounce Hallertauer hops (aromatic hops)
- 1 teaspoon Irish moss
- 1 Bavarian wheat liquid yeast
- 1 teaspoon gelatin
- ¾ cup bottling sugar

BREWING PROCEDURES

1. Put the crushed crystal into the boiling bag. Add 1½ to 2½ gallons of cold water and bring to a near boil (160°F). Shut off heat and let grain steep for 30 minutes. Remove grain bag and drain it completely.
2. Dissolve in extract and return to heat. Bring to a boil and add Northern Brewer boiling hops. Boil 30 minutes. Add Cascade hops. Boil 15 minutes. Add Irish moss. Boil 15 minutes. Turn off heat and add Hallertauer

aromatic hops. Cover and steep for 15 minutes.

3. Cold-break wort by placing into a sink full of cold water. When the wort is below 100°F, strain into primary fermenter. Add cold water to make 5½ gallons. When cooled below 85°F pitch yeast. (Note: You must start the yeast 1–2 days ahead of time. Follow the instructions on the back of the yeast package.)

4. Also mix the dry hops in 1 cup of hot water. Stir into cooled wort. Ferment in cool, dark place (65–75°F) for 5–7 days.

5. Rack into secondary leaving all the hops and sediment behind. Dissolve gelatin in 1 cup hot water. Stir into secondary and replace airlock. When clear (3–5 days) rack again, leaving sediment behind.

6. Dissolve bottling sugar in 1 cup hot water. Stir into cleared beer. Bottle and cap.

7. Age a minimum of 3–4 weeks.

SCHWARZRITTER DUNKELWEIZEN
▥ ▥ ▥

STEPHEN SNYDER

In a traditional all-grain dunkelweizen, the dark color is derived mainly from an intensive decoction mash. In an extract brew, coloring malts are needed to bring the classic maltiness and dark color expected of this brew. If your water lacks temporary hardness, add a half teaspoon of calcium carbonate in the steep to compensate for the acidity of the dark malts being used.

ORIGINAL GRAVITY: 1.056

FINAL GRAVITY: 1.106

POTENTIAL ALCOHOL: 5.25% ABV

IBUs: 15

INGREDIENTS

    6 gallons bottled spring water
    ½ cup light crystal malt
    1 cup Vienna amber malt
    1 cup chocolate malt
    1 cup Munich dark malt
    3.3 pounds Ireks Weizen extract (½ of a 3 kilogram can)
    2 pounds Dutch light DME
    2 pounds Dutch amber DME
    ½ ounce Styrian Goldings plug 5.3% AA (boil) 90 minutes
    ½ ounce Saaz plug 3.1% AA (boil) 30 minutes
    ½ ounce Hallertauer plug 2.9% AA (flavor) 10 minutes
    1 Yeast Lab Bavarian Weizen W51 (with starter)
    ¾ cup corn sugar for priming

BREWING PROCEDURES

1. Add cracked malts to ½ gallon cold water. Let sit for 15–20 minutes. Bring slowly to 158°F, then remove from heat. Steep 30 minutes then sparge to brew kettle.

2. Add 2½ gallons of cold water, wheat extract, and DME. Dissolve thoroughly.

3. Boil vigorously for 90 minutes, adding hops as noted above.

4. Hot-break trub should be skimmed throughout the boil.

5. Let hot wort sit for 30 minutes (covered) in ice-water bath before straining into settling bucket (a regular plastic fermenter, carboy, or bottling bucket will do) containing 3 gallons ice-cold water (33–40°F).

6. Take temperature and hydrometer readings.

7. Temperature should be below 75°F before pitching yeast. Stir gently to aerate. Cover with clean towel and move to dark, quiet, draft-free space.

8. After 3 to 5 days, rack off of trub to another closed plastic fermenter or carboy.

9. Fit with airlock and ferment 3–5 more days.

10. When fermentation is complete, prime with ¾ cup corn sugar and bottle.

11. Warm-condition 10–14 days at room temperature (68°F). Store cold (40–45°) 2–3 weeks and serve at 45–50°.

STUMBLING BILLY GOAT WHEATBOCK
🍺 🍺

BEER & WINEMAKING SUPPLIES, INC.— NORTHAMPTON, MASSACHUSETTS

"A wheat doppelbock of super-premium quality. Made for spring tapping and celebrating. Uses German-type hops and authentic German grains. Best typified by Aventinus from Schneider in Germany."

ORIGINAL GRAVITY: 1.072–76

FINAL GRAVITY: 1.016–18

POTENTIAL ALCOHOL: 7.6% ABV

INGREDIENTS

> 2 pounds German Munich malt (cracked)
>
> ¾ pound light German crystal malt (cracked)
>
> ¼ pound dextrine malt (cracked)
>
> 6 pounds wheat malt extract syrup
>
> 2 pounds wheat dry malt extract
>
> 2.5 ounces Liberty hop pellets (bittering and aroma)

> 10–14 grams dry lager yeast or Wyeast lager yeasts 3056, 3068, or 3333; Wyeast wheat yeasts 3056, 3068, or 3333; or Wyeast ale yeasts 1007 or 1338
>
> ¾ cup corn sugar for bottling and optional bottling yeast

BREWING PROCEDURES

Note: If using a liquid culture, activate 12–24 hours prior to brew session.

1. Place your three crushed, blended grains in a 6–8 quart pan and stir in 3 quarts of 168°F water. Mix well. Grain should bring temperature down to approximately 150–154°F. Steep for 45 minutes in oven, small insulated cooler, or on stovetop at that temperature. While grain is steeping, bring 2 gallons of water up to 165°F in an 8–12-quart pot. Place strainer or colander over large kettle, then pour and spoon all grains and liquid in. Rinse with 1.5–2 gallons of 165°F water. Allow liquid to drain into kettle. Discard grains and bring liquid to a boil. Momentarily remove from heat.

2. Pour the 6 pounds of malt extract into the pot, making sure to rinse out the container to get all the malt. Stir well.

3. Resume boiling (total time: 1 hour). When boil begins, add ½-ounce portions of hops at the following intervals for a total boil of 1 hour: 60 minutes, 45 minutes, 30 minutes, and 15 minutes.

4. Shut off the heat, add the last ½ ounce of hops, and let stand for 15 minutes.

5. Put 3 gallons of very cold water into your sterilized primary fermenter, then carefully pour the hot wort into it. Top up to 5 gallons with more cold water if necessary. If still above 85°F, run a cold water bath around your fermenter. The fermenter

should then be stirred or swirled to aerate the wort. Take a hydrometer reading and write it down.

6. Wort should now be 70–85°F. Activate dry yeast by putting in 1 cup of sterile water at 75–95°F for 15 minutes, then stir well.

7. Now add the yeast and stir or swirl to aerate. Pitch yeast solution into fermenter. Put lid and airlock on. Fill airlock halfway with water.

8. Ferment at room temperature (60–70°F) for 4 days, then siphon over to a glass secondary fermenter for another 4–7 days. Take a hydrometer reading, and if low enough, bottle the beer into 53 reusable bar bottles (12-ounce size) or equivalent.

9. Bottling procedure: Make a priming syrup on the stove with 1 cup water and ¾ cup corn sugar, bring to a boil, and then shut heat off immediately, stirring well. Transfer beer back to primary or bottling bucket, mixing the priming syrup in well to distribute evenly. Siphon into bottles and cap them.

10. Remember to sanitize everything you use after the boil with a good chlorinated alkaline cleanser.

11. Allow bottles to sit at room temperature for 1–2 weeks before cooling down.

WEINACHTEN WEIZEN-BOCK
🍺 🍺 🍺

STEPHEN SNYDER

The use of traditional malts used in German brewing in conjunction with classic hop varieties and a weizen yeast will produce a truly authentic brew. I recommend soft water for this recipe along the lines of Munich's water profile. This beer will improve greatly with age, so make it in early fall and save it for Christmas. (Frequent testing over the fall is allowable for quality control, of course.)

ORIGINAL GRAVITY: 1.069

FINAL GRAVITY: 1.020

POTENTIAL ALCOHOL: 6.5% ABV

IBUs: 12

INGREDIENTS

    ¼ cup German dark crystal malt
    6.6 pounds (3 kilograms) Ireks Weizen extract
    4 pounds Laaglander dark DME
    ¼ ounce Hallertauer whole hops at 5.2% AA (boil) 60 minutes
    ¼ ounce Hallertauer whole hops at 5.2% AA (boil) 45 minutes
    ¼ ounce Hallertauer whole hops at 5.2% AA (flavor) 15 minutes
    Yeast Lab liquid Bavarian weizen yeast (requires starter)
    1.2 cups Dutch light DME for priming

BREWING PROCEDURES

1. Add cracked crystal malt to 1 pint of cold water. Bring slowly to boil. Remove from heat immediately and strain liquid into brew kettle.

2. Add 3 gallons of cold water and bring to a boil.

3. Remove brew kettle from heat before adding extract and DME to avoid sticking or burning.

4. Boil for 60 minutes, adding hops as noted above.

5. Hot trub should be skimmed at end of boil.

6. Let hot wort sit for 30 minutes (covered) in ice-water bath before pouring into single-stage fermenters containing 2.5 gallons ice-cold water (33–40°F).

7. Should be below 75°F before pitching yeast. Stir gently to minimally aerate. Cover with clean towel and move to dark, quiet, draft-free space and ferment at 65–70°F.

8. Ferment for 7–10 days or until fermentation ceases.

9. Prime with DME and bottle.

10. Warm-condition 7 days at room temperature (68–72°F). Store cold (33–40°F) 3 months and serve at 45–50°F.

WITBIER

"Belgian beer" is possibly the hardest beer term in the world to define because it is not a single style but a vast array of unique styles, including dubbel, tripel, saison, oud bruin, and witbier, to name but a few. Pierre Rajotte's *Belgian Ale* is an excellent source of recipes and historical information, Michael Jackson's *The Great Beers of Belgium* is required reading for those seeking more in-depth knowledge of commercial brands, and Tim Webb's *Good Beer Guide to Belgium and Holland* is a mandatory travel guide for those visiting this beer lover's paradise. A few classic Belgian beers to emulate include: Rodenbach Grand Cru, Dubuisson Scaldis, Frank Boon Kriek, Celis White, Liefmans Frambozenbier, Cantillon Super Gueuze, Chimay Cinq Cents, Orval, and Moortgat Duvel.

Belgian witbier, also known as "bière blanche" or "white beer," has its origins in the Flemish region of Belgium, particularly around the town of Louvain. Historically, these beers were made with certain portions of raw wheat and raw oats, but because of the difficulty in milling and mashing these, new brewers might be better served using malted wheat, whole wheat flour, and/or precooked oats instead. These beers should be tart, slightly acidic, and well carbonated. The aroma should be of malt and wheat, and "noble" hop varieties are recommended. White beer is often spiced, with coriander and Curaçao bitter orange peel being the clear favorites.

WITBIER BASICS

ORIGINAL GRAVITY: 1.044–50

FINAL GRAVITY: 1.006–10

IBUs: 15–20

COLOR (SRM): 2–4

ALCOHOL BY VOLUME: 4.5–5.2%

BELGIAN WHITE
⚏ ⚏ ⚏

DICK FOEHRINGER

THE BREWMEISTER—FAIR OAKS,
    CALIFORNIA

"Belgian White is an awesome ale with malted wheat, barley, and oats. The style is enhanced by the addition of coriander seed and spicy Hallertauer hops. This delicious brew comes from Belgium, which is sometimes called 'the Disneyland of Beer.'"

ORIGINAL GRAVITY: 1.042

FINAL GRAVITY: 1.010

POTENTIAL ALCOHOL: 4.1% ABV

INGREDIENTS

1 pound steel cut oats

4 pounds Alexander's wheat malt extract

2 pounds English light dry extract

1½ ounce Hallertauer hops (60 minutes) boiling

½ ounce Hallertauer hops (15 minutes) aromatic

1 ounce crushed coriander seed (5 minutes)

1 teaspoon Irish moss (15 minutes)

1 teaspoon gelatin

1 Wyeast Belgian Ale liquid yeast

¾ cup priming sugar

BREWING PROCEDURES

1. Put the steel-cut oats into a grain bag. Add 1½ to 2½ gallons of cold water and bring to a near boil (160–170°F). Shut off heat and let grain steep for 30 minutes. Remove grain bag and drain it completely.

2. Dissolve in extract and return to heat. Bring to a boil. Add the first addition of Hallertauer hops and boil for 45 minutes. Add the second addition of hops and the Irish moss and boil for 10 minutes. Add the crushed coriander seed and boil for 5 minutes.

3. Cold-break wort by placing into a sink full of cold water. When the wort is below 100°F, strain into primary fermenter. Add cold water to make 5½ gallons. When cooled to below 85°F, pitch yeast. (Note: You must start the yeast 1–2 days ahead of time. Follow the instructions on the back of the yeast package.)

4. Ferment in cool (65–75°F), dark place. When fermentation has ceased, rack into secondary, leaving all the hops and sediment behind. Dissolve gelatin in 1 cup hot water and stir into secondary. Allow beer to clear, typically (3–5 days).

5. Rack again, leaving sediment behind. Dissolve bottling sugar in 1 cup hot water. Stir into cleared beer. Bottle and cap.

6. Allow to age/carbonate in the bottles a minimum of 2–4 weeks.

BELGIAN WITBIER
⚏ ⚏

JOE & BRYAN TIMMONS

BOSTON BREWERS SUPPLY CO.—
    JAMAICA PLAIN, MASSACHUSETTS

"Our Belgian Witbier is made up of about 40 percent malted wheat, 60 percent malted barley, has a single hop addition for bittering purposes, and uses a special Belgian yeast culture to add authenticity. We hope you enjoy it!"

ORIGINAL GRAVITY: 1.048

FINAL GRAVITY: 1.010

POTENTIAL ALCOHOL: 4.9% ABV

IBUs: approximately 22

Ingredients

> 8 ounces flaked oats
>
> 4 pounds Alexander's wheat extract
>
> 3 pounds light malt extract syrup
>
> 2 ounces Hallertauer hop pellets
>
> 1 ounce ground coriander seed
>
> ½ ounce dried Curaçao orange peel
>
> Wyeast 3944 Belgian Witbier yeast
>
> ¾ cup corn sugar for priming

Yeast Preparation

The liquid yeast should be prepared a few days prior to your brewing session. To start the incubation, simply follow the instructions on the back of the package. We suggest that you increase the pitching rate by preparing a starter; it's easy. Boil 2 cups of water with 5 tablespoons of dry malt for 15 minutes. Sterilize a quart-size beer bottle and fill with the wort. To avoid shocking the yeast, make sure that both the wort and the yeast are room temperature. Aerate the starter by swirling the wort and attach an airlock with a 2-drilled stopper. Leave at room temperature and when the starter activity subsides, it is ready to pitch. Remember to sanitize the neck of the bottle again before pitching.

Brewing Procedures

1. Secure the flaked oats in the muslin straining bag. Pour 2 gallons of cold water into your brewpot, apply heat, and add the grain bag. Heat to a near boil (about 155°F), turn off the heat, cover the pot, and allow the oats to steep for 30 minutes. Remove the grain bag, drain, and discard.

2. Thoroughly dissolve the malt extract, apply heat, and bring to a boil. Add the Hallertauer pellets and start timing the boil; the total elapsed time will be 45 minutes. After 40 minutes, add half of the Curaçao orange peel and half of the ground coriander seed. Continue to boil for an additional 5 minutes, then cover and remove pot from heat.

3. After 20 minutes, add all of the remaining hops and the Irish moss flakes. Continue to boil for an additional 25 minutes, then cover and remove the pot from the heat.

Remember that after the wort has cooled, it is highly vulnerable to contamination; everything that comes into contact with it from this point on must be thoroughly sanitized!

4. Cool the wort as quickly as possible. A wort chiller works best, but if you haven't got one yet a cold water bath will do the trick. Place the covered pot in your kitchen sink and fill with ice and cold water. When the temperature has fallen to about 90°F, transfer the wort, through a strainer if possible, into your fermenter. Top off with enough cold water to reach a 5-gallon level and stir or shake well. Draw off a small sample and take both a hydrometer and a temperature reading; always discard the sample used.

5. When the wort has cooled to 65–70°F, you are ready to add the yeast. Once the yeast has been added, attach an airlock and keep the fermenter in a cool, dark location where temperature fluctuations are minimal, ideally 68°F. Active fermentation should become visible in the next 12 to 24 hours and will continue for about 3 to 5 days.

6. When visible signs of fermentation have ceased, gently transfer the beer to a sanitized secondary fermenter (ideally a 5-gallon glass carboy), leaving all sediment behind. Add the remaining spices, attach an

airlock, and allow the beer to settle for an additional 10 to 14 days at the same temperature of primary fermentation. At the end of this period, draw off a small sample and check the final gravity. By now it should be within the range stated above; if not wait another couple of days and check again. Prepare to bottle.

BOTTLING AND CONDITIONING

1. Sanitize all of your siphoning and bottling equipment, bottles, and caps.
2. Boil the 6 ounces of corn sugar in about a cup of water and pour it into your bottling bucket. Gently siphon the beer out of the fermenter into the bucket, making sure the flow is directed to the bottom of the bucket; avoid splashing or agitating the beer.
3. Using your siphon tubing and bottle filler, fill each bottle to within an inch from the top and cap immediately. Store the bottles upright for 3 to 4 weeks at 60°F, chill, and enjoy.

WIT BIER
⫴ ⫴ ⫴ ⫴
STEPHEN SNYDER

I based this recipe on an amalgamation of some of my favorite Belgian wits, one American and two Belgian, but used some flaked adjuncts because of the extremely low extract yields I have often experienced with raw grains in a homebrew setting. The flaked ingredients are pregelatinized and offer somewhat of a hedge against the difficulty of using raw wheat and oats. The preboil in conjunction with an extended protein rest helps to avoid many of the problems of low yields and sluggish runoff but may reduce some the traditional haziness expected of this beer style.

ORIGINAL GRAVITY: 1048

FINAL GRAVITY: 1.013

POTENTIAL ALCOHOL: 4.5% ABV

IBUs: 18

INGREDIENTS (FOR 5.5 GALLONS)

> 6 pounds Belgian Pils malt (crushed)
> 2 pounds flaked wheat
> 3 pounds raw soft white wheat (crushed)
> 1 pound flaked oats
> 1 ounce EKG plugs at 3.3% AA (boil 60 minutes)
> 1 ounce Saaz aroma hops (boil 2 minutes)
> 1 ounce crushed coriander
> 1 ounce Curaçao bitter orange peel
> 1 teaspoon sweet orange peel
> 1 liter starter Wyeast 3944 Belgian Witbier yeast
> 0.75 cup corn sugar for priming

BREWING PROCEDURES

1. Preboil the 3 pounds of crushed raw wheat in 1 gallon of water for 15 minutes to gelatinize the starch prior to mashing. After the boil add the raw wheat and the water they were boiled in to the mash tun.
2. Protein rest. Mash in the wheat, oats, and malted barley at 104°F in approximately 2 gallons of hard brewing liquor; stir well. Immediately raise temperature to 122°F with bottom heat or boiling water. Rest 45 minutes. Stir occasionally.
3. Saccharification rest. Raise temperature with bottom heat or boiling water. Rest 90 minutes at 150°F. Test for remaining starches

with iodine tincture. If negative (wort no longer turns purplish/black), mash out.

4. Mash out. Raise temperature to 165–170°F. Rest 10 minutes to decrease viscosity.

5. Transfer to lauter tun. Slowly sparge with 5.5 gallons 170°F water over 45–60 minutes and collect wort into brew kettle.

6. Collect 6.5 gallons of wort.

7. Boil for 90 minutes, adding hops as noted above. Add the sweet and bitter orange peels and the 1 ounce of coriander with 2 minutes remaining in the boil. Add the cumin and cardamom at knockout.

8. Force cool with wort chiller.

9. Rack into fermenter through sanitized strainer bag or sieve to remove spices and hops.

10. Pitch 1 liter of yeast starter. Aerate well. Cover fermenter and attach airlock.

11. Rest beer for 2–3 hours or until trub settles. (Optional.)

12. Rack off of trub into another fermenter and ferment under airlock at 60–65°F for 7 days.

13. Rack to secondary and ferment under airlock for 1 week at 60°F.

14. Rack to bottling bucket, prime, add fresh yeast (optional), and bottle.

15. Condition at 65–70°F for 7–10 days.

16. Cellar for 3 weeks at 55–60°F.

17. Serve at 47°F.

"Diable Blanche" Wit Bier

▥ ▥ ▥

MARK RICHMOND, HEAD BREWER, GREAT LAKES BREWING CO.—CLEVELAND, OHIO

Many Belgian white brewers have a "secret" spice they use that veteran beer writers like Michael Jackson and Roger Protz are unable to coax out of them. Mark Richmond has chosen not to be so coy and reveals that he uses chamomile in this impressively aromatic all-grain formulation.

ORIGINAL GRAVITY: 1.046

FINAL GRAVITY: 1.012

POTENTIAL ALCOHOL: 4.6% ABV

INGREDIENTS

    6 pounds Belgian Pils malt
    4 pounds raw wheat flakes
    0.5 pound oats
    1 ounce Hallertau (5.2 AAU) (60 minutes)
    1 ounce Tettnang (5.5 AAU) (20 minutes)
    1 ounce Hallertau (5.2 AAU) (10 minutes)
    1 ounce Saaz (4.8 AAU) after boil
    1 ounce crushed coriander seed (60 minutes)
    1 ounce chamomile (30 minutes)
    0.5 ounce sweet orange peel (10 minutes)
    Wyeast 3944 Belgian White Beer yeast
    1 ounce crushed coriander seed and 0.5 ounce sweet orange peel added to secondary
    ¾ to 1 cup priming sugar

BREWING PROCEDURES

1. Crush malt and perform a 1-hour infusion mash at 152°F.

2. Boil for 90 minutes, adding hops as noted above.

3. Cool, pitch yeast, and ferment as normal.

4. Transfer to secondary after 1 week, add spices, and bottle after 1 more week.

EAST COAST WIT

⧗ ⧗ ⧗ ⧗

EAST COAST BREWING SUPPLY—STATEN ISLAND, NEW YORK

The brewer of this recipe needs experience and confidence in reserve to successfully pull off the lactic acid mash called for. A small picnic cooler or Styrofoam box is sometimes used for this purpose, but do your research first. If done properly, the result will be an amazingly tart and refreshing wit on par with the best craft-brewed versions.

ORIGINAL GRAVITY: 1.045

FINAL GRAVITY: 1.012

POTENTIAL ALCOHOL: 4.3% ABV

INGREDIENTS (FOR 5.5 GALLONS)

Lactic Mash:
>   0.50 pound Belgian 2-row
>   0.50 pound Belgian 6-row

Main Mash:
>   2.25 pounds Belgian 2-row
>   2.25 pounds Belgian 6-row
>   4 pounds unmalted, hard red wheat (ground fine)
>   5 HBUs bittering hops, equal portions of Willamette and Cascade
>   0.25 ounce bitter orange quarters, milled (boil 15 minutes)
>   0.25 ounce fresh whole coriander, milled (boil 15 minutes)
>   Wyeast 3944 Belgian White beer yeast
>   ¾ to 1 cup corn sugar for priming

BREWING PROCEDURES

1. Prepare lactic mash 48 hours prior to start. Hold at 120°F.

   Main Mash:

1. Dough in and perform acid rest at 95°F for 30 minutes; add sour mash.

2. Protein rest at 122°F for 30 minutes.

3. Saccharification rest at 150°F for 45 minutes.

4. Saccharification rest at 161°F for 15 minutes.

5. Mash out at 168°F for 10 minutes.

6. Ferment in primary for 1 week at 64–75°F.

7. Ferment in secondary for 4 weeks at 54–59°F.

8. Bottle or keg, correcting pH to 3.9 with lactic acid, if necessary.

WHITE'S BIER

⧗ ⧗ ⧗ ⧗

PAUL WHITE, HEAD BREWER, THE SEVEN BARREL BREWERY—WEST LEBANON, NEW HAMPSHIRE

Brewer's Notes: "Do not use 'wheat beer' yeast. I have tried various liquid yeasts with this recipe, but I like what I get with the Edme best."

ORIGINAL GRAVITY: 1.040–42

FINAL GRAVITY: 1.010–12

POTENTIAL ALCOHOL: 3.8–3.9% ABV

INGREDIENTS

>   4 pounds 6-row malt
>   4 pounds flaked wheat
>   6 AAUs of Hallertau whole flower hops
>   1 teaspoon of Irish moss
>   ¾ ounce freshly crushed coriander seed
>   Edme ale yeast
>   ¾ cup corn sugar for priming

BREWING PROCEDURES

1. Dough into 3 gallons of water at 132–135°F and rest at 122–125°F for 30 minutes. Boost temperature to 150°F for 2-hour rest, boost-

ing back to 150°F whenever the temperature falls to 144°F.

2. Mash-out and sparge to collect 6 gallons. After boiling the wort 15 minutes, add 6 AAUs of Hallertau flowers and boil 45 minutes. Add 1 teaspoon of Irish moss and ¾ ounce freshly crushed coriander seed, boil 15 minutes, then shut off heat.

3. Stir in another ¾ ounce crushed coriander, cover, and let stand 10 minutes. Chill to 70°F, top up to 5 gallons if necessary, and pitch rehydrated Edme ale yeast.

4. Primary ferment for 5 days; transfer to secondary for 7 days or more. Keg or bottle. Age for at least 2 weeks.

BELGIUM WIT

⑪ ⑪ ⑪ ⑪

DAVID GOURLEY

THE MAD CAPPER—GLASTONBURY, CONNECTICUT

Here's a recipe designed to help the witbier lover stock up with a 10-gallon all-grain batch. The cardamom lends a spicy-herbally touch that will blend with an extended maturation phase into a soft blend of fruit and wheat flavors.

ORIGINAL GRAVITY: 1.052

FINAL GRAVITY: 1.006

POTENTIAL ALCOHOL: 5.9% ABV

INGREDIENTS (FOR 10 GALLONS)

    10 pounds lager malt

    8 pounds cracked bulgar wheat

    1 pound rolled oats

    2 ounces Tettnang hop pellets (boil 60 minutes)

    1.5 ounces Tettnang hop pellets (boil 30 minutes)

    2 teaspoons Irish moss (boil 30 minutes)

    30 grams coriander (finishing)

    15 grams orange peel (finishing)

    3 grams cardamom (finishing)

    Wyeast 3944 Belgian White Beer yeast

    20 ml lactic acid at kegging

    1.5 cups corn sugar for priming (or force carbonate)

BREWING PROCEDURES

1. Mash in with 135°F water for an initial temperature of 122°F.

2. Rest 45 minutes at 122°F.

3. Raise to 150°F and rest 90 minutes.

4. Raise to 162°F and rest 15 minutes.

5. Mash out, lauter, and sparge as you normally do.

6. Boil wort for 90 minutes, adding hops and Irish moss as noted above. Add spices and orange peel with 2 minutes remaining.

7. Cool with wort chiller, rack to primary, then pitch yeast.

8. Ferment 7 days in the glass primary and 7 days in the glass secondary fermenter.

9. Adjust acidity with lactic acid, then keg or prime and bottle using your favorite methods.

BELGIAN WIT

⑪ ⑪ ⑪ ⑪

DAN SOBOTI

U-BREW—MILLBURN, NEW JERSEY

Flaked wheat is used in this well-designed recipe as an alternative to the use of troublesome raw wheat. Flaked adjuncts also cut down on your milling time and require no preboiling. The six-row adds surplus enzymes for an easy step mash. The spicing here is done subtly for a balance of wheat, malt, and yeast aromatics.

ORIGINAL GRAVITY: 1.043

FINAL GRAVITY: 1.011

POTENTIAL ALCOHOL: 4.2% ABV

IBUs: 11

COLOR: 3 SRM

INGREDIENTS

4.5 pounds flaked wheat
2.5 pounds American 2-row
2 pounds American 6-row
0.5 ounce Willamette hops 4.9% AA
¼ ounce of sweet orange peel
¼ ounce of bitter orange peel
¾ ounce coriander
Yeast Lab Belgian Wheat or Wyeast Belgian White yeast
¾ cup corn sugar for priming

BREWING PROCEDURE

1. Use your favorite mashing technique. I used a step-infusion mash with a protein rest of 30 minutes.
2. Boil for 60 minutes, adding hops at the beginning. All spices are crushed and added for last 15–20 minutes of the boil.
3. Force-cool and pitch yeast from a healthy starter. No fining agents are used with this beer because a cloudiness is desired. Ferment, prime, and bottle using your favorite methods.

ABBEY BEERS

When brewing an abbey style, the home-brewer should aim for a strong, dark-amber (or golden when brewing a tripel) beer that is lightly hopped, bottle-conditioned, brewed with medium to soft water and, of course, top-fermented. Belgian specialty grains such as Cara-Vienne, CaraMunich, and biscuit malt are suggested, as well as mild European hop varieties such as East Kent Goldings, Saaz, Hallertauer, and Styrian Goldings. These can be used for bittering as well as flavor, but go easy on the hop bouquet; aroma should be malty or neutral. But, of course, there are always exceptions—the pale ale–like Orval Trappist Ale, for example, is famous for its hop bouquet. Also important is the use of an alcohol-tolerant Belgian ale yeast if you are brewing high-gravity styles.

Belgian brewing law freely allows the use of up to 40 percent adjuncts, including such unlikely ingredients as raw wheat, candi sugar, coriander, and orange peel as previously mentioned, as well as stale hops and wild yeast. Just a few of the many unique commercial brands include the imported St. Sixtus, Grimbergen, Affligem, Corsendonk, Orval, and Chimay, as well as a variety of new American brews including New Belgium Brewing's Abbey Trappist Style Ale, Celis White and Grand Cru, and GABF medal winner Tripel Threat from Cambridge Brewing Company.

DUBBEL BASICS

ORIGINAL GRAVITY: 1.063–70

FINAL GRAVITY: 1.012–16

IBUs: 18–25

COLOR (SRM): 10–14

ALCOHOL BY VOLUME: 6–7.5%

TRIPEL BASICS

ORIGINAL GRAVITY: 1.070–95

FINAL GRAVITY: 1.016–24

IBUs: 20–25

COLOR (SRM): 3.5–5.5

ALCOHOL BY VOLUME: 7–10%

ABBEY ALE

THE HOME BREWERY—OZARK, MISSOURI

The strong molasses-like flavor of sorghum would be out of place in most beer styles, but it can find a good home in the rich, fruity, and intense flavor profile of a Belgian dubbel. The result here is a profound complexity that blends together with the other flavors over time. Let this one age a few months at cellar temperatures.

ORIGINAL GRAVITY: 1.054

FINAL GRAVITY: 1.014

POTENTIAL ALCOHOL: 5.1% ABV

INGREDIENTS

> 6.6 pounds (2 packs) Belgian Abbey malt extract syrup
>
> 1 pound sorghum syrup, in boil
>
> ¼ pound crushed medium crystal malt
>
> ¼ pound crushed Belgian CaraVienne malt
>
> ¼ pound crushed Belgian Special B malt
>
> 1½ ounces Perle pellet hops (7.4% AA) in boil
>
> ¾ ounce Hallertau pellets (4.5% AA) flavoring
>
> 1 pack Wyeast 1214 Belgian ale yeast
>
> ¾ cup corn sugar for priming

BREWING PROCEDURES

1. Heat 5 gallons of water in a large kettle. Add crushed grains. Many people don't have a kettle that large, but heat as much as you can (at least 2 gallons). Remove grains from kettle at 170°. When the water is boiling, turn off the heat and add the malt extract to the water. Use a spoon and stir until you are sure no malt extract is sticking to the bottom of the kettle. Then turn the heat back on.

2. Bring the kettle back to a boil and stir occasionally so the ingredients won't burn on the bottom of the kettle. When your recipe calls for bittering hops, now is the time to add them and stir them in. Watch out for a boilover. In the early part of the boil, the kettle usually tries to boil over once or twice, so control this by adjusting the heat. Later in the boil, the surface tension changes and boiling over is not a problem. Keep stirring occasionally and let the beer (wort) boil hard for 1 hour.

3. When finishing hops are called for in your recipe, stir them in 2 minutes before the end of the boil. Using finishing hops at the end of the boil adds a fresh aroma and flavor to the beer, and the use of finishing hops is appropriate in most beer styles.

4. Pour the hot beer (wort) into the primary fermenter. It is not necessary to strain the wort if you used hop pellets. Add cold water to bring the total volume up to 5 gallons. Cover the fermenter and wait until the temperature is down to 75°F. If you have a wort chiller, use it to bring the temperature down quickly. At 75° or less, add the yeast in your recipe. Just tear open the pack(s) and sprinkle it on the wort. Close the fermenter with the lid, stopper, and airlock. Remember to put water (or vodka) in the airlock. Vodka evaporates more quickly, but bacteria won't live in it.

5. Pitch yeast and ferment at room temperature. Fermentation should start within 24 hours, and should continue for 2 weeks. Leave the beer alone and don't open the lid. After 2 weeks, transfer to a secondary fermenter for 3 weeks.

6. To bottle, siphon about 1 pint of beer into a pan and warm it on the stove. Add exactly ¾ cup of corn sugar to the pan and stir until it is dissolved. Pour this back into the beer and stir gently but well to distribute the sugar. Siphon or tap into clean sanitized bottles and cap. Keep the bottles at room temperature. The flavor of this beer will change dramatically with extended aging.

PIRATES BREW TRAPPIST ALE
🏛 🏛 🏛

JAY GARRISON, HEAD BREWER, PIRATE BREWERY

BREWBUDDYS—REDONDO BEACH, CALIFORNIA

A medium-bodied beer with a deep reddish brown color. When brewed with the Wyeast Belgian Abbey yeast and allowed to age at least a month or so, the slight bitterness goes away and a very pleasant, sharp fruity taste ensues.

ORIGINAL GRAVITY: 1.045

FINAL GRAVITY: 1.012

POTENTIAL ALCOHOL: 4.3% ABV

INGREDIENTS

    6 pounds pale liquid extract
    12 ounces Scottish crystal malt
    4 ounces Special B malt
    4 ounces CaraMunich malt
    2 ounces chocolate malt
    1 pound wheat malt
    ½ ounce Galena hops
    ½ ounce Brewers Gold hops
    ½ ounce Styrian Goldings hops
    ½ ounce Fuggles hops
    Wyeast 1214 Belgian Abbey or English dry ale yeast
    ¾ cup corn sugar for bottling

BREWING PROCEDURES

1. If you selected the Wyeast liquid yeast, you must break the inner packet before you begin to brew. Allow 1 day for each month after the manufacture date printed on the front. If you're using the dry yeast that came with the Pirates Brew Kit, go ahead and get to it.

2. Prepare the grain. The grain should be crushed; if you did not get the grain crushed at the shop, crush it with some sort of rolling pin. Heat 1 gallon of water to about 165°F, turn off the heat, add the grains, and steep for about 15 minutes.

3. Strain the grain, collecting the liquid into

your brewpot. Rinse the grain (sparge) with 4 quarts of hot (165°F) water.

4. Add the extract and 1 gallon of water to the "grain tea," then stir to dissolve. (You might want to rest the bag of extract in hot water for a while to soften it up.) Bring the wort to a soft rolling boil.

5. Add the Galena hops to the wort and boil for 45 minutes. Stir occasionally.

6. Add the Brewers Gold hops to the wort and boil for 10 minutes. Stir occasionally.

7. Add the Styrian Goldings hops and continue to boil for 5 minutes. Add the Fuggles hops to the wort and turn off the heat; stir and let sit (covered, if possible) for 10 minutes.

8. Add the boiled wort to your sanitized, rinsed fermenter. Add ice-cold water to make 5 gallons. When the temperature drops to 75°F or less, add the yeast.

9. If you use liquid yeast, open the swollen packet and add to the wort. If you use dry yeast, add the yeast to 1 cup of 90°F water for a few minutes before adding to the wort. (You can add the yeast directly to the wort and let it sit for a few minutes also, but rehydrating the yeast in warm water will improve the fermentation.) Stir the wort thoroughly with a sanitized spoon.

10. Put the lid on the fermenter tightly, insert the fermentation lock with the stopper into the hole in the lid, and fill it up about ¾ of the way with water or vodka. Let the wort ferment for a week or two until the fermentation ceases.

11. When fermentation is complete, siphon the beer into a sanitized bottling bucket. Boil the corn sugar in about a cup of water; cool; stir gently into the beer. This provides the nutrients necessary for the yeast to carbonate the beer in the bottle.

12. Insert one end of the sanitized and rinsed hose into the bottling spigot and the other end to the bottle filler. Push the bottle filler down onto the bottom of the bottle and open the bottling spigot. Five gallons of beer will make about 2 cases, so make sure you sanitize this amount beforehand. Leave about ½–¾ inch of space at the top of the bottle. Cap the bottles.

13. Let the beer age for 3 weeks to 6 months. Chill and enjoy.

BELGIAN DOUBLE
▥ ▥ ▥
BOSTON BREWERS SUPPLY CO.—
JAMAICA PLAIN, MASSACHUSETTS

"We use a blend of CaraMunich, biscuit, and Special B malts with a small quantity of authentic Belgian candi sugar to achieve the correct color and maltiness. Hallertau hops are used for bittering, and fermentation is conducted by a pure Belgian yeast culture that contributes to the complexity of this ale."

ORIGINAL GRAVITY: 1.058–60

FINAL GRAVITY: 1.015–17

POTENTIAL ALCOHOL: 6% ABV

IBUs: 20 to 22

INGREDIENTS

6 pounds light malt extract syrup

1 pound light dry malt extract

1 pound dark Belgian candi sugar

1 pound CaraMunich malt

4 ounces biscuit malt

4 ounces Special B malt

2 ounces Hallertau hop pellets

0.5 ounce Saaz hop pellets

1 teaspoon Irish moss

Belgian Abbey yeast culture

¾ cup corn sugar for priming

BREWING PROCEDURES

1. Secure the grains in the muslin straining bag. Pour 2 gallons of cold water into your brewpot, apply heat, and add the grain bag. Heat to a near boil (about 155–158°F). Cover the pot, remove from the heat, and allow the grains to steep for 30 minutes. After 30 minutes, remove and discard the grain bag.

2. Turn off the heat and, while stirring constantly, dissolve all of the malt extract and candi sugar. As soon as the boil begins, add all of the Hallertau hops and start timing the boil; the total elapsed time will be 60 minutes. Maintain a good rolling boil and stir occasionally. After 40 minutes add the Irish moss flakes; 15 minutes later add the Saaz hops; 5 minutes later cover and remove the pot from the heat.

Remember that after the wort has cooled, it is highly vulnerable to contamination; everything that comes into contact with it from this point on must be thoroughly sanitized!

3. Cool the wort as quickly as possible. A wort chiller works best, but if you haven't got one yet a cold water bath will do the trick. Place the covered pot in your kitchen sink and fill with ice and cold water. When the temperature has fallen to about 90°F, transfer the wort, through a strainer if possible, into your fermenter. Top off with enough cold water to reach a 5-gallon level and stir or shake well. If you are using a glass carboy for fermentation, it is a good idea to add the cold water first. Draw off a small sample and take both a hydrometer and a temperature reading; this will indicate your original gravity. Always discard the sample used.

4. When the wort has cooled to 65–70°F, you are ready to add the yeast. Once the yeast has been added, attach an airlock and keep the fermenter in a cool, dark location where temperature fluctuations are minimal, ideally 68–70°F. Active fermentation should become visible in the next 12 to 24 hours and will continue for about 3 to 5 days. This ale can be bottled immediately but will benefit from a week of secondary fermentation. If you choose to bottle right away, take both a temperature and a hydrometer reading. If the terminal gravity is within the range stated above, proceed directly to the bottling instructions below; if not, wait another couple of days and check again.

5. When visible signs of fermentation have ceased, gently siphon the beer to the sanitized secondary fermenter (ideally a 5-gallon glass carboy), leaving all sediment behind. Attach an airlock and allow the beer to settle for an additional 5 to 7 days at the same temperature of primary fermentation.

6. At the end of this period, draw off a small sample and check the final gravity. By now it should be within the range stated above; if not, wait another couple of days and check again. Prepare to bottle.

BOTTLING AND CONDITIONING

1. Sanitize all of your siphoning and bottling equipment, bottles, and caps.

2. Boil the 6 ounces of corn sugar in about a pint of water and pour it into your bottling bucket. Gently siphon the beer (again leaving sediment behind) out of the fermenter into the bucket, making sure the flow is directed to the bottom of the bucket; avoid splashing or agitating the beer. Reserve the last remnants to take thermometer and hydrometer readings; this will be your final gravity.

3. Using your siphon tubing and bottle filler, fill each bottle to within an inch from the top and cap immediately. Store the bottles upright at room temperature, about 65–70°F for a minimum of 3 weeks; chill and enjoy. When kept at cellar temperatures, this ale will gracefully mature over several months. Serve cool, not cold. Enjoy!

ABBEY NORMAL

⊞ ⊞ ⊞

STEPHEN SNYDER

Perhaps I went a little overboard with the ingredient list for this recipe, but I wanted to make this extract beer as complex as possible. It worked almost too well, since I had to age this beer for almost a year before the flavors balanced out into an organized profile. It seems even better when packaged in large 22 ounce or 750 ml bottles.

ORIGINAL GRAVITY: 1.070

FINAL GRAVITY: 1.017

POTENTIAL ALCOHOL: 7.5% ABV

IBUs: 30.5

HBUs: 8.25

INGREDIENTS

- 7 gallons cold, soft water (bottled spring water is ideal)
- 3 pounds English amber DME
- 3 pounds Dutch light DME
- $\frac{1}{2}$ pound turbinado (raw brown sugar)
- $\frac{1}{2}$ pound cane sugar
- 1 cup ($\frac{1}{4}$ pound) CaraVienne Belgian light crystal malt
- 1 cup CaraMunich Belgian medium crystal malt
- 4 cups (1 pound) Munich malt
- 1 cup Vienna malt
- 1 cup ($\frac{1}{4}$ pound) Belgian biscuit malt
- 2 cups ($\frac{1}{2}$ pound) Belgian aromatic malt
- 5 heaping tablespoons whole wheat flour
- $\frac{1}{2}$ cup chocolate malt
- $\frac{1}{2}$ teaspoon calcium carbonate added to mash water to reduce acidity
- $\frac{1}{2}$ ounce Styrian Goldings hop plug at 5.3% AA (boil)—90 minutes
- $\frac{1}{2}$ ounce Saaz hop plug at 3.1% AA (boil)—90 minutes
- $\frac{1}{2}$ ounce Kent Goldings hop plug at 5.0% AA (boil)—60 minutes
- $\frac{1}{2}$ ounce Saaz hop plug at 3.1% AA (boil)—30 minutes
- 1 teaspoon Irish moss
- $\frac{1}{2}$ ounce Saaz hop plug at 3.1% AA (flavor)—10 minutes
- 1 ounce Hallertau whole flowers (aroma)—steeped 30 minutes
- Yeast Lab Trappist Ale yeast (requires starter)
- 1 cup corn sugar for priming

BREWING PROCEDURES

1. Add cracked specialty grains and calcium carbonate to 1 gallon soft water. Sprinkle whole wheat flour over top and gently mix in.
2. Bring slowly to 158°F, steep 45 minutes, then sparge to brew kettle with 170°F water.
3. Add 6 gallons cold, soft water. Dissolve in malt extracts. Bring to boil.
4. Boil for a total of 3 hours, adding hops as noted above.
5. Add Irish moss at 15 minutes before knockout. Add 1 ounce Hallertauer hops in a muslin bag at knockout.
6. Cool wort with wort chiller or ice-water bath.
7. Rack cooled, strained wort gently into primary fermenter.
8. Pitch yeast at 75°F or less.
9. Open-ferment between 68–72°F for 5–7 days.
10. Bottle with DME first boiled in 1 pint water, then filtered. Warm-condition (at 70°–80°F) 14 days.
11. Cellar condition (50–55°F) 3–6 months.

OUD-TURNHOUT BROWN
🍺 🍺 🍺
DAN SOBOTI
U-BREW—MILLBURN, NEW JERSEY

Don't substitute ingredients for this dubbel; the candi sugar and the Special B malt in particular lend a truly authentic character reminiscent of the classic Corsendonk Monk's Brown Ale.

ORIGINAL GRAVITY: 1.056

FINAL GRAVITY: 1.014

POTENTIAL ALCOHOL: 5.4% ABV

IBUs: 20.9

COLOR: 37.5 SRM

INGREDIENTS

> 500 grams Belgian candi sugar (amber)
> 0.5 pound Belgian CaraVienne malt
> 0.5 pound Belgian Special B malt
> 6.6 pounds light malt extract syrup
> 1 ounce German Hallertau hops 5.0% AA boil 60 minutes
> 0.5 ounce East Kent Goldings hops 5.0% AA boil 15 minutes
> Liquid Belgian Ale yeast
> Priming sugar: $1\frac{1}{4}$ cup wheat DME (for a creamy head)

BREWING PROCEDURES

1. Start with 3 gallons of water. Put the milled grains in a grain bag and put it into the cold water. Heat the water until it is simmering.
2. Take the grains out of the water and add the DME and the candi to the water. Bring it to a boil and continue to boil for 60 minutes, adding the hops at the appropriate time. Add 2 teaspoons of Irish moss for the last 15 minutes.
3. At the end of the boil, force-cool and add enough water to make a total of 5 gallons. Add the yeast from a healthy starter and ferment.
4. When fermentation is complete, bottle with priming sugar and condition for at least 4 weeks.

CLOISTER DUBBEL
🍺 🍺 🍺 🍺
STEPHEN SNYDER

You can add some refined sugar to boost the gravity on this one if you like but keep the fermentation temperature below 70°F and make sure you have a healthy yeast starter for a strong fermentation. Because of the makeup of my water supply, I have added 2 teaspoons of calcium carbonate to counteract the acidity of the dark malts used. If your water is high in temporary hardness already, you may not need this adjustment.

ORIGINAL GRAVITY: 1.064

FINAL GRAVITY: 1.016

POTENTIAL ALCOHOL: 6.4% ABV

IBUs: 25

INGREDIENTS (FOR 5.5 GALLONS)

- 11 pounds Belgian pils malt (crushed)
- 0.75 pound Special B malt (crushed)
- 1 pound Munich malt (crushed)
- 1 pound dextrine malt (crushed)
- 0.25 pound German dark crystal malt (crushed)
- 0.25 pound Belgian chocolate malt (crushed)
- 2 teaspoons calcium carbonate
- 0.5 ounce Styrian hop plugs at 7.1% AA (boil 60 minutes)
- 1 ounce Fuggles hop plugs at 4.1% AA (boil 45 minutes)
- 0.5 ounce Saaz hop plugs at 3.3% AA (boil 10 minutes)
- Wyeast 1214 Belgian Ale yeast in a 1 liter starter
- ¾ cup corn sugar for bottling

BREWING PROCEDURES

1. Saccharification rest. Rest 90 minutes at 155°F. Stir occasionally. Test for remaining starches with iodine tincture as noted above. If negative (wort no longer turns purplish/black), mash out.
2. Mash out. Raise to 165–170°F. Rest 5–10 minutes to decrease viscosity.
3. Transfer to lauter tun. Slowly sparge with 165–170°F water over 45–60 minutes and collect wort into brew kettle.
4. Collect 6.5 gallons of wort.
5. Boil for 90 minutes, adding hops as noted above.
6. Force-cool with wort chiller.
7. Rack through sanitized sieve or strainer bag into carboy or other fermenter.
8. Pitch 1 liter yeast starter. Aerate well.
9. Rest beer for 2–3 hours or until trub settles. (Optional.)
10. Rack into primary fermenter and open-ferment or ferment under airlock at 58–68°F for 5 to 7 days.
11. Rack to secondary for 7 to 10 days.
12. Rack to bottling bucket, prime, add fresh yeast (optional), and bottle or keg.
13. Condition at 65–68°F for 10 to 14 days.
14. Cellar for 6 to 8 weeks.
15. Serve at 55–60°F.

DUBBEL 'EM UP
⫼ ⫼ ⫼ ⫼

DAN SOBOTI

U-BREW—MILLBURN, NEW JERSEY

This recipe allows the all-grain brewer a lot of latitude in using preferred yeasts and brewing techniques. The ingredient list is simple and straightforward but produces a dubbel in the classic tradition with the chocolaty-raisiny quality of the Special B malt dominating.

ORIGINAL GRAVITY: 1.057

FINAL GRAVITY: 1.014

POTENTIAL ALCOHOL: 5.5% ABV

IBUs: 22.1

Color: 43.5 SRM

INGREDIENTS

> 8 pounds Belgian pale malt
>
> 0.75 pound Belgian CaraMunich malt
>
> 0.5 pound Belgian Special B malt
>
> 0.5 kilogram Belgian candi sugar (dark)
>
> 1 ounce Liberty hops 4.5% AA boil 60 minutes
>
> 0.5 ounce Styrian Golding 4.5% AA boil 15 minutes
>
> 1–2 teaspoons of Irish moss
>
> Belgian ale yeast
>
> ¾ cup of corn sugar or 1¼ cup of DME for priming

BREWING PROCEDURES

1. Use your favorite mashing technique for this. I used a single-infusion mash with a strike temperature of about 158°F. I like a full-bodied dubbel. Sparge until you have between 5.5 and 6 gallons.

2. Do a 60-minute boil, adding the hops at the appropriate time. Add 1–2 teaspoons of Irish moss for the last 15 minutes.

3. Force-cool, aerate well, and pitch a healthy yeast starter. There are many Belgian ale yeasts on the market today. Use your favorite.

4. Prime with ¾ cup of corn sugar or 1¼ cup of DME.

EAST COAST ABBEY DUBBEL

▥ ▥ ▥ ▥

EAST COAST BREWING SUPPLY—STATEN ISLAND, NEW YORK

Once again, East Coast Brewing Supply provides a recipe tailored to the needs of the large-scale all-grain brewer. The table and corn sugars called for are essential to lighten the body a touch of this delicious reddish brown dubbel and are good substitutes for Belgian candi and invert sugar.

ORIGINAL GRAVITY: 1.065

FINAL GRAVITY: 1.017

POTENTIAL ALCOHOL: 6.4% ABV

INGREDIENTS (FOR 12.5 GALLONS)

> 19.5 pounds Klages malt
>
> 1 pound 90 °L crystal malt
>
> 1.25 pounds chocolate malt
>
> 3 pounds wheat malt
>
> 3.5 ounces Mt. Hood hops (3.4% AA) for 60 minutes
>
> 1 ounce Saaz hop plugs for 2 minutes
>
> 1 pound corn sugar
>
> 1 pound table sugar
>
> 2 teaspoons Irish moss
>
> Wyeast Belgian Ale (2 quart starter)
>
> 1¾ to 2 cups corn sugar for priming

Water Requirements:

> Mash: 6⅛ gallons
>
> Raise: 3 gallons
>
> Sparge: 12¼ gallons

BREWING PROCEDURES

1. Dough in crushed malts at 130°F, rest at 120°F. Hold for 35 minutes.

2. Add raise water to bring temperature to 150°F. Hold for 1 hour. Raise heat to 167°F, then mash out and start sparge. Sparge water should be at 176°F.

3. Collect about 14¼ gallons of wort. Boil for 90 minutes, adding bittering hops after 30 minutes. Add finishing hops in last 2 minutes.

4. Chill, pitch yeast and ferment as normal. Rack to secondary after 2 weeks.

5. Prime with corn sugar and bottle-condition for 3–5 weeks.

Note: Color good, chocolate malt comes through nicely. Good malt-to-hop balance. You might experiment with a higher gravity.

Tripple

THE HOME BREWERY—OZARK, MISSOURI

The Home Brewery is noted for developing accurate recipes that expose novice brewers to some of the world's more challenging and lesser-known beer styles. This is one such simple recipe that produces a very good tripel with lots of real Belgian character. You can use this formulation to build upon in the future, adding light candi sugar to lighten the body or experimenting with different fermentation temperatures to alter the flavor profile.

ORIGINAL GRAVITY: 1.074

FINAL GRAVITY: 1.025

POTENTIAL ALCOHOL: 6.5% ABV

INGREDIENTS

¼ **pound whole light crystal malt**

¼ **pound Belgian dextrine malt**

9.9 pounds (3 packs) Belgian Abbey malt extract syrup

2 ounces Kent Goldings pellets (5.5% AA) in boil

1 ounce Saaz pellets (4.2% AA) in last 5 minutes

½ teaspoon Irish moss in last 15 minutes of boil

1 pack Wyeast 1214 ale yeast

¾ **cup corn sugar for priming**

BREWING PROCEDURES

1. Heat 5 gallons of water in a large kettle. Add crushed grains. Many people don't have a kettle that large, but heat as much as you can (at least 2 gallons). Remove grains from kettle at 170°F. When the water is boiling, turn off the heat and add the malt extract to the water. Use a spoon and stir until you are sure no malt extract is sticking to the bottom of the kettle. Then turn the heat back on.

2. Bring the kettle back to a boil and stir occasionally so the ingredients won't burn on the bottom of the kettle. If your recipe calls for bittering hops, now is the time to add them and stir them in. Watch out for a boilover. In the early part of the boil, the kettle usually tries to boil over once or twice, so control this by adjusting the heat. Later in the boil, the surface tension changes and boiling over is not a problem. Keep stirring occasionally and let the beer (wort) boil hard for 1 hour. Stir in the ½ teaspoon of Irish moss in your recipe about 15 minutes before the end of the boil.

3. If finishing hops are called for in your recipe, stir them in 2 minutes before the end of the boil. Using finishing hops at the end of the boil adds a fresh aroma and flavor to the beer, and the use of finishing hops is appropriate in most beer styles.

4. Pour the hot beer (wort) into the primary fermenter. It is not necessary to strain the wort if you used hop pellets. Add cold water to bring the total volume up to 5 gallons. Cover the fermenter and wait until the temperature is

down to 75°F. If you have a wort chiller, use it to bring the temperature down quickly. At 75° or less, add the yeast in your recipe. Just tear open the pack(s) and sprinkle it on the wort. Close the fermenter with the lid, stopper, and airlock. Remember to put water (or vodka) in the airlock. Vodka evaporates more quickly, but bacteria won't live in it.

5. Pitch yeast and ferment at room temperature. Fermentation should start within 24 hours, and may continue for 2 weeks. Leave the beer alone and don't open the lid. When the airlock has not bubbled for several days and the beer is flat, still, and clearing, transfer to a secondary fermenter for 1 to 2 weeks.

6. To bottle, siphon about 1 pint of beer into a pan and warm it on the stove. Add exactly ¾ cup of corn sugar to the pan and stir until it is dissolved. Pour this back into the beer and stir gently but well to distribute the sugar. Siphon or tap into clean sanitized bottles and cap. Keep the bottles at room temperature. After a week, put a bottle in the refrigerator and try it. It will be best in about 3 months in the bottle.

"DEMISE" BELGIAN TRIPLE
⏚ ⏚ ⏚ ⏚

MARK RICHMOND, HEAD BREWER, GREAT LAKES BREWING CO.—CLEVELAND, OHIO

Like many strong, pale Belgian ales, Mark Richmond's formulation for a 9.5% ABV Belgian tripel deserves its ominous moniker, especially if you have more than one. The recipe and the techniques are simple but require brewing

equipment capable of handling such a large quantity of mashed malt. Try to find the real candi sugar used by Belgian brewers. It lends an authentic quality to this fine ale.

ORIGINAL GRAVITY: 1.096

FINAL GRAVITY: 1.025

POTENTIAL ALCOHOL: 9.5% ABV

INGREDIENTS

18 pounds Belgian Pils malt
2 pounds candi sugar
2 ounces Crystal hops (4.1 AAU) (60 minutes)
1 ounce Tettnang hops (4.6 AAU) after boil
Wyeast 1214 Belgian Ale yeast
¾ cup corn sugar for priming

BREWING PROCEDURES

1. Infusion-mash crushed grains for 1 hour at 155°F.
2. Perform a 90-minute boil, adding hops as noted above.
3. Add candy sugar 30 minutes into boil.
4. Chill wort and transfer to fermenter. Pitch with Wyeast 1214.
5. Ferment at 65°F.
6. Rack, bottle, and condition as normal.

TRIPEL PLAY
⏚ ⏚ ⏚ ⏚

DAN SOBOTI

U-BREW—MILLBURN, NEW JERSEY

This tripel is designed to be full-bodied, a good quality for a strong ale, especially if you let this one age for a year or more. As in the previous tripel recipes, try to use an authentic Belgian candi sugar.

ORIGINAL GRAVITY: 1.077

FINAL GRAVITY: 1.019

POTENTIAL ALCOHOL: 7.4% ABV

IBUs: 23.8

COLOR: 7.6 SRM

INGREDIENTS

> 12 pounds Belgian Pils malt
>
> 0.75 kilogram Belgian candi (amber)
>
> 3 ounces German Hallertau 2.0% AA boil for 60 minutes
>
> Wyeast 1388 Belgian Strong Ale
>
> ¾ cup corn sugar or 1¼ cup DME

BREWING PROCEDURES

1. Use your favorite mashing technique for this. I used a single-infusion mash with a saccharification temperature of about 158°F. I like a full-bodied tripel. Sparge until you have between 5.5 and 6 gallons.

2. Do a 60-minute boil, adding all of the hops at the beginning of the boil. Add 1–2 teaspoons of Irish moss for the last 15 minutes.

3. Force-chill (I use an immersion chiller), aerate well, and pitch a healthy yeast starter. There are many Belgian ale yeasts on the market today. I think Wyeast 1388, Belgian Strong Ale, is a very good choice.

4. Prime with ¾ cup corn sugar or 1¼ cup DME.

Notes:

Boil temperature of water: 212°F

Grain starting temperature: 68°F

Desired grain/water ratio: 1.3 quarts per pound

Strike water: 3.36 gallons of water at 175°F

First mash temperature: 158°F

"THE TRUMPET OF DEATH" BELGIAN PALE ALE

🛢 🛢 🛢 🛢

MARK RICHMOND, HEAD BREWER, GREAT LAKES BREWING CO.—CLEVELAND, OHIO

Don't let the name scare you; this recipe is of much lower gravity than Mark's other Belgian brews and produces a delightfully quaffable ale with that classic LaChouffe complexity and a nice hop nose.

ORIGINAL GRAVITY: 1.056

FINAL GRAVITY: 1.008

POTENTIAL ALCOHOL: 6.25% ABV

INGREDIENTS

> 10 pounds Belgian Pils malt
>
> 8 ounces CaraMunich malt
>
> 2 ounces chocolate malt
>
> 2 ounces Crystal hops (4.1 AAU) 60 minutes
>
> 1 ounce Tettnang hops (4.6 AAU) 30 minutes
>
> 1 ounce Tettnang hops (4.6 AAU) 10 minutes
>
> 0.5 ounces Tettnang hops (4.6 AAU) after boil
>
> 0.5 ounces crystal hops (4.6 AAU) after boil
>
> LaChouffe yeast
>
> Priming sugar

BREWING PROCEDURES

1. 1-hour infusion mash at 152°F.

2. 90-minute boil.

3. Pitch with cultured up LaChouffe yeast.

4. Ferment at 65°F.

5. Ferment, prime, and bottle using your preferred methods.

"Afterglow" Grand Cru Style Strong Ale 🛢🛢🛢🛢

Mark Richmond, Head Brewer, Great Lakes Brewing Co.—Cleveland, Ohio

This recipe produces a classic example of a Belgian category S or "Superior" style of beer often rolled out by the artisanal brewers seasonally or for the Christmas holidays. Served young it is an explosion of fruit, hops, and spice. If allowed to mature a year or two you'll have an ale of immense complexity and depth.

Original Gravity: 1.084

Final Gravity: 1.020

Potential Alcohol: 8.5% ABV

Ingredients

12 pounds Belgian Pils malt

1.5 pounds aromatic malt

2 pounds light dry malt extract

2 ounces Hallertau hops (5.2 AAU) (60 minutes)

1 ounce Tettnang hops (5.5 AAU) (20 minutes)

1 ounce Hallertau hops (5.2 AAU) (10 minutes)

1 ounce Saaz hops (4.8 AAU) after boil

1 ounce crushed coriander seed (60 minutes)

0.5 ounce sweet orange peel (10 minutes)

1 ounce crushed coriander seed and 0.5 ounce sweet orange peel added to secondary

Wyeast 3944 Belgian Witbier yeast

¾ to 1 cup priming sugar

Brewing Procedures

1. Infusion-mash crushed grains for 1 hour at 155°F.
2. Perform a 90-minute boil, adding hops as noted above.
3. Add extract 30 minutes into boil.
4. Pitch with Wyeast 3944.
5. Ferment at 65°F.
6. Bottle and condition as normal.

LAMBIC

The origins of the name of this beer are lost to history, but most modern authorities agree that it probably came from the town Lembeek located in the area around Brussels where lambics are brewed. As an appellation, albeit a very general one, lambic is a beer of at least 1.020 original gravity made from as much as 40 percent unmalted wheat and spontaneously fermented by wild, airborne microorganisms. The true lambics are spontaneously fermented by microbes that exist in a small area around Brussels in the Belgian province of Brabant called the Payottenland. Lambics are distinguished for their tart, acidic, and quenching nature produced by strains of *Brettanomyces bruxellensis* and *Brettanomyces lambicus* yeasts and lactic acid–producing bacteria such as *Pediococcus damnosus* that are dreaded contaminants in most other beer styles. Out of respect for the appellation, what you will be making as a homebrewer should rightfully be called "lambic-style."

Unblended lambic is much rarer on the retail market than gueuze, a bottle-conditioned blend of old (two- to three-year-old) and young (one-year-old) lambic. Gueuze is often composed of a blend of many lambics ranging in age from one to three years old. These blends can be of equal portions or can sometimes contain a majority of young lambic. Gueuze should be conditioned for at least three months and some suggest at least nine months in the bottle with a period of warm conditioning at up to 75°F. Faro was once considered an "everyday" lambic blended with Mars beer or some light ale, served on draft and sweetened with a lump or two of sugar. Faro has become increasingly rare, and bottled versions are often pasteurized to retain that trademark candi sugar sweetness.

To brew a lambic-style ale you must be ready to embark on what will probably be the most difficult and challenging experience a homebrewer can undertake. You must forget all the things you've learned about "proper" brewing techniques and overcome the obstacles of mashing raw wheat, using stale hops, fermenting in oak, and keeping the beer for over a year while simultaneously juggling mixed cultures of wild yeasts and beer-spoiling bacteria. High-enzyme malts such as domestic six-row are recommended to convert the 30–40 percent of raw soft white wheat. A high-temperature sugar rest is employed to provide a dextrinous wort that will sustain the long, slow ferment. A high-temperature sparge at up to 200°F is used to extract astringent tannins that are part of the classic lambic profile. Lambics are typically "oversparged" in the normal brewing sense to facilitate a large volume of wort that can be boiled for as much as six hours. Two- to three-year-old

aged European aroma hops are used so that only the preservative properties, not the bitterness, flavor, or aroma, are present. One traditional technique that I would avoid, however, is the practice of cooling the wort overnight in a shallow, open vessel. This is intended to introduce native Payottenland microflora for spontaneous fermentation and, therefore, has little value to the American homebrewer. Fermentation in an oak cask or on oak chips is recommended for true lambic flavor, and this fermentation should last for at least nine months to a year. If you choose to further ferment your lambic on fruit, add these whole to another oak cask or secondary fermenter and allow them to ferment for several more months before bottling. You can expect the classic lambic fruits like raspberry and sour cherry to contribute 1.008–1.010 points per pound per gallon. Eight to ten pounds per five-gallon batch will tend to produce the proper fruit character. Because of the long fermentation periods, a new culture of lambic yeast and bacteria is suggested at bottling. Above all else, keep lambic yeast and bacteria strains away from your normal brewing operations and fermentation equipment.

Some of the classic brewers of commercial examples of lambic, gueuze, and faro include Brouwerij Frank Boon, Brouwerij Lindemans, and Brasserie Cantillon.

LAMBIC BASICS

ORIGINAL GRAVITY: 1.047–54

FINAL GRAVITY: 1.004–10

IBUs: 15–21

COLOR (SRM): 5–10

ALCOHOL BY VOLUME: 5–7%

EAST COAST PINEAPPLE LAMBIC

⫿ ⫿ ⫿ ⫿

EAST COAST BREWING SUPPLY—STATEN ISLAND, NEW YORK

The variety of fruit used in Belgian lambics has broadened rapidly in recent years to attract a wider-range audience of craft beer lovers. Lambics can be found featuring banana, plums, and yes, pineapple. If you are a lambic purist, you can substitute the more traditional cherries or raspberries if you like, but don't forget that it is a homebrewer's duty to break with convention once in a while.

ORIGINAL GRAVITY: 1.042 (before fruit addition)

FINAL GRAVITY: 1.011 (before fruit addition)

POTENTIAL ALCOHOL: 4% ABV (before fruit addition)

INGREDIENTS (FOR 12 GALLONS)

- 14 pounds Klages malt
- 6 pounds raw wheat
- 2 ounces Northern Brewer hops (3-year-old crushed plugs) 60 minutes
- 16 pounds fresh crushed pineapple
- Wyeast 1056 American Ale. Starter stepped up 3 times to 1.4 liters for each primary.
- 1 quart of Wyeast Bruxellensis blend
- ¾ to 1 cup priming sugar

Water Requirements:
- Decoct: 2.8 gallons
- Mash: 3.2 gallons
- Raise: 7.0 gallons
- Sparge: 10 gallons

BREWING PROCEDURES

1. Add all wheat and 10% (1.4 pounds Klages) to boiler. Strike heat 163°. Hold at 158°F for 10 minutes, then boil for 30 minutes.

2. Mash in at 130°. Bring to 140° for 15 minutes, then add boiled wheat to bring temperature to 158°F. Hold for 30 minutes. Mash out at 170°F and sparge.

3. Collect approximately 14 gallons of wort. Boil for 90 minutes, adding hops after 30 minutes.

4. Boil down to 12.25 gallons. Rack chilled wort into 2 primary fermenters and pitch yeast.

5. Rack into two 6-gallon secondary fermenters after 4 days.

6. After 2 weeks in secondary fermenters, add pineapple to two 6-gallon glass carboys. Rack beer onto fruit. Pitch 1 quart of Wyeast Bruxellensis into each carboy.

7. Keep beer on fruit and yeast for at least 3 months.

8. Prime, bottle, then condition for 2–12 months.

LAMBIC-STYLE KRIEK/FRAMBOISE

⫿ ⫿ ⫿ ⫿

STEPHEN SNYDER

Besides patience, good luck, and attention to traditional recipes, I think the secret to brewing lambic-style beer is a primary fermentation in an oak barrel. I use a 10-gallon oak barrel found at an antique shop. It is very old and required intense cleaning and conditioning to remove years of residue, so you'd probably be better off buying a new one and breaking it in yourself. Remember to keep this brew away from your normal brewing and fermenting area.

ORIGINAL GRAVITY: 1.048

FINAL GRAVITY: 1.013

POTENTIAL ALCOHOL: 4.5% ABV (before addition of fruit)

IBUs: 16

INGREDIENTS (FOR 10 GALLONS)

> 13 pounds domestic 6-row malt (crushed)
>
> 7 pounds raw soft white wheat (crushed)
>
> 1 ounce East Kent Goldings hop plugs at 4.7% AA (boiled 60 minutes)
>
> 10 pounds whole raspberries and 10 pounds whole sour cherries
>
> 2 liter starter of Wyeast 1214 Belgian Ale yeast
>
> 1 liter starter of Wyeast 3278 Belgian Lambic (*Brettanomyces* blend) yeast
>
> 1.5 cups corn sugar for priming

BREWING PROCEDURES

1. Mash in at 100°F with 6 gallons of soft to moderate brewing liquor.
2. Immediately raise the temperature approximately 2°F per minute to 122°F.
3. Maintain protein rest for 20 minutes.
4. Ladle 25% of the mash into a second kettle and bring to 158°F.
5. Keep original "rest mash" temperature constant at 122°F.
6. Maintain a saccharification rest for 15 minutes.
7. Bring to a boil for 15 minutes.
8. Recombine with the "rest mash" to yield a temperature of 147°F (64°C), applying bottom heat or cold water if necessary to adjust temperature up or down.
9. Rest 15 minutes.
10. Pull a second decoction and perform exactly as in the first. Recombine with the main mash to raise the temperature to about 158–160°.
11. Raise to 158°F with boiling water if necessary and rest for 60 minutes.
12. Raise to 170°F with boiling water. Rest for 15 minutes and mash out. Transfer to lauter tun.
13. Sparge with 10 gallons of 200°F water. Recirculate the first gallon of runoff.
14. Collect 12 gallons of wort.
15. Boil for 180 minutes, adding hops as noted above.
16. Force-cool with a wort chiller.
17. Rack through a sanitized strainer bag or sieve into 2 carboys or other 2 fermenters to remove hops.
18. Pitch 2 liter ale yeast starter evenly between batches. Aerate well. Cover and attach airlocks.
19. Rest beer for 2–3 hours or until trub settles. (Optional.)
20. Rack off of trub into a sanitized 10-gallon oak cask up to the bung hole. Ferment for 14 days at 63–68°F. Add the lambic blend in a 1 liter starter; fit bung hole with drilled stopper and blowoff hose.
21. Continue to ferment in the oak cask for 12–24 months, then rack into two 5-gallon carboys with crushed fruit.
22. Ferment another 2–3 months.
23. Add fresh cultures of both 3278 and 1214, prime with 1.5 cups corn sugar, bottle, and condition 4–8 weeks at 65–75°F.
24. Cellar for 6–12 months at 50–60°F.

OUD BRUIN

Often classified as "Flanders brown," the name of this beer in Flemish translates to "old brown," a self-explanatory sobriquet for a medium-bodied, reddish brown ale of Belgium that is aged for up to a year. These beers are generally bottle-conditioned and unlike British beers of similar character, exhibit no roast or hop aromas but a rather a gentle malty, fruity, or acidic quality. The most highly acclaimed commercial versions are quite acidic (with pH as low as 3.5) and tart from the presence of various bacteria introduced in the maturation process. As you might gather from the name, old brown's character is largely a part of the aging process.

Commercially, the older well-aged beers are sometimes blended with younger beers to temper their acidity and to create a complex mix of flavors. These are excellent keeping beers and after bottling, can be kept for years. These beers are challenging for the home brewer not only because of the proper balancing of bacteria cultures needed for correct acidity levels but also because of the patience needed to age these beers for several months in a secondary fermenter or cask and again in the bottle. However, if you have become as infatuated with these beers as most who have tried them, you will no doubt be tempted to try brewing one yourself at least once.

A basic grist of Belgian pils or pale ale malt is advised with your coloring derived from a long wort boil and just a small portion of crystal malt. Hops play a subordinate role and should be barely perceptible. Classic aroma varieties are suggested. The fruitiness contributed by yeast is a common hallmark of oud bruins, but diacetyl, which often accompanies the esters in British ales, is inappropriate. Therefore, a cleaner brown ale yeast is suggested for the primary ferment, or at the very least a cool ferment at the lower end of the optimum temperature is advised. Open fermentation is certainly an option for the homebrewer and may produce more of the fruity qualities true to this style. A long secondary fermentation is mandatory, and if the budget allows, aging in oak pays huge dividends for your trouble. To obtain the lactic acid quality, homebrewers sometimes culture up the residue from classic bottle-conditioned brands, often with unpredictable results. Use of some of the newer lambic-style cultures on the market in the secondary may be a safer alternative. Water should be soft in order to avoid extracting intense Burton-style dryness or bitterness from the hops.

Liefmans produces the mostly widely available commercial versions, a classic oud bruin named Goudenband and raspberry- and cherry-flavored versions titled Frambozenbier and Kriekbier, respectively.

OUD BRUIN BASICS

ORIGINAL GRAVITY: 1.044–56

FINAL GRAVITY: 1.008–10

IBUs: 15–25

COLOR (SRM): 12–18

ALCOHOL BY VOLUME: 4.8–5.2%

OUD BRUIN

▦ ▦ ▦ ▦

STEPHEN SNYDER

You can use a variety of primary yeasts for this one. Just try to pick an ale strain with a fairly clean profile or ferment at the lower end of the optimum temperature when using yeasts that produce a lot of diacetyl or esters. As an alternative to the Wyeast Lambic yeast and the BrewTek Pediococcus you can try your hand at culturing up a secondary yeast from a bottle of commercial oud bruin such as the Liefmans Goudenband. One caveat, though: Yeast harvested from old bottles may contain living microbes of only a few if any of the many strains of yeasts and bacteria necessary for an authentic profile. Partial mash brewers can substitute 6.5 pounds of light to amber dry malt extract or 7.5 pounds of light to amber malt extract syrup for the 11 pounds of Belgian Pils malt and brew as normal, then begin from step 10 below.

ORIGINAL GRAVITY: 1.056

FINAL GRAVITY: 1.015

POTENTIAL ALCOHOL: 5.4% ABV (before addition of fruit)

IBUs: 22

INGREDIENTS (FOR 5.5 GALLONS)

11 pounds Belgian 2-row Pils malt (crushed)

1 pound Munich malt (crushed)

0.5 pound German dark crystal malt (crushed)

1 ounce Hallertau hop plugs at 3% AA

1 ounce Saaz hop plugs at 3.3% AA

2 teaspoons Irish Moss (boil 15 minutes)

BrewTek CL–320 Belgian Ale 2 or Wyeast 1084 Irish Ale yeast

Wyeast 3278 Belgian Lambic blend (BrewTek CL–5600 Pediococcus Damnosus may

also be used after the primary ferment but prior to the addition of the lambic blend)

1 ounce oak chips

¾ cup corn sugar for priming

BREWING PROCEDURES

1. Saccharification rest. Mash in, stir well. Rest 15 minutes at 140°F.

2. Saccharification rest. Raise temperature and rest 15 minutes at 148°F. Stir occasionally.

3. Saccharification rest. Rest 30–45 minutes at 158°F. Test for remaining starches with iodine tincture. If negative (wort no longer turns purplish/black), mash out.

4. Mash out. Raise to 165–170°F. Rest 10 minutes to decrease viscosity.

5. Transfer to lauter tun. Slowly sparge with 165–168°F water over 45–60 minutes and collect wort into brew kettle.

6. Collect 7 gallons of wort.

7. Boil for 3 hours, adding hops and Irish moss as noted above.

8. Force-cool with wort chiller.

9. Rack through sanitized sieve or strainer bag into carboy or other fermenter.

10. Pitch 1 liter yeast starter. Aerate well.

11. Rest beer for 2–3 hours or until trub settles. (Optional.)

12. Rack into primary fermenter and open-ferment at 62–65°F for 5 to 7 days.

13. Rack to secondary, add sanitized oak chips, and ferment under airlock for 8–16 weeks. Add lambic yeast package and ferment under airlock for another 8–12 weeks.

14. Rack to bottling bucket, prime, add fresh yeast, and bottle or keg.

15. Condition at 65°F for 10 days.

16. Cellar at 55°F for 1–6 months.

17. Serve at 55–60°F.

NORTH AMERICAN ALES

Many ales brewed in the United States are creative variations of European classics, often reflecting a combination of German and British brewing traditions. Some of these variations are close enough to their European counterparts to be included in the prior recipe sections under the respective classic style. Others, such as American amber ale, American brown, and American wheat have been newly defined by America's craft brewers. These are individualistic enough to stand on their own and are included here along with older American classics like cream ale. We have lumped together many styles of "American Ale" for simplicity. Ingredients and water profiles for American-style ales depend largely on the style being brewed, but generally consist of American-grown malts and hops and a fairly clean, neutral yeast strain, with water that is medium-hard or soft due to the higher hopping rates and the lighter-colored malts of American brews.

Thankfully, the list of fine microbrews in this category is enormous. Good American ales can be found in several style categories including brown, amber, wheat, and cream ale. A minuscule list of the more popular and acclaimed standouts includes North Coast's Ruedrich's Red Seal Ale, Harpoon Ale, New York Harbor Ale, Little Kings Cream Ale, Brooklyn Brown, and Genessee Cream Ale.

CREAM ALE BASICS

ORIGINAL GRAVITY: 1.044–55

FINAL GRAVITY: 1.008–10

IBUs: 10–22

COLOR (SRM): 2–4

ALCOHOL BY VOLUME: 4.5–5.75%

AMBER ALE BASICS

ORIGINAL GRAVITY: 1.050–60

FINAL GRAVITY: 1.012–14

IBUs: 30–40

COLOR (SRM): 8–18

ALCOHOL BY VOLUME: 5–6%

AMERICAN WHEAT BASICS

ORIGINAL GRAVITY: 1.030–50

FINAL GRAVITY: 1.004–18

IBUs: 15–25

COLOR (SRM): 2–8

ALCOHOL BY VOLUME: 3.5–4.5%

CREAMY BROWN ALE
🍺 🍺 🍺

RIC GENTHNER

WINE BARREL PLUS—LIVONIA, MICHIGAN

This brown ale is a rich, malty brew that has the taste and aroma of fresh hops. A thick, creamy head tops this well-balanced beer.

ORIGINAL GRAVITY: 1.069

FINAL GRAVITY: 1.020

POTENTIAL ALCOHOL: 6.5% ABV

INGREDIENTS

> ¼ pound chocolate malt
> ¼ pound black patent malt
> ⅛ pound roasted barley malt
> 1 pound crystal malt
> 8 pounds amber and light (mixed) malt extract
> 1 ounce Fuggles hops
> ½ ounce Northern Brewer hops (boiling)
> 1 teaspoon Irish moss
> 1 package Wyeast 3056 Bavarian Wheat
> 2 ounces Cascade hops (dry hopping)
> ¾ cup corn sugar

BREWING PROCEDURES

1. Add the chocolate, crystal, roasted, and black patent malt to 2 gallons of water that is at 158°F. Leave for 1 hour.
2. Remove the grain and rinse.
3. Add the malt extracts and the Fuggles and Northern Brewer hops and boil for 45 minutes.
4. Add the Irish moss to the boil for the last 15–20 minutes.
5. Pour immediately into primary fermenter with cold water and top up to 5 gallons.
6. Add yeast when cool.
7. After primary fermentation add whole Cascade hops. Leave for 2 weeks.
8. Bottle with ¾ cup of corn sugar.

CASCADES ALE
🍺

THE CELLAR HOMEBREW—SEATTLE, WASHINGTON

"The explosion of microbreweries here in the Northwest has resulted in a pale ale style that has somewhat digressed from the English style. Usually hopped at a higher rate than the British pales, and with American-bred hop varieties like Cascade and Centennial. Our recipe features the distinctive citrusy flavor of the Cascade hops."

ORIGINAL GRAVITY: 1.038

FINAL GRAVITY: 1.010

POTENTIAL ALCOHOL: 3.6% ABV

INGREDIENTS (FOR 5.5 GALLONS)

> 6 pounds Alexander's light bulk malt syrup
> 1 ounce Perle or Northern Brewer hops (boiling)
> 1½ ounce Cascade hops (finishing)
> 1 package Edme dry ale or American Ale liquid yeast
> ¾ cup corn sugar for priming

BREWING PROCEDURES

Note: If you are using the American Ale liquid yeast with this recipe, be sure to start that yeast at least 1 to 3 days before doing any of the brewing steps below. Follow the package directions and use the yeast in step 4 below.

1. Bring 2 to 2½ gallons brewing water to a boil in your brewing kettle.

2. Remove the brewing kettle from the burner and add the 6 pounds Alexander's light malt syrup. The syrup is easier to pour if the can has been previously placed in hot water. Also, rinse the can with hot water to ensure that all the syrup goes into the kettle. Stir the mixture, now called "wort," until it boils. Watch carefully at this time because the wort may boil over. You can prevent this by pouring a cup of cold water into the overboiling wort.

3. At boiling point, add the Perle boiling hops. Hops can be placed in a hop bag or added loose, to be later strained out after the boil using a strainer bag. Time the boil for about 1 hour, stirring occasionally. After the first 10 minutes of this boil, remove 2 cups of wort in measuring cup and cover with foil or plastic. Cool to 90°F for use in step 4.

4. Making the yeast starter: For dry yeast, use ½ cup warm tap water (90–100°F). Sprinkle the contents of yeast packet into that water, cover for at least 15 minutes, and then add to the 2 cups of wort you prepared in step 3. Cover and set aside for use in step 8. For liquid yeast, prepare 1 to 3 days ahead of brewing time per package instructions. Open the swollen package and add the contents to the 2 cups of wort as prepared in step 3.

5. After the wort has boiled for that 1 hour, add finishing hops. Place them in the hop bag, which has been emptied of the spent boiling hops, and place them in the boiling kettle or just add the Cascade finishing hops directly to the brewing kettle. They will be strained later in step 7.

6. Let the boil continue for 5 minutes. This gives the beer its hop aroma. Remove the pot from the burner and let it cool, covered, for about 20 minutes.

7. Pour 3 gallons of cold water into the sanitized open fermenter fitted with strainer bag. If loose finishing hops were used in step 5, strain the warm wort from step 6 into the cold water. Top up the fermenter to 5½ gallons using cold tap water. Cover the fermenter and cool the wort as rapidly as possible.

8. When the wort has cooled to about 80°, add the yeast starter and ferment as you usually do.

GOLDEN ALE

THE VINEYARD—UPTON, MASSACHUSETTS
The ease of this recipe and the familiar light American flavor make this recipe a terrific choice for the beginning brewer. Simple additions of American hops lend a recognizable micro character perfect for enjoying with food.

ORIGINAL GRAVITY: 1.050–53

FINAL GRAVITY: 1.010–12

POTENTIAL ALCOHOL: 5.3% ABV

INGREDIENTS

½ pound light crystal malt grain
3.3 pounds English extra light malt extract
3 pounds Dutch light dry malt extract
1½ ounces Willamette hop pellets (boiling)
½ ounce Willamette hop pellets (last 15 minutes)
1 teaspoon Irish moss (15 minutes)
1 package Whitbread ale yeast
½ cup corn sugar for priming

BREWING PROCEDURES

1. Crush and put all grains into 1 quart cold water for 10 minutes. Slowly bring to a boil.

Once boiling commences, remove from heat. Strain liquid into brewpot.

2. Add 1½ gallons water, malt extract, and bring to a boil. At start of boil add 1½ ounces Willamette hop pellets. Last 15 minutes of boil time, add ½ ounce Willamette hop pellets and one teaspoon Irish moss.

3. Strain into sanitized primary fermenter and add cold water to make 5 gallons; let cool. Pitch yeast when temperature drops below 80°F. Primary fermentation: 4 days at 70°F. Secondary fermentation: 8 days at 70°F.

4. At bottling time boil ½ cup priming sugar with 1 cup water for bulk priming.

McDermott's Golden Ale

⫿

Northeast Brewers Supply—
Providence, Rhode Island

"This is a great beer for those who say homebrew *tastes* like it has been brewed at home or that it's too rich for them. This brilliantly clear, golden ale is a favorite at the shop because it's dry and crisp, with a wonderful floral aroma from dry-hopping."

Original Gravity: 1.046

Final Gravity: 1.012

Potential Alcohol: 4.4% ABV

Ingredients

> Two 3.3-pound cans John Bull light unhopped extract
> 2 ounces Northern Brewer whole boiling hops
> 1 teaspoon Irish moss

1½–2 ounces Northern Brewer whole hops for dry-hopping
Wyeast 1007 German Ale yeast
¾ cup corn sugar

Brewing Procedures

1. Boil water; add cans of extract.

2. Add boiling hops in boiling bag and the teaspoon of Irish moss.

3. Boil wort for 25 minutes (short boil keeps beer very clear).

4. Sparge into fermenter.

5. When cool, add yeast. After kräusen, put in secondary fermenter.

6. Add dry-hops to secondary and let sit for 2 weeks.

7. Bottle or keg.

Yaller Beer

⫿ ⫿ ⫿ ⫿

Andrew Tveekrem, Brewmaster,
Great Lakes Brewing Co.—
Cleveland, Ohio

"This beer, as the name indicates, is a pale and wimpy summer beer brewed expressly for picnics and weddings. It is suitable for old ladies, children, dogs, and any other typical light beer drinkers."

Original Gravity: 1.050

Final Gravity: 1.010

Potential Alcohol: 5.1% ABV

Ingredients (for 10 Gallons)

> 18 pounds DeWolf Cosyns pilsner malt
> 2 pounds dextrine malt

Hops: Boy, this is the hard part. You really have to restrain yourself. Stick to the lower-alpha varieties like Hallertau or Kent. One or two handfuls up front, then just little additions of two at a time until done. The real trick is to get just enough hop bitterness and flavor to make it drinkable without blowing away the target audience (kids, dogs, etc.).

1 quart thick yeast slurry of Wyeast 1028 London Ale

1½ cups corn sugar for priming

BREWING PROCEDURES

1. Mash crushed malt at 154–156°F for 1 hour, stirring occasionally.

2. Lauter to collect 12 gallons of wort and bring to a boil.

3. Add Hallertau or Kent hop pellets at the beginning of the boil.

4. Boil for 75 minutes, adding handfuls of hop pellets at 30 minutes prior to the end. Add more handfuls of hop pellets at 15 minutes prior to the end.

5. At the end of the boil add more handfuls of hops.

6. Swirl, cool, and ferment at 65°F.

7. Rack, prime, and bottle as you normally do.

RAUCOUS RED ALE
🍺 🍺 🍺

THE HOME BEER, WINE, & CHEESEMAKING SHOP—WOODLAND HILLS, CALIFORNIA

The meteoric rise of American microbrews has spawned a style called "amber ale" that still has yet to be narrowly defined. This gives craft brewers (homebrewers included) great latitude in choosing ingredients to fill the grain bill.

The Belgian malts as used in this recipe are a smart choice. They lend a warm, bready character beneath the contrasting fruitiness of Cascade hops. This could be a classic.

ORIGINAL GRAVITY: 1.059

FINAL GRAVITY: 1.013

POTENTIAL ALCOHOL: 6% ABV

IBUs: 28

COLOR: 13 SRM

INGREDIENTS

8 ounces Gambrinus honey malt

4 ounces Belgian biscuit malt

4 ounces Belgian aromatic malt

8 ounces Belgian CaraMunich malt

4 ounces Belgian Special B 220 °L malt

6 pounds Royal light DME

0.75 ounce Cluster hop pellets at 6.6% AA (60 minutes)

1.25 ounces Crystal hop pellets at 3.2% AA (20 minutes)

1 ounce Cascade hop pellets at 5.8% AA (0 minutes—at knockout)

1 teaspoon Irish moss

1 teaspoon gypsum

Wyeast 1272 American Ale II

¾ cup corn sugar for priming

BREWING PROCEDURES

1. Steep (soak) the grains in 2 quarts of 150°F water for 30–40 minutes. Sparge (rinse) with 2.5 quarts of 150°F water into your boiling pot. Discard grain. No water over 170°F with grain. Do not oversparge. Do not squeeze grain bag.

2. After adding 2.5 gallons of water and dissolving the malt, bring pot to a gentle but rolling boil. Skim all foam before starting

the hop sequence. Add Irish moss the last 20 minutes to remove the protein missed in steps 1 and 2. Add the gypsum into the boil. It adds hardness, accentuating the crisp hop character.

3. Ferment at an average of 62–66°F. This keeps the fruity esters to a minimum. Pitch (add) yeast when your water bath around the fermenter reads 70–80°F. Maintain this temperature until the first signs of fermentation (about 10–12 hours). If using a yeast starter (highly recommended), fermentation can start in 2–3 hours. Use ¾ cup sugar for priming.

AMBER ALE

JOE & BRYAN TIMMONS
BOSTON BREWERS SUPPLY CO.–
JAMAICA PLAIN, MASSACHUSETTS

"Our Amber Ale is a quick-maturing ale that is excellent just three to four weeks after brewing. It is deep amber in color and has a beautiful floral/spicy hop aroma from the late addition of Cascade hops. The generous amount of crystal malt used adds a rich caramel/malty flavor that is balanced by a firm hop bitterness."

ORIGINAL GRAVITY: 1.040–42

FINAL GRAVITY: 1.010–12

POTENTIAL ALCOHOL: 4% ABV

IBUs: approximately 37

INGREDIENTS

    6 pounds English light extract syrup
    1.5 pounds English crystal malt
    2 ounces Cascade hop pellets (bittering)
    1 ounce Cascade hop pellets (aroma)
    1 teaspoon Irish moss flakes
    1 package dry ale yeast
    6 ounces corn sugar for priming

BREWING PROCEDURES

1. Secure the grains in the muslin straining bag. Pour 2 gallons of cold water into your brewpot, apply heat, and add the grain bag. Heat to a near boil (about 155°F), turn off the heat, cover the pot, and allow the grains to steep for 15 minutes. Remove the grain bag, drain, and discard.

2. Thoroughly dissolve the malt extract, apply heat, and bring to a boil. As soon as the wort (unfermented beer) begins to boil, add the 2 ounces of Cascade hops. Start timing the boil; the total elapsed time will be 60 minutes. Maintain a good rolling boil.

3. After 45 minutes, add the Irish moss flakes. Ten minutes later, add the remaining ounce of Cascade pellets. Continue to boil for an additional 5 minutes, then cover and remove the pot from the heat. Allow the aroma hops to steep in the wort for about 15 minutes.

Remember that after the wort has cooled, it is highly vulnerable to contamination; everything that comes into contact with it from this point on must be thoroughly sanitized!

4. Cool the wort as quickly as possible. A wort chiller works best, but if you haven't got one yet a cold water bath will do the trick. Place the covered pot in your kitchen sink and fill with ice and cold water. When the temperature has fallen to about 90°F, transfer the wort, through a strainer if possible, into your fermenter. Top off with enough cold

water to reach a 5-gallon level and stir or shake well. Draw off a small sample and take both a hydrometer and a temperature reading; always discard the sample used.

5. When the wort has cooled to 65–70°F, you are ready to add the yeast. Once the yeast has been added, attach an airlock and keep the fermenter in a cool, dark location where temperature fluctuations are minimal, ideally 68°F. Active fermentation should become visible in the next 12 to 24 hours and will continue for about 3 to 5 days.

6. When visible signs of fermentation have ceased, gently transfer the beer to a sanitized secondary fermenter (ideally a 5-gallon glass carboy) leaving all sediment behind. Attach an airlock and allow the beer to settle for an additional 5 to 7 days at the same temperature of primary fermentation. At the end of this period, draw off a small sample and check the final gravity. By now it should be within the range stated above; if not, wait another couple of days and check again. Prepare to bottle.

Bottling and Conditioning

1. Sanitize all of your siphoning and bottling equipment, bottles, and caps.

2. Boil the 6 ounces of corn sugar in about a cup of water and pour it into your bottling bucket. Gently siphon the beer out of the fermenter into the bucket, making sure the flow is directed to the bottom of the bucket; avoid splashing or agitating the beer.

3. Using your siphon tubing and bottle filler, fill each bottle to within an inch from the top and cap immediately. Store the bottles upright for 3 to 4 weeks, chill, and enjoy.

Rhino Horn Amber Ale

Mountain Malt and Hop Shoppe— Lake Katrine & Poughkeepsie, New York

"This recipe was first brewed on a snowy winter's day with ingredients that were on hand. The result: a smooth, well-balanced amber ale with toasted overtones. It never had a name until I drank a Rhino Chasers Amber Ale. I wonder how they got my recipe."

Original Gravity: 1.051

Final Gravity: 1.014

Potential Alcohol: 4.8% ABV

Ingredients

- 1 teaspoon gypsum
- 1/2 pound 40 °L crystal malt
- 1 /2 ounces Liberty hop pellets at 5% AA (bittering)
- 1/4 pound toasted malt
- 1/2 ounce Tettnang hop plug (flavor)
- 1/4 pound Munich malt
- 1/2 ounce Tettnang hop plug (aroma)
- 3 pounds English extra light DME
- 1 teaspoon Irish moss
- 3 pounds English extra amber DME
- 1 package Glenbrew ale yeast
- 3/4 cup of priming sugar

Brewing Procedures

1. In a 12-quart or larger stainless-steel pot, heat 1 gallon of water to 160°F and add 1 teaspoon of gypsum. Stir until dissolved and turn off heat. Place cracked grains in a nylon bag and immerse in water. Cover pot and allow grain to steep for 30 minutes. Remove grain bag and bring the "tea" to a

boil. (If you do not have a nylon bag, add grains directly to water and strain.)

2. When boil is attained, turn off heat and add the dry malt. (Putting DME in a bowl first makes it easier to add.) Turn on heat and return to a boil.

3. When the danger of a messy boilover has passed, add 1½ ounces of Liberty hop pellets and cook at a low, rolling boil for 30 minutes.

4. Add 1 teaspoon of Irish moss and boil for 5 more minutes.

5. Take one half-ounce Tettnang hop plug and slice it up. Place pieces in a muslin hop bag and immerse in wort. Boil for 8 more minutes.

6. Take the remaining half-ounce Tettnang hop plug and repeat the same process. Boil for 2 more minutes, then turn off heat. Immediately remove both hop bags.

7. Take the brewpot from the stove and place it in a sink partially filled with cold water. Add 1 gallon of sanitary, refrigerated water (40°F) to the brewpot, then cover and place ice in the water around the brewpot. Never add ice directly to the wort! Let stand 15 minutes. Place 2 gallons of refrigerated water into the fermenter, then add the wort. Check the temperature (65–75°F is ideal). Top off to 5½ gallons with either more cold or room-temperature water.

8. With a sanitized measuring cup, scoop out ¾ cup and take a hydrometer reading. Discard sample.

9. Add the package of Glenbrew yeast to the fermenter when the temperature of the wort is between 65–75°F, let sit 10 minutes, then stir vigorously to aerate. Snap the fermenter lid on, fill the airlock halfway with water, and place in lid. Place fermenter in a spot where the temperature will remain a constant 65–70°F.

10. Ferment in the primary for 5–6 days, then rack into a glass carboy for 2 weeks.

11. When brew is clear, siphon into a bottling bucket. Dissolve priming sugar into 1 cup boiling water, cool, and gently stir into beer with a sanitized spoon. CAUTION: If finished volume is less than 5 gallons, scale proportionately (e.g., 4½ gallons = ⅔ cup sugar).

12. Keep in a warm place for 7–10 days, then move to a cool place to age for 2 weeks.

YELLOW DOG PALE ALE
⎯ ⎯ ⎯

THE HOME BREWERY—OZARK, MISSOURI
This old reliable has long been The Home Brewery's most famous recipe, as it has won countless awards for its customers. Best described as having a classic American brewpub character, this produces an exceptionally clean, well-balanced ale.

ORIGINAL GRAVITY 1.047

FINAL GRAVITY: 1.012

POTENTIAL ALCOHOL: 4.6% ABV

INGREDIENTS

1 cup whole crystal malt

6.6 pounds (2 packs) Yellow Dog malt extract

1 pack Burton water salts

1 pack yeast Nutrient/Heading salts

¾ ounce Chinook hop pellets (12.2% AA) in boil

¾ ounce Kent Goldings hop pellets (5.5% AA) in last 5 minutes

¾ ounce Willamette hop pellets (5.5% AA) when heat is off

½ teaspoon Irish moss added 15 minutes before the end of the boil

2 packs Doric ale yeast *or* 1 Wyeast Liquid Ale

¾ cup corn sugar for priming

BREWING PROCEDURES

1. Heat 5 gallons of water in a large kettle. Add crushed grains. Many people don't have a kettle that large, but heat as much as you can (at least 2 gallons). Remove grains from kettle at 170°. When the water is boiling, turn off the heat and add the malt extract to the water. Use a spoon and stir until you are sure no malt extract is sticking to the bottom of the kettle. Then turn the heat back on.

2. Bring the kettle back to a boil and stir occasionally so the ingredients won't burn on the bottom of the kettle. If your recipe calls for bittering hops, now is the time to add them and stir them in. Watch out for a boilover. In the early part of the boil, the kettle usually tries to boil over once or twice, so control this by adjusting the heat. Later in the boil, the surface tension changes and boiling over is not a problem. Keep stirring occasionally, and let the beer (wort) boil hard for 1 hour. Stir in the ½ teaspoon of Irish moss in your recipe about 15 minutes before the end of the boil.

3. If finishing hops are called for in your recipe, stir them in 2 minutes before the end of the boil. Using finishing hops at the end of the boil adds a fresh aroma and flavor to the beer, and the use of finishing hops is appropriate in most beer styles.

4. Pour the hot beer (wort) into the primary fermenter. It is not necessary to strain the wort if you used hop pellets. Add cold water to bring the total volume up to 5 gallons. If you are using our B3a Fermenter (the one in the kits), the 5-gallon mark is the bottom ring. Cover the fermenter and wait until the temperature is down to 75°F. If you have a wort chiller, use it to bring the temperature down quickly. At 75° or less, add the yeast in your recipe. Just tear open the pack(s) and sprinkle it on the wort. Close the fermenter with the lid, stopper, and airlock. Remember to put water (or vodka) in the airlock. Vodka evaporates more quickly, but bacteria won't live in it.

5. Fermentation should start within 24 hours, and may continue for between 1 day and 2 weeks, depending on the type of yeast, the recipe, and the temperature. Leave the beer alone and don't open the lid. When the airlock has not bubbled for several days and the beer is flat, still, and clearing, it is ready to bottle.

6. To bottle, siphon about 1 pint of beer into a pan and warm it on the stove. Add exactly ¾ cup of corn sugar to the pan and stir until it is dissolved. Pour this back into the beer and stir gently but well to distribute the sugar. Siphon or tap into clean sanitized bottles and cap. Keep the bottles at room temperature. After a week, put a bottle in the refrigerator and try it. It will be best in about 3 weeks.

MAINSAIL ALE
⫟ ⫟ ⫟

DICK FOEHRINGER

THE BREWMEISTER—FAIR OAKS, CALIFORNIA

"Mainsail Ale offers a reasonably complex (a hint of sweetness along with medium-strong hops and a rich malty flavor) taste and aroma in a medium-bodied ale."

ORIGINAL GRAVITY: 1.053

FINAL GRAVITY: 1.014

POTENTIAL ALCOHOL: 5% ABV

INGREDIENTS

> 1 pound crystal malt
>
> 7 pounds light malt extract syrup
>
> 1¾ ounce Chinook hops (boiling)
>
> 1 ounce malto-dextrin
>
> 2 teaspoons gypsum
>
> ¼ ounce Chinook hops (aromatic)
>
> ¼ ounce Cascade hops (aromatic)
>
> 1 teaspoon Irish moss
>
> 1 ale yeast
>
> 1 teaspoon gelatin
>
> ¾ cup bottling sugar

BREWING PROCEDURES

1. Put the crushed crystal into the boiling bag. Add 1½ gallons of cold water and slowly bring to a near boil. Shut off heat and let the grain steep for 30 minutes. Remove grain bag and drain it completely.

2. Stir in and dissolve completely the extract syrup. Return to heat and add the boiling hops, gypsum, and malto-dextrin. Boil for 45 minutes; add Irish moss and aromatic hops. Boil for 15 minutes.

3. Cool the wort and strain into primary fermenter. Add cold water to make 5½ gallons. When cooled below 85°F, pitch yeast and ferment in cool place (70°F).

4. Rack into secondary and add dissolved gelatin. When clear (3–5 days), rack and add dissolved bottling sugar. Bottle and cap.

5. Age a minimum of 3–4 weeks. (Hop bitterness will diminish with age.)

SWEETHEART WHEAT
⊞ ⊞

THE CELLAR HOMEBREW—SEATTLE, WASHINGTON

"A style growing in popularity among many Northwest microbreweries. The character of wheat is coupled with sweet notes of honey in this uniquely refreshing treat. No finishing hops are used in this brew to allow the appealing aromatics of the honey to shine through."

ORIGINAL GRAVITY: 1.038

FINAL GRAVITY: 1.010

POTENTIAL ALCOHOL: 3.5% ABV

INGREDIENTS (FOR 5.5 GALLONS)

> ¼ pound German light crystal malt (crushed)
>
> ¼ pound 50–60 °L English crystal malt (crushed)
>
> 1 can English wheat malt syrup
>
> 1 pound wheat DME
>
> 2 pounds high-quality honey
>
> 2 ounces Hallertau Hersbrucker hops
>
> Edme dry ale yeast or German Ale liquid yeast
>
> ¾ cup corn sugar for priming

BREWING PROCEDURES

Note: If you are using the German Ale liquid yeast with this recipe, be sure to start that yeast at least 1 to 3 days before doing any of the brewing steps below. Follow the package directions and use the yeast in step 5.

1. Place the crushed German light crystal and English crystal malts in a strainer bag. Add

this bag of grain to your brewing kettle, which contains 2 to 2½ gallons brewing water. Bring the brewing water to a boil, then remove the bag of grains. It is not a good idea to boil these specialty grains for any length of time, as they may contribute a bitter or grainy taste to the finished beer.

2. Sparge (rinse) the bag of grains with about 1 quart of hot tap water into the brewing kettle; dispose of the spent grains.

3. Remove the brewing kettle from the burner and add 1 can of English wheat malt extract, the 1-pound bag of dry wheat extract, and the 2 pounds of honey. The syrup is easier to pour if the can has been previously placed in hot water. Also, rinse the can with hot water to ensure that all the syrup goes into the kettle. Stir the mixture, now called "wort," until it boils. Watch carefully at this time because the wort may boil over. You can prevent this by pouring a cup of cold water into the overboiling wort.

4. At boiling point, add the Hallertau Hersbrucker boiling hops. Hops can be placed in a hop bag or added loose, to be later strained out after the boil using a strainer bag. Time the boil for about 1 hour, stirring occasionally. After the first 10 minutes of this boil, remove 2 cups of wort in measuring cup, and cover with foil or plastic. Cool to 90°F for use in step 5.

5. Making the yeast starter: For dry yeast, use ½ cup warm tap water (90–100°F). Sprinkle the contents of yeast packet into that water, cover for at least 15 minutes, and then add to the 2 cups of wort you prepared in step 4. Cover and set aside for use in step 8 below. For liquid yeast, prepare 1 to 3 days ahead of brewing time per package instructions.

Open the swollen package and add the contents to the 2 cups of wort as prepared in step 4.

6. After the wort has boiled for that 1 hour, remove the pot from the burner and let it cool, covered, for about 20 minutes.

7. Pour 3 gallons of cold water into the sanitized open fermenter followed by the warm wort from step 6. Top up the fermenter to 5½ gallons using cold tap water. Cover the fermenter and cool the wort as rapidly as possible.

8. When the wort has cooled to about 80°, add the yeast starter and ferment as you usually do.

HONEY WEISS BEER

▥ ▥ ▥

E. C. KRAUS—INDEPENDENCE, MISSOURI

"While not a defined AHA beer style, this is certainly a beer that brings its own reward. It is very similar to the summertime weisse of Germany. Light fluorescent yellow with a distinct clovey aroma, which is further enhanced by the addition of honey. The hops are detectable but remain subdued by other characteristics."

ORIGINAL GRAVITY: 1.050–55

FINAL GRAVITY: 1.013–14

POTENTIAL ALCOHOL: 4.8–5.3% ABV

IBUs: 13–17

COLOR: 3–8 SRM/4–12 °L

INGREDIENTS:

   1 pound 6-row barley (mini-mashed)
   1 pound malted wheat (mini-mashed)

3.3 pounds barley/wheat mix malt extract syrup

1 pound light dried malt extract (2½ cups)

1 pound honey (clove spun preferred)

1¼ ounces Hallertau pellet hops (45-minute boil time)

¼ ounce Hallertau pellet hops (finish)

1 tablespoon Irish moss (15-minute boil time)

⅓ ounce Burton water salts

1 package Wyeast 3068 Weihenstephan Wheat

¾ cup priming sugar (bottling time)

BREWING PROCEDURES

1. Lightly crack malted grains and put with 1½ gallons of warm water in a cooking pan. Bring temperature to 122–125°F and hold for 30 minutes, then bring the same mixture to 155–160°F and hold for 45 minutes.

2. Strain the grains out by use of a colander and discard.

3. Bring the liquid back to a boil and add both the liquid and dried malt extracts. Bring back to a boil again.

4. Once boiling, add Hallertau hops and boil for 45 minutes. During the last 15 minutes of boil, add Irish moss and honey. During the last 1 minute of the boil, add the finishing hops and Burton salts.

5. Once the boiling is complete, add the wort to your fermenter with cold water up to 5 gallons. Make sure it has cooled below 80°F and add yeast.

6. Attach airlock to fermenter and allow to ferment for 7–10 days or until finished.

7. Bottle with priming sugar as normal and allow to condition for 4–6 weeks.

BARLEY-WHEAT "RED" ALE

DICK FOEHRINGER

THE BREWMEISTER—FAIR OAKS, CALIFORNIA

"For all of you "red" ale drinkers, this recipe is for you. Barley-Wheat Red Ale is, as its name implies, reddish in color due to the roasted barley. The half-wheat/barley combination gives excellent body with high-alcohol strength. The Fuggles hops provide a good balanced bitterness in the brew. This brew is patterned after Australian Red Back Ale."

ORIGINAL GRAVITY: 1.057

FINAL GRAVITY: 1.014

POTENTIAL ALCOHOL: 5.6% ABV

INGREDIENTS

¼ pound roasted barley

4 pounds Alexander's pale malt extract

4 pounds Alexander's wheat malt extract

1½ ounce Fuggles hops (60 minutes) boiling

½ ounce Fuggles hops (5 minutes) aromatic

1 teaspoon Irish moss (15 minutes)

1 Doric dry ale yeast

1 teaspoon gelatin

¾ cup bottling sugar

BREWING PROCEDURES

1. Put the roasted barley into a grain bag. Place 1½ to 2 gallons of cold water in your brewpot. Place grain bag in water and bring to a near boil (160°F). Turn off heat and allow grains to steep for 30 minutes. Drain and remove grain.

2. Dissolve extract thoroughly and then return

mixture to heat. Bring to a boil. Add the 1½ ounce of hops and boil for 45 minutes. Add Irish moss and boil for 10 minutes. Add the remaining ½ ounce of aromatic hops and boil for 5 minutes. Cold-break the wort to below 100°F by setting your pan of wort into a sink full of cold water.

3. Put the cooled wort into your primary fermenter and add cold water to make 5½ gallons. When cooled below 85°F, pitch your yeast. (Note: Rehydrate your yeast by dissolving it in 1 cup warm water and allowing it to sit for 10 minutes before pitching.) Ferment in a cool (65–75°F), dark place.

4. When fermentation has ceased, transfer to the secondary, leaving all the sediment behind.

5. Dissolve gelatin in 1 cup hot water and stir into secondary. Allow beer to clear, typically 3–5 days. Rack again, leaving sediment behind.

6. Dissolve bottling sugar in 1 cup of hot water and stir into beer. Bottle and cap.

7. Allow to age/carbonate in the bottles for 2–4 weeks. Enjoy!

KILLER WHEATEN ALE

THE CELLAR HOMEBREW—SEATTLE, WASHINGTON

"Wheat beers are made by replacing a substantial portion of the malted barley in a recipe with malted wheat, lending a distinctive flavor, especially to lighter beers."

ORIGINAL GRAVITY: 1.036

FINAL GRAVITY: 1.009

POTENTIAL ALCOHOL: 3.5% ABV

INGREDIENTS (FOR 5.5 GALLONS)

- ¼ pound German light crystal malt (crushed)
- ¼ pound dextrine malt (crushed)
- 1 can Alexander's wheat malt syrup
- 1 can Alexander's wheat "Kicker"
- 1 ounce Hallertauer hops (boiling)
- 1 ounce Hallertauer hops (finishing)
- 1 package Whitbread dry ale or American Ale liquid yeast
- ¾ cup corn sugar for priming

BREWING PROCEDURES

Note: If you are using the American Ale liquid yeast with this recipe, be sure to start that yeast at least 1 to 3 days before doing any of the brewing steps below. Follow the package directions and use the yeast in step 5.

1. Place the crushed German light crystal and dextrine malts in a strainer bag. Add this bag of grain to your brewing kettle, which contains 2 to 2½ gallons brewing water. Bring the brewing water to a boil, then remove the bag of grains. It is not a good idea to boil these specialty grains for any length of time as they may contribute a bitter or grainy taste to the finished beer.

2. Sparge (rinse) the bag of grains with about 1 quart of hot tap water into the brewing kettle; dispose of the spent grains.

3. Remove the brewing kettle from the burner and add the 1 can of Alexander's wheat malt syrup and the 1 can of Alexander's wheat "Kicker." The syrup is easier to pour if the can has been previously placed in hot water. Also, rinse the can with hot water to ensure that all the syrup goes into the kettle. Stir the mixture, now called "wort," until

it boils. Watch carefully at this time because the wort may boil over. You can prevent this by pouring a cup of cold water into the over-boiling wort.

4. At boiling point, add the Hallertau boiling hops. Hops can be placed in a hop bag or added loose, to be later strained out after the boil using a strainer bag. Time the boil for about 1 hour, stirring occasionally. After the first 10 minutes of this boil, remove 2 cups of wort in measuring cup and cover with foil or plastic. Cool to 90°F for use in step 5.

5. Making the yeast starter: For dry yeast, use ½ cup warm tap water (90–100°F). Sprinkle the contents of yeast packet into that water, cover for at least 15 minutes, and then add to the 2 cups of wort you prepared in step 4. Cover and set aside for use in step 7. For liquid yeast, prepare 1 to 3 days ahead of brewing time per package instructions. Open the swollen package and add the contents to the 2 cups of wort as prepared in step 4.

6. After the wort has boiled for that 1 hour, add the Hallertau finishing hops. Place them in the hop bag, which has been emptied of the spent boiling hops, and place them in the boiling kettle, or just add the finishing hops directly to the brewing kettle. They will be strained later in step 8.

7. Let the boil continue for 5 minutes. This gives the beer its hop aroma. Remove the pot from the burner and let it cool, covered, for about 20 minutes.

8. Pour 3 gallons of cold water into the sanitized open fermenter fitted with strainer bag; if loose finishing hops were used in step 6, strain the warm wort from step 7 into the cold water. Top up the fermenter to 5½ gallons using cold tap water. Cover

the fermenter and cool the wort as rapidly as possible.

9. When the wort has cooled to about 80°, add the yeast starter and ferment as you usually do.

WHEAT BEER
🍺 🍺 🍺 🍺

TONY LUBOLD, HEAD BREWER, CATAMOUNT BREWING CO.—WHITE RIVER JUNCTION, VERMONT

This is a classic example of a clean and fresh-tasting American style wheat for the all-grain brewer. You can use a variety of different yeasts for this one. Just remember to "keep it clean" for an authentic profile.

ORIGINAL GRAVITY: 1.040

FINAL GRAVITY: 1.011

POTENTIAL ALCOHOL: 3.6% ABV

INGREDIENTS

- 6 pounds 6-row malt
- 4 pounds malted wheat
- 1 ounce Hallertau (60 minutes)
- Irish moss (20 minutes)
- Ale yeast
- 2 ounces Cascade (in primary fermenter)
- ¾ cup corn sugar

BREWING PROCEDURES

1. Mix all malt in 8 quarts of water. Rest for 1 hour at 155°F.

2. Sparge with 12 quarts of water. Boil for 1 hour with the Hallertau hops.

3. Pitch yeast and ferment at 50–55°F for 4 days. Transfer to a carboy to age for 14 days with the Cascade hops.

4. Bottle as usual using ¾ cup of corn sugar.

5. Allow to age at about 50–55°F for 5 to 6 weeks.

High Sierras Pale Ale

▥ ▥ ▥

Jim Livingston
The Home Brewery—Riverside, California

This award-winning recipe features a formulation that produces a beer amazingly similar to one of America's best and has become one of The Home Brewery's favorites. The flavor is clean, hoppy, and well-balanced with a fresh Cascades aroma.

Original Gravity: 1.060

Final Gravity: 1.014

Potential Alcohol: 6% ABV

Ingredients

- 8 ounces 2-row Klages malt
- 8 ounces dextrine malt
- 8 ounces 40 °L crystal malt
- 8 pounds Alexander's pale malt extract
- 1½ ounces Perle hop pellets (bittering)
- 1½ ounces Cascade hop pellets (aroma)
- ½ ounce Cascade hop pellets (dry hops)
- Wyeast 1056 American ale yeast
- ¾ cup dextrose (corn sugar) or 1 cup light dry malt extract for priming

Brewing Procedures

1. Heat 5 gallons of water in a large kettle. Add crushed grains. Many people don't have a kettle that large, but heat as much as you can (at least 2 gallons). Remove grains from kettle at 170°. When the water is boiling, turn off the heat and add the malt extract to the water. Use a spoon and stir until you are sure no malt extract is sticking to the bottom of the kettle. Then turn the heat back on.

2. Bring the kettle back to a boil and stir occasionally so the ingredients won't burn on the bottom of the kettle. If your recipe calls for bittering hops, now is the time to add them and stir them in. Watch out for a boilover. In the early part of the boil, the kettle usually tries to boil over once or twice, so control this by adjusting the heat. Later in the boil, the surface tension changes and boiling over is not a problem. Keep stirring occasionally, and let the beer (wort) boil hard for 1 hour.

3. If finishing hops are called for in your recipe, stir them in 2 minutes before the end of the boil. Using finishing hops at the end of the boil adds a fresh aroma and flavor to the beer, and the use of finishing hops is appropriate in most beer styles.

4. Pour the hot beer (wort) into the primary fermenter. It is not necessary to strain the wort if you used hop pellets. Add cold water to bring the total volume up to 5 gallons. Add dry hops. Cover the fermenter and wait until the temperature is down to 75°F. If you have a wort chiller, use it to bring the temperature down quickly. At 75° or less, add the yeast in your recipe. Just tear open the pack(s) and sprinkle it on the wort. Close the fermenter with the lid, stopper, and airlock. Remember to put water (or vodka) in the airlock. Vodka evaporates more quickly, but bacteria won't live in it.

5. Fermentation should start within 24 hours, and may continue for between 1 day and 2 weeks, depending on the type of yeast, the recipe, and the temperature. Leave the beer alone and don't open the lid. When the air-lock has not bubbled for several days and the beer is flat, still, and clearing, it is ready to bottle.

6. To bottle, siphon about 1 pint of beer into a pan and warm it on the stove. Add exactly ¾ cup of corn sugar to the pan and stir until it is dissolved. Pour this back into the beer and stir gently but well to distribute the sugar. Siphon or tap into clean sanitized bottles and cap. Keep the bottles at room temperature. After a week, put a bottle in the refrigerator and try it. It will be best in about 3 weeks.

EAST COAST AMERICAN PALE ALE
⌸ ⌸ ⌸ ⌸

EAST COAST BREWING SUPPLY—STATEN ISLAND, NEW YORK

This recipe is designed for the all-grain brewer who wants to get more than the usual 5 gallons of beer for his efforts. If you don't have the facilities or equipment to handle this much wort, cut the ingredients in half for a six-gallon batch. The end result for either recipe will be a citrusy, microbrewery-style pale ale with a big hop character.

ORIGINAL GRAVITY: 1.051

FINAL GRAVITY: 1.013

POTENTIAL ALCOHOL: 4.9% ABV

INGREDIENTS (FOR 12 GALLONS)

17 pounds Klages 2-row malt

1 pound 90 °L crystal malt

2 ounces Cluster hops boiled for 60 minutes

2.5 ounces Cascade hops boiled for 60 minutes

1.5 ounces Cascade hops boiled for 20 minutes

1 ounce Cascade hops steeped for 30 minutes after boil

1 ounce Cascade hops—dry-hopped in secondary

4 teaspoons gypsum in the boil

2 teaspoons Irish moss for 30 minutes

Wyeast 1056 American Ale yeast

1.8 cups corn sugar for priming (0.75 cup per 5 gallons)

BREWING PROCEDURES

1. Dough in grain at 127°F in 4.5 gallons.
2. Hold protein rest for 30 minutes.
3. Raise temperature to 148°F with 2.25 gallons of 200°F water. Heat to 150–152°F. Mash for 1 hour.
4. In 10 minutes mash out at 168°F. Sparge with 9 gallons of 170°F water. Collect 13 to 13.5 gallons.
5. Boil for 1.5 hours. Add hops as listed.
6. Settle trub for 30 minutes. Cool with counterflow chiller.
7. Collect 12 gallons in 2 fermenters. Pitch yeast.
8. Ferment in primary for 3–4 days at 64–73°F.
9. Ferment in secondary for 2 weeks at 64–73°F.
10. Keg or bottle with 0.75 cup corn sugar per 5 gallons.

PACIFIC PALE ALE

⫸ ⫸ ⫸

DON BRETON

MARYLAND HOMEBREW—COLUMBIA,
  MARYLAND

The growing recognition of the merits of America's pale ales has helped make this recipe Maryland Homebrew's most popular. The wide variety of specialty malts lends complexity and a perfect balance between sweetness and dryness underneath a big hop presence.

ORIGINAL GRAVITY: 1.065

FINAL GRAVITY: 1.016

POTENTIAL ALCOHOL: 6.5% ABV

INGREDIENTS

  ½ pound Munich malt

  ½ pound dextrine malt

  ½ pound wheat malt

  ½ pound CaraVienne

  Two 4-pound cans Alexander's pale
    unhopped malt extract

  2 ounces Mt. Hood hops

  1 ounce Liberty hops

  1 ounce Willamette hops

  Wyeast 1056 American Ale yeast

  ¾ cup priming sugar or 1¼ cups dry malt
    extract

BREWING PROCEDURES

1. Steep crushed grains at 160°F for 30 minutes in 1 to 2 gallons of water. Be very careful not to let the water get too hot.

2. Remove grains and bring pot to boil. Add 2 cans of Alexander's malt extract, stirring and being careful not to scorch on bottom.

3. After boil begins, add 1 ounce of Mt. Hood hops. Twenty minutes later, add 1 ounce of Liberty hops. Twenty minutes later, add second ounce of Mt. Hood hops. Five minutes later, add 1 ounce of Willamette hops and turn off heat.

4. Cover and steep for 20 minutes.

5. Chill wort, adding enough water to make 5.5 gallons.

6. When wort is chilled to less than 80°F, add Wyeast 1056 American Ale yeast. Stir vigorously for 3 minutes, giving full aeration to the wort.

7. Ferment in primary for 5 days at 68–70°F. Transfer to secondary fermenter on day 5 and prime with ¾ cup of priming sugar or 1¼ cups DME. Bottle on day 14.

8. Age in bottle at 65°F for 14 days and enjoy.

WEST COAST IPA

⫸ ⫸

JOE & BRYAN TIMMONS

BOSTON BREWERS SUPPLY CO.—
  JAMAICA PLAIN, MASSACHUSETTS

"Although India pale ale originated in London during the eighteenth century, it seems to be gaining much greater popularity here in the States. Almost every microbrewery and brewpub now have their own version of this well-hopped, high-gravity pale ale. A favorite of ours comes from a famous West Coast brewery that came into existence in the 1960s. Despite intense competition, their ale is still one of the finest available and has been described by many as an American classic. Here is our best shot at it. A more authentic taste profile will be achieved if you use a liquid yeast culture; we suggest Wyeast 1056 American Ale."

ORIGINAL GRAVITY: 1.058–62

Final Gravity: 1.015–18

Potential Alcohol: 6% ABV

IBUs: approximately 45

Ingredients

> 8 ounces light crystal malt
> 9 pounds light malt extract syrup
> 1 ounce Chinook hop pellets
> 3 ounces Cascade hop pellets
> 1 teaspoon Irish moss
> 1 package dry ale yeast
> 6 ounces corn sugar for priming

Brewing Procedures

1. Secure the grains in the muslin straining bag. Pour 2 gallons of cold water into your brewpot, apply heat, and add the grain bag. Heat to a near boil (about 155°F), then remove the grain bag, drain, and discard.

2. Turn off the heat and, while stirring constantly, dissolve all of the malt extract. Bring to a boil and add the 1 ounce of Chinook hop pellets. Immediately start timing the boil; the total elapsed time will be 45 minutes. The following additions should be made according to the schedule below:

   30 minutes into the boil, add 1 ounce of Cascade pellets and the Irish moss.
   40 minutes into the boil add an additional 1 ounce of Cascade pellets.
   5 minutes after the last addition, cover and remove the pot from the heat.

   Remember that after the wort has cooled, it is highly vulnerable to contamination; everything that comes into contact with it from this point on must be thoroughly sanitized!

3. Cool the wort as quickly as possible. A wort chiller works best, but if you haven't got one

yet a cold water bath will do the trick. Place the covered pot in your kitchen sink and fill with ice and cold water. When the temperature has fallen to about 90°F, transfer the wort, through a strainer if possible, into your fermenter. Top off with enough cold water to reach a 5-gallon level and stir or shake well. Draw off a small sample and take both a hydrometer and a temperature reading; always discard the sample used.

4. When the wort has cooled to 65–70°F, you are ready to add the yeast. Once the yeast has been added, attach an airlock and keep the fermenter in a cool, dark location where temperature fluctuations are minimal, ideally 65–70°F. Active fermentation should become visible in the next 12 to 24 hours and will continue for about 3 to 5 days.

5. When visible signs of fermentation have ceased, it is time to transfer and dry-hop the beer. Secure the remaining 1 ounce of Cascade pellets in the second muslin bag and place it in your "secondary fermenter." Gently siphon the beer to the sanitized secondary fermenter (ideally a 5-gallon glass carboy), leaving all sediment behind. Attach an airlock and allow the beer to settle for an additional 5 to 7 days at the same temperature of primary fermentation.

6. At the end of this period, draw off a small sample and check the final gravity. By now it should be within the range stated above; if not, wait another couple of days and check again. Prepare to bottle.

Bottling and Conditioning

1. Sanitize all of your siphoning and bottling equipment, bottles, and caps.

2. Boil the 6 ounces of corn sugar in about a

pint of water and pour it into your bottling bucket. Gently siphon the beer (again leaving sediment behind) out of the fermenter into the bucket, making sure the flow is directed to the bottom of the bucket; avoid splashing or agitating the beer.

3. Using your siphon tubing and bottle filler, fill each bottle to within an inch from the top and cap immediately. Store the bottles upright for a minimum of 3 weeks, chill, and enjoy.

EAST COAST IPA

⫪⫪⫪⫪⫪

EAST COAST BREWING SUPPLY—STATEN ISLAND, NEW YORK

This recipe is for a classic American IPA bursting with Cascade hop bitterness, flavor, and aroma. The Wyeast 1056 lends a clean microbrewery profile.

ORIGINAL GRAVITY: 1.060

FINAL GRAVITY: 1.014

POTENTIAL ALCOHOL: 6% ABV

INGREDIENTS (FOR 12 GALLONS)

> 20 pounds Klages 2-row malt (crushed)
>
> 1 pound 40 °L crystal malt (crushed)
>
> 2 ounces Cluster (60 minutes)
>
> 3.5 ounces Cascade (60 minutes)
>
> 1.5 ounces Cascade (20 minutes)
>
> 1 ounce Cascade (steeped 30 minutes after boil)
>
> 1 ounce Cascade (dry-hopped in secondary)
>
> 2 teaspoons gypsum in boiler
>
> 2 teaspoons Irish moss with 30 minutes left in boil
>
> Wyeast 1056 American Ale yeast

BREWING PROCEDURES

1. Mash, 2-step infusion. Protein rest at 122°F with 4 gallons of water for 25 minutes. Raise to 154°F with 2.5 gallons of 200°F water for 1 hour.

2. Sparge with 10 gallons of 170°F water. Yield: 13 gallons of wort.

3. Boil 1 hour to reduce to 12 gallons. Allow hot break to settle for 30 minutes

4. Use counterflow chiller to cool to 76°F. Collect in two 6-gallon carboys. Pitch yeast.

5. Ferment 3 days in primary and rack to secondary for 3 weeks.

6. Keg and artificially carbonate.

BIG BERTHA PALE ALE

⫪⫪⫪⫪⫪

TOM SWEENEY, BREWMASTER, AMERICA'S BREWING COMPANY AT WALTER PAYTON'S ROUNDHOUSE COMPLEX, AURORA, ILLINOIS

BREW & GROW—CHICAGO, ILLINOIS

Would this be an American IPA? When you are as busy as this Chicago area brewmaster, you need to make large quantities of a great pale ale. Here is a recipe for very strong pale ale with a robust American-English character and a big Cascade hop aroma.

ORIGINAL GRAVITY: 1.070

FINAL GRAVITY: 1.018

POTENTIAL ALCOHOL: 6.9% ABV

INGREDIENTS (FOR 10 GALLONS)

> 20 pounds English pale malt
>
> 1 pound 6-row malt
>
> 1 pound 40 °L caramel malt

½ pound wheat malt

½ pound 10 °L Munich

½ pound dextrine malt

1 teaspoon Burton salts

1 teaspoon gypsum

5½ ounces Northern Brewer hops (boiling)

1 ounce Cascade hops (boiling)

1 ounce Willamette hops (finishing)

500 ml slurry of Wyeast 1056 American Ale

1.5 cups corn sugar for priming

BREWING PROCEDURES

1. Crush grains, add water salts, and dough in. Infusion mash at 156°F until conversion plus 15 minutes. Raise temperature to 165°F and hold 10 minutes. Rest for 20 minutes. Sparge at 165°F.

2. Hop schedule: Boil 10 minutes and add Northern Brewer hops. Boil another 70 minutes and add Cascade hops. Boil another 10 minutes and add Willamette hops.

3. Rest for 30 minutes. Chill to 70°F. Aerate wort and pitch yeast. Ferment at 60–65°F.

4. Prime and bottle using your favorite techniques.

Notes: Very hoppy Northwest-type pale ale.

AMERICAN CREAM ALE
⚜ ⚜

THE HOME BREWERY—OZARK, MISSOURI

Novice brewers who happen to be fans of Genessee Cream Ale or Little Kings will love this simple but authentic recipe. You'll soon have a clean, bright, and dry cream ale that improves dramatically with a couple weeks of cold lagering.

ORIGINAL GRAVITY: 1.055

FINAL GRAVITY: 1.013

POTENTIAL ALCOHOL: 5.5% ABV

INGREDIENTS

3.3 pounds (1 pack) Home Brewery hopped amber malt extract

3.3 pounds (1 pack) Home Brewery unhopped light malt extract

1 pound corn sugar, added to the boil

1 ounce Northern Brewer hop pellets (bittering)

½ teaspoon Irish moss added 15 minutes before the end of the boil

¾ ounce Cascade hop pellets (finishing)

2 packs Doric ale yeast

¾ cup corn sugar for priming

BREWING PROCEDURES

1. Heat 5 gallons of water in a large kettle. Many people don't have a kettle that large, but heat as much as you can (at least 2 gallons). When the water is boiling, turn off the heat and add the malt extract to the water. Use a spoon and stir until you are sure no malt extract is sticking to the bottom of the kettle. Then turn the heat back on.

2. Bring the kettle back to a boil and stir occasionally so the ingredients won't burn on the bottom of the kettle. If your recipe calls for bittering hops, now is the time to add them and stir them in. Watch out for a boilover. In the early part of the boil, the kettle usually tries to boil over once or twice, so control this by adjusting the heat. Later in the boil, the surface tension changes and boiling over is not a problem. Keep stirring occasionally and let the beer (wort) boil hard for 1 hour. Stir in the ½ teaspoon of Irish moss in your recipe about 15 minutes before the end of the boil.

3. If finishing hops are called for in your recipe, stir them in 2 minutes before the end of the boil. Using finishing hops at the end of the boil adds a fresh aroma and flavor to the beer, and the use of finishing hops is appropriate in most beer styles.

4. Pour the hot beer (wort) into the primary fermenter. It is not necessary to strain the wort if you used hop pellets. Add cold water to bring the total volume up to 5 gallons. If you are using our B3a Fermenter (the one in the kits), the 5-gallon mark is the bottom ring. Cover the fermenter and wait until the temperature is down to 75°F. If you have a wort chiller (C44), use it to bring the temperature down quickly. At 75° or less, add the yeast in your recipe. Just tear open the pack(s) and sprinkle it on the wort. Close the fermenter with the lid, stopper, and airlock. Remember to put water (or vodka) in the airlock. Vodka evaporates more quickly, but bacteria won't live in it.

5. Fermentation should start within 24 hours, and may continue for between 1 day and 2 weeks, depending on the type of yeast, the recipe, and the temperature. Leave the beer alone and don't open the lid. When the airlock has not bubbled for several days and the beer is flat, still, and clearing, it is ready to bottle.

6. To bottle, siphon about 1 pint of beer into a pan and warm it on the stove. Add exactly ¾ cup of corn sugar to the pan and stir until it is dissolved. Pour this back into the beer and stir gently but well to distribute the sugar. Siphon or tap into clean sanitized bottles and cap. Keep the bottles at room temperature. After a week, put a bottle in the refrigerator and try it. It will be best in about 3 weeks.

ALL-AMERICAN CREAM ALE

🍺 🍺 🍺

BEER & WINEMAKING SUPPLIES, INC.— NORTHAMPTON, MASSACHUSETTS

The use of flaked maize and rice may seem like the ingredients used by the megabreweries and out of place in the repertoire of a homebrewer. On the contrary, cream ale is one of a few rare exceptions where these adjuncts have historically been used and are important to the unique flavor and body of this style, which should be light, clean, and low in flavor profile.

ORIGINAL GRAVITY: 1.042–44

FINAL GRAVITY: 1.010–12

POTENTIAL ALCOHOL: 4–4.25% ABV

INGREDIENTS

- 8 ounces American pale malt (cracked)
- 8 ounces flaked maize
- 8 ounces flaked rice
- 6 pounds American light malt extract syrup
- 2 teaspoon Burton water salts or gypsum
- 1 ounce American Liberty hops (bittering)
- 1 ounce American Columbus hops (aroma)
- 10–14 grams dry ale yeast or Wyeast 1056 American Ale yeast*
- ¾ cup corn sugar for bottling

BREWING PROCEDURES

Note: If using a liquid culture, activate 12–24 hours prior to brew session.

1. Place your three blended grains in a 2–4-quart pan and stir in 1.5 quarts of 168°F water. Mix well. Grain should bring temperature down to approximately 150–154°F. Steep for 45 minutes in oven, small insulated cooler, or on stovetop at that temperature. While grain is steeping, bring 2 gallons of water up to 165°F in an 8–12-quart pot. Place strainer or colander over large kettle, then pour and spoon all grains and liquid in. Rinse with 2 gallons of 165°F water. Allow liquid to drain into kettle. Discard grains and bring liquid to a boil. Momentarily remove from heat.

2. Pour the 6 pounds of malt extract into the pot, making sure to rinse out the container to get all the malt. Stir well, then add the gypsum or Burton salts and stir well again.

3. Resume boiling (total time: 1 hour). Split the Liberty hops into two equal portions and add half; at the 30-minute mark, add the second half.

4. Shut off the heat, add the one ounce of Columbus hops, and let stand for 15 minutes.

5. Put 3 gallons of very cold water into your sterilized primary fermenter, then carefully pour the hot wort into it. Top up to 5 gallons with more cold water if necessary. If still above 85°F, run a cold water bath around your fermenter. The fermenter should then be stirred or swirled to aerate the wort. Take a hydrometer reading and write it down.

6. Wort should now be 70–85°F. Activate dry yeast by putting in 1 cup of sterile water at 75–95°F for 15 minutes, then stir well.

7. Now add the yeast and stir or swirl to aerate. Pitch yeast solution into fermenter. Put lid and airlock on. Fill airlock halfway with water.

8. Ferment at room temperature (60–70°F) for 4 days, then siphon over to a glass secondary fermenter for another 4–7 days. Take a hydrometer reading, and if low enough, bottle the beer into 53 reusable bar bottles (12-ounce size) or equivalent.

9. Bottling procedure: Make a priming syrup on the stove with 1 cup water and ¾ cup corn sugar, bring to a boil, and then shut heat off immediately, stirring well. Transfer beer back to primary or bottling bucket, mixing the priming syrup in well to distribute evenly. Siphon into bottles and cap them.

10. Remember to sanitize everything you use after the boil with a good chlorinated alkaline cleanser.

11. Allow bottles to sit at room temperature for 1–2 weeks before cooling down.

CREAM ALE

DICK FOEHRINGER

THE BREWMEISTER—FAIR OAKS, CALIFORNIA

"Cream ale's character is reminiscent of a hoppier, slightly stronger, slightly fruitier cousin to an American light beer. Well carbonated and refreshing on a hot day. Similar to Little Kings or Genessee Cream Ale."

ORIGINAL GRAVITY: 1.060

FINAL GRAVITY: 1.010

POTENTIAL ALCOHOL: 6.5% ABV

INGREDIENTS

½ pound crystal malt

½ pound CaraPils malt

½ dextrine malt

8 pounds Alexander's pale malt extract syrup

½ ounce Willamette hops—60 minutes (boiling)

⅓ ounce Hallertauer hops—60 minutes (boiling)

⅓ ounce Cascade hops—60 minutes (boiling)

½ ounce Hallertauer—2 minutes (aromatic)

1 teaspoon Irish moss—15 minutes

1 ale yeast

1 teaspoon gelatin

¾ cup bottling sugar

BREWING PROCEDURES

1. Put the crystal and CaraPils into the boiling bag. Add 1½ to 2½ gallons of cold water and bring to a near boil. Shut off heat and let grain steep for 30 minutes. Remove grain bag and drain it completely.

2. Stir in and thoroughly dissolve extract syrup. Return to heat and add the 3 boiling hops. Boil wort for 45 minutes. Add Irish moss, boil for 15 minutes, then during the last 2 minutes of the boil, add the aromatic hops. Remove from heat.

3. Cool the wort and strain into the primary fermenter. Add cold water to make 5½ gallons. Rehydrate the yeast by dissolving into ½ cup warm water. Let the yeast mixture sit for 15 minutes before pitching.

4. When below 85°F pitch the yeast. Ferment at 75°F.

5. Rack to secondary and stir in dissolved gelatin. When clear (3–5 days) rack and add dissolved bottling sugar. Bottle and cap.

6. Age a minimum of 3–4 weeks.

MUNICH PALE ALE

🍺 🍺 🍺 🍺

ANDREW TVEEKREM, BREWMASTER, GREAT LAKES BREWING CO.— CLEVELAND, OHIO

"Here's a fun one that makes for a neat twist on the pale ale theme, more Germanic in profile with a deep malt flavor and noble hop aroma. It can also be brewed as a lager with the appropriate yeast and temperature."

ORIGINAL GRAVITY: 1.062

FINAL GRAVITY: 1.016

POTENTIAL ALCOHOL: 6.1% ABV

INGREDIENTS (FOR 10 GALLONS)

30 pounds Belgian Munich malt

8 or 9 handfuls of Hallertau hop pellets

A dash of Irish moss

1 quart thick yeast slurry of Wyeast 1028 London Ale

1.5 cups corn sugar for priming

BREWING PROCEDURES

1. Mash crushed malt at 154–156°F for 1 hour, stirring occasionally.

2. Lauter to collect 12 gallons of wort and bring to a boil.

3. Add 2 or 3 handfuls of Hallertau hop pellets at the beginning of the boil.

4. Boil for 75 minutes, adding 3 more handfuls of hop pellets at 30 minutes prior to the end. Add 3 more handfuls of hop pellets at 15 minutes prior to the end and a dash of Irish moss.

5. At the end of the boil add 3 more handfuls of hops.
6. Swirl, cool, and ferment at 65°F.
7. Rack, prime, and bottle as you normally do.

PALE RYE ALE

🍺 🍺 🍺 🍺

CHETT SCHAFF & PAUL HEALY
MOUNTAIN MALT AND HOP SHOPPE— LAKE KATRINE & POUGHKEEPSIE, NEW YORK

If you have enjoyed the bottle-conditioned Red-hook Rye from Seattle, you'll at last be able to imitate it with this recipe. The result is a fruity, clean, and dry ale that balances between the refreshing spiciness of a wheat beer and the complexity of an English bitter.

ORIGINAL GRAVITY: 1.052

FINAL GRAVITY: 1.014

POTENTIAL ALCOHOL: 5.2% ABV

INGREDIENTS

> 4 pounds Belgian 2-row biscuit malt
> 1 teaspoon gypsum
> 1.5 ounces Perle hops
> 3.5 pounds Klages malt
> 1.5 ounces Willamette hops
> 2 pounds flaked rye
> 1/3 ounce Burton water salts
> 1 pound flaked barley
> Wyeast 1968 ESB ale yeast
> 1/2 pound dextrine malt
> 3/4 cup corn sugar for priming

BREWING PROCEDURES

1. Mash Schedule:

Mash in—2.75 gallons of water. Stir in 1 teaspoon of gypsum.

Protein rest—30 minutes at 128°F.

Saccharification rest—30 minutes at 149°F.

Saccharification rest—30 minutes at 158°F.

Mash out—5 minutes at 170°F.

Sparge with 5 gallons of 170°F water at pH 5.5.

2. Collect wort in a 12-quart or larger stainless-steel pot and bring to a boil.
3. When the danger of a messy boilover has passed, add 1½ ounces of Perle hops (13 HBU) and cook at a rolling boil for 30 minutes.
4. Add 1 teaspoon of Irish moss and ½ ounce Willamette hops; boil for 5 more minutes.
5. Add ½ ounce Willamette hops. Boil for 8 more minutes.
6. Add the remaining ½ ounce Willamette hops. Boil for 2 more minutes, then turn off heat.
7. Take the brewpot from the stove and place it in a sink partially filled with cold water. Add 1 gallon of sanitary, refrigerated water (40°F) to the brewpot, then cover and place ice in the water around the brewpot. Never add ice directly to the wort! Let stand 15 minutes. Place 2 gallons of refrigerated water into the fermenter, then add the strained wort. Check the temperature (65–75°F is ideal). Top off to 5½ gallons with either more cold or room-temperature water.
8. With a sanitized measuring cup, scoop out ¾ cup and take a hydrometer reading. Discard sample.

9. Add the package of yeast to the fermenter when the temperature of the wort is between 65–75°F, then stir vigorously to aerate. Snap the fermenter lid on, fill the airlock halfway with water and place in lid. Place fermenter in a spot where the temperature will remain a constant 65–70°F.

10. Ferment in the primary for 5–6 days, then rack into a glass carboy for 2 weeks.

11. When brew is clear, siphon into a bottling bucket. Dissolve priming sugar into 1 cup boiling water, cool, and gently stir into beer with a sanitized spoon. CAUTION: If finished volume is less than 5 gallons, scale proportionately (e.g., 4½ gallons = ⅔ cup sugar).

12. Keep in a warm place for 7–10 days, then move to a cool place to age for 2 weeks.

DOWN UNDER ALE
🍺 🍺

PAUL HEALY

MOUNTAIN MALT AND HOP SHOPPE— LAKE KATRINE & POUGHKEEPSIE, NEW YORK

For the lovers of the great Australian beers, here's an authentic but simple formulation for a bold, refreshing brew. The Pride of Ringwood hops are universal in Australian craft brewing and are essential for capturing that classic Aussie quality.

ORIGINAL GRAVITY: 1.050

FINAL GRAVITY: 1.017

POTENTIAL ALCOHOL: 4.5% ABV

INGREDIENTS

1 teaspoon gypsum
4 ounces amber crystal malt
1 ounce Northern Brewer at 7.5% AA (boil)
1 ounce Pride of Ringwood hops 8% AA (boil)
1 can Coopers light
1 can Coopers amber
1 ounce Pride of Ringwood hops (aroma)
1 teaspoon Irishmoss
Coopers ale yeast
¾ cups corn sugar

BREWING PROCEDURES

1. In a 12-quart or larger stainless-steel pot, heat ½ gallon of water to 155°F and add 1 teaspoon of gypsum. Stir until dissolved and turn off heat. Place cracked grains in a nylon bag and immerse in water. Cover pot and allow grain to steep for 30 minutes. Remove grain bag and bring the "tea" to a boil. (If you do not have a nylon bag, add grains directly to water and strain.)

2. When boil is attained, turn off heat and add the liquid malt extracts. Turn on heat and return to a boil.

3. When the danger of a messy boilover has passed, add 1 ounce of Pride of Ringwood hops and 1 ounce of Northern Brewer hops and cook at a rolling boil for 30 minutes.

4. Add 1 teaspoon of Irish moss and boil for 13 more minutes.

5. Add 1 ounce of Pride of Ringwood hops. Boil for 2 more minutes.

6. Take the brewpot from the stove and place it in a sink partially filled with cold water. Add 1 gallon of sanitary, refrigerated water (40°F) to the brewpot, then cover and place ice in the water around the brewpot. Never add ice directly to the wort! Let stand 15 minutes. Place 2 gallons of refrigerated water into the fermenter, then add the wort. Check the temperature (65–75°F is ideal).

Top off to 5½ gallons with either more cold or room temperature water.

7. With a sanitized measuring cup, scoop out ¾ cup and take a hydrometer reading. Discard sample.

8. Add the package of Coopers ale yeast to the fermenter when the temperature of the wort is 65–75°F, let sit 10 minutes, then stir vigorously to aerate. Snap the fermenter lid on, fill the airlock halfway with water, and place in lid. Place fermenter in a spot where the temperature will remain a constant 65–70°F.

9. Ferment in the primary for 5–6 days, then rack into a glass carboy for 2 weeks.

10. When brew is clear, siphon into a bottling bucket. Dissolve priming sugar into 1 cup boiling water, cool, and gently stir into beer with a sanitized spoon. CAUTION: If finished volume is less than 5 gallons, scale proportionately (e.g., 4½ gallons = ⅔ cup sugar).

11. Keep in a warm place for 7–10 days, then move to a cool place to age for 2 weeks.

XX CERVESA

⫸ ⫸ ⫸

DICK FOEHRINGER

THE BREWMEISTER—FAIR OAKS,
    CALIFORNIA

"This beer is similar in taste and color to the commercial beer Dos Equis. It should have a slightly sweet, malty taste. If you taste our version with hot salsa and chips, it makes an even more sweeter and maltier taste. XX Cervesa is designed to go well with hot Mexican food. Enjoy."

ORIGINAL GRAVITY: 1.053

FINAL GRAVITY: 1.014

POTENTIAL ALCOHOL: 5% ABV

INGREDIENTS

   ½ pound crystal malt

   6 pounds light malt extract syrup

   1 pound dark Australian dry extract

   ½ teaspoon citric acid

   4 ounces lactose

   2 teaspoons gypsum

   1½ ounces Cascade hops (boiling)

   1 teaspoon Irish moss

   ½ ounce Cascade hops (aromatic)

   1 ale yeast

   1 teaspoon gelatin

   ¾ cup bottling sugar

BREWING PROCEDURES

1. Put the crystal into the boiling bag. Add 1½ to 2½ gallons of cold water and bring to a near boil (160°F). Shut off heat and let grain steep for 30 minutes. Remove grain bag and drain it completely.

2. Dissolve in dry extract, syrup extract, lactose, citric acid, and gypsum. Return to heat and boil for 15 minutes. Add the boiling hops and boil for 30 minutes. Add Irish moss; boil 15 minutes. Turn off heat and add aromatic hops. Cover and let steep for 15 minutes.

3. Cold-break wort by placing into a sink full of cold water. When the wort is below 100°F, strain into primary fermenter. Add cold water to make 5½ gallons. When cooled below 85°F, pitch yeast. (Note: Rehydrate your yeast by dissolving in 1 cup warm water. Let stand for 15 minutes.) Also mix the dry hops in 1 cup of hot water. Stir into cooled wort.

4. Ferment in cool, dark place (65–75°F). Rack into secondary, leaving all the hops and sediment behind. Dissolve gelatin in 1 cup hot water.

5. Stir into secondary and replace airlock. When clear (3–5 days) rack again, leaving sediment behind.

6. Dissolve bottling sugar in 1 cup hot water. Stir into cleared beer. Bottle and cap.

7. Age a minimum of 2–3 weeks.

QUINOA BALLS ALE
⫿ ⫿ ⫿
PAUL HEALY & KURT ULRICH
MOUNTAIN MALT AND HOP SHOPPE—
LAKE KATRINE & POUGHKEEPSIE,
NEW YORK

Frustrated that they could not find a recipe using this native grain of the Andes (pronounced "keen-wah"), Kurt and Paul decided to come up with their own. Using some more traditional ingredients in conjunction with the quinoa, they've produced a light-bodied pale ale with a distinct, nutty flavor. You should try this at least once.

ORIGINAL GRAVITY: 1.035

FINAL GRAVITY: 1.009

POTENTIAL ALCOHOL: 3.5% ABV

INGREDIENTS

2 pounds quinoa
1 pound Munich malt
½ pound light crystal malt
1 teaspoon gypsum
1.5 ounces Polischner Lublin (bittering)
1 ounce East Kent Goldings (aroma)

1 ounce East Kent Goldings (bittering)
1 can Edme DMS
10 grams Nottingham ale yeast
¾ cup corn sugar for priming

BREWING PROCEDURES

1. In a 12-quart or larger stainless steel pot, boil quinoa in 1.5 gallons of water for 30 minutes. Let cool 15 minutes. Add specialty grains, gypsum, and DMS. Stabilize at 153°F and hold for 1 hour. Sparge with 1 gallon of 170°F water. Collect wort in brewpot and bring to a boil.

2. When the danger of a messy boilover has passed, add 1 ounce of East Kent Goldings (10 HBU) and 1½ ounces of Lublin hops and cook at a rolling boil for 45 minutes.

3. Add 1 teaspoon of Irish moss and boil for 13 more minutes.

4. Add 1 ounce of East Kent Goldings for aroma. Boil 2 minutes more.

5. Turn off the heat. Take the brewpot from the stove and place it in a sink partially filled with cold water. Add 1 gallon of sanitary, refrigerated water (40°F) to the brewpot, then cover and place ice in the water around the brewpot. Never add ice directly to the wort! Let stand 15 minutes. Place 2 gallons of refrigerated water into the fermenter, then add the strained wort. Check the temperature (65–75°F is ideal). Top off to 5½ gallons with either more cold or room-temperature water.

6. With a sanitized measuring cup, scoop out ¾ cup and take a hydrometer reading. Discard sample.

7. Add the package of yeast to the fermenter when the temperature of the wort is 65–75°F, let sit 10 minutes, then stir vigor-

ously to aerate. Snap the fermenter lid on, fill the airlock halfway with water, and place in lid. Place fermenter in a spot where the temperature will remain a constant 65–70°F.

8. Ferment in the primary for 5–6 days, then rack into a glass carboy for 2 weeks.

9. When brew is clear, siphon into a bottling bucket. Dissolve priming sugar into 1 cup boiling water, cool, and gently stir into beer with a sanitized spoon. CAUTION: If finished volume is less than 5 gallons, scale proportionately (e.g., $4\frac{1}{2}$ gallons = $\frac{2}{3}$ cup sugar).

10. Keep in a warm place for 7–10 days, then move to a cool place to age for 2 weeks.

LAGER
RECIPES

PILSNER

Those who are lucky enough to enjoy a twenty-five-cent Budweiser Budvar or a Pilsner Urquell in a café in Prague's Old Town will often insist that these are the best beers they have ever experienced. Unfortunately, Budvar is restricted from import to the United States because of its similarity (in name only) to Anheuser-Busch's Budweiser, and the green-bottled Pilsner Urquell you get at the local supermarket can be months past its prime, or "light-struck." However, the microbrewed Weeping Radish's Corolla Gold, Stoudt's Pilsener, August Schell Pils, Frankenmuth German-style Pilsener or Garten Bräu Special, if you are fortunate enough to have access to them, are award-winning and much fresher alternatives that will give you good examples to judge your homebrewed pilsner against.

Suggested ingredients of these all-malt lagers are pale Belgian pils, two-row German, or "Moravian" pilsner malt, light crystal malt, Saazer and Styrian Goldings hops, a Bohemian yeast strain such as Wyeast 2124 or BrewTek CL–600, and very soft water. The same is true for brewing the less malty, hoppier German version called "pils," but a cleaner yeast strain, such as Wyeast 2042, BrewTek CL-660, or Yeast Lab L31, should be substituted along with slightly harder water.

PILSNER BASICS

ORIGINAL GRAVITY: 1.043–49

FINAL GRAVITY: 1.014–20

IBUs: 30–43

COLOR (SRM): 4–4.5

ALCOHOL BY VOLUME: 4–4.5%

BOHEMIAN PILSNER
▥ ▥ ▥

DICK FOEHRINGER

THE BREWMEISTER—FAIR OAKS, CALIFORNIA

"The original pilsner beer was brewed in Plzen (which means 'Green Meadows'), Bohemia, in 1842. Bohemian was the original style, which is pale, golden, and alluring. A creamy, dense head tops a well-carbonated brew with an accent on the rich, sweet malt. The medium-bodied Bohemian style gets its aromatic character from the Czech Saaz hops."

ORIGINAL GRAVITY: 1.050

FINAL GRAVITY: 1.012

POTENTIAL ALCOHOL: 4.9% ABV

INGREDIENTS

$\frac{1}{2}$ pound 20 °L crystal malt

$\frac{1}{4}$ pound dextrine malt

$\frac{1}{4}$ pound flaked barley

4 pounds Alexander's pale malt extract

2 pounds light dry malt extract

1 ounce Saaz hops (60 minutes) boiling

1$\frac{1}{2}$ ounces Saaz hops (30 minutes) boiling

1 ounce Saaz hops (15 minutes) flavor

$\frac{1}{2}$ ounce Saaz hops (2 minutes) aroma

½ teaspoon citric acid

1 teaspoon calcium carbonate

1 teaspoon Irish moss (15 minutes)

1 Wyeast Bohemian Lager liquid yeast

Gelatin

¾ cup bottling sugar

BREWING PROCEDURES

1. Put the crystal, dextrine, and barley malted grains into a grain bag. Place 1½ to 2 gallons of cold water in your brewpot. Place grain bag in water and bring to a near boil. Steep grains for 30 minutes. Remove grains.

2. Dissolve liquid and dry extract, citric acid, and calcium carbonate thoroughly and return mixture to heat. Bring to a boil. Add 1 ounce hops and boil 30 minutes. Add 1½ ounces of hops and boil 15 minutes. Add 1 ounce hops and the Irish moss and boil 15 minutes. Add last ½ ounce hops, boil 2 minutes, then turn off heat and steep for an additional 5 minutes.

3. Cold-break the wort to below 100°F. Put the cooled wort into your primary fermenter and add cold water to make 5½ gallons. When cooled to below 85°F, pitch your yeast.

Note: You must start the liquid yeast 1–2 days prior to brewing to allow it to culture up. Follow the instructions on the package for preparation.

4. Ferment in a cool (55–65°F), dark place. When fermentation has ceased, transfer to the secondary. Dissolve gelatin in 1 cup hot water and stir into secondary. Allow beer to clear, typically 3–5 days.

5. Rack again and stir in dissolved bottling sugar. Bottle and cap.

6. Allow to age/carbonate in the bottles for 2–4 weeks. Enjoy!

CLASSIC PILSNER

JOE & BRYAN TIMMONS

BOSTON BREWERS SUPPLY CO.—
JAMAICA PLAIN, MASSACHUSETTS

"This medium-bodied Bohemian lager is clean, crisp, hop-spicy, and bitter with rich malty overtones. Our pilsner's rich mouthfeel and pleasant malty sweetness are obtained by combining Alexander's light syrup with a dextrinous Dutch dry malt and a touch of light crystal, while the generous use of Czech Saaz hops provide a clean, refreshing bitterness and a spicy/floral aroma. Use a liquid yeast for a more authentic taste profile."

ORIGINAL GRAVITY: 1.044–46

FINAL GRAVITY: 1.010–12

POTENTIAL ALCOHOL: 4.7% ABV

IBUs: 30 to 33

INGREDIENTS

4 ounces dextrine malt

4 ounces light crystal malt

4 pounds Alexander's light extract syrup

2 pounds Dutch light dry malt

4 ounces Czech Saaz hop pellets

1 teaspoon Irish moss flakes

1 package Superior dry lager yeast or
Wyeast 2124 Bohemian Lager yeast

6 ounces corn sugar for priming

BREWING PROCEDURES

1. Secure the grains in the muslin straining bag. Pour 2 gallons of cold water into your brewpot, apply heat, and add the grain bag. Heat to a near boil (about 155º), turn off the heat, cover the pot, and allow the grains to steep for 30 minutes. Remove the grain bag, drain, and discard.

2. Thoroughly dissolve the malt extract, apply heat, and bring to a boil. As soon as the wort (unfermented beer) begins to boil, add 2 ounces of the Saaz hops. Start timing the boil; the total elapsed time will be 60 minutes. Maintain a good rolling boil. Periodically stir the wort, and skim the brown, resinous scum (hot break) that forms on the top.

3. After 40 minutes, add another ounce of the Saaz hops and the Irish moss flakes. Fifteen minutes later, add the remaining ounce of Saaz hops and continue to boil for an additional 5 minutes, then cover and remove the pot from the heat.

   Remember that after the wort has cooled, it is highly vulnerable to contamination; everything that comes into contact with it from this point on must be thoroughly sanitized!

4. Cool the wort as quickly as possible. A wort chiller works best, but if you haven't got one yet a cold water bath will do the trick. Place the covered pot in your kitchen sink and fill with ice and cold water. When the temperature has fallen to about 90°F, transfer the wort, through a strainer if possible, into your fermenter. Top off with enough cold water to reach a 5-gallon level and stir or shake well. Draw off a small sample and take both a hydrometer and a temperature reading; always discard the sample used.

5. When the wort has cooled to 65–70°F, you are ready to add the yeast. Once the yeast has been added, attach an airlock and keep the fermenter at room temperature for 12 to 18 hours (until fermentation becomes visible), then transfer the fermenter to the coolest location you have access to, ideally 50–55°F until fermentation is complete.

6. When visible signs of fermentation have ceased, gently transfer the beer to a sanitized secondary fermenter (ideally a 5-gallon glass carboy), leaving all sediment behind. Attach an airlock and allow the beer to settle for an additional 10 to 14 days at the same temperature of primary fermentation or colder. At the end of this period, draw off a small sample and check the final gravity. By now it should be within the range stated above; if not, wait another couple of days and check again. Prepare to bottle.

BOTTLING AND CONDITIONING

1. Sanitize all of your siphoning and bottling equipment, bottles, and caps.

2. Boil the 6 ounces of corn sugar in about a cup of water and pour it into your bottling bucket. Gently siphon the beer out of the fermenter into the bucket, making sure the flow is directed to the bottom of the bucket; avoid splashing or agitating the beer.

3. Using your siphon tubing and bottle filler, fill each bottle to within an inch from the top and cap immediately. Store the bottles upright for 1 week at room temperature and for an additional 2 to 3 weeks as cold as you can get it, ideally 35–45°F.

CHEXO PILSNER
⫴ ⫴
JIM STOCKTON
HOME FERMENTER CENTER—EUGENE, OREGON

The Saaz hops are the essential component of this recipe for the beginning-to-intermediate brewer venturing into lager brewing. They lend that trademark aroma that graces the classic pilsners. The Dutch malt brings a good level of maltiness and residual sweetness.

ORIGINAL GRAVITY: 1.043

FINAL GRAVITY: 1.012

POTENTIAL ALCOHOL: 4% ABV

INGREDIENTS

> ¼ pound light crystal malt (crushed)
> 5 pounds Dutch light dry malt extract
> 5 ounces malto-dextrin
> 2½ ounce Cascade hops, boiling
> ½ ounce Saaz hops, flavoring
> 1¼ Saaz hops, aromatic
> 2 packages lager yeast or Wyeast liquid lager yeast
> ¾ cup corn sugar for bottling

BREWING PROCEDURES

1. When adding flavoring grains, such as crystal or black patent malt, a smoother-tasting brew will be attained by extracting the flavor and color before the boil. To do this add the grain to cold water and bring almost to a boil. Do not boil the grains!

2. Turn off the heat, cover, and steep the grains for approximately 20 minutes. Strain and rinse (sparge) the grains with 1–2 quarts of hot water (170°F). Do not over-sparge. Add the resulting extract to the boil and discard the spent grains.

3. Mix the dry malt and malto-dextrin with cool water, at least 2½ to 3 gallons, and boil for 30 minutes, add the Cascade hops and grain extract, and continue the boil for 30 minutes.

4. Add the Saaz hops at about 15 minutes. Remove the boiling hops at the end of the hour boil, then add the aromatic hops. Boil for 2–3 minutes to sanitize. For extra hop aroma save ¼ ounce of the Saaz to add during the third day of fermentation.

5. Ferment at 45–55°F and in a 2-stage glass fermenter. Bottle and prime using your favorite methods.

SMUGGLER'S SOCKS PILSNER
▥ ▥

THE CELLAR HOMEBREW—SEATTLE, WASHINGTON

A simple-to-brew recipe that is in the classic Continental pilsner style. A light-bodied beer with plenty of signature Saaz hops in the finish. The mass-produced American beers can trace their evolution back to this style, though few of the flavor characteristics remain in those brands.

ORIGINAL GRAVITY: 1.049

FINAL GRAVITY: 1.015

POTENTIAL ALCOHOL: 4.5% ABV

INGREDIENTS (FOR 5.5 GALLONS)

> ½ pound German light crystal malt
> 5 pounds light dry malt extract
> 1 can Alexander's pale "Kicker"
> 3 ounces Saaz hops (boiling)
> 1 ounce Saaz hops (finishing)
> Dry lager yeast or Wyeast Bohemian Lager liquid yeast
> ¾ corn sugar for priming

BREWING PROCEDURES

Note: If you are using the Bohemian Lager liquid yeast with this recipe, be sure to start that yeast at least

1 to 3 days before doing any of the brewing steps below. Follow the package directions and use the yeast in step 5.

1. Place the crushed German light crystal malt in a strainer bag. Add this bag of grain to your brewing kettle, which contains 2 to 2½ gallons brewing water. Bring the brewing water to a boil, then remove the bag of grains. It is not a good idea to boil these specialty grains for any length of time, as they may contribute a bitter or grainy taste to the finished beer.

2. Sparge (rinse) the bag of grains with about 1 quart of hot tap water into the brewing kettle; dispose of the spent grains.

3. Remove the brewing kettle from the burner and add the 5 pounds of light dry malt and the 1 can of Alexander's pale "Kicker." The syrup is easier to pour if the can has been previously placed in hot water. Also, rinse the can with hot water to ensure that all the syrup goes into the kettle. Stir the mixture, now called "wort," until it boils. Watch carefully at this time because the wort may boil over. You can prevent this by pouring a cup of cold water into the overboiling wort.

4. At boiling point, add the Saaz boiling hops. Hops can be placed in a hop bag or added loose, to be later strained out after the boil using a strainer bag. Time the boil for about 1 hour, stirring occasionally. After the first 10 minutes of this boil, remove 2 cups of wort in measuring cup and cover with foil or plastic. Cool to 90°F for use in step 5.

5. Making the yeast starter: For dry yeast, use ½ cup warm tap water (90–100°F). Sprinkle the contents of the yeast packet into that water, cover for at least 15 minutes, and then add to the 2 cups of wort you prepared in step 4. Cover and set aside for use in step 7. For liquid yeast, prepare 1 to 3 days ahead of brewing time per package instructions. Open the swollen package and add the contents to the 2 cups of wort as prepared in step 4.

6. After the wort has boiled for that 1 hour, add the Saaz finishing hops. Place them in the hop bag, which has been emptied of the spent boiling hops, and place them in the boiling kettle or just add the finishing hops directly to the brewing kettle. They will be strained later in step 8.

7. Let the boil continue for 5 minutes. This gives the beer its hop aroma. Remove the pot from the burner and let it cool, covered, for about 20 minutes.

8. Pour 3 gallons of cold water into the sanitized open fermenter fitted with strainer bag; if loose finishing hops were used in step 6, strain the warm wort from step 7 into the cold water. Top up the fermenter to 5½ gallons using cold tap water. Cover the fermenter and cool the wort as rapidly as possible.

9. When the wort has cooled to about 80°, add the yeast starter and ferment as you usually do.

GERMAN PILSENER

THE HOME BREWERY—OZARK, MISSOURI
This formulation for beginning brewers utilizes a minimum of ingredients to keep things simple but produces a smooth dry pils in the German tradition with plenty of hop bitterness.

This would make a good candidate for your first foray into this style.

ORIGINAL GRAVITY: 1.048

FINAL GRAVITY: 1.013

POTENTIAL ALCOHOL: 4.6% ABV

INGREDIENTS

> 6.6 pounds (2 packs) Home Brewery unhopped light malt extract
>
> 3 ounces Tettnanger hop pellets (bittering)
>
> ½ teaspoon Irish moss added 15 minutes before the end of the boil
>
> ½ ounce Hallertauer hop pellets (finishing)
>
> 1 pack European lager yeast
>
> ¾ cup corn sugar for priming

BREWING PROCEDURES

1. Heat 5 gallons of water in a large kettle. Many people don't have a kettle that large, but heat as much as you can (at least 2 gallons). When the water is boiling, turn off the heat and add the malt extract to the water. Use a spoon and stir until you are sure no malt extract is sticking to the bottom of the kettle. Then turn the heat back on.

2. Bring the kettle back to a boil and stir occasionally so the ingredients won't burn on the bottom of the kettle. If your recipe calls for bittering hops, now is the time to add them and stir them in. Watch out for a boilover. In the early part of the boil, the kettle usually tries to boil over once or twice, so control this by adjusting the heat. Later in the boil, the surface tension changes and boiling over is not a problem. Keep stirring occasionally, and let the beer (wort) boil hard for 1 hour. Stir in the ½ teaspoon of Irish moss in your recipe about 15 minutes before the end of the boil.

3. If finishing hops are called for in your recipe, stir them in 2 minutes before the end of the boil. Using finishing hops at the end of the boil adds a fresh aroma and flavor to the beer, and the use of finishing hops is appropriate in most beer styles.

4. Pour the hot beer (wort) into the primary fermenter. It is not necessary to strain the wort if you used hop pellets. Add cold water to bring the total volume up to 5 gallons. If you are using our B3a Fermenter (the one in the kits), the 5-gallon mark is the bottom ring. Cover the fermenter and wait until the temperature is down to 75°F. If you have a wort chiller, use it to bring the temperature down quickly. At 75° or less, add the yeast in your recipe. Just tear open the pack(s) and sprinkle it on the wort. Close the fermenter with the lid, stopper, and airlock. Remember to put water (or vodka) in the airlock. Vodka evaporates more quickly, but bacteria won't live in it.

5. Fermentation should start within 24 hours, and may continue for between 1 day and 2 weeks, depending on the type of yeast, the recipe, and the temperature. (Ideally, this beer should ferment at 42°F.) Leave the beer alone and don't open the lid. When the airlock has not bubbled for several days and the beer is flat, still, and clearing, it is ready to bottle.

6. To bottle, siphon about 1 pint of beer into a pan and warm it on the stove. Add exactly ¾ cup of corn sugar to the pan and stir until it is dissolved. Pour this back into the beer and stir gently but well to distribute the sugar. Siphon or tap into clean sanitized bottles and cap. Keep the bottles at room temperature. After a week, put a bottle in

the refrigerator and try it. It will be best in about 3 weeks.

BOHEMIAN PILSNER
⫼ ⫼

BEER & WINE HOBBY—WOBURN, MASSACHUSETTS

The Saaz and Hallertauer hops have a long tradition of blending well together, especially in light lagers such as this Czech-style pilsner. The choice of yeasts suggested allows you to choose either a malt-accented or a somewhat drier beer.

ORIGINAL GRAVITY: 1.040–42

FINAL GRAVITY: 1.012–14

POTENTIAL ALCOHOL: 3.6% ABV

INGREDIENTS

> One 4-pound can Alexander's pale malt extract
> 3 pounds extra light DME
> 2 ounces Hallertauer hop plugs (boiling)
> 1 ounce Saaz plugs (finishing)
> 1 teaspoon Irish moss
> Wyeast 2278 Czech Pils or 2007 Pilsen Lager liquid yeast
> ¾ cup corn sugar to prime

BREWING PROCEDURES

1. Crack crystal malt, place in a muslin bag, and tie. Add cracked grains to 2 gallons cold water and bring to a boil. When water comes to a boil, remove from heat and let steep for 10 minutes. Remove and discard grains.
2. Add can of liquid malt and dried malt. Be sure to save 1¼ cups of the dried malt for bottling! Add the Hallertauer hop plugs tied in a muslin bag. Boil for 45 minutes. Add Irish moss, boil for 10 more minutes. During the last 5 minutes, add the Saaz hop plugs tied in a muslin bag. Remove all hops.
3. Have a primary fermenter prepared with 3½ gallons of cold water. Add hot wort to cold water to make up to a total of 5¼ gallons. When wort has cooled to 65–75°F, pitch prepared yeast.
4. Ferment for 2 weeks in primary, 2 weeks in secondary at recommended fermentation temperature.
5. Bottle with corn sugar priming and condition for 2–3 weeks.

PIRATES BREW PILSNER
⫼ ⫼

JAY GARRISON, HEAD BREWER, PIRATE BREWERY

BREWBUDDYS—REDONDO BEACH, CALIFORNIA

This medium-bodied, light-colored beer leans more toward the malty side than the bitter like a true Czech pilsner. It finishes with a smooth, mellow hop aftertaste. For a variety of flavor profiles you might try brewing this one with Wyeast 2206, 2042, or 2278.

ORIGINAL GRAVITY: 1.047

FINAL GRAVITY: 1.014

POTENTIAL ALCOHOL: 4.3% ABV

INGREDIENTS

> 1 pound dextrine malt
> 6 pounds light liquid extract

1 ounce Cluster hops

1 ounce Cascade whole flower hops

1 teaspoon Irish moss

Wyeast 2124 Bohemian, 2007 Pilsen, or dry lager yeast

¾ cup corn sugar for bottling

BREWING PROCEDURES

1. If you selected the Wyeast liquid yeast, you must break the inner packet before you begin to brew. Allow 1 day for each month after the manufacture date printed on the front. If you're using the dry yeast that came with the Pirates Brew Kit, go ahead and get to it.

2. Prepare the grain. The grain should be crushed; if you did not get the grain crushed at the shop, crush it with some sort of rolling pin. You can either mix the grain with 2 quarts of water and heat it until it starts to boil, or heat it to about 165°F and steep for about 15 minutes.

3. Strain the grain, collecting the liquid into your brewpot. Rinse the grain (sparge) with 2 quarts of hot (170–180°F) water.

4. Add the bag of extract and 1 gallon of water to the brewpot. (You might want to rest the bag of extract in hot water for a while to soften it up.) Bring the wort to a soft rolling boil.

5. Add the Cluster hops to the wort and boil for 40 minutes. Stir occasionally.

6. Add the Irish moss, then place the Cascade leaf hops in the hop bag and add to the wort; boil for 20 minutes. Stir occasionally.

7. Add the boiled wort to your sanitized, rinsed fermenter. Add ice-cold water to make 5 gallons. When the temperature drops to 75°F or less, add the yeast.

8. If you use liquid yeast, open the swollen packet and add to the wort. If you use dry yeast, add the yeast to 1 cup of 90°F water for a few minutes before adding to the wort. (You can add the yeast directly to the wort and let it sit for a few minutes also, but rehydrating the yeast in warm water will improve the fermentation.) Stir the wort thoroughly with a sanitized spoon.

9. Put the lid on the fermenter tightly, insert the fermentation lock with the stopper into the hole in the lid, and fill it up about ¾ of the way with water or vodka. Let the wort ferment for a week at 55°F.

10. Transfer to a secondary fermenter, and ferment another 2 weeks at 40°F. (Note: If you have no means to control the fermentation temperature, just ferment at room temperature for a week or two; you will still have a fine beer.)

11. When fermentation is complete, siphon the beer into a sanitized bottling bucket. Boil the corn sugar in about a cup of water; cool; stir gently into the beer. This provides the nutrients necessary for the yeast to carbonate the beer in the bottle.

12. Insert one end of the sanitized and rinsed hose into the bottling spigot and the other end to the bottle filler. Push the bottle filler down onto the bottom of the bottle and open the bottling spigot. Five gallons of beer will make about 2 cases, so make sure you sanitize this amount beforehand. Leave about ½–¾ inch of space at the top of the bottle. Cap the bottles.

13. Let the beer age for 2 weeks to 6 months. Chill and enjoy.

BOHEMIAN PILSENER
⬛ ⬛ ⬛

STEPHEN SNYDER

Because of the simplicity of Bohemian Pilsener, very few ingredients are needed to produce a great homebrewed version, even with malt extract. I made it a little more complicated by adding the hops in five additions to bring out as much Saaz character as possible.

ORIGINAL GRAVITY: 1.043–45

FINAL GRAVITY: 1.008–10

POTENTIAL ALCOHOL: 4.5% ABV

IBUs: 31

HBUs: 15.5

INGREDIENTS

> ¼ pound German light crystal malt
>
> 5 pounds Dutch extra light DME
>
> 1½ ounces Saaz plugs at 3.1% AA (boil) 60 minutes
>
> ½ ounce Saaz plugs at 3.1% AA (boil) 45 minutes
>
> ½ ounce Saaz plugs at 3.1% AA (boil) 30 minutes
>
> 1 ounce Saaz plugs at 3.1% AA (flavor) 10 minutes
>
> 1 ounce Saaz plugs 3.1% AA (aroma) steep 30 minutes
>
> 2 teaspoons Irish moss
>
> 2.5 gallons bottled spring water at 40°F
>
> 2 packages Wyeast 2124 Bohemian liquid yeast
>
> 1.4 cups Dutch light DME for priming

BREWING PROCEDURES

1. Add cracked crystal malt in nylon hop bag to 1 quart of cold tap water. Bring slowly just to boil. Remove from heat immediately and strain liquid into brew kettle.

2. Add 3 gallons of cold water and bring to a boil.

3. Remove brew kettle from heat before adding extract and DME to avoid sticking or burning.

4. Boil for 60 minutes, adding hops as noted above.

5. Hot trub should be skimmed throughout the boil. Add Irish moss 15 minutes before end of boil.

6. Let hot wort sit for 30 minutes (covered) in ice water bath before straining into primary fermenter containing 2.5 gallons of ice-cold water.

7. Should be below 76°F before pitching first package of yeast. Stir *vigorously* to aerate. Fit with blowoff hose and move to dark, quiet, draft-free space.

8. Leave at room temperature until fermentation activity is evident (24 hours), then cool to 46–50°F.

9. Attach airlock after kräusen falls (48 hours). Ferment for 10–12 more days.

10. Rack to secondary (preferably a 5-gallon glass carboy) fermenter for 2 more weeks.

11. Prime with DME dissolved in 1 pint boiling water and bottle with contents of second yeast package stirred into bottling bucket.

12. Store cool at fermentation temperature (46–50°F) for 7–10 days or until carbonation level is correct. Store cold (32–35°F) 8–12 weeks and serve at 45–50°F.

Note: Laaglander/Dutch malt extract is less fermentable than most English malt extracts, which will leave higher final gravities and more residual sweetness, and also requires upward adjustment of amounts used for priming.

SOUTH SEA PILS

🏛 🏛 🏛 🏛 🏛

FAL ALLEN, HEAD BREWER, PIKE PLACE BREWERY—SEATTLE, WASHINGTON

This recipe demonstrates the relative simplicity of brewing a traditional pilsner, even in a nine-gallon, all-grain batch. As this recipe also shows, even though there are but a few ingredients, using the correct malts and hop varieties is of even greater importance in such a beer, as is careful monitoring of fermentation temperature and sufficient lagering.

ORIGINAL GRAVITY: 1.047

FINAL GRAVITY: 1.013

POTENTIAL ALCOHOL: 4.5% ABV

INGREDIENTS (FOR 9 GALLONS)

> 12 pounds pilsner malt
> 2.5 pounds dextrine malt
> ¼ teaspoon gypsum (added to mash)
> 2 ounces Perle hops (boiling)
> 1 ounce Mt. Hood hops (boiling)
> 1 ounce Mt. Hood hops (finishing)
> 2 ounces Saaz or Tettnang (finishing)
> Wyeast 2124 Bohemian Lager
> 1.4 cups corn sugar for priming

MASH PROGRAM AND FERMENTATION PROCEDURE

1. Mash in (dough in) at 122–124°F and rest for 25 minutes.
2. Remove thickest one-third of the mash, add 1 pint of water, and decoct (bring to a boil).
3. Return to main mash body. This should raise temperature to 142–144°F. Rest for 20 minutes.
4. Remove thickest one-third of the mash, add 1 pint of water, and decoct (second decoction).
5. Add back to the main body of the mash. Temperature should be 150–154°F.
6. Rest for 1 hour, then remove thickest one-third of the mash, adding 6 to 16 ounces of water as needed and decoct (third decoction).
7. Add back to the main body of the mash. This should raise temperature to 170°F.
8. Begin runoff, sparging with 168–170°F water.
9. Boil for 1.5 hours, adding 2 ounces Perle and 1 ounce Mt. Hood hops after 30 minutes.
10. Add 1 ounce Mt. Hood and 2 ounces Saaz or Tettnang hops when there are 5 minutes remaining in the boil.
11. Chill wort to 55°F and pitch yeast.
12. Lower temperature over the next 48 hours to 45°F.
13. At the end of the primary fermentation (4–7 days), rack to the secondary and lager for 60–90 days at 40–45°F.
14. Rack, prime, and bottle as you normally do.

DORTMUNDER EXPORT

Originally brewed in the North Rhine–Westphalia region of western Germany in and around Dortmund, a city with very hard water (TDS over 1,000 mg/l), Dortmunder (now called "Export" in Germany) was one of the four great beers to arise in continental Europe during the lagering revolution, along with Vienna, pilsner, and Munich dunkel. Dortmunder is ordinarily a pale but full-bodied lager occupying the middle ground between the clean, hoppy dryness of German pils and the sweeter maltiness of Munich helles.

Original gravities are usually in the 1.056 range. Use hard water, but beware of high hopping levels, as severe bitterness may result. Aim for an original gravity between 1.048–1.060, IBUs between 23–37, and alcohol ABV from 5–6%. Esters and diacetyl should not be evident, and final gravity should be kept very low by highly attenuative yeasts such as Wyeast 2042, BrewTek CL-660, or Yeast Lab L31. Ayinger Jahrhundert is one of the few genuine examples brewed in accordance with the Reinheitsgebot that is exported to the United States. Stoudt's Export Gold, Hübsch Lager, and Los Gatos Lager are excellent American microbrewed examples to sample while brewing your first batch.

DORTMUNDER BASICS

ORIGINAL GRAVITY: 1.048–55

FINAL GRAVITY: 1.010–14

IBUs: 20–30

COLOR (SRM): 3–5

ALCOHOL BY VOLUME: 5–6%

NORTHWESTERN LAGER

PAUL WHITE, HEAD BREWER, THE SEVEN BARREL BREWERY—WEST LEBANON, NEW HAMPSHIRE

Rare German lager styles don't have to be the domain of the advanced brewer. This is an extract recipe with only the simplest hop additions of European hops for authenticity. If you feel like venturing into liquid yeasts to improve this brew, try one of the North German—style lager yeasts found in the yeast profiles section on pages 80–82.

ORIGINAL GRAVITY: 1.055

FINAL GRAVITY: 1.014

POTENTIAL ALCOHOL: 5.3% ABV

INGREDIENTS

6.6 pounds Northwestern Gold malt extract

1 ounce Perle or Northern Brewer—bittering at 7–9 AAU

1 ounce Saaz or Hallertau—flavoring

1 ounce Saaz or Hallertau—finishing

Lager yeast

¾ cup priming sugar

BREWING PROCEDURES

1. Mix extract well with hot water, then bring

to a boil. When the boil is under control, add bittering hops and start timing. Total length of boil will be 60 minutes.

2. If using Irish moss, add 2 teaspoons 20 minutes before the end of the boil.

3. Add flavoring hops 15 minutes before the end of boil.

4. Add finishing hops 1–2 minutes before the end of boil.

5. Cool to achieve 70–80º after topping up in the fermenter, and pitch yeast.

6. Ferment, prime, and bottle using your favorite methods.

GERMAN DORTMUNDER
⫿ ⫿

THE VINEYARD—UPTON, MASSACHUSETTS
This recipe is a very simple and straightforward way to brew an accurate Dortmunder using the proper ingredients. The challenge comes in keeping your fermentation temperatures low and steady and maintaining a good six- to eight-week lagering stage at or close to 32°F.

ORIGINAL GRAVITY: 1.052

FINAL GRAVITY: 1.013

POTENTIAL ALCOHOL: 5% ABV

INGREDIENTS

½ pound light crystal malt grain

4 pounds Heidelberg light malt extract

3 pounds light dry malt extract

1 ounce German Hallertau hop pellets (40 minutes)

1 ounce Tettnanger hop pellets (30 minutes)

½ ounce Styrian Goldings hop plug (10 minutes)

1 teaspoon Irish moss (15 minutes)

2 packages Amsterdam lager yeast

¾ cup corn sugar for priming

BREWING PROCEDURES

1. Crush and steep grain in 1 quart cold water for 10 minutes, then bring to a boil slowly, stirring occasionally. Once boiling commences, remove from heat and strain liquid into boiling pot.

2. Add 1.5 gallons water, Heidelberg malt, 3 pounds light dry malt, and bring to boil. Once boiling, add 1 ounce German Hallertau hop pellets and start timer for 40 minutes. Add 1 ounce Tettnanger hop pellets last 30 minutes. Add Irish moss last 15 minutes. Add ½ ounce plug of Styrian Goldings hops last 10 minutes.

3. Strain into primary fermenter and add up to 5 gallons with cold water. Let cool and add yeast. Primary fermentation: 6–8 days at 55°F.

4. After 6–8 days, siphon into secondary fermenter. Secondary fermentation: 8–10 days at 55°F. Add priming sugar at bottling time.

5. After bottling, maintain 55°F for 1 week, then place bottles in refrigerator for lagering.

EXPORT LAGER
⫿ ⫿

THE CELLAR HOMEBREW—SEATTLE, WASHINGTON
"Try to use the lightest crystal malt available and use a yeast for this one that doesn't leave

too much residual maltiness. Give this one time to lager in the secondary at 32° to promote a smoother, drier profile. The outcome will be a gently aromatic and cleanly satisfying German-style lager."

ORIGINAL GRAVITY: 1.046

FINAL GRAVITY: 1.012

POTENTIAL ALCOHOL: 4.5% ABV

INGREDIENTS (FOR 5.5 GALLONS)

- 1/2 **pound German light crystal malt (crushed)**
- 1 **can Coopers Lager malt extract syrup**
- 3 **pounds extra light dry malt extract**
- 1 **ounce Tettnang hops (boiling)**
- 1 **ounce Hallertau Hersbrucker hops (finishing)**
- 1 **package dry lager or German liquid lager yeast**
- 1 1/4 **teaspoon yeast nutrient**
- 3/4 **cup priming sugar**

BREWING PROCEDURES

1. Place crushed crystal malt in a strainer bag. Add this bag of grain to your brewing kettle, which contains 2 to 2 1/2 gallons brewing water.
2. Bring the brewing water to a boil, then remove the bag of grains.
3. Remove the brewing kettle from the burner and add any malt syrup and dry malt extract. Stir thoroughly and return the kettle to the burner. Continue heating and stirring this wort until it boils.
4. At boiling point, add any yeast nutrient, water salts, and boiling hops. Hops can be placed in a hop bag or added loose, to be later strained out after the boil using a strainer bag. Time the boil for about 1 hour, stirring occasionally. After the first 10 minutes of this boil, remove 2 cups of wort in measuring cup and cover with foil or plastic. Cool to 90°F for use in step 5.
5. Making the yeast starter: For dry yeast, use 1/2 cup warm tap water (90–100°F). Sprinkle the contents of yeast packet into that water, cover for at least 15 minutes, and then add to the 2 cups of wort you prepared in step 4. Cover and set aside for use in step 9. For liquid yeast, prepare 1 to 3 days ahead of brewing time per package instructions.
6. After the wort has boiled for that 1 hour, add finishing hops. Place them in the hop bag, which has been emptied of the spent boiling hops, and place them in the boiling kettle, or just add the finishing hops directly to the brewing kettle.
7. Let the boil continue for 5 minutes. Remove pot from burner and let cool, covered, for about 20 minutes.
8. Pour 3 gallons of cold water into the sanitized open fermenter fitted with strainer bag; if loose finishing hops were used in step 6, strain the warm wort from step 7 into the cold water. Top up the fermenter to 5 1/2 gallons using cold tap water. Cover the fermenter and cool the wort as rapidly as possible.
9. When the wort has cooled to about 80°, add the yeast nutrient and ferment, prime, and bottle as you usually do.

MUNICH HELLES

Helles means "light" in German. This refers to the beer's color, not its body, alcoholic strength, or caloric content. Also called "Munich light" or "hell bier," helles characteristics include a medium malty flavor, smooth mouthfeel, thirst-quenching bitterness, and subtle hop aroma and flavor. For the home brewer, a Wissenschaftliche yeast strain is recommended, as are original gravities around 1.050, very pale lager malt or extract, and Hallertau hops. Often considered a blue-collar beer, helles is one of southern Germany's number one best-sellers and what you're most likely to be served by the liter in a beer hall such as the Hofbräuhaus. Kloster Andechs Hell, Paulaner Premium Lager, and Spaten Premium Lager are prime imported versions. Old Dominion's Hard Times Select and Pennsylvania Brewing's Helles Gold are both award-winning American microbrews to enjoy while you're waiting for your own to mature.

HELLES BASICS

ORIGINAL GRAVITY: 1.044–47

FINAL GRAVITY: 1.008–12

IBUs: 20–25

COLOR (SRM): 3–4.5

ALCOHOL BY VOLUME: 4.5–5.5%

MCHALE'S BEST (MUNICH HELLES)

BEER UNLIMITED—MALVERN, PENNSYLVANIA

This simple recipe for the German beer hall favorite is designed for those who must ferment at warmer-than-normal lager temperatures. After the beer is bottled, then you can do your cold lagering for a few weeks in the refrigerator a few bottles at a time if necessary.

ORIGINAL GRAVITY: 1.048

FINAL GRAVITY: 1.015

POTENTIAL ALCOHOL: 4.3% ABV

INGREDIENTS

    1 can Mountmellick light lager malt extract
    1 can English extra light malt extract
    3 ounces Tettnang hops
    1 teaspoon Irish moss
    Wyeast 2042 Danish Lager yeast
    2 tablespoons gelatin
    ¾ cup corn sugar for priming

BREWING PROCEDURES

1. Boil extracts with 1½ ounce Tettnang for 1 hour.
2. At 30 minutes—add Irish moss.
3. 10 minutes before the end—add ½ ounce Tettnang.
4. Last 2 minutes—add ½ ounce Tettnang.
5. Dry-hop with the final ½ ounce Tettnang.
6. Ferment at 58–68°F for 1 week.
7. Rack to secondary fermenter and add 1 tablespoon gelatin in a water solution.
8. Ferment at cooler temperatures for 1–4 weeks.

9. Prime with ¾ cup corn sugar and 1 table-spoon gelatin, both in a water solution.

MUNICH HELLES LAGER
⫶ ⫶ ⫶

DICK FOEHRINGER

THE BREWMEISTER—FAIR OAKS, CALIFORNIA

"Munich helles is a mildly hopped, malty, pale-colored beer. It is the mainstay of Bavarian festive beer drinking. This lager is traditional to southern German style and is lower in alcohol, but superb for everyday quaffing!"

ORIGINAL GRAVITY: 1.045

FINAL GRAVITY: 1.010

POTENTIAL ALCOHOL: 4.5% ABV

INGREDIENTS

- ½ pound 20 °L crystal malt
- ¼ pound flaked malted barley
- 6 pounds pale malt extract
- 1½ ounce Tettnanger hops (60 minutes) boiling
- ½ ounce Tettnanger hops (end of boil) aromatic
- 1 teaspoon Irish moss (15 minutes)
- 1 Wyeast Munich Lager liquid yeast
- 1 teaspoon gelatin
- ¾ cup bottling sugar

BREWING PROCEDURES

1. Put the crushed crystal malt and flaked barley malt grains into a grain bag. Place 1½ to 2 gallons of cold water in your brewpot. Place grain bag in water and bring to a near boil (160°F). Turn off heat and allow grains to steep for 30 minutes. Drain and remove grain.

2. Dissolve liquid extract thoroughly and then return mixture to heat. Bring to a boil. Add the 1½ ounce of hops and boil for 45 minutes. Add Irish moss and boil for 15 minutes. Add the end-of-boil ½ ounce of aromatic hops. Turn off heat and steep for 15 minutes. Cold-break the wort to below 100°F by setting your pan of wort into a sink full of cold water.

3. Put the cooled wort into your primary fermenter and add cold water to make 5½ gallons. When cooled below 85°F, pitch your yeast. (Note: You must start the liquid yeast 1–2 days prior to brewing to allow it to culture up. Follow the instructions on the package for preparation.)

4. Ferment in a cool (50–60°F), dark place. When fermentation has ceased, transfer to the secondary, leaving all the sediment behind.

5. Dissolve gelatin in 1 cup hot water and stir into secondary. Allow beer to clear, typically 3–5 days. Rack again, leaving sediment behind. Dissolve bottling sugar in 1 cup of hot water and stir into beer.

6. Bottle and cap.

7. Allow to age/carbonate in the bottles for 2–4 weeks. Enjoy!

LIGHT LAGER
⫶ ⫶

THE FLYING BARREL—FREDERICK, MARYLAND

This light, easy-drinking lager is perfect for warm summer days with a gentle hop aroma and a subtle malt sweetness underneath ideal for complementing summer foods.

ORIGINAL GRAVITY: 1.038

FINAL GRAVITY: 1.010

POTENTIAL ALCOHOL: 3.5% ABV

INGREDIENTS

> One 4-pound can Alexander's pale
>
> One 1.4 pound Alexander's pale "Kicker"
>
> 2 ounces Kent Golding hops, alpha acid 5 to 5.5% (we prefer plugs)
>
> 1 ounce German Hallertau hops, alpha acid 3 to 3.5%
>
> 1 teaspoon Irish moss
>
> 1 pack Wyeast 2308 Munich Lager
>
> ¾ cup corn sugar for priming

BREWING PROCEDURES

1. Break yeast pack a day before you are ready to brew (may need more than one day . . . check date and instructions).
2. Boil malt and Kent Goldings hops for about 30 minutes in about 1½ gallons of water.
3. After 15 minutes of the boil, put the Irish moss in the wort.
4. After 25 minutes of the boil, put the Hallertau hops in the wort.
5. Put boiling wort into a fermenter with 3½ gallons of cold water.
6. When temperature drops to below 75 degrees, pitch yeast.
7. Take hydrometer reading, airlock fermenter, and watch the yeast do its thing.
8. After 4 days, rack into a clean fermenter (glass if possible), airlock, and watch the yeast do its thing for another 20 days or until fermentation is complete.
9. Prime and bottle.

BIERGARTEN HELLES
🍺 🍺 🍺

STEPHEN SNYDER

I designed this recipe with traditional ingredients to achieve a real Munich helles flavor. Getting the color right in an extract brew is much harder. To achieve the proper color, be careful not to caramelize your wort; try to cool the wort as fast as possible, and if you can, do a full wort boil using medium-high heat instead of a hard, rolling boil.

ORIGINAL GRAVITY: 1.047

FINAL GRAVITY: 1.012

POTENTIAL ALCOHOL: 4.5% ABV

IBUs: 24

INGREDIENTS

> ¼ pound German light crystal malt (10 ˚L)
>
> 6.6 pounds light extract syrup (unhopped)
>
> 1 ounce Hallertauer pellets 3.3% AA (boil) 60 minutes
>
> 1 ounce Hallertauer pellets 3.3% AA (boil) 30 minutes
>
> 1 ounce Hallertauer pellets 3.3% AA (flavor) 15 minutes
>
> ½ ounce Hallertau Hersbrucker plug 2.9% AA (aroma) steep 30 minutes
>
> ½ ounce Saaz plug 3.1% AA (aroma) steep 30 minutes
>
> Wyeast 2206 Bavarian Lager liquid yeast
>
> ¾ cup corn sugar for priming

BREWING PROCEDURES

1. Place cracked crystal malt in hop bag, then put into 1 quart of cold water. (I boiled, then cooled ½ gallon of water beforehand to remove chlorine.) Bring slowly to boil. Remove from heat immediately when boil

begins. Strain liquid into brew kettle. Sparge grains with hot water.

2. Add 3 gallons of cold water and malt extract and stir gently until completely dissolved. (I also boiled, then cooled, 3 gallons of water beforehand to remove chlorine.)

3. By dissolving extract before boiling water, wort color will be much lighter. I also used a heat diffuser under my kettle to prevent scorching and to keep the boil gentle, which will also keep the wort lighter in color.

4. Boil for 60 minutes, adding hops as noted above. Avoid stirring the wort excessively after dissolving in extract.

5. Hot-break trub should be skimmed throughout the boil. Be careful not to remove the boiling hops.

6. Use wort chiller or let hot wort sit for 30 minutes (covered) in an ice-water bath before straining into a *secondary* fermenter containing 2.5 gallons ice-cold water (33–40°F). Wort should now be ready for pitching yeast.

7. Make certain wort is below 75°F before pitching yeast. Stir vigorously to aerate.

8. After 8–12 hours, rack off cold-break trub to *primary* fermenter. Cover and fit with airlock (or blowoff hose if using a carboy; then use an airlock after blowoff ceases) and move to dark, quiet, draft-free space.

9. Keep at room temperature until signs of fermentation activity are evident, then move to 46–51°F space. Ferment for 10–14 days or until primary fermentation ceases.

10. Rack back to *secondary* and ferment for 1–2 weeks more.

11. Prime with sugar dissolved in 1 pint boiling water and bottle.

12. Condition 7–14 days at fermentation temperature (46°F). Store cold (33–34°F) 8 weeks and serve at 45–47°F.

VIENNA

Just prior to Josef Grolle's invention of pilsner lager in 1842, legendary brewer Anton Dreher began brewing a malty, amber-red lager in Vienna in late 1840–early 1841 using industrial age brewing techniques of refrigeration, malting, and yeast management. Early records of this beer do not offer specific details of gravity and color, but it is believed that it was similar to the Märzen style. It is known, however, that over the past 150 years since its invention in Vienna, original gravities of the commercial Vienna style fell in relation to the Bavarian fest biers, which are now generally accepted as being stronger and darker than the original auburn-hued Vienna. There are several American microbrews in the Vienna style, such as Brooklyn Lager, Old West Amber, Rhomberg Classic Amber, and others, but true Vienna is fairly rare in Europe.

VIENNA BASICS

ORIGINAL GRAVITY: 1.048–56

FINAL GRAVITY: 1.012–18

IBUs: 22–28

COLOR (SRM): 8–12

ALCOHOL BY VOLUME: 4.4–6%

4. Cool to achieve 70–80° after topping up in the fermenter, and pitch yeast.

5. Ferment, prime, and bottle using your favorite methods.

NORTHWESTERN VIENNA

PAUL WHITE, HEAD BREWER, THE SEVEN BARREL BREWERY—WEST LEBANON, NEW HAMPSHIRE

Vienna is one of the best beers to match with food, especially zesty, spicy dishes. This recipe is designed to allow even the first-time brewer the joys of making and tasting this landmark style.

ORIGINAL GRAVITY: 1.042

FINAL GRAVITY: 1.014

POTENTIAL ALCOHOL: 3.6% ABV

INGREDIENTS

6.6 pounds Northwestern amber malt extract

1½ ounce Hallertau or Saaz bittering at 5–6 AAUs

1 ounce Hallertau or Saaz flavoring hops

Lager yeast

¾ cup priming sugar

BREWING PROCEDURES

1. Mix extract well with hot water, then bring to a boil. When the boil is under control, add bittering hops and start timing. Total length of boil will be 60 minutes.

2. If using Irish moss, add 2 teaspoons 20 minutes before the end of the boil.

3. Add flavoring hops 15 minutes before the end of boil.

VIENNA LAGER

JOE & BRYAN TIMMONS

BOSTON BREWERS SUPPLY CO.— JAMAICA PLAIN, MASSACHUSETTS

A blend of light and dark crystal malts contributes to our Vienna's beautiful amber-red color, toasted malt aroma, and rich, complex, malty taste. A multiple hopping schedule with the finest Saaz and Hallertau hops provides a clean, smooth bitterness and a subtle hop flavor. A liquid yeast culture will add a more authentic taste profile.

ORIGINAL GRAVITY: 1.050–54

FINAL GRAVITY: 1.014–16

POTENTIAL ALCOHOL: 5% ABV

IBUs: 24 to 26

INGREDIENTS

6 ounces German Vienna malt

6 ounces German light crystal malt

6 ounces British dark crystal malt

6.6 pounds Ireks light extract syrup

1 pound Dutch dry malt

2 ounces Czech Saaz hop pellets

1 ounce Hallertauer hop pellets

1 teaspoon Irish moss

1 package Superior dry lager yeast or Wyeast 2308 Munich Lager yeast

6 ounces corn sugar for priming

BREWING PROCEDURES

1. Secure the crushed grains in the muslin straining bag. Pour 2 gallons of cold water into your brewpot, apply heat, and add the grain bag. Heat to a near boil (about 155°), turn off the heat, cover the pot, and allow the grains to steep for 30 minutes. Remove the grain bag, drain, and discard.

2. Thoroughly dissolve the malt extract, apply heat, and bring to a boil. As soon as the wort (unfermented beer) begins to boil, add 1 ounce of the Saaz hops and start timing the boil; the total elapsed time will be 60 minutes. Maintain a good rolling boil, stirring occasionally and skimming the brown resinous scum from the top of the wort.

3. After 25 minutes, add the 1 ounce of Hallertau hops; 20 minutes later, add the Irish moss flakes. After 10 more minutes, add the remaining ounce of Saaz hops. Continue to boil for an additional 5 minutes, then cover and remove the pot from the heat.

   Remember that after the wort has cooled, it is highly vulnerable to contamination; everything that comes into contact with it from this point on must be thoroughly sanitized!

4. Cool the wort as quickly as possible. A wort chiller works best, but if you haven't got one yet a cold water bath will do the trick. Place the covered pot in your kitchen sink and fill with ice and cold water. When the temperature has fallen to about 90°F, transfer the wort, through a strainer if possible, into your fermenter. Top off with enough cold water to reach a 5-gallon level and stir or shake well. Draw off a small sample and take both a hydrometer and a temperature reading; always discard the sample used.

5. When the wort has cooled to 65–70°F, you are ready to add the yeast. Once the yeast has been added, attach an airlock and keep the fermenter at room temperature for 12 to 18 hours (until fermentation becomes visible), then transfer the fermenter to the coolest location you have access to, ideally 50–55°F, until fermentation is complete.

6. When visible signs of fermentation have ceased, gently transfer the beer to a sanitized secondary fermenter (ideally a 5-gallon glass carboy), leaving all sediment behind. Attach an airlock and allow the beer to settle for an additional 10 to 14 days at the same temperature of primary fermentation or colder. At the end of this period, draw off a small sample and check the final gravity. By now it should be within the range stated above; if not, wait another couple of days and check again. Prepare to bottle.

BOTTLING AND CONDITIONING

1. Sanitize all of your siphoning and bottling equipment, bottles, and caps.

2. Boil the 6 ounces of corn sugar in about a cup of water and pour it into your bottling bucket. Gently siphon the beer out of the fermenter into the bucket, making sure the flow is directed to the bottom of the bucket; avoid splashing or agitating the beer.

3. Using your siphon tubing and bottle filler, fill each bottle to within an inch from the top and cap immediately. Store the bottles upright for 1 week at room temperature and for an additional 2 to 3 weeks as cold as you can get it, ideally 35–45°F.

WINTER LAGER

🍺 🍺

THE VINEYARD—UPTON, MASSACHUSETTS

This malty, amber-red lager is also just as welcome in the other three seasons, as it provides a wonderful accompaniment to a wide range of hearty foods. The toasted lager malt lends a warm, bready aroma to the gentle Saaz hop nose.

ORIGINAL GRAVITY: 1.042

FINAL GRAVITY: 1.012

POTENTIAL ALCOHOL: 3.9% ABV

INGREDIENTS

> 8 ounces toasted lager malt
> 8 ounces lager malt
> 8 ounces crystal malt
> 3.3 pounds John Bull hopped light
> 4 pounds Dutch light dry malt
> 1 teaspoon Irish moss (last 15 minutes)
> ½ ounce Saaz hop plug (last 10 minutes)
> 1 packet Whitbread lager yeast
> 1 teaspoon ascorbic acid (add at bottling)
> ¾ cup priming sugar

BREWING PROCEDURES

1. Crush all grains (toasted lager malt, lager malt, and crystal malt) with rolling pin or short spurts in the blender.
2. Put all crushed grains in 1½ gallons cold water and bring to a boil.
3. Strain liquid into brew boiling pot, add ½ gallon water, John Bull hopped light, and 4 pounds dry malt, and bring to a boil for 40 minutes. Last 15 minutes add Irish moss. Last 10 minutes add ½ ounce Saaz hop plug. Strain into primary fermenter and bring to 5 gallons with cold water.

4. Let cool, pitch yeast. Primary fermentation: 4 days at 60–65°F.
5. Rack off solids after 4 days into secondary fermenter. Secondary fermentation: 8 days at 60–65°F.
6. Add priming sugar and ascorbic acid at bottling time. Lager at 55°F for 8 days.

VIENNA AMBER

🍺 🍺 🍺

STEPHEN SNYDER

The traditional ingredients and generous hopping have produced rave reviews for this extract beer in the past, although the Munich yeast, which is one of my favorites, can be a little unpredictable. Because it can leave high final gravities, I've offered a second choice, the drier but more stable Pilsen Lager yeast.

ORIGINAL GRAVITY: 1.048

FINAL GRAVITY: 1.014

POTENTIAL ALCOHOL: 4.4% ABV

INGREDIENTS

> 6 gallons bottled spring water
> ½ pound cracked 40 °L crystal malt (2 cups)
> ½ cup Munich malt
> 1.5 kilograms Heidelberg light unhopped extract (3.3 pounds)
> 3.5 pounds Dutch light spray malt
> 1½ ounce Styrian Goldings 6% AA plug hops (boil) 60 minutes
> ½ ounce Styrian Goldings 6% AA plug hops (boil) 30 minutes
> 1 ounce Hallertau plugs 3% AA (flavor) 10 minutes
> 1 ounce Saaz plugs 3% AA (aroma) 1 minute

1 package Wyeast 2308 Munich or 2007
    Pilsen Lager yeast
¾ cup corn sugar for priming

BREWING PROCEDURES

1. Crack and add grains to 1 quart of cold tap water in large pot. Bring slowly almost to boil, remove from heat, then pour strained wort into brew kettle.
2. Add 2½ gallons cold water. Bring to boil. Remove brew kettle from heat before adding extract and DME to avoid sticking or burning.
3. Boil vigorously for a total of 1 hour, adding hops as noted above.
4. Immerse covered brewpot in sink filled with ice water for 30 minutes.
5. Rack cooled wort into primary fermenter containing 3 gallons ice-cold water to equal 5 gallons.
6. Pitch yeast at 75°F, cool to 46–58°F and ferment 10–14 days in primary, then rack and ferment at least 2 more weeks in secondary (preferably a 5-gallon glass carboy).
7. Rack to bottling bucket and add 1 package of rehydrated lager yeast and DME dissolved in 1 pint boiling water. Stir well.
8. Bottle with sugar dissolved in 1 pint boiling water, then condition at fermentation temperature for 1 week.
9. Cold-lager 4–8 weeks at 32–34°F.

EINBECK STYLE LAGER
🍺 🍺 🍺 🍺

TONY LUBOLD, HEAD BREWER, CATA-
MOUNT BREWING CO.—WHITE RIVER
JUNCTION, VERMONT

If you are new to all-grain brewing, this should be one of your first stepped-mash recipes. It is amazingly simple and will result in a wonderfully malty, well-balanced lager with a reddish gold color. The small addition of chocolate malt lends color and a very subtle roastiness.

ORIGINAL GRAVITY: 1.047

FINAL GRAVITY: 1.012

POTENTIAL ALCOHOL: 4.5% ABV

INGREDIENTS

6 pounds English lager malt
2 pounds English pale malt
5 ounces chocolate malt
1½ ounces Styrian Goldings pellets (60 minutes)
Irish moss (20 minutes)
½ ounce Hallertau (primary fermenter)
2 packages dried lager yeast
¾ cup corn sugar

BREWING PROCEDURES

1. Mix all crushed malt in 10 quarts of 150°F water. The temperature should drop to about 135°F. Rest 30 minutes.
2. Raise the temperature to 155°F, hold for 45 minutes. Raise the temperature to 170°F.
3. Sparge with 12 quarts of water. Boil for 1 hour, adding hops and Irish moss as noted above.
4. Pitch and ferment at 55–60°F for 5 days. Transfer to the carboy and age for 7 days.
5. Bottle as usual using ¾ cup corn sugar. Place in a room-temperature area for one week. Remove to a cooler place to mature for at least 5 more weeks.

MÄRZEN/OKTOBERFEST

Taken from the German word "März" for the month of March, Märzen (or Maerzen) is a fest bier believed to have been brewed first by monks during the month of March and laid down during the summer months. In the Middle Ages, these were probably strong, dark ales brewed in anticipation of the late summer/early autumn harvest festivals, but were eclipsed in 1858 when Gabriel Sedlmayr II's brother Joseph introduced Vienna-style beer to Munich's Oktoberfest and in 1872 when Gabriel unveiled his classic Märzen.

Originally, the nineteenth-century version of this beer was the same as Vienna, a reddish amber lager, and many purists still consider it so. But, in reality, the original gravities and colors of these beers have diverged over the years to the point where the seasonal Oktoberfest/Märzen is now generally accepted as darker and stronger than the traditional Vienna lager as brewed by its inventor, Anton Dreher. Both, however, are increasingly lower in gravity than their predecessors, particularly in Munich, where more brewers are offering a golden, standard-gravity lager as their fest bier.

Märzen should be a well-carbonated, deep-amber lager, featuring a sweet malt aroma and flavor balanced with the crisp bitterness and subtle finish of German hops. Medium to soft water is recommended, as is a "Munich" or "Bavarian-style" lager yeast (you can use a clean ale yeast in a pinch, but ferment at the lower range of ale-fermenting temperatures). Authentic Bavarian versions are usually much sweeter and, therefore, more heavily hopped than their American counterparts. Good commercial examples include Spaten Ur Maerzen, Paulener Oktoberfest, Hacker Pschorr Oktoberfest, Weeping Radish Fest, Catamount Octoberfest, and Samuel Adams Octoberfest.

MÄRZEN BASICS

ORIGINAL GRAVITY: 1.050–60

FINAL GRAVITY: 1.012–20

IBUs: 20–25

COLOR (SRM): 8–12

ALCOHOL BY VOLUME: 5–6%

KRAUT DOG OKTOBERFEST

◀▌

THE HOME BREWERY—OZARK, MISSOURI

If you are a new homebrewer, you will discover that one of the great joys of becoming a brewer is the greater significance that celebrations like Oktoberfest take on. There is no need to achieve master brewer status to contribute your own beers to these fests. Here is a very, very simple formulation for a robust and malty Oktoberfest of your own.

ORIGINAL GRAVITY 1.048

FINAL GRAVITY: 1.013

POTENTIAL ALCOHOL: 4.6% ABV

INGREDIENTS

> **6.6 pounds (2 packs) Yellow Dog malt extract**
>
> **1 ounce Hersbrucker pellets (5.3% AA) in boil**
>
> **No finishing hops**
>
> **1 pack Wyeast lager yeast (your choice)**
>
> **¾ cup corn sugar for priming**

BREWING PROCEDURES

1. Heat 5 gallons of water in a large kettle. Many people don't have a kettle that large, but heat as much as you can (at least 2 gallons). When the water is boiling, turn off the heat and add the malt extract to the water. Use a spoon and stir until you are sure no malt extract is sticking to the bottom of the kettle. Then turn the heat back on.

2. Bring the kettle back to a boil and stir occasionally so the ingredients won't burn on the bottom of the kettle. If your recipe calls for bittering hops, now is the time to add them and stir them in. Watch out for a boilover. In the early part of the boil, the kettle usually tries to boil over once or twice, so control this by adjusting the heat. Later in the boil, the surface tension changes and boiling over is not a problem. Keep stirring occasionally, and let the beer (wort) boil hard for 1 hour. Stir in the ½ teaspoon of Irish moss in your recipe about 15 minutes before the end of the boil.

3. If finishing hops are called for in your recipe, stir them in 2 minutes before the end of the boil. Using finishing hops at the end of the boil adds a fresh aroma and flavor to the beer, and the use of finishing hops is appropriate in most beer styles.

4. Pour the hot beer (wort) into the primary fermenter. It is not necessary to strain the wort if you used hop pellets. Add cold water to bring the total volume up to 5 gallons. If you are using our B3a Fermenter (the one in the kits), the 5-gallon mark is the bottom ring. Cover the fermenter and wait until the temperature is down to 75°F. If you have a wort chiller, use it to bring the temperature down quickly. At 75° or less, add the yeast in your recipe. Just tear open the pack(s) and sprinkle it on the wort. Close the fermenter with the lid, stopper, and airlock. Remember to put water (or vodka) in the airlock. Vodka evaporates more quickly, but bacteria won't live in it.

5. Fermentation should start within 24 hours, and may continue for between 1 day and 2 weeks, depending on the type of yeast, the recipe, and the temperature. (Ideally, this beer should ferment at 42°F.) Leave the beer alone and don't open the lid. When the airlock has not bubbled for several days and the beer is flat, still, and clearing, it is ready to bottle.

6. To bottle, siphon about 1 pint of beer into a pan and warm it on the stove. Add exactly ¾ cup of corn sugar to the pan and stir until it is dissolved. Pour this back into the beer and stir gently but well to distribute the sugar. Siphon or tap into clean, sanitized bottles and cap. Keep the bottles at room temperature. After a week, put a bottle in the refrigerator and try it. It will be best in about 3 weeks.

BAVARIAN PRIDE

⫘ ⫘

THE CELLAR HOMEBREW—SEATTLE, WASHINGTON

"This Oktoberfest style of amber German beer, also known as Vienna or Märzen, is the best known of the "fest" beers. Smooth and malty, with a hop bite that does not linger. A great treat anytime."

ORIGINAL GRAVITY: 1.056

FINAL GRAVITY: 1.015

POTENTIAL ALCOHOL: 5.5% ABV

INGREDIENTS (FOR 5.5 GALLONS)

- 1/2 pound German light crystal malt (crushed)
- 1/4 pound chocolate malt (crushed)
- 1 can Cooper's Lager syrup
- 1 can Alexander's amber "Kicker"
- 3 pounds English amber dry malt
- 2 ounces Tettnang hops (boiling)
- 1 ounces Tettnang hops (finishing)
- 1 package Cooper's dry yeast or Munich Lager liquid yeast
- 3/4 cup corn sugar for priming

BREWING PROCEDURES

Note: If you are using the Munich Lager liquid yeast with this recipe, be sure to start that yeast at least 1 to 3 days before doing any of the brewing steps below. Follow the package directions and use the yeast in step 5.

1. Place the crushed German light crystal and chocolate malts in a strainer bag. Add this bag of grain to your brewing kettle, which contains 2 to 2½ gallons brewing water. Bring the brewing water to a boil, then remove the bag of grains. It is not a good idea to boil these specialty grains for any length of time, as they may contribute a bitter or grainy taste to the finished beer.

2. Sparge (rinse) the bag of grains with about 1 quart of hot tap water into the brewing kettle; dispose of the spent grains.

3. Remove the brewing kettle from the burner and add the 1 can of Cooper's lager syrup, the 1 can of Alexander's amber "Kicker," and the 3 pounds of English amber dry malt. The syrup is easier to pour if the can has been previously placed in hot water. Also, rinse the can with hot water to ensure that all the syrup goes into the kettle. Stir the mixture, now called "wort," until it boils. Watch carefully at this time because the wort may boil over. You can prevent this by pouring a cup of cold water into the over-boiling wort.

4. At boiling point, add the Tettnang boiling hops. Hops can be placed in a hop bag or added loose, to be later strained out after the boil using a strainer bag. Time the boil for about 1 hour, stirring occasionally. After the first 10 minutes of this boil, remove 2 cups of wort in measuring cup and cover with foil or plastic. Cool to 90°F for use in step 5.

5. Making the yeast starter: For dry yeast, use 1/2 cup warm tap water (90–100°F). Sprinkle the contents of yeast packet into that water, cover for at least 15 minutes, and then add to the 2 cups of wort you prepared in step 4. Cover and set aside for use in step 9. For liquid yeast, prepare 1 to 3 days ahead of brewing time per package instructions. Open the swollen package and add the contents to the 2 cups of wort as prepared in step 4.

6. After the wort has boiled for that 1 hour, add the Tettnang finishing hops. Place

them in the hop bag, which has been emptied of the spent boiling hops, and place them in the boiling kettle or just add the finishing hops directly to the brewing kettle. They will be strained later in step 8.

7. Let the boil continue for 5 minutes. This gives the beer its hop aroma. Remove the pot from the burner and let it cool, covered, for about 20 minutes.

8. Pour 3 gallons of cold water into the sanitized open fermenter fitted with strainer bag. If loose finishing hops were used in step 6, strain the warm wort from step 7 into the cold water. Top up the fermenter to 5½ gallons using cold tap water. Cover the fermenter and cool the wort as rapidly as possible.

9. When the wort has cooled to about 80°, add the yeast starter and ferment as you usually do.

MR. MARTY'S MERRY MARZENFEST
🍺🍺🍺

E. C. KRAUS HOME WINE AND BEER MAKING SUPPLIES—INDEPENDENCE, MISSOURI

"A full-bodied malty brew. Orange-copper colored with a sweetness that only succumbs to the well-balanced but limited edge of hops."

ORIGINAL GRAVITY: 1.052–57

FINAL GRAVITY: 1.013–14

POTENTIAL ALCOHOL: 5–5.6% ABV

IBUs: 20–30

COLOR: 8–14 SRM/12–23 °L

INGREDIENTS

- 8 ounces crystal malt
- 2 ounces chocolate malt
- 3.3 pounds light unhopped malt syrup
- 2.5 pounds light dried malt extract (6.2 cups)
- 8 ounces malto-dextrin
- 2 ounces Hallertau pellet hops (45 minutes boil time)
- 1 tablespoon Irish moss (15 minutes boil time)
- ½ ounce Saaz pellet hops (finishing)
- 14 grams dry Munich lager or Wyeast 2565 Kölsch yeast (for warm-temperature brewing)
- ¾ cup priming sugar

BREWING PROCEDURES

1. Lightly crack malted barleys and put with 1½ gallons of cold water in a cooking pot. Slowly bring to a boil over a 30–45-minute period.

2. Once the liquid is boiling, strain the grains out by the use of a colander or the like and discard.

3. Bring liquid back to a boil and add the malt extracts. Bring back to a boil again.

4. Once boiling, add Hallertau hops and boil for 45 minutes. During the last 15 minutes of the boil, add the Irish moss. During the last 5 minutes of the boil, fold in the malto-dextrin.

5. Once the boiling is complete, add the Saaz hops; turn off the burner and allow to steep for 15 minutes with a lid on.

6. Now add the wort to your fermenter along with cold tap water up to 5 gallons. Make sure the wort has cooled to below 80°F and pitch yeast.

7. Attach airlock to fermenter and allow to fer-

ment for 7–10 days or until finished and bottle with priming sugar as normal.

OKTOBERFEST
🍺 🍺 🍺

BEER & WINE HOBBY–WOBURN, MASSACHUSETTS

This advanced extract recipe uses many different malts and multiple hop additions to create a complex, balanced, and authentic fest beer suitable for brewing competitions. If you lack cold fermenting and lagering facilities, try the Düsseldorf yeast, but keep it as cool as you can.

ORIGINAL GRAVITY: 1.050–52

FINAL GRAVITY: 1.010–16

POTENTIAL ALCOHOL: 4.6–5.1% ABV

INGREDIENTS

$\frac{1}{4}$ **pound chocolate malt**

$\frac{1}{2}$ **pound dark German crystal malt**

$\frac{1}{4}$ **pound victory malt**

One 6.6 pound can Ireks light malt extract syrup

1 pound Dutch amber dry malt

4 ounces malto-dextrin

2 ounces Hallertau hops (boil)

1 ounce Tettnang hops (boil)

$\frac{1}{2}$ **teaspoon sodium chloride**

$\frac{1}{2}$ **ounce plug Saaz hops (finish)**

1 teaspoon Irish moss

Dry German lager yeast or Yeast Lab A06 German Düsseldorf yeast (requires starter)

$\frac{3}{4}$ **cup priming sugar**

BREWING PROCEDURES

1. Add 2 gallons of cold water to your pot; put

$\frac{1}{4}$ pound crushed chocolate malt, $\frac{1}{2}$ pound crushed German crystal malt, and $\frac{1}{4}$ pound crushed victory malt into your muslin bag and tie. Place bag in cold water and bring to a boil.

2. When water comes to a boil, remove from heat and let grains steep for 5 minutes. Remove grains and discard.

3. Return pot to heat and bring to a boil; add Ireks malt, 1 pound Dutch amber malt, 4 ounces malto-dextrin, 2 ounces Hallertau, 1 ounce Tettnang hops and $\frac{1}{2}$ teaspoon sodium chloride. Boil for 45 minutes. During the last 15 minutes of your boil, add $\frac{1}{2}$ ounce Saaz plug. Remove from heat and cool.

4. Add to your primary fermenter containing enough water to bring to $5\frac{1}{4}$ gallons.

5. Pitch prepared yeast when wort has cooled to between 65°F and 75°F. Proceed as usual. Finish fermenting.

6. Prime with $\frac{3}{4}$ cup corn sugar and bottle.

BAVARIAN OKTOBERFEST
🍺 🍺 🍺

STEPHEN SNYDER

Because this beer is bottle-conditioned, I did the lagering after it was packaged with no adverse effects. It reached its peak after about six months, becoming mellower, smoother, and clearer. I would recommend oxygen-absorbing bottle caps and a refrigerator where the temperature can be strictly controlled.

ORIGINAL GRAVITY: 1.060

FINAL GRAVITY: 1.014

POTENTIAL ALCOHOL: 6% ABV

INGREDIENTS

- 1 pound German light crystal malt (4 cups)
- ¼ pound Munich malt (1 cup)
- ¼ pound Vienna malt (1 cup)
- 1.5 kg BierKeller amber unhopped malt extract syrup (3.3 pounds)
- 4 pounds Dutch light spray malt
- 1 ounce Northern Brewer whole hops 7.7% AA (bittering) 90 minutes
- 1 ounce Northern Brewer whole hops 7.7% AA (bittering) 60 minutes
- 1 ounce Hallertauer plug 2.9% AA (flavor) 15 minutes
- 1 ounce Hallertauer plug (aroma) 2 minutes
- 2 packages Wyeast Bavarian lager yeast (or 1 package with starter)
- ½ cup corn sugar for priming

BREWING PROCEDURES

1. Add cracked crystal, Vienna, and Munich to ½ gallon of cold tap water in large pot. Bring slowly to 155°F, steep 30 minutes, then sparge grains and add wort to brew kettle. Add 2 gallons of water.
2. Bring to boil. Remove brew kettle from heat before adding malt extract and DME to avoid sticking or burning.
3. Boil for a total of 1½ hours, adding hops as noted above. Remove from heat at 1½ hours and let sit covered in a sink or tub of ice-cold water for ½ hour.
4. Rack wort through sanitized strainer into primary fermenter containing 3.5 gallons ice-cold water—filtering trub through hops. Wort should now be cool enough to pitch yeast immediately.
5. Pitch yeast at 75°F, then cool to 45–58°F after fermentation activity begins. Ferment 10–14 days in primary, 10–14 days in secondary.
6. Bottle with corn sugar dissolved in 1 pint boiling water. Leave at fermentation temperature for 1–2 weeks, then cold-lager (at 32–35°F) 6–8 weeks or up to 6 months.

MÄRZEN

🍺 🍺 🍺

DICK FOEHRINGER

THE BREWMEISTER–FAIR OAKS, CALIFORNIA

"Our Märzen is a German Oktoberfest-style lager that has a rich amber-red color with mild, sweet malt character. The aroma is assertively malty, but appropriately balanced with the spiciness of the plentiful Hallertauer and Saaz hops."

ORIGINAL GRAVITY: 1.053

FINAL GRAVITY: 1.014

POTENTIAL ALCOHOL: 5% ABV

INGREDIENTS

- ½ pound 60 °L crystal malt
- ¼ pound CaraPils malt
- ¼ pound chocolate malt
- 7 pounds amber malt extract
- 1 ounce Hallertauer hops (60 minutes) boiling
- 1 ounce Hallertauer hops (30 minutes) boiling
- 2 ounce Saaz hops (5 minutes) aromatic
- 1 teaspoon Irish moss
- 1 dry lager yeast
- 1 teaspoon gelatin
- ¾ cup bottling sugar

BREWING PROCEDURES

1. Put the crushed crystal malt, dextrine malt, and chocolate malt grains into a grain bag. Place 1½ to 2 gallons of cold water in your brewpot. Place grain bag in water and bring to a near boil (160–170°F). Turn off heat and allow grain to steep for 30 minutes. Remove grain.

2. Dissolve liquid extract thoroughly and then return mixture to heat. Bring to a boil. Add the first addition of the Hallertauer boiling hops and boil for 30 minutes. Add the second addition and boil for 15 minutes. Add Irish moss and boil for 10 minutes. Add the aromatic hops and boil 5 minutes.

3. Cold-break the wort to below 100°F. Put the cooled wort into your primary fermenter and add cold water to make 5½ gallons. When cooled below 85°F, pitch your yeast. Note: You should rehydrate the yeast by dissolving the packet in ½ cup warm water. Let it stand for 15 minutes, stir, and add to the wort.

4. Ferment in a cool (45–65°F), dark place. When fermentation has ceased, transfer to the secondary, leaving all the sediment behind.

5. Dissolve gelatin in 1 cup hot water and stir into secondary. Allow beer to clear, typically 3–5 days. Rack again, leaving sediment behind and stir in dissolved bottling sugar.

6. Dissolve the bottling sugar in 1 cup hot water and thoroughly stir into cleared beer. Bottle and cap.

7. Allow to age/carbonate in the bottles for 2–4 weeks. Enjoy!

ALTSTADT MÄRZEN

STEPHEN SNYDER

Malty, ruddy, and slightly sweet, this double-decoction recipe for the traditional style of Märzen is rapidly disappearing from Munich's Oktoberfest. Although this can be ready to drink after 6–8 weeks of lagering and 2 to 4 weeks conditioning, tradition dictates that it be stored from March to late September to wear the sobriquet "Märzen."

ORIGINAL GRAVITY: 1058

FINAL GRAVITY: 1.015

POTENTIAL ALCOHOL: 5.6% ABV

IBUs: 25

INGREDIENTS (FOR 5.5 GALLONS)

> 6 pounds Munich malt (crushed)
>
> 6 pounds 2-row pilsner malt (crushed)
>
> 0.5 pound German dark crystal malt (crushed)
>
> 2.5 ounces Hersbrucker hop plugs at 3% AA (boil 60 minutes)
>
> Wyeast 2206 Bavarian Lager yeast in a 1 liter starter
>
> 1.5–1.75 quarts of unfermented wort or 0.75 cup corn sugar for priming

BREWING PROCEDURES

1. Mash in at 122°F with 4 gallons of brewing liquor (see Munich water profile) for proper adjustment.

2. Maintain protein rest 15 minutes before pulling first decoction.

3. Pull first decoction of the thickest one-third of the mash.

4. Ladle into second kettle and raise heat 2°F per minute to 155°F.

5. Hold saccharification rest for 15 minutes.

6. Bring to a boil over 10–15 minutes and boil for 20 minutes.

7. Recombine decocted portion slowly into pot with main mash over 10–15 minutes, while stirring.

8. The main mash should now be around 147°F. Adjust with bottom heat if necessary.

9. Immediately pull a second decoction and perform exactly as in the first.

10. Recombine with main rest mash. If necessary, raise temperature with bottom heat to 155°F.

11. Hold for 10–30 minutes or until iodine test is negative.

12. Mash out. Raise to 165–168°F. Rest 5–10 minutes to decrease viscosity.

13. Transfer to lauter tun and sparge with 172° water.

14. Collect 6.5–7 gallons of wort.

15. Boil for 90 minutes, adding hops as noted above. Skim hot break for the first 30 minutes of the boil.

16. Force-cool with wort chiller.

17. Rack through sanitized sieve or strainer bag into carboy or other fermenter to remove hops and trub.

18. Pitch 1 liter yeast starter. Aerate well.

19. (Optional step): Rest beer for 2–24 hours to settle trub, then rack to primary.

20. Rack into primary fermenter and ferment under airlock at 48–58°F for 10 to 14 days.

21. Rack to secondary and lager under airlock for 6 to 26 weeks at 31–35°F.

22. Rack to bottling bucket, prime, add fresh yeast, and bottle or keg.

23. Condition at 48–58°F for 10–14 days.

24. Mature for 3 to 4 weeks at 32–40°.

25. Serve at 45–50°F.

BAVARIAN DARK

Bavarian dark is an umbrella for many more distinct regional styles such as the chocolaty, coffee-ish schwarzbier and the soft, malty Münchner dunkel (pronounced "doonk'l").

Munich's water profile proved a perfect match for the dark malts in use in Bavaria; and with the isolation of lager yeast strains and the development of refrigeration technology in the mid-1800s, Munich's brewers were able to create the benchmark of dark lagers. Traditional recipes start with light European two-row lager malts, pilsner malts, or very light extracts, then add roasted malts such as Vienna, Munich, and black prinz for color. The darker malts used require some degree of temporary hardness in the brewing liquor. A smooth, malty, and slightly fruity yeast strain is good for the Munich version; a Danish or other clean lager yeast can be substituted for the other Bavarian darks, with Bavarian hops or their derivatives to provide bitterness (20–30 IBUs), flavor, and aroma. Dunkels should not be black, but a deep, garnet brown.

There are regrettably few imports in the schwarzbier/dunkel categories, but such standouts as Köstritzer Schwarzbier and Ayinger Altbairisch Dunkel are available. Notable microbrews to compare your version to include Franken-muth German Style Dark and Schwarz Hacker. If you are ever in Germany, be sure to try Spaten Dunkel on draft.

BAVARIAN DARK BASICS

ORIGINAL GRAVITY: 1.044–54

FINAL GRAVITY: 1.012–18

IBUs: 20–30

COLOR (SRM): 14–30

ALCOHOL BY VOLUME: 3.8–6%

MUNICH DUNKEL

DICK FOEHRINGER

THE BREWMEISTER–FAIR OAKS,
    CALIFORNIA

"Our Munich dunkel has a distinctively roasted and chocolate character complemented by malty sweetness and low hop bitterness. A truly great German dark lager!"

ORIGINAL GRAVITY: 1.061

FINAL GRAVITY: 1.015

POTENTIAL ALCOHOL: 6.2% ABV

INGREDIENTS

> $\frac{1}{2}$ pound 60 °L crystal malt
>
> $\frac{1}{2}$ pound chocolate malt
>
> 8 pounds pale malt extract syrup
>
> $1\frac{1}{2}$ ounces Tettnanger hops (60 minutes) boiling
>
> $\frac{1}{2}$ ounce Tettnanger hops (5 minutes) aromatic
>
> 1 teaspoon Irish moss (15 minutes)
>
> Wyeast 2308 Munich Lager yeast
>
> 1 teaspoon gelatin
>
> $\frac{3}{4}$ cup bottling sugar

BREWING PROCEDURES

1. Put the crushed crystal and chocolate malts into a grain bag. Place bag and $1\frac{1}{2}$ to $2\frac{1}{2}$ gallons of cold water in your brewpot. Bring to a near boil (160–170°F). Shut off heat and steep the grain for 30 minutes. Remove grains.

2. Stir in extract and thoroughly dissolve. Return to heat. Bring to a boil. Add the first addition of the Tettnanger boiling hops and boil for 45 minutes. Add the Irish moss and boil for 10 minutes. Add the second addition of Tettnanger hops (aromatic) and boil for 5 minutes.

3. Cold-break by placing the pan into a sink full of cold water. When wort is below 100°F, strain the wort into your primary fermenter. Add enough cold water to make $5\frac{1}{2}$ gallons.

4. When wort is cool (below 85°F), pitch your yeast. (Note: You must start your liquid yeast 1–2 days prior to brewing. Follow the instructions for yeast prep on the back of the foil bag.)

5. Ferment in a cool (45–65°F), dark place. When fermentation is complete, rack into secondary, leaving all sediment behind.

6. Prepare gelatin by dissolving in 1 cup hot water and stir into secondary. When clear (3–5 days), rack again, leaving sediment

behind. Prepare bottling sugar by dissolving in 1 cup hot water.

7. Stir dissolved bottling sugar into clear beer.

8. Bottle and cap. Allow to age/carbonate in the bottles for 2–4 weeks.

BAHNHOFF DUNKEL
⫼ ⫼ ⫼

STEPHEN SNYDER

This dunkel is strictly Reinheitsgebot and features an authentic Münchener flavor, but the use of DME as a primer requires a little extra effort. It should be boiled in a quart of water with a couple of pellet hops in order to cause a hot break. Skim the break off as well as possible, then chill it down and pour through a filter bag or strainer into your bottling bucket to remove the hop residue and as much cold break as you can.

> ORIGINAL GRAVITY: 1.058
>
> FINAL GRAVITY: 1.012
>
> POTENTIAL ALCOHOL: 5.5%ABV

INGREDIENTS

- ½ cup chocolate malt
- 2 cups German light crystal malt
- 3.3 pounds BierKeller Dark unhopped malt extract syrup
- 4 pounds Dutch extra light DME
- ½ ounce Northern Brewer whole hops at 7.7% AA 90 minutes (boil)
- ½ ounce Spalter pellets at 4.5% AA 60 minutes (boil)
- ½ ounce Hallertauer whole hops at 4% AA 15 minutes (flavor)
- ½ ounce Spalter pellets at 4.5% AA 10 minutes (flavor)
- 1 ounce Hallertauer whole hops steeped 30 minutes (aroma)
- 1 package Wyeast 2308 Munich lager yeast with starter
- 1.2 cups light DME for priming

BREWING PROCEDURES

1. Crack and add grains to 2 quarts of cold tap water in large pot. Bring almost to boil, then steep 20 minutes before sparging grains as wort is poured into brew kettle.

2. Add 3 gallons cold water. Bring to boil. Remove brew kettle from heat before adding extract and DME to avoid sticking or burning.

3. Boil for a total of 2 hours, adding hops as noted above.

4. Let covered brew kettle sit in ice-water bath 30 minutes.

5. Rack wort into primary fermenter containing 2 gallons ice-cold water.

6. Pitch yeast at 75°F. After fermentation activity becomes evident, cool to 48–58°F and ferment 10–14 days in primary, 10–14 days in secondary.

7. Bottle with light DME, leave at fermentation temperature 7 days, then cold-lager 6–8 weeks at 32–35°F.

CONTINENTAL DARK LAGER
⫼ ⫼ ⫼ ⫼ ⫼

TONY LUBOLD, HEAD BREWER, CATAMOUNT BREWING CO.—WHITE RIVER JUNCTION, VERMONT

This all-grain recipe utilizes the tried-and-true decoction method for producing that elusive maltiness mandatory in this classic beer style.

The flavor will be full and malty, but clean and not at all heavy or cloying—an easy beer to fall in love with.

ORIGINAL GRAVITY: 1.046

FINAL GRAVITY: 1.012

POTENTIAL ALCOHOL: 4.4% ABV

INGREDIENTS

> 8 pounds English lager malt
> ½ pound English crystal malt
> 1 ounce English chocolate malt
> 1½ ounces Saaz pellets (60 minutes)
> ½ ounce Styrian Goldings pellets (15 minutes)
> ½ ounce Hallertau pellets (in primary fermenter)
> Irish moss (20 minutes)
> 2 packages dried lager yeast
> ¾ cup corn sugar

BREWING PROCEDURES

1. Mix 6½ pounds lager malt with 8 quarts of 140°F water and rest for 20–25 minutes (temperature should be about 125°F).
2. Mix all other malt in 1½ quarts of 150°F water to make a thick mash, then bring to a boil, stirring constantly. Add this hot mash to the main mash.
3. Remove 2 quarts of the main mash and bring to a boil. Return to the main mash and hold 1 hour.
4. Raise the temperature of the whole mash to 170°F.
5. Sparge with 10 quarts of water. Boil 1 hour, adding hops and Irish moss as noted above.
6. Pitch yeast and ferment for 12 days at 45–50°F.
7. Transfer to the carboy to age for 7 days.

8. Bottle as usual with ¾ cup corn sugar. Place in a room-temperature area for 1 week.
9. Remove to a cooler location to mature for at least 5 more weeks.

GRUNWALD DUNKEL

STEPHEN SNYDER

This all-grain recipe shows how simple the ingredients are for this much neglected beer style. The decoction mashing is where the trouble comes in but is not nearly as hard as people think. After you've done it once you'll swear by it for the increased extraction rates and the malt flavor that is very hard to produce in a step mash.

ORIGINAL GRAVITY: 1.049

FINAL GRAVITY: 1.012

POTENTIAL ALCOHOL: 4.6% ABV

IBUs: 25

INGREDIENTS (FOR 5.5 GALLONS)

> 6 pounds Munich malt (crushed)
> 4 pounds 2-row pilsner malt (crushed)
> 0.5 pound German dark crystal malt (crushed)
> 2.5 ounces Hersbrucker hop plugs at 3% AA (boil 60 minutes)
> Wyeast 2308 Munich Lager yeast in a 1 liter starter
> 1.5–1.75 quarts of unfermented wort or 0.75 cup corn sugar for priming

BREWING PROCEDURES

1. Mash in at 122°F with 3.5 gallons of brewing liquor (see Munich water profile) for proper adjustment.

2. Maintain protein rest 15 minutes before pulling first decoction.

3. Pull first decoction of the thickest 40% of the mash.

4. Ladle into second kettle and raise heat 2°F per minute to 150°F.

5. Hold saccharification rest for 15 minutes.

6. Bring to a boil over 10–15 minutes and boil for 20 minutes.

7. Recombine decocted portion slowly into pot with main mash over 10–15 minutes, while stirring.

8. The main mash should now be around 147°F. Adjust with bottom heat if necessary.

9. Immediately pull a second decoction and perform exactly as in the first.

10. Recombine with main rest mash. If necessary, raise temperature with bottom heat to 150°F.

11. Hold for 30 minutes or until iodine test is negative.

12. Mash out. Raise to 165–168°F. Rest 5–10 minutes to decrease viscosity.

13. Transfer to lauter tun and sparge with 172° water.

14. Collect 6.5–7 gallons of wort.

15. Boil for 90 minutes, adding hops as noted above. Skim hot break throughout boil.

16. Force-cool with wort chiller.

17. Rack through sanitized sieve or strainer bag into carboy or other fermenter to remove hops and trub.

18. Pitch 1 liter yeast starter. Aerate well.

19. (Optional step:) Rest beer for 2–24 hours to settle trub, then rack to primary.

20. Rack into primary fermenter and ferment under airlock at 45–52°F for 10–14 days.

21. Rack to secondary and lager under airlock for 6 weeks at 31–35°F.

22. Rack to bottling bucket, prime, add fresh yeast, and bottle or keg.

23. Condition at 48–58°F for 10–14 days.

24. Mature for 3 to 4 weeks at 32–40°.

25. Serve at 45–50°F.

BOCK

Traditionally brewed in winter for spring consumption, bock beer's history is shrouded in myth. Many believe that bock derives its name from its city of origin, Einbeck, Germany. Others believe that bock takes its name directly from the German word for male goat because it is often brewed under the sign of Capricorn. In any event, Munich malt, with small portions of roasted and crystal malt, should dominate the recipe to provide a sweet, malty character. Hop bitterness, flavor, and aroma should be kept low but evident, and "noble" or Hallertau hybrids are preferred, as are long, cold ferments to keep diacetyl and esters low. Some bicarbonate hardness is desirable to counteract the acidity of the dark malts. Deep copper to dark brown in color, alcoholically strong (6%+ ABV), and very malty in flavor, bocks taste best when cold-lagered several months. When low on homebrew, look for the renowned German originals such as Einbecker Ur Bock and the acclaimed (and easier to find)

American versions, such as Frankenmuth German Style Bock, Catamount Bock, or Otter Creek Brewing's Mud Bock (a very convincing bock fermented with ale yeast).

BOCK BASICS

ORIGINAL GRAVITY: 1.064–72

FINAL GRAVITY: 1.018–24

IBUs: 20–25

COLOR (SRM): 9.5–22

ALCOHOL BY VOLUME: 6.6–7.5%

OLD BILLY'S BEARD
⊞ ⊞ ⊞

THE CELLAR HOMEBREW—SEATTLE, WASHINGTON

"Get your malt here! A generous sweetness dominates this German lager, hailing originally from Einbeck. A bock's malt flavor is not disguised by hops or roasted grains as it is in most stouts and other hefty brews. Some say it was brewed under Capricorn, the sign of the billy goat (or 'bock' in German). We say brew it anytime."

ORIGINAL GRAVITY: 1.063

FINAL GRAVITY: 1.016

POTENTIAL ALCOHOL: 6.3% ABV

INGREDIENTS (FOR 5.5 GALLONS)

$\frac{1}{2}$ **pound English crystal malt (crushed)**

$\frac{1}{4}$ **pound chocolate malt (crushed)**

6 pounds British light bulk malt syrup

3.3 pound can English light malt syrup

3 ounces Tettnang hops (boiling)

1 ounce Tettnang hops (finishing)

2 packages dry lager yeast or Bavarian Lager liquid yeast

$\frac{3}{4}$ **cup corn sugar for priming**

BREWING PROCEDURES

Note: If you are using the Bavarian Lager liquid yeast with this recipe, be sure to start that yeast at least 1 to 3 days before doing any of the brewing steps below. Follow the package directions and use the yeast in step 5.

1. Place the crushed English crystal and chocolate malts in a strainer bag. Add this bag of grain to your brewing kettle, which contains 2 to 2½ gallons brewing water. Bring the brewing water to a boil, then remove the bag of grains. It is not a good idea to boil these specialty grains for any length of time, as they may contribute a bitter or grainy taste to the finished beer.

2. Sparge (rinse) the bag of grains with about 1 quart of hot tap water into the brewing kettle; dispose of the spent grains.

3. Remove the brewing kettle from the burner and add the 6 pounds of British light malt syrup and the 3.3-pound can of English light malt syrup. The syrup is easier to pour if the can has been previously placed in hot water. Also, rinse the can with hot water to ensure that all the syrup goes into the kettle. Stir the mixture, now called "wort," until it boils. Watch carefully at this time because the wort may boil over. You can prevent this by pouring a cup of cold water into the overboiling wort.

4. At boiling point, add the Tettnang boiling hops. Hops can be placed in a hop bag or added loose, to be later strained out after the boil using a strainer bag. Time the boil for about 1 hour, stirring occasionally. After the first 10 minutes of this boil, remove 2 cups of wort in measuring cup and cover with foil or plastic. Cool to 90°F for use in step 5.

5. Making the yeast starter: For dry yeast, use ½ cup warm tap water (90–100°F). Sprinkle the contents of yeast packet into that water, cover for at least 15 minutes, and then add to the 2 cups of wort you prepared in step 4. Cover and set aside for use in step 7 below. For liquid yeast, prepare 1 to 3 days ahead of brewing time per package instructions. Open the swollen package and add the contents to the 2 cups of wort as prepared in step 4.

6. After the wort has boiled for that 1 hour, add the Tettnang finishing hops. Place them in the hop bag, which has been emptied of the spent boiling hops, and place them in the boiling kettle or just add the finishing hops directly to the brewing kettle. They will be strained later in step 8.

7. Let the boil continue for 30 minutes. Remove the pot from the burner and let it cool, covered, for about 20 minutes.

8. Pour 3 gallons of cold water into the sanitized open fermenter fitted with strainer bag. If loose finishing hops were used in step 6, strain the warm wort from step 7 into the cold water. Top up the fermenter to 5½ gallons using cold tap water. Cover the fermenter and cool the wort as rapidly as possible.

9. When the wort has cooled to about 80°, add the yeast starter and ferment as you usually do.

AMERICAN BOCK

DICK FOEHRINGER

THE BREWMEISTER—FAIR OAKS, CALIFORNIA

The name says "American" but this simple recipe has all the right stuff for a Bavarian-style bock and is tailor-made for the extract brewer who wants to experience the joys of brewing this classic. The specialty malts and Bavarian hops bring a real authenticity to the brew. Lager this one as long as you can stand it. You will be greatly rewarded.

ORIGINAL GRAVITY: 1.062

FINAL GRAVITY: 1.018

POTENTIAL ALCOHOL: 5.9% ABV

INGREDIENTS

½ pound crystal malt

¼ pound black patent malt

¼ pound Munich malt

7 pounds amber malt extract

1 pound dark dry malt extract

1½ ounces Hallertauer hops (60 minutes) boiling

½ ounce Hallertauer hops (end of boil) aromatic

1 teaspoon Irish moss (15 minutes)

German dry lager yeast or Bavarian Lager liquid yeast

1 teaspoon gelatin

¾ cup bottling sugar

BREWING PROCEDURES

1. Put the crushed crystal, black malt, and Munich malt grains into a bag. Place 1½ to 2 gallons of cold water in your brewpot. Place grain bag in water and bring to a near boil (160°F). Turn off heat and allow grains

to steep for 30 minutes. Drain and remove grains.

2. Dissolve liquid extract thoroughly and then return mixture to heat. Bring to a boil. Add the 1½ ounce of hops and boil for 45 minutes. Add Irish moss and boil for 15 minutes. Add the end-of-boil aromatic hops, turn off heat, and steep for 15 minutes.

3. Cold-break the wort to below 100°F by setting your pan of wort into a sink full of cold water. Put the cooled wort into your primary fermenter and add cold water to make 5½ gallons. When cooled below 85°F, pitch your yeast. (Note: Rehydrate your yeast by dissolving it in warm water and allowing it to sit for 10 minutes before pitching.) Ferment in a cool (55–65°F), dark place.

4. When fermentation has ceased, transfer to the secondary, leaving all the sediment behind. Dissolve gelatin in 1 cup hot water and stir into secondary. Replace airlock and allow beer to clear, typically 3–5 days.

5. Rack again, leaving sediment behind. Dissolve bottling sugar in 1 cup of hot water and stir into beer. Bottle and cap.

6. Allow to age/carbonate in the bottles for 2–4 weeks. Enjoy!

BIG BAD BOCK

⫼ ⫼

THE VINEYARD—UPTON, MASSACHUSETTS
Much of the secret to a good bock is patience. Give this robust brew time to mature, and its flavors will blend and evolve into a complex mix of fruitiness, roast, and malt with the hops elusively in the background. Good lager yeast

strains with starters are also recommended for ensuring a strong, healthy ferment.

ORIGINAL GRAVITY: 1.066–70

FINAL GRAVITY: 1.016–20

POTENTIAL ALCOHOL: 6.6% ABV

INGREDIENTS

   ½ **pound dextrine malt**
   ½ **pound chocolate malt**
   ½ **pound toasted malt**
   6.6 pounds Premier pale malt extract
   2 pounds amber dry malt extract
   1 ounce Nugget hop pellets (boiling)
   ½ **ounce U.S. Hallertau (boiling)**
   ½ **ounce U.S. Hallertau (last 15 minutes)**
   1 teaspoon Irish moss (last 15 minutes)
   1 packet Vierka lager yeast
   ½ **cup corn sugar for priming**

BREWING PROCEDURES

1. Crush and put all grains into 1½ quarts cold water for 10 minutes. Slowly bring to a boil. Once boiling commences remove from heat. Strain liquid into boiling pot.

2. Add 1½ gallons water, malt extract, dry malt, and bring to a boil. At start of boil, add Nugget hop pellets and ½ ounce U.S. Hallertau pellets. Last 15 minutes of boil time add ½ ounce U.S. Hallertau pellets and Irish moss.

3. Strain into sanitized primary fermenter and add cold water to make 5 gallons. Let cool. Pitch yeast when temperature drops below 80°F. Primary fermentation: 8 days at 55–60°F. Secondary fermentation: 10 days at 55–60°F, slowly raising temperature to 65°F. Lager in bulk when fermentation is complete, as cold as 32°F for at least 1 week.

4. At bottling time, boil 1 cup water with ½ cup priming sugar for bulk priming.

BOCK TO THE BASICS
▥ ▥ ▥

WIND RIVER BREWING COMPANY—EDEN PRAIRIE, MINNESOTA

This recipe doles out the kettle hops in three "gifts," as the German brewmeisters say. The dry-hopping, which is only occasionally used in Bavaria, is a nice touch, providing a delicate hop bouquet amidst the roasted malt aroma.

ORIGINAL GRAVITY: 1.074

FINAL GRAVITY: 1.019

POTENTIAL ALCOHOL: 7.3% ABV

INGREDIENTS

⅛ pound toasted barley

1/16 pound chocolate malt

½ pound dextrine malt

½ pound 40 °L caramel malt

6 pounds dark malt extract syrup

4 pounds amber malt extract syrup

½ ounce each, Tettnang/Mt. Hood hops— 90 minutes

½ ounce each, Tettnang/Mt. Hood hops— 60 minutes

½ ounce each, Tettnang/Mt. Hood hops— 30 minutes

1 ounce each, Tettnang/Mt. Hood hops for dry-hopping (4 days in secondary)

Wyeast Bavarian Lager liquid yeast

1½ cups DME for priming

BREWING PROCEDURES

1. Steep cracked grains in 150–160°F water (5½ gallons) for 30 minutes.

2. Remove grain; add and dissolve liquid malt extract. Slowly bring to boil. At 90 minutes add hops. At 60 minutes add hops. At 30 minutes add hops.

3. Finish the boil. Use wort chiller. When wort is below 75°F, transfer to carboy and pitch the yeast.

4. Allow primary to continue for 10–14 days at 40°–45°F. Transfer into secondary for 6–8 weeks.

5. At fourth week add your dry hops for 4 days and then remove.

6. At kegging/bottling add 1½ cups dry malt extract that has been boiled in 3 cups of water for at least 10 minutes.

7. Bottle/keg condition for 7 days, then chill and drink. Enjoy!

GENTHNER BOCK
▥ ▥ ▥

RIC GENTHNER

WINE BARREL PLUS—LIVONIA, MICHIGAN

This is one of Wine Barrel Plus's favorite and most popular recipes. It follows a simple formulation of using Bavarian hops and what the Germans call "farbesmalz" to provide color and roast malt character. The use of malt extract instead of sugar to prime adds to the authenticity and encourages a dense, creamy head and mellow maltiness if allowed to slowly mature.

ORIGINAL GRAVITY: 1.066–70

FINAL GRAVITY: 1.014–20

POTENTIAL ALCOHOL: 6.6% ABV

INGREDIENTS

- ½ pound chocolate malt
- 1 pound CaraMunich malt
- 8 pounds amber plain malt extract
- 2 ounces German Hallertauer hops (boiling)
- 2 ounces Tettnang whole hops (dry-hopping)
- 1 teaspoon Irish moss
- 1 Wyeast Bavarian Lager liquid yeast
- 1¼ cup amber dry malt extract (for bottling)

BREWING PROCEDURES

1. Add the chocolate malt and the CaraMunich malt to 1½ gallons of water, bring to 158°, and hold for 60 minutes. Bring the grain to a boil. Remove the grain when the boiling starts.
2. Add the malt extract and the Hallertauer hops and boil for 60 minutes.
3. Add Irish moss to the boil for the last 15–20 minutes.
4. Pour immediately into primary fermenter with cold water and top up to 5 gallons.
5. Add yeast when cool.
6. After initial fermentation, rack into secondary and add 2 ounces of Tettnang hops.
7. Lager at 31°.
8. Bottle with 1¼ cup of malt when fermentation is complete.

PIRATES BREW BOCK
🍺 🍺 🍺

JAY GARRISON, HEAD BREWER, PIRATE BREWERY

BREWBUDDYS—REDONDO BEACH, CALIFORNIA

"A heavy-bodied and dark beer perfect for early spring enjoyment. If lagered and allowed to age, the slight bitterness that initially exists disappears, leaving a very smooth and mellow-drinking beer that will complement any meal."

ORIGINAL GRAVITY: 1.073

FINAL GRAVITY: 1.018

POTENTIAL ALCOHOL: 7.3% ABV

INGREDIENTS

- 8 ounces Klages malt (toasted)
- 6 ounces 80 °L crystal malt
- 5 ounces chocolate malt
- 7.5 pounds dark liquid extract
- 2 ounces Hallertau hops
- 1 ounce Mt. Hood hops
- Wyeast 2206 Bavarian, 2308 Munich, 2124 Bohemian Lager, or dry lager yeast
- ¾ cup corn sugar for priming

BREWING PROCEDURES

1. If you selected the Wyeast liquid yeast, you must break the inner packet before you begin to brew. Allow 1 day for each month after the manufacture date printed on the front. If you're using the dry yeast that came with the Pirates Brew Kit, go ahead and get to it.
2. Prepare the grains. First, toast the pale malt in the oven for 20 minutes at 350°F, then crush them; if you did not get the other grains crushed at the shop, crush them with some sort of rolling pin. You can either mix the grains with 2 quarts of water and heat it until it starts to boil, or heat it to about 165°F and steep for about 15 minutes.
3. Strain the grains, collecting the liquid into your brewpot. Rinse the grains (sparge) with 2 quarts of hot (170–180°F) water.

4. Add the bag and can of extract and 1 gallon of water to the brewpot. (You might want to rest the bag of extract in hot water for a while to soften it up.) Bring the wort to a soft rolling boil.

5. Add the Hallertau hops to the wort and boil for 40 minutes. Stir occasionally.

6. Add half of the Mt. Hood hops to the wort and boil for 20 minutes. Stir occasionally.

7. Add the last half of the Mt. Hood hops to the wort and turn off the heat; stir and let sit (covered, if possible) for 10 minutes.

8. Add the boiled wort to your sanitized, rinsed fermenter. Add ice-cold water to make 5 gallons. When the temperature drops to 75°F or less, add the yeast.

9. If you use liquid yeast, open the swollen packet and add to the wort. If you use dry yeast, add the yeast to 1 cup of 90°F water for a few minutes before adding to the wort. (You can add the yeast directly to the wort and let it sit for a few minutes also, but rehydrating the yeast in warm water will improve the fermentation.) Stir the wort thoroughly with a sanitized spoon.

10. Put the lid on the fermenter tightly, insert the fermentation lock with the stopper into the hole in the lid, and fill it up about ¾ of the way with water or vodka. Let the wort ferment for a week at 55°F.

11. Transfer to a secondary fermenter and ferment another 2 weeks at 40°F. (Note: If you have no means to control the fermentation temperature, just ferment at room temperature for a week or two; you will still have a fine beer.)

12. When fermentation is complete, siphon the beer into a sanitized bottling bucket. Boil the corn sugar in about a cup of water; cool; stir gently into the beer. This provides the nutrients necessary for the yeast to carbonate the beer in the bottle.

13. Insert one end of the sanitized and rinsed hose into the bottling spigot and the other end to the bottle filler. Push the bottle filler down onto the bottom of the bottle and open the bottling spigot. Five gallons of beer will make about 2 cases, so make sure you sanitize this amount beforehand. Leave about ½–¾ inch of space at the top of the bottle. Cap the bottles.

14. Let the beer age for 2 weeks to 6 months. Chill and enjoy.

Mai/Helles Bock

These are full-flavored, but pale, bock beers. These lagers are brewed in the dead of winter and aged until May—hence the name. Helles bocks have a big, rich malt flavor balanced by Bavarian hops, but lack the dark roasted or crystal malts that deeply color the better-known styles of bock. The seasonal Mai bock of the Stoudt Brewing Company represents the rare American-made version of this German classic. Würzburger Hofbräu May Bok, Spaten Premium Bock, and Ayinger Maibock represent notable imports. If cold lagering is a problem, these can be homebrewed success-fully with a clean, mild ale yeast strain; however, it is recommended that these beers be aged a minimum of two months if using ale yeast and a minimum of three months if using lager yeast.

MAI BOCK BASICS

ORIGINAL GRAVITY: 1.064–72

FINAL GRAVITY: 1.012–20

IBUs: 20–35

COLOR (SRM): 4.5–6

ALCOHOL BY VOLUME: 6–7.5%

HELLES BOCK
🍺 🍺 🍺
BEER & WINE HOBBY—WOBURN, MASSACHUSETTS

Who would expect that such an intimidating beer style could be so easy? Use the ale yeast if you don't have the ability for a cold ferment or the patience to lager before trying this one. Just try to ferment as cool as possible. Keep your boil to 1 hour and you'll have a beer perfect in taste and color to please those certified beer judges out there.

ORIGINAL GRAVITY: 1.067

FINAL GRAVITY: 1.018

POTENTIAL ALCOHOL: 6.5% ABV

INGREDIENTS

½ pound light German crystal malt

¼ pound victory malt

2 cans of Australian light plain malt

2 pounds English light dry malt

2 ounces Hallertau hop pellets (boil)

1 ounce Saaz hop pellets (boil)

½ ounce Saaz plug (finish)

3-inch licorice stick

1 teaspoon Irish moss

½ teaspoon sodium chloride

Yeast Lab L32 Bavarian Lager yeast (requires starter) or Wyeast 1007 German Ale yeast

¾ cup priming sugar

Note: Prepare yeast starter 24 hours in advance.

BREWING PROCEDURES

1. Add 2 gallons of cold water to your pot, put ½ pound of crushed German crystal malt and ¼ pound crushed victory malt into muslin bag, and tie. Place bag in cold water and bring to a boil.

2. When water comes to a boil, remove from heat and let steep for 5 minutes. Remove grains and discard, return pot to heat, and bring to a boil.

3. Add 2 cans of light malt extract, 2 pounds of light dry malt, 2 ounces of Hallertau pellets, 1 ounce Saaz pellets, and 3-inch licorice stick. Boil for 45 minutes. During the last 15 minutes of your boil add ½ ounce Saaz plug, 1 teaspoon Irish moss, and ½ teaspoon of sodium chloride. Remove from heat and cool.

4. Add to your primary fermenter containing enough cold water to bring total volume to 5¼ gallons. Pitch prepared yeast when wort has cooled to between 65° and 75°F.

5. Finish fermenting, prime with ¾ cup corn sugar, and bottle.

HELLES BOCK
🍺 🍺 🍺
DANIEL SOBOTI JR.
U-BREW—MILLBURN, NEW JERSEY

"I used Yeast Lab L32 (Munich Lager) for this batch. It is supposed to ferment with a rich, clean flavor and leave a slight malty sweetness. It came out tasting very good and there was a nice residual sweetness."

ORIGINAL GRAVITY: 1.066

FINAL GRAVITY: 1.016

POTENTIAL ALCOHOL: 6.5% ABV

IBUs: 24

COLOR: 5.3 SRM

INGREDIENTS

- 1.25 pounds 10 °L crystal malt
- 11.5 pounds 2-row pilsner malt
- 1 ounce Hallertauer-German 5.0% AA boiled for 60 minutes
- 0.25 ounce Hallertauer-German 5.0% AA boiled for 2 minutes
- Yeast Lab L32 Munich Lager

BREWING PROCEDURES

1. Step-infusion used. Mash in at 120°F for 30 minutes.
2. Raise to 155°F until iodine test comes up negative (about 45 minutes).
3. Sparge, boil, force-cool, then pitch yeast from a starter. Ferment, prime, and bottle as usual.
4. Age beer 2 months; better after 4 months.

DOPPELBOCK

Originated in Bavaria in the form of Paulener's Salvator, these "double bocks" are required to be brewed at original specific gravities of 1.074 or above. Homebrewers should try to keep fruitiness and diacetyl as low as possible, with the malty sweetness from high final gravities dominating hop bitterness, flavor, and aroma. Although lighter, copper-colored examples do exist, dark brown is the most common color. Munich malt and dark German crystal malt are traditional ingredients, as well as the obligatory German hops. Not for the impatient brewer, these beers will need at least three months of lagering at close to 32°F to achieve their true potential. Besides Salvator, Spaten's Optimator is a good, widely available import as is Celebrator Doppelbock. Samuel Adams Double Bock represents the rare American-made version that is widely distributed.

DOPPELBOCK BASICS

ORIGINAL GRAVITY: 1.072–80

FINAL GRAVITY: 1.020–28

IBUs: 17–27

COLOR (SRM): 12–30

ALCOHOL BY VOLUME: 6.5–8%

BAVARIAN DOPPELBOCK

THE HOME BREWERY—OZARK, MISSOURI

This extract recipe will help ease the neophyte into lager brewing and more specifically, into the wonderful world of Bavarian bocks. You continue to build on your brewing skills by using this recipe and adding fresh yeasts, specialty grains, and extended lagering. The possibilities are endless. Be forewarned, it will be hard to go back to brewing simple pale ales after this.

ORIGINAL GRAVITY: 1.075

FINAL GRAVITY: 1.019

POTENTIAL ALCOHOL: 7.4% ABV

INGREDIENTS

- 3.3 pounds (1 pack) Home Brewery hopped dark malt extract
- 3.3 pounds (1 pack) Home Brewery hopped amber malt extract
- 3.3 pounds (1 pack) Yellow Dog malt extract
- 1 ounce Hallertauer hop pellets (bittering)
- ½ teaspoon Irish moss added 15 minutes before the end of the boil
- No finishing hops
- 2 packs European Lager yeast
- ¾ cup corn sugar for priming

BREWING PROCEDURES

1. Heat 5 gallons of water in a large kettle. Many people don't have a kettle that large, but heat as much as you can (at least 2 gallons). When the water is boiling, turn off the heat and add the malt extract to the water. Use a spoon and stir until you are sure no malt extract is sticking to the bottom of the kettle. Then turn the heat back on.

2. Bring the kettle back to a boil and stir occasionally so the ingredients won't burn on the bottom of the kettle. If your recipe calls for bittering hops, now is the time to add them and stir them in. Watch out for a boilover. In the early part of the boil, the kettle usually tries to boil over once or twice, so control this by adjusting the heat. Later in the boil, the surface tension changes and boiling over is not a problem. Keep stirring occasionally and let the beer (wort) boil hard for 1 hour. Stir in the ½ teaspoon of Irish moss in your recipe about 15 minutes before the end of the boil.

3. If finishing hops are called for in your recipe, stir them in 2 minutes before the end of the boil. Using finishing hops at the end of the boil adds a fresh aroma and flavor to the beer, and the use of finishing hops is appropriate in most beer styles.

4. Pour the hot beer (wort) into the primary fermenter. It is not necessary to strain the wort if you used hop pellets. Add cold water to bring the total volume up to 5 gallons. If you are using our fermenter (the one in the kits), the 5-gallon mark is the bottom ring. Cover the fermenter and wait until the temperature is down to 75°F. If you have a wort chiller, use it to bring the temperature down quickly. At 75° or less, add the yeast in your recipe. Just tear open the pack(s) and sprinkle it on the wort. Close the fermenter with the lid, stopper, and airlock. Remember to put water (or vodka) in the airlock. Vodka evaporates more quickly, but bacteria won't live in it.

5. Fermentation should start within 24 hours, and may continue for between 1 day and 2

weeks, depending on the type of yeast, the recipe, and the temperature. (Ideally, this beer should ferment at 42°F.) Leave the beer alone and don't open the lid. When the airlock has not bubbled for several days and the beer is flat, still, and clearing, it is ready to bottle.

6. To bottle, siphon about 1 pint of beer into a pan and warm it on the stove. Add exactly ¾ cup of corn sugar to the pan and stir until it is dissolved. Pour this back into the beer and stir gently but well to distribute the sugar. Siphon or tap into clean sanitized bottles and cap. Keep the bottles at room temperature. After a week, put a bottle in the refrigerator and try it. It will be best in about 3 weeks.

Note: This beer should be aged at least 3 months before drinking.

GUTENACHT DOPPELBOCK
🍺 🍺 🍺

JIM WILLENBECHER

CROSSFIRE BREWING SUPPLY—BROAD BROOK, CONNECTICUT

"Gutenacht is a duplication of a famous Bavarian monastery's bock. This double bock is very dark, very high in alcohol, and is brewed in accordance with the Reinheitsgebot. It is an excellent example of a German Christmas bock."

ORIGINAL GRAVITY: 1.086–96

FINAL GRAVITY: 1.019–23

POTENTIAL ALCOHOL: 9.8% ABV

IBUs: 28

INGREDIENTS

1 pound dark German crystal malt

8 ounces chocolate malt

13.2 pounds amber German malt extract

10 ounces wheat malt syrup

½ ounce German blend* at 75 minutes

¼ ounce German blend at 25 minutes

¼ ounce German blend at 23 minutes

¼ ounce German blend at 21 minutes

¼ ounce German blend at 20 minutes

¼ ounce German blend at 19 minutes

¼ ounce German blend at 17 minutes

¼ ounce German blend at 15 minutes

¼ ounce German blend at 13 minutes

¼ ounce German blend at 11 minutes

⅛ ounce German blend at 7 minutes

⅛ ounce German blend at 4 minutes

⅛ ounce German blend at 1 minute

1 pack German lager yeast, 1 pack Champagne yeast

⅞ cup light dry malt for priming

German blend: Equal parts Hallertau, Tettnang, Saaz, Northern Brewer, Styrian Goldings, and Gold. All imported pellets (whole flowers will get in your way).

GRAIN PREPARATION

1. Crush grain fresh. Never buy already crushed grain; it will be stale.
2. Add 1 gallon of water.
3. Add 1 teaspoon gypsum.
4. Bring to 175°F and stir.
5. Stir well, let settle.
6. Draw off liquid, siphon.
7. Rinse with 175°F water.

BREWING PROCEDURES

1. Boil for 30 minutes before starting timer shown in ingredients.
2. When last hops are in boil, cool very rapidly

by adding cold water and placing brewpot in tub of ice water. Transfer to sterile fermenter. Do not remove hop pellets. They will settle with yeast.

3. Make up fermenter volume to 4.5 U.S. gallons and aerate with a passion.

4. When cooled to 86°F to 94°F rehydrate both yeasts together in 1 quart of water at 93°F to 97°F. After 5 to 10 minutes pitch yeast.

5. After kräusen falls, boil 1 quart of water and add ½ ounce of German blend in thirds at 7, 4, and 1 minute. Cool and pour into beer. Do not strain.

6. Let ferment out (3 to 4 weeks).

7. At bottling add priming malt to 1 quart of boiling water. Add ½ ounce of German blend in thirds at 7, 4, and 1 minute. Cool and pour into bottling bucket through tea strainer to remove all traces of hop pellets. Transfer beer into bottling bucket and stir gently. Bottle immediately.

BREWER'S DOPPLEBOCK

⊞ ⊞ ⊞

NORTHEAST BREWERS SUPPLY—
PROVIDENCE, RHODE ISLAND

This brew is distinguished by a strong malt character that is required to support its hefty alcoholic content. The use of the American Lager yeast allows you to ferment at higher temperatures and still maintain a nice, clean profile.

ORIGINAL GRAVITY: 1.075

FINAL GRAVITY: 1.019

POTENTIAL ALCOHOL: 7.4% ABV

INGREDIENTS

1.5 pounds doppelbock grain mix— crushed (½ pound crystal malt, ½ pound pale malt, ½ pound chocolate malt)

6 pounds Dutch dark dry malt extract

2 pounds Dutch light dry malt extract

4 ounces Hallertau hop pellets (boiling, 16 HBUs)

1.5 ounces Hallertau whole hops (finishing, 6 HBUs)

½ teaspoon Irish moss

Wyeast 2035 American Lager yeast

1 sterile starter mix

¾ cup corn sugar for priming

BREWING PROCEDURES

1. Three days before you're ready to brew, take the liquid yeast out of the refrigerator and prepare according to instructions on the package. In about 24 hours, the foil pouch will expand. Prepare a yeast starter according to the instructions on page 11. Add the yeast from the expanded foil pouch. Cover the opening with tin foil and shake well to aerate the starter solution. You'll have a ton of yeast to pitch into your doppelbock in about a day and a half.

2. Add water to the largest (up to 5-gallon capacity) stainless-steel or enameled-steel pot you can find, leaving space for the malt (approx. ¾ gallon) and a couple of inches at the top for the boil. Put the grain mix into one of the boiling bags and drop it into the pot while the water is still cool. Apply heat. Remove the grains just before the water starts to boil.

3. When the water starts to boil, stir in the malt extract (to avoid scorching, turn off heat before adding malt—turn it back on after

malt is well mixed). Put the boiling hops (pellets) into the pot. When the water starts boiling again, set your timer for *25 minutes*.

4. After 25 minutes, add the Irish moss and set your timer for an additional *20 minutes*.

5. After you've boiled the wort for a total of 45 minutes, put the finishing hops into a hop boiling bag, drop them in, and boil for an additional *2 minutes*. Remove from heat.

6. Cool the wort. There are a couple of ways to do this. If you have a wort chiller, this process takes about 10 minutes. If you're boiling a small quantity of wort (1½ to 3 gallons) you can add it to cold water in your primary fermenter to make up 5 gallons. Whatever method you use, remember the time between the end of the boil and pitching the yeast is when your brew is most susceptible to contamination. Therefore, extra care is warranted during this time to protect the wort from exposure to undesirable microorganisms. Be sure to sanitize everything that comes into contact with your beer with boiling water, chlorine, or iodophor.

7. When the wort has been added to the primary fermenter and cooled to 70–80°F, add the yeast.

8. To reduce lag time, fermentation should be initiated at room temperature (65–70°F). When signs of fermentation are visible, move to a cooler place (preferably 50–55°F).

9. After about 2 weeks, rack to a secondary fermenter. Most of the yeast will be on the bottom, so be sure to suck some up into secondary fermenter.

10. After another week or two, measure the specific gravity. If it's between 1.024–1.030 and

holding steady, it's ready to bottle or keg. Cheers!

BOCK AND WHITE
▥ ▥ ▥

PAUL WHITE, HEAD BREWER, THE SEVEN BARREL BREWERY—WEST LEBANON, NEW HAMPSHIRE

In true craft-brewer fashion, brewmaster Paul White breaks from convention by adding a little wheat malt to this terrific doppelbock formulation. The end result is a very subtle dryness to balance the richness of the Ireks malt extract and a great head of foam atop your stein.

ORIGINAL GRAVITY: 1.076 (estimated)

FINAL GRAVITY: 1.020

POTENTIAL ALCOHOL: 7.6% ABV

INGREDIENTS

>   3 pounds 2-row pale malt
>   1 pound Munich malt
>   1 pound malted wheat
>   4 ounces chocolate malt
>   4 ounces crystal malt
>   4 ounces dextrine malt
>   6.6 pounds Ireks Munich light malt extract
>   10 AAUs of Northern Brewer whole flower hops
>   1 teaspoon Irish moss
>   1 ounce Hallertau whole flower hops
>   Munich Lager yeast
>   ¾ cup corn sugar for priming

BREWING PROCEDURES

1. Mash in 2 gallons of water at 152°F for 1½ hours.

2. Mash out and sparge with 2 gallons of water.

Add 6.6 pounds Ireks Munich light extract and bring to a boil. Add 10 AAUs of Northern Brewer flowers and boil for 45 minutes. Add 1 teaspoon Irish moss and 1 ounce Hallertau flowers; boil 15 minutes more.

3. Chill, bring volume up to 5 gallons, and pitch a Munich Lager yeast. Ferment as a lager.

4. Bottle with corn sugar and age 4 months or more.

   Brewer's Notes: "Original gravity was not recorded; final gravity was 1.020." The only other recorded notes were, "Wow! Great! Do it again!"

NORTH AMERICAN LAGERS

This designation once referred to the products of the giant breweries such as Bud, Coors, Stroh's, and Miller, especially in the beer-judging arena. However, the recipes listed here are more pre-Prohibition in character than the adjunct-heavy, mass-produced versions and are more in spirit the quality of craft-brewed varieties such as Anchor Steam, Brooklyn Lager, and Harpoon Lager.

CALIFORNIA COMMON BASICS

ORIGINAL GRAVITY: 1.040–55

FINAL GRAVITY: 1.012–18

IBUs: 30–45

COLOR (SRM): 8–17

ALCOHOL BY VOLUME: 3.6–5%

PRE-PROHIBITION AMERICAN PILSNER BASICS

ORIGINAL GRAVITY: 1.044–60

FINAL GRAVITY: 1.010–16

IBUs: 20–40

COLOR (SRM): 2–5

ALCOHOL BY VOLUME: 5–6%

AMERICAN BACKYARD DRY

🍺 🍺

E. C. KRAUS–INDEPENDENCE, MISSOURI

"A good quenching beer for the warm months ahead. Similar to the larger brewery beers. It is very light in both color and taste, and also has a clean, dry finish. The hops, while noticeable, are not predominant by any means. You may want to add some heading powder for additional foam retention."

ORIGINAL GRAVITY: 1.033–39

FINAL GRAVITY: 1.009–11

POTENTIAL ALCOHOL: 3–3.5% ABV

IBUs: 15–20

COLOR: 2–4 SRM/3–6 °L

INGREDIENTS

> 2.2 pounds extra pale hopped malt syrup
>
> 2.2 pounds plain rice syrup
>
> 1 pound light dried malt extract (2½ cups)
>
> ½ ounce Cascade pellet hops (30-minute boil time)
>
> 1 tablespoon Irish moss (15-minute boil time)
>
> 2 teaspoons organic yeast nutrient (end of boil)
>
> 2 teaspoons amylase enzyme (add to fermenter)
>
> 14 grams dry lager or Wyeast 2278 Czech Pils yeast
>
> 1 cup priming sugar (bottling time)

BREWING PROCEDURES

1. Start with 1½ to 2½ gallons of water. Add to that the malt syrup, rice syrup, and the dried malt and bring to a boil.

2. Once boiling, add the Cascade pelletized hops and boil for 30 minutes. During the last 5 minutes of boil, add the Irish moss. At the end of the boil, stir in the organic yeast nutrient.

3. Once the boiling is complete, transfer the wort to your fermenter and add water to equal 5 gallons. Make sure it has cooled below 80°F and add the yeast and the amylase enzyme.

4. Attach airlock to fermenter and allow to ferment for 7–10 days or until finished fermenting.

5. Bottle with priming sugar as normal and allow to condition for 3–5 weeks.

INDUSTRIAL LAGER

THE CELLAR HOMEBREW—SEATTLE, WASHINGTON

"A light American pilsner style that will satisfy drinkers of standard American fare and turn off the beer snob. This recipe has just a bit more body and flavor than the commercial American lagers, and remains a refreshing thirst quencher for those warm summer afternoons."

ORIGINAL GRAVITY: 1.032

FINAL GRAVITY: 1.008

POTENTIAL ALCOHOL: 3% ABV

INGREDIENTS (FOR 5.5 GALLONS)

> One 4-pound can Alexander's light malt syrup
>
> 1 pound dry rice extract
>
> 1 cup honey (optional)
>
> 1 ounce Hallertauer hops (boiling)
>
> 1 ounce Hallertauer hops (finishing)
>
> 1 package dry lager yeast or American Lager liquid yeast
>
> ¾ cup corn sugar for priming

BREWING PROCEDURES

Note: If you are using the American Lager liquid yeast with this recipe, be sure to start that yeast at least 1 to 3 days before doing any of the brewing steps below. Follow the package directions and use the yeast in step 4.

1. Pour 2½ gallons of water into your brew kettle and bring to a boil.

2. Remove the brewing kettle from the burner and add the 4-pound can of Alexander's light malt syrup, the 1 pound of dry rice extract, and the *optional* 1 cup of honey. The syrup is easier to pour if the can has been previously placed in hot water. Also, rinse the can with hot water to ensure that all the syrup goes into the kettle. Stir the mixture, now called "wort," until it boils. Watch care-

fully at this time because the wort may boil over. You can prevent this by pouring a cup of cold water into the overboiling wort.

3. At boiling point, add the Hallertauer boiling hops. Hops can be placed in a hop bag or added loose, to be later strained out after the boil using a strainer bag. Time the boil for about 1 hour, stirring occasionally. After the first 10 minutes of this boil, remove 2 cups of wort in measuring cup and cover with foil or plastic. Cool to 90°F for use in step 4.

4. Making the yeast starter: For dry yeast, use ½ cup warm tap water (90–100°F). Sprinkle the contents of yeast packet into that water, cover for at least 15 minutes, and then add to the 2 cups of wort you prepared in step 3. Cover and set aside for use in step 8 below. For liquid yeast, prepare 1 to 3 days ahead of brewing time per package instructions. Open the swollen package and add the contents to the 2 cups of wort as prepared in step 3.

5. After the wort has boiled for that 1 hour, add the Hallertauer finishing hops. Place them in the hop bag, which has been emptied of the spent boiling hops, and place them in the boiling kettle, or just add the finishing hops directly to the brewing kettle. They will be strained later in step 7.

6. Let the boil continue for 5 minutes. This gives the beer its hop aroma. Remove the pot from the burner and let it cool, covered, for about 20 minutes.

7. Pour 3 gallons of cold water into the sanitized open fermenter fitted with strainer bag. If loose finishing hops were used in step 5, strain the warm wort from step 6 into the cold water. Top up the fermenter to 5½ gallons using cold tap water. Cover the fermenter and cool the wort as rapidly as possible.

8. When the wort has cooled to about 80°F, add the yeast starter and ferment as you usually do.

AMERICAN LIGHT

THE HOME BREWERY—OZARK, MISSOURI
A lawn-mower beer extraordinaire can be found with this simple formulation. Make a batch or two in spring and save for summertime enjoyment. The Cascade hops give it a fruity, fresh aroma. Perfect for warm weather!

ORIGINAL GRAVITY: 1.032

FINAL GRAVITY: 1.008

POTENTIAL ALCOHOL: 3.1% ABV

INGREDIENTS

> 3.3 pounds (1 pack) Home Brewery hopped light malt extract
> 1.1 pounds (⅓ pack) Home Brewery unhopped light malt extract
> No bittering hops
> ½ teaspoon Irish moss added 15 minutes before the end of the boil
> ¾ ounce Cascade hop pellets (finishing)
> 1 pack European Lager yeast
> ¾ cup corn sugar for priming

BREWING PROCEDURES

1. Heat 5 gallons of water in a large kettle. Many people don't have a kettle that large, but heat as much as you can (at least 2 gallons). When the water is boiling, turn off the heat and add the malt extract to the water. Use a spoon and stir until you are sure no malt extract is sticking to the bottom of the kettle. Then turn the heat back on.

2. Bring the kettle back to a boil and stir occasionally so the ingredients won't burn on the bottom of the kettle. If your recipe calls for bittering hops, now is the time to add them and stir them in. Watch out for a boilover. In the early part of the boil, the kettle usually tries to boil over once or twice, so control this by adjusting the heat. Later in the boil, the surface tension changes and boiling over is not a problem. Keep stirring occasionally, and let the beer (wort) boil hard for 1 hour. Stir in the 1/2 teaspoon of Irish moss in your recipe about 15 minutes before the end of the boil.

3. If finishing hops are called for in your recipe, stir them in 2 minutes before the end of the boil. Using finishing hops at the end of the boil adds a fresh aroma and flavor to the beer, and the use of finishing hops is appropriate in most beer styles.

4. Pour the hot beer (wort) into the primary fermenter. It is not necessary to strain the wort if you used hop pellets. Add cold water to bring the total volume up to 5 gallons. If you are using our B3a Fermenter (the one in the kits), the 5-gallon mark is the bottom ring. Cover the fermenter and wait until the temperature is down to 75°F. If you have a wort chiller (C44), use it to bring the temperature down quickly. At 75° or less, add the yeast in your recipe. Just tear open the pack(s) and sprinkle it on the wort. Close the fermenter with the lid, stopper, and airlock. Remember to put water (or vodka) in the airlock. Vodka evaporates more quickly, but bacteria won't live in it.

5. Fermentation should start within 24 hours, and may continue for between 1 day and 2 weeks, depending on the type of yeast, the recipe, and the temperature. (Ideally, this beer should ferment at 42°F.) Leave the beer alone and don't open the lid. When the airlock has not bubbled for several days and the beer is flat, still, and clearing, it is ready to bottle.

6. To bottle, siphon about 1 pint of beer into a pan and warm it on the stove. Add exactly 3/4 cup of corn sugar to the pan and stir until it is dissolved. Pour this back into the beer and stir gently but well to distribute the sugar. Siphon or tap into clean sanitized bottles and cap. Keep the bottles at room temperature. After a week, put a bottle in the refrigerator and try it. It will be best in about 3 weeks.

AMERICAN PILSNER

TONY LUBOLD, HEAD BREWER, CATAMOUNT BREWING CO.—WHITE RIVER JUNCTION, VERMONT

This nearly forgotten style had almost vanished in the wake of the insipid megabrewery versions. Today, there is a major revival afoot spurred by homebrewed versions such as this. Like the pre-Prohibition brews, this one is robust, well hopped, and an excellent thirst quencher.

ORIGINAL GRAVITY: 1.055

FINAL GRAVITY: 1.007

POTENTIAL ALCOHOL: 6.1% ABV

INGREDIENTS

7 pounds English lager malt
2 pounds English light dried malt extract
1 1/2 ounces Cascade (60 minutes)
1 ounce Saaz (30 minutes)

1 teaspoon Irish moss (20 minutes)
2 packages dried lager yeast
¾ cup priming sugar

BREWING PROCEDURES

1. Dough in 7 pounds of lager malt in 4 quarts of water at 110°F by mixing with clean hands. Rest for 15 minutes.
2. Add 2 quarts of boiling water, stirring constantly. This should bring the temperature up to about 130°F.
3. Hold that temperature for 40 minutes (I had to apply some gentle heat on occasion, stirring constantly).
4. Add 2 more quarts of boiling water and raise the temperature to 155°F (I had to apply heat here also).
5. Hold 155°F for 50 minutes. Sparge with 10 quarts water.
6. Pitch yeast and ferment for 11 days at 40–45°F. Transfer to the carboy to age for 7 days, then bottle.
7. Add ¾ cup sugar to 1 pint of water and bring to a boil. Cool and add to the beer and bottle as usual.
8. Place the bottles in a room temperature area for 1 week, then remove to a cooler location to age for at least 5 weeks more.

AMERICAN AMBER LAGER

BOB FRANK

THE FLYING BARREL—FREDERICK, MARYLAND

It's hard to find a more straightforward and highly rewarding recipe for the first-time lager brewer. This malty, well-balanced beer is close enough to a Märzen in strength and authenticity to save for your Oktoberfest party.

ORIGINAL GRAVITY: 1.056

FINAL GRAVITY: 1.015

POTENTIAL ALCOHOL: 5.4% ABV

INGREDIENTS

1 pound 10 °L crystal malt
1 pound 10 °L Munich malt
Two 3.3-pound boxes of Northwestern light unhopped malt syrup
4 ounces Liberty hop pellets
1 package Wyeast 2007 Pilsen Lager yeast
¾ cup corn sugar for priming

BREWING PROCEDURES

1. Steep crushed grains in 2–3 quarts of water for approximately 30 minutes at 158°F.
2. Strain wort into brewpot and bring to a boil.
3. Add malt syrup and 3.5 ounces of hops.
4. Boil for 45 minutes.
5. Add the remaining ½ ounce of hops and boil for an additional 2 minutes.
6. Cool, pitch yeast (that you started the day before).
7. Ferment for 21 days at 48–56°F.
8. Bottle with ¾ cup of corn sugar dissolved in 1 pint boiling water.
9. Condition at fermentation temperature for 3–4 weeks.

THE HOME BREWERY "FAMOUS" AMBER LAGER

⏣ ⏣ ⏣

JAMIE P. STEPHENS

THE HOME BREWERY—RIVERSIDE, CALIFORNIA

This great recipe might be classified as a hybrid of American amber ale and Vienna lager. Or maybe it's a new style altogether? Time will tell. Either way, this is a beer that is unparalleled for matching with food, especially spicy California cuisine.

ORIGINAL GRAVITY: 1.055

FINAL GRAVITY: 1.014

POTENTIAL ALCOHOL: 5.3% ABV

INGREDIENTS

> ½ cup 20° L crystal malt
> ½ cup 60° L crystal malt
> ½ cup 90° L crystal malt
> 3 pounds Dutch light dry malt extract
> 3.3 pounds Yellow Dog malt extract
> 1.5 ounce Kent Goldings hop pellets (bittering)
> 0.5 ounce Cascade hop pellets (bittering)
> 0.5 ounce Tettnanger hop pellets (Finishing)
> ½ teaspoon Irish moss
> 2 packs lager yeast
> ¾ corn sugar for priming

BREWING PROCEDURES

1. Add cracked crystal malt to 2 quarts cold water and raise to a boil. Remove grains when boil commences.
2. Turn off heat; dissolve in dry malt extracts and 2 gallons water. Return to boil, add Kent Goldings hops, and boil for 1 hour.

Add Cascade hops after 30 minutes. Add Irish moss after 45 minutes. Add Tettnanger hops after 50 minutes.

3. Cool wort with a wort chiller or place brewpot in ice-water bath for 20 minutes. Strain into primary fermenter. Pitch yeast when temperature is below 75°F.
4. When signs of fermentation are evident, move to cool, dark place and ferment to completion at 46–58°F. Rack to secondary for 1 to 2 weeks.
5. Bottle with ¾ cup corn sugar dissolved in 1 pint boiling water.
6. Condition at fermentation temperature for 1 week, then cold-lager 3 to 4 weeks.

SIMPLY SUMPTUOUS STEAM BEER

⏣ ⏣ ⏣

THE HOME BEER, WINE, & CHEESEMAKING SHOP—WOODLAND HILLS, CALIFORNIA

The title of this recipe is a mouthful, but so is the beer. The mixture of malts and hop varieties makes for quite a mélange of flavors with a citrusy Cascade bouquet. A few weeks of lagering will greatly repay your patience.

ORIGINAL GRAVITY: 1.045

FINAL GRAVITY: 1.012

POTENTIAL ALCOHOL: 4.3% ABV

IBUs: 45

COLOR: 10 SRM

INGREDIENTS

> 4 ounces Belgian aromatic malt
> 4 ounces Belgian biscuit malt

4 ounces Gambrinus honey malt

8 ounces Scottish 80 °L malt

5 pounds Aussie light dry malt extract

1 ounce Northern Brewer hop pellets at
8.5% AA (60 minutes)

0.5 ounce Centennial hop pellets at 9.9%
AA (20 minutes)

0.5 ounce Cascade hop pellets at 5.8% AA
(0 minutes—at knockout)

1 teaspoon Irish moss

1 teaspoon gypsum

Wyeast 2112 California Lager yeast

¾ cup corn sugar for priming

BREWING PROCEDURES

1. Steep (soak) the grains in 2 quarts of 150°F
   water for 30–40 minutes. Sparge (rinse)
   with 2.5 quarts of 150°F water into your boiling pot. Discard grain. No water over 170°F
   with grain. Do not oversparge. Do not
   squeeze grain bag.

2. After adding 2.5 gallons of water and dissolving the malt, bring pot to a gentle but
   rolling boil. Skim all foam before starting
   the hop sequence. Add Irish moss the last
   20 minutes to remove the protein missed in
   steps 1 and 2. Add the gypsum into the boil.
   It adds hardness, accentuating the crisp hop
   character.

3. Ferment at an average of 55–58°F. This
   keeps the fruity esters to a minimum. Pitch
   (add) yeast when your water bath around
   the fermenter reads 70–80°F. Maintain this
   temperature until the first signs of fermentation (about 10–12 hours). If using a yeast
   starter (highly recommended), fermentation can start in 2–3 hours. Use ¾ cup sugar
   for priming.

SHORELINE STEAMER

THE CELLAR HOMEBREW—SEATTLE,
WASHINGTON

A California common or "steam" beer is a beer
brewed with lager yeast at ale temperatures,
usually with an ample supply of hops. The
warmer temperature lends more fruity overtones to the beer, while the lager yeast provides
a crisper finish. This unique combination
defines the California common style.

ORIGINAL GRAVITY: 1.068

FINAL GRAVITY: 1.021

POTENTIAL ALCOHOL: 6.3% ABV

INGREDIENTS (FOR 5.5 GALLONS)

¾ pound English crystal malt (crushed)

½ pound light German crystal malt
(crushed)

¼ pound chocolate malt (crushed)

6 pounds Alexander's light bulk malt syrup

3 pounds English light dry malt extract

1 ounce Cascade and 1 ounce Chinook
hops (boiling)

1 ounce Cascade and 1 ounce Chinook
hops (finishing)

Burton water salts (optional, add during
step 4)

1 package dry lager yeast or California
Lager liquid yeast

¾ cup corn sugar for priming

BREWING PROCEDURES

Note: If you are using the California Lager liquid
yeast with this recipe, be sure to start that yeast at least
1 to 3 days before doing any of the brewing steps
below. Follow the package directions and use the yeast
in step 5.

1. Place the crushed English crystal, German

light crystal, and chocolate malts in a strainer bag. Add this bag of grain to your brewing kettle, which contains 2 to 2½ gallons brewing water. Bring the brewing water to a boil, then remove the bag of grains. It is not a good idea to boil these specialty grains for any length of time as they may contribute a bitter or grainy taste to the finished beer.

2. Sparge (rinse) the bag of grains with about 1 quart of hot tap water into the brewing kettle; dispose of the spent grains.

3. Remove the brewing kettle from the burner and add the 6 pounds of Alexander's light malt syrup and the 3 pounds of English light dry malt. The syrup is easier to pour if the can has been previously placed in hot water. Also, rinse the can with hot water to ensure that all the syrup goes into the kettle. Stir the mixture, now called "wort," until it boils. Watch carefully at this time because the wort may boil over. You can prevent this by pouring a cup of cold water into the over-boiling wort.

4. At boiling point, add the Cascade and Chinook boiling hops. Hops can be placed in a hop bag or added loose, to be later strained out after the boil using a strainer bag. Time the boil for about 1 hour, stirring occasionally. After the first 10 minutes of this boil, remove 2 cups of wort in measuring cup and cover with foil or plastic. Cool to 90°F for use in step 5.

5. Making the yeast starter: For dry yeast, use ½ cup warm tap water (90–100°F). Sprinkle the contents of yeast packet into that water, cover for at least 15 minutes, and then add to the 2 cups of wort you prepared in step 4. Cover and set aside for use in step 9 below.

For liquid yeast, prepare 1 to 3 days ahead of brewing time per package instructions. Open the swollen package and add the contents to the 2 cups of wort as prepared in step 4.

6. After the wort has boiled for that 1 hour, add the Cascade and Chinook finishing hops. Place them in the hop bag, which has been emptied of the spent boiling hops, and place them in the boiling kettle or just add the finishing hops directly to the brewing kettle. They will be strained later in step 8.

7. Let the boil continue for 5 minutes. This gives the beer its hop aroma. Remove the pot from the burner and let it cool, covered, for about 20 minutes.

8. Pour 3 gallons of cold water into the sanitized open fermenter fitted with strainer bag; if loose finishing hops were used in step 6, strain the warm wort from step 7 into the cold water. Top up the fermenter to 5½ gallons using cold tap water. Cover the fermenter and cool the wort as rapidly as possible.

9. When the wort has cooled to about 80°, add the yeast starter and ferment as you usually do.

CALIFORNIA COMMON BEER
▥ ▥

BOSTON BREWERS SUPPLY CO.— JAMAICA PLAIN, MASSACHUSETTS

"Our Anchor Steam look-alike may surprise a few of your friends. The beer's original gravity of 1.050, terminal gravity of 1.014, and a bitterness level of 30 IBUs are all very close to those of the original. The Northern Brewer and Cascade hop varieties we have chosen have been Anchor's signature for many years, and in keeping with tradition we use lager yeast, ferment at ale temperatures, and cold-condition the finished beer. We hope that you enjoy our representation of this world classic."

ORIGINAL GRAVITY: 1.050–52

FINAL GRAVITY: 1.012–14

POTENTIAL ALCOHOL: 5% ABV

IBUs: 30 to 32

INGREDIENTS

> 8 ounces English crystal malt
> 6 pounds light malt extract syrup
> 1 pound light dry malt extract
> 2 ounces Northern Brewer hop pellets
> 1 ounce Cascade hop pellets
> 1 teaspoon Irish moss
> 1 package Superior dry lager yeast
> 6 ounces corn sugar for priming

BREWING PROCEDURES

1. Secure the crushed grains in the muslin straining bag. Pour 2 gallons of cold water into your brewpot, apply heat, and add the grain bag. Heat to a near boil (about 155–158°F). Cover the pot, remove from the heat, and allow the grains to steep for 30 minutes. After 30 minutes remove the grain bag, drain, and discard.

2. Turn off the heat and, while stirring constantly, dissolve all of the malt extract. As soon as the boil begins add the 1 ounce of Northern Brewer hops and start timing the boil; the total elapsed time will be 45 minutes. Maintain a good rolling boil and stir

occasionally. After 20 minutes add the other ounce of Northern Brewer hop pellets; 10 minutes later add the Irish moss flakes; 40 minutes into the boil add the 1 ounce of Cascade hop pellets for the last 5 minutes, then cover and remove from the heat.

Remember that after the wort has cooled, it is highly vulnerable to contamination; everything that comes into contact with it from this point on must be thoroughly sanitized!

3. Cool the wort as quickly as possible. A wort chiller works best, but if you haven't got one yet a cold water bath will do the trick. Place the covered pot in your kitchen sink and fill with ice and cold water. When the temperature has fallen to about 90°F, transfer the wort, through a strainer if possible, into your fermenter. Top off with enough cold water to reach a 5-gallon level and stir or shake well. If you are using a glass carboy for fermentation, it is a good idea to add the cold water first. Draw off a small sample and take both a hydrometer and a temperature reading; always discard the sample used.

4. When the wort has cooled to 65–70°F, you are ready to add the yeast. Once the yeast has been added, attach an airlock and keep the fermenter in a cool, dark location where temperature fluctuations are minimal, ideally 65–70°F. Active fermentation should become visible in the next 12 to 24 hours and will continue for about 3 to 5 days. This ale can be bottled immediately but will benefit from a week of secondary fermentation. If you choose to bottle right away, take both a temperature and a hydrometer reading. If the terminal gravity is within the range stated above, proceed directly to the bot-

tling instructions below; if not, wait another couple of days and check again.

5. When visible signs of fermentation have ceased, gently siphon the beer to the sanitized secondary fermenter (ideally a 5-gallon glass carboy), leaving all sediment behind. Attach an airlock and allow the beer to settle for an additional 5 to 7 days at the same temperature of primary fermentation.

6. At the end of this period, draw off a small sample and check the final gravity. By now it should be within the range stated above; if not, wait another couple of days and check again. Prepare to bottle.

BOTTLING AND CONDITIONING

1. Sanitize all of your siphoning and bottling equipment, bottles, and caps.

2. Boil the 6 ounces of corn sugar in about a pint of water and pour it into your bottling bucket. Gently siphon the beer (again leaving sediment behind) out of the fermenter into the bucket, making sure the flow is directed to the bottom of the bucket; avoid splashing or agitating the beer. Reserve the last remnants to take thermometer and hydrometer readings; this will be your final gravity.

3. Using your siphon tubing and bottle filler, fill each bottle to within an inch from the top and cap immediately. Store the bottles upright for 1 week at room temperature, about 65–70°F, and for an additional 2 weeks to 4 weeks as cold as you can get it. Enjoy!

AMERICAN BOCK
⫿ ⫿ ⫿

THE HOME BREWERY—OZARK, MISSOURI

The American influence in this bock is its modest gravity, which makes it easier to enjoy more than one on a chilly spring evening. Although the strength is more at home in Texas, the taste is authentically Bavarian with German hops and a malty Munich yeast strain.

ORIGINAL GRAVITY: 1.040

FINAL GRAVITY: 1.011

POTENTIAL ALCOHOL: 3.6% ABV

INGREDIENTS

- ½ pound crushed light crystal malt
- ¼ pound crushed black patent malt
- ¼ pound crushed victory malt
- 5½ pounds (1 large pack) Yellow Dog malt extract
- 1½ ounces Hallertauer pellets (4.5% AA) at start of boil
- ½ ounce Tettnanger pellets (4.2% AA) in last 5 minutes
- ½ teaspoon Irish moss in last 15 minutes of boil
- Wyeast 2308 Munich Lager yeast
- ¾ cup corn sugar for priming

BREWING PROCEDURES

1. Heat 5 gallons of water in a large kettle. Add crushed grains. Many people don't have a kettle that large, but heat as much as you can (at least 2 gallons). Remove grains from kettle at 170°. When the water is boiling, turn off the heat and add the malt extract to the water. Use a spoon and stir until you are sure no malt extract is sticking to the bottom of the kettle. Then turn the heat back on.

2. Bring the kettle back to a boil and stir occasionally so the ingredients won't burn on the bottom of the kettle. If your recipe calls for bittering hops, now is the time to add them and stir them in. Watch out for a boilover. In the early part of the boil, the kettle usually tries to boil over once or twice, so control this by adjusting the heat. Later in the boil, the surface tension changes and boiling over is not a problem. Keep stirring occasionally, and let the beer (wort) boil hard for 1 hour. Stir in the ½ teaspoon of Irish moss in your recipe about 15 minutes before the end of the boil.

3. If finishing hops are called for in your recipe, stir them in 2 minutes before the end of the boil. Using finishing hops at the end of the boil adds a fresh aroma and flavor to the beer, and the use of finishing hops is appropriate in most beer styles.

4. Pour the hot beer (wort) into the primary fermenter. It is not necessary to strain the wort if you used hop pellets. Add cold water to bring the total volume up to 5 gallons. Cover the fermenter and wait until the temperature is down to 75°F. If you have a wort chiller, use it to bring the temperature down quickly. At 75° or less, add the yeast in your recipe. Just tear open the pack(s) and sprinkle it on the wort. Close the fermenter with the lid, stopper, and airlock. Remember to put water (or vodka) in the airlock. Vodka evaporates more quickly, but bacteria won't live in it.

5. Pitch yeast at room temperature; ferment at 42°F. Fermentation should start within 24 hours, and may continue for 2 weeks. Leave the beer alone and don't open the lid. When the airlock has not bubbled for several days and the beer is flat, still, and clearing, it is ready to bottle.

6. To bottle, siphon about 1 pint of beer into a pan and warm it on the stove. Add exactly ¾ cup of corn sugar to the pan and stir until it is dissolved. Pour this back into the beer and stir gently but well to distribute the sugar. Siphon or tap into clean sanitized bottles and cap. Keep the bottles at room temperature. After a week, put a bottle in the refrigerator and try it. It will be best in about 3 weeks.

SPECIALTY
BEER RECIPES

BAVARIAN SPECIALTY BEERS

Bavaria is well known for the world-classic beers it produces in abundance: bock, dunkel, weizen, helles. Less famous but equally well crafted and steeped in brewing tradition are its specialty beers brewed in lesser-known locales, primarily in Franconia, beyond the overshadowing powerhouse breweries of Munich. These beers include rauchbier, steinbier, kellerbier, Erlanger, Kulmbacher, kräusenbier, dampfbier, roggenbier, and the elusive zoigl. We have provided recipes for roggen, rauch, and kellerbiers below. For the rest, specialty Bavarian brewers have been slow to reveal their secrets—you will have to undertake a pioneering adventure into the world of Bavaria's rare styles on your own. Perhaps for future editions of this book, you will share what you have learned in the form of a classic recipe. Prost!

Classic commercial examples of Bavarian specialties include: Aecht Schlenkerla Rauchbier, Kaiserdom Rauchbier, Schierlinger Roggen, Rauchenfels Steinbier and Steinweizen, and St. Georgen Bräu Kellerbier.

ROCKIN' ROGGEN

BEER & WINEMAKING SUPPLIES, INC.— NORTHAMPTON, MASSACHUSETTS

This style of beer is fairly new on the craft-brewing scene. The well-known Thurn und Taxis commercial example, Schierlinger Roggen, bears a striking similarity to a Bavarian dunkelweizen, but has its own unique dryness, as does this recipe. The combination of ingredients used here really brings out the distinct rye flavor, and the weizen yeast lends a complementary fruitiness. Finding all the ingredients, however, may take some scavenger hunting, but it's worth it. Good luck!

ORIGINAL GRAVITY: 1.046–48

FINAL GRAVITY: 1.010–12

POTENTIAL ALCOHOL: 4.5% ABV

INGREDIENTS

    4 ounces malted rye (cracked)

    4 ounces flaked rye

    8 ounces dark German crystal malt (cracked)

    2 teaspoon gypsum or Burton salts

    7 pounds light malt extract

    2 ounces German Select hops for bittering

    1 ounce German Spalt hops for aroma

    10–14 grams dry ale yeast, Wyeast 3056 Bavarian Wheat, or Wyeast 3068 Weihenstephan Wheat*

    ¾ cup corn sugar for bottling

BREWING PROCEDURES

Note: If using a liquid culture, activate 12–24 hours prior to brew session.

1. Place your three blended grains in a 3–4-quart pan and stir in 1 quart of 168°F water. Mix well. Grain should bring temperature down to approximately 150–154°F. Steep for 45 minutes in oven, small insulated cooler, or on stovetop at that temperature. While grain is steeping, bring 2 gallons

of water up to 165°F in an 8–12-quart pot. Place strainer or colander over large kettle, then pour and spoon all grains and liquid in. Rinse with 1.5–2 gallons of 165°F water. Allow liquid to drain into kettle. Discard grains and bring liquid to a boil. Momentarily remove from heat.

2. Pour the 7 pounds of malt extract into the pot, making sure to rinse out the container to get all the malt. Stir well, then add the gypsum or Burton salts and stir well again.

3. Resume boiling (total time: 1 hour). Split the 2 ounces of Select hops into two equal portions. At the 15-minute mark, add 1 ounce; at the 30-minute mark, add the second ounce. At 60 minutes, add the 1 ounce of Spalt hops.

4. Shut off the heat and let stand for 15 minutes.

5. Put 3 gallons of very cold water into your sterilized primary fermenter, then carefully pour the hot wort into it. Top up to 5 gallons with more cold water if necessary. If still above 85°F, run a cold water bath around your fermenter. The fermenter should then be stirred or swirled to aerate the wort. Take a hydrometer reading and write it down.

6. Wort should now be 70–85°F. Activate dry yeast by putting in 1 cup of sterile water at 75–95°F for 15 minutes, then stir well.

7. Now add the yeast and stir or swirl to aerate. Pitch yeast solution into fermenter. Put lid and airlock on. Fill airlock halfway with water.

8. Ferment at room temperature (60–70°F) for 4 days, then siphon over to a glass secondary fermenter for another 4–7 days. Take a hydrometer reading, and if low enough, bottle the beer into 53 reusable bar bottles (12-ounce size) or equivalent.

9. Bottling procedure: Make a priming syrup on the stove with 1 cup water and ¾ cup corn sugar, bring to a boil, and then shut heat off immediately, stirring well. Transfer beer back to primary or bottling bucket, mixing the priming syrup in well to distribute evenly. Siphon into bottles and cap them.

10. Remember to sanitize everything you use after the boil with a good chlorinated alkaline cleanser.

11. Allow bottles to sit at room temperature for 1–2 weeks before cooling down.

Bavarian Kellerbier
🍺🍺🍺

Stephen Snyder

I tried to pattern this beer after St. Georgen Kellerbier using the German method of packaging before terminal gravity is reached in order to produce carbonation. You avoid the hassle of priming, but there is a lot of trial and error involved. I first tried 80 percent of total expected attenuation as some brewing texts have suggested and that was too much carbonation, especially if you plan to lager for several months. I recommend at least 85 percent, but your results may differ with different ingredients or methods. Either way, the resulting conditioning is uncommonly smooth, creamy, and long-lasting. Perfect for a kellerbier! I used minikegs for this beer and dispensed with a hand pump because this beer is traditionally served *vom fass* (on draft) by gravity feed, but you can use any other kegging system or bottles.

ORIGINAL GRAVITY: 1.055

FINAL GRAVITY: 1.014

POTENTIAL ALCOHOL: 5.5% ABV

IBUs: 35

INGREDIENTS

- ¼ pound light crystal malt
- 3 pounds Munich malt
- ¾ pound Vienna malt
- ¼ pound dextrine malt
- 5 pounds Dutch extra light DME
- 2 ounces Tettnang bittering hops 4.5% AA—60 minutes
- 1 ounce Hersbrucker flavor hops, 15-minute boil
- 1 ounce Hersbrucker aroma hops, 2-minute boil
- Wyeast 2308 Munich Lager yeast in 1.5 liter starter

BREWING PROCEDURES

(Refer to General Lager Brewing Procedures beginning on page 16.)

SPECIAL BREWING PROCEDURES

1. Mash grains 1 hour at 155°F. Sparge with 168°F water.
2. Ferment at 46–54°F. Check specific gravity regularly and keg when 85% of total expected attenuation is reached. If bottling, ferment to completion, then prime with speise.
3. Cool to 39° for 24 hours to settle yeast when fermentation is at 85% complete, or approximately 1.020.
4. Rack off sediment and into kegs and bung. Allow to ferment for 10–14 more days at normal fermentation temperature.
5. Slowly reduce temperature approximately 1° per day down to 32°F.
6. Lager 1 to 2 months.
7. Serve at 45–48°F.

BAMBERGER STYLE RAUCHBIER

FAL ALLEN, HEAD BREWER, PIKE PLACE BREWERY—SEATTLE, WASHINGTON

Not long ago, homebrewers had to rely on liquid smoke or home-smoked malt to brew their own rauchbier. Luckily, homebrewer demand has made some excellent German smoked malts increasingly available. Don't forget the lagering phase, especially when brewing Märzen-strength versions.

ORIGINAL GRAVITY: 1.050

FINAL GRAVITY: 1.014

POTENTIAL ALCOHOL: 4.75% ABV

INGREDIENTS (FOR 8 GALLONS)

- 8 pounds pilsner malt
- 4 pounds Weyerman rauch malt
- 1 pounds biscuit malt
- ½ pound dextrine malt
- ½ pound Munich malt
- 3 ounces Spalt (boil)
- 3 ounces Saaz (finish)
- ¼ teaspoon gypsum (depending on your water) in mash
- ¼ teaspoon Irish moss
- Wyeast 2124 Bohemian Lager yeast
- 1.2 cups corn sugar for priming

BREWING PROCEDURES

1. Dough in at 124°F for 20 minutes.
2. Remove thickest third of the mash, add 1 pint of water, and decoct (bring to a boil).
3. Add back to the rest of the mash (temperature should be 140–144°F).
4. Rest for 20 minutes, then pull second decoction using the same method as before.

5. Add to the main mash. Temperature should be 149–151°F (ideally 150°F).

6. Rest for 1 hour, run off, and sparge with 170–174°F water.

7. Boil for 1.5 hours, adding Spalt hops after 30 minutes.

8. Add Irish moss when 10 minutes remain in the boil.

9. Add Saaz hops when 5 minutes remain in the boil.

10. Chill wort to 55°F and pitch yeast.

11. Hold for 24 hours, then lower temperature over the next 48 hours to 45°F.

12. At the end of the primary fermentation, rack to the secondary and lager for 60 days at 40–45°F.

EAST COAST RAUCH BIER

East Coast Brewing Supply—Staten Island, New York

After you've acquired a taste (or is it an addiction?) for Bamberg-style smoked lagers, you'll surely want more than the usual five-gallon batch on hand. This recipe is for you. Thankfully, the new availability of authentic German smoked malts makes quantities of this size much easier to brew now that you don't have to home-smoke your own malts. After you've brewed this great beer once, try bumping up the gravity to 1.060 the next time for a wonderfully smoky Oktoberfest beer.

ORIGINAL GRAVITY: 1.046

FINAL GRAVITY: 1.013

POTENTIAL ALCOHOL: 4.3% ABV

INGREDIENTS (FOR 13.5 GALLONS)

- 4.5 pounds Klages malt
- 12 pounds Ireks rauch malt
- 2 pounds Munich 20 °L malt
- 0.5 pound chocolate malt
- 4 ounces Mt. Hood hops (3.4% AA) for 60 minutes
- 0.5 ounce Mt. Hood hops for 2 minutes
- Wyeast 2278 Czech Pils yeast (with 600 ml starter)
- 2 cups priming sugar

Water Requirements:
- Mash: 4.75 gallons
- Raise: 2.9 gallons
- Sparge: 8.5 gallons

BREWING PROCEDURES

1. Dough in at 129°F, resting at 119°. Hold for 35 minutes.

2. Add raise water to bring temperature to 150°F. Hold for 1 hour. Raise heat to 168°F, then mash out and start sparge.

3. Collect about 14¼ gallons of wort. Boil for 90 minutes, adding bittering hops after 30 minutes. Add finishing hops in last 2 minutes.

4. Pitch yeast and ferment at 55°F. Rack to secondary fermenters after 2 weeks and ferment in glass carboys 2 more weeks.

5. Prime, bottle, and condition as normal.

CHRISTMAS AND HOLIDAY BEERS

These beers enjoy a long and proud tradi- tion and are usually heavier, darker, and with a more unusual character than the every- day beer. These beers were brewed with the finest ingredients and saved especially for the holiday season. For decades, we Americans had to rely on Europe for such a beer as Affligem Super Noel, Würzburger Bavarian Holiday,

Aass Jule Øl, Scaldis Noel, Samichlaus Bier, Felinfoel Festive Ale, or Samuel Smith's Winter Welcome. Thankfully for us, there are now a wealth of specially crafted holiday beers in America, such as Geary's Hampshire Special Ale, Sierra Nevada Celebration Ale, Catamount Christmas Ale, and Anchor's Our Special Ale.

YULE FUEL

MOUNTAIN MALT AND HOP SHOPPE— LAKE KATRINE & POUGHKEEPSIE, NEW YORK

"The following winter warmer recipe was cre- ated to warm you without a fire on those cold and blustery nights. It gently blends a high- alcohol, malty beer with the unique flavors of demerara sugar, black treacle, cinnamon, and orange. This one's not for weenies!"

ORIGINAL GRAVITY: 1.100

FINAL GRAVITY: 1.027

POTENTIAL ALCOHOL: 9.9% ABV

INGREDIENTS

> 1 can Brewferm Christmas
>
> 2 teaspoons gypsum
>
> 2 cans Edme Strong Ale malt extract
>
> 1 teaspoon Irish moss
>
> 1 pound English light DME
>
> ½ ounce sweet orange peel
>
> One 3-inch stick of cinnamon
>
> Wyeast 1728 Scottish Ale yeast
>
> 5 ounces black treacle

> 1 box of demerara cubes (save 30 cubes for priming)

BREWING PROCEDURES

1. In a 16-quart or larger stainless-steel pot, heat 1¼ gallons of water to a boil and add 2 teaspoons of gypsum.
2. When boil is attained, turn off heat and add the 3 cans of malt and the dry malt. (Putting DME in a bowl first makes it easier to add.) Turn on heat and return to a boil.
3. When the danger of a messy boilover has passed, add the black treacle and all but 30 of the demerara cubes (you'll need 30 cubes to prime 5 gallons).
4. Add 1 teaspoon of Irish moss and boil for 10 more minutes.
5. Add the 3-inch stick of cinnamon and the ½ ounce of sweet orange peel. Boil 5 more minutes and turn off the heat.
6. Take the remaining ½ ounce Tettnang hop plug and repeat the same process. Boil for 2 more minutes, then turn off heat. Immedi- ately remove both hop bags.
7. Take the brewpot from the stove and place it in a sink partially filled with cold water.

Add 1 gallon of sanitary, refrigerated water (40°F) to the brewpot, then cover and place ice in the water around the brewpot. Never add ice directly to the wort! Let stand 15 minutes. Place 2 gallons of refrigerated water into the fermenter, then add the wort. Check the temperature (65–75°F is ideal). Top off to 5½ gallons with either more cold or room-temperature water.

8. With a sanitized measuring cup, scoop out ¾ cup and take a hydrometer reading. Discard sample.

9. Add the package of yeast to the fermenter when the temperature of the wort is 65–75°F, then stir vigorously to aerate. Snap the fermenter lid on, fill the airlock halfway with water, and place in lid. Place fermenter in a spot where the temperature will remain a constant 65–70°F.

10. Ferment in the primary for 5–6 days, then rack into a glass carboy for 3 weeks.

11. When brew is clear, siphon into a bottling bucket. Dissolve remaining demerara sugar into 1 cup boiling water, cool, and gently stir into beer with a sanitized spoon. CAUTION: If finished volume is less than 5 gallons, scale proportionally (e.g., 4½ gallons = ⅔ cup sugar).

12. Keep in a warm place for 14 days, then move to a cool place to age and store.

13. Suggestion: Start a tradition. Have a Christmas party and make a batch of this beer. Serve at next year's party when you are brewing the batch for the following year. Cheers!

SPICED WINTER ALE
🍺 🍺
BOSTON BREWERS SUPPLY CO.–
JAMAICA PLAIN, MASSACHUSETTS

"Those of you who enjoy a broad variety of beer styles will certainly agree that this is one of the more exciting periods of the year. A few minutes in your favorite package store will reveal a multitude of wonderful seasonal specialties: Anchor Our Special Ale, Sierra Nevada Celebration Ale, Shipyard Prelude, Harpoon Winter Warmer; the choices seem endless. Who could resist brewing their own? Our spiced ale has become our largest-selling specialty ale. It is deep brown in color, has an enticing citrusy aroma, and a complex spicy flavor that follows through to the finish. Be forewarned, this one usually goes fast so you may want to consider a double batch!"

ORIGINAL GRAVITY: 1.058–60

FINAL GRAVITY: 1.014–16

POTENTIAL ALCOHOL: 6% ABV

INGREDIENTS

> 8 ounces English crystal malt
> 2 ounces black patent malt
> 6 pounds light extract syrup
> 1 pound light dry malt extract
> 1 pound clover honey
> 2.5 ounces Cascade hop pellets
> 1 ounce dried ginger root
> 2 whole cinnamon sticks
> 2 whole nutmeg
> 0.5 ounce dried orange peel
> 1 teaspoon Irish moss
> 1 package dry ale yeast or Wyeast 1056 American Ale
> 6 ounces corn sugar for priming

BREWING PROCEDURES

1. Secure the grains in the muslin straining bag. Pour 2 gallons of cold water into your brewpot, apply heat, and add the grain bag. Heat to a near boil (about 160°F). Cover the pot, remove from the heat, and allow the grains to steep for 30 minutes. After 30 minutes remove and discard the grain bag.

2. Turn off the heat and, while stirring constantly, dissolve all of the malt extract and the honey. As soon as the boil begins add the 2 ounces of Cascade hops and start timing the boil; the total elapsed time will be 45 minutes. Maintain a good rolling boil and stir occasionally. Crush the whole nutmeg, break up the cinnamon sticks, and chop up both the dried ginger root and orange peel; set aside. After 30 minutes add all of the spices and the Irish moss flakes. Ten minutes later add the ½ ounce of Cascade hops and continue to boil for an additional 5 minutes, then cover and remove the pot from the heat.

   Remember that after the wort has cooled, it is highly vulnerable to contamination; everything that comes into contact with it from this point on must be thoroughly sanitized!

3. Cool the wort as quickly as possible. A wort chiller works best, but if you haven't got one yet a cold water bath will do the trick. Place the covered pot in your kitchen sink and fill with ice and cold water. When the temperature has fallen to about 90°F, transfer the wort, through a strainer if possible, into your fermenter. Top off with enough cold water to reach a 5-gallon level and stir or shake well. If you are using a glass carboy for fermentation, it is a good idea to add the cold water first. Draw off a small sample and take both a hydrometer and a temperature reading; always discard the sample used.

4. When the wort has cooled to 65–70°F, you are ready to add the yeast. Once the yeast has been added, attach an airlock and keep the fermenter in a cool, dark location where temperature fluctuations are minimal, ideally 65–70°F. Active fermentation should become visible in the next 12 to 24 hours and will continue for about 3 to 5 days.

5. On the fifth or sixth day, gently siphon the beer to a sanitized secondary fermenter (ideally a 5-gallon glass carboy), leaving all sediment behind. Attach an airlock and allow the beer to settle for an additional 5 to 7 days at the same temperature as primary fermentation.

6. At the end of this period, draw off a small sample and check the final gravity. By now it should be within the range stated above; if not, wait another couple of days and check again. Prepare to bottle.

BOTTLING AND CONDITIONING

1. Sanitize all of your siphoning and bottling equipment, bottles, and caps.

2. Boil the 6 ounces of corn sugar in about a pint of water and pour it into your bottling bucket. Gently siphon the beer (again leaving sediment behind) out of the fermenter into the bucket, making sure the flow is directed to the bottom of the bucket; avoid splashing or agitating the beer. Reserve the last remnants to take thermometer and hydrometer readings; this will be your final gravity.

3. Using your siphon tubing and bottle filler, fill each bottle to within an inch from the

top and cap immediately. Store the bottles upright at room temperature, about 65–70°F, for a minimum of 3 weeks, chill, and enjoy.

HOLIDAY BEER
🍺🍺
THE VINEYARD—UPTON, MASSACHUSETTS
The pound of honey adds a subtle touch of residual sweetness to this brew, which is perfect for a little wassailing.

ORIGINAL GRAVITY: 1.045

FINAL GRAVITY: 1.012

Potential Alcohol: 4.3% ABV

INGREDIENTS

- ½ pound crystal malt
- 2 ounces black patent malt
- 6.6 pounds Premier unhopped pale malt extract
- 1 pound honey
- 2 ounce Cascade hop pellets (40 minutes)
- ½ ounce Saaz hop plug (5 minutes)
- 1 ounce grated ginger root
- Two 3-inch cinnamon sticks
- Grated peels of 4 oranges
- 1 packet Whitbread ale yeast
- ¾ cup priming sugar

BREWING PROCEDURES

1. To 1½ gallons cold water add crushed crystal and black patent malts; bring to a boil and remove from heat.
2. Strain out grains, add ½ gallon water, malt extract, honey, and Cascade hops, and boil for 40 minutes. Add ginger, cinnamon, and orange peels for last 10 minutes of boil. Add

Saaz hops last 5 minutes of boil.
3. Strain into primary fermenter, top up to 5 gallons with cold water, let cool, pitch yeast. Primary fermentation: 5 days at 65°F.
4. Rack off solids after 5 days into secondary fermenter. Secondary fermentation: 8 days at 65°F.
5. Add priming sugar at bottling time.

CHRISTMAS ALE
🍺🍺🍺
BEER & WINE HOBBY—WOBURN, MASSACHUSETTS
Besides the blend of spices, the secret to this recipe is the use of a Trappist or other Belgian ale yeast. Try making this one many months before Christmas, then let it age.

ORIGINAL GRAVITY: 1.045–52

FINAL GRAVITY: 1.008–12

POTENTIAL ALCOHOL: 5.1% ABV

INGREDIENTS

- ½ pound German dark crystal malt
- ⅛ pound chocolate malt
- 2 cans light liquid malt extract
- 2 pounds wildflower honey
- 2 ounces Cascade pellets (boil)
- 1 teaspoon Irish moss
- ½ ounce Hallertau Plug (finish)
- 1 package Beer & Wine Hobby Special Spice Blend (contains: sweet orange peel, cinnamon, cloves, and allspice)
- 1 package Burton water salts
- 1 package liquid Trappist Ale yeast in a 1 liter starter
- ¾ cup priming sugar

BREWING PROCEDURES

1. Add 2 gallons of cold water to your pot; put ½ pound crushed German crystal malt and ⅛ pound crushed chocolate malt into muslin bag and tie. Place bag in cold water and bring to a boil. When water comes to a boil, remove from heat and let steep for 5 minutes. Remove grains and discard.

2. Return pot to heat and bring to a boil. Add 2 cans of light liquid malt extract, 2 pounds honey, and 2 ounces Cascade hop pellets. Boil for 45 minutes. During the last 15 minutes of your boil, add ½ ounce Hallertau plug, 1 teaspoon Irish moss, and 1 package Burton water salts. Remove from heat and cool; strain out hops.

3. Add to your primary fermenter enough water to bring total volume to 5¼ gallons. Place special spice blend in muslin bag, tie, and place in primary fermenter.

4. Pitch prepared yeast (instructions included) when wort has cooled to between 65° and 75°F. Proceed as usual.

5. After 4 days in primary, siphon into secondary, leaving spices behind—or take spices out if you are doing it as single stage. Finish fermenting.

6. Prime with ¾ cup of corn sugar and bottle.

FRUIT- AND SPICE-FLAVORED BEERS

There is no strict definition of this style, although beers made with fruit and other natural flavoring agents probably predate the use of barley in most regions of the world. When formulating your own recipes, the best rule of thumb is to use the fruits and spices you like to eat. Raspberries and sour cherries are perennial favorites. The fruit can be added to the kettle, the primary, or the secondary, but should be crushed only after any large seeds or pits are removed to avoid harsh, bitter tastes being extracted. Macerated fruits such as cherries and raspberries that are to receive a long fermentation time are often left intact, as in Belgian kriek and framboise, for example. At most they should only be lightly crushed. *Macerate* means to soften or separate into component parts by steeping, as opposed to "masticate," which implies reducing to pulp by crushing and grinding. You can estimate that fresh fruit yields an average of 1.010 specific gravity points per pound per gallon of water. This will vary depending on the type of fruit, the freshness, the ripeness, and the length of the ferment. As for quantity, one and a half pounds of fruit per gallon of beer is a good minimum. Adjust up or downward in subsequent batches to suit your taste.

Fermenting with fruit provides a few challenges to the normal brewing procedure, however, in that unsanitized fruits can introduce wild yeast and bacteria into your beer and the pulp, skins, and seeds can block airlocks and blowoff hoses during fermentation, particularly during high kräusen. The sanitation question is not so much a problem when the fruit is incorporated into the hot wort at the end of the boil and allowed to sit for 20–30 minutes with the heat off. Fresh or fresh-frozen whole fruits intended for brewing should never be boiled, since pectins in the fruit, which are responsible for turning boiled fruit juice into fruit jelly, will produce a gelatinous haze in your beer.

Fruits can also be sterilized with chemical additives such as potassium or sodium metabisulfite in the form of campden tablets. These are used primarily in preventing bacterial growth in winemaking and I do not recommend their use for beer making for a number of reasons. The first is that many people, especially asthmatics, are severely allergic to the sulfites in these products; the second is that any sulfites remaining on the fruit can seriously inhibit yeast growth. Pasteurization at a temperature of 145°F for 30 minutes, then quickly chilling to 40°F before adding to the fermenter, is perhaps preferable to a chemical solution.

Many of the problems of brewing with fruit relate to their tendency to clog airlocks and blowoff hoses. This can be overcome by allowing greater headspace above the beer in a primary fermenter. Use a 7.5-gallon barrel for a 5-gallon batch, for example. Using a larger-diameter blowoff hose when carboy brewing can also alleviate the problem of fruit residue blockage. Please remember that the hole in the drilled stopper for the carboy must also have a larger opening than normal or you've gained nothing by adding a larger hose. The best method in my opinion is the traditional method of adding fruits, as demonstrated in Belgian brewing. Simply add pasteurized fruits to the secondary fermenter. The fruit fermentation will be much less vigorous on its own and less likely to cause a blockage, much more of the subtle fruit flavor and aroma will be retained, and the pH and alcohol level of the fermented beer will provide added protection against the dangers of spoilage.

Many microbreweries have taken a shot at fruit-flavored beers, and some of the standouts are Pyramid Apricot Ale, Marin Brewing's Bluebeery Ale, Tied House Cafe & Brewery's Passion Pale, and Buffalo Bill's Pumpkin Ale.

APRICOT WHEAT ALE
🍺🍺
OLD WEST HOMEBREW—COLORADO SPRINGS, COLORADO

Try this refreshing fruit beer if you enjoy the taste of the award-winning Pyramid Apricot Ale. It comes pretty darn close.

ORIGINAL GRAVITY: 1.049

FINAL GRAVITY: 1.012

POTENTIAL ALCOHOL: 4.8% ABV

INGREDIENTS

7 pounds English wheat extract (in bulk)

8 ounces malto-dextrin

2 ounces Hallertau whole hops (60 minutes)

Wyeast 1056 American Ale yeast

4 ounces apricot extract

¾ cup corn sugar

BREWING PROCEDURES

1. This is a very simple recipe to put together. Boil the extract, malto-dextrin, and hops together for 60 minutes. There are no flavor or finish hop additions.

2. Cool to 70°F and pitch the liquid yeast that you have started at least 1 day prior.

3. Ferment for 7–10 days.

4. Prime with ¾ cup corn sugar or 1¼ cup DME. Add the apricot extract to your bottling bucket along with the corn sugar and beer.

5. Gently stir the mixture and bottle or keg. Enjoy in 10 days.

Tree-Top Ale
⫴ ⫴ ⫴

Beer & Wine Hobby—Woburn, Massachusetts

With its use of spruce, a traditional Christmas spice, this recipe could also fit just as easily into the Holiday Beers section. Either way the spruce is a spicy and aromatic palate cleanser, just right for a hot summer day.

Original Gravity: 1.035

Final Gravity: 1.008

Potential Alcohol: 3.4% ABV

Ingredients

> 6.6 pounds light plain malt extract
> 1 ounce spruce essence or 1 cup freshly picked spruce tips
> 1 ounce Hallertauer hop pellets (boil)
> 1 package Burton water salts
> 1 teaspoon Irish moss
> 1 ounce Tettnang pellets (aromatics)
> 1 ounce loose finishing hops
> Yeast Lab A02 American Ale (starter required)
> ¾ cup corn sugar for priming

Brewing Procedures

1. Bring 2 gallons of water to a boil. Add 6.6 pounds light plain malt extract, 1 ounce spruce essence (½ bottle), and 1 ounce Hallertauer hop pellets; boil for 35 minutes. Add Burton water salts and 1 teaspoon Irish moss. Boil for 5 minutes, then add Tettnang hops and boil for 10 minutes more.

2. Remove from heat and add hot liquid wort to primary fermenter containing 3 gallons of cold water. Make up to total volume of 5¼ gallons. Place finishing hops in muslin bag and add to primary fermenter.

3. Pitch prepared and actively fermenting yeast starter into wort and ferment as usual.

4. If using single-stage fermentation, remove finishing hops after 2 days of fermentation; if using 2-stage fermentation, remove when transferring to secondary fermenter. Finish fermenting.

5. Prime with ¾ cup priming sugar.

6. For best results, age at least 4 weeks. This recipe will produce a wonderful, clean and refreshing, crisp beer.

Raspberry Weizen Beer
⫴

The Vineyard—Upton, Massachusetts

This is a very easy recipe for one of the most refreshing and flavorful variations on a wheat beer. If you don't care for raspberries, any of your favorite summer berries will do. Long Trail makes a terrific Blackberry Wheat that might be a good source of inspiration.

Original Gravity: 1.045

Final Gravity: 1.010

Potential Alcohol: 4.5% ABV

INGREDIENTS

- **3.3 pounds Northwestern Gold hopped malt extract**
- **3.3 pounds Northwestern Weizen unhopped malt extract**
- **6 pounds raspberries (fresh or frozen)**
- **1 teaspoon Irish moss (last 15 minutes)**
- **2 packages Doric ale yeast**
- **¾ cup corn sugar for priming**

BREWING PROCEDURES

1. Bring as much water as possible (up to 5 gallons) to a boil and remove from heat.
2. Add the malt extract and stir to dissolve completely and place back on heat to bring to a boil. Boil for 20 minutes after 5 minutes add Irish moss.
3. Crush raspberries on the bottom of a sanitized primary fermenter. Pour the hot beer wort over the raspberries, cover, and allow to cool.
4. When the temperature drops below 80°F add yeast. Primary fermentation: 5 days at 70°F. Secondary fermentation: 10 days at 70°F.
5. At bottling time boil ¾ cup corn sugar in 1 cup water for bulk priming.

EASY FRUIT BEER

LIZ BLADES

BLADES HOME BREWERY—BOLTON, ENGLAND

"I've also used this recipe to produce a reasonable smoke beer by fermenting as per 1–8 and at stage 9 adding around 20 ml of liquid smoke per 5 liters instead of the fruit. The secondary ferment under airlock took around 2 weeks and then I bottled. Do take care with the smoke; otherwise it can be like drinking the residue of the barbecue!"

ORIGINAL GRAVITY: 1.045

FINAL GRAVITY: 1.011

POTENTIAL ALCOHOL: 4.4% ABV

INGREDIENTS (FOR 5 IMPERIAL GALLONS)

- **1.8 kilograms English Wheat Beer kit**
- **500 grams light dried malt extract**
- **0.9 kilogram Edme Diastatic malt syrup**
- **1 kilogram of fruit per 5 liters of beer, e.g., peaches, raspberries, strawberries, blackberries, apricots—let your imagination go!**
- **1 packet of your own favorite yeast**
- **1 cup corn sugar for priming**

BREWING PROCEDURES

1. Sterilize equipment in the normal way.
2. Remove labels from both cans and place in warm water for 5–10 minutes (this makes contents easier to pour).
3. Place contents of both cans in a large pan, rinse out cans with hot (not boiling) water, and empty into pan. Bring the pan to a boil and allow to simmer for 5–10 minutes to sterilize the wort.
4. In the meantime, rehydrate the yeast in a cup of tepid water.
5. Add the sterilized wort and the light dried malt extract to your primary fermenter together with 15 liters of very hot water and stir vigorously until all malt is dissolved.
6. Make up to 22.5 liters with cool water.
7. Pitch in yeast when temperature of wort is around 65°F.
8. Cover and allow to ferment at around 65°F for 1 week.

9. Transfer to secondary fermenter under air-lock with chosen fruit(s) and allow to ferment for around 4 weeks. I like the temperature at this stage to be around 50–55°F.

10. Bottle in usual way and *try* to resist drinking for at least 3 months. Remember, patience is a virtue!

STRAWBERRY PATCH ALE

🍺 🍺

E. C. KRAUS–INDEPENDENCE, MISSOURI

"This brew will win the hearts of many non–beer drinkers as well as the veteran beer connoisseur. The strawberry aroma is very noticeable upon pouring; amber in color with a brilliant red hue. It has a distinct, fruity strawberry flavor that blends perfectly with the tinge of hops, producing a uniquely rounded flavor seldom found in beers."

ORIGINAL GRAVITY: 1.047–53

FINAL GRAVITY: 1.013–17

POTENTIAL ALCOHOL: 4.5% ABV

IBUs: 14–18

COLOR: 4–7 SRM/6–10 °L

INGREDIENTS

    3.3 pounds light unhopped malt syrup

    2 pounds light dried malt extract (5 cups)

    8 pounds fresh chopped strawberries

    8 ounces malto-dextrin (5-minute boil time)

    1 ounce Tettnanger pellet hops (45-minute boil time)

    $\frac{1}{2}$ ounce Hallertau pellet hops (finishing)

    1 tablespoon Irish moss (15-minute boil time)

    1 campden tablet (crushed)

    $\frac{1}{4}$ teaspoon pectic enzyme

    14 grams ale yeast or Wyeast 1968 London ESB

    1 cup priming sugar (bottling time)

BREWING PROCEDURES

1. Start by adding the chopped strawberries in an open container with 1 gallon of tap water. Add to it 1 campden tablet (crushed) and the pectic enzyme. Allow mixture to sit in the open for a 24-hour period.

2. The next day, take $1\frac{1}{2}$ to $2\frac{1}{2}$ gallons of water and add the malt syrup and the dried malt. Bring to a boil.

3. Once boiling, add the Tettnanger pelletized hops and boil for 45 minutes. During the last 15 minutes of the boil, add the Irish moss. At the last 5 minutes of the boil, add the malto-dextrine, and at the end of the boil, add the Hallertau pelletized hops and allow to steep for 10 minutes with the lid on and the burner off.

4. Once the boiling and steeping is complete, add the wort to your fermenter, then pour in the prepared strawberries. Then add water to equal $5\frac{1}{2}$ gallons. Be sure the mixture has cooled down to below 80°F before adding the yeast.

5. Attach airlock to fermenter and allow to ferment for 3–4 days, then rack the beer off of the strawberry pulp into a clean fermenter and allow to finish fermentation and clearing.

6. Bottle with priming sugar as normal and allow to condition for 4–6 weeks.

Apple Ale

⫟⫟

Beer & Wine Hobby—Woburn,
   Massachusetts

"This recipe makes a pretty good amber ale before the fruit is added. After the addition of the apple flavoring you've got a great alternative to apple cider or a wonderful summer refresher."

ORIGINAL GRAVITY: 1.038–42

FINAL GRAVITY: 1.008–10

POTENTIAL ALCOHOL: 4.1% ABV

Ingredients

- ½ pound light German crystal malt
- 1 can Mountmellick amber plain malt
- 2 pounds English dry malt
- 2 ounce Lublin hops (boil)
- ½ ounce Hallertau plug (last 10 minutes)
- 1 package Burton water salts
- 1 teaspoon Irish moss
- Wyeast 1056 American Ale or 1098 British Ale
- ¾ cup corn sugar (priming)
- 2 bottles Beer & Wine Hobby Apple Fruit Natural Fruit flavoring—add before bottling

Brewing Procedures

1. Add 2 gallons of cold water to your pot; put ½ pound crushed German crystal malt into muslin bag and tie. Place bag in cold water and bring to boil. When water comes to a boil, remove grains and discard.

2. Add 1 can Mountmellick amber liquid malt, 2 pounds English dry malt, and 2 ounces Lublin hops. Boil for 30 minutes. During the last 10 minutes of your boil, add Irish moss, Burton water salts, and ½ ounce Hallertau plug.

3. Remove from heat and cool. Strain out Hallertau hops. Add to your primary fermenter containing enough water to bring total volume to 5¼ gallons.

4. Pitch prepared yeast when wort has cooled to between 75°F and 80°F. Proceed as usual. Finish fermenting.

5. When beer is done fermenting, siphon into bottling container, add 2 bottles of Apple Natural Fruit flavoring and ¾ cup of corn sugar, and bottle.

"Your Favorite" Fruit Ale

⫟⫟

Dick Foehringer

The Brewmeister—Fair Oaks,
   California

"Have you ever tried a raspberry or cranberry ale? How about cherry, strawberry, blackberry, or peach? Well, this is a basic ale recipe to which you add 6–8 pounds of your favorite fruit. Lightly hopped so the fruit aroma and taste come through. Relatively high in alcohol with 7 pounds of extract plus the fermentables from the fruit! Try one and you'll make many, many more."

ORIGINAL GRAVITY: 1.073 (estimated)

FINAL GRAVITY: 1.018

POTENTIAL ALCOHOL: 7.3% ABV

Ingredients

- 7 pounds pale malt extract syrup
- 6–8 pounds fresh or frozen fruit of your choice
- 1½ ounces Hallertauer hops (boiling)

½ ounce Hallertauer hops (aromatic)

1 teaspoon Irish moss

1 Windsor Ale dry yeast

1 teaspoon gelatin

¾ cups corn sugar for bottling

Fruit Prep: Depending upon the type of fruit you are using, there are two methods of preparation. If you are using fruit without big seeds like raspberries, you can prepare them in a blender. Add a small amount of water and blend to a soft, creamy pulp. If the fruit has seeds like cherries, you do not want to grind up the seeds, as they are bitter. With this type of fruit, simply mash to a pulp mixture with a potato masher. Collect the fruit in a large bowl and set aside till the end of the boil.

BREWING PROCEDURES

1. Put 1½ to 2½ gallons of cold water in your brewpot. Bring to a near boil (160°F). Shut off heat, stir in extract, and thoroughly dissolve.

2. Return to heat, add boiling hops, and boil 45 minutes. Add Irish moss and boil 15 minutes. Turn off heat and add the bowl of fruit pulp and aromatic hops.

3. Cover and steep 30 minutes. Cold-break the wort by placing the pan into a sink full of cold water. When wort is cooled below 75°F, pour the entire contents into your primary fermenter.

4. Add enough cold water to make 6 gallons. Rehydrate yeast by dissolving in 1 cup warm water and let it sit for 10 minutes.

5. When wort is cool (below 75°F), pitch yeast. Ferment in a cool, dark place. When fermentation is complete, rack into secondary, leaving all fruit pulp and sediment behind.

6. Prepare gelatin by dissolving in 1 cup hot water and stir into secondary. (Note: With some fruits, you may have to repeat the secondary/gelatin-clearing procedure a second time to obtain a crystal-clear result.)

7. When clear (3–5 days) rack again, leaving sediment behind. Prepare bottling sugar by dissolving in 1 cup hot water. Stir dissolved bottling sugar into clear beer, bottle, and cap.

8. Age a minimum of 2–3 weeks. The fruitiness will be more dominant at first, but will mellow with further aging. Enjoy!!! We know you will!

HARVEST PUMPKIN ALE
⊞ ⊞ ⊞
JOE & BRYAN TIMMONS
BOSTON BREWERS SUPPLY CO.—
JAMAICA PLAIN, MASSACHUSETTS

"As you know, traditional ales and lagers are categorized by established brewing parameters characteristic of the style being reproduced. According to the Association of Brewers, our Harvest Pumpkin Ale would fall into the specialty beer category and that's where the fun begins, since there are no set guidelines within this category. Just remember that, like hops, the aromatic oils of most spices will evaporate during the boil. Late or multiple additions of fresh spices to the brewpot or the secondary fermenter will yield better results."

ORIGINAL GRAVITY: 1.046–48

FINAL GRAVITY: 1.010–12

POTENTIAL ALCOHOL: 5% ABV

IBUs: approximately 29

INGREDIENTS

> 1 pound British crystal malt
>
> 6 pounds light malt extract syrup
>
> 1 pound light dry malt
>
> 2 ounces Willamette hop pellets
>
> 4 pounds fresh pumpkin
>
> 2 whole nutmeg
>
> 3 cinnamon sticks
>
> 4 whole cloves
>
> 1 teaspoon Irish moss flakes
>
> 1 package dry ale yeast
>
> 6 ounces corn sugar for priming

BREWING PROCEDURES

1. To prepare the pumpkin for this recipe you have to slice it into 6 or 8 equal-size wedges, remove the seeds, and rinse well. Place the wedges skin-side down in a roasting pan, cover with aluminum foil, and cook in a 350°F preheated oven for about 30 minutes, or until flesh is soft. When it has cooled, divide it into 2 equal portions. Scoop out the pumpkin meat from one portion and set aside. The clean pumpkin meat will be added to the brewpot and the remaining wedges added to the fermenter.

2. While the pumpkin is cooking, secure the grains in the muslin straining bag. Pour 2 gallons of cold water into your brewpot, apply heat, and add the grain bag. Heat to a near boil (about 155°F), turn off the heat, then remove the grain bag, drain, and discard.

3. Thoroughly dissolve the malt extract, apply heat, and bring to a boil. As soon as the wort (unfermented beer) begins to boil, add the 2 ounces of Willamette hops and the clean pumpkin meat; stir well. Start timing the boil; the total elapsed time will be 50 minutes. Maintain a good rolling boil.

4. After 30 minutes, add the Irish moss flakes; 15 minutes later, add 2 broken cinnamon sticks, 1 crushed nutmeg, and all of the cloves. Continue to boil for an additional 5 minutes, then cover and remove the pot from the heat, allowing the spices to steep for 5 to 10 minutes.

Remember that after the wort has cooled, it is highly vulnerable to contamination; everything that comes into contact with it from this point on must be thoroughly sanitized!

5. Cool the wort as quickly as possible. A wort chiller works best, but if you haven't got one yet a cold water bath will do the trick. Place the covered pot in your kitchen sink and fill with ice and cold water. When the temperature has fallen to about 90°F, transfer the wort, through a strainer if possible, into your fermenter. Top off with enough cold water to reach a 5-gallon level and stir or shake well. Draw off a small sample and take both a hydrometer and a temperature reading; always discard the sample used. Add the remaining pumpkin wedges to the fermenter.

6. When the wort has cooled to 65–70°F, you are ready to add the yeast. Once the yeast has been added, attach an airlock and keep the fermenter in a cool, dark location where temperature fluctuations are minimal, ideally 68°F. Active fermentation should become visible in the next 12 to 24 hours and will continue for about 3 to 5 days.

7. On the fifth or sixth day, gently transfer the beer to a sanitized secondary fermenter (ideally a 5-gallon glass carboy), leaving all sediment behind. Add the remaining cinnamon and nutmeg to the fermenter, attach an airlock, and allow the beer to settle for

an additional 7 to 10 days at the same temperature of primary fermentation. At the end of this period, draw off a small sample and check the final gravity. By now it should be within the range stated above; if not, wait another couple of days and check again. Prepare to bottle.

BOTTLING AND CONDITIONING

1. Sanitize all of your siphoning and bottling equipment, bottles, and caps.
2. Boil the 6 ounces of corn sugar in about a cup of water and pour it into your bottling bucket. Gently siphon the beer out of the fermenter into the bucket, making sure the flow is directed to the bottom of the bucket; avoid splashing or agitating the beer.
3. Using your siphon tubing and bottle filler, fill each bottle to within an inch from the top and cap immediately. Store the bottles upright for 3 to 4 weeks, chill, and enjoy.

PAUL'S PUMPKIN ALE
⊞ ⊞ ⊞

PAUL HEALY

MOUNTAIN MALT AND HOP SHOPPE— LAKE KATRINE & POUGHKEEPSIE, NEW YORK

"The following was created by the manager of our Lake Katrine store (Paul was a chef in a former life). It revels in spices and will have the brewer thinking he is in the kitchen when Mom is making a pumpkin pie."

ORIGINAL GRAVITY: 1.056

FINAL GRAVITY: 1.016

POTENTIAL ALCOHOL: 5.3% ABV

INGREDIENTS

$1/2$ pound amber crystal malt

One 12-inch-diameter pumpkin

3.3 pounds John Bull plain light malt extract

1 ounce whole nutmeg

3.3 pounds John Bull plain amber malt extract

$1/8$ ounce whole allspice

1 pound English Wheat DME

Three 3-inch cinnamon sticks

2 ounces Tettnang hop pellets (bittering)

$2^1/2$ teaspoons pectic enzyme

$1/2$ ounce Cascade hop plug (flavor)

2 teaspoons gypsum

1 ounce Tettnang hop plug (aroma)

1 teaspoon Irish moss

2 packages Nottingham ale yeast

$3/4$ cup priming sugar

BREWING PROCEDURES

1. Remove the pith and seeds from the center of the pumpkin and carefully cut off the hard outside skin. Cut the clean meat into 1-inch by 1-inch cubes and boil them in a 12-quart or larger stainless-steel pot with 1 gallon of water for 2 hours (cover pot to prevent liquid loss).
2. Strain out the pumpkin meat, keeping the cooking liquid. Put meat in strainer bag and place in sanitized fermenter with 1 gallon of cold water. Cover with lid and airlock until later.
3. In your 12-quart or larger stainless-steel pot, heat $1^1/4$ gallon of water to 160°F and add 1 teaspoon of gypsum. Stir until dissolved and turn off heat. Place cracked grains in a nylon bag and immerse in water. Cover pot and allow grain to steep for 30 minutes.

Remove grain bag and bring the "tea" to a boil. (If you do not have a nylon bag, add grains directly to water and strain.)

4. When boil is attained, turn off heat and add the cans of malt extract and the dry malt. (Putting DME in a bowl first makes it easier to add.) Turn on heat and return to a boil.

5. When the danger of a messy boilover has passed, add 2 ounces of Tettnang hop pellets and cook at a rolling boil for 45 minutes.

6. Add 1 teaspoon of Irish moss and boil for 5 more minutes.

7. Take one ½-ounce Cascade hop plug and slice it up. Place pieces in a muslin hop bag and immerse in wort. Boil for 5 more minutes.

8. Crack spices and place in a muslin sack. Add to wort; boil 3 more minutes.

9. Take the 2 remaining Tettnang hop plugs and repeat the same process. Boil for 2 more minutes, then turn off heat. Immediately remove both hop bags.

10. Take the brewpot from the stove and place it in a sink partially filled with cold water. Add 1 gallon of sanitary, refrigerated water (40°F) to the brewpot, then cover and place ice in the water around the brewpot. Never add ice directly to the wort! Let stand 15 minutes. Place 2 gallons of refrigerated water into the fermenter, then add the strained wort. Check the temperature (65–75°F is ideal). Top off to 6 gallons with either more cold or room-temperature water.

11. With a sanitized measuring cup, scoop out ¾ cup and take a hydrometer reading. Discard sample.

12. Add the 2½ teaspoons of pectic enzyme and the 2 packs of yeast to the fermenter when the temperature of the wort is 65–75°F; let sit 10 minutes, then stir vigorously to aerate. Snap the fermenter lid on, fill the airlock halfway with water, and place in lid. Place fermenter in a spot where the temperature will remain a constant 65–70°F.

13. Ferment in the primary for 10 days, then rack into a glass carboy for 2 weeks.

14. When brew is clear, siphon into a bottling bucket. Dissolve priming sugar into 1 cup boiling water, cool, and gently stir into beer with a sanitized spoon. CAUTION: If finished volume is less than 5 gallons, scale proportionately (e.g., 4½ gallons = ⅔ cup sugar).

15. Keep in a warm place for 7–10 days, then move to a cool place to age for 2 weeks.

GINGER ALE
🍺 🍺 🍺 🍺

PAUL WHITE, HEAD BREWER, THE SEVEN BARREL BREWERY—WEST LEBANON, NEW HAMPSHIRE

You can forget the soda-pop version that shares the same name after you brew this fairly easy all-grain batch. It features freshly grated ginger for a uniquely spicy, refreshing flavor.

ORIGINAL GRAVITY: 1.040–42

FINAL GRAVITY: 1.010–12

POTENTIAL ALCOHOL: 3.9% ABV

INGREDIENTS

    4 pounds 6-row malt
    4 pounds flaked wheat
    8 AAUs of Hallertau whole hops
    1 teaspoon of Irish moss
    1 ounce freshly grated ginger root

2 packages Edme ale yeast

¾ cup corn sugar

BREWING PROCEDURES

1. Dough crushed malt and flaked wheat into 3 gallons of water at 132–135°F and rest at 122–125°F for 30 minutes.
2. Boost temperature to 150°F for a 2-hour rest, boosting back to 150°F whenever the temperature falls to 144°F.
3. Mash out and sparge to collect 6 gallons. Bring wort to a boil.
4. After boiling the wort 15 minutes, add 8 AAUs of Hallertau flowers and boil 45 minutes. Add 1 teaspoon of Irish moss and 1 ounce freshly grated ginger root, boil 15 minutes, then shut off heat.
5. Chill to 70°F, top up to 5 gallons if necessary, and pitch rehydrated Edme ale yeast.
6. Primary ferment for 5 days; transfer to secondary for 7 days or more.
7. Keg or bottle with corn sugar. Age for at least 2 weeks.

RASPBERRY WHEAT

⊕ ⊕

JOE & BRYAN TIMMONS

BOSTON BREWERS SUPPLY CO.–

JAMAICA PLAIN, MASSACHUSETTS

This is a simple intermediate recipe for what is becoming a favorite microbrewery seasonal. Try using a liquid Belgian or Bavarian wheat yeast or a neutral American Ale yeast for the ultimate summer refresher.

ORIGINAL GRAVITY: 1.043–45

FINAL GRAVITY: 1.010–12

POTENTIAL ALCOHOL: 4% ABV

IBUs: approximately 20

INGREDIENTS

0.5 pound light crystal malt

3.3 pounds Northwestern wheat extract

3 pounds English light extract

1.5 ounces Hallertau hop pellets (bittering)

0.5 ounces Hallertau hop pellets (aroma)

1 teaspoon Irish moss flakes

4 pounds fresh or frozen raspberries

1 package dried ale yeast

6 ounces corn sugar for priming

BREWING PROCEDURES

1. Secure the grains in the muslin straining bag. Pour 2 gallons of cold water into your brewpot, apply heat, and add the grain bag. Heat to a near boil (about 155º); turn off the heat. Remove the grain bag, drain, and discard.
2. Thoroughly dissolve the malt extract, apply heat, and bring to a boil. As soon as the wort begins to boil, add the 1.5 ounces of Hallertau bittering hops. Start timing the boil; the total elapsed time will be 60 minutes. Prepare the raspberries according to the directions below. After 45 minutes, add the Irish moss and continue to boil for an additional 15 minutes. Turn off the heat and add the 0.5 ounce of Hallertau aroma hops. Cover the pot and steep for 5 minutes.
3. In another pot, bring 1 gallon of water to a boil, remove the pot from the heat, and add the frozen raspberries. Stabilize the temperature between 155° and 160°F. Cover the pot and allow the fruit to steep until the wort has been cooled. Do not boil the fruit!

Remember that after the wort has cooled, it is highly vulnerable to contamination; everything that comes into contact with it from this point on must be thoroughly sanitized!

4. Cool the wort as quickly as possible. A wort chiller works best, but if you haven't got one yet a cold water bath will do the trick. Place the covered pot in your kitchen sink and fill with ice and cold water. While the wort is cooling, funnel the fruit and water mixture into your fermenter. When the temperature has fallen to about 90°F, transfer the wort, through a strainer if possible, into your fermenter. Top off with enough cold water to reach a 5-gallon level and stir or shake well. Draw off a small sample and take both a hydrometer and a temperature reading; always discard the sample used.

5. When the wort has cooled to 65–70°F, you are ready to add the yeast. Once the yeast has been added, attach a blowoff tube and keep the fermenter in a cool, dark location where temperature fluctuations are minimal, ideally 68°F. Active fermentation should become visible in the next 12 to 24 hours and will continue for about 3 to 5 days.

6. After 5 days of primary fermentation, gently transfer the beer to a sanitized secondary fermenter (ideally a 5-gallon glass carboy), leaving all sediment behind. Attach an airlock and allow the beer to ferment for an additional 10 to 14 days at the same temperature of primary fermentation. At the end of this period, draw off a small sample and check the final gravity. By now it should be within the range stated above; if not, wait another couple of days and check again. Prepare to bottle.

BOTTLING AND CONDITIONING

1. Sanitize all of your siphoning and bottling equipment, bottles, and caps.

2. Boil the 6 ounces of corn sugar in about a cup of water and pour it into your bottling bucket. Gently siphon the beer out of the fermenter into the bucket, making sure the flow is directed to the bottom of the bucket; avoid splashing or agitating the beer.

3. Using your siphon tubing and bottle filler, fill each bottle to within an inch from the top and cap immediately. Store the bottles upright for 3 to 4 weeks, chill, and enjoy.

THANKSGIVING CRANBERRY ALE

JOE & BRYAN TIMMONS
BOSTON BREWERS SUPPLY CO.— JAMAICA PLAIN, MASSACHUSETTS

"Here's a truly unique ale that utilizes one of our state's most bountiful crops, the cranberry. At first you might think that adding cranberries to beer is a little odd, but cranberries and beer are perfectly suited for each other. The tartness of this fruit balances especially well with the light, crisp characteristics of wheat as well as the sweetness of malt. Our cranberry ale is a beautiful pale amber-red color with a complex fruity, faintly spicy aroma. The cranberry presence is more evident on the pallet, contributing a pronounced tartness and refreshing finish."

ORIGINAL GRAVITY: 1.044–46

FINAL GRAVITY: 1.008–10

POTENTIAL ALCOHOL: 4.6% ABV

IBUs: 20 to 22

INGREDIENTS

> 6 ounces torrefied wheat
>
> 6.6 pounds Northwestern Weizen extract
>
> 1 ounce Hallertau hop pellets
>
> 1 ounce Tettnanger hop pellets
>
> 2 pounds whole cranberries
>
> 1 teaspoon Irish moss
>
> 1 package dry ale yeast
>
> 6 ounces corn sugar for priming

BREWING PROCEDURES

1. Secure the torrefied wheat in the muslin straining bag. Pour 2 gallons of cold water into your brewpot, apply heat, and add the grain bag. Heat to a near boil (about 155°F), turn off the heat, cover the pot, and allow the grains to steep for 15 minutes. Remove the grain bag, drain, and discard.

2. While the grains are steeping, you must prepare the cranberries. Rinse the berries with cold water and then drain in a strainer. Using a food processor, chopper, or blender, finely grind or puree the berries and set aside for future use.

3. Thoroughly dissolve the malt extract, apply heat, and bring to a boil. As soon as the wort (unfermented beer) begins to boil, add the Hallertau and Tettnang hops. Start timing the boil; the total elapsed time will be 50 minutes. Maintain a good rolling boil. After 20 minutes, add the cranberry puree; 10 minutes later add the Irish moss flakes. Continue to boil for an additional 20 minutes, then cover and remove the pot from the heat.

Remember that after the wort has cooled, it is highly vulnerable to contamination; everything that comes into contact with it from this point on must be thoroughly sanitized!

4. Cool the wort as quickly as possible. A wort chiller works best, but if you haven't got one yet a cold water bath will do the trick. Place the covered pot in your kitchen sink and fill with ice and cold water. When the temperature has fallen to about 90°F, transfer the wort, through a strainer if possible, into your fermenter. Top off with enough cold water to reach a 5-gallon level and stir or shake well. Draw off a small sample and take both a hydrometer and a temperature reading; always discard the sample used.

5. When the wort has cooled to 65–70°F, you are ready to add the yeast. Once the yeast has been added, attach an airlock and keep the fermenter in a cool, dark location where temperature fluctuations are minimal, ideally 65–70°F. Active fermentation should become visible in the next 12 to 24 hours and will continue for about 3 to 5 days.

6. When visible signs of fermentation have ceased, gently transfer the beer to a sanitized secondary fermenter (ideally a 5-gallon glass carboy), leaving all sediment behind. Attach an airlock and allow the beer to settle for an additional 7 to 10 days at the same temperature of primary fermentation. At the end of this period, draw off a small sample and check the final gravity. By now it should be within the range stated above; if not, wait another couple of days and check again. Prepare to bottle.

BOTTLING AND CONDITIONING

1. Sanitize all of your siphoning and bottling equipment, bottles, and caps.

2. Boil the 6 ounces of corn sugar in about a cup of water and pour it into your bottling

bucket. Gently siphon the beer out of the fermenter into the bucket, making sure the flow is directed to the bottom of the bucket; avoid splashing or agitating the beer.

3. Using your siphon tubing and bottle filler, fill each bottle to within an inch from the top and cap immediately. Store the bottles upright for 3 to 4 weeks, chill, and enjoy.

BELGIAN KRUIDENBIER
🛢 🛢 🛢
STEPHEN SNYDER

I threw everything but the kitchen sink into this recipe in trying to recreate a Belgian spiced beer such as those often produced seasonally by small artisinal brewers. It turned out well, I thought, and the spices can be varied infinitely to suit your personal taste. Leave out the oak chips for a mellower character. This recipe also makes for an excellent Christmas beer.

ORIGINAL GRAVITY: 1.064

FINAL GRAVITY: 1.014

POTENTIAL ALCOHOL: 6.5% ABV

INGREDIENTS

- ½ pound German light crystal malt
- ½ pound victory malt
- ½ pound Vienna malt
- 3 pounds English amber DME
- 3 pounds Dutch light DME
- ½ pound corn sugar
- ¼ pound sucrose
- ¼ pound brown sugar
- 1 ounce hop bittering blend (¼ ounce Styrian Goldings, ¼ ounce Hallertauer, ½ ounce Saaz)
- ¾ ounce hop flavoring blend (¼ ounce each Golding, Hallertauer, Saaz)
- ¾ ounce hop aromatic blend (¼ ounce each Golding, Hallertauer, Saaz)
- 1 teaspoon Irish moss
- Spice blend (3 ounces—cinnamon, nutmeg, allspice, cloves, orange peel, dried apple, star anise, cardamom, coriander)
- 1 package Wyeast 1214 liquid Belgian ale yeast with starter
- 1 ounce oak chips
- 1.25 cups DME for priming

BREWING PROCEDURES

1. Crack and add malts to 2½ quarts of 155°F brewing liquor. Steep 60 minutes.
2. Bring slowly to 170°F, rest 10 minutes, then immediately sparge into brew kettle.
3. Add 2 gallons soft water. Bring to boil. Remove brew kettle from heat before adding extract and DME to avoid sticking or burning.
4. Boil for a total of 2 hours, adding hops at 30, 110, and 118 minutes.
5. Add Irish moss at 105 minutes.
6. Immerse covered brewpot in sink filled with ice water for 30 minutes.
7. Put spices in a hop bag and boil separately for 5 minutes in 1 pint of water.
8. Rack cooled, strained wort into primary fermenter bucket containing 2½ to 3 gallons ice-cold, soft water to equal 6 gallons.
9. Pitch yeast at 75°F, then add spice sack with water it was boiled in to fermenter and 1 ounce of sanitized oak chips.
10. Ferment between 68° and 75°F for 7–14 days.
11. Bottle with DME primer, warm-condition (68°F) 7 days.
12. Cellar-condition (56°F) 4–6 weeks.

Weights and Measures

(All measures are in U.S. equivalents unless otherwise noted.)

Liquid Measures

1 gallon = 3.785 liters

1 gallon = 4 quarts = 128 fluid ounces

1 gallon of water weighs 8.35 pounds

1 Imperial (British) gallon × 0.833 = 1 U.S. gallon

1 Imperial gallon = 1.20095 U.S. gallons

1 quart = 2 pints = 4 cups = 32 fluid ounces = .95 liter

1 pint = 16 fluid ounces = 2 cups = 1/2 quart

1 barrel = 31 1/2 gallons

1/2 barrel = 1 keg = 15.5 gallons = approximately 7 cases

1/4 barrel (pony keg) = 7.75 gallons

1 tablespoon = 3 teaspoons = 1/2 fluid ounce

1 cup = 16 tablespoons = 8 fluid ounces

1 teaspoon = 1/3 tablespoon or 1/8 fluid ounce

1 fluid ounce = 2 tablespoons or 6 teaspoons

1 liter = 100 centiliters = 1,000 milliliters

1 liter = 2.11 pints = 1.057 quarts = .264 gallons

1 hectoliter = 100 liters

Gallons × 3.8 = liters

Liters × 0.26 = gallons

British Beer Cask Sizes (in Imperial Gallons)

1 hogshead = 54 gallons (1.5 barrels)

1 barrel = 36 gallons

1 kilderkin = 18 gallons

1 firkin = 9 gallons

1 pin = 4.5 gallons

Belgian Beer Cask Sizes

1 foudre = 25 barrels (3,000 liters)

1 pipe = 5.5 barrels (650 liters)

1 tonne = 2.2 barrels (267 liters)

Dry Weight Measures

1 pound = 16 ounces = 454 grams

1 ounce = 28.349 grams

1 kilogram = 1,000 grams = 35.27 ounces = 2.21 pounds

1 gram = 100 centigrams = 1,000 milligrams

1,000 milligram = 0.35 ounce

Pounds × 0.45 = kilos

Kilos × 2.2 = pounds

Measurement Conversion

Known Quantity	To Find	Mutiply By
Teaspoons	Milliliters	4.93
Teaspoons	Tablespoons	0.33
Tablespoons	Milliliters	14.79
Tablespoons	Teaspoons	3.00
Cups	Liters	0.24
Cups	Pints	0.50
Cups	Quarts	0.25
Pints	Cups	2.00
Pints	Liters	0.47
Pints	Quarts	0.50
Quarts	Cups	4.00
Quarts	Gallons	0.25
Quarts	Liters	0.95
Quarts	Pints	2.00
Gallons	Liters	3.79
Gallons	Quarts	4.00

Temperature Conversion

Celsius = 0.556 × (F° − 32). Subtract 32 from Fahrenheit degrees, then multiply by five-ninths (0.556).

Fahrenheit = (1.8 × C°) + 32. Multiply Celsius degrees by nine-fifths (1.8), then add 32.

Conversion of Some Common Temperatures

Mashing—148–158°F = 64–70°C

Sparging—160–170°F = 71–77°C

Boiling—212°F = 100°C

Pitching (Ale)—65–75°F = 18–24°C

Pitching (Lager)—55–60°F = 13–16°C

Fermenting (Ale)—60–80°F = 16–27°C

Fermenting (Lager)—40–60°F = 4–16°C

Lagering—32–45°F = 0–7°C

Cellaring—50–55°F = 10–13°C

Serving (Ale)—50–55°F = 10–13°C

Serving (Lager)—45–50°F = 7–10°C

Sugar and Malt Conversions

Dry malt extract (DME) and Brewer's (corn) sugar:

  1 pound = 2.4 cups

  1 cup = 6.5 ounces

Cane sugar:

  1 pound = 2 cups

  1 cup = 8 ounces = 1/2 pound

  1 ounce = 2 level tablespoons

NOTE: 3/4 cup corn sugar for priming = 1.20–1.5 cups light DME—depending on fermentability. For example: Dutch DME is typically 55% fermentable; English is typically 75%.

FORMULAS

DETERMINING SPECIFIC GRAVITY USING MALT EXTRACT

Brewers Resource of Camarillo, California, offers this simple formula for determing how much malt you will need to produce the original specific gravity of your wort before you start to brew, especially if you intend to brew a specific style of beer. Dry malt extract (DME) produces about 44 degrees per pound/per gallon of water. Liquid malt extract produces approximately 35 degrees. To predetermine the original gravity of your beer when designing recipes, use this simple formula to determine how much malt extract to use: (degrees of extract) times pounds of malt used divided by gallons of beer to be brewed. For instance, if we use 4 1/2 pounds of DME to make 5 gallons of beer we would have 44 × 4.5 = 198 . . . so, 198 divided by 5 (gallons of beer to be made) = 39.6, or an original gravity of about 1.040.

DETERMINING ALPHA ACID UNITS (AAUs)

This commonly used formulation was made famous by Dave Line in The Big Book of Brewing (Amateur Winemaker, Andover, UK, 1974). This is not as accurate as determining IBUs but provides a very good estimation for home brewers. Add the alpha acid percent per ounce of hops you will be boiling for more than 15 minutes and then divide by the number of gallons to be made. For instance: 1 1/2 ounces of hops with 5.5% AA + 1 ounce hops with 4% AA = 12.25 total alpha acid units. Divide the AAUs by the gallons of beer to be made; 5 gallons would yield 2.5 AAUs per gallon of beer.

DETERMINING HOME-BREW BITTERING UNITS (HBUs)

Homebrew bittering units, or HBUs, is a formulation used by the American Homebrewers Association based on Dave Line's AAU formula, and equals the total ounces of hops to be boiled for 15 minutes or more multiplied by their alpha acid rating.

Example: 3 ounces of 4.4% AA hops = 3 × 4.4 (not 4.4%!) = 13.2 HBUs.

DETERMINING INTERNATIONAL BITTERNESS UNITS (IBUs)

This formulation is based on a model used by Byron Burch in *Brewing Quality Beers: The Home Brewer's Essential Guidebook*, ounces of hops times alpha acid times percent utilization (as a function of boil time) divided by 7.25. For instance, if we brew a pale ale with 1 1/2 ounces of Fuggles (4.8 AA) boiled 60 minutes for bittering, and 3/4 ounce of Goldings (5.5 AA) boiled 15 minutes for flavor, we would have the following: 1.5 × 4.8 = 7.2 and 7.2 × 30 = 216. 216 ÷ 7.25 = 29.79 IBUs. Add to this the flavoring hops; .75 × 5.5 = 4.13; 4.13 × 8 = 33.04; 33.04 ÷ 7.25 = 4.56 IBUs for a total of 34.35 IBUs. Percent utilizations are:

Up to 5 minutes 5%
6 to 10 minutes 6%
11 to 15 minutes 8%
16 to 20 minutes 10.1%
21 to 25 minutes 12.1%
26 to 30 minutes 15.3%
31 to 35 minutes 18.8%
36 to 40 minutes 22.8%
41 to 45 minutes 26.9%
46 to 50 minutes 28.1%
51 to 60 minutes 30%

Note: Although professional brewers and some homebrewers can achieve hop utilization rates as high as 40 percent with hop pellets, it is safer to assume that you will only achieve a maximum of 30 percent with pellets and 25 percent when using plugs or whole flowers. Using these figures, as well as aiming for the midrange of IBUs in the style you are brewing, will improve your chances of achieving appropriate bitterness. Some of the other factors that increase hop bitterness utilization, according to Gerard W. C. Lemmens in his treatise "Hop Utilisation," include:

1. High wort pH
2. Long boil times
3. Low wort gravity
4. Using "fresh" hops
5. Strain of yeast used

Conversely, it also should be noted that the factors that decrease hop utilization include:

1. Low wort pH
2. Short boil times
3. High wort gravity
4. Hop bags
5. Stale hops
6. Strain of yeast used

DETERMINING PERCENTAGE OF ALCOHOL BY VOLUME (ABV)

Subtract the alcohol percentage of the final gravity reading from the alcohol percentage of the original gravity reading:

Example: 7% (1.055) − 1% (1.010) = 6%

Or original gravity minus final gravity (without decimal points) divided by 7.5:

Example: 1055 − 1010 = 45 ÷ 7.5 = 6%

Converting ABV to Percentage of Alcohol by Weight (ABW)

Mutiply the ABV figure by .80, or 80 percent:

Example: ABV = 6% × .80 = 4.8%

Conversely, to determine ABV when you know ABW, multiply by 1.25.

Example: ABW = 4.8% × 1.25 = 6%

Hydrometers

The specific gravity scale refers to the weight of a liquid in relation to the weight of water, which is set at 1.000, or 1,000. This is the scale used by British brewers and is the scale used by the majority of American homebrewers.

The Balling or Brix scale (a saccharometer) expresses the percentage of sugar in the liquid (by weight) and is expressed in degrees Plato (°P). This is the scale used by many American and all German brewers.

The alcohol scale measures the approximate amount of alcohol expressed as a percentage that will be present in the beer when fermentation is complete. Two readings must be taken—one before yeast is pitched, and one when fermentation has ceased. (See example 2 below.)

Temperature Corrections for Standard Hydrometers

Most hydrometers are calibrated to read specific gravity accurately at 60°F. If your wort is not at this temperature, you'll need to adjust your readings according to the correction figures below (see example 1). Temperatures are in degrees Fahrenheit. Caution: Do not immerse a cold hydrometer into hot or boiling liquid. It may break. Temperature readings should be taken in cool liquid or after the hydromter has been preheated in hot water.

TEMPERATURE / CORRECTION

Temperature	Correction
40	Subtract 1
50	Subtract 1/2
60	Add 0
70	Add 1
77	Add 2
84	Add 3
88	Add 4
95	Add 5
100	Add 6
105	Add 7
115	Add 9
120	Add 11
140	Add 16
150	Add 19
170	Add 26
212	Add 42

Example 1:
Wort temperature is 77° F.
Specific Gravity: 1.053
Correction Figure: +2
Actual Specific Gravity: 1.055

Determining potential alcohol: Subtract the second alcohol reading (young beer) from the first alcohol reading (wort).

Example 2:
1st Reading (Original Gravity:):1.055
Corresponding alcohol %: 7.0
2nd Reading (Final Gravity:): 1.014
Corresponding alcohol %: 1.5
Therefore, 7.0 – 1.5 = 5.5% alcohol ABV (ABV)

TRIPLE SCALE HYDROMETER READINGS

Potential / ALCOHOL %	Specific / GRAVITY	Degrees / PLATO	Potential / ALCOHOL %	Specific / GRAVITY	Degrees / PLATO
0.00%	1.002	0.50	3.750	1.032	8.00
0.125	1.003	0.75	3.875	1.033	8.25
0.250	1.004	1.00	4.000	1.034	8.50
0.375	1.005	1.25	4.125	1.035	8.75
0.500	1.006	1.50	4.250	1.036	9.00
0.625	1.007	1.75	4.375	1.037	9.25
0.750	1.008	2.00	4.500	1.038	9.50
0.875	1.009	2.25	4.625	1.039	9.75
1.000	1.010	2.50	4.750	1.040	10.00
1.125	1.011	2.75	5.000	1.041	10.25
1.250	1.012	3.00	5.125	1.042	10.50
1.375	1.013	3.25	5.250	1.043	10.75
1.500	1.014	3.50	5.375	1.044	11.00
1.625	1.015	3.75	5.500	1.045	11.25
1.750	1.016	4.00	5.625	1.046	11.50
1.875	1.017	4.25	5.750	1.047	11.75
2.000	1.018	4.50	5.875	1.048	12.00
2.125	1.019	4.75	6.000	1.049	12.25
2.250	1.020	5.00	6.125	1.050	12.50
2.375	1.021	5.25	6.250	1.051	12.75
2.500	1.022	5.50	6.375	1.052	13.00
2.625	1.023	5.75	6.500	1.053	13.25
2.750	1.024	6.00	6.625	1.054	13.50
2.875	1.025	6.25	6.750	1.055	13.75
3.000	1.026	6.50	7.000	1.056	14.00
3.125	1.027	6.75	7.125	1.057	14.25
3.250	1.028	7.00	7.250	1.058	14.50
3.375	1.029	7.25	7.375	1.059	14.75
3.500	1.030	7.50	7.500	1.060	15.00
3.625	1.031	7.75	7.750	1.061	15.25

Potential / *Specific* / *Degrees*				*Potential* / *Specific* / *Degrees*				*Potential* / *Specific* / *Degrees*		
ALCOHOL %	/	GRAVITY	/ PLATO	ALCOHOL %	/	GRAVITY	/ PLATO	ALCOHOL %	/ GRAVITY	/ PLATO
7.875		1.062	15.50	10.500		1.082	20.50	13.250	1.102	25.50
8.000		1.063	15.75	10.625		1.083	20.75	13.375	1.103	25.75
8.125		1.064	16.00	10.750		1.084	21.00	13.500	1.104	26.00
8.250		1.065	16.25	10.875		1.085	21.25	13.750	1.105	26.25
8.375		1.066	16.50	11.000		1.086	21.50	13.875	1.106	26.50
8.500		1.067	16.75	11.125		1.087	21.75	14.000	1.107	26.75
8.625		1.068	17.00	11.250		1.088	22.00	14.125	1.108	27.00
8.750		1.069	17.25	11.375		1.089	22.25	14.250	1.109	27.25
8.875		1.070	17.50	11.500		1.090	22.50	14.375	1.110	27.50
9.000		1.071	17.75	11.625		1.091	22.75	14.500	1.111	27.75
9.125		1.072	18.00	11.750		1.092	23.00	14.625	1.112	28.00
9.250		1.073	18.25	12.000		1.093	23.25	14.750	1.113	28.25
9.375		1.074	18.50	12.125		1.094	23.50	14.875	1.114	28.50
9.500		1.075	18.75	12.250		1.095	23.75	15.000	1.115	28.75
9.750		1.076	19.00	12.375		1.096	24.00			
9.875		1.077	19.25	12.500		1.097	24.25			
10.000		1.078	19.50	12.750		1.098	24.50			
10.125		1.079	19.75	12.875		1.099	24.75			
10.250		1.080	20.00	13.000		1.100	25.00			
10.375		1.081	20.25	13.125		1.101	25.25			

NOTE: As you can see from the above figures, there are roughly 4 points of specific gravity per degree of Plato. Example: .5°P × 4 = SG 1.002.

DIRECTORY

ASSOCIATIONS

American Homebrewers Association
736 Pearl Street
P.O. Box 1679
Boulder, Colorado 80306–1679
(303) 447–0816
FAX (303) 447–2825
Brewlab—The Life Science Building
University of Sunderland
Chester Road
Sunderland SR1 3SD
England
0 (1) 91 515 2535
CAMRA Ltd. (Campaign For Real Ale)
230 Hatfield Road, St. Albans
Hertfordshire AL1 4LW, England
727–867201 (from the U.S., first dial 011–44)
FAX 727–867670 (from the U.S., first dial 011–44)
De Objectieve Bierproevers (OBP)
(Belgian Beer Consumer's Organization)
Postbus 32

2600 Berchem 5
Belgium
Home Wine and Beer Trade Association
604 N. Miller Road
Valrico, Florida 33594
813–685–4261
Association of Bottled Beer Collectors
c/o Bob Heath
4 Woodhall Road, Penn,
Wolverhampton WV4 4DJ
England
0 (1) 902 342 672
British Beermat Collectors Society
c/o Brian West
10 Coombe Hill Crescent
Thame
Oxfordshire OX9 2EH
The Brewer's Society
(Brewers and Licensed Retailers Association)
42 Portman Square
London W1H OBB
0 (1) 71 486 4831

The Inn Sign Society
2 Mill House, Mill Lane
Countess Wear, Exeter
Devonshire EX2 6LL
0 (1) 392 70728
Institute of Brewing
33 Clarges Street
London W14 8EE
England
Promotie Informatie Traditioneel Bier (PINT)
(Dutch Beer Consumer's Organization)
Postbus 3757
1001 AN Amsterdam
Netherlands
Siebel Institute of Technology
4055 W. Peterson
Chicago, Illinois 60646
312–463–3400
FAX 312–463–4962
Society for the Preservation of Beers from the Wood (SPBW)
61 De Frene Road
London SE26 4AF

Svenska Ölfrämjandet (SO)
(Swedish Beer Consumer's Organization)
Box 16244
S–10325 Stockholm
Sweden

MAGAZINES

Zymurgy/New Brewer
736 Pearl Street
P.O. Box 1679
Boulder, Colorado 80306–1679
(303) 447–0816
FAX (303) 447–2825
Brewing Techniques
P.O. Box 3222
Eugene, Oregon 97403
(541) 687–2993
FAX (541) 687–8534
Suds 'n Stuff
Bosak Publishing Co.
4764 Galicia Way
Oceanside, California 92056
(619) 724–4447
FAX (619) 940–0549
American Brewer—The Business of Beer
P.O. Box 510
Hayward, California 94543–0510
(510) 538–9500
Brew Your Own
P.O. Box 1504
Martinez, California 94553
FAX (510) 372–8582
E-Mail: BYOmag@mother.com
Brew
1120 Mulberry Street
Des Moines, Iowa 50309
(515) 243–4929
FAX (515) 243–4517
All About Beer
Chautauqua, Inc.
1627 Marion Ave.
Durham, North Carolina 27705
(919) 490–0589
FAX (919) 490–0865
American Breweriana Journal
American Breweriana Association
P.O. Box 11157
Pueblo, Colorado 81001

Malt Advocate
3416 Oak Hill Road
Emmaus, Pennsylvania 18049
(610) 967–1083
E-Mail: maltman999@aol.com
Beer Magazine
102 Burlington Cr.
Ottawa, Ontario K1T 3K5
Canada
613–737–3715

NEWSPAPERS

Ale Street News
P.O. Box 1125
Maywood, New Jersey 07607
(201) 368–9100
FAX (201) 368–9101
E-Mail: alestreet@aol.com
BarleyCorn
P.O. Box 549
Frederick, Maryland 21705
(301) 831–3759
FAX (301) 831–6376
Brew Hawaii
P.O. Box 852
Hauula, Hawaii 96717–9998
808–259–6884
Celebrator Beer News
P.O. Box 375
Hayward, California 94543
(510) 670–0121
FAX (510) 670–0639
CompuServe 70540,1747
Midwest Beer Notes
339 6th Avenue
Clayton, Wisconsin 54004
715–948–2990
E-Mail: beernote@realbeer.com
Rocky Mountain Brews
251 Jefferson
Fort Collins, Colorado 80524
303–224–2524
Southern Draft Brew News
702 Sailfish Rd.
Winter Springs, Florida 32708
407–327–9451
Southwest Brewing News
11405 Evening Star Drive
Austin, Texas 78739
512–467–2225
512–282–4935

What's Brewing
(CAMRA Newspaper)
230 Hatfield Road, St. Albans
Hertfordshire AL1 4LW, England
727–867201 (from the U.S., first dial 011–44)
FAX 727–867670 (from the U.S., first dial 011–44)
E-Mail: camra@camra.org.uk
Home Page: www.camra.org.uk
What's Brewing
(CAMRA—Canada Newspaper)
P.O. Box 30101
Saanich Centre Postal Outlet
Victoria, B.C. V8X 5E1
Canada
604–386–2818
Yankee Brew News
P.O. Box 520250
Winthrop, Massachusetts 02152
Home Page: realbeer.com:80/ybn/
Beer & Tavern Chronicle
244 Madison Ave., Suite 164
New York, New York 10016
(212) 685–8334

NEWSLETTERS

Alephenalia
140 Lakeside Ave.—Suite 300
Seattle, Washington 98122–6538
(206) 448–1228
Northwest Brew News
22833 Bothell-Everett Hwy, Suite 1139
Bothell, Washington 98021–9365
206–742–5327
On Tap: The Newsletter
P.O. Box 71
Clemson, South Carolina 29633
803–654–3360
The Pint Post
12345 Lake City Way N.E. 159
Seattle, Washington 98125
206–365–5812
What's On Tap
P.O. Box 7779
Berkeley, California 94709
1–800–434–7779

CONTRIBUTORS

MICROBREWERS

Fal Allen, Head Brewer—Pike Place Brewery, Seattle, Washington

Clay Biberdorf, Head Brewer—Hart Brewing, Pyramid Ales, Kalama, Washington

Jay Garrison, Head Brewer—Pirate Brewery, Redondo Beach, California

Mike Knaub, Head Brewer—Chickies Rock Beers, Starview Brewing Company, Mt. Wolf, Pennsylvania

Tony Lubold, Head Brewer—Catamount Brewing Company, White River Junction, Vermont

Jim Quilter, Assistant Brewmaster—Sierra Nevada Brewing Co. Inc., Chico, California

Mark Richmond, Head Brewer—Great Lakes Brewing Company, Cleveland, Ohio

Tom Sweeney, Brewmaster—America's Brewing Company at Walter Payton's Roundhouse Complex, Aurora, Illinois

Andrew Tveekrem, Head Brewer—Great Lakes Brewing Company, Cleveland Ohio

Paul White, Head Brewer—The Seven Barrel Brewery, West Lebanon, New Hampshire

HOMEBREW SUPPLY SHOPS

The Brewmeister
4249 Winding Woods Way
Fair Oaks, California 95628
916–985–7299

The Home Brewery
1506 Columbia Avenue #12
Riverside, California 92507
909–796–0699
1–800–622–7393 (orders)
E-mail: acmebrew@empirenet.com

Brewer's Resource
404 Calle San Pablo, No. 104
Camarillo, California 93012
805–445–4100
1–800–827–3983 (orders)
FAX (805) 443–4130

RCA Distributors
9229 Allano Way St.
Santee, California 92701
619–448–6688
FAX 603–445–2018

BrewBuddys
1509 Aviation Boulevard
Redondo Beach, California 90278
310–798–2739
1–800–372–3433 (orders)

William's Brewing
2594 Nicholson Street
P.O. Box 2195
San Leandro, California 94577
510–895–2739
1–800–759–6025 (orders)

The Home Beer, Wine, & Cheesemaking Shop
22836 Ventura Blvd., #2
Woodland Hills, California 91364
818–884–8586
FAX 818–224–3812

The Beverage People
840 Piner Road, #14
Santa Rosa, California 95403
707–544–2520
1–800–544–1867 (orders)

Old West Homebrew Supply
303 East Pikes Peak Avenue
Colorado Springs, Colorado 80903
719–635–2443
1–800–ILV–BREW (orders)

The Mad Capper
P.O. Box 161
Glastonbury, Connecticut 06033
860–659–8588

Crossfire Brewing Supplies
17 Kreyssig Road
Broad Brook, Connecticut 06016
860–623–6537

The Home Brewery
416 S. Broad St.
P.O. Box 575

Brooksville, Florida 34601
904–799–3004
1–800–245–BREW (orders)

Brew & Grow
2379 Bode Road
Schaumburg, Illinois 60194
847–885–8282
1–800–444–2837
FAX 847–885–8634

Brew & Grow
1824 N. Besly Ct.
Chicago, Illinois 60622
(733) 395–1500

Sheaf & Vine Brewing Supply
5425 S. LaGrange Rd.
Countryside, Illinois 60525
708–430–HOPS

The Home Brewery
1446 N. 3rd Street
Bardstown, Kentucky 40004
502–349–1001
FAX (Same)
1–800–992-BREW (orders)

Brew Masters, Ltd.
12266 Wilkins Avenue
Rockville, Maryland 20852
1–800–466–9557 (orders)
301–984–9557
FAX (301) 881–9250

Brew Masters, Ltd.
1017 Light Street
Baltimore, Maryland 21230
410–783–1258
FAX 410–783–0145

The Flying Barrel
111 South Carroll Street
Frederick, Maryland 21701
301–663–4491

Maryland Homebrew
6770 Oak Hall Lane, Suite 115
Columbia, Maryland 21045
410–290–3768
FAX 410–290–6795
Home Page: www.mdhb.com

The Vineyard
123 Glen Avenue
P.O. Box 80
Upton, Massachusetts 01568
1–800–626–2371

FAX 508–529–2448
E-mail: winegrower@aol.com
Beer & Winemaking Supplies, Inc.
154 King Street
Northampton, Massachusetts 01060
1–800–473–BREW (orders)
413–586–0150 (advice)
(413) 584–5674
The Modern Brewer
99 Dover Street
Somerville, Massachusetts 02144
617–629–0400
1–800–SEND ALE
Beer & Wine Hobby
180 New Boston Street
Woburn, Massachusetts 01801–6206
1–800–523–5423 (orders)
617–933–8818 (info)
FAX 617–662–0872
Boston Brewers Supply
48 South Street
Jamaica Plain, Massachusetts 02130
617–983–1710
Wine Barrel Plus
30303 Plymouth Road
Livonia, Michigan 48150
313–522–9463
Wind River Brewing Company
7212 Washington Ave. South
Eden Prairie, Minnesota 55344
1–800–266–4677 (orders)
612–942–0589 (advice)
FAX 612–942–0635
E-mail: windrvr@bitstream.net
Home Page: www.windriverbrew.com
The Home Brewery
P.O. Box 730
Ozark, Missouri 65721
581–485–0963
1–800–321–BREW (orders)
FAX 417–485–0965
E. C. Kraus
733 S. Northern Boulevard
P.O. Box 7850
Independence, Missouri 64054
816–254–0242
The Home Brewery
4300 N. Pecos Road, 13
North Las Vegas, Nevada 89115
702–644–7002
1–800–288–DARK (orders)
RCA Distributors
10 North St.
North Walpole, New Hampshire
03609

603–445–2018
1–800–RCA–BREW
FAX 603–445–2018
The Home Brewery
56 W. Main Street
Bogota, New Jersey 07603
201–525–1833
1–800–426–BREW (orders)
U-Brew
319 1/2 Millburn Avenue
Millburn, New Jersey 07041
201–376–0973
FAX 201–376–0493
East Coast Brewing Supply
124 Jacques Avenue
P.O. Box 060904
Staten Island, New York 10306
718–667–4459
FAX 718–987–3942
Mountain Malt and Hop Shoppe
54 Leggs Mills Road
Lake Katrine, New York 12449
914–336–7688
1–800–295–MALT (orders)
Mountain Malt and Hop Shoppe
29 Vassar Road
Poughkeepsie, New York 12603
(914) 463–HOPS
The Home Brewery
P.O. Box 1662
Grand Forks, North Dakota 58201
701–772–2671
1–800–367–BREW (orders)
Starview Brew
51 Codorus Furnace Road
Mt. Wolf, Pennsylvania 17347
717–266–5091
Beer Unlimited
Routes 30 and 401
Great Valley Shopping Center
Malvern, Pennsylvania 19355
610–889–0905
Beer Unlimited
515 Fayette Street
Conshohocken, Pennsylvania
19428
610–397–0666
Home Fermenter Center
123 Monroe Street
Eugene, Oregon 97402
(503) 485–6238
Northeast Brewers Supply, Inc.
745 Branch Avenue
Providence, Rhode Island 02904
401–521–4262

The Cellar Homebrew
14411 Greenwood Avenue North
P.O. Box 33525
Seattle, Washington 98133
206–365–7660
1–800–342–1871 (orders)
FAX 206–365–7677
E-mail: homebrew@aa.net
Home Page: www.aa.net/
~homebrew/catalog.html
Brewing Supplies
13 Oxford Road
Altrincham WA14 2DY
England
161 9282347
Brewing Supplies
48 Buxton Road
Stockport SK2 3NB
England
161 4804880
Blades Home Brewery
115 Market Street
Farnworth, Bolton
Lancashire BL4 8EX
England
1204 72130
The Cellars
114–116 Albany Road
Cardiff CF2 3RU
Wales
1222 493567
Jolly Brewer
1 College Street
Wrexham Clwyd LL13 8NA
Wales
1978 263338

The recipes of these professional brewers in no way reflect on their affiliation with, or the beers of, their respective breweries and are taken purely from their personal homebrew recipe collections.

Glossary

Adjunct. An unmalted cereal grain or other fermentable product used for brewing. An adjunct must rely on surplus enzymes in the mash to convert its starch to sugar.

Aerate. In brewing practice, to forcibly introduce air or pure oxygen into wort to facilitate yeast growth.

Airlock. A simple one-way valve fitted to a fermenter that allows the escape of CO_2 but prevents entry of outside air.

Ale. Originally, the designation for a malt beverage brewed with bittering herbs other than hops but now a broad term for any top-fermented beer.

Alpha Acid. A hop flower resin that contributes bitterness to beer.

Alpha Acid Units (AAU). Ounces of hops being boiled multiplied by their alpha acid percentage. Two ounces of 5% alpha acid hops would yield 10 alpha acid units.

Attenuation. The lowering of the fermentables in a wort as the result of yeast metabolism.

Autolysis. The process in which yeast cells metabolize each other in a nutrient-depleted beer.

Beer. Any top- or bottom-fermented malt beverage.

Beta Acid. A largely insoluble hop flower resin that contributes bitterness only when oxidized.

Bottle-Conditioned. A beer whose carbonation has been produced by natural processes in the bottle by the action of living yeast.

Bottom Fermentation. Fermentation by *Saccharomyces uvarum* or so-called lager yeast that settles at the bottom of the fermenter during the fermentation process.

Burtonizing. The addition of gypsum or calcium sulfate in order to replicate the brewing liquor of Burton-on-Trent in the brewing of pale ale.

Carbonation. The carbon dioxide dissolved in a liquid. Also, the process of producing dissolved carbon dioxide by a variety of methods.

Cask. A barrel of various sizes, traditionally made of wood, and generally containing living yeast sediment as opposed to a keg in which the beer is filtered and force-carbonated artificially. Also, an oak barrel used as a fermentation or maturation vessel.

Cask-Conditioned. Beer, generally an ale, that derives its carbonation from a natural refermentation in the barrel from which it is dispensed.

Chill Haze. Cloudiness in the finished beer resulting from undegraded protein and tannins that coagulate at cold temperatures.

Chlorophenols. Chlorine-based compounds that contribute an unpleasant chemical taste and smell. In beer, they are usually the result of using a chlorinated sanitizer.

Cold-Break. The coagulation of protein and other molecules when the wort is chilled.

Condition. The dissolved carbon dioxide in a beer.

Decoction. To extract by boiling. In brewing parlance, the mashing process whereby a portion of the mash is removed, boiled, then returned to the main mash in order to raise the temperature. Decoction is primarily thought of as a German method designed to work with undermodified malts for consistent temperature control before the invention of the thermometer.

Degrees of Extract. A measurement of specific gravity degrees yielded by one pound of fermentables in one gallon of water.

Dextrines. Unfermentable or slowly fermentable carbohydrates that give body to beer.

Diacetyl. A chemical compound produced during fermentation recognized by a buttery or butterscotch aroma. Perceptible diacteyl aroma is considered a fault in most beer styles and in excessive amounts in beers such as pale ale, where it is appropriate.

Diastase. Starch-degrading enzymes, primarily beta- and alpha-amylase.

DMS (Dimethyl Sulfide). A chemical compound produced during malting that produces a cooked corn or vegetable aroma. A fault in most beer styles and in large amounts in beers such as pilsner, where it is appropriate.

Dropping Bright. Yeast settlement in packaged beer.

Dry-Hopping. Addition of unboiled aroma hops into an airtight beer container such as a cask or secondary fermenter for ten or more days to produce hop bouquet.

EBC. Abbreviation for European Brewing Convention. A widely used measurement of color.

Esters. Compounds primarily produced during warm fermentations, principally by wild or top-fermenting yeast strains, that are responsible for fruity aromas in beer. These esters often suggest aromas of banana, cloves, apples, and vanilla.

Final Gravity. The density of a beer relative to the density of water at the end of the main fermentation.

Finings. Substances used to clarify beer after the fermentation process primarily by settling out suspended yeast and proteins.

Finishing Hops. Hops added in the final stages of a wort boil or as dry hops for the purpose of lending flavor and/or aroma to the finished beer.

Flocculation. The coagulation of suspended matter in a liquid into a mass. Hot- and cold-break flocculate, but the term "flocculation" is primarily used in reference to the coagulation of yeast during fermentation.

Force-Carbonate. To forcibly dissolve carbon dioxide into fermented beer under pressure.

Germination. The phase of the malting process where the grain kernel is soaked in water until it forms a tiny sprout called an acrospire. Germination initiates enzyme development and the preliminary conversion of starches.

Grist. The grains or adjuncts crushed for mashing.

HBU (Homebrew Bittering Units). Another name for AAUs, HBUs are an approximate measurement of the total alpha acids contributed to the beer obtained by multiplying alpha acid by ounces of hops boiled for more than fifteen minutes. This measurement only approximates actual bitterness, as hops boiled sixteen minutes contribute less bitterness than hops boiled sixty minutes.

Hop Back. From the French "bac à houblons," a vessel used to strain loose hops from the wort at the end of the boil. The hop back is also used as a container where wort is strained through unboiled aroma hops on the way to the fermenter.

Hot-Break. Protein that is coagulated during the wort boil.

Hydrometer. A device used to measure the percent of sugars in a wort, its relative density compared to water, and its potential alcohol content.

IBU. Also known as EBU, a measurement of a beer's bitterness based on the estimated alpha acid percentage of the hops used and the length of time they are boiled.

Initial Heat. The first stabilized temperature of the mash once the grist is mixed with the brewing liquor.

Keg. Usually a metal barrel used to hold beer that is force-carbonated.

Kräusen. The thick, foamy head of yeast that forms at the peak of fermentation.

Kräusening. Introduction of actively fermenting beer at the stage of "high kräusen" to more thoroughly fermented beer, usually in order to condition the beer.

Lager. Literally, to store. More specifically, in brewing practice, "lager" means to gradually lower a beer to near freezing temperatures after primary fermentation. Once a temperature of 32–35°F is attained, the lagering phase often lasts for two to three weeks with top-fermented beers or one to six months for bottom-fermented beers.

Lauter. To separate the sweet wort from the spent grains (draff) after the completion of the mash. The lauter tun is a vessel with a slotted false bottom above a tap to allow the wort to be drawn off.

Liquor. A professional brewer's term for water used for brewing.

Lovibond. A measurement of color used primarily in Great Britain.

Lupulin. The powdery, yellowish substance in female hop flowers containing the resins and essential oils that give hops their flavor, bitterness, and aroma.

Malt. A cereal grain, usually barley, that has undergone a period of germination and drying.

Mash. *n.* A mixture of crushed grains and hot water. *v.* The process of mixing crushed grains with hot water to cause a conversion of starch to sugar.

Maturation. The process of aging the beer after fermentation is complete to mellow and blend strong flavors. Maturation may be carried out at a variety of temperatures and in bottles, casks, or tanks, depending on the style of beer.

Modification. The changes in a cereal grain brought about by germination during the malting process.

Original Gravity. The first specific-gravity reading taken with the hydrometer to calculate the beer's potential strength before the onset of fermentation.

Oxidation. The negative effects of air on brewing ingredients, wort, and fermented beer that lends stale, almond-like, or wet cardboard tastes and aromas.

pH. The relative measurement of alkalinity and acidity on a scale of 1 to 14 with 7 being neutral. One represents the most acidic value, 14 represents the most alkaline.

Pitching. The addition of yeast to unfermented wort.

Priming. The addition of sugars or wort to fermented beer for the purpose of producing carbonation through a secondary fermentation.

Rack. To transfer beer or wort.

Rest. A length of time the mash is kept at a particular temperature.

Retorrefication. Heating of the grist prior to mashing in in order to lessen the loss of heat in the mash liquor.

Rousing. The act of stirring or redistributing prematurely settled yeast. This is usually only done with quickly flocculating English ale yeasts and when fermenting high-gravity worts.

Saccharification. The breakdown of complex carbohydrates into simple sugars that can be readily fermented by beer yeast.

Secondary Fermenter. An airtight vessel used after the primary fermentation for lagering, maturation, or the settling of suspended matter in beer.

Sparging. The act of rinsing wort out of the spent grains after the mash with hot water.

SRM (Standard Reference Method). A measurement of beer and grain color analogous to Lovibond degrees used by American brewers.

Starter. A small and usually weak wort used to build up small quantities of yeast to larger volumes for pitching into unfermented wort in the primary fermenter. The larger quantities spur a faster and more vigorous fermentation.

Step-Mash. A mash schedule that features upward steps in rest temperatures to accommodate a variety of optimum enzyme-operating temperatures.

Stillage. A cradle for holding a horizontal beer cask for dispensing or storage purposes.

Strike Heat. The temperature of the hot liquor when it is mixed with the grist in a mash.

Tannin. Compounds naturally occurring in cereal grains that can contribute to haziness or astringent bitterness in beer.

Trub. Precipitated proteins, oils, and tannins suspended in wort either by boiling or cooling.

Ullage. Also known as "headspace" or "airspace," ullage is the area between the surface of the beer and its container occupied by air or gas.

Wort. The sweet liquid that comes from mashing. Unfermented beer.

Yeast. Simple, single-celled microscopic fungi responsible for the fermentation process.

BIBLIOGRAPHY

BOOKS

Burch, Byron. *Brewing Quality Beers: The Home Brewer's Essential Guidebook,* 2nd ed. Fulton, CA: Joby Books, 1994.

Collins, Marie and Virginia Davis. *A Medieval Book of Seasons.* New York: HarperCollins Publishers, 1992.

Eckhardt, Fred. *The Essentials of Beer Styles.* Portland, OR: Fred Eckhardt Communications, 1989.

Evans, Jeff, ed. *Good Beer Guide 1996.* St. Albans, England: CAMRA Books, Campaign for Real Ale, 1996.

Fargis, Paul and Sheree Bykofsky, ed. directors. *The New York Public Library Desk Reference.* New York: Webster's New World, 1989.

Fix, George. *Principles of Brewing Science.* Boulder, CO: Brewers Publications, 1989.

Fix, George and Laurie Fix. *Vienna, Märzen, Oktoberfest, Classic Beer Style Series.* Boulder, CO: Brewers Publications, 1991.

Foster, Terry. *Pale Ale, Classic Beer Style Series.* Boulder, CO: Brewers Publications, 1990.

Foster, Terry. *Porter, Classic Beer Style Series.* Boulder, CO: Brewers Publications, 1992.

Garetz, Mark. *Using Hops: The Complete Guide to Hops for the Craft Brewer.* Danville, CA: HopTech, 1994.

Graves, M. *A Modern Herbal.* New York: Dover Publications, 1971.

Guinard, Jean-Xavier. *Lambic, Classic Beer Style Series.* Boulder, CO: Brewers Publications, 1990.

Hajn, Ivo. *Budejovicky Budvar 1895–1995.* AGES Agency, Ceské Budejovice, C.R., 1995.

Hutchens, Alma R. *Native American Herbalogy.* Boston: Shambhala Publications, 1973.

Jackson, Michael. *The Great Beers of Belgium,* 2nd ed., London, England: Duncan Baird Publishers, 1994.

Jackson, Michael. *Michael Jackson's Beer Companion.* Philadelphia: Running Press, 1993.

Jackson, Michael. *The New World Guide to Beer.* Philadelphia: Running Press, 1988.

Jackson, Michael. *The Simon & Schuster Pocket Guide to Beer,* 4th ed. New York: Fireside/Simon & Schuster, 1994.

La Pensee, Clive. *The Historical Companion to House-Brewing.* Beverley, U.K.: Montag Publications, 1990.

Lees, Graham. *Good Beer Guide to Munich and Bavaria.* St. Albans, England: CAMRA Books, the Campaign for Real Ale, 1994.

Miller, David. *Continental Pilsener, Classic Beer Style Series.* Boulder, CO: Brewers Publications, 1989.

Miller, David. *The Complete Handbook of Homebrewing.* Pownal, VT: Garden Way Publishing, Storey Communications, 1988.

Noonan, Gregory J. *Brewing Lager Beer.* Boulder, CO: Brewers Publications, 1986.

Noonan, Gregory J. *Scotch Ale, Classic Beer Style Series.* Boulder, CO: Brewers Publications, 1993.

O'Neill, P.J., ed. *Cellarmanship—Caring for Real Ale.* St. Albans, England: CAMRA, the Campaign for Real Ale, 1994.

Papazian, Charlie. *The New Complete Joy of Homebrewing.* New York: Avon Books, 1984.

Protz, Roger. *The European Beer Almanac.* Moffat, Scotland: Lochar Publishing Ltd., 1991.

Rajotte, Pierre. *Belgian Ale, Classic Beer Style Series.* Boulder, CO: Brewers Publications, 1992.

Richman, Darryl. *Bock, Classic Beer Style Series.* Boulder, CO: Brewers Publications, 1994.

Roberston, James D. *The Connoisseur's Guide to Beer.* Aurora, IL: Caroline House Publishers, 1982.

Rombauer, Irma S. and Marion R. Becker. *The Joy of Cooking.* Indianapolis: Bobbs-Merrill, 1975.

Snyder, Stephen. *The Beer Companion.* New York: Simon & Schuster, 1996.

Snyder, Stephen. *The Brewmaster's Recipe Manual.* Guttenberg, NJ: The Beer Garden Press, 1994.

Warner, Eric. *German Wheat Beer, Classic Beer Style Series.* Boulder, CO: Brewers Publications, 1992.

Webb, Tim. *Good Beer Guide to Belgium and Holland.* St. Albans, England: CAMRA Books, the Campaign for Real Ale, 1994.

Wheeler, Graham. *Home Brewing— The CAMRA Guide.* St. Albans, England: CAMRA Books, 1993.

Willenbecher, James F. *Concoction of a Beer Engineer.* Broad Brook, CT: CEI Publications, 1992.

Yenne, Bill. *Beers of the World.* Secaucus, NJ: Chartwell Books, 1994.

PERIODICALS

Busch, Jim. "Cask-Conditioned Ales." *Zymurgy* 16, no. 4 (1993).

Busch, Jim. "Stepping Up to Advanced Techniques." *Brewing Techniques* 3, no. 2 (March/April 1995).

"The CAMRA Fact Sheet," published by *What's Brewing,* Iain Loe, research manager, Roger Protz, editor, St. Albans, Herts, England.

Dalldorf, Thomas E. ed. "Festivals, Tastings, & Brew Ha Ha." *Celebrator* 6, no. 4 (August/ September 1993).

Davison, Dennis. "Eisbock: The Original Ice Beer." *Zymurgy* 18, no. 5 (winter 1995).

Eames, Alan D. "Beer, Women, and History—Part I." *Yankee Brew News,* Fall 1993.

Eden, Karl J. "History of German Brewing." *Zymurgy* 16, no. 4 (1993).

Frane, Jeff. "How Sweet It Is—Brewing with Sugar." *Zymurgy* 17, no. 1 (spring 1994).

Gold, Elizabeth, ed. "1994 Homebrew Competition Rules and Regulations—Style Guidelines." *Zymurgy* 16, no. 5 (winter 1993).

Gordon, Dan. "The Lagering of Lagers." *Zymurgy* 16, no. 4 (1993).

Haiber, Rob. "Hops: The Brewer's Bitter Balancer." *Ale Street News* 2, no. 2 (April/May 1993).

Haiber, Rob. "Beer Styles No. 1— Pilsener." *Ale Street News* 2, no. 4 (August/September 1993).

Hall, Michael L. "Brew by the Numbers—Add Up What's in Your Beer." *Zymurgy* 18, no. 2 (summer 1995).

Hanbury, David C. "The British Brewing Scene." *Zymurgy* 16, no. 4 (1993).

Haunold, Alfred, and Gail B. Nickerson. "Mt. Hood, a New American Noble Aroma Hop." *American Society of Brewing Chemists Journal* (1990).

Haunold, Alfred, and Gail B. Nickerson. "Factors Affecting Hop Production, Hop Quality, and Brewer Preference." *Brewing Techniques* 1, no. 1 (May/June 1993).

Hersh, Jay. "Brewing in Styles— Bavaria's Dark Secret." *Brewing Techniques* 4, no. 1 (January/February 1996).

Jean, Paul Jr., ed. "Off the Lees." *Better Winemaking* 5, no. 1 (winter 1994).

Kenneally, Christopher. "A Lambic Beer Tour Through Payottennland." *Yankee Brew News* 4, no. 4 (winter 1993–94).

Lees, Graham. "Nibbling Away at Bavaria's Great Heritage." *What's Brewing,* June 1994.

Lemmens, Gerard W. C. "Hop Utilisation." *American Brewer—The Business of Beer,* no. 55 (spring 1993).

"Letters," *What's Brewing,* June 1994.

McMaster, Charles. "Why Stout Was Once the Fat Man of Brewing." *What's Brewing,* March 1994.

McMaster, Charles. "Scots Light: Beer Burns Raved About." *What's Brewing,* May 1994.

Metzger, Bill. "Witbier, A Belgian Specialty." *All About Beer* 14, no. 2 (May 1993).

Metzger, Bill. "The Celis Brewery—A Belgian Oasis in Texas." *Ale Street News* 2, no. 4 (August/September 1993).

Miller, Dave. "Ask the Trouble Shooter." *Brewing Techniques* 2, no. 5 (September/October 1994).

Narziss, Ludwig. "Special Malts for Greater Beer Type Variety." *Zymurgy* 16, no. 5 (winter 1993).

Protz, Roger. "Old Spanish Custom Is at the Root of Shep's Dark Brew." *What's Brewing,* March 1994.

Protz, Roger. "Why Old Black Magic Still Casts a Spell." *What's Brewing,* May 1994.

Rivers, George, ed. "Beer of the Month: Saison DuPont." *BarleyCorn,* July/August 1993.

Robertson, James. "Holiday & Winter Beers." *All About Beer* 14, no. 6 (January 1994).

Smith, Gregg. "The Brews of Ski Country." *All About Beer* 15, no. 1 (March 1994).

Street, Tobin, ed. "Beer and Brewing in Boston." *The Improper Bostonian* 2, no. 4 (January 20, 1993).

Warner, Eric. "The Art and Science of Decoction Mashing." *Zymurgy* 16, no. 4 (1993).

Wheeler, Graham. "Back from the Dead." *What's Brewing,* May 1994.

INDEX

Abbey Ale, 226–27
abbey beers, 48, 225–26
    Abbey Ale, 226–27
    Abbey Normal, 230–31
    "Afterglow" Grand Cru Style
        Strong Ale, 237
    Belgian Double, 228–29
    Cloister Dubbel, 231–32
    "Demise" Belgian Triple, 235
    Dubbel'em Up, 232–33
    East Coast Abbey Dubbel,
        233–34
    Oud-Turnhout Brown, 231
    Pirates Brew Trappist Ale,
        227–28
    Tripel Play, 235–36
    Tripple, 234–35
    "Trumpet of Death" Belgian
        Pale Ale, 236
Abbey Normal, 230–31
acid malt, 59
acid rests, 31
additives, 90–91, 95
adjuncts, 29, 59, 95, 225
aeration, 18, 83
"Afterglow" Grand Cru Style
    Strong Ale, 237
aging, 12, 38
airlock, 3
alcohol content
    alcohol by volume, calculating,
        353–54
    hydrometer scale, 3, 354
    sugar addition and, 9
ale, x
    fermentation time, 34–35, 38
    maturation time, 12, 38, 45
    partial mash brewing, 14–16
    priming, 36, 38
    serving temperature, 12
    yeast varieties, xx, 74–80, 83

ale recipes
    Abbey Ale, 226–27
    abbey beers, 225–37
    Abbey Normal, 230–31
    "Afterglow" Grand Cru Style
        Strong Ale, 237
    All-American Cream Ale,
        263–64
    Altbier, 199–200
    altbiers, 197–203
    Amber Ale, 248–49
    American Cream Ale, 262–63
    Apple Ale, 343
    Apricot Wheat Ale, 339–40
    Bacchus' Ale, 191–92
    Barley-Wheat "Red" Ale,
        254–55
    Barley Wine, 192–93
    barley wines, 189–97
    Bavarian Wheat Beer, 208–9
    Belgian Double, 228–29
    Belgian White, 219
    Belgian Wit, 224–25
    Belgian Witbier, 219–21
    Belgium Wit, 224
    Big Ben's Bitter, 143–44
    Big Bertha Pale Ale, 261–62
    bitters, 142–50
    Black Dog Porter, 159–60
    Black Dragon Export Stout,
        169–70
    Black Heart Porter, 158–59
    Brass Rale, 126–27
    Brewmaster's Entire Butt,
        157–58
    British Pub Porter, 161
    Brown Ale, 110–11
    brown ales, 108–17
    Brown & British, 115
    Brutus, 196–97
    California Barley Wine, 193–94

Cardiff Dark, 122–23
Cascades Ale, 244–45
Christmas Ale, 337–38
Classic English Pale Ale, 129–30
Cloister Dubbel, 231–32
Colonial Honey Porter, 154–55
"Colonial" IPA, 138–39
Cream Ale, 264–65
Creamy Brown Ale, 244
Deep Winter Stout, 166
"Demise" Belgian Triple, 235
"Diable Blanche" Wit Beer, 222
Down Under Ale, 267–68
Dry Irish Stout, 167–68
Dubbel'em Up, 232–33
Dunkel Weissbier, 214–15
East Coast Abbey Dubbel,
    233–34
East Coast American Pale Ale,
    258
East Coast IPA, 261
East Coast Newcastle Brown
    Ale, 116–17
East Coast Pineapple Lambic,
    239
East Coast Weizen, 213–14
East Coast Wit, 223
Ein Alt Bitte, 203
Elephant Chaser India Pale Ale,
    141–42
English Real Ale, 125–26
Erin-Go-Braugh Pale Ale,
    132–33
Far Out ESB, 147–48
Fire Breathing Stout, 164–65
Fooler's Wonton Pride, 130–31
German Alt, 201–2
German Altbier, 200–201
Ginger Ale, 347–48
Glastonbury ESB, 150
Golden Ale, 245–46

ale recipes (*cont.*)

Hail to the "India Pale Ale," 141

Happy Jerry Strong Ale, 119–20

Harvest Pumpkin Ale, 344–46

Hefe Weizen, 212–13

High Sierras Pale Ale, 257–58

Honey Weiss Beer, 253–54

How Now Brown Ale, 113–15

India Pale Ale, 139

India pale ales, 135–42

Inspiration Stout, 170–71

Irish Cream Stout, 171–72

Irish Red Ale, 133–34

Irish red ales, 132–35

Jolly Brewer's Best Bitter, 144–45

Killer Wheaten Ale, 255–56

Kölsch, 204–5

kölsch ales, 204–5

Kölsch-German Pale Ale, 205

lambics, 237–40

Lambic-Style Kriek/Framboise, 239–40

London Calling Ordinary Bitter, 146–47

Londoner's Brown Ale, 116

London Porter, 151–54

McCellar's Stout, 165–66

McDermott's Golden Ale, 246

Mainsail Ale, 251–52

Mark's Rye Stout, 173–74

Maryland Style India Pale Ale, 136

mild ales, 121–23

Ms. Bessy's Moo-Moo Milk Stout, 172

Munich Pale Ale, 265–66

New Alt Bier, 198–99

New York-Shire Bitter, 145–46

90 Shilling Scotch Ale, 187–88

North American ales, 243–70

Northwestern Wheat, 206–7

Nut Brown Ale, 109–10, 111–12

Oatmeal Stout, 176, 179–80, 181–82

oatmeal stouts, 175–82

Off-Kilter Ale, 184–85

old ales, 117–20

Old Pick & Muler, 118–19

Orfordville Porter Revisited, 161–62

oud bruin, 241–42

Oud Bruin, 242

Oud-Turnhout Brown, 231

Pacific Pale Ale, 259

Pale Ale, 127–28, 131–32

Pale Ale (Partial Mash), 128–29

pale ales, 124–32

Pale Rye Ale, 266–67

Paul's Pumpkin Ale, 346–47

Pirates Brew Bitter, 186–87

Pirates Brew Irish Stout, 168–69

Pirates Brew Nut Brown Ale, 112–13

Pirates Brew Oatmeal Stout, 176–77

Pirates Brew Porter, 156–57

Pirates Brew Trappist Ale, 227–28

Ploughman's Barleywine, 194–95

Pole-Tossin' Scottish Export, 183

Porter, 155, 162

porters, 150–62

Public House Mild, 122

Quaker's Stout, 177–79

Quilter's Irish Death, 196

Quinoa Balls Ale, 269–70

Rainy Day IPA, 140–41

Raspberry Weizen Beer, 340–41

Raspberry Wheat, 348–49

Raucous Red Ale, 247–48

"Red" Zeppelin Ale, 134–35

Rhine Castle Alt, 202–3

Rhino Horn Amber Ale, 249–50

Russian Imperial Stout, 174–75

Salzburger Kristall-Weizen, 211

Schwarzritter Dunkelweizen, 215–16

Scotch Ale, 188–89

Scots Brown Ale, 108–9

Scottish Ale, 187

Scottish Light 60°/-, 183–84

Scottish and Scotch ales, 182–89

Shout It Out Oatmeal Stout, 180–81

Snake Rock IPA, 136–37

Spiced Winter Ale, 335–37

Spring Pale Ale, 124–25

Stockport Style Bitter, 148

stouts, 163–75

Strawberry Patch Ale, 342

Strong English Bitter, 148–49

Stumbling Billy Goat Wheat-bock, 216–17

Sweetheart Wheat, 252–53

Sweet Stout, 173

Thanksgiving Cranberry Ale, 349–51

Tree-Top Ale, 340

Tripel Play, 235–36

Tripple, 234–35

Trouble, 195–96

"Trumpet of Death" Belgian Pale Ale, 236

Walt's Gnarly Barley Wine, 190–91

Weinachten Weizenbock, 217–18

weizenbiers, 206–18

West Coast IPA, 259–61

Wheat Beer, 207–8, 211–12, 256–57

White's Bier, 223–24

Wit Bier, 221–22

witbiers, 218–25

XX Cervesa, 268–69

Yaller Beer, 246–47

Yeasty Beasty Wheat, 209–10

Yellow Dog Pale Ale, 250–51

"Your Favorite" Fruit Ale, 343–44

Ale Yeast Blend, 80

All-American Cream Ale, 263–64

all-grain brewing, xiii, 19–24
alpha acid percentages, x, xviii, xix, 72, 353
Altbier, 199–200
altbiers, x, 48, 95, 197–98
    Altbier, 199–200
    Ein Alt Bitte, 203
    German Alt, 201–2
    German Altbier, 200–201
    New Alt Bier, 198–99
    Rhine Castle Alt, 202–3
Altbier yeast, 74
Altstadt Märzen, 299–300
Amber Ale, 248–49
amber ales, 48, 95, 243, 247
    Amber Ale, 248–49
    Rhino Horn Amber Ale, 249–50
amber lagers
    American Amber Lager, 321
    Home Brewery "Famous" Amber Lager, 322
    Vienna Amber, 291–92
amber malt, 59
American Ale yeast, 75
American Ale yeast (Chico), 74
American Amber Lager, 321
American Backyard Dry, 317–18
American beer styles
    amber ale, 48, 95, 243
    lager, 95
    microbrewed ale, 48
    microbrewery lager, 48–49
    pilsner, 49
    premium lager, 49
    wheat, 206, 243
American Bock, 306–7, 326–27
American Cream Ale, 262–63
American Homebrewing Association, 143
American Lager yeast (New Ulm), 80
American Light, 319–20
American Megabrewery Lager yeast, 80

American Microbrewery Ale yeast, 75
American Microbrewery Lager yeast, 80
American Pilsner, 320–21
American Society of Brewing Chemists (ASBC), 59
American White Ale yeast, 75
amino acids, 28
amylase enzymes, 23, 90
Anchor Brewing Company, 55
Apple Ale, 343
Apricot Wheat Ale, 339–40
aromatic malt, 59
ascorbic acid (vitamin C), 90
Australian Ale yeast, 75
Australian beers, 49

Bacchus' Ale, 191–92
bacterial cultures, 82
Bahnhoff Dunkel, 302
Balling scale, 3
Bamberger Style Rauchbier, 332–33
barley, xvii
    flaked, 62
    raw, 65
    roasted, 65
    syrup, 59–60
Barley-Wheat "Red" Ale, 254–55
Barley Wine, 192–93
barley wines, 12, 49, 95, 189
    Bacchus' Ale, 191–92
    Barley Wine, 192–93
    Brutus, 196–97
    California Barley Wine, 193–94
    Ploughman's Barleywine, 194–95
    Quilter's Irish Death, 196
    Trouble, 195–96
    Walt's Gnarly Barley Wine, 190–91
Bavarian Beer Purity Law, xx
Bavarian dark lagers, 300–301
    Bahnhoff Dunkel, 302

    Continental Dark Lager, 302–3
    Grunwald Dunkel, 303–4
    Munich Dunkel, 301–2
Bavarian Doppelbock, 31, 313–14
Bavarian Kellerbier, 331–32
Bavarian Lager yeast, 80
Bavarian Oktoberfest, 297–98
Bavarian Pride, 295–96
Bavarian specialty beers, 330
    Bamberger Style Rauchbier, 332–33
    Bavarian Kellerbier, 331–32
    East Coast Rauch Bier, 333
    Rockin' Roggen, 330–31
Bavarian weissbiers, 31
Bavarian Weizen yeast, 75
Bavarian Wheat Beer, 208–9
Bavarian Wheat yeast, 75
B-Brite solution, 6, 91
beer history, xiv–xvi
beer styles, x, 49–58
beet sugar, 61
Belgian Abbey yeast, 75
Belgian Ale (Rajotte), 218
Belgian Ale yeast, 75–76
Belgian beer styles, 218, 225
    abbey beers, 225
    ales, 9
    oud bruin, 241
    red ale, 49
    strong ale, 49, 96
    witbier, 218
Belgian Double, 228–29
Belgian Kruidenbier, 351
Belgian Lambic Blend yeast, 82
Belgian pils malt, 60
Belgian Strong Ale yeast, 76
Belgian Trappist yeast, 76
Belgian Wheat yeast, 76
Belgian White, 219
Belgian White Beer yeast, 76
Belgian Wit, 224–25
Belgian Witbier, 219–21
Belgian Wit yeast, 76
Belgium Wit, 224

Berliner weisse, 96
bière de garde, 49–50, 96
bière de Mars, 50
bière de Paris, 49–50
Biergarten Helles, 287–88
Big Bad Bock, 307–8
Big Ben's Bitter, 143–44
Big Bertha Pale Ale, 261–62
biscuit malt, 60
bitter ales, 50, 96, 97, 124, 142–43
   Big Ben's Bitter, 143–44
   Far Out ESB, 147–48
   Glastonbury ESB, 150
   Jolly Brewer's Best Bitter, 144–45
   London Calling Ordinary Bitter, 146–47
   New York-Shire Bitter, 145–46
   Pirates Brew Bitter, 186–87
   Stockport Style Bitter, 148
   Strong English Bitter, 148–49
bittering hops, xix, 10, 15, 17, 68
bitterness, xviii, 45
black barley, 60
Black Dog Porter, 159–60
Black Dragon Export Stout, 169–70
Black Heart Porter, 158–59
black patent malt (black malt), 60
bleach, 40, 91
bock beers, 12, 31, 50, 97, 304–5
   American Bock, 306–7, 326–27
   Big Bad Bock, 307–8
   Bock to the Basics, 308
   Genthner Bock, 308–9
   Helles Bock, 311–12
   Old Billy's Beard, 305–6
   Pirates Brew Bock, 309–10
Bock to the Basics, 308
Bock and White, 316–17
Bohemian Lager yeast, 80
Bohemian Pilsener, 280
Bohemian Pilsner, 51, 272–73, 278
boiling, 6, 9, 15, 17, 44, 94
   and chlorine removal, 6, 9, 86
   and tannin flavors, 11

boiling kettle, 19
Bösken-Diebels, Paul, 197
bottle capper, 4
bottled water, 10
bottle filler, 4, 8
bottles, 4, 36
   glass color, 11–12
   sanitizing, 7–8, 36
bottling, 7–8, 11, 35–37
   caps, 4, 45
   equipment, 3–4
bottling bucket, 3, 37
Bramling Cross hops, 68
Brass Rale, 126–27
Brettanomyces Lambicus yeast, 82
Brewer's Dopplebock, 315–16
Brewers Gold hops, 68
brewer's sugar, 60, 62
brewing
   degree of difficulty, xii–xiii
   equipment, 2–3, 5–6
   procedures, 5–8
   record and evaluation form, 41–42
Brewing Lager Beer (Noonan), 19, 86
brew kettle, 2
Brewmaster's Entire Butt, 157–58
BrewTek yeasts, 74
Briess Malting Company, 61
British Ale yeast, 76–77
British Ale yeast (Whitbread), 76
British Columbia Goldings hops, 68
British Draft Ale yeast, 77
British Microbrewery Ale yeast, 77
British Pale Ale yeast, 77
British Pub Porter, 161
British Real Ale yeast, 77
Brown Ale, 110–11
brown ales, 50, 97, 108
   Brown Ale, 110–11
   Brown & British, 115
   East Coast Newcastle Brown Ale, 116–17
   How Now Brown Ale, 113–15
   Londoner's Brown Ale, 116

   Nut Brown Ale, 109–10, 111–12
   Pirates Brew Nut Brown Ale, 112–13
   Scots Brown Ale, 108–9
Brown & British, 115
brown malt, 60
brumalt, 60–61
Brutus, 196–97
BTF-Iodophor, 91
Bullion hops, 68–69
Burch, Byron, xvi
Burton-style pale ale, 86
Burton water salts, 85, 90

calcium, 85
calcium carbonate, 86, 90
calcium chloride, 86
California Barley Wine, 193–94
California Common Beer, 50, 97, 323, 324–26
California Gold yeast, 80
California Lager yeast, 80–81
California Pub Brewery Ale yeast, 77
Campaign for Real Ale (CAMRA), xvi, 143
Campden tablets, 91
Canadian Ale yeast, 77
Canadian beers, 50
candi sugar, 61
cane sugar, 9, 61, 352
caps, bottle, 4, 45
caramel malts, 61, 62
caramel sugar, 61
CaraMunich malt, 61
CaraPils malt, 61
CaraVienne malt, 61
carbonate hardness, 9, 84, 85
carbonating, 38–39, 40
carbonation chart, 43
carboy, 3, 15, 44
Cardiff Dark, 122–23
Cascade hops, 5, 69
Cascades Ale, 244–45
casks, 45, 352

cellars, 45
Centennial hops, 69
Challenger hops, 69
Champagne yeast, 82
Chexo Pilsner, 274–75
Chinook hops, 69
chloride ions, 84
chlorine, 6, 9, 86, 91
chocolate malt, 61–62
Christmas Ale, 337–38
Christmas and holiday beers, 334
    Christmas Ale, 337–38
    Holiday Beer, 337
    Spiced Winter Ale, 335–37
    Yule Fuel, 334–35
citric acid, 90
city water analyses, 88
clarifying, 35
clarity, 9, 44
Classic British Ale yeast, 77
Classic English Pale Ale, 129–30
Classic Pilsner, 273–74
CL–9 sanitizer, 92
Cloister Dubbel, 231–32
Cluster hops, 69
cold trub removal, 44
colloidal stability, 28
Colonial Honey Porter, 154–55
"Colonial" IPA, 138–39
color measurements, 59
Columbus hops, 69
commercial beers, xvi
competitions, homebrewing, 12
Complete Handbook of Home Brewing
    (Miller), 19
conditioning, 12, 38, 96
Continental Dark Lager, 302–3
Continental Pilsener (Miller), 44
cooling, wort, 7, 11, 15, 16, 17–18,
    20–21
"Cornelius" kegs, 39
corn sugar, 5, 7, 9, 36, 38, 40, 62
"craft-brewed" beers, 48
Cranberry Ale, Thanksgiving,
    349–51

Cream Ale, 264–65
cream ales, 51, 98, 243
    All-American Cream Ale,
      263–64
    American Cream Ale, 262–63
    Cream Ale, 264–65
Creamy Brown Ale, 244
Crystal hops, 69
crystal malt, 14, 17, 61
    dark, 62
    German, 63
Czech pilsner, 51, 98
Czech Pils yeast, 81

Danish Lager yeast, 81
dark crystal malt, 62
decoction mashing, 31–33
Deep Winter Stout, 166
deionization, 87
demerara sugar, 62
"Demise" Belgian Triple, 235
dextrine malt, 16–17, 62
dextrines, 23, 26, 28
dextrose-glucose, 62
"Diable Blanche" Wit Beer, 222
diacetyl, 34
dimethyl sulfide (DMS), 15
disinfectants, 6
distilled water, 10, 87
doppelbocks, 50, 98, 312
    Bavarian Doppelbock, 31,
      313–14
    Bock and White, 316–17
    Brewer's Dopplebock, 315–16
    Gutenacht Doppelbock,
      314–15
Dortmunder export lagers, 51, 86,
    98, 282
    Export Lager, 283–84
    German Dortmunder, 283
    Northwestern Lager, 282–83
double decoction, 33
doughing in, 22
Down Under Ale, 267–68
Dreher, Anton, 288

dried malt extract (DME), 4–5, 62,
    93, 352, 353
"dry-hopping," 15, 35
Dry Irish Stout, 167–68
"dry stout," 12, 55, 163
dry yeasts, xii, xxi, 7, 10
    rehydrating, 11, 15–16, 18
dubbel, 51, 99
Dubbel'em Up, 232–33
Dunkel Weissbier, 214–15
dunkelweizen, 56, 99
Dusseldorf Ale yeast, 77
Düsseldorfer alt, 48

East Coast Abbey Dubbel, 233–34
East Coast American Pale Ale, 258
East Coast IPA, 261
East Coast Newcastle Brown Ale,
    116–17
East Coast Pineapple Lambic, 239
East Coast Rauch Bier, 333
East Coast Weizen, 213–14
East Coast Wit, 223
East European Lager yeast, 81
East Kent Goldings hops, 69
Easy Fruit Beer, 341–42
EBC color scale, 59
Eckhardt, Fred, xvi
Ein Alt Bitte, 203
Einbeck Style Lager, 292
eis bock, 51
Elephant Chaser India Pale Ale,
    141–42
English ales, 48–49, 108, 117, 121,
    124, 142–43
English Ale yeast, 77
English Barleywine Ale yeast, 77
English pale malt, 62
English Real Ale, 125–26
enzymes, 23, 31, 90
    starch-degrading, xxi, 84
Epsom salts, 85, 90
equipment
    all-grain brewing, 19–22
    bottling, 3–4

equipment (*cont.*)
 brewing, 2–3
 sanitizing of, 5–6
Erin-Go-Braugh Pale Ale, 132–33
Erlanger, 51
Eroica hops, 69
European Ale (Alt) yeast, 77–78
European Brewing Convention
  (Congress), 59
Export Lager, 283–84

faro, 51, 238
Far Out ESB, 147–48
Fermax, 90
fermentation, 7, 83, 96
 fruits and, 338
 length of time, 34–35
 secondary, 11, 35, 44, 96
 temperatures, 11, 34, 83
fermenter, 2–3
final gravity, 7, 34, 35–36, 38–39, 94
fining agents, 9
finishing hops, xix, 68
Fire Breathing Stout, 164–65
Fix, George, 19
"Flanders brown," 53, 241
flavor, xxi, 11, 44–45, 84
flavoring hops, xix, 15, 17
Fooler's Wonton Pride, 130–31
framboise, 51
fruit- and spice-flavored beers,
  338–39
 Apple Ale, 343
 Apricot Wheat Ale, 339–40
 Belgian Kruidenbier, 351
 East Coast Pineapple Lambic,
  239
 Easy Fruit Beer, 341–42
 Ginger Ale, 347–48
 Harvest Pumpkin Ale, 344–46
 Lambic-Style Kriek/Framboise,
  239–40
 Paul's Pumpkin Ale, 346–47
 Raspberry Weizen Beer, 340–41
 Raspberry Wheat, 348–49

Strawberry Patch Ale, 342
 Thanksgiving Cranberry Ale,
  349–51
 Tree-Top Ale, 340
 "Your Favorite" Fruit Ale,
  343–44
Fuggles hops, 69

Galena hops, 69
gelatin, 9, 90
Genthner Bock, 308–9
German Ale yeast, 78
German Alt, 201–2
German Altbier, 200–201
German beers, 31
German crystal malt, 63
German Dortmunder, 283
German Lager yeast, 81
German/North European pils, 51
German pale malt, 65
German Pilsener, 276–78
German roasted raw wheat, 63
German Weiss yeast, 78
German Wheat yeast, 78
Ginger Ale, 347–48
Glastonbury ESB, 150
glucose, 63
Golden Ale, 245–46
golden syrup, 66
*Good Beer Guide to Belgium and Hol-
  land* (Webb), 218
grain mill, 21
grand cru, 51
Great Beers of Belgium (Jackson), 218
Great British Beer Festival, 142–43
"green beer," 38
Green Bullet hops, 69
green glass, 11–12
grist, xviii, 22, 26, 95
grits, 63
Grolle, Josef, 288
Grunwald Dunkel, 303–4
gueuze, 52, 238
Gutenacht Doppelbock, 314–15
gypsum, 85, 90

Hail to the "India Pale Ale," 141
Hallertauer Hersbrucker hops, 70
Hallertauer Mittelfrüh hops, 70
Hallertauer Tradition hops, 70
Hallertau hops, 69–70
Happy Jerry Strong Ale, 119–20
Harvest Pumpkin Ale, 344–46
heading agents, 90
Hefe Weizen, 56, 212–13
helles beers, 285. *See also* Munich
  helles
Helles Bock, 311–12
helles hefe, 103
Hersbrucker hops, 70
high-kräusen stage, 34, 83
High Sierras Pale Ale, 257–58
*Historical Companion to House-
  Brewing* (La Pensee), 86
Holiday Beer, 337
homebrew bittering units (HBU),
  xx, 353
Home Brewery "Famous" Amber
  Lager, 322
Honey Weiss Beer, 253–54
hop bags, 2
hops, xii, xviii–xx, 45, 93
 adding to wort, 6, 10, 15, 17
 alpha acid percentages, x, xviii,
  xix, 72, 353
 bittering, xix, 10, 15, 17, 68
 "dry-hopping," 15, 35
 finishing, xix, 68
 flavoring, xix, 15, 17
 pellets, xix–xx, 5, 15, 17
 plugs, xix, 15, 17
 storing, 10
 varieties, 68–74
 whole flowers, xviii, xix, 10, 15,
  17
How Now Brown Ale, 113–15
hydrometers, 3, 354

ice beer, 52
"imperial stout," 163
India Pale Ale, 139

India pale ales (IPA), 52, 99, 124, 135, 259
  "Colonial" IPA, 138–39
  East Coast IPA, 261
  Elephant Chaser India Pale Ale, 141–42
  Hail to the "India Pale Ale," 141
  India Pale Ale, 139
  Maryland Style India Pale Ale, 136
  Rainy Day IPA, 140–41
  Snake Rock IPA, 136–37
  West Coast IPA, 259–61
  see also pale ales
Industrial Lager, 318–19
infusion mashing, single-temperature, 25–27
ingredients, 4–5, 22, 93
Inspiration Stout, 170–71
international bittering units (IBU), xx, 353
International Bottled Water Association, 87
invert sugar, 63
iodine tincture, 21, 27
ions, water, xxi, 84–85
Irish Ale yeast, 78
Irish Cream Stout, 171–72
Irish Dry Stout yeast, 78
Irish moss, 9, 40, 90
Irish Red Ale, 133–34
Irish red ales, 52, 132
  Erin-Go-Braugh Pale Ale, 132–33
  Irish Red Ale, 133–34
  "Red" Zeppelin Ale, 134–35
"Irish" stout, 55, 163
isinglass, 9, 90

Jackson, Michael, xvi, 117, 218, 222
Jolly Brewer's Best Bitter, 144–45
jumper cable, 40
juniper berries, 90

keg beer, xvi
kegging, 39–40

kellerbier, 52
Kellerbier, Bavarian, 331–32
Killer Wheaten Ale, 255–56
klosterbier, 52
Kölsch, 204–5
Kölsch-German Pale Ale, 205
kölsch-style ales, 52, 99, 204
  Kölsch, 204–5
  Kölsch-German Pale Ale, 205
Kölsch yeast, 78
"kräusening," 36
Kraut Dog Oktoberfest, 293–94
kriek, 52
kristall, 56
Kulmbacher, 52

Labatt's Brewery, 52
lactic acid, 90
lactose (milk sugar), 90
lager, x
  fermentation time, 34, 35, 38
  maturation time, 12, 35, 38, 45
  partial mash brewing, 16–18
  priming, 36–37, 38
  serving temperature, 12
  yeast varieties, xx, 80–82, 83
lagering, 35, 38
lager malt, 63–64
lager recipes
  Altstadt Märzen, 299–300
  American Amber Lager, 321
  American Backyard Dry, 317–18
  American Bock, 306–7, 326–27
  American Light, 319–20
  American Pilsner, 320–21
  Bahnhoff Dunkel, 302
  Bavarian dark lagers, 300–304
  Bavarian Doppelbock, 313–14
  Bavarian Oktoberfest, 297–98
  Bavarian Pride, 295–96
  Biergarten Helles, 287–88
  Big Bad Bock, 307–8
  bock beers, 304–10
  Bock to the Basics, 308

Bock and White, 316–17
Bohemian Pilsener, 280
Bohemian Pilsner, 272–73, 278
Brewer's Dopplebock, 315–16
California Common Beer, 324–26
Chexo Pilsner, 274–75
Classic Pilsner, 273–74
Continental Dark Lager, 302–3
doppelbocks, 312–17
Dortmunder export lagers, 282–84
Einbeck Style Lager, 292
Export Lager, 283–84
Genthner Bock, 308–9
German Dortmunder, 283
German Pilsener, 276–78
Grunwald Dunkel, 303–4
Gutenacht Doppelbock, 314–15
Helles Bock, 311–12
Home Brewery "Famous" Amber Lager, 322
Industrial Lager, 318–19
Kraut Dog Oktoberfest, 293–94
Light Lager, 286–87
McHale's Best (Munich Helles), 285–86
Mai/helles bocks, 310–12
Märzen, 298–99
Märzen/Oktoberfest lagers, 293–300
Mr. Marty's Merry Marzenfest, 296–97
Munich Dunkel, 301–2
Munich helles, 285–88
Munich Helles Lager, 286
North American lagers, 317–27
Northwestern Lager, 282–83
Northwestern Vienna, 289
Oktoberfest, 297
Old Billy's Beard, 305–6
pilsners, 272–81
Pirates Brew Bock, 309–10
Pirates Brew Pilsner, 278–79
Shoreline Steamer, 323–24

lager recipes (*cont.*)
   Simply Sumptuous Steam Beer, 322–23
   Smuggler's Socks Pilsner, 275–76
   South Sea Pils, 281
   Vienna Amber, 291–92
   Vienna Lager, 289–90
   Vienna-style lagers, 288–92
   Winter Lager, 291
Lager Yeast Blend, 81
lambics, 12, 45, 52–53, 100, 237–38
   East Coast Pineapple Lambic, 239
   Lambic-Style Kriek/Framboise, 239–40
Lambic-Style Kriek/Framboise, 239–40
La Pensee, Clive, 86
lauter tun, 20, 24
Liberty hops, 70
licorice sticks, 90
Light Lager, 286–87
liquid measures, 352
liquid yeasts, xii, xx–xxi, 5, 10
   advance preparation, 7, 16
   quantity to use, 11
"liquor," xxi, 22, 84, 86
London Ale yeast, 78–79
London Calling Ordinary Bitter, 146–47
Londoner's Brown Ale, 116
London Porter, 151–54
Lovibond color scale, 59
Lublin hops, 70

McCellar's Stout, 165–66
McDermott's Golden Ale, 246
macerated fruits, 338
McHale's Best (Munich Helles), 285–86
magnesium, 85
Mai/helles bocks, 100, 310–11
   Helles Bock, 311–12
Mainsail Ale, 251–52

maize, flaked, 62–63
malt, xvii–xviii, 93
   types of, 59–68
malted grains, 22
malt extract, xi, xii, 4–5, 9, 95
   priming solution, 36
   and specific gravity, 93, 353
   syrup, 2, 4–5, 6, 64, 93
malto-dextrin, 90
Mark's Rye Stout, 173–74
Maryland Style India Pale Ale, 136
Märzen, 298–99
Märzen/Oktoberfest lagers, 31, 53, 100, 293
   Altstadt Märzen, 299–300
   Bavarian Oktoberfest, 297–98
   Bavarian Pride, 295–96
   Kraut Dog Oktoberfest, 293–94
   Märzen, 298–99
   Mr. Marty's Merry Marzenfest, 296–97
   Oktoberfest, 297
mash extract brewing, 14
mashing, 22–23, 95–96
   decoction, 31–33
   single-temperature infusion, 25–27
   step-mashing, 27–30
mash paddle, 19–20
mash tuns, 19
maturation time, 12
measurement conversion, 352
Mexican beer, 53
microbreweries, xvi, 48–49
mild ale, 53, 100, 121
   Cardiff Dark, 122–23
   Public House Mild, 122
mild ale malt, 64
Miller, David, 19, 44
mineral water, 10, 87
mini-mashing, 14
Mr. Marty's Merry Marzenfest, 296–97
Mittelfrüh hops, 70
modification, xvii–xviii

molasses, 64, 66
Mount Hood hops, 70
Ms. Bessy's Moo-Moo Milk Stout, 172
Münchner dunkel, 53, 84
Munich Dunkel, 301–2
Munich helles, 53, 101, 285
   Biergarten Helles, 287–88
   Light Lager, 286–87
   McHale's Best (Munich Helles), 285–86
   Munich Helles Lager, 286
Munich Helles Lager, 286
Munich Lager yeast, 81
Munich malt, 64
Munich Pale Ale, 265–66

natural water, 87
New Alt Bier, 198–99
New Complete Joy of Homebrewing (Papazian), 86
New York-Shire Bitter, 145–46
New Zealand beers, 49
90 Shilling Scotch Ale, 187–88
Noonan, Gregory, 19, 86
North American ales, 243
   All-American Cream Ale, 263–64
   Amber Ale, 248–49
   American Cream Ale, 262–63
   Barley-Wheat "Red" Ale, 254–55
   Big Bertha Pale Ale, 261–62
   Cascades Ale, 244–45
   Cream Ale, 264–65
   Creamy Brown Ale, 244
   Down Under Ale, 267–68
   East Coast American Pale Ale, 258
   East Coast IPA, 261
   Golden Ale, 245–46
   High Sierras Pale Ale, 257–58
   Honey Weiss Beer, 253–54
   Killer Wheaten Ale, 255–56
   McDermott's Golden Ale, 246
   Mainsail Ale, 251–52
   Munich Pale Ale, 265–66

Pacific Pale Ale, 259
Pale Rye Ale, 266–67
Quinoa Balls Ale, 269–70
Raucous Red Ale, 247–48
Rhino Horn Amber Ale, 249–50
Sweetheart Wheat, 252–53
West Coast IPA, 259–61
Wheat Beer, 256–57
XX Cervesa, 268–69
Yaller Beer, 246–47
Yellow Dog Pale Ale, 250–51
North American lagers, 317
    American Amber Lager, 321
    American Backyard Dry,
        317–18
    American Bock, 326–27
    American Light, 319–20
    American Pilsner, 320–21
    California Common Beer,
        324–26
    Home Brewery "Famous"
        Amber Lager, 322
    Industrial Lager, 318–19
    Shoreline Steamer, 323–24
    Simply Sumptuous Steam Beer,
        322–23
North American Lager yeast, 81
Northdown hops, 70
Northern Brewer hops, 70–71
North German Lager yeast, 81
Northwestern Lager, 282–83
Northwestern Vienna, 289
Northwestern Wheat, 206–7
Nugget hops, 71
Nut Brown Ale, 109–10, 111–12

oak chips, 90–91
Oatmeal Stout, 176, 179–80,
    181–82
oatmeal stouts, 175
    Oatmeal Stout, 176, 179–80,
        181–82
    Pirates Brew Oatmeal Stout,
        176–77
    Quaker's Stout, 177–79

Shout It Out Oatmeal Stout,
    180–81
    see also stout
oats, flaked, rolled, and steel cut, 63
Off-Kilter Ale, 184–85
Oktoberfest lagers, 53, 100, 293
    Altstadt Märzen, 299–300
    Bavarian Oktoberfest, 297–98
    Bavarian Pride, 295–96
    Kraut Dog Oktoberfest, 293–94
    Märzen, 298–99
    Mr. Marty's Merry Marzenfest,
        296–97
    Oktoberfest, 297
old ales, 53, 117–18
    Happy Jerry Strong Ale,
        119–20
    Old Pick & Muler, 118–19
Old Bavarian Lager yeast, 81
Old Billy's Beard, 305–6
Old German Ale yeast, 79
Old Pick & Muler, 118–19
Omega hops, 71
One-Step sanitizer, 6, 92
open fermentation, 34
Orfordville Porter Revisited, 161–62
original gravity, xx, 7, 38–39, 94
Original Pilsner yeast, 81–82
Orval Trappist Ale, 225
Oud Bruin, 53–54, 101, 241–42
Oud-Turnhout Brown, 231

Pacific Pale Ale, 259
Pale Ale, 127–28, 131–32
Pale Ale (Partial Mash), 128–29
pale ale malt, 64
pale ales, 54, 101, 124, 142, 199
    Big Bertha Pale Ale, 261–62
    Brass Rale, 126–27
    Classic English Pale Ale, 129–30
    East Coast American Pale Ale,
        258
    English Real Ale, 125–26
    Fooler's Wonton Pride, 130–31
    High Sierras Pale Ale, 257–58

Kölsch-German Pale Ale, 205
Munich Pale Ale, 265–66
Pacific Pale Ale, 259
Pale Ale, 127–28, 131–32
Pale Ale (Partial Mash), 128–29
Pale Rye Ale, 266–67
Spring Pale Ale, 124–25
Yellow Dog Pale Ale, 250–51
    see also India pale ales
Pale Ale yeast, 79
pale malt, 64–65
Pale Rye Ale, 266–67
papain, 91
Papazian, Charlie, xvi, 20, 86
partial mash brewing
    ale, 14–16
    lager, 16–18
Pasteur, Louis, xv
Pasteur Champagne yeast, 82
pasteurization, 339
Paul's Pumpkin Ale, 346–47
pectic enzyme, 91
Pediococcus Cerevisiae culture, 82
Pediococcus Damnosus culture, 82
pellet hops, xix–xx, 5, 15, 17
Perle hops, 71
permanent hardness, 85
pH scale, xv
pH test papers, 21
pH values, 21, 22, 23, 84, 85, 86
Pilsen Lager yeast, 82
Pilsner Lager yeast, 82
pilsner malt, 30, 65
pilsners, 51, 272
    American Pilsner, 320–21
    Bohemian Pilsener, 280
    Bohemian Pilsner, 272–73, 278
    Chexo Pilsner, 274–75
    Classic Pilsner, 273–74
    German Pilsener, 276–78
    Pirates Brew Pilsner, 278–79
    Smuggler's Socks Pilsner, 275–76
    South Sea Pils, 281
Pirates Brew Bitter, 186–87
Pirates Brew Bock, 309–10

Pirates Brew Irish Stout, 168–69
Pirates Brew Nut Brown Ale, 112–13
Pirates Brew Oatmeal Stout,
    176–77
Pirates Brew Pilsner, 278–79
Pirates Brew Porter, 156–57
Pirates Brew Trappist Ale, 227–28
Ploughman's Barleywine, 194–95
plug hops, xix, 15, 17
Pole-Tossin' Scottish Export, 183
Polyclar, 9, 91
Porter, 155, 162
porters, 54, 101, 150–51
    Black Dog Porter, 159–60
    Black Heart Porter, 158–59
    Brewmaster's Entire Butt,
        157–58
    British Pub Porter, 161
    Colonial Honey Porter, 154–55
    London Porter, 151–54
    Orfordville Porter Revisited,
        161–62
    Pirates Brew Porter, 156–57
    Porter, 155, 162
porter's ale, 121, 150
potassium metabisulfite, 92
pressure bleeder, 40
pressure checker, 40
Pride of Ringwood hops, 71
primary grist, 95
priming, 5, 36–37, 38, 96
Principles of Brewing Science (Fix), 19
Progress hops, 71
Prohibition, xvi
protein rests, 23, 28, 29, 30, 32, 33
proteins, 23, 44
Protz, Roger, 222
Public House Mild, 122
Pumpkin Ale, Harvest, 344–46
Pumpkin Ale, Paul's, 346–47
PureSeal bottle caps, 45

Quaker's Stout, 177–79
Quilter's Irish Death, 196
Quinoa Balls Ale, 269–70

racking stem and tip, 4, 8
Rainy Day IPA, 140–41
Rajotte, Pierre, 218
Raspberry Weizen Beer, 340–41
Raspberry Wheat, 348–49
rauchbier, 54
    Bamberger Style Rauchbier,
        332–33
    East Coast Rauch Bier, 333
Raucous Red Ale, 247–48
"Red" Zeppelin Ale, 134–35
refrigeration, xv–xvi, 45
rests, 23
reverse osmosis, 87
Rhine Castle Alt, 202–3
Rhino Horn Amber Ale, 249–50
rice extract syrup, 65
Richmond, Mark, 222
roasted malt, 65
Rockin' Roggen, 330–31
roggenbier, 54
running off, 24
Russian Imperial Stout, 163,
    174–75
rye, 65
    flaked, 63
rye beer, 54

Saaz (Zatec) hops, 71
saccharification rests, 23, 25, 26,
    29, 30, 32, 33
St. Louis Lager yeast, 82
saison ale, 54
Saison yeast, 79
salt, 85
Salzburger Kristall-Weizen, 211
sanitizing, 5–6
    of bottles, 7–8, 36
    fruits and, 338–39
    solution, 2, 4, 91–92
schwarzbier, 54
Schwarzritter Dunkelweizen,
    215–16
Scotch Ale, 188–89
Scotch Ale yeast, 79

Scots Brown Ale, 108–9
Scottish Ale, 187
Scottish Ale yeast, 79
Scottish Bitter yeast, 79
Scottish 80/- ale, 102
Scottish Light 60°/-, 183–84
Scottish and Scotch ales, 54–55,
    102, 182
    90 Shilling Scotch Ale, 187–88
    Off-Kilter Ale, 184–85
    Pirates Brew Bitter, 186–87
    Pole-Tossin' Scottish Export, 183
    Scotch Ale, 188–89
    Scottish Ale, 187
    Scottish Light 60°/-, 183–84
secondary fermentation, 11, 35,
    44, 94
Sedlmayr, Gabriel, II, 53
serving temperature, 12, 96
Shoreline Steamer, 323–24
Shout It Out Oatmeal Stout, 180–81
Simply Sumptuous Steam Beer,
    322–23
single decoction, 32
single-temperature infusion mash-
    ing, 25–27
siphon hose, 4, 8
siphoning, 37
six-row barley, xvii, 32, 64–65
"slap packs," 5, 83
"Smartcaps," 45
smoke beer, 54, 332–33, 341
Smuggler's Socks Pilsner, 275–76
Snake Rock IPA, 136–37
soda ash, 92
sodium, 84
sodium metabisulfite, 92
Sørenson, S. P. L., xv
South Sea Pils, 281
Spalter hops, 71
Spalter Select hops, 71
sparging, 23–24, 26, 44–45
Special B malt, 65
Special London yeast, 79
special-purpose yeasts, 82

specialty beer recipes
    Apple Ale, 343
    Apricot Wheat Ale, 339–40
    Bamberger Style Rauchbier,
        332–33
    Bavarian Kellerbier, 331–32
    Bavarian specialty beers, 330–33
    Belgian Kruidenbier, 351
    Christmas Ale, 337–38
    Christmas and holiday beers,
        334–38
    East Coast Rauch Bier, 333
    Easy Fruit Beer, 341–42
    fruit- and spice-flavored beers,
        338–51
    Ginger Ale, 347–48
    Harvest Pumpkin Ale, 344–46
    Holiday Beer, 337
    Paul's Pumpkin Ale, 346–47
    Raspberry Weizen Beer, 340–41
    Raspberry Wheat, 348–49
    Rockin' Roggen, 330–31
    Spiced Winter Ale, 335–37
    Strawberry Patch Ale, 342
    Thanksgiving Cranberry Ale,
        349–51
    Tree-Top Ale, 340
    "Your Favorite" Fruit Ale,
        343–44
    Yule Fuel, 334–35
specialty grains, 11, 14, 16–17, 44,
    59
specialty malts, 44, 95
specific gravity, 3, 7, 24, 353
"speise," 36, 37
Spiced Winter Ale, 335–37
spray malt, 65
Spring Pale Ale, 124–25
spring water, 10, 15, 87, 89
spruce essence, 91
SRM color scale, 59
Standard Research (Reference)
    Method, 59
starch-degrading enzymes, xxi, 84
steam beers, 50, 55, 323

Shoreline Steamer, 323–24
Simply Sumptuous Steam Beer,
    322–23
steinbier, 55
step-mashing, 27–30
Sticklebract hops, 71
Stockport Style Bitter, 148
stout, 12, 55, 102, 163
    Black Dragon Export Stout,
        169–70
    Deep Winter Stout, 166
    Dry Irish Stout, 167–68
    Fire Breathing Stout, 164–65
    Inspiration Stout, 170–71
    Irish Cream Stout, 171–72
    McCellar's Stout, 165–66
    Mark's Rye Stout, 173–74
    Ms. Bessy's Moo-Moo Milk
        Stout, 172
    Pirates Brew Irish Stout,
        168–69
    Russian Imperial Stout,
        174–75
    Sweet Stout, 173
    see also oatmeal stouts
Stout Ale yeast, 79
"stout porter," 150, 163
Straight-A sanitizer, 92
Strawberry Patch Ale, 342
strike heat, 23, 26, 28
Strissel Spalt hops, 71
Strong English Bitter, 148–49
"stuck mash," 24
Stumbling Billy Goat Wheatbock,
    216–17
Styrian (Savinja) Goldings hops,
    71–72
sugars, residual, 38
sulfate, 84–85
sulfites, 339
Swedish Ale yeast, 79
Sweetheart Wheat, 252–53
"sweet stout," 175
Sweet Stout, 173
Swiss Lager yeast, 82

tannins, 11, 12, 24, 25, 32, 44
Target hops, 72
temperatures, 3, 20
    conditioning, 8, 38, 45
    conversion charts, 352
    fermentation, 11, 34, 83
    hydrometer corrections, 3, 354
    lagering, 35
    mashing, 11, 23, 26, 30, 32
    resting, 23
    serving, 12, 96
    single-temperature infusion
        mashing, 25–27
    sparging, 23–24
    step-mashing, 27–30
    strike heat, 23, 26, 28
temporary hardness, 85
Tettnanger hops, 72
Thames Valley yeast, 79
Thanksgiving Cranberry Ale,
    349–51
thermometers, 3, 20
toasted malt, 66
torrefied grains, 66
total dissolved solids (TDS), 85
Trappe Ale yeast, 79
Trappist ale, 48, 55
Trappist Ale yeast, 80
treacle, 66
Tree-Top Ale, 340
tripel, 55, 102
Tripel Play, 235–36
triple decoction, 33
Tripple, 234–35
Trouble, 195–96
trub sediment, 44
"Trumpet of Death" Belgian Pale
    Ale, 236
turbinado sugar, 62, 66
two-row barley, xvii, 26, 32, 64

Ultra hops, 72

victory malt, 66
Vienna Amber, 291–92

Vienna Lager, 289–90
Vienna malt, 66
Vienna-style lagers, 55–56, 103, 288–89
   Einbeck Style Lager, 292
   Northwestern Vienna, 289
   Vienna Amber, 291–92
   Vienna Lager, 289–90
   Winter Lager, 291

Walt's Gnarly Barley Wine, 190–91
water, xii, 5, 9–10, 86–89
   and flavor, xxi, 84
   hardness, 9, 84, 85, 95
   ions in, xxi, 84–85
   treatments, 22, 85–86
   and yeast nutrients, xxi, 84
water crystals, 91
"water salts," 86, 91
Webb, Tim, 218
weighing grains, 21–22
weights and measures, 352
Weihenstephan Wheat yeast, 80
Weinachten Weizenbock, 217–18
weizen (wheat) beers, x, 56, 103, 206
   Apricot Wheat Ale, 339–40
   Bavarian Wheat Beer, 208–9
   Dunkel Weissbier, 214–15
   East Coast Weizen, 213–14
   Hefe Weizen, 212–13
   Honey Weiss Beer, 253–54
   Killer Wheaten Ale, 255–56
   Northwestern Wheat, 206–7
   Raspberry Weizen Beer, 340–41
   Raspberry Wheat, 348–49
   Salzburger Kristall-Weizen, 211
   Schwarzritter Dunkelweizen, 215–16

Stumbling Billy Goat Wheat-bock, 216–17
Sweetheart Wheat, 252–53
Weinachten Weizenbock, 217–18
Wheat Beer, 207–8, 211–12
Wheat Beer (American-style), 256–57
Yeasty Beasty Wheat, 209–10
weizenbock, 50, 103
West Coast IPA, 259–61
wheat
   flaked, 63
   German roasted raw, 63
   malt, 66
Wheat Beer, 207–8, 211–12, 256–57
wheat beers. *See* weizen beers
Whitbread Golding Variety (WGV) hops, 72
"white beer," 56, 206, 218
White's Bier, 223–24
whole flower hops, xviii, xix, 10, 15, 17
Willamette hops, 72
Winter Lager, 291
Wit Bier, 221–22
witbiers, 56, 103, 218
   Belgian White, 219
   Belgian Wit, 224–25
   Belgian Witbier, 219–21
   Belgium Wit, 224
   "Diable Blanche" Wit Beer, 222
   East Coast Wit, 223
   White's Bier, 223–24
   Wit Bier, 221–22
wort, xi
   adding hops to, 6, 10, 15, 17
   adding yeast to, 7, 16, 18, 83

boiling, 6, 9, 17, 44, 96
cooling, 7, 11, 15, 16, 17–18, 20–21
wort chiller, 20–21
Wyeast Brewer's Choice yeast, 74
Wyeast yeasts, 5, 74

XX Cervesa, 268–69

Yaller Beer, 246–47
yeast, xii, 5, 10, 96
   adding to wort, 7, 16, 18, 83
   ale varieties, xx, 74–80, 83
   dry, rehydrating of, 11, 15–16, 18
   fermentation process, xvii, 34, 83
   and flavor, xx–xxi
   lager varieties, xx, 80–82, 83
   liquid, advance preparation, 7, 16
   nutrients, xxi, 15, 17, 84, 91
   quantity to use, xxi, 11, 83
   sediment, 8, 34–35, 44
   storing, 83
   wort pH and, 87
Yeast Culture Kit Company, 74
Yeast Lab yeasts, 74
Yeasty Beasty Wheat, 209–10
Yellow Dog Pale Ale, 250–51
Yeoman hops, 72
Yorkshire bitters, 142
"Your Favorite" Fruit Ale, 343–44
Yule Fuel, 334–35

"Zapap" lauter tun, 20
Zenith hops, 72
zoigl, 56